Lecture Notes in Computer Science 3235

Commenced Publication in 1973
Founding and Former Series Editors:
Gerhard Goos, Juris Hartmanis, and Jan van Leeuwen

T0223558

David de Frutos-Escrig   Manuel Núñez (Eds.)

Formal Techniques for Networked and Distributed Systems – FORTE 2004

24th IFIP WG 6.1 International Conference
Madrid, Spain, September 27-30, 2004
Proceedings

 Springer

Volume Editors

David de Frutos-Escrig
Manuel Núñez
Universidad Complutense de Madrid
Dept. Sistemas Informáticos y Programación
Madrid 28040, Spain
E-mail:{defrutos/mn}@sip.ucm.es

Library of Congress Control Number: Applied for

CR Subject Classification (1998): C.2.4, D.2.2, C.2, D.2.4-5, D.2, F.3, D.4

ISSN 0302-9743
ISBN 3-540-23252-4 Springer Berlin Heidelberg New York

Springer is a part of Springer Science+Business Media

springeronline.com

© Springer-Verlag Berlin Heidelberg 2004
Printed in Germany

Typesetting: Camera-ready by author, data conversion by DA-TeX Gerd Blumenstein
Printed on acid-free paper   SPIN: 11321293   06/3142   5 4 3 2 1 0

Preface

This volume contains the proceedings of the 24th IFIP TC 6/WG 6.1 International Conference on Formal Techniques for Networked and Distributed Systems (FORTE 2004), held in Madrid, Spain, September 27–30, 2004. FORTE denotes a series of international working conferences on formal description techniques applied to computer networks and distributed systems. The conference series started in 1981 under the name PSTV. In 1988 a second series under the name FORTE was set up. Both series were united to FORTE/PSTV in 1996. Three years ago the conference name was changed to its current form. The last five meetings of this well-established conference series were held in Beijing, China (1999), Pisa, Italy (2000), Cheju Island, Korea (2001), Houston, USA (2002), and Berlin, Germany (2003).

The scope of the papers presented at FORTE 2004 covered semantic models and application of formal description languages (in particular, automata and Petri Nets), as well as the verification and testing of communication and distributed systems. The conference was preceded by 2 half-day tutorials by Roberto Gorrieri and Farn Wang. The proceedings contain the 20 regular papers accepted and presented at the conference. They were selected from 54 submitted papers in a careful selection procedure based on the assessment of three referees for each paper. The proceedings also include the papers contributed by the three invited speakers: Martín Abadi, Tommaso Bolognesi, and Juan Quemada.

FORTE 2004 was organized under the auspices of IFIP TC 6 by Universidad Complutense de Madrid. We would like to express our gratitude to the numerous people who contributed to the success of FORTE 2004. The reviewing process was one of the major efforts during the preparation of the conference, including not only PC members but additional reviewers. Finally, we would like to thank the local organizers for the excellent running of the conference. In particular, Luis Llana (as Web master), Natalia López (as organizing chair), and Fernando Rubio (as publicity chair) deserve a special mention. Last, but not least, we are in debt to Richard van de Stadt, the author of CyberChair, the tool we used to deal with the whole organization process.

We would like to mention that this is the first time that FORTE had three colocated workshops:

- TheFormEMC: 1st International Workshop on Theory Building and Formal Methods in Electronic/Mobile Commerce
- EPEW: 1st European Performance Engineering Workshop
- ITM: 1st International Workshop on Integration of Testing Methodologies

The proceedings of these workshops, which took place on the 1st and 2nd of October in Toledo, are also published by Springer in the LNCS series.

September 2004   David de Frutos-Escrig
                                                     Manuel Núñez

Organizing Entities

UNIVERSIDAD
COMPLUTENSE
DE MADRID

UNIVERSIDAD
DE CASTILLA
LA MANCHA

INTERNATIONAL
FEDERATION
FOR
INFORMATION
PROCESSING

Other Sponsors

Ministerio de Educación y Ciencia, Junta de Comunidades de Castilla–La Mancha, Excmo. Ayuntamiento de Madrid, Comunidad Autónoma de Madrid, Facultad de Informática (UCM).

Executive Committee

Conference Chairs   David de Frutos-Escrig
    Manuel Núñez
Publicity Chair   Fernando Rubio
Organizing Chair   Natalia López
Workshops Chair   Valentín Valero

Organizing Committee

Alberto de la Encina   Luis Llana   Ismael Rodríguez
Carlos Gregorio   Natalia López   Fernando Rubio
Mercedes Hidalgo   Olga Marroquín   Alberto Verdejo

Steering Committee

Gregor v. Bochmann	University of Ottawa, Canada
Tommaso Bolognesi	Istituto di Elaborazione della Informazione, Italy
Guy Leduc	University of Liege, Belgium
Kenneth Turner	University of Stirling, UK

We want to express our gratitude for the collaboration of the former members of the Steering Committee: Ed Brinksma, Stan Budkowski, Elie Najm, and Richard Tenney.

Program Committee

Gregor von Bochmann	Univ. of Ottawa, Canada
Tommaso Bolognesi	IEI Pisa, Italy
Mario Bravetti	University of Bologna, Italy
Ana Cavalli	INT Evry, France
Jean Pierre Courtiat	LAAS Toulouse, France
David de Frutos-Escrig	Complutense University of Madrid, Spain
Rachida Dssouli	Concordia University, Montreal, Canada
Reinhard Gotzhein	University of Kaiserslautern, Germany
Holger Hermanns	Saarland University, Germany
Teruo Higashino	Osaka University, Japan
Dieter Hogrefe	University of Göttingen, Germany
Gerard J. Holzmann	Bell Labs, USA
Claude Jard	IRISA, France
Myungchul Kim	ICU Taejon, Korea
Hartmut König	Brandenburg University of Technology, Germany
Maciej Koutny	University of Newcastle upon Tyne, UK
Guy Leduc	University of Liege, Belgium
David Lee	Bell Labs, China
Elie Najm	ENST, France
Manuel Núñez	Complutense University of Madrid, Spain
Doron A. Peled	University of Warwick, UK
Alexandre Petrenko	CRIM Montreal, Canada
Kenji Suzuki	Kennisbron Co., Japan
Ken Turner	University of Stirling, UK
Hasan Ural	University of Ottawa, Canada
Ümit Uyar	City University of New York, USA
Valentín Valero	Universidad Castilla-La Mancha, Spain
Farn Wang	National Taiwan University, Taiwan
Jianping Wu	Tsinghua University, Beijing, China
Nina Yevtushenko	Tomsk State University, Russia

Additional Reviewers

Baptiste Alcalde
Gerd Behrmann
Bernard Berthomieu
Sergiy Boroday
Diego Cazorla
Robert Clark
Fernando Cuartero Gómez
Raymond Devillers
Chen Dongluo
Nicola Dragoni
A. Dury
Michael Ebner
Abdeslam En-Nouaary
Xiaoming Fu
Stefania Gnesi
Cyril Grepet
Claudio Guidi
Serge Haddad
Hesham Hallal
Toru Hasegawa
Klaus Havelund
May Haydar
Loïc Hélouët
Jia Le Huo
Akira Idoue
David N. Jansen
Thierry Jéron
Cai Jianpeng
Sungwon Kang
Tatjana Kapus
Victor Khomenko
Hanna Klaudel
Anton Kolomeets
Vitali Kozioura
Jean Leneutre

Keqin Li
Natalia López
Roberto Lucchi
Luis Llana
Hermenegilda Macià Soler
Savi Maharaj
Olga Marroquín Alonso
Narciso Martí-Oliet
Michael Meier
Nicola Mezzetti
Gethin Norman
Tomohiko Ogishi
Jean-Marie Orset
Miguel Palomino
Juan José Pardo Mateo
Svetlana Prokopenko
Ismael Rodríguez
Elisangela Rodriguez Vieira
Fernando Rubio
Vlad Rusu
Claudio Sacerdoti Coen
Joern Schneider
Christel Seguin
Koushik Sen
Soonuk Seol
Leslie Smith
Rene Soltwisch
Natalia Spitsyna
Alexandre Tauveron
Dong Wang
Yin Xia
Shi Xingang
Wang Zhiliang
Li Zhongjie
Bachar Zouari

Table of Contents

A Logical Account of NGSCB

Martín Abadi[1] and Ted Wobber[2]

[1]University of California at Santa Cruz
[2]Microsoft Research, Silicon Valley

Abstract. As its name indicates, NGSCB aims to be the "Next-Generation Secure Computing Base". As envisioned in the context of Trusted Computing initiatives, NGSCB provides protection against software attacks. This paper describes NGSCB using a logic for authentication and access control. Its goal is to document and explain the principals and primary APIs employed in NGSCB.

1 Introduction

NGSCB ("Next-Generation Secure Computing Base", formerly known as "Palladium") integrates hardware and software components that aim to help in protecting data and processes against software attacks [8,9,14,15]. The hardware includes a cryptographic co-processor that contains keys and offers basic cryptographic services. The software includes new, trusted operating system components.

While the architecture and the implementation of NGSCB continue to evolve, quite a few of its features have been discussed in public. We believe that it is worthwhile to elucidate them further. Many of these features seem likely to remain important as NGSCB matures, and also appear in other projects and research efforts in the area of Trusted Computing [1,10,12,13,16].

In this paper, we present an attempt to understand the fundamentals of NGSCB in terms of a logic for authentication and access control. This formalism had its origins in the context of the Taos operating system and of the Digital Distributed System Security Architecture [11,12,18]. In this application to NGSCB, we use the logic for describing relationships between principals while abstracting away most of the details of the underlying cryptographic protocols. Although it may be feasible and perhaps attractive, we do not relate the logic to concrete implementations, nor base new implementations on the logic. Our goal is to document the components and primary APIs employed in NGSCB, and to provide concise and principled explanations for them.

At present, one may view all work on NGSCB as "work in progress". This paper is no exception. Because the specifics of NGSCB remain subject to change, we are less concerned with giving a detailed and up-to-the-minute account than with providing a consistent explanation of important concepts and techniques.

The next section reviews the logic. Section 3 reviews the basics of NGSCB. Sections 4, 5, and 6 describe principals, derived authorities, and the certification infrastructure (which is external to NGSCB but necessary for its applications).

D. de Frutos-Escrig and M. Núñez (Eds.): FORTE 2004, LNCS 3235, pp. 1-12, 2004.

Section 7 deals with the main system services in logical terms. Section 8 briefly addresses privacy. Section 9 discusses an example. Section 10 concludes.

2   A Brief Logic Review

The logic enables us to describe a system in terms of principals and their statements. The logical formula P *says s* means that principal P makes or supports statement s. The principal may for example be a user, a piece of hardware, the combination of some hardware and some software, or a cryptographic key.

We also allow compound principals, particularly of the form $P \mid C$. The meaning of $P \mid C$ is "P quoting C"; we have that $P \mid C$ says s when P says that C says s. For instance, P may represent a piece of hardware, and C a piece of code or a user.

In addition, the logical formula $P \Rightarrow Q$ means that P speaks for Q, so if P *says s* then Q *says s*, for every s. We generally assume the *hand-off axiom* which says that if Q *says* $P \Rightarrow Q$ then indeed $P \Rightarrow Q$. We use the "speaks for" relation for many purposes. For instance, we often write that a key K speaks for a principal P when K is P's public signature key. Typically only P knows the corresponding signing key (K's inverse) and can produce signatures that can be checked with K. We may also write that a principal speaks for any group of which it is a member; thus, when we write that P speaks for a group we typically mean that P is or speaks for some member of the group, not necessarily all members of the group. (It would be easy to extend the logic with a membership relation, and to replace "speaks for" with membership in these uses; whether this extension is worth the trouble remains open to debate.) We may represent an access control list (ACL) as the group of the principals authorized by the list. If G_X is the ACL for accessing an object X, then P speaks for G_X when P is authorized to access X.

Although the logic does not lead to correctness proofs of the kind expected in high-assurance systems, this logic and its relatives have been useful in several ways in the past. Much as in this paper, the logic has served for describing and documenting the workings of a system, what the system achieves, and on what assumptions it relies, after the fact or in the course of development. In this respect, formal notations do not accomplish anything beyond the reach of careful, precise prose, but they are helpful. The logic has also served in validating particular techniques for authorization, reducing them to logical reasoning, and also as a basis for new techniques; research on stack inspection and proof-carrying authorization exemplify this line of work [3,6,17,18]. Finally, the logic has served as a foundation for languages for writing general security policies [7].

We refer to previous papers for more detailed descriptions of the logic and its applications.

3   Assumptions on NGSCB

We assume that at the root of any NGSCB node there exists a hardware-based security facility that implements cryptosystems, random number generation, and key storage. We use the term *Security Support Component (SSC)* to describe this facility since it has been previously used in related literature. The Trusted Platform Module (TPM) from the Trusted Computing Group [16] may be the main current example of an SSC.

We further assume that the hardware has the capability to load an operating system that can be reliably identified by taking a hash (or *code-id*) of the initial operating system image and data. This operating system, so loaded, will reside in a protected area of memory that cannot be accessed by untrusted code that the operating system might load. Therefore, the hardware has reason to believe that the statements made by the securely loaded operating system can be attributed to the principal identified by the code-id. In turn, the operating system can load a child process and attribute statements made by that child process to the principal identified by the hash of its code and data. Following one existing nomenclature for NGSCB, we call the securely loaded operating system the *Nexus*, and we call any child process that it loads a *Nexus Computing Agent* (*NCA*). The Nexus may be implemented, for example, by combining a virtual-machine hypervisor with a trusted guest operating system [10,15]. For simplicity, we focus on situations with one distinguished Nexus and one distinguished NCA; of course, other software may be running on the hardware at the same time.

Finally, we assume trusted input and output paths for communication with users. In particular, the hardware may guarantee that only a particular Nexus receives input from the keyboard and can send output to a display. The Nexus may in turn provide a similar guarantee to a particular NCA.

These assumptions are consistent with previous, public descriptions of NGSCB, such as the ones found in papers and on the Web. Those descriptions, like most informal descriptions, are however incomplete and imprecise in some respects. One of the goals of the present logical account is to complement those descriptions, with additional details (some of them validated in private conversations with the NGSCB team, and some of them conjectured rather than based on an official NGSCB design), and with a partial rationale for the workings of NGSCB.

4   Principals

Next we enumerate principals relevant for NGSCB security.

The following principals are particular to each NGSCB node. Each node will have different instances of them.

K_0	the permanent public key of the SSC
K_T	a per-boot public key of the SSC
S_0	the master symmetric key of the SSC
S_T	a per-boot symmetric key derived from S_0

The inverse of the key K_0 and the symmetric key S_0 never leave the SSC hardware; the inverse of the key K_T and the symmetric key S_T may or may not leave the hardware, as discussed below. We rely on asymmetric cryptography (public-key operations with K_0, K_T, and their inverses) primarily for digital signatures, rather than for public-key encryption. When encryption is needed, we indicate it explicitly. The symmetric key S_0 may be replaced with a pair of keys for asymmetric encryption, with only minor changes.

The following principals represent software images. There can, of course, be many different images in which we might be interested. For simplicity of exposition, we will be concerned with only two:

C_{NEX} the code-id of a particular Nexus
C_{NCA} the code-id of a particular NCA

The following principals complete the cast; they provide the context outside an NGSCB system:

M	a manufacturer of SSC hardware
V	a vendor or author of Nexus software
A	a vendor or author of NCA software
K_M	M's public signature key
K_V	V's public signature key
K_A	A's public signature key
G_M	a group of public signature keys for SSCs produced by M
G_V	a group of code-ids for Nexus software images produced by V
G_A	a group of code-ids for NCA software images produced by A
CA	a trusted certification authority

5   Derived Authorities

It would be possible for an SSC to make statements only with its permanent public key K_0. However, it is desirable to sign as few certificates as possible with this key. Therefore, we assume that, at boot time, the SSC generates a temporary key pair, consisting of the public key K_T and its inverse. Then K_0 transfers all of its authority to K_T. This hand-off of authority is captured in the following statement:

$$K_0 \; says \; K_T \Rightarrow K_0$$

The certificate described here, and all subsequent certificates mentioned in this paper, should be considered valid only for a limited period of time. The logic does not directly model time, so we do not represent time formally; one could probably add it with a modest effort.

In this formulation, we assume that the SSC holds the temporary secret key (the inverse of K_T) in hardware and uses the key for signing statements on behalf of other principals on the local machine. This key could instead reside in the Nexus and be accessed through a similar interface. In this case, the key would no longer be protected within the SSC, so the two arrangements entail different security properties.

Because of the secure loading steps described above, a successfully loaded Nexus will have the authority of the compound principal $K_T \mid C_{NEX}$. An SSC can run any Nexus software, but the rights of a specific Nexus instance are exactly those of the SSC parameterized by the code-id of the Nexus. Similarly, an NCA loaded on top of a Nexus would speak as $K_T \mid C_{NEX} \mid C_{NCA}$.

6   Certification Infrastructure

In order to deduce anything useful about statements made by the software running on an NGSCB node, we must have trust assumptions. We hypothesize the presence of a certification authority CA that makes statements that are globally trusted. In particular, we trust CA to specify the set of acceptable NGSCB nodes and the set of trusted Nexus and NCA software images; we express this trust as follows:

$$CA \Rightarrow G_M$$
$$CA \Rightarrow G_V$$
$$CA \Rightarrow G_A$$

We simplify a bit here: in practice, CA will almost always be implemented by a hierarchy of certification authorities and there will be multiple subgroups of G_M, G_V, and G_A, according to the intended applications and trust relationships.

Next, we must give some key (or set of keys) the authority to certify membership in the groups G_M, G_V, and G_A. We represent such statements in the following certificates:

$$CA \; says \; K_M \Rightarrow G_M$$
$$CA \; says \; K_V \Rightarrow G_V$$
$$CA \; says \; K_A \Rightarrow G_A$$

Finally, we use the signing keys that correspond to K_M, K_V, and K_A for making membership certificates for the specific hardware/software stack that we intend to construct:

$$K_M \; says \; K_0 \Rightarrow G_M$$
$$K_V \; says \; C_{NEX} \Rightarrow G_V$$
$$K_A \; says \; C_{NCA} \Rightarrow G_A$$

Combining the certificates and trust assumptions, we can derive:

$$K_0 \Rightarrow G_M$$
$$C_{NEX} \Rightarrow G_V$$
$$C_{NCA} \Rightarrow G_A$$

Note that if K_0 is a member of G_M (so $K_0 \Rightarrow G_M$ in our model) then K_0 can also define new group members of G_M. In particular, $K_0 \Rightarrow G_M$ and $K_0 \; says \; K_T \Rightarrow K_0$ imply that $K_T \Rightarrow G_M$. Using a primitive membership relation rather than "speaks for" would remove this possibility.

7   Programmatic Interface

The programmatic interface of NGSCB supports the sealing of information and hardware-based attestation. Next we explain those functions in terms of the logic and of the definitions of the previous sections.

7.1 Sealing

Seal(X,C). The Seal function stores the data X in such a way that it can be retrieved later by the same SSC, and only by that SSC. Furthermore, a code-id C is bound into the result so that the SSC can restrict subsequent access to that code-id. For example, an NCA might seal data under its own code-id for later retrieval, or the Nexus might seal data under the code-id of a subsequent Nexus version as part of a version migration strategy. The sealed data might be private user information, and the goal of the sealing might be to protect this information from viruses on the same machine.

Sealing amounts to setting up an access control rule, which we model with the following statement:

$$S_0 \ says \ C \Rightarrow G_X$$

This means that the hardware asserts that C is a member of the group G_X of principals that can access an object with the data X. Nothing here precludes the possibility that other objects also contain the data X and that code other than C may access those objects.

In practice, the SSC does not store the data, but rather encrypts it with its private key and returns the sealed data item. Here we can use the symmetric key S_0 instead of K_0 since the statement is always evaluated in the context of the local machine. So this kind of sealing can be accomplished through authenticated encryption using symmetric ciphers and message authentication codes (MACs).

In order to limit the exposure of S_0, the use of a per-boot symmetric secret, S_T, might be desirable. (Indeed, the TPM design goes further in permitting chains of intermediate keys.) Suppose that we generate a per-boot nonce, N, and derive S_T as a function of S_0 and N for example by setting $S_T = \text{HMAC}(S_0, N)$. This definition implies that N must be stored in plaintext with the sealed content in order to allow the recovery of S_T. In the logic, the access control rule for the sealed object can be expressed with the following statements:

$$S_0 \ says \ S_T \Rightarrow S_0$$
$$S_T \ says \ C \Rightarrow G_X$$

The *Seal* function might be offered to NCAs by the Nexus, or NCAs might be given direct access to the SSC's *Seal* function. In the former case, a symmetric key held by the Nexus would be used for sealing instead of S_T. This design has the advantage of allowing more straightforward migration to different hardware, but the disadvantage of exposing temporary keys within the memory system.

Unseal(X,C). The Unseal function retrieves data held under seal. Conceptually, access to the sealed data is granted on the basis of the result of evaluating the corresponding ACL using the code-id of the caller. When *Seal* relies on encryption, the SSC implements *Unseal* by decrypting data that it previously sealed under its own secret.

PKSeal(X,K). The PKSeal function is similar to Seal except that a target key K is used instead of a code-id. In this case the unsealer is not assumed to be the same SSC as the sealer. Therefore, *PKSeal* can be used to seal data for retrieval on another machine.

We can describe *PKSeal* by an access control rule, much as we did for *Seal*:

$$K_T \, says \, K \Rightarrow G_X$$

If *PKSeal* is implemented by placing X on a storage server operated by a trusted third party, then the certificate $K_T \, says \, K \Rightarrow G_X$ can be directly useful as input to the reference monitor on that server: when K requests access to X, the reference monitor grants it.

Alternatively, as its name suggests, the implementation *PKSeal* can perform public-key encryption on X. For this purpose, the public key K should be an encryption key (and not just a key for checking signatures).

PKUnseal(X,K). Much like Unseal, PKUnseal implements the corresponding access control rule. When PKUnseal relies on encryption, the implementation of PKUn*seal* relies on decryption. In this case, whoever holds the inverse of the public key used for sealing will have de facto access to X.

7.2 Attestation

Quote(ST). The Quote function allows the SSC to attest to statements made by principals under its control. For example, the SSC may attest that a particular, trusted application (not a virus) is making a request to write a file.

Suppose that an NCA wishes to utter the statement *ST* and have the SSC attest to this statement over a network. As described in Section 5, the NCA speaks with the authority:

$$K_T \mid C_{NEX} \mid C_{NCA}$$

Since only cryptographic keys can securely make statements over an otherwise unprotected network, the SSC encodes the uttered statement as:

$$K_T \, says \, (C_{NEX} \mid C_{NCA} \, says \, ST)$$

According to the definition of quoting in the logic, this formula can be written more straightforwardly:

$$K_T \mid C_{NEX} \mid C_{NCA} \, says \, ST$$

In particular, *Quote* can be used to attest that a key speaks for a principal. For example, suppose that an NCA wishes to indicate that a key K is authorized to make statements on its behalf. In this case, the quoted statement *ST* is:

$$K \Rightarrow K_T \mid C_{NEX} \mid C_{NCA}$$

and the certificate that the SSC would form in order to attest to this hand-off of authority would be:

$$K_T \, says \, (C_{NEX} \mid C_{NCA} \, says \, (K \Rightarrow K_T \mid C_{NEX} \mid C_{NCA}))$$

which reduces to:

$$K_T \mid C_{NEX} \mid C_{NCA} \; says \; K \Rightarrow K_T \mid C_{NEX} \mid C_{NCA}$$

Here the key K may be a public key, but it may also be a symmetric key that underlies an authenticated communication channel from the NCA.

This kind of quoting might be used by the Nexus directly as well. In this case, the SSC would produce:

$$K_T \; says \; (C_{NEX} \; says \; K \Rightarrow K_T \mid C_{NEX})$$

which implies:

$$K_T \mid C_{NEX} \; says \; K \Rightarrow K_T \mid C_{NEX}$$

Verify(ST). The Verify function must decode a statement generated by Quote and check the consistency of its cryptographic evidence. Furthermore, the results of Verify should enable reasoning about the principal that made the statement in question.

Often, the receiver of a statement interprets the statement in a different trust environment (and in a different machine) than the sender. The receiver must come to conclusions based on its own trust assumptions. For example, if the receiver sees:

$$K_T \; says \; (C_{NEX} \mid C_{NCA} \; says \; ST)$$

and believes:

$$K_0 \; says \; K_T \Rightarrow K_0$$

then the receiver can conclude:

$$K_0 \mid C_{NEX} \mid C_{NCA} \; says \; ST$$

Suppose that the receiver has the certificates and trust assumptions introduced in Section 6. Then the receiver can deduce:

$$G_M \mid G_V \mid G_A \; says \; ST$$

The receiver may trust $G_M \mid G_V \mid G_A$ on ST. For example, when ST represents a request for access to an object X, the ACL for X may include $G_M \mid G_V \mid G_A$, granting access to a member of G_M quoting a member of G_V quoting a member of G_A. (In other words, the receiver may have that $G_M \mid G_V \mid G_A \Rightarrow G_X$.) Thus, the receiver can reason about the principal that said ST and use the identity of that principal as the basis for access control decisions.

8   Privacy

It may be undesirable for all certification chains associated with the statements from a given SSC to be rooted at a single key K_0. If this were the case, then an observer might be able to track the activity of specific machines and use this information to compromise user privacy. In light of such concerns, several privacy-enhancing mechanisms have been developed.

Upon boot, the Nexus might communicate with an anonymization service that would be trusted to issue semi-permanent key pairs to trusted system components, and also trusted to respect privacy. In this case, the Nexus carries out a secure transaction with the anonymization service, using the authority $K_T \mid C_{NEX}$. After establishing that $K_T \mid C_{NEX} \Rightarrow G_M \mid G_V$, the service returns a collection of public keys K_i, their inverses, and certificates of the following form:

$$K_{ANON} \text{ says } K_i \Rightarrow G_M \mid G_V$$
$$CA \text{ says } K_{ANON} \Rightarrow G_M \mid G_V$$

where K_{ANON} is the public key of the anonymization service. The inverse of any key K_i can be used by the Nexus to sign subsequent statements. Since neither K_i nor K_{ANON} are linked to any single user, SSC, or Nexus, this indirection provides some anonymity for the holder of the inverse of K_i.

Variants of this scheme can provide keys K_i that speak for G_M or for $G_M \mid G_V \mid G_A$ (rather than for $G_M \mid G_V$). The inverse of a key that speaks for G_M should not be under the control of the Nexus; therefore, the anonymization service should return the key sealed in such a way that only the SSC itself can access it.

More sophisticated schemes rely on group cryptography [2,4,5]. Using group cryptography, an SSC may issue signatures that cannot be distinguished from signatures generated by some set of other SSCs. Instead of K_0, each SSC has a share of the group key $K_{NODE\text{-}GROUP}$. The manufacturer M makes K_M says $K_{NODE\text{-}GROUP} \Rightarrow G_M$. Then the SSC can produce a certificate for a temporary key K_T:

$$K_{NODE\text{-}GROUP} \text{ says } K_T \Rightarrow K_{NODE\text{-}GROUP}$$

Although this certificate does not identify a particular SSC, shares of the group key can be revoked; the specifics of revocation vary across schemes.

9   An Example

In this section we exercise the logic on a practical example of an application of NGSCB, due to Butler Lampson and Paul Leach. In this application, an NCA presents an image (perhaps of a sales order or an online-banking transfer) to the user of a machine, and attests to the fact that the user clicked "OK" to accept the consequences implied by the image. For this application, we have to assume that there is a trusted path between the NCA and the keyboard and display in front of the user. We also assume that an untrusted banking or purchasing application is running (perhaps in a web browser) on the user's machine outside the context of NGSCB. This untrusted application uses the trusted NCA to carry out security-critical aspects of online transactions directly with the merchant or bank.

There are many different protocols that could support this sort of scenario. We will assume a simple model in which the NCA establishes an authenticated channel to a bank, and uses that channel to assert that a specific user has confirmed the contents of a specific image. For these purposes, we assume that the user can present a password known to the bank.

Although the Nexus and NCA might depend on an untrusted operating system to communicate with the network, the cryptography used to establish and maintain a secure channel can be implemented within a trusted NCA. Let us say that the NCA establishes an SSL channel to the bank and authenticates the bank using a certificate chain in the usual style. The NCA can also authenticate itself to the bank in that SSL exchange. In the logic, this authentication can be written as:

$$K_T \mid C_{NEX} \mid C_{NCA} \text{ says } Channel \Rightarrow K_T \mid C_{NEX} \mid C_{NCA}$$

where

$$K_0 \text{ says } K_T \Rightarrow K_0$$

Much as in Section 7.2, the bank can now deduce that *Channel* speaks for a trusted NGSCB node running a trusted NCA. Using *Channel* or by other means, the bank can transmit an appropriate image for the user to accept. The image is received by the NCA and shown on the user's display via the trusted path to the hardware. Perhaps the target window is distinguished with a specialized border that indicates secured images of this form. If the image is acceptable to the user, then the user is asked to provide a password and click "OK". Gathering this input on the trusted path from the keyboard, the NCA can now make the following statement on the trusted channel to the bank:

$$Password \text{ says } OK\text{-}Image$$

Here, the image might be represented by its hash. If all is in order, the bank can deduce:

$$Channel \mid User \text{ says } OK\text{-}Image$$

then

$$K_0 \mid C_{NEX} \mid C_{NCA} \mid User \text{ says } OK\text{-}Image$$

and hence

$$G_M \mid G_V \mid G_A \mid User \text{ says } OK\text{-}Image$$

Now the bank may conclude that the user (or at least an NCA holding the user's password) authorized the consequences represented by *Image*. Furthermore, the bank may also conclude that the transaction took place over a channel from a trusted NGSCB node and a trusted NCA.

The bank may impose restrictions on the set of machines and software that can serve as origin of the channel. These restrictions may thwart certain types of attacks. For example, even if the password is compromised, it cannot be used directly by just any application.

10 Conclusion

This paper describes NGSCB in terms of a logic for authentication and access control. Its goal is to document and explain NGSCB's principals and primary APIs. It aims to complement previous descriptions of NGSCB, with additional design elements, and with a (partial) formal rationale for the workings of NGSCB.

As discussed in the introduction, NGSCB is still "work in progress". We will not venture predictions on its future evolution or applications. It is possible that some or all of the features of NGSCB described in this paper will change. That represents a risk, but an inevitable one whenever one applies formal techniques in the course of the development process. We believe that, in any case, those features and their principles will be valuable beyond the context of NGSCB.

Acknowledgements

We wish to thank Butler Lampson, John Manferdelli, Fred Schneider, and Jeannette Wing for discussions on this work and encouragement, and Marcus Peinado for information on NGSCB. Martín Abadi's work was done at Microsoft Research, Silicon Valley.

References

[1]   Abadi, M.: Trusted computing, trusted third parties, and verified communications. To appear in Proceedings of the 19th IFIP International Security Conference (SEC 2004), Kluwer, 2004.

[2]   Ateniese, G., Camenisch, J., Joye, M., and Tsudik, G.: A practical and provably secure coalition-resistant group signature scheme. In Proceedings of Crypto 2000, pages 255–270, Springer-Verlag, 2000.

[3]   Appel, A., and Felten, E.: Proof-carrying authentication. In Proceedings of the 5th ACM Conference on Computer and Communications Security, pages 52–62, 1999.

[4]   Boneh, D., Boyen, X., and Shacham, H.: Short group signatures. To appear in Proceedings of Crypto 2004, Springer-Verlag, 2004.

[5]   Brickell, E.: An efficient protocol for anonymously providing assurance of the container of a private key. Submitted to the Trusted Computing Group, 2003.

[6]   Bauer, L., Schneider, M., and Felten, E.: A general and flexible access control system for the Web. In Proceedings of the 11th USENIX Security Symposium 2002, pages 93–108, 2002.

[7]   DeTreville, J.: Binder, a logic-based security language. In Proceedings of the IEEE Symposium on Security and Privacy, pages 105–113, 2002.

[8]   England, P., Lampson, B., Manferdelli, J., Peinado, M., and Willman, B.: A trusted open platform. IEEE Computer, 36(7):55–62, 2003.

[9]   England, P., and Peinado, M.: Authenticated operation of open computing devices. In Proceedings of the 7th Australasian Conference on Information Security and Privacy, pages 346–361, Springer-Verlag, 2002.

[10]   Garfinkel, T., Pfaff, B., Chow, J., Rosenblum, M., and Boneh, D.: Terra: A virtual machine-based platform for trusted computing. In Proceedings of the 19th Symposium on Operating System Principles (SOSP 2003), pages 193–206, 2003.

[11]   Gasser, M., Goldstein, A., Kaufman, C., Lampson, B.: The Digital distributed system security architecture. In Proceedings of 12th National Computer Security Conference, pages 305–319, NIST/NCSC, 1989.

[12]   Lampson, B., Abadi, B., Burrows, M., and Wobber, E.: Authentication in distributed systems: Theory and practice. ACM Transactions on Computer Systems, 10(4):265–310, 1992.

[13]   Lie, D., Thekkath, C., Mitchell, M., Lincoln, P., Boneh, D., Mitchell, J., and Horowitz, D.: Architectural support for copy and tamper resistant software. In Ninth International ACM Conference on Architectural Support for Programming Languages and Operating Systems (ASPLOS-IX), pages 168–177, 2000.

[14]   Microsoft Corporation: Next-generation secure computing base. Archive Product Information, http://www.microsoft.com/resources/ngscb/archive.mspx.

[15]   Peinado, M., Chen, Y., England, P., and Manferdelli, J.: NGSCB: A trusted open system. To appear in Proceedings of the 9th Australasian Conference on Information Security and Privacy (ACISP 2004), Springer-Verlag, 2004.

[16]   Trusted Computing Group: Home page, http://www.trustedcomputinggroup.org.

[17]   Wallach, D., Appel, A., and Felten, E.: SAFKASI: a security mechanism for language-based systems. ACM Transactions on Software Engineering and Methodology, 9(4):341–378, 2000.

[18]   Wobber, E., Abadi, M., Burrows, M., and Lampson, B.: Authentication in the Taos operating system. ACM Transactions on Computer Systems, 12(1):3–32, 1994.

Composing Event Constraints in State-Based Specification

Tommaso Bolognesi

CNR - ISTI
t.bolognesi@isti.cnr.it
http://fmt.isti.cnr.it/

Abstract. Event-based process algebraic specification languages support an elegant specification technique by which system behaviours are described as compositions of constraints on event occurrences and event parameters. This paper investigates the possibility to export this specification paradigm to a state-based formalism, and discusses some deriving advantages in terms of verification.

1 Introduction

Process-algebraic specification languages have received much attention in the eighties and nineties, with emphasis, in the first decade, on theoretical foundations and semantics, and with various experiments and projects, in the second decade, for their application to the development of large-scale software systems.

Many people involved in software production, and several researchers from academia as well, agree today in observing that most of the early, ambitious goals of process algebra have not been met. The diffusion of process-algebraic languages within software companies, as a routine tool for design and verification activities, is quite limited.

Process-algebras and related methods represent just a portion of the articulated area of Formal Methods (FM). It is fair to admit that, so far, FM's in general have gained only limited acceptance in industry. Typically, they are applied in the development of safety-critical (sub-)systems, for which formal verification becomes crucial; but their popularity does not compare with that reached by more 'practical' approaches such as the object-oriented UML.

The reasons for these difficulties have been already discussed quite extensively in the past; we only mention, below, those that have more directly motivated the work presented in this paper.

- The offer of FM's appears still too wide and fragmented. The WWW Virtual Library on Formal Methods, as of today, provides a list of 92 individual notations and associated tools (http://vl.fmnet.info/#notations). While some techniques are fairly stable, others keep evolving, and new ones appear, although less frequently than in the past; making choices in such a wide and dynamic set is hard, also considering the high training costs associated with the adoption of a FM.

D. de Frutos-Escrig and M. Núñez (Eds.): FORTE 2004, LNCS 3235, pp. 13–32, 2004.

- 'Political' concerns and parochial attitudes have often obstructed the recognition of similarities among formal languages and the convergence towards fewer stable proposals. FM's would greatly benefit from some unification effort, as it happened with the definition of the Unified Modelling Language. Some steps in this direction have been already taken, as indicated, for example, by the recently established Integrated Formal Methods (IFM) series of international conferences, by the work on the Unified Theories of Programming [1], and by proposals such as *Circus* [2], but much remains to be done, also in the sense discussed in the next bullet.
- Perhaps more specifically in the area of process algebraic FM's, there has often been a mismatch between the offers from FM developers, and the real needs of perspective FM users, with the former emphasizing on the meta-level of formal semantic definition, on axiomatisations, on countless semantic relations, and the latter emphasizing on ease of use, expressive flexibility, pragmatic guidelines, tool support. The well known work on Design Patterns is an important factor for the wide acceptance of Object Oriented technology (note that patterns are language-independent!): this is, again, a lesson from O-O technology that the FM community might want to take into serious consideration.

Formal approaches to the behavioural specification are often partitioned into state-based (e.g. Abstract State Machines [3, 4], B [5], TLA [6, 7], or Z [8]), usually rooted in logics, and event-based (e.g. CSP [9], CCS [10], or LOTOS [11, 12]), with algebraic roots. Today, software engineers seem to look more favourably at state-based FM's: they better relate with other traditional and well understood engineering methods, they have proven to be quite effective in hardware design, and they lend themselves to increasingly effective analytical techniques. And yet, event-oriented thinking keeps playing an important role, at least in the early phases of system development; for example, use case diagrams, scenarios, message sequence charts are widely used in requirements analysis.

This paper is an attempt to promote some cross-fertilisation and convergence in the area of FM and, in particular, between the event-based and state-based specification paradigms: in line with the remarks above, we wish to address aspects of language pragmatics, namely specification style, structuring principles, and tool-supported verification, rather than semantic foundations.

Fifteen years have passed since the publication of the LOTOS specification of Al's Node by Quemada and Azcorra, [13] which has represented a tiny but very effective example of the so called 'Constraint-Oriented' specification style. We believe that, while several results of theoretical interest from process algebra have failed to scale up to realistic-size system development, some expressive tools from this area of FM's have shown to be very effective. We wish to list three of them, in order of increasingly complexity:

- The basic notion of 'event'. This is an abstraction that process-oriented specification languages regard as equally important as the notion of 'state variable', but conveniently distinguished from it.

– Parallel composition operators. These are the most typical among the ad-hoc, high level behavioural operators of process algebras. In particular, *selective synchrony* (i.e., the general LOTOS parallel operator '|[S]|', where S is a list of synchronization gates), fundamentally based on the gate/event concept, is crucial for compactly specifying interaction patterns simultaneously involving interleaving and synchronized events from different system components.
– The constraint-oriented specification style mentioned above. This way of structuring specifications is in turn based on the use of the selective synchrony parallel operator.

In this paper we investigate the extent to which the three expressive tools above, typical of process-algebraic specification, can be imported into state-based specification. For fixing ideas, we select one representative language from each paradigm: we choose LOTOS and TLA+. For space reasons, we have to assume some familiarity with both of them, but the uninitiated reader should still be able to follow our discussion on specification structuring principles, without being distracted by the details of the two concrete languages.

The key question addressed by the paper can be summarized as follows.

– Assume you want to adopt a state-based formalism such as TLA+ for specifying systems, being attracted by:
  • the simplicity and universality of its constructs, which are based on first order logic, and on few temporal logic operators – no need to learn ad-hoc, process-algebraic behavioural operators;
  • the conceptual simplicity of the verification technique it supports (implementation is pure logical implication);
  • the free availability of tools (most notably, the model checker TLC).
– Assume also you have an inclination towards structuring some behavioural specifications as collections of constraints insisting on partially overlapped sets of events (deriving from a possibly unconfessed past experience in the community of 'LOTOS-eaters').

Should you give up your way to conceive specifications? In this paper we try to justify a negative answer to this question.

In Section 2 we recall Al's Node, we introduce two abstract, monolithic formal specifications of it, in LOTOS and in TLA+, and show one way to model 'events' in TLA+.

In Section 3 we address constraint-oriented specification. We show that the behaviour of Al's Node can be conveniently expressed in terms of three constraints, and that their interplay can be compactly expressed in LOTOS. We then illustrate two ways in which we can approximate that structuring in TLA+.

In Section 4 we take advantage of the translations into TLA+ by conducting some verification activity. We prove, by the TLC model checker, that the two TLA+ constraint-oriented specifications of Al's Node are equivalent, and that they implement the initial, monolithic specification.

In Section 5 we present our conclusions and identify items for further work.

2 Event-Based, Monolithic Specification

In this section we introduce Al's Node by providing an informal, monolithic (one process) description and a formalisation in LOTOS. We then illustrate a very similar formalization in TLA+, based on a simple idea for preserving the notion of observable event. This TLA+ specification provides the reference against which the subsequent, structured, constraint-oriented TLA+ specifications are formally verified.

2.1 Informal Description of Al's Node

Al's Node is a switching device for controlling message traffic in a network. The node keeps the following data structures:

- a bag of messages,
- a set of active ports,
- a set of (*route, port*) pairs, defining the active routings.

Messages can be accepted by the system at any active port, and stored in the node. An incoming messages consist of a (*data, route*) pair: the *data* item has to be re-directed to the associated *route*. Stored messages can be lost, or output, not necessarily in FIFO order, at some active port that is paired, according to the current active routings, to the route indicated in the message.

For keeping specifications concise, and in accordance with the original example, we allow elements to be only added to, not removed from the set of active ports and the set of (*route, port*) pairs. We omit the treatment of timeouts.

2.2 Monolithic Specification in LOTOS

The LOTOS specification makes use of three predefined sets: *Data, Ports, Routes*. For representing data structures we depart from the LOTOS standard, and use plain mathematical structures; besides being more convenient, they can be re-used in TLA+. The specification consists in a single process, called *AlsNode-Monol*. This process insists on gates DATA_IN, DATA_OUT, DATA_LOSS, CTL, and is parameterized by the three variables:

msgBag: a bag of (*data, route*) pairs, of size at most N,
activePorts: a set of *Ports*,
activeRoutes: a set of (*route, port*) pairs.

Process *AlsNodeMonol* is structured as a set of alternatives, each consisting of an event, controlled by a guard (a 'selection predicate', in LOTOS terminology), and followed by a recursive process instantiation with updated parameters. In the specification we omit gate lists in recursive process instantiations: they are the same that appear in the enclosing process definition. We use symbol '(+)' for bag union and '(-)' for bag subtraction.

```
PROCESS AlsNodeMonol
   [DATA_IN, DATA_OUT, DATA_LOSS, CTL]
   (msgBag: BagOf(Data x Routes),
   activePorts: SubsetOf(Ports),
   activeRoutes: SubsetOf(Routes x Ports))
:=
   DATA_IN ?d: Data ?r: Routes ?p: Ports
      [p in activePorts, Size(msgBag) < N];
      LET msgBag' = msgBag (+) {<d, r>} IN
      AlsNodeMonol [---] (msgBag', activePorts, activeRoutes)
   []
   DATA_OUT ?d: Data ?r: Routes ?p: Ports
      [p in activePorts, <d, r> in msgBag, <r, p> in activeRoutes)];
      LET msgBag' = msgBag (-) {<d, r>} IN
      AlsNodeMonol [---] (msgBag', activePorts, activeRoutes)
   []
   DATA_LOSS ?d: Data ?r: Routes   [<d, r> in msgBag];
      LET msgBag' = msgBag (-) {<d, r>} IN
      AlsNodeMonol [---] (msgBag', activePorts, activeRoutes)
   []
   CTL ?p: Ports    [p notin activePorts];
      LET activePorts'= activePorts union {p} IN
      AlsNodeMonol [---] (msgBag, activePorts', activeRoutes)
   []
   CTL ?r: Routes ?p: Ports    [<r, p> notin activeRoutes];
      LET activeRoutes'= activeRoutes union {<r, p>} IN
      AlsNodeMonol [---] (msgBag, activePorts, activeRoutes')
ENDPROC (* AlsNodeMonol *)
```

The interpretation of the events at the process gates is as follows. An event at gate DATA_IN, with parameters (d, r, p) represent the input of message (d, r) at port p. Events at gate DATA_OUT have a similar interpretation, while those at DATA_LOSS do not need a *port* parameter. Gate CTL is used only for adding elements to *activePorts* and *activeRoutes*. The complete set of possible events is explicitly defined in TLA+ module *AlsNodeInterface* in the next subsection.

2.3   Monolithic Specification in TLA+ and Event Representation

A monolithic specification of Al's Node in TLA+ with the same structure of the above LOTOS specification can be provided quite easily, since the latter matches a *state-oriented* style, and makes use of a restricted number of operators, namely *action prefix* with *guards, choice* and *process instantiation*. We only have to decide about the representation of events. TLA+ does not offer a primitive notion of event. It offers *actions*. A TLA+ action is logical formula that includes primed and unprimed variables, and may or may not be satisfied by a *step*. A step is a pair of successive *states*. A state is an assignment of values to all state variables.

LOTOS events occur at *gates*. A gate is a location at which processes atomically synchronize and agree on tuples of values. A gate cannot be assimilated to a normal state variable because it is intrinsically unable to retain any value. Processes may be thought of as writing values at gates, but these values are immediately lost. They can only be retained by using local process variables (as in '?d: Data').

Thus, we model events in TLA+ by a write-only state variable that we conventionally call e, and that shall only appear in primed form in action predicates, so that it never contributes to pre-conditions. Event e shall be a tuple (or a record), in which the first component is a sort of event type, and is the equivalent of a LOTOS gate identifier, while the remaining components represent the event parameters. The advantages of introducing the special event variable become more apparent with constraint oriented specification, as discussed in the next section.

A TLA+ specification is formed by a set of modules. Our first module, presented below, is called *AlsNodeInterface*. It introduces the basic components of the specification, that shall be imported by the subsequent TLA+ specifications. The interface introduces the node capacity N, the predefined sets *Data*, *Ports* and *Routes*, the special event variable e, and the set where it is supposed to range. These are also the events of the LOTOS specification.

─────────── MODULE *AlsNodeInterface* ───────────

VARIABLE e

CONSTANTS N, *Data*, *Ports*, *Routes*

$EventSet \triangleq$
$\qquad \{\langle \text{"DATA\_IN"}, d, r, p\rangle : d \in Data, r \in Routes, p \in Ports\}$
$\qquad \cup \{\langle \text{"DATA\_OUT"}, d, r, p\rangle : d \in Data, r \in Routes, p \in Ports\}$
$\qquad \cup \{\langle \text{"DATA\_LOSS"}, d, r\rangle : d \in Data, r \in Routes\}$
$\qquad \cup \{\langle \text{"CTL"}, p\rangle : p \in Ports\}$
$\qquad \cup \{\langle \text{"CTL"}, r, p\rangle : r \in Routes, p \in Ports\}$

$EventTypeInvariant \triangleq e \in EventSet \cup \{\langle\rangle\}$

The monolithic TLA+ specification of Al's Node is provided in two steps, by modules *InternalAlsNodeMonol* and *AlsNodeMonol* below. The attribute 'internal' refers to the fact that the specification in that module makes use of variables *msgBag*, *activePorts*, *activeRoutes*, that should not be regarded as contributing to the reference, observable behaviour of the system. Adopting the process-algebraic view, the only observable behaviour should be that expressed by events, that is, by variable e (which is contributed by module *AlsNodeInterface*). Thus, in module *AlsNodeMonol* all variables except e are hidden, by means of temporal existential quantification.

─────────────── MODULE *InternalAlsNodeMonol* ───────────────

EXTENDS *AlsNodeInterface, Naturals, Bags*

VARIABLES   to be internalized
> $msgBag$,   bag of messages in transit
> $activePorts$,   set of active ports
> $activeRoutes$ the dynamic association route-port

───

$TypeInvariant \triangleq$
> $\wedge\ EventTypeInvariant$
> $\wedge\ IsABag(msgBag)$
> $\wedge\ BagToSet(msgBag) \in$ SUBSET $(Data \times Routes)$
> $\wedge\ activePorts \in$ SUBSET $Ports$
> $\wedge\ activeRoutes \in$ SUBSET $(Routes \times Ports)$

───

$DataIn(d,\ route,\ port) \triangleq$
> $\wedge\ e' = \langle$ "DATA_IN", $d,\ route,\ port \rangle$
> $\wedge\ port \in activePorts$
> $\wedge\ msgBag' = msgBag \oplus SetToBag(\{\langle d,\ route \rangle\})$
> $\wedge$ UNCHANGED $\langle activePorts,\ activeRoutes \rangle$

$DataOut(d,\ route,\ port) \triangleq$
> $\wedge\ e' = \langle$ "DATA_OUT", $d,\ route,\ port \rangle$
> $\wedge\ port \in activePorts$
> $\wedge\ \langle d,\ route \rangle \in BagToSet(msgBag)$
> $\wedge\ \langle route,\ port \rangle \in activeRoutes$
> $\wedge\ msgBag' = msgBag \ominus SetToBag(\{\langle d,\ route \rangle\})$
> $\wedge$ UNCHANGED $\langle activePorts,\ activeRoutes \rangle$

$DataLoss(d,\ route) \triangleq$
> $\wedge\ \exists\, x \in BagToSet(msgBag) : x = \langle d,\ route \rangle$
> $\wedge\ e' = \langle$ "DATA_LOSS", $d,\ route \rangle$
> $\wedge\ msgBag' = msgBag \ominus SetToBag(\{\langle d,\ route \rangle\})$
> $\wedge$ UNCHANGED $\langle activePorts,\ activeRoutes \rangle$

$AddPort(port) \triangleq$
> $\wedge\ e' = \langle$ "CTL", $port \rangle$
> $\wedge\ port \notin activePorts$
> $\wedge\ activePorts' = activePorts \cup \{port\}$
> $\wedge$ UNCHANGED $\langle msgBag,\ activeRoutes \rangle$

$AddRoutePort(route,\ port) \triangleq$
> $\wedge\ e' = \langle$ "CTL", $route,\ port \rangle$
> $\wedge\ \langle route,\ port \rangle \notin activeRoutes$
> $\wedge\ activeRoutes' = activeRoutes \cup \{\langle route,\ port \rangle\}$
> $\wedge$ UNCHANGED $\langle msgBag,\ activePorts \rangle$

───

$Init \quad \overset{\Delta}{=}$
$\qquad \land e = \langle \rangle$
$\qquad \land msgBag = EmptyBag$
$\qquad \land activePorts = \{\}$
$\qquad \land activeRoutes = \{\}$

$Next \quad \overset{\Delta}{=}$
$\qquad \lor \exists\, d \in Data,\, r \in Routes,\, p \in Ports : DataIn(d,\, r,\, p)$
$\qquad \lor \exists\, d \in Data,\, r \in Routes,\, p \in Ports : DataOut(d,\, r,\, p)$
$\qquad \lor \exists\, d \in Data,\, r \in Routes : DataLoss(d,\, r)$
$\qquad \lor \exists\, p \in Ports : AddPort(p)$
$\qquad \lor \exists\, r \in Routes,\, p \in Ports : AddRoutePort(r,\, p)$

$Spec \quad \overset{\Delta}{=} \qquad Init \land \Box[Next]_{\langle e,\, msgBag,\, activePorts,\, activeRoutes \rangle}$

$BagConstraint \overset{\Delta}{=} BagCardinality(msgBag) \leq N$
THEOREM $TypeInvariant$

──────────── MODULE $AlsNodeMonol$ ────────────

EXTENDS $AlsNodeInterface$

$Inner(msgBag,\, activePorts,\, activeRoutes) \overset{\Delta}{=}$
$\qquad$ INSTANCE $InternalAlsNodeMonol$

$Spec \overset{\Delta}{=} \qquad \exists\, msgBag,\, activePorts,\, activeRoutes :$
$\qquad\qquad Inner(msgBag,\, activePorts,\, activeRoutes)!Spec$

The central part of module *InternalAlsNodeMonol* consists in the definition of five basic actions: *DataIn, DataOut, DataLoss, AddPort, AddRoutePort*. Each manipulates in a different way parts of the global state, and accounts at the same time for one event type which, in the first three cases, has the same name as the action predicate. These five actions appear as disjuncts in the global action *Next*. Finally, formula *Spec* defines all legal behaviours of Al's Node: these are infinite sequence of global states in which the first element satisfies the *Init* formula, and any pair of adjacent states satisfies the *Next* action, or leaves all variables unchanged (*stuttering step*). Note that, although in principle a step could simultaneously satisfy more than one basic action, this never happens because the actions end up being mutually exclusive, if not for the incompatibility of their pre-conditions, because of the disjoint event sets that they support (post-conditions).

The correspondence between the LOTOS and TLA+ specifications is clear. In particular: LOTOS choice corresponds to disjunction; selection predicates and the updated process parameters reflect pre- and post-conditions in TLA+

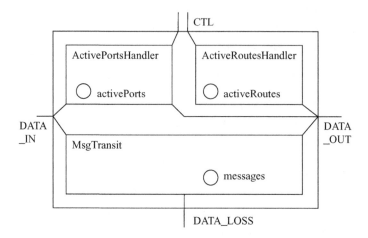

Fig. 1. Constraint-composition for Al's Node

actions; the LOTOS symbol '?' corresponds to existential quantification, which generalizes disjunction.

3   Event-Based, Constraint-Oriented Specification

In this section we first provide an informal, constraint-oriented description of Al's Node and its LOTOS formalisation, essentially following [QA89]. Then we introduce two TLA+ specifications meant to approximate, in two different ways, the compact structure of the LOTOS specification.

3.1   Informal

The behaviour of Al's Node is captured by the three constraints illustrated in Figure 1. This diagram reflects the key ideas of event-based, constraint-oriented specification. The behaviour of a system is conceived as the composition of some constraints, each insisting on some subset of the externally visible events. Typically, these subsets are partially overlapped. A constraint C may encapsulate data structures; these are not directly accessible by the other constraints. Based on their values, C expresses pre-conditions that concur in determining the 'when' (ordering constraints) and the 'what' (constraints on parameters) of its controlled events. On other parameters of these events, as well as on the other events, C has no influence. An event occurrence has an impact on the data structures of all the constraints that support the event (post-conditions).

Informally, the constraints for Al's Node are as follows:

MsgTransit Messages consisting of a (*data, route*) pair are input by the system and stored. Each of the stored messages is eventually lost or output.

ActivePorts Messages can be input and output only at one of the currently active ports. The set of currently active ports can be updated, by adding one new port at a time.

ActiveRoutes A (*data, route*) stored message can be output only at a port which is associated, according to the current active routings, to the message's route. The current active routings can be updated, by adding one new (*route, port*) pair at a time.

The above description contains the same information as the previous, monolithic, informal description of the system, but organizes it into three partial behavioural views according to a principle of separation of concerns intended to favour both the writing and the reading of this type of documentation.

3.2   Constraint-Oriented Specification in LOTOS

The three constraints of Al's Node behaviour are directly expressed, in LOTOS, by the following three processes. We use the same constants, predefined sets and events of the monolithic specification, and a constant *NoMsg*, that is required to be different from any message. Note that process *MsgTransit* is in turn defined in terms of an auxiliary process *OneMsg*. Ultimately, *MsgTransit* is formed by N interleaved instances of process *OneMsg*, each temporarily holding one message, or no message. We write $msg[1]$ and $msg[2]$ for denoting the two components of a message.

```
PROCESS MsgTransit[DATA_IN, DATA_OUT, DATA_LOSS] (k: Nat)
:=
    [] [k > 1] -> OneMsg[DATA_IN, DATA_OUT, DATA_LOSS](NoMsg, Empty)
                  |||
                  MsgTransit[DATA_IN, DATA_OUT, DATA_LOSS](k-1)
    [] [k = 1] -> OneMsg[DATA_IN, DATA_OUT, DATA_LOSS](NoMsg, Empty)


WHERE

PROCESS OneMsg[DATA_IN, DATA_OUT, DATA_LOSS]
    (msg: Data x Routes, status: {Empty, Full})
:=
    [] [status = Empty] -> DATA_IN ?d: Data ?r: Routes ?p: Ports;
        LET msg' = <d, r>, status' = Full IN  OneMsg[---] (msg', status')
    [] [status = Full] -> DATA_OUT !msg[1] !msg[2] ?p: Ports;
        LET msg' = NoMsg, status' = Empty IN  OneMsg[---] (msg', status')
    [] [status = Full] -> DATA_LOSS !msg[1] !msg[2];
        LET msg' = NoMsg, status' = Empty IN  OneMsg[---] (msg', status')
ENDPROC (* OneMsg *)

ENDPROC (* MsgTransit *)


PROCESS ActivePortsHandler[DATA_IN, DATA_OUT, CTL]
```

```
    (ActivePorts: SUBSET of Ports)
:=
    [] DATA_IN ?d: Data ?r: Routes ?p: Ports [port in activePorts]
        ActivePortsHandler[---](---)
    [] DATA_OUT ?d: Data ?r: Routes ?p: Ports [port in activePorts]
        ActivePortsHandler[---](---)
    [] CTL ?p: Ports [port in activePorts]
        LET activePorts' = activePorts \union {p} IN
        ActivePortsHandler[---](activePorts')
ENDPROC (* ActivePortsHandler *)

PROCESS ActiveRoutesHandler[DATA_IN, DATA_OUT, CTL]
    (ActiveRoutes: SUBSET of (Routes X Ports))
:=
    [] DATA_OUT ?d: Data ?r: Routes ?p: Ports [<d, r> in ActiveRoutes];
        ActiveRoutesHandler[---](---)
    [] CTL ?r: Routes ?p: Ports [<r, p> notIn in ActiveRoutes];
        LET activeRoutes' = activeRoutes \union {<r, p>} IN
        ActiveRoutesHandler[---](activePorts')
ENDPROC (* ActivePortsHandler *)
```

Once the three constraints are defined as processes, their composition is described by a parallel expression, which directly reflects the cooperation pattern of Figure 1. This if found in the body of process *AlsNodeCO* ('CO' stands for constraint-oriented).

```
PROCESS AlsNodeCO[DATA_IN, DATA_OUT, DATA_LOSS, CTL]
    (n: Nat)
:=
            MsgTransit[DATA_IN, DATA_OUT, DATA_LOSS](n)
      |[DATA_IN, DATA_OUT]|
            (ActivePortsHandler[DATA_IN, DATA_OUT, CTL](EmptySet)
            |[DATA_OUT]|
             ActiveRoutesHandler[DATA_OUT, CTL](EmptySet)
            )
ENDPROC (* AlsNodeCO *)
```

3.3   First Constraint-Oriented Specification in TLA+

The challenge we pose now, in moving to state-based specification, and to TLA+ in particular, is to try and preserve the three-fold structure of the constraint-oriented specification, first by independently describing the three constraints, and then by trying to combine them in a compact expression.

Even more ambitiously, we try to do that by using only what we might call 'basic TLA+'. In the introduction of [7] Lamport indicates that the basic concepts introduced in Part I of his book should enable the reader to handle most of the specification problems one is likely to encounter in ordinary engineering practice. Thus, we stick to those basic concepts and investigate the extent to which constraint-oriented specification fits into this picture. An additional, pragmatic reason for this restriction is that we want to verify our specifications by the TLC tool, which currently does not handle the composite specifications discussed in Part II of that book ('More advanced topics').

In basic TLA+ one models a complex component by writing a complex action. The action consists of a disjunction of more elementary actions, each describing some event possibility. For writing our constraint-oriented specification we use the conventional, write-only, event variable e, and set two requirements:

- Each constraint must be described by a separate action, handling a disjoint portion of the global state, namely the bag of messages, the set of active ports, and the set of active routes; these actions must share only the generic event variable, and must cooperate in defining its value, according to constraint groupings that depend on the type of event, as illustrated in Figure 1.
- The global system (action *Next*) must only refer to those three actions, not to their sub-components.

Composition can only be logical conjunction or disjunction; disjunction is readily excluded – it is too weak – and we are left with the tentative definition:

$$Next \triangleq MsgTransit \land ActivePortsHandler \land ActiveRoutesHandler$$

The problem now is one of defining the three component actions in such a way that the global behaviour is as expected. Since each component is going to be a disjunction of sub-components, and some sub-components contain only partial descriptions of events, to be conjoined with complementary, partial descriptions of the same event in other constraints, we need to make sure that the global conjunction induce all the desired pairings among the disjuncts, but *only* those pairings.

To this purpose, we design our first TLA+ specification according to the following three criteria:

- We explicitly identify, for each constraint, the subset of events of primary interest (called *KeyEvents*): these are events that involve the reading and/or writing of the state variables the constraint is in charge of.
- Each constraint C is described as the disjunction of two cases: if the occurring global event is one of the key events, then C contributes to it by a disjunction of sub-components, say C_1, ..., C_n, each one describing a different type or subtype of event; if the global event is not a key event, then C contributes by 'neutrally' allowing the event to occur ('don't care') and by simply making sure that its own state variables are unaffected.
- As required, the sub-components C_1, ..., C_n of constraint C shall only manipulate the set, say C_{vars}, of state variables controlled by the constraint. However, if some C_i updates only *some* of these variables, it will also make sure that the other variables of C_{vars} are unaffected.

The need to preserve the value of some variables across a step is a consequence of the fact that in TLA+ the variables not explicitly controlled by an action can assume arbitrary values.

TLA+ module *AlsNodeCO1* below directly reflects the requirements and criteria above.

────────────── MODULE *AlsNodeCO1* ──────────────

EXTENDS *AlsNodeInterface*, *Naturals*, *FiniteSets*, *TLC*

VARIABLES

$\quad msg,$ array of N messages in transit
$\quad ctl,$ array of N control states
$\quad activePorts,$ set of active ports
$\quad activeRoutes$ the dynamic association route-port

$TypeInvariant \triangleq$
$\quad \wedge\ EventTypeInvariant$
$\quad \wedge\ msg \in [1 .. N \rightarrow ((Data \times Routes) \cup \{\langle\rangle\})]$
$\quad \wedge\ ctl\ \in [1 .. N \rightarrow \{\text{"empty"}, \text{"full"}\}]$
$\quad \wedge\ activePorts \in \text{SUBSET}\ Ports$
$\quad \wedge\ activeRoutes \in \text{SUBSET}\ (Routes \times Ports)$

$EventSubset(key) \triangleq \{ ee \in EventSet : ee \neq \langle\rangle \wedge ee[1] = key\}$

$MsgTransit\_In \triangleq$
$\quad \exists\, i \in 1 .. N,\, d \in Data,\, route \in Routes,\, port \in Ports :$
$\qquad \wedge\ ctl[i] = \text{"empty"}$
$\qquad \wedge\ ctl' = [ctl\ \text{EXCEPT}\ ![i] = \text{"full"}]$
$\qquad \wedge\ e' = \langle\, \text{"DATA\_IN"},\, d,\, route,\, port\rangle$
$\qquad \wedge\ msg' = [msg\ \text{EXCEPT}\ ![i] = \langle d,\, route\rangle]$

$MsgTransit\_Out \triangleq$
$\quad \exists\, i \in 1 .. N,\, d \in Data,\, route \in Routes,\, port \in Ports :$
$\qquad \wedge\ ctl[i]\ \ = \text{"full"}$
$\qquad \wedge\ msg[i] = \langle d,\, route\rangle$
$\qquad \wedge\ ctl' = [ctl\ \text{EXCEPT}\ ![i] = \text{"empty"}]$
$\qquad \wedge\ e' = \langle\, \text{"DATA\_OUT"},\, msg[i][1],\, msg[i][2],\, port\rangle$
$\qquad \wedge\ msg' = [msg\ \text{EXCEPT}\ ![i] = \langle\rangle]$

$MsgTransit\_Loss \triangleq$
$\quad \exists\, i \in 1 .. N,\, d \in Data,\, route \in Routes :$
$\qquad \wedge\ ctl[i]\ \ = \text{"full"}$
$\qquad \wedge\ msg[i] = \langle d,\, route\rangle$
$\qquad \wedge\ ctl' = [ctl\ \text{EXCEPT}\ ![i] = \text{"empty"}]$
$\qquad \wedge\ e' = \langle\, \text{"DATA\_LOSS"},\, msg[i][1],\, msg[i][2]\rangle$
$\qquad \wedge\ msg' = [msg\ \text{EXCEPT}\ ![i] = \langle\rangle]$

$MsgTransit \stackrel{\Delta}{=}$
   LET $KeyEvents \stackrel{\Delta}{=}$
         $EventSubset(\text{"DATA\_IN"})$
         $\cup\ EventSubset(\text{"DATA\_OUT"})$
         $\cup\ EventSubset(\text{"DATA\_LOSS"})$
   IN
         $\vee\quad \wedge\quad e' \in KeyEvents$
               $\wedge\quad \vee\ MsgTransit\_In$
                      $\vee\ MsgTransit\_Out$
                      $\vee\ MsgTransit\_Loss$
         $\vee\quad \wedge\quad e' \in EventSet \setminus KeyEvents$
               $\wedge\quad \text{UNCHANGED}\ \langle msg,\ ctl \rangle$

$ActivePortsHandler\_ControlIn \stackrel{\Delta}{=} \ldots$
$ActivePortsHandler\_DataIn \stackrel{\Delta}{=} \ldots$
$ActivePortsHandler\_DataOut \stackrel{\Delta}{=} \ldots$
$ActivePortsHandler \stackrel{\Delta}{=} \ldots$

$ActiveRoutesHandler\_ControlIn \stackrel{\Delta}{=} \ldots$
$ActiveRoutesHandler\_DataOut \stackrel{\Delta}{=} \ldots$
$ActiveRoutesHandler \stackrel{\Delta}{=} \ldots$

$Init \stackrel{\Delta}{=}$
      $\wedge\ e = \langle \rangle$
      $\wedge\ msg = [i \in (1 \mathrel{..} N) \mapsto \langle \rangle]$
      $\wedge\ ctl\ = [i \in (1 \mathrel{..} N) \mapsto \text{"empty"}]$
      $\wedge\ activePorts = \{\}$
      $\wedge\ activeRoutes = \{\}$

$Next \stackrel{\Delta}{=}$
      $\wedge\ MsgTransit$
      $\wedge\ ActivePortsHandler$
      $\wedge\ ActiveRoutesHandler$

$Spec \stackrel{\Delta}{=}\ Init \wedge \square[Next]_{\langle e,\, msg,\, ctl,\, activePorts,\, activeRoutes \rangle}$

$AlsNodeCO2Instance \stackrel{\Delta}{=} \text{INSTANCE}\ AlsNodeCO2$
$AlsNodeCO2Spec \stackrel{\Delta}{=} AlsNodeCO2Instance!Spec$

THEOREM $Spec \Rightarrow \square TypeInvariant$
THEOREM $Spec \Rightarrow AlsNodeMonol!Spec$
THEOREM $Spec \Rightarrow AlsNodeCO2Spec$

3.4   Second Constraint-Oriented Specification in TLA+

A second approach to the constraint-oriented specification of Al's Node in TLA+ is suggested by considering the two-step procedure introduced in [14] for transforming a LOTOS multiple parallel expression into a set of algebraic expressions describing explicitly the process groupings that support the events at the different gates.

Let us apply the first step of that simple procedure to the top behaviour expression of LOTOS process *AlsNodeCO*. For every gate G we rewrite the parallel expression as follows: we replace a process instantiation by the plain process name, if G is in the gate list of that process, and by a zero otherwise; and we replace a parallel operator by a product operator, if G is in the list of synchronization gates, and by a sum operator, if it is not. We thus obtain the following set of gate-labelled algebraic expressions:

```
DATA_IN:     MsgTransit * (ActivePortsHandler + 0)
DATA_OUT:    MsgTransit * (ActivePortsHandler * ActiveRoutesHandler)
DATA_LOSS:   MsgTransit + (0 * 0)
CTL:         0 + (ActivePortsHandler + ActiveRoutesHandler)
```

By the second transformation step, these expressions are flattened into SOP (sum of products) form:

```
DATA_IN:     MsgTransit * ActivePortsHandler
DATA_OUT:    MsgTransit * ActivePortsHandler * ActiveRoutesHandler
DATA_LOSS:   MsgTransit
CTL:         ActivePortsHandler + ActiveRoutesHandler
```

Each gate-labelled SOP represents now the possible groupings of processes that support the events at that gate (see [14] for details).

Module *AlsNodeCO2* below represents an alternative, constraint-oriented specification of Al's Node in which the global *Next* action is formed by exactly the five disjuncts above (interpreting sum and product as disjunction and conjunction, respectively). Each disjunct refers to a specific event type, as identified by the different gates. Notice that we could make use of the same elementary actions used in module *AlsNodeCO1*, which is instantiated with name *CO1*.

─────────── MODULE *AlsNodeCO2* ───────────

EXTENDS *AlsNodeInterface, Naturals, FiniteSets*

VARIABLES

msg,	array of N messages in transit
ctl,	array of N control states
activePorts,	set of active ports
activeRoutes	the dynamic association route-port

$CO1 \triangleq$ INSTANCE *AlsNodeCO1*

$Init \triangleq CO1!Init$

$TypeInvariant \triangleq CO1!TypeInvariant$

$EventSubset(x) \triangleq CO1!EventSubset(x)$

$MsgTransit \triangleq$

$\qquad\qquad \lor CO1!MsgTransit\_In$
$\qquad\qquad \lor CO1!MsgTransit\_Out$
$\qquad\qquad \lor CO1!MsgTransit\_Loss$

$ActivePortsHandler \triangleq$

$\qquad\qquad \lor\quad CO1!ActivePortsHandler\_ControlIn$
$\qquad\qquad \lor\quad CO1!ActivePortsHandler\_DataIn$
$\qquad\qquad \lor\quad CO1!ActivePortsHandler\_DataOut$

$ActiveRoutesHandler \triangleq$

$\qquad\qquad \lor CO1!ActiveRoutesHandler\_ControlIn$
$\qquad\qquad \lor CO1!ActiveRoutesHandler\_DataOut$

$Next \triangleq$

$\qquad \lor \quad \land\ e' \in EventSubset(\text{"DATA\_IN"})$
$\qquad\qquad\quad \land\ MsgTransit$
$\qquad\qquad\quad \land\ ActivePortsHandler$
$\qquad\qquad\quad \land\ \text{UNCHANGED}\ activeRoutes$

$\qquad \lor \quad \land\ e' \in EventSubset(\text{"DATA\_OUT"})$
$\qquad\qquad\quad \land\ MsgTransit$
$\qquad\qquad\quad \land\ ActivePortsHandler$
$\qquad\qquad\quad \land\ ActiveRoutesHandler$

$\qquad \lor \quad \land\ e' \in EventSubset(\text{"DATA\_LOSS"})$
$\qquad\qquad\quad \land\ MsgTransit$
$\qquad\qquad\quad \land\ \text{UNCHANGED}\ activePorts$
$\qquad\qquad\quad \land\ \text{UNCHANGED}\ activeRoutes$

$\qquad \lor \quad \land\ \exists\, p \in Ports : e' = \langle\text{"CTL"}, p\rangle$
$\qquad\qquad\quad \land\ \text{UNCHANGED}\ \langle msg,\, ctl\rangle$
$\qquad\qquad\quad \land\ ActivePortsHandler$
$\qquad\qquad\quad \land\ \text{UNCHANGED}\ activeRoutes$

$\qquad \lor \quad \land\ \exists\, r \in Routes,\ p \in Ports : e' = \langle\text{"CTL"}, r, p\rangle$
$\qquad\qquad\quad \land\ \text{UNCHANGED}\ \langle msg,\, ctl\rangle$
$\qquad\qquad\quad \land\ \text{UNCHANGED}\ activePorts$
$\qquad\qquad\quad \land\ ActiveRoutesHandler$

$Spec \triangleq Init \land \Box[Next]_{\langle e,\, msg,\, ctl,\, activePorts,\, activeRoutes\rangle}$

$AlsNodeCO1Spec \triangleq CO1!Spec$

THEOREM $Spec \Rightarrow \Box\, TypeInvariant$
THEOREM $Spec \Rightarrow AlsNodeMonol!Spec$
THEOREM $Spec \Rightarrow AlsNodeCO1Spec$

Care should be taken in preventing uncontrolled behaviour of state variables that are not explicitly handled by a product of elementary actions. Thus, the disjuncts in the body of *Next*, derived from the SOP's, are enriched by UNCHANGED clauses that handle those excluded variables: in this way, each disjunct covers the complete global state.

4   Verification

Are the two constraint-oriented TLA+ specifications correct implementations of the more abstract, monolithic specification of Al's Node? In TLA, implementation is implication. Thus, let us start by verifying, using the TLC model checker, that the *Spec* in module *AlsNodeCO1* implies the *Spec* in module *AlsNodeMonol*. Recall that the latter is obtained from module *InternalAlsNodeMonol* by hiding all variables except the event variable *e*. The proof consists then in exhibiting a *refinement mapping* that relates the variables of *AlsNodeCO1* to those of *InternalAlsNodeMonol*. Module *MCAlsNodeCO1* below (MC stands for 'Model Checker') extends module *AlsNodeCO1* by adding the definition of the desired refinement mapping.

— MODULE *MCAlsNodeCO1* —

EXTENDS $Bags,\ AlsNodeCO1$

$omsgBag\ \triangleq$ a state function of $\langle ctl,\ msg \rangle$
   LET $f[k \in (0\,..\,N)]\ \triangleq$
      IF $k\ > 0$
         THEN
            IF $ctl[k] =$ "full"
               THEN $SetToBag(\{msg[k]\}) \oplus f[k-1]$
               ELSE $f[k-1]$
         ELSE $EmptyBag$
   IN $f[N]$

$AN\ \triangleq$ INSTANCE $InternalAlsNodeMonol$ WITH $msgBag \leftarrow omsgBag$

$ImplementationProperty\ \triangleq AN!Spec$

THEOREM $Spec \Rightarrow ImplementationProperty$

The theorem at the end of the module states that if the tuple of variables (e, msg, ctl, $activePorts$, $activeRoutes$) behaves as specified by the *Spec* in module *AlsNodeCO1*, then the tuple (e, $omsgBag$, $activePorts$, $activeRoutes$) behaves as specified by the *Spec* in module *InternalAlsNode*, with $omsgBag$ playing the role of $msgBag$. The refinement mapping provides 'witnesses' for the hidden variables $msgBag$, $activePorts$, $activeRoutes$ of the *Spec* in module *AlsNodeMonol*; in particular, the implementation handles exactly the same data structures *activePorts* and *activeRoutes* of the internal, abstract specification, so that the refinement mapping for them is just the identity function (see [7] for further discussion on refinement mappings, and on the way TLC supports these proofs). The module required for proving that also our second TLA+ constraint-oriented specification implements the initial, monolithic specification, is identical to the module above, except that the EXTENDS clause has to refer to *AlsNodeCO2*.

Although the two constraint-oriented specifications of Al's Node have been developed by following different intuitions, a closer comparison of the definitions of *MsgTransit*, *ActiveRoutesHandler*, *ActivePortsHandler*, and *Next* in the two modules suggests that they might be logically equivalent. Rather than manually rewriting one into the other, we run again TLC, and prove their equivalence by showing that they imply each other (note that they manipulate exactly the same state variables). The two relevant theorems appear at the bottom of modules *AlsNodeCO1* and *AlsNodeCO2*. (For convenience of exposition, the two modules we show end up instantiating each other; of course TLC cannot handle this circularity, and before running the tool, one has to edit them so that they refer to each other in turns.)

5   Conclusions

We have investigated the possibility to export what we consider an elegant, event-based specification style, based on constraint composition, to a state-based formalism such as TLA+. For doing so, we have introduced in our TLA+ specifications a special purpose, write-only variable, conventionally called e, which plays the role of LOTOS gates and events. When composing TLA+ actions by logical conjunction, this variable plays a crucial role in selecting the desired pairings of disjuncts, while filtering out the undesired ones.

The main advantage of using a process-algebraic formalism for writing specifications in constraint-oriented style is one of conciseness: the ad-hoc specialized operator of selective synchrony allows one to capture constraint composition by compact parallel composition expressions. Not surprisingly, using the more generic, logical conjunction operator generally leads to longer specifications. In particular, one has to split the specification effort between two complementary concerns: describing the changes of some variables, and making sure that other variables preserve their values. This feature, known as the 'frame problem', is shared by other logic-based formalisms, e.g. Z, while is completely absent in event-based formalisms.

However, moving to a state-based, and logic-based setting, while retaining event-oriented thinking, may offer some benefits:

- The formalism is more basic, more general, and can be learnt more easily.
- Specifications can be manipulated and transformed by simple and universally recognized laws of logics, rather than by specialized algebraic laws for behavioural operators.
- When events are assimilated to state variables, they inherit all the manipulation techniques available for the latter. For example, one can express different levels of visibility, for a given specification, by simultaneously hiding some components of the global state and some components of the event.

This last circumstance enables interesting expressive and analytical possibilities that we have only started to explore.

Acknowledgments

I express my gratitude to Leslie Lamport and Egon Boerger, for various stimulating discussions on the state-based vs. event-based diatribe.

References

[1] Hoare, T., He, J.: Unifying Theories of Programming. Prentice Hall (1998) 14
[2] Woodcock, J.C.P., Cavalcanti, A.L.C.: The semantics of Circus. In Bert, D., Bowen, J., Henson, M.C., Robinson, K., eds.: ZB 2002: Formal Specification and Development in Z and B, Springer-Verlag (2002) 184–203 Lecture Notes in Computer Science, 2272. 14
[3] Gurevich, Y.: Evolving Algebras 1993 - Lipari Guide. In Boerger, E., ed.: Specification and Validation Methods, Oxford Univ. Press (1995) 9–36 14
[4] Boerger, E., Staerk, R.: Abstract State Machines - A Method for High-Level System Design and Analysis. Springer (2003) 14
[5] Abrial, J.R.: The B-Book - Assigning Programs to Meanings. Cambridge Univ. Press (1996) 14
[6] Lamport, L.: The temporal logic of actions. ACM Transactions on Programming Languages and Systems 16 (1994) 872–923 14
[7] Lamport, L.: Specifying Systems - The TLA+ Language and Tools for Hardware and Software Engineers. Addison-Wesley (2003) 14, 23, 30
[8] Spivey, J.M.: The Z Notation - A Reference manual. Prentice-Hall (1989) 14
[9] Hoare, C.A.R.: Communicating Sequential Processes. Prentice-Hall (1985) 14
[10] Milner, R.: A Calculus of Communicating Systems. Volume 92 of Lecture Notes in Computer Science. Springer-Verlag (1980) 14
[11] Bolognesi, T., Brinksma, E.: Introduction to the ISO specification language LOTOS. Computer Networks and ISDN Systems 14 (1987) 25–59 14
[12] Brinksma, E.: ISO, Information Processing Systems, Open Systems Interconnection, LOTOS, a formal description technique based on the temporal ordering of observational behaviour - IS8807. Technical report, Geneva (1989) 14

[13] Quemada, J., Azcorra, A.: A constraint oriented specification of al's node. In van Eijk, P.H.J., Vissers, C.A., Diaz, M., eds.: The Formal Description Technique LOTOS, North-Holland (1989) 83–88   14

[14] Bolognesi, T.: Deriving graphical representations of process networks from algebraic expressions. Information Processing Letters **46** (1993) 289–294   27

Formal Description Techniques
and Software Engineering:
Some Reflections after 2 Decades of Research

Juan Quemada

Dept. of Telematic Engineering, Universidad Politécnica de Madrid
Ciudad Universitaria s/n, 28040, Madrid, Spain
jquemada@dit.upm.es
http://www.dit.upm.es/~quemada

Abstract. Software engineering is based today to a large extend on rapid prototyping languages or design environments which are high level, very expresive, executable and enabling the quick production of running prototypes, whereas formal methods emphasices the preciseness and proper mathematical foundations which eanble the production of unambiguous references needed in protocol engineering. The goals of formal methods and rapid prototyping are not in contradiction, but have very rarely been considered together. This paper analyzes the evolution, background and main divergence points, in order to highligh how convergence could be achieved.

1 Introduction

Mathematical models and techniques are at the core of many engineering disciplines and physical sciences. Those mathematical models usually define abstract views or properties of systems allowing a better understanding of the main parameters and elements. Traditionally, engineering disciplines have made use of mathematical models to highlight the relevant parameters of a given design problem, while hiding the irrelevant aspects to reduce the complexity of the design process.

Computer science and engineering differs from most engineering disciplines because it focusses in the design of digital systems which are discrete, as opposed to the analog nature of the systems addressed by most other engineering disciplines. Telecomunnication engineering dealt originally with analog radio or electrical signals, but the strong trend in last decades towards unification of information representation in digital multimedia formats has transformed most telecomunication systems into highly specialised computers for switching or processing some kind of multimedia information in digital format. For example telephone exchanges or packet routers. Therefore telecom engineering deals today also to a large extend with digital systems.

Digital systems are implemented directly as hardware systems when the complexity is low and the higher cost of the design is justified by large productions. But most digital system designs are implementated as software. Software based systems have usually a huge complexity and therefore research has focussed

D. de Frutos-Escrig and M. Núñez (Eds.): FORTE 2004, LNCS 3235, pp. 33-42, 2004.
© IFIP International Federation for Information Processing 2004

intensively during the last decades in methods and techniques able to cope with complexity.

Mathematical models of discrete systems have been used since the beginnings of computer science. Digital systems are modelled with various types of finite state machines, also called automata. But the huge number of states that most systems have, makes this model more a conceptual tool than a real engineering tool. Therefore automata were extended with standard programming variables to achieve a more understandable representation of large state spaces, leading to "extended automata" as a more powerfull mathematical model of discrete systems.

The programs of the first processors were coded directly in the machine language of the processor. The reference which defined the semantics of the machine language and the programs was the processor itself and there was not a need of a mathematical model of the processor for program designers.

High level languages, such as Fortran, Cobol, Pascal or C, appeared soon and provided mathematical abstractions of digital states in the form of variables and of program control in the form of high level program instructions. High level languages have a much higher expressive power than machine language and allow more productive and effective designs of programs. High level language programming is based on a set of software tools (compilers, debuggers, etc.) which allow execution of high level programs. High level languages have been also applied to the design of hardware systems.

High level languages created the need for new mathematical models, because tools for high level programming languages have to be implemented usually in many different processors and operating systems. Therefore a precise definition of the syntax and semantics of programming languages was needed, as a reference for compiler implementation, because all compilers should generate a code executing in the same way in each different processor or operating system.

There exists also a large community of more practmatic computer scientists that claim that the most effective way of defining semantics is having reference implementations. Reference implementations are implementations which have been extensively validated and agreed within a given community or committee to be the reference towards which correctness will be determined. Reference implementation are usually based on open software to facilitate product generation.

About two decades ago a big community of researchers and engineers started to apply mathematical modelling languages as a means to precisely define the semantics and behaviour of complete computer systems or parts of them, because they claimed that many problems of existing software or systems were due to the lack of a precise mathematical definition of the languages, procedures and tools used.

This community was especially important in computer networking [8], because network protocols are algorithms which have to be implemented in any machine to be connected to a network and mathematical models were considered the most precise way of specifying the protocols which should form the reference architecture of the standardized computer networks which were being designed at that time.

This community was named the "formal methods" or "formal techniques" community and had as it main objective the development of rigorous and precise mathematical techniques able to support the development of programs, computers systems, communication protocols, etc. The ultimate goal of this community was the development of a complete mathematical formalization of the software and systems design process, covering from the initial requirements specification phases to the final implementation of the running systems, which assured the correctness by construction of the implementation with respect to all the requirements and design decisions imposed during the development process.

To achieve this goal many new elements are needed such as, precise description languages, abstraction, stepwise refinement, correctness verification and validation techniques, transformation techniques, implementation generation techniques, testing tools and theories, etc. All this new developments should have a well defined mathematical semantics and should enable a new era of rigorous and fail save software and systems design.

The paper will focuss in the rest on the analysis of the achievements and failures and especially in the relation with techniques which have been accepted in industry for performing software engineering. The paper focusses also only in the use of formal methods in protocol engineering, communication networks and distributed applications, although many of the conclusions can be applied to a more general context.

2   Software Engineering and Formal Methods

Software engineering is the discipline concerned with creating and maintaining software applications by applying computer science, project management, domain knowledge, and other skills and technologies. Cost-effectivenes, product development lead-times, existance of proper design tools or environments and availability of trained people are mandatory issues for industry to accept new methods or tools.

Most protocol implementations are software developments and therefore, formal methods research should address industry priorities and should fully integrate into software engineering practices to be successfully incorporated. Lets analyze how formal methods and software engineering have evolved to try to understand better how formal methods research should be incorporated in software engineering practices.

Formal methods based processes rely on the vision that the main characteristics and features of a system can be specified in the first phase of the design process and that the rest of this design process refines this initial specification introducing design decisions which lead at the end of the process to a correct implementation which fulfills the initial requirements.

The design process may consist of more than one step, where each step takes as input a given partial definition of the system and generates a more complete definition of the system which should be proven correct with respect to the previous design steps, by some kind of mathematical correctness proof. In networking architectures the input specification is usually called the service and the implementation of the service is called the protocol.

This design model is very much in line with the waterfall model proposed in 1970 by W. Royce [1], which is considered somehow obsolete. It has been considered by several authors as the "dream of the western manager" because it would allow managers to precisely specify their objectives, strategies and requirements, which the rest of the organisation should just implement. Such a model would provide the project manager with an absolute amd rigorous control of the developments made.

During all those years of intensive research in formal methods, the software engineering community and industry has evolved and developed different approaches which have proven very effective, such as rapid prototyping, the spiral model, extreme programming, agile methods, etc [2, 3, 4], which have been widely accepted by industry.

Those methods are based on the vision that the main features of a complex system can not be properly understood in the first phases of the design process. Designers know at the beginning only the problem they have to solve.

The design process should be therefore an incremental learning and design process based on rapid prototyping. Early prototypes must be produced of the least understood parts, to gain a better understanding, as well as to obtain early user/customer feedback and allow testing.

As the "Manifesto for Agile Software Development" [3] states, the emphasis is put, in those approaches, much more on frequent software prototypes, adaptation to changes and direct interaction/collaboration among designers and/or customers, than on requiremments, planning or documentation.

In prototyping based software engineering approaches the emphasis is put on rapid prototyping languages or design environments which are high level, very expresive and executable, enabling the quick production of running prototypes, rather than in preciseness or proper mathematical foundations as formal methods emphasice.

The goals of formal methods and of rapid prototyping are not in contradiction, but have very rarely been considered together. The formal methods community should probably take into account the main trends of software engineering and try to provide solutions for the problems that software engineering has, rather than trying to develop a complete independent design framework.

2.1 Dealing with Complexity and Reusability of Software

Management of complexity has been one of the main challenges in software engineering. Abstraction is the main conceptual tool for dealing with complexity and most programming and specification languages include abstraction mechanisms such as, procedures as abstractions of operations, variables/records/structures as abstractions of state, objects as abstractions of program modules with clear usage interfaces, processes as abstractions of behaviour, etc.

There exist a large consensus that the object oriented model is the right abstraction mechanism in sequential programming languages, for building well structured programs, as well as reusable libraries of software components. On the process side there is not such a consensus and several models exist especially for interprocess communication.

Todays design and programming languages, as well as, software engineering tools have evolved to support the needs of both, software engineering practices and mangement of complexity. Nevertheless, the abstraction mechanisms supported in programing languages provide only syntactic support for the abstraction mechanisms.

Formal methods should have provided semantic support for abstractions and have produced interesting results in this direction, but the languages and mechanisms used do not fulfill the software engineering needs.

Providing support for semantic abstraction in a framework which is applicable in todays software engineering practices is one of the still unrealized main promises of formal methods.

3   Protocol Engineering and FDT Standards (Formal Description Techniques)

The advent of computer networking led to the proposal of protocol engineering as somehow different form software engineering [5, 6, 7, 8]. Protocol engineering considered the following vision and goals, especially within the community which considered that the use of formal methods was the only way of creating a rigorous engineering discipline.

- Protocol standards should be legal or defacto standards which provide an unambiguous reference for deriving implementations, as well as conformance test which could assess in practice the correctness of implementations with respect to the protocol standard.
- Protocols standards should be correct. As correctness can only be determined with respect to a given set of requirements, the service definition was considred the requirements to be met by a given protocol.

This vision and goals led to some specific challenges which have guided researchers in the formal protocol engineering community during the last two decades, such as

- Challenge 1. Development of a language for unambiguosly representing protocol standards: To achieve this challenge FTDs (Formal Description Techniques) should be developed and standardized to provide a unambigous means for describing protocol standards.
- Challenge 2. Protocol representations should be proven correct: To achieve this challenge each protocol should be accompanied by a service specification and a proof that states that the protocol is a correct implementation of the service. As there are some properties about correctness, such as deadlock or starvation absence, which are independent of the service specification an additional validation of such properties was required.
- Challenge 3. Protocols should also provide the best performance: To achieve this challenge automatic derivation of analytic or simulation models should be possible where protocol performance could be anlyzed and optimized.
- Challenge 4. Protocol representations should allow automatic derivation of correct protocol imlementations: To achieve this challenge automatic derivation of implementations using correctness preserving transformations were needed.
- Challenge 5. There should exist a procedure to verify or validate the correctness of protocol implementations: This procedure was assumed to be

based in conformance testing of implementations under test. To achieve this challenge automatic test suite derivation from the protocol description should be possible with sufficient coverage of the protocol behaviour and state space.

The first formal description technique was IBMs FAPL [5] which was used to deploy early IBM network architectures to a wide range of system, soon followed by other proposals. The advantages of having standardized FDT became clear soon. The first standardized FDT (or semi, becuase it was not fully formal at the beginning) was CCITTs SDL [6] which is based on an extended finite state machine model. SDL has been also the most successfull standardized FDT due to it's use for defining several CCITT/ITU standards, although the core of the software industry has not adapted it. The definition of the ISO-OSI reference model during the eighties and nineties led to the definition of two additional FDTs, which where competing with each other and with SDL as well. The first one was Estelle [6], which was based on an extended finite state machine model and standard Pascal data types. The second one was LOTOS [6], which was based on an algebraic calculus of processes and algebraic data types.

There were therefore 2 FDTs (SDL, ESTELLE) based on the less abstract "extended automata" model and one FDT (LOTOS) based on the more abstract mathematical theories of algebraic calculi of processes and algebraic data types. SDL and Estelle are much like programming languages and have more or less the same level of abstraction than C, Pascal, ADA or Java, although they were better suited for protocol representation. LOTOS on the other hand is more abstract, but it's main drawback for application in software engineering is the ACT ONE data definition language which has an algebraic semantics and is not executable. The behaviour part, based on a mixture of CCS [9] and CSP [10], was extremely powerfull and provided solutions for dealing with semantic abstraction which do not exist in todays design languages and tools. But the lack of executability of the data part made LOTOS difficult to apply.

Although protocols and network architectures have some minor distinguishing features with respect to other software developments, the mayority of the elements of the discipline are comon to software engineering and in my opinion, it would have been wiser to consider protocol engineering as a specialization of software engineering which inherits all it's elements and procedures. The design of the Internet was done following many of the software engineering principles explained before and its success was probably due to the higher effectiveness of rapid prototyping approach as compared to the more waterfall oriented approaches based on formal methods, which were used by standards organisations (ISO, CCITT/ITU) and the formal methods community.

4   Protocol Engineering and the Internet

The success of the Internet was due to many factors. The most important factor was probably the early availability of running implementations of the TCP/IP stack, as well as the availability of a large variety of applications. When ISO was starting work on developing FDTs, the Internet was already operational. Nevertheless, the development and of course the success of the Internet would not have been possible if the designers would not have provided effective solutions to the challenges of protocol engineering. The protocol engineering behind the Internet was not based in formal methods, but provided quite effective solutions which could align in many cases even with the agile software development manifesto.

The working procedures of the IETF, the Internet Engineering Task Force, where all Interent standards are produced since it was created in 1886, are close to the sofware engineering practices based on rapid prototyping described before. The working procedures of the IETF are also much more democratic than those of most standard organisations and have had a big impact in the way technology is produced today. The effectiveness of the procedures used for developing protocols and applications in the IETF led to the early availability of many running services, which had been properly tunned and adapted to users needs, even if many of the components used where not properly optimized. Lead times were more important than quality of the result.

The IETF promoted from the beginning the open participation of researchers into standardization committees, where participants could attend on a personal basis without any accreditation or fee as it is usually necessary in official standard bodies. IETF has also not avoided the existance of competing standards proposals, accepting only the proposals which were widely accepted by the user community. A standard was never accepted without two or more running implementations. Those implementations were used as references and were usually open software which could be used in the implementation of the standards on other machines. Those practices motivated a large community of researchers and developers to contribute to the production of the IETF standards.

The Internet designers dealt as follows with the challenges of protocol engineering

- Challenge 1. Development of a language for unambiguosly representing protocol standards: IETF standards are described as informal textual descriptions to facilitate the understandability. The use of ASCII text has been promoted to facilitate editing. Nevertheless, textual description of standards are complemented by reference implementations in C, Java, PERL, ..., which are the real references with which implementations must interwork.

- Challenge 2. Protocol representations should be proven correct: Correctness was substituted by rapid prototyping and user evaluation. Proposed standards had to have several running implementations interworking among them. User acceptance substituted proofs of correctness. This makes a lot of sense, because a correctness proof of a protocol implementation with respect to a service does not mean anything. The important issue is to have services which are accepted and usefull for users.

- Challenge 3. Protocols should also provide the best performance: Protocols were optimized using standard simulation techniques. Running prototypes provided also a lot of early feedback to improve the performance problems of the first versions of the standards.

- Challenge 4. Protocol representations should allow automatic derivation of correct protocol imlementations: Reference implementations did provide an effective way of deriving implementations, because most of them are based in open software. They were ported and easily recompiled in new machines.

Reference implementations were written in high level languages for which compilers existed in most machines such as C, Java, PERL, etc. Only the small part of the code which was hardware or O.S. dependant had to be rewritten.

- Challenge 5. There should exist a procedure to verify or validate the correctness of protocol implementations: Interworking of implementations substituted conformance testing. As most implementation were derived from the same reference implementation interworking was not difficult to achieve.

The solutions given to the challenges of protocol engineering were not very innovative, but were cost effective and ready to apply. Therefore innovation focussed in providing new services, new networking technologies or improved versions of the protocols. Most services were not optimized, but were providing a nice service, were running and were ready to deploy.

On the other hand, in the development of the ISO-OSI reference model and in CCITT/ITU FDTs were defined from scratch and as no agreement could be reached there were three FDTs competing. No tools were available at the beginning and a lot of time and research effort was necesary to have the first prototypes of the compilers and design environments ready. The first implementations of the protocols had to be therefore handcoded. In addition the ISO-OSI protocol stack had a lower performance than the Internet stack due to the fact that the protocols were first specified and then implemented. The design life-cycle was very in line with the waterfall model and did not assure a proper and well tunned result in time. When this was detected it was too late to produce a better version of the OSI protocols. There were many other causes for this delay, especially of political nature, but the use of a different methodological approach would have led very likely to a better technical result. The Internet had started deployment and as it was the only widely available working solution, it was adopted by industry despite of the big political support in favour of OSI.

5   Opportunities and Challenges for Formal Methods Today

Research in formal methods has not taken into account software engineering practices and methodologies as used in industry and therefore the results obtained are difficult to apply in real software developments. Software engineering practices need several features as mandatory, such as

- *Support for rapid prototyping.* The development of early prototypes plays a crucial role in todays systems design because it enables an early user or customer evaluation, which verification, validation or formal proof systems can not support by any means. Early prototyping allows to validate the usability, functionality or friendliness and enables early tuning or redisgn. Effective rapid prototyping languages must be executable and be very expressive:

  o *Executability.* Non executable mathematical modelling languages do not seem to have applicability in todays software engineering because they do not allow prototyping.
  o *Being high level.* Design languages must allow prototype development with a minimum effort and should have therefore powerfull instructions which

allow prototype implementation with a minimum number of instructions or statements.

- *Support reusability of classes and objects.* Design languages must facilitate reusability. As object oriented languages are considered as the ones which provide the best support for reusability, formal design languages should support object orientation.

- *Support for reusability of behaviour definitions.* The behaviour or process part of the existing design languages needs probably still substantial research, because no consensus exist about the best formalism. Algebraic calculi of process theory has provided executable process models with very high expressive power and nice abstraction features, although integration into conventional design languages should be done.

- *Support for semantic abstractions.* Design languages for complex systems need to have some kind of semantic abstractions which allow to decompose the design process into a sequence of understandable steps. Most design languages provide some support, but without providing a formal semantics, where abstraction mechanisms just perform syntax matching of interfaces. This is probably one of the places where formal methods can provide better design methods. For example the hiding operation of CCS [9] and LOTOS [6] is a very powerfull abstraction mechanism. The testing or conformance relations [11, 12] of CCS and LOTOS are formal notions of implementation which can be integrated quite smothly into software engineering practices.

Protocol implementations are like other hardware or software implementations and therefore protocol engineering should fully align with software engineering practices. The need for a more formal approach to systems and application design still exists, but must not ignore all the pragmatic lessons learned in large software developments in industry.

Formal methods researchers should try to develop design languages with support for rapid prototyping, with a high expresive power and also with support for semantic abstractions for classes and behaviours. This would allow a much smoother design process by stepwise refinement where, instead of having the usual sequence of non executable formal descriptions, a sequence of executable prototypes would be generated, where each prototype can be proven as a correct implementation of the previous one, but which can also be evaluated and validated by users/customers.

The LOTOS formal description technique [6] got very near to this approach at the behaviour part, providing semantic abstraction mechanisms which do not exist in the design languages used today in software engineering. But the algebraic data part made it unusable for software engineering. A language based on the LOTOS behaviour part and a conventional executable data typing would have been a very powerfull design language at that time. Some industrial trials performed in the nineties validated this approach [13]. It was a pitty that this opportunity was missed.

An expressive and executable language providing formal support to design by stepwise refinement can enhance todays state of the art. This language should incorporate all the features which today are mandatory in software engineering such as, object orientation or module and interface constructs, and of course should support semantic abstractions for objects and behaviour in a way which can be easily mapped in todays engineering practices.

There exist opportunities for using formal methods research results to enrich existing design languages and methodologies. For example: The new Web architectural framework with all the new XML based languages and tools; or to enhance well accepted design languages such as Java of C#.

References

[1]   Royce, W.W., Managing the Development of Large-Scale Software: Concepts and Techniques Proceedings, Wescon, August 1970.

[2]   Zave, P., The Operational versus the Conventional Approach to Software Development, Com. Of the ACM, 27 (2), 1984, pp.104-118.

[3]   Boehm, B.W., Anchoring the Software Process, IEEE Software, July 1996, pp.73-82.

[4]   Agile Processes, http://www.c2.com/cgi/wiki?AgileProcesses.

[5]   Schultz, G.D., Rose, D.B., West, C.H., Gray, J.P. Executable Description and Validation of SNA, IEEE Transactions on Communications, April 1980, pp. 661-677.

[6]   Turner, K. J. (Editor), Using Formal Description Techniques, An Introduction to Estelle, LOTOS and SDL, John Wiley and Sons, 1993, ISBN 0-471-93455-0.

[7]   Bowman, H., Derrick, J., Formal Methods for Distributed Processing: A Survey of Object Oriented Approaches, Cambridge University Press, 2001, ISBN 0-521-77184-6.

[8]   Special issue on Protocol Engineering, IEEE Transactions on Computers, Volume 40 , Issue 4 , April 1991.

[9]   Milner, R., A Calculus of Communicating Systems, Lecture Notes in Computer Science 92, Springer-Verlag 1980.

[10]   Hoare, C. A. R., Communicating Sequential Processes, Prentice Hall International, Englewood Cliffs, New Jersey, 1985.

[11]   De Nicola, R., Hennesy, M., Testing Equivalences for Processes, Theoretical Computer Science, 34:83-133, 1984.

[12]   Brinksma, E., Scollo, P., Formal Notions of Implementation and Conformance in LOTOS.

[13]   Fernandez, A., Miguel, C., Vidaller, L., Quemada, J., Development of a Satellite Communication Network Based on LOTOS, IFIP Transactions C-8: Protocol Specification, Testing and Verification XII, pp. 179-193, North-Holland, June 1992, ISSN 0926-549X.

Parameterized Models
for Distributed Java Objects

Tomás Barros, Rabéa Boulifa, and Eric Madelaine

INRIA Sophia-Antipolis
{tomas.barros,rabea.boulifa,eric.madelaine}@sophia.inria.fr

Abstract. Distributed Java applications use remote method invocation as a communication means between distributed objects. The ProActive library provides high level primitives and strong semantic guarantees for programming Java applications with distributed, mobile, secured components. We present a method for building finite, parameterized models capturing the behavioural semantics of ProActive objects. Our models are symbolic networks of labelled transition systems, whose labels represent (abstractions of) remote method calls. In contrast to the usual finite models, they encode naturally and finitely a large class of distributed object-oriented applications. Their finite instantiations can be used in classical model-checkers and equivalence-checkers for checking temporal logic properties in a compositional manner. We are building a software tool set for the analysis of ProActive applications using these methods.

1 Introduction

We aim at developing methods for the analysis and verification of behavioural properties of distributed applications, that would be applicable in automatic tools, on a real language. At the heart of such tools lie sophisticated static analysis techniques, and abstraction principles, that enable the generation of finitary models of the behaviour from the source code of the application. A good candidate as a behavioural model would be a process algebra with at least value-passing features, or even encoding dynamic process and channel creation and reconfiguration. Still, despite the very important development in the last 20 years of value-passing and high-order process theories, most of them are just too expressive to be subject to decision procedures, and would not give us models and algorithms usable in practical tools.

At the same time, a number of analysis tools, model-checkers, equivalence checkers have been developed, using input formats, in their respective areas; that have some of the desired features for our work. For example the Promela language, input of the SPIN model-checker, can describe value-passing processes and channels with data values of simple types or the NTIF format [1] that encodes the sophisticated communication between E-LOTOS processes. However, few of them include compositional structures that would allow to take advantage of the congruence properties of process algebra models. Outside the value-passing area, it is worth citing the seminal work by Arnold [2], and the MEC language

D. de Frutos-Escrig and M. Núñez (Eds.): FORTE 2004, LNCS 3235, pp. 43–60, 2004.
© IFIP International Federation for Information Processing 2004

and analysis tool, that permits a direct and finite representation of the synchronisation constraint between processes.

Our approach aims at combining the value-passing and the synchronisation product approaches. We define a model featuring parameterized processes, value-passing communication, behaviours expressed as symbolic labelled transition systems, and data-values of simple countable types. We have developed a graphical language close to this model, that is powerful and natural enough to serve as a specification language for distributed applications [3]. We argue that the same model is adequate as the target for automatic model generation for distributed applications. As an illustration of the approach, we define the generation procedure [4] for the Java/ProActive framework. One key feature is that the design of the model ensures that it can be automatically and finitely produced from an "abstract" version of the application code, in which data have been abstracted to simple types. Then, given a finite instantiation of the variables in the model, we have an automatic procedure producing a (hierarchical) finite instantiation of the model, suitable for use e.g. in a standard model-checker.

Our method can be applied in the following way: starting with the source code of a real application, the developer would specify an abstraction of its data-types, and transform his code accordingly. The work in the Bandera tool set [5] shows how this step can be largely assisted by the tool. At this level, the design of the abstraction can be tuned specifically to the properties one wishes to verify, in order to reduce the size of the generated models. From this abstract code, static analysis techniques, plus our model generation procedure, produces automatically a parameterized network. Then the developer, for each property he wants to prove, will produce a finite network, using a notion of instantiation that is again an abstract interpretation in the style of [6], before checking the property (or its corresponding instantiation) with a model-checker. The instantiation could even be performed on-the-fly, if the checker offers this possibility. The properties can be themselves specified as parameterized scenarios in our graphical language, or as parameterized formulas in a temporal logics.

In section 2, we define parameterized labelled transition systems and synchronisation networks, their instantiations to pure LTS and networks, and the corresponding synchronisation product. Then we sketch a generic way of defining finite instantiations as abstract interpretations of the parameterized models. In section 3, we specialise this model for representing the behaviours of Java distributed applications built using the ProActive framework, and give an algorithm for computing the models from static analysis of the code. In section 4, we give an example of model generated for a small ProActive application. Finally, we conclude about our work and future research directions.

2   Parameterized Models

We give the behavioural semantics of programs in terms of labelled transition systems. We specify the composition of LTSs by synchronisation networks [2], and give their semantics in term of a synchronisation product.

2.1   Theoretical Model

We start with an unspecified set of communications **Actions** *Act*, that will be refined later.

We model the behaviour of a process as a Labelled Transition System (LTS) in a classical way [7]. The LTS transitions encode the actions that a process can perform in a given state.

Definition 1 LTS. *A labelled transition system is a tuple* $(S, s_0, L, \rightarrow)$ *where* S *is the set of states,* $s_0 \in S$ *is the initial state,* $L \subseteq Act$ *is the set of labels,* $\rightarrow$ *is the set of transitions:* $\rightarrow \subseteq S \times L \times S$. *We write* $s \xrightarrow{\alpha} s'$ *for* $(s, \alpha, s') \in \rightarrow$.

Then we define **Nets** in a form inspired by [2], that are used to synchronise a finite number of processes. A Net is a form of generalised parallel operator, and each of its arguments are typed by a **Sort** that is the set of its possible observable actions.

Definition 2 Sort. *A Sort is a set* $I \subseteq Act$ *of actions.*

A LTS $(S, s_0, L, \rightarrow)$ can be used as an argument in a Net only if it agrees with the corresponding Sort $(L \subseteq I_i)$. In this respect, a Sort characterises a family of LTSs which satisfy this inclusion condition.

Nets describe dynamic configurations of processes, in which the possible synchronisations change with the state of the Net. They are Transducers, in a sense similar to the open Lotos expressions of [8]. They are encoded as LTSs which labels are synchronisation vectors, each describing one particular synchronisation of the process actions:

Definition 3 Net. *A Net is a tuple* $< A_G, I, T >$ *where* A_G *is a set of global actions,* I *is a finite set of Sorts* $I = \{I_i\}_{i=1,\ldots,n}$, *and* T *(the transducer) is a LTS* $(T_T, s_{0_t}, L_T, \rightarrow_T)$, *such that* $\forall \vec{v} \in L_T$, $\vec{v} = < l_t, \alpha_1, \ldots, \alpha_n >$ *where* $l_t \in A_G$ *and* $\forall i \in [1, n], \alpha_i \in I_i \cup \{idle\}$.

We say that a Net is *static* when its transducer vector contains only one state. Note that a synchronisation vector can define a synchronisation between one, two or more actions from different arguments of the Net. When the synchronisation vector involves only one argument, its action can occur freely.

The semantics of the Net construct is given by the synchronisation product:

Definition 4 Synchronisation Product. *Given a set of LTS* $\{LTS_i = (S_i, s_{0_i}, L_i, \rightarrow_i)\}_{i=1\ldots n}$ *and a Net* $< A_G, \{I_i\}_{i=1\ldots n}, (S_T, s_{0_T}, L_T, \rightarrow_T) >$, *such that* $\forall i \in [1, n], L_i \subseteq I_i$, *we construct the product LTS* $(S, s_0, L, \rightarrow)$ *where* $S = S_T \times \prod_{i=1}^{n}(S_i)$, $s_0 = s_{0_T} \times \prod_{i=1}^{n}(s_{0_i})$, $L = A_G$, *and the transition relation is defined as:*

$$\rightarrow \stackrel{def}{=} \{s \xrightarrow{l_t} s' \mid s = < s_t, s_1, \ldots, s_n >, s' = < s'_t, s'_1, \ldots, s'_n >,$$
$$\exists s_t \xrightarrow{\vec{v}} s'_t \in \rightarrow_T, \vec{v} = < l_t, \alpha_1, \ldots, \alpha_n >, \forall i \in [1, n], (\alpha_i \neq idle \wedge s_i \xrightarrow{\alpha_i} s'_i \in \rightarrow_i$$
$$) \vee (\alpha_i = idle \wedge s_i = s'_i)$$

Note that the result of the product is a LTS, which in turn can be synchronised with other LTSs in a Net. This property enables us to have different levels of synchronisations, i.e. a hierarchical definition for a system.

Next, we introduce our parameterized systems which are an extension from the above definitions to include parameters. These definitions are connected to the semantics of Symbolic Transition Graph with Assignment (STGA) [9].

Parameterized Actions have a rich structure, for they take care of value passing in the communication actions, of assignment of state variables, and of process parameters. In order to be able to define variable instantiation as an *abstraction* of the data domains (in the style of [6]), we restrict these domains to be **simple (countable) types**, namely: booleans, enumerated sets, integers or intervals over integers and finite records, arrays of simple types.

Definition 5 Parameterized Actions *are:* τ *the non-observable action,* $\mathcal{M}$ *encoding an observable local sequential program (with assignment of variables),* $?m(P, \overline{x})$ *encoding the reception of a call to the method* m *from the process* P *(* $\overline{x}$ *will be affected by the arguments of the call) and* $!P.m(\overline{e})$ *encoding a call to the method* m *of a remote process* P *with arguments* $\overline{e}$.

A parameterized LTS is a LTS with parameterized actions, with a set of parameters (defining a family of similar LTSs) and variables attached to each state. Parameters and variables types are simple. Additionally, the transitions can be guarded and have a resulting expression which assigns the variables associated to the target state:

Definition 6 pLTS. *A parameterized labelled transition system is a tuple* $pLTS = (K, S, s_0, L, \rightarrow)$ *where:*
$K = \{k_i\}$ *is a finite set of parameters,*
S *is the set of states, and each state* $s \in S$ *is associated with a finite set of variables* $\overrightarrow{v_s}$,
$s_0 \in S$ *is the initial state,*
$L = (b, \alpha(\overrightarrow{x}), \overrightarrow{e})$ *is the set of labels (parameterized actions), where* b *is a boolean expression,* $\alpha(\overrightarrow{x})$ *is a parameterized action, and* $\overrightarrow{e}$ *is a finite set of expressions.*
$\rightarrow \; \subseteq S \times L \times S$ *is the set of transitions:*

Definition 7 Parameterized Sort. *A Parameterized Sort is a set* pI *of parameterized actions.*

Definition 8 *A* **pNet** *is a tuple* $< pA_G, H, T >$ *where:* pA_G *is the set of global parameterized actions,* $H = \{pI_i, K_i\}_{i=1..n}$ *is a finite set of holes (arguments). The transducer* T *is a pLTS* $(K_G, S_T, s_{0_T}, L_T, \rightarrow_T)$, *such that* $\forall \overrightarrow{v} \in L_T, \overrightarrow{v} = < l_t, \alpha_1^{k_1}, \ldots, \alpha_n^{k_n} >$ *where* $l_t \in pA_G$, $\alpha_i \in pI_i \cup \{idle\}$ *and* $k_i \in K_i$.

The K_G of the transducer is the set of global parameters of the pNet. Each hole in the pNet has a sort constraint pI_i and a parameter set K_i, expressing that

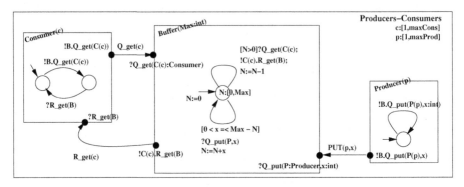

Fig. 1. Graphical representation of parameterized networks

this "parameterized hole" corresponds to as many actual arguments as necessary in a given instantiation. In a synchronisation vector $\overrightarrow{v} =< l_t, \alpha_1^{k_1}, \ldots, \alpha_n^{k_n} >$, each $\alpha_i^{k_i}$ corresponds to the α_i action of the k_i-nth corresponding argument LTS.

In the framework of this paper, we do not want to give a more precise definition of the language of parameterized actions, and we shall not try to give a direct definition of the synchronisation product of pNets/pLTSs. Instead, we shall instantiate separately a pNet and its argument pLTSs (abstracting the domains of their parameters and variables to finite domains, before instantiating for all possible values of those abstract domains), then use the non-parameterized synchronisation product (Definition 4). This is known as the early approach to value-passing systems [7, 10].

2.2 Graphical Language

We provide a graphical syntax for representing *static* Parameterized Networks, that is a compromise between expressiveness and user-friendliness. We use a graphical syntax similar to the Autograph editor [11], augmented by elements for parameters and variables: a *pLTS* is drawn as a set of circles representing states and edges representing transitions, where the states are labelled with their set of variables $(\overrightarrow{v_s})$ and the edges are labelled by $[b] \ \alpha(\overrightarrow{x}) \rightarrow \overrightarrow{e}$ (see Definition 6).

An *static pNet* is represented by a set of boxes, each one encoding a particular Sort of the pNet. These boxes can be filled with a pLTS satisfying the Sort inclusion condition. Each box has ports on the border, represented by bullets, each one encoding a particular parameterized action of the Sort.

Fig. 1 shows an example of such a parameterized system. It is a simple consumer-producer system with a single buffer and an arbitrary number of consumers and producers. In Fig. 1, the right-most link is a communication name **Q_put** from process **Producer(p)** to the buffer **B**, carrying a value **x:int** that the developer has chosen to observe as the event **PUT(p,x)**.

The edges between ports in Figure 1 are called links. Links express synchronisation between internal boxes or to external processes. Each link encodes a transition in the Transducer LTS of the *pNet*.

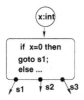 The sequential code encoding the control and data-flow within a process is carried by macro-transitions, with multiple output states. We restrict them to sequential programs without communication events. This way, we avoid duplicating code in sequential transitions and at the same time avoid the extra interleaving that would be created by macro-transitions containing visible events.

We have used this language extensively in [3] to specify and verify a large distributed system from a realistic case study.

2.3   Instantiations as Abstractions

From a parameterized network, we want to construct abstract models, with parameters in abstract domains simpler than the original (concrete) domains. Ultimately the parameter domains should be finite, allowing us to use standard model-checking tools on the abstract model. And we want this abstraction to be consistent, in the sense that some families of properties (typically reachability) are preserved by the abstraction. Thus from the reachability of some abstract event in the abstract domain, we can conclude to the reachability of some concrete representative of this event in the original model.

In a slightly different settings, [6] have shown how to define abstractions on value domains, in such a way that they induce safe abstractions on value-passing processes (preserving safety and liveness properties). We shall use a similar construction to define instantiations as safe abstractions of our simple data types: an instantiation is a partition (a total subjection) from a simple data type onto an abstract domain; lifting the instantiation to sets of values yields a Galois connection.

3   Application: Models for Distributed Active Objects

We now specialise our parameterized models, for representing the behaviour of distributed applications. We choose a specific framework providing high-level distribution and communication primitives for distributed objects, namely the ProActive library. ProActive is also endowed with a formal semantics, and the library services provide strong guarantees on the communication mechanism, that helps a lot in defining our model generation method.

It should be clear that our parameterized models could also be used for other languages or other frameworks. However, providing a similar work for languages with weaker semantical properties (like Java with standard RMI, or C with basic sockets) would definitely be more difficult, and the various properties of our approach (finiteness, abstraction, compositionality) would not be guaranteed.

3.1   Java and ProActive

ProActive [12] is a pure Java implementation of distributed active objects with asynchronous remote method calls and replies by means of future references. A distributed application built using PROACTIVE is composed of a quantity of active objects (or activities), each one having a distinguished entry point, the *root*, accessible from anywhere. All the other members of an active object (they are called *passive objects*) can not be referenced directly from outside. Each active object owns its own and unique thread of control and the programmer decides the order to serve (or not) incoming calls to its methods. Each active object has a pending queue where are dropped the incoming requests to be served by the control thread. The requests are done via a *rendez-vous* phase so there is a guaranty of delivery and a conservation of the order of incoming calls. The responses (when relevant) are always asynchronous with replies by means of future references; their synchronisation is done by a mechanism of *wait-by-necessity*.

ProActive provides primitives to dynamically create and migrate active objects. Dynamic creation is naturally represented in our parameterized models. Migration is not treated in this work: the semantics of *ProActive* ensures transparent active object migration and remote creation.

3.2   Data Abstraction

The aim in this work is to generate parameterized models encoding the behaviour of ProActive distributed objects. The events that we want to observe in these models are naturally the communication between activities, plus eventually specific local events that the user will specify.

Being interested in automatic procedure for generating finitely representations of the behaviours, and working with a real language, we have a problem with the representation of potentially infinite data objects (including user-defined classes). So we require that the source code be first transformed by abstraction of the data-types of the application into the "simple types" of our model.

This transformation cannot be fully automatic, and it will require some input from the user to specify the abstraction of all types in the code (Fig. 2). Furthermore, it will be interesting at this step to abstract away from any data information that would not be significant for the properties that the user wants to prove. It has been shown, e.g. in the Bandera tool [5], how such data abstraction can be implemented as code transformation, either at source code or intermediate code level.

3.3   Code Analysis

The generation of our behavioural models from the source code requires sophisticated analysis, starting with usual static analysis functions. Class analysis determines the possible class(es) of each variable in the program, and the possible

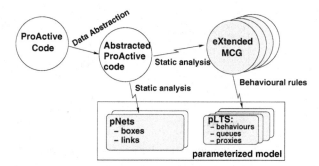

Fig. 2. Building models of distributed active objects

identiti(es) of the method called at each invocation point. Then we use Control Flow analysis to compute the Method Call Graph, and Data Flow analysis to track the values of parameters. The adaptation of these methods to ProActive code are not trivial, in particular because the proxy mechanism of the library include a lot of dynamic code generation, and we must emulate its effects during static analysis.

Language restrictions: For the sake of this paper, we shall not consider the treatment of exceptions and arrays. Other aspects, such as Java concurrency features (threads, monitors), reflection and dynamic class loading, will not be allowed. These features are important indeed in the implementation of the library, but are not needed for the library user.

The rest of this section describes the steps of the model construction. Starting from the Abstract ProActive code, we build a (static and finite) network description, an eXtended Method Call Graph (XMCG) for each active object class, a local pNet for each activity, and finally a pLTS for each method.

3.4   Step 1: Topology and Communication, Extraction of the Global Network

Static Topology: In general the topology of a distributed ProActive application is dynamic and unbounded, because active objects can be created dynamically. We compute a static approximation of this topology, in the form of a parameterized network based on: the (finite) set of active object classes, the (finite) set of active object creation points, and the (finite) set of program points where an active object emits a remote request.

Boxes: Given a set of active object classes, a set of creation points, we obtain a set of (parameterized) active objects $\{O_i\}$. For each active object creation point, we build a Box $B(O_i(params))$.

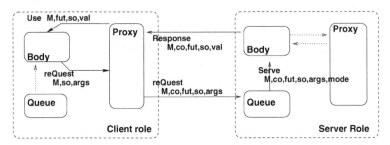

Fig. 3. Communication between two activities

Communication Protocol: Fig. 3 illustrates the communication corresponding to a request addressed to a remote activity, its processing and the return of its result. A method call to a remote activity goes through a proxy, that locally creates a "future" object, while the request goes to the remote request queue. The request arguments include the references to the caller and callee objects, but also to the future. It also contains a deep copy of the method's arguments, because there is no sharing between remote activities. Later, the request may eventually be served, and its result value will be sent back and used to update the future value.

Building the Communication Links: In the following we denote m a message containing: the (fully qualified) method name, references to the caller, future, callee (parameterized) objects, and either the parameters or the return value of the message.

For each active object class, we analyse the relevant source code to compute its ports and the corresponding links:

1. The set of public methods of the active object main class gives us the set of "receive request" ports $?Q\_m$ of its box, and their response ports (when applicable) $!o.R\_m$.
2. We then identify in the code the variables carrying "active objects" values, using data flow analysis techniques, and taking into account their creation parameters.
3. For each call to a method of a remote object, we add a "send request" port $!o.Q\_m$ to the current box, linked to the corresponding port of the remote object box, and if this method expects a result, a "response" port $?R\_m$.
4. For each local event that we want to observe (e.g. some local method call), we add a "local" port $Call\_m$ to the current box.
5. For each pair of opposite actions such as $?Q\_m$ - $!o.Q\_m$, we build a link (in this case labelled Q_m).

Fig. 4 gives an example of such a pNet, computed from the ProActive code presented in section 4.

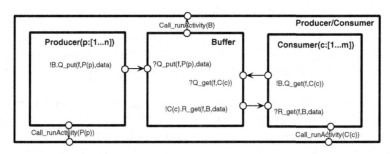

Fig. 4. Producers/Consumers: global network

3.5   Step 2: eXtended Call Graphs

For each active object class, we define an eXtended Method Call Graph (XMCG) structure containing the results of usual class and control flow analysis (on all classes used by this activity), sequential code encoding the data-flow, and specific constructs relative to the ProActive features namely: active objects, future objects, remote requests and responses, mechanism for the selection of requests in a request queue.

An Extended Method Call Graph is a tuple: $\left\langle M, m_0, V, \xrightarrow{calls}_C, \xrightarrow{succs}_T \right\rangle$ where M is a set of fully qualified methods names, $m_0 \in M$ is the initial method name, V is a set of nodes, and the two transition relations are respectively the inter-procedural (method calls) and intra-procedural (sequential control) transfer relations.

The nodes in V are typed as:

- *ent* $(c, m, args)$ the entry node of method $m \in M$, called by object c,
- *call* $(calls)$ encoding method calls (local or remote),
- *pp* (lab) encoding an arbitrary program point with label lab,
- *ret* (val) encoding the return node of a method with result value val,
- *serve* $(calls, mset, pred, mode)$ encoding the selection of the request $m \in mset$ from the local request queue,
- *use* (fut, val) encoding the point of utilisation of a future value.

All nodes have at most one outgoing transfer edge $< succs(n) = MT, N >$, with $< n, MT, N > \in \xrightarrow{succs}_T$ in which the meta-transition MT is a sequential program with a non-empty set of resulting states N.

Call and Serve nodes have a set of nondeterministic outgoing method call edges, $calls(n)$, with $\forall c$ in $calls(n), \exists n'. < n, c, n' > \in \xrightarrow{calls}_C$, each call being either:

- *Remote* $(o.m, args, var, fut)$ for a call to method m of a remote object o through the proxy fut,
- *Local* $(o.m, args, var)$ for a call to method m of a local object o,
- *Unknown* $(o.m, args, var, fut)$ when it cannot be decided statically whether the call is local or remote.

3.6   Step 3: A pNet for the Behaviour of Each Active Object Class

An activity is composed of a body (itself decomposed as we shall see later), a model of its queue, and a model of the proxies (future objects) for each remote method call in its code. The activity model is a pNet synchronising these 3 parts.

Methods structure The essential choice for modelling the behaviour of programs is to get a finite, parameterized representation that take into account the parameters of recursive methods, and the representation of objects in the store. We give the rational for these two points, before describing the procedure for building the model of an activity behaviour.

We choose here to consider each method as a parameterized process, method calls being local synchronisation between specific instantiations of the processes. This simple scheme trivially ensures that we get a finite parameterized network. For each method call and for each return from a call, we generate in the activity pNet a synchronisation event between the 2 processes involved.

Objects and Stores There is one common store for each activity. Each object creation point in the code corresponds to a number of objects in the store. If the static analysis can determine precisely this number, we shall use it, otherwise, we index the object by an integer denoting its creation rank.

Queues The request queue of an active object runs independently of its body, and is always accepting arriving requests (of correct type) encoded by Q_m actions. It is synchronised with the object body through the services (S_m) actions produced by rule DO-SERVE.

There are several primitives for selecting requests from the queue. The most frequent way to filter the requests is by the request name, but the programmer

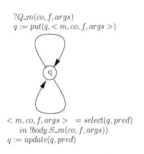

$?Q\_m(co, f, args)$
$q := put(q, < m, co, f, args >)$

$< m, co, f, args > \quad = select(q, pred)$
    $in \; !body.S\_m(co, f, args))$
$q := update(q, pred)$

can also build more complex selection filters, using the request arguments and/or the sender identity. He can also decide to serve the requests in various order or to do some global treatment on the queue after selection e.g.: *serve Oldest* (foo), *serve Oldest* $(foo(i), i < 10)$, *serve Newest* (foo, bar) or *serve flushNewest* $(Move(x, y))$.

The various primitives used in a given active object define statically a finite partition of the requests domain. We also collect all selection/operation modes used in the active object code, within: $Modes = \{serve, serveAndFlush\} \times \{Oldest, Newest, Nth\}$.

The idea is that we can now model the queue as a product of independent processes, each encoding one set in the partition, and implementing the relevant operation modes. The model for each part is built in a generic way, as an instantiation of the figure above, in which $m, args, pred$ must be replaced by the corresponding possible values.

The most beneficial optimisation comes from the factorisation in separate queues, and is computed from static analysis by collecting all service primitives used in a specific active object.

Those queues will be coordinated by the automaton encoding the activity behaviour. The benefits come from the fact that we avoid to compute this interleaved product independently from its context.

3.7   Step 4: A Model for the Activity Behaviour

The procedure for building the model of a (parameterized) activity is:

1. Compute the set of required static object classes, the XMCG, and the set of object instances in the store (static object creation points with their parameters).
2. Build the activity pNet, with one box for each method in the XMCG, and one-to-one links for method calls. The activity behaviour is functional, because there is a single thread of execution in the activity; this means that only one of those boxes has an initial transition that can be fired alone while others will have to wait to be called.
3. For each method m in the activity, use the Procedure Method-Behav (m, n, XMCG), where n is the entry node of m in the XMCG, to compute the corresponding parameterized LTS.

```
1    Method-Behav (m, n, < M, V, --calls-->C, --succs-->T>) :
2      Aut.init = {fresh s₀}; Map = ∅; Caller = ∅; ToDo = {< n, s₀ >}
3      while ToDo ≠ ∅
4        ToDo.choose < n, s >
5        if Map(n) then DO-LOOP-JOIN
6        else
7          select~n in
8            Ent(c,m,args)                        : DO-ENTRY
9            Call(calls(n))                       : DO-CALL
10           PP(lab)                              : DO-PP
11           Serve(calls(n),mset,pred,mode)       : DO-SERVE
12           Use(fut,val)                         : DO-FUTURE
13           Ret(val)                             : DO-RETURN
14         unless~n=Ret
15           let MT, N = succs(n) in
16           foreach~nᵢ in~N do
17             fresh~sᵢ; ToDo.Add < nᵢ, sᵢ >
18           Aut.add~s₁  --MT-->  S = {sᵢ}ᵢ
```

The ToDo set collects all pending MCG nodes, that need to be processed later, with the corresponding LTS node. Map is the mapping between nodes of the XMCG, and the corresponding nodes in the created LTS. For all nodes, MT is a meta-transition encoding the sequential intra-procedural flow. It carries a piece of sequential program (possibly empty) and has a number (≥ 1) of target nodes $\mathcal{N}$, from which we create an equal number of LTS nodes $\mathcal{S}$. The s_1 LTS node in line 18 is the terminal node created by each of the specific DO-* procedures (joining all branches created by the procedure when necessary).

Each of the following node-specific procedures sets the s_1 for branching the subsequent transitions, and updates the mapping Map.

Initialisation : The *Caller* object is memorised and will be used by the return nodes.

```
DO-ENTRY (c, m, args) =
    fresh s₁; Caller =˜c, Map  =  Map ∪ {n ↦  s₁}
              ?Call_m(c,args)
    Aut.add s  ───────────────→  s₁
```

Sequential nodes : PP nodes in the XMCG correspond to program points, e.g. a label in the source code corresponding to a loop or a join in the program structure, or a specific passage point that the user has designated. This event can be made visible in the LTS if we need it for a given proof.

```
DO-PP (lab) =
                                    Obs(lab)
    if observable(lab) then Aut.add s ───────→ (fresh s₁), Map  =  Map ∪ {n ↦  s₁}
    else˜s₁ =˜s
```

Call nodes : A call node has one or more call transitions, each of them can be remote or local, and each of them have an optional [Mix] guard, meaning that its true (remote or local) nature will only be determined at instantiation time.

```
DO-CALL (calls(n)) =
    fresh˜s₁, Map  =  Map ∪ {n ↦  s₁}
    foreach call in calls(n)
      match call with
                                            !fut.Q_m(o,args)
        "Remote(o.m,args,var,fut)":  Aut.add s ────────────────→  s₁
                                            !o.Call_m(args)
        "Local(o.m,args,var)":       Aut.add s ────────────────→ (fresh s₂)
                                            [Mix]!fut.Q_m(o,args)
        "Unknown(o.m,args,var,fut)": Aut.add s ────────────────→  s₁
                                            [Mix]!o.Call_m(args)
                                     Aut.add s ────────────────→ (fresh s₂)
    if local-or-unknown ∩ non-void-result(m) then
                      ?Ret_m(o,val)                   var:= val
      Aut.add˜s₂ ────────────────→ (fresh s₃) ────────────────→ s₁
```

Return nodes : Return nodes are not marked in the node mapping: each return node of a method is treated separately, and generates its own !Ret action. The return value *val* is absent for void-result methods.

```
DO-RETURN (val) =
              !Caller.Ret_m(val)
    Aut.add s ────────────────→ (fresh s₁)
```

Request Service nodes : Serving a request from the local queue is similar to calling a method, but we have to encode the request selection mechanism. Call arcs from a serve node are only of Local type, and for each request m in *mset*, we have such one call arc, expressing one of the possible selection in the queue. The activity model is synchronised with the queue model through the ?S_m message (with guard *pred* if needed); then the method m is started with the arguments gathered from the queue, it waits for the computation to terminate and if necessary sends back the return value to the caller (object o, proxy f, that were stored with the request).

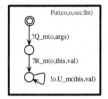
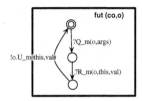

Fig. 5.   Automata for futures' proxies (without or with recycling)

```
DO-SERVE (calls(n),mset,pred,mode) =
 fresh˜s₁, Map = Map ∪ {n ↦ s₁}
 foreach call in calls(n)
   match call with "Local(o.m,args,var)"
   if m ∈ mset do
     fresh˜s₂, s₃
     Aut.add s  ──[pred]?S_m(f,o,args,mode)──→  s₂  ──!body.Call_m(this,args)──→  s₃
     if null-result(m) then Aut.add˜s₃  ──?Ret_m(val)──→  s₁
     else                     Aut.add˜s₃  ──?Ret_m(val)──→  (fresh s₄)  ──!o.R_m(f,this,val)──→  s₁
```

Loops : The (LOOP-JOIN rule) applies to all types of nodes that already have been visited. Then the corresponding LTS node is substituted to the current LTS node, eventually creating loops or joins in the LTS.

```
DO-JOIN-LOOP () = s₁ = Map(n)
    Aut.replace(s,s₁)
```

Future values and utilisation : We create a future object at each remote invocation point with a non-void result type. This future object provides the value to its potential use points. Thereby, we have as many "future objects" automatas as invocation points, and we synchronise those with their use points in the future rule. There are cases when static information garanties that a future value is consumed at a particular point, in which case we can recycle the corresponding future object (then a single automaton can be used, instead of a family indexed by its occurence in the store, see Fig. 5).

```
DO-FUTURE (fut,val) =
    Aut.add s  ──?U_m(fut,val)──→  (fresh s₁)
    Map = Map ∪ {n ↦ s₁}
```

4   Example

We use here a part of the Producer/Consumer example from section 1 to illustrate the model generation.

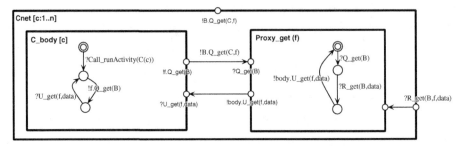

Fig. 6. Resulting Consumer model

4.1 ProActive Code and Extended MCG

The consumer and corresponding XMCG:

```
public void runActivity(Body myBody) {

    { ...
    while (true) {
    Type data = Buffer.get();
    System.out.println("The value is " + data);
    }
    }
}
```

runActivity()
enr(runActivity)
while (true)
call(data, Buffer.get, Consumer)
use(data)
PP (println (data))

The buffer and corresponding XMCG:

```
public void runActivity(Body body) {
    int bound;
    Type [] tab;
    {
    while (true) {
    if (bound==0)
            service.serveOldest("put");
        else
            service.serveOldest();
}}}

void put (Type data) {
    tab[bound]=data;
    bound++;
    }

Type get(){
    return(tab[bound--]);}
```

runActivity()
ent(runActivity)
PP
if (i==0)
serve({put}, args, oldest)   serve({put,get},args,oldest)
PP   PP
Local(put,args)   Local(get)
put(data)   get()
ent(put, args)   ent(get)
tab[i]=data   data=tab[i]
i++   i--
ret   ret(data)

4.2 The Generated Nets

We illustrate the model construction with two examples: the Buffer pNet in Fig. 7 illustrates the model of local method calls, and its interaction with the queue, while the Consumer pNet in Fig. 6 illustrates the interaction with a proxy. For each of the methods LTSs, we have applied a simple optimisation after completion of the Method-Behav procedure, removing all empty transitions that where not part of a non-deterministic choice (removal of tau-prefix).

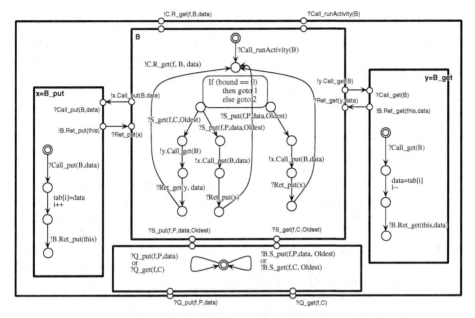

Fig. 7. Resulting Buffer model

Fig. 6 shows the pNet modelling the Consumer behaviour. Note that the data accessed by the Consumer is immediately consumed (the Use node in the MCG follows immediately the Request node). This implies that there can be only one "get" future active at any time, so we use a single future in the proxy instead of an indexed family of futures.

An interesting feature is that the Q_get synchronisation between the consumer root and its proxy is directly visible as a message addressed to the buffer process (thanks to the expressivity of synchronisation vectors); this technique enables us to avoid an explicit encoding of a rendez-vous protocol, that would introduce unnecessary interleavings.

5   Conclusion and Directions

We have introduced a language to describe the behaviour of communicating distributed systems using parameterized models. The parameters in our model are variables that encode both: data value (such as in the theories of value-passing systems), and process identifiers (such as in the theories of channel-passing systems). We argue that our models are suitable as a specification language for distributed systems behaviour, and for models resulting from static analysis of source code. We also gave a graphical representation of those models that aims to be used by non-specialist in formal methods; we have shown in [3] how our graphical models can be used to specify and verify large distributed applications.

Our models enable us to have a finite representation of infinite systems. They naturally encode the semantics of languages for distributed applications. In fact, we have sketched a method for constructing parameterized models for distributed applications built with the PROACTIVE library. This method has been described in terms of algorithms, and use an extension of method call graphs obtained by flow analysis. Our methodology was illustrated guided by a Producer-Consumer system.

We have developed a tool that makes automatic instantiations of our parameterized models, we have developed a prototype of a graphical editor to design parameterized systems and we will integrate, in a short-term, these parameterized systems to on-the-fly model checking tools.

Having a specification and the models generated from the source code, we want to check the correctness of the implementation. This check will need a refinement pre-order, which allows the implementation to make some choices amongst the possibilities left by the specification, and it should be compatible with the composition by synchronisation networks.

We shall also extend the approach to take into account other features of the middleware, and in particular the primitives for group communication, and for specifying distributed security policies. Last but not least, ProActive active objects are also viewed as *distributed components* in a component framework. In the next version, it will be possible to assemble distributed objects to form more complex components. This will increase the impact of the compositionality of our model, and the importance of being able to prove that a component agrees with its (behavioural) specification.

References

[1] Garavel, H., Lang, F.: NTIF: A general symbolic model for communicating sequential processes with data. In: Proceedings of FORTE'02 (Houston), LNCS 2529 (2002) 43

[2] Arnold, A.: Finite transition systems. Semantics of communicating sytems. Prentice-Hall (1994) 43, 44, 45

[3] Barros, T., Madelaine, E.: Formalisation and proofs of the chilean electronic invoices system. Technical Report RR-5217, INRIA (2004) 44, 48, 58

[4] Boulifa, R., Madelaine, E.: Model generation for distributed Java programs. In N. Guelfi, E. A., Reggio, G., eds.: Workshop on scientiFic engIneering of Distributed Java applIcations, Luxembourg, Springer-Verlag, LNCS 2952 (2003) 44

[5] Corbett, J., Dwyer, M., Hatcliff, J., Pasareanu, C., Laubach, S., Zheng, H.: Bandera: Extracting finite-state models from java source code. Int. Conference on Software Engineering (ICSE) (2000) 44, 49

[6] Cleaveland, R., Riely, J.: Testing-based abstractions for value-passing systems. In: International Conference on Concurrency Theory. (1994) 417–432 44, 46, 48

[7] Milner, R.: Communication and Concurrency. Prentice Hall (1989) ISBN 0-13-114984-9. 45, 47

[8] Lakas, A.: Les Transformations Lotomaton: une contribution à la pré-implémentation des systémes Lotos. PhD thesis (1996) 45

 [9] Lin, H.: Symbolic transition graph with assignment. In Montanari, U., Sassone, V., eds.: CONCUR '96, Pisa, Italy, LNCS 1119 (1996) 46
[10] Milner, R., Parrow, J., Walker, D.: A calculus of mobile processes. Information and Computation **100** (1992) 47
[11] Bouali, A., Ressouche, A., Roy, V., de Simone, R.: The fc2tools set. In Dill, D., ed.: Computer Aided Verification (CAV'94), Standford, Springer-Verlag, LNCS (1994) 47
[12] Caromel, D., Klauser, W., Vayssière, J.: Towards seamless computing and meta-computing in Java. Concurrency Practice and Experience **10** (1998) 1043–1061 49

Towards the Harmonisation of UML and SDL

Rüdiger Grammes and Reinhard Gotzhein

Department of Computer Science
University of Kaiserslautern
67653 Kaiserslautern, Germany
{grammes,gotzhein}@informatik.uni-kl.de

Abstract. UML and SDL are languages for the development of software systems that have different origins, and have evolved separately for many years. Recently, it can be observed that OMG and ITU, the standardisation bodies responsible for UML and SDL, respectively, are making efforts to harmonise these languages. So far, harmonisation takes place mainly on a conceptual level, by extending and aligning the set of language concepts. In this paper, we argue that harmonisation of languages can be approached both from a syntactic and semantic perspective. We show how a common basis can be derived from the analysis of the UML meta-model and the SDL abstract grammar. For this purpose, conceptually sound and well-founded mappings from meta-models to abstract grammars and vice versa are defined and applied. The long term objective is the syntactic and semantic integration of UML and SDL. The key to achieving this objective is a common language core, which can then be extended in different ways to cover further, more specific language concepts, and is sufficiently flexible to support future language add-ins.

1 Introduction

UML (Unified Modeling Language [1], [2]) is a graphical language for specifying, modelling and documenting software systems with widespread use in industry, standardised by the Object Management Group (OMG). It is a family of notations (e.g., use case diagrams, class diagrams, sequence diagrams, statechart diagrams, deployment diagrams) supporting different views of a system throughout the software life cycle. Recently, the UML 2.0 standard was finalised. The new standard is a major revision of UML 1.x, and introduces, amongst other things, better support for system structure and components.

SDL (System Design Languages [3]) is a graphical specification language for distributed systems and, in particular, communication systems, standardised by the International Telecommunications Union (ITU). It is widely used in telecommunications industry. SDL is a sophisticated set of notations (e.g., MSC-2000, SDL-2000, ASN.1, TTCN), supporting different system views on different levels of abstraction.

With SDL-2000, several important steps towards its future harmonisation with UML were made. For instance, classes and associations including aggregation, composition, and specialisation were added to the language. Furthermore,

D. de Frutos-Escrig and M. Núñez (Eds.): FORTE 2004, LNCS 3235, pp. 61–78, 2004.
© IFIP International Federation for Information Processing 2004

composite states that are similar to submachines in UML statecharts were incorporated. In turn, UML 2.0 introduced structured classes, which extend classes by an internal structure consisting of nested structured classes, ports and connectors. This makes it possible to model architectural aspects of systems in a fashion similar to SDL.

First attempts to harmonise UML and SDL have already been made. The Z.109 standard [4] defines a subset of UML 1.3 [2] that has a mapping to SDL-2000. The UML subset is used in combination with SDL, with the semantics based on SDL-2000. In [5], Selic and Rumbaugh define a transformation from SDL-92 to UML 1.3 extended with the Rational Rose real-time profile.

Ultimately, these efforts are directed towards an integration of both languages and the corresponding notations. However, at the time being, UML and SDL still deviate in many ways, making it hard to see whether and when integration might actually be achieved. Differences range from pure syntactic aspects to semantic concepts, resulting from the origin of the languages. Also, it is not clear whether different views of a system even if expressed in notations belonging to the same family are consistent.

A true integration of both languages and the corresponding notations will require a common syntactic and semantic core. This basis may then be extended in different ways, yielding a variety of language profiles. This way, the system developer will be enabled to model different parts of a system using different notations, and to combine them into a single view.

In order to derive a common syntactic and semantic basis, the existing language definitions of UML and SDL should be taken as a starting point. In this paper, we present the results of analysing several corresponding excerpts of UML and SDL, compare them, and derive a common subset. This is done on the syntactical level, by defining conceptually sound and well-founded mappings from meta-models (used to define the abstract syntax of UML, see Section 2) to abstract grammars (used by SDL, see Section 2) and vice versa (Section 3), and by extracting common production rules (Section 4). Results are discussed in Section 5.

2   UML Meta-Model and SDL Abstract Grammar

The definition of a language consists of its syntax and semantics. The concrete syntax of a language includes separators and other constructs needed for parsing the language. The abstract syntax omits these details and contains only the elements relevant for the definition of the semantics. Both the concrete and the abstract syntax of a language can be defined in terms of a grammar, consisting of a set of production rules that define the syntactically correct sentences.

For SDL, a concrete (textual and graphical) syntax and two abstract syntaxes, AS0 and AS1, are defined. The AS0 is obtained from the concrete syntax by omitting details such as separators and lexical rules. Otherwise, is very similar to the concrete syntax of SDL. The abstract syntax AS1 is obtained from the abstract syntax AS0 through a step of transformations followed by a mapping.

During the transformation, additional concepts are translated into core concepts of SDL as described in the standard.

The abstract syntax of SDL is described in terms of an abstract grammar, similar to BNF. It consists of two kinds of production rules, namely concatenations and synonyms. A *concatenation* 'lhs ::=(::) rhs' describes the non-terminal lhs (left hand side) as a composite object consisting of the elements denoted by rhs (right hand side). Optional elements are enclosed in square brackets, and alternatives are separated by vertical bars. The suffix '*' describes a possibly empty list of elements, '+' a non-empty list and '-set' a set of distinguishable elements. A *synonym* 'lhs ::=(=) rhs' describes that the non-terminal lhs is an element of the kind rhs and can not be syntactically distinguished from other elements of this kind.

For the mapping described in Section 3, we assume a normal form of the abstract grammar, where concatenations have no alternatives on the right hand side. The SDL abstract grammar can be easily transformed into this normal form by introducing new synonyms for these alternatives.

Below an excerpt of the AS1, the production rule State-node, is shown. State nodes are composite objects consisting of a state name, a save signalset, and sets of input nodes, spontaneous transitions, continuous signals and connect nodes. Optionally, a state node can have a composite state type identifier (in that case, the state represents a composite state of the respective type).

```
State-node ::=(::) State-name
               [On-exception]
               Save-signalset
               Input-node-set
               Spontaneous-transition-set
               Continuous-signal-set
               Connect-node-set
               [Composite-state-type-identifier]
```

A meta-model is a model used to define a language for the specification of models. In UML, this meta-model approach is used to define the language syntax. In particular, the abstract syntax of the language is defined using UML class diagrams. This approach is reflective, since class diagrams are UML models, and therefore described in terms of themselves. On top of the model and the meta-model, more layers can exist (meta-meta-models, etc.). UML uses a four layer meta-model structure: user objects (M0), model (M1), meta-model (M2) and meta-meta-model (M3). Every element in a layer is an instance of an element of the direct superordinate layer.

The UML class diagrams used for the description of the abstract syntax comprise packages, classes, attributes, associations and specialisation. Classes in the UML meta-model describe language elements. An occurrence of the language element in the model (M1) is an instance of the meta-model class. Classes in the meta-model can be parameterised by attributes. Attributes describe properties of the language element described by a class. Composition between meta-model classes describes that a language element contains another. General associations relate language elements with each other, e.g., a transition with a trigger. The meta-model uses packages, abstract classes and specialisation to structure the abstract syntax.

3 Defining Mappings Between UML Meta-Model and SDL Abstract Grammar

In this section, we define precise, conceptually sound mappings from meta-models to abstract grammars, and vice versa. The examples for the reverse mapping can be found in [6]. As it turns out, not every element of the UML meta-model can be mapped. Also, several meta-model elements may have the same representation in the abstract grammar. Therefore, the mapping is not completely reversible. However, it is possible to map every element of an abstract grammar to a meta-model representation. In Section 4, these mappings will be applied to UML and SDL to extract a common syntactical basis.

3.1 Classes and Enumerations

map(MM): A *concrete class* of the meta-model represents a language element of the model. E.g., the meta-model class State represents all state descriptions in a UML statemachine. In an abstract grammar, a language element is represented by a specific production rule, namely a concatenation. Therefore, a concrete class in the meta-model is mapped to a concatenation of the abstract grammar. The name of the non-terminal is derived from the class name and the package structure of the meta-model (see below). The right hand side of the concatenation is derived from the class definition (attributes) and context (associations) as defined below (see 3.2, 3.3).

An *abstract class* of the meta-model describes properties that are common to its subclasses. E.g., the meta-model class Vertex describes properties that are common to states and pseudo-states (initial states, ...). Since an abstract class can not be instantiated, it does not represent a language element of the model. Therefore, no concatenation is used in the mapping. Instead, we have decided to map an abstract class of the meta-model to another kind of production rule, namely a synonym, of the abstract grammar. In an abstract grammar, a synonym replaces the element on its left hand side with an element of the right hand side. This is a similar to abstract classes in the meta-model, which must be replaced by one of their concrete subclasses in a model. The name of the non-terminal is selected as in the case of a concrete class. The right hand side is derived from the context (specialisation) as described below (see 3.5).

An *enumeration* in the meta-model is a set of values used to parameterise meta-model classes. E.g., the meta-model class Pseudostate describes different language elements (entry point, exit point, ...) of the model depending on the value of the attribute 'kind' of the enumeration type PseudostateKind. Enumerations do not directly describe language elements of the model. Therefore, as in the case of abstract classes, no concatenation is used in the mapping. Instead,

MM		map(MM)
Vertex	<<enumeration>> TransitionKind	BehSM_StateMachine ::=(::)
	internal local	BehSM_Vertex ::=(=)
StateMachine	external	BehSM_TransitionKind ::=(=)

enumerations are also mapped to synonyms of the abstract grammar. This production rule replaces the enumeration by one of its values.

The name of the non-terminals introduced by the mappings described above is the qualified name of the class or enumeration. The qualified name is a sequence of the packages the class or enumeration is contained in (from outermost to innermost) and the name of the class or enumeration, each separated by underscores. E.g., Kernel_Element is the name of the non-terminal introduced by the class Element in the package Kernel. The qualified name is used in order to avoid name clashes between equally named classes in different packages.

Example: The following example comes from the meta-model of UML state machines. It describes two classes, an abstract class *Vertex* and a concrete class StateMachine. Furthermore, there is an enumeration TransitionKind. All of these elements are contained in the package BehaviorStatemachines (not shown), that we will shortly refer to as BehSM.

StateMachine is a concrete class, and is therefore mapped to a concatenation. The name BehSM_StateMachine comes from the package structure and the name of the class. The abstract class *Vertex* and the enumeration TransitionKind are mapped to synonyms.

map(AG): As mentioned in the mapping from meta-models to abstract grammars, concrete classes and *concatenations* both represent language elements of the model. Therefore, concatenations of the abstract grammar are mapped to concrete classes in the meta-model. The name of the concrete class is derived from the production rule (see below).

A *synonym* of the abstract grammar represents a language element that does not appear in the model, but stands for other language elements. E.g., a Data-type-definition in the SDL abstract grammar is a synonym for a Value-data-type-definition, an Object-data-type-definition or an Interface-definition. This is a similar concept to abstract classes in the meta-model, which we have mapped to synonyms in the abstract grammar. However, it is also similar to an enumeration, where the enumeration stands for one of its values. Therefore, we map a synonym in the abstract grammar either to an abstract class or an enumeration. The exact mapping depends on the right hand side of the synonym (see 3.2, 3.3). The name

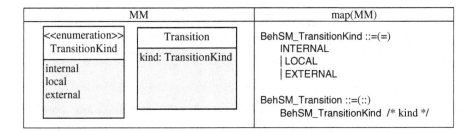

MM	map(MM)
<<enumeration>> TransitionKind / internal / local / external Transition / kind: TransitionKind	BehSM_TransitionKind ::=(=) INTERNAL | LOCAL | EXTERNAL BehSM_Transition ::=(::) BehSM_TransitionKind /* kind */

of the class or enumeration is the name of the non-terminal on the left hand side of the production rule.

3.2   Attributes

map(MM): In the meta-model, *attributes* of a class represent properties of a language element of the model. E.g., the attribute 'kind' of the meta-model class Transition describes if the transition is internal, local or external. In an abstract syntax tree, an attribute is represented as a sub-node of the non-terminal and corresponds to a class. We have mapped concrete classes to concatenations of the abstract grammar. Therefore, an attribute of a concrete class is mapped to a terminal on the right hand side of the concatenation. We map attributes to terminals since they do not need to be refined any further. The only exception is an enumeration type; in that case we map the attribute to a non-terminal, since we have mapped enumerations to synonyms and non-terminals. The name of the terminal is the name of the type (e.g. Boolean). The name of the non-terminal is derived from the name of the enumeration and the package structure, as defined in 3.1.

Attributes that are marked as *derived* carry no additional information and can be omitted. E.g., the attribute 'isComposite' of State can be derived from the number of associated regions. If they are not omitted, additional static conditions are needed to define the dependencies between the original and the derived attributes. Default values of attributes can not be mapped to the abstract grammar. They can be described by static conditions.

Elements of an enumeration represent values of the enumeration type. A value in an abstract grammar is represented by a terminal. Therefore, enumeration elements are mapped to terminals of the abstract grammar. The name of the terminal is the name of the enumeration element. An enumeration is mapped to a synonym of the abstract grammar. Therefore, we map the terminals to the right hand side of the synonym corresponding to the enumeration.

Example: The following example (again from BehaviorStatemachines) contains a concrete class Transition and the enumeration TransitionKind. The classes are mapped as described in the previous section. The attribute 'kind' of Transition is an element on the right hand side of BehSM_Transition. In this special case ('kind' is an enumeration), it is a non-terminal that refers to the mapping of the enumeration TransitionKind. The name of the attribute is appended as a comment. The enumeration literals of TransitionKind appear as an alternative of terminals on the right hand side of the production rule, written in all caps for better distinction.

map(AG): A *terminal* on the right hand side of a concatenation represents a property of the language element. In the meta-model, an attribute represents a property of a language element. The terminal is therefore mapped to an attribute of the concrete class corresponding to the concatenation. The type of the attribute is the name of the terminal. The name of the terminal can be chosen arbitrarily as long as it does not conflict with other attribute names of the class.

A synonym with only terminals on the right hand side represents an enumeration of values. E.g., the synonym Agent-kind of the SDL abstract grammar is an enumeration of the values SYSTEM, BLOCK and PROCESS. Therefore, the terminals are mapped to enumeration values of the enumeration corresponding to the synonym.

3.3 Associations

map(MM): An *aggregation* or *composition* between two classes means that one language element contains or is made up of other language elements. E.g., a Region in a statechart contains vertices and transitions. In the same way, a node in an abstract syntax tree can have sub-nodes. E.g., a State-transition-graph of the SDL abstract grammar has a set of State-nodes as sub-nodes. Therefore, we map aggregation and composition to the abstract grammar so that the definition of the aggregated class is a sub-node of the aggregating class. This is achieved by adding the non-terminal corresponding to the aggregated class on the right hand side of the concatenation corresponding to the aggregating concrete class.

A *general association* between two classes is an association between language elements, in which the elements play a certain role. E.g., a State is associated with a number of triggers, the triggers playing the role of deferrable triggers. In the SDL abstract grammar, two language elements are associated by identifiers. E.g., an Input-node is associated with a Signal by a Signal-identifier on the right hand side of the concatenation corresponding to the Input-node. Therefore, a directed general association is mapped to an identifier on the right hand side of the concatenation corresponding to the concrete class the association originates from. An undirected general association is split into two directed general associations.

An associations with the *union* property is the union of the associations that subset it. This is expressed by the property *subsets*. As in the case of derived attributes, associations with the union property are not mapped to the abstract grammar.

MM	map(MM)

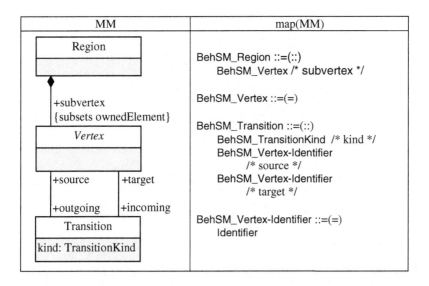	BehSM_Region ::=(::)
	  BehSM_Vertex /* subvertex */
	
	BehSM_Vertex ::=(=)
	
	BehSM_Transition ::=(::)
	  BehSM_TransitionKind /* kind */
	  BehSM_Vertex-Identifier
	    /* source */
	  BehSM_Vertex-Identifier
	    /* target */
	
	BehSM_Vertex-Identifier ::=(=)
	  Identifier

Example: The following example shows the abstract class *Vertex* and the concrete classes Transition and Region. Region is composed of a *Vertex* called subvertex. This composition is a subset of the association 'ownedElement' between two Elements. In the AST, BehSM_Region thus has BehSM_Vertex on the right hand side, with the name appended as a comment. Between Vertex and Transition there are two bidirectional associations, which are split into two unidirectional associations respectively. Attributes and associations of an abstract class are not mapped to the corresponding synonym in the AST, since an abstract class is not a synonym for one of its attributes or associations. Instead, they are copied into the respective subclasses, as described in Section 3.5. In this example, *Vertex* has no subclasses. Therefore, we only have to map the two general associations 'source' and 'target'. To distinguish between general association and composition, an association is mapped to an identifier (in this case, BehSM_Vertex-Identifier) on the right hand side of the corresponding production rule. How the identifier looks like is not further specified. It could be a qualified name like in the case of SDL.

map(AG): *Non-terminals* on the right hand side of a *concatenation* can stand for an enumeration or a class in the meta-model. In case they represent an enumeration they represent an attribute of the class (see 3.2). In case they represent a class, this class is a sub-node of the class corresponding to the concatenation. This is similar to a class in the meta-model that is composed of other classes. Therefore, in this case we map a non-terminal on the right hand side of a concatenation to a composition in the meta-model. The composing class is the class corresponding to the concatenation; the composed class is the class corresponding to the non-terminal on the right hand side. The role of the classes can be chosen arbitrarily.

Table 1. Mapping of Multiplicities

MM	AG
0..1	*[Name]*
0..n, 1 < n	(as 0..*)
0.. *	*Name **
0.. * {unique}	*Name-**set***
1	*Name*
1..n, 1 < n	(as 1..*)
1.. *	*Name +*
1..* {unique}	(as 0..* {unique})
n	(as 0..*)
n..m, 1 < n < m	(as 1..*)
n..*, 1 < n	(as 1..*)

An *identifier* on the right hand side of a concatenation identifies a language element that is associated with the language element described by the concatenation. E.g., in the SDL abstract grammar, an Input-node is associated with a Signal by a Signal-identifier. Therefore, we map an identifier on the right hand side of a concatenation to a directed general association in the meta-model. The source of the association is the concrete class corresponding to the concatenation, according to the mapping in 3.1. The target is the concrete class corresponding to the language element referenced by the identifier. The role of the classes can be chosen arbitrarily.

3.4 Multiplicity

The following table defines a mapping between multiplicities in the meta-model and the abstract grammar. In UML, multiplicities consist of a lower bound and an optional upper bound, which can be infinite. The property *ordered* expresses that there is a linear order for the elements. The property *unique* expresses that no element appears more than once. In the abstract grammar, an optional element is enclosed by square brackets. A possibly empty list of elements is marked by a '*' behind the element, a non empty list by a '+'. A set of distinct elements is marked by the suffix '-set'.

Table 1 shows the mapping of multiplicities between meta-model and abstract grammar. If we use lists in the abstract grammar, the elements are ordered and not necessarily unique. If we use sets, they are not ordered and unique. Therefore, we can only map one of the properties to the abstract grammar. In this case, the property *ordered* is omitted from the mapping.

3.5 Specialisation

In the UML meta-model, abstract classes and specialisation are used frequently to capture common aspects of different classes, and as part of a meta-language core reused in several standards (see UML: Infrastructure [1]). For the abstract syntax, abstract classes are not directly interesting, since they can not be instantiated and therefore do not appear in a model, except through their subclasses. Nonetheless we map them to the abstract grammar, to preserve as much of the structure of the meta-model as possible.

map(MM): We have to map specialisation to the abstract grammar, and the fact that a specializing class inherits properties of the specialised class. The easiest way to do this is to copy these properties into the specializing classes before the mapping. This has the advantage that redefinition of properties is easy to realise. They are not copied to subclasses that overwrite them.

This is done as follows:

1. For every class that has subclasses, copy all attributes of the class and all associations that originate from this class to each of its direct subclasses.
   (a) An attribute is only copied to a subclass if no attribute of the same name already exists, i.e., if the attributed is not redefined.
   (b) An association is only copied to a subclass if it is not redefined in the subclass.
2. Repeat step 1 for all subclasses that have new attributes and associations after the last execution of step 1.

In the meta-model, an abstract class can take part in an association. In the model, an instance of a concrete class that specialises the abstract class takes part in the association instead. E.g., a Vertex is associated with Transitions as the source of these transitions. In the model, the source of these transitions is either a State or a Pseudostate. In the abstract grammar, we can express this using a synonym. We have already mapped an abstract class to a non-terminal and a synonym (see 3.1). To map the specialisation to the abstract grammar, we add the non-terminals corresponding to the direct sub-classes of the abstract class to the right hand side of the synonym. This means that every occurrence of the non-terminal (the abstract class) is replaced by a non-terminal (one of the subclasses) in the abstract syntax tree.

To map specialisation to the abstract grammar, we need synonyms. On the other hand, a concrete class can have subclasses, but is mapped to a concatenation (see 3.1). In this case, we transform the meta-model before we perform the mapping. The concrete class with subclasses is replaced by an abstract class of the same name. The concrete class is renamed, e.g. by adding a special prefix, and added as a subclass of the new abstract class. The subclasses of the concrete class are now subclasses of the new abstract class and the mapping can be performed. However, we still have to copy the attributes of the concrete class to its former subclasses, as described above.

Example: The following example is taken from the package Kernel and covers classifiers, classes and associations. *Classifier* is an abstract class with the

MM	map(MM)

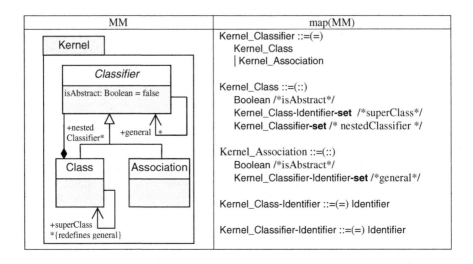	Kernel_Classifier ::=(=)
	  Kernel_Class
	  | Kernel_Association
	
	Kernel_Class ::=(::)
	  Boolean /*isAbstract*/
	  Kernel_Class-Identifier-**set** /*superClass*/
	  Kernel_Classifier-**set** /* nestedClassifier */
	
	Kernel_Association ::=(::)
	  Boolean /*isAbstract*/
	  Kernel_Classifier-Identifier-**set** /*general*/
	
	Kernel_Class-Identifier ::=(=) Identifier
	
	Kernel_Classifier-Identifier ::=(=) Identifier

attribute 'isAbstract'. A classifier can be generalised by another classifier, described by the association named 'general'. Concrete subclasses of *Classifier* are Class and Association. The association 'superClass' between two classes redefines the association 'general'.

Before mapping to the abstract grammar, we have to copy the attributes and associations of the abstract class *Classifier* to its subclasses. The attribute 'isAbstract' is copied to the classes Class and Association, since no attribute of the same name exists. A new association 'general' from Association to *Classifier* is added. The association 'superClass' redefines 'general', therefore no new association is added to Class.

The abstract class *Classifier* is mapped to a synonym. Class and Association are direct subclasses of *Classifier*; therefore, we add the non-terminals corresponding to these classes on the right hand side of the synonym.

map(AG): *Non-terminals* of the abstract grammar represent language elements. A synonym of the abstract grammar with non-terminals on the right hand side replaces a language element by another. E.g., a Return-node in the abstract grammar of SDL is replaced by an Action-return-node, a Value-return-node or a Named-return-node. We map synonyms to abstract classes in the meta-model. Abstract classes can not be instantiated, but can have instances through their subclasses. Therefore, we map a synonym with non-terminals on the right hand side in the abstract grammar to a specialisation relationship. The specialised class is the class corresponding to the non-terminal on the left hand side. The specialising classes are the classes corresponding to the non-terminals on the right hand side.

3.6   Meta-Model Approach vs. Abstract Grammar Approach

From the discussion so far, it is quite obvious that the meta-model approach to defining an abstract syntax is more expressive than the (context free) grammar approach. As a consequence, the mapping from the SDL abstract grammar to a meta-model is completely reversible. However, this is not the case for the mapping from the UML meta-model to an abstract grammar. Several elements of the UML meta-model can not be expressed in the abstract grammar. They are described in [6]. In consequence, the meta-model approach seems to be preferable as a basis for the harmonisation of UML and SDL. It covers and extends the expressiveness of abstract grammars, and thus seems to be the right choice. However, when it comes to implementing a language by providing tool support, an abstract grammar is still needed. With the mapping defined above, such an abstract grammar can be systematically derived.

4   Extracting a Common Abstract Syntax from SDL and UML

Translating the meta-model of UML 2.0 into an abstract grammar supports the comparison of the abstract syntax of UML 2.0 and SDL-2000. In particular, it enables us to examine how the common constructs of SDL and UML are reflected in common parts of the abstract syntax of both languages, and to extract a common abstract grammar.

As it has turned out, some information of the meta-model is lost when it is mapped to an abstract grammar (see Section 3.6). However, the information lost is not important for the extraction, because it is not present in the abstract syntax of SDL.

Instead of mapping the UML meta-model to an abstract grammar, we could apply the mapping from the SDL abstract grammar to a meta-model. This way, no information would be lost, as the meta-model is more expressive. However, the extraction process would not benefit from this choice. Even worse, the extraction would be harder, since the UML meta-model defines a large number of abstract classes with attributes and associations, which would not show up in the SDL meta-model. It would be necessary to either copy the attributes of abstract classes to their subclasses in the UML meta-model (as described in Section 3.5), or to identify common attributes and associations, and shift them to super-classes in the SDL meta-model.

To relate language elements of SDL-2000 and UML 2.0 on a syntactical level, substantial knowledge of both languages is required. In particular, it is necessary to take the semantics of language elements into account. E.g., we need knowledge of the semantics of the language elements to relate the Package-name of a Package-definition in the abstract syntax of SDL with the String of a structured class in the abstract syntax of UML. Also, it can be expected that for some of the common constructs the abstract syntax will be different, although the semantic is the same. In some cases, there might even be a common abstract syntax, although the semantics is different.

To extract the common abstract syntax of the two languages, we take the production rules for language elements that are similar in UML and SDL, e.g. packages, as a starting point, and compare their right hand sides. For corresponding elements in both sets of production rules that represent similar concepts, the production rules for these elements are compared. If they overlap, we can relate the two elements with each other and include them in the common abstract syntax. We start the extraction with very high level language elements, namely packages and agents/classes, before moving to language elements with a finer granularity.

4.1   Packages

Both SDL and UML have a concept of packages for grouping and reuse of elements of the specification. Both support the nesting of packages (2). The abstract syntax of UML describes the contents of a package as a set of PackageableElements, a synonym for all elements that can be contained in a package. SDL describes sets of the elements that can be contained in a package, e.g. Signal-definition-**set**. Common packageable elements in SDL and UML are agents/classes (3), signals (4) and composite states/statemachines (5).

SDL-2000 (AS1)	Common AS	UML 2.0 (derived AS)
Package-definition ::=(::)	Package-definition ::=(::)	Kernel_Package ::=(::)
1 Package-name	1 Package-name	1 [String]
2 Package-definition-**set**	2 Package-definition-**set**	2 Kernel_Package-**set**
Data-type-definition-**set**	3 Signal-definition-**set**	Kernel_PackageableElement-**set**
Syntype-definition-**set**	4 Agent-type-definition-**set**	Kernel_PackageMerge-**set**
3 Signal-definition-**set**	5 Statemachine-**set**	Kernel_ElementImport-**set**
Exception-definition-**set**		Kernel_PackageImport-**set**
4 Agent-type-definition-**set**		Kernel_PackageableElement ::=(=)
5 Composite-state-type-		4 StructuredClasses_Class
definition-**set**		5 BehStateMachines_StateMachine
Procedure-definition-**set**		3 Communications_Signal

4.2   Signals

Signal types exist in SDL and UML to describe communication between agents/ objects. Signals have a name (1) and parameters, which are represented by sorts in SDL and properties in UML. While representing similar concepts, the abstract syntax of sorts and properties are different, therefore signals in the common abstract grammar have no parameters.

SDL-2000 (AS1)	Common AS	UML 2.0 (derived AS)
Signal-definition ::=(::)	Signal-definition ::=(::)	Communications_Signal ::=(::)
1 Signal-name	1 Signal-name	Kernel_Property *
Sort-reference-identifier *		1 [String]
		...

4.3   Agent-type/Class

UML 2.0 introduces structured classes, which are classes extended with internal structure and ports. Structured classes are semantically and syntactically similar to Agent-types in SDL. Both have an internal structure of properties (respectively agents, 9), connectors (channels, 7) and gates (ports, 6). Both agent-types and structured classes can specialise other agent-types and structured classes (2), however SDL only supports single inheritance while UML supports multiple inheritance. Behaviour is associated with an Agent-type as a State-machine-definition, which consists of a name and a Composite-state-type-identifier (8). Behaviour is associated with structured classes by a Behavior-Identifier (8). Behaviour in the abstract syntax of UML is a synonym for statemachines and other behaviour models. Statemachines are syntactically similar to composite-state-types in SDL. The abstract syntax of the two languages differs slightly, since UML does not have a State-machine-definition. In the common abstract grammar, we include the State-machine-definition but discard the name associated with it, since it does not exist in UML.

SDL-2000 (AS1)	Common AS	UML 2.0 (derived AS)
Agent-type-definition ::=(::)	Agent-type-definition ::=(::)	StructuredClasses_Class ::=(::)
1 Agent-type-name	1 Agent-type-name	1 [String]
Agent-kind	2 [Agent-type-identifier]	...
2 [Agent-type-identifier]	3 Signal-definition-**set**	Kernel_Classifier-Identifier-**set**
Agent-formal-parameter *	4 Agent-type-definition-**set**	2 StructClasses_Class-Identifier-**set**
Data-type-definition-**set**	5 Statemachine-**set**	[Kernel_Type]
Syntype-definition-**set**	9 Agent-definition-**set**	Kernel_ElementImport-**set**
3 Signal-definition-**set**	6 Port-definition-**set**	Kernel_PackageImport-**set**
Timer-definition-**set**	7 Channel-definition-**set**	Kernel_Constraint-**set**
Exception-definition-**set**	8 [Agent-behaviour]	Kernel_Behavior-**set**
Variable-definition-**set**		8 [Kernel_Behavior-Identifier]
4 Agent-type-definition-**set**	Agent-behaviour ::=(::)	Boolean /*isActive*/
5 Composite-state-type-	8 Statemachine-identifier	Communications_Reception-**set**
definition-**set**		6 Ports_Port-**set**
Procedure-definition-**set**		7 CompStruct_Connector-**set**
9 Agent-definition-**set**		9 IntStruct_Property-**set**
6 Gate-definition-**set**		Kernel_Property *
7 Channel-definition-**set**		Kernel_Classifier-**set**
8 [State-machine-definition		Kernel_Operation *
]		
State-machine-definition ::=(::)		Kernel_Classifier ::=(=)
State-name		4 StructuredClasses_Class
8 Composite-state-type-		5 BehStateMachines_StateMachine
identifier		3 Communications_Signal
		...

4.4   Channel/Connector

Channels/connectors connect gates/ports. In SDL, a channel has one or two channel-paths. In case of two channel-paths, the channel is bi-directional and the originating gate of the first path is the destination gate of the second path and vice versa. In UML, the connector connects two or more ports. In the common AS, a channel is a set of channel-ends (2), which is a pair of ports (3). No direction is specified.

SDL-2000 (AS1)	Common AS	UML 2.0 (derived AS)
Channel-definition ::=(::)	Channel-definition ::=(::)	IntStruct_Connector ::=(::)
1 Channel-name	1 Channel-name	IntStruct_Connector-Identifier
[NODELAY]	2 Channel-end-**set**	2 Ports_ConnectorEnd * /* 2..* */
2 Channel-path-**set**		[Kernel_Association-Identifier]
	Channel-end ::=(::)	...
Channel-path ::=(::)	3 Port-identifier	1 [String]
3 Originating-gate	3 Port-identifier	[Kernel_Type]
3 Destination-gate		Ports_ConnectorEnd ::=(::)
Signal-identifier-**set**		3 [IntStruct_ConnectableElement-Identifier]

4.5   Gate/Port

Gates/ports are endpoints for channels/connectors. Gates specify valid signals for both directions, while ports have required and provided interfaces (2, 3).

SDL-2000 (AS1)	Common AS	UML 2.0 (derived AS)
Gate-definition ::=(::)	Port-definition ::=(::)	Ports_Port ::=(::)
1 Gate-name	1 Port-name	3 Interfaces_Interface-Identifier-**set**
2 In-signal-identifier-**set**	2 Signal-identifier-**set**	2 Interfaces_Interface-Identifier-**set**
3 Out-signal-identifier-**set**	3 Signal-identifier-**set**	Ports_Port-Identifier-**set**
		IntStruct_ConnectorEnd-**set**
		1 [String]
		...

4.6   Composite-state-type/Statemachine

Composite-state-types as well as statemachines have a name (1), a sequence of parameters (3) and an identifier of the composite-state-type/statemachine that they specialise (2), if any. In UML, a statemachine has one or more regions that contain states and transitions. The equivalent in SDL is a Composite-state-graph (one region) or a State-aggregation-graph (two or more regions).

A Composite-state-graph contains a State-transition-graph which contains the states of the Composite-state-type. A Region in UML maps to a State-transition-graph in SDL. Both contain the states (5) and transitions of the composite-state-type/statemachine. Multiple regions are not included in the common AS, because of the different syntax and semantics in SDL and UML. The common AS for Statemachines can be found in [6].

4.7   Agent/Property

Agents and properties are both instances of a type (2) (agent-type in SDL, structured class in UML). Both specify upper and lower bounds for the number of instances (3). While the lower bound in UML is optional, it is required in SDL.

SDL-2000 (AS1)	Common AS	UML 2.0 (derived AS)
Agent-definition ::=(::)	Agent-definition ::=(::)	IntStruct_Property ::=(::)
1 Agent-name	1 Agent-name	Kernel_AggregationKind
Number-of-instances	2 [Agent-type-identifier]	Kernel_Property* /*subset*/
2 Agent-type-identifier	Number-of-instances	Kernel_Property* /*refined*/
		[Kernel_ValueSpecification]
Number-of-instances ::=(::)	Number-of-instances ::=(::)	[Kernel_Association-Identifier]
3 Initial-number	3 [Initial-number]	1 [String]
3 [Maximum-number]	3 [Maximum-number]	2 [Kernel_Type-Identifier]
		3 [Kernel_ValueSpecification]
Initial-number ::=(=) Nat	Initial-number ::=(=) Nat	3 [Kernel_ValueSpecification]
Maximum-number ::=(=)	Maximum-number ::=(=)	3 ...
Nat	Nat	

4.8   State-node/State

State-nodes in SDL are similar to states in UML, however the syntax is different. Both have a name (1) and an identifier of the composite-state-type/statemachine that is the submachine of this state (2), if any. States are the source of transitions, but in SDL these transitions are associated with the trigger of the transition (Input-node) and in UML with the state itself. The common AS for States can be found in [6].

5   Conclusions and Outlook

With regard to recent language developments, harmonisation and finally integration of languages are becoming urgent topics. With more notations being used during the development of a given system, the question whether these views are consistent is gaining importance. Also, in the context of large systems, the use of a mix of notations is getting more likely. Standardisation work to harmonise

UML and SDL is an important effort towards the objective of having a set of languages that can be used together.

In this paper, we have argued that the harmonisation of languages requires a common syntactic and semantic basis. Following this line, we have first defined conceptually sound and well-founded mappings from meta-models – used to define the abstract syntax of UML – to abstract grammars – used by SDL –, and vice versa. By applying these mappings, we have then extracted common production rules, arriving at a common abstract grammar for several language constructs. While the results were encouraging for structural language elements, it turned out that the coverage was below expectations for behavioural constructs. From this experience, we have drawn the conclusion that an extraction on a purely syntactical basis is not sufficient.

In [6], we have therefore compared language elements on a semantic basis. For this comparison, we chose UML statecharts and SDL process graphs, respectively. UML statecharts have a complete semantics with few variation points. Several attempts to formally define the behaviour of statecharts exist, e.g. [7]. The syntactic comparison of UML and SDL revealed that the abstract syntax of statecharts and process graphs is very different. However, there are several language elements in both languages that have a similar notation and represent similar concepts, despite major syntactic differences. The semantic comparison showed that there is indeed potential for the harmonisation of UML and SDL. However, it also revealed that without a common formal basis, the results that can be obtained are of limited value.

We finally conclude that future work should be directed towards a common semantic core for UML and SDL, with the intention of having extensions of this core to cover further, language specific concepts. Both languages are complex and sophisticated, so this will definitely not be a simple task. However, our experience with the definition of the SDL formal semantics [8] has shown that this kind of work provides valuable feedback to the language designers, finally leading to an even better language.

In a related work, Fischer et al [9] describe a way to generate meta-models from BNF grammars and demonstrate their approach for the abstract syntax of SDL-2000. To capitalise on the advantages of meta-models, they introduce abstract concept definitions and transform generated concrete elements to specialisations of abstract elements.

References

[1] OMG Unified Modelling Language Specification: Version 2.0 (2003) 61, 70
[2] OMG Unified Modelling Language Specification: Version 1.3 (1999) 61, 62
[3] ITU Recommendation Z.100: Specification and Description Language. Geneva (1999) 61
[4] ITU Recommendation Z.109: SDL combined with UML. Geneva (2000) 62
[5] Selic, B., Rumbaugh, J.: Mapping SDL to UML. Rational Software Whitepaper. (1999) 62

[6] Grammes, R., Gotzhein, R.: Towards the Harmonisation of UML and SDL - Syntactic and Semantic Alignment -. Technical Report 327/03, Technical University of Kaiserslautern (2003) 64, 72, 76, 77

[7] Börger, E., Cavarra, A., Riccobene, E.: Modeling the dynamics of UML State Machines. In Gurevich, Y., Kutter, P., Odersky, M., Thiele, L., eds.: Abstract State Machines. Theory and Applications, Springer-Verlag (2000) pp. 223–241 77

[8] Glässer, U., Gotzhein, R., Prinz, A.: The Formal Semantics of SDL-2000 - Status and Perspectives. Computer Networks **42** (2003) pp. 343–358 77

[9] Fischer, J., Piefel, M., Scheidgen, M.: A Metamodel for SDL-2000 in the Context of Metamodelling ULF. In: SAM'04. (2004) 77

Localizing Program Errors
for Cimple Debugging

Samik Basu[1], Diptikalyan Saha[2], and Scott A. Smolka[2]

[1] Department of Computer Science
Iowa State University, Ames, IA 50014
sbasu@cs.iastate.edu
[2] Department of Computer Science
State University of New York at Stony Brook, Stony Brook, NY 11794
{dsaha,sas}@cs.sunysb.edu

Abstract. We present automated techniques for the explanation of counter-examples, where a counter-example should be understood as a sequence of program statements. Our approach is based on variable dependency analysis and is applicable to programs written in Cimple, an expressive subset of the C programming language. Central to our approach is the derivation of a focus-statement sequence (FSS) from a given counter-example: a subsequence of the counter-example containing only those program statements that directly or indirectly affect the variable valuation leading to the program error behind the counter-example. We develop a ranking procedure for FSSs where FSSs of higher rank are conceptually easier to understand and correct than those of lower rank. We also analyze constraints over uninitialized variables in order to localize program errors to specific program segments; this often allows the user to subsequently take appropriate debugging measures. We have implemented our techniques in the FocusCheck model checker, which efficiently checks for assertion violations in Cimple programs on a per-procedure basis. The practical utility of our approach is illustrated by its successful application to a fast, linear-time median identification algorithm commonly used in statistical analysis and in the Resolution Advisory module of the Traffic Collision Avoidance System.

1 Introduction

Model checking [22, 7] has recently made significant inroads in the domain of software verification [12, 18, 3, 11, 16, 4]. In this setting, model checking typically follows a three-step iterative process of abstraction, verification and refinement [24, 2, 17, 6]. First, given a system S, a finite-state abstraction S' of S is generated. Then, S' is verified with respect to the given property and a counter-example (sequence of program statements) is generated should a violation occur. Finally, S' is refined in case the counter-example is spurious (infeasible in S). The three steps are iterated until a feasible counter-example is identified or the abstract system satisfies the property.

D. de Frutos-Escrig and M. Núñez (Eds.): FORTE 2004, LNCS 3235, pp. 79–96, 2004.
© IFIP International Federation for Information Processing 2004

```
                                      FSS₁ Assumptions: gotlock == 1
                                   4:    lock=0
1: int gotlock, lock;   13: void getlock() {   5:                    12:
2: bool error = false; 14:  if (lock == 0)     6:                    18:   lock==1:false
3: int main() {        15:    lock++;                11:        got-  20:    error=true
4:   lock = 0;         16:  else error = true; lock==1:true
5:   if (*) {          17: void rellock() {    FSS₂ Assumptions: gotlock != 0
6:     while (*) {     18:  if (lock == 1)
7:       if (*) {      19:    lock-;           4:    lock=0      9:    gotlock++;
8:         getlock();  20:  else error = true; }        5:             11:        got-
9:         gotlock++;  21: void bigProcedure() { 5:   lock==1:false
10:        bigProcedure();}        22:  ... }    6:            6:
11:      if (gotlock == 1)                       7:            7:
12:        rellock();}}                           8:           8:
                                     14:  lock==0:true   14:  lock==0:false
                                     15:  lock++         16:  error=true
           (a)                                    (b)
```

Fig. 1. Simple locking program from [17]

In the event a feasible counter-example is generated, the user is left with the task of identifying the cause of the counter-example and taking appropriate corrective or debugging measures. However, the complex behavior of software systems, owing to the presence of complicated data and control structures, makes the process of decoding counter-examples extremely tedious, if not impossible.

To address this state of affairs, we present two automated techniques for effective error-reporting. The first of these is aimed at ranking counter-examples such that those counter-examples of higher rank are easier to understand and debug than those of lower rank. The second is a technique for localizing errors in programs to specific program regions, again allowing for effective identification and correction of program errors.

Our approach is based on variable dependency analysis and is applicable to programs written in Cimple, an expressive subset of the C programming language. Central to our approach is the notion of a *focus-statement sequence* (FSS), introduced by us in [5]. A FSS is a subsequence of a counter-example containing only those program statements that directly or indirectly affect the variable valuation leading to the program error behind the counter-example. As discussed further in Section 2, our FSS technique can thus be seen as an application of program slicing. Besides making counter-examples easier to understand by eliminating unnecessary details, FSSs can also be used to efficiently determine the feasibility of counter-examples, as the feasibility of the sequence of operations in an FSS implies the existence of a feasible counter-example.

Being based on variable dependency analysis, our approach also successfully identifies the constraints or *assumptions* over uninitialized or input variables necessary for the feasibility of a FSS. Such information can be used to understand program behavior in the context of different variable initializations. We have also developed the FocusCheck model checker for Cimple. It identifies all feasible counter-examples in a given Cimple program and presents these to the user in a precise and informative manner in terms of their FSSs and assumption sets.

Consider first our technique for ranking counter-examples. The basic idea behind this technique is to *rank* FSSs in terms of their length and the number of variables in their assumption sets. In [10], Engler and Ashcraft alluded to the importance of ranking counter-examples for easy inspection of deadlock errors in multi-threaded programs. In a similar vein, we order FSSs such that those of higher rank correspond to errors that are conceptually easier to understand and debug than those of lower rank.

Figure 1(a) presents a simple locking program correct behavior of which requires strict alternation between invocations of `getlock()` and `rellock()`; a violation occurs if `error=true` in any execution sequence of the program. The conditional construct `if(*)` is semantically equivalent to non-deterministic choice, required for representing conditional expressions whose variables are abstracted away to obtain finite data domain program. The `FocusCheck` model checker identifies two counter-examples in terms of their FSSs and assumption sets (Figure 1(b)). The FSSs returned by `FocusCheck` are significantly smaller than the counter-examples from which they are derived as it discards program segments (e.g. the statements of `bigProcedure()`) that do not affect the valuation `error=true`. Variable dependency analysis tells us that in this case, the focus statements are those involving variables `gotlock`, `lock` and `error`. For each FSS returned by `FocusCheck`, the line numbers of the program statements in the FSS are given; the program statement itself is also given if it represents an operation on a variable of interest; e.g., statement `lock=0` at line 4 of FSS_1.

Our ranking procedure identifies the shorter of the two FSSs—FSS_1 comprising seven program statements, four of which are operations on the variables of interest—as the higher-ranked FSS. This directs the user to inspect FSS_1 before FSS_2. The user is also provided with the corresponding assumption set which reveals that the program behaves incorrectly if `gotlock` is initialized to 1; i.e., the error manifests when the condition at line 11 evaluates to true. Corrective measures therefore involve the appropriate initialization of `gotlock` (negate the assumption) in one of the statements leading to the statement at line 11. Ranking FSSs and their assumption sets narrows down the erroneous region in the program under investigation, and assist the user in taking corrective measure by inserting the assignment `gotlock=0` after line 5 or line 6.

Consider next our technique for localizing errors to specific program regions. This technique is based on the observation that in many practical scenarios, a single error in a program can lead to multiple counter-examples, owing to the program's branching behavior. Given a set of FSS, we generate a *reduced set of focus-statement sequences* by discarding the differences and analyzing the commonalities among the FSSs.

To illustrate our technique for localizing errors in programs, consider the `Cimple` program of Figure 2(a). The program is intended to compute the minimum and maximum of three integer variables but contains an obvious typo at line 6 (marked in the figure): the assignment `max=y` should instead be `min=y`. The error condition is satisfied if the minimum or the maximum is set to an incor-

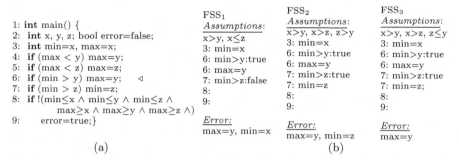

Fig. 2. MinMax example from [13]

rect value. FocusCheck produces three FSSs corresponding to the three possible erroneous program behaviors (Figure 2(b)).

Our technique for localizing program errors is based on the elimination of a constraint and its negation, should they appear in two different assumption sets; it is easily shown that such a pair of constraints is irrelevant to the cause of the error. In the example, our technique first eliminates the constraints z>y and z≤y from the assumption sets of FSS$_2$ and FSS$_3$, respectively. FSS$_3$ is then discarded, being now identical to FSS$_2$ in terms of its assumption set and line numbers. FSS$_1$ and FSS$_2$ contain x≤z and x>z, and we delete these constraints from their respective assumption sets. The remaining constraint in the assumption sets of FSS$_1$ and FSS$_2$ is x>y. We project x>y on both the FSSs and identify the if-block at line 6 as the region containing the error.

An important aspect of our technique for generating FSSs is that it proceeds in a modular fashion, handling each procedure in the program independently of the others. Specifically, our technique seeks to minimize the overhead of analyzing a procedure if it has been invoked from multiple call sites and each of these call sites are present in the counter-example sequence. Central to our technique is the summarization of each procedure with respect to the valuation of global variables.

Our techniques for ranking FSSs and for localizing program errors allow the user to view counter-examples at different levels of granularity and detail (Figure 3). At the lowest level, the user is presented with the entire counter-example sequence. At the intermediate levels, the user sees the FSS of the counter-examples, ordered in terms of their relative complexity. At the highest level, reduced sets of focus statements are identified on the basis of the constraints in their assumption sets. As one moves to higher levels, information is organized and/or minimized without compromising its usefulness.

Contributions and Organization of the Paper. In summary, the main contributions of the paper may be seen as follows:

Fig. 3. Viewing counter-examples at different levels of detail

1. We present a hierarchy of automated techniques aimed at allowing users to effectively ascertain the root cause of a program error. To the best of our knowledge, this is the first effort to organize error explanation at different levels of granularity.
2. Focus-statement sequences, introduced in [5] and reviewed in Section 2, use variable dependency analysis to make counter-examples much easier to comprehend by discarding unnecessary details. We introduce in Section 3.1 a procedure for ranking FSSs such that FSSs higher in the ranking correspond to errors that are conceptually easier to understand and debug than those lower in the ranking.
3. Our technique for generating a reduced set of FSS from a given set of FSSs and their assumptions proceeds by discarding the differences and analyzing the commonalities among the given FSSs (Section 3.2). It can significantly aid the user in localizing the region within a program containing the error under investigation.
4. We have implemented our error-localization technique in the `FocusCheck` model checker. At its core, the model checker performs reachability analysis of programs to generate all possible feasible counter-examples in terms of their FSSs (Section 4). Reachability analysis is performed in a modular fashion by summarizing the effects of a given procedure independently of all other procedures (Section 3.3).
5. We demonstrate the effectiveness of our technique by analyzing the resolution advisory module (RA) of the traffic collision avoidance system (TCAS) (Section 5).

2   Preliminaries

In this section, we provide a brief overview of our technique for extracting focus-statement sequences from counter-examples [5]. Given a program and a correctness assertion, a *counter-example* is a sequence of statements executed by the program leading to a violation of the assertion. A *focus-statement sequence* (FSS) is a subsequence of a counter-example such that each statement in the subsequence directly or indirectly affects the variable valuations responsible for the assertion violation in the program.

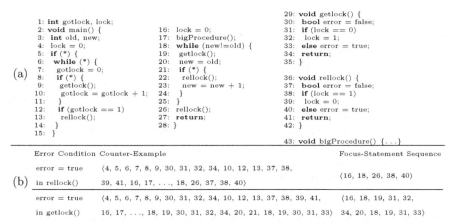

Fig. 4. (a) The locking example (expanded version) (b) Counter-Examples and FSS

Focus-Statement Sequences: Slicing Counter-Examples. Our technique for identifying FSSs, which are semantically dependent, possibly noncontiguous, program segments, is based on *program slicing* [9, 19]. Counter-examples are generated during model checking via reachability analysis from the start state of the program to a state violating the correctness condition. Reachability analysis is also used to record the dynamic control and data dependencies at each statement. Note that the last statement of a counter-example is responsible for the violation of correctness condition. A statement in a counter-example is classified as focus statement if it directly or indirectly affects the last statement in the counter-example. That is, a FSS is obtained from a counter-example sequence S by slicing S, using the last statement in S as the slicing criterion.

Definition 1 (Focus Statement). *Given a counter-example sequence $S = \langle s_1, s_2, \ldots, s_n \rangle$ where s_i denotes the i-th program statement along with its line number and s_n is the last statement in the counter-example, s_j is said to be a focus statement if any one of the following holds:*

1. *s_j is in the slice of S w.r.t. slicing criterion s_n;*
2. *s_j is a call or return statement with at least one focus statement in the body of the called procedure.*

Our slicing method for extracting FSSs from counter-examples works as follows. We perform backward exploration from the last statement s_n of a counter-example sequence S. A set Error is maintained during the analysis, containing the line numbers of the statements and variables that affect s_n. Error is generated from the sets control(s_i) and data(s_i) for each statement s_i in S, representing control and data dependencies at s_i, respectively. Statement s_i is control-dependent on those conditional statements whose line numbers are present in control(s_i), while s_i depends on the variables in data(s_i).

For the first of the two counter-example sequences given in Figure 4(b), the set Error is initialized to {38}, as the last statement at line 40 of the counter-example has control(40) = {38}. As backward analysis proceeds, the statement at line 38 is encountered with Error = {38}; therefore, the statement at line 38 is classified as a focus statement and Error is updated by removing 38 and introducing the variable lock (lock ∈ data(38)). The next statement reached in the backward exploration is the one at line 37 (error=true). However, the variable error ∉ Error. Therefore the statement at line 37 is not a focus statement and the Error set is unaltered. Backward exploration terminates if set Error is empty or all the statements in the counter-example have been analyzed. The focus-statement sequences identified in this manner are given in Figure 4(b) alongside their corresponding counter-example sequences.

Feasibility of Counter-Example Sequences. The behavior of a program typically depends upon the valuation of variables that are inputs to the program. If an input variable has an infinite domain, say the integers, reachability analysis is typically performed by leaving the operations on these variables uninterpreted. For example, the operations at lines 18, 20 and 23 in Figure 4(a) are uninterpreted and forward reachability is performed by considering all possible (boolean) valuations of the conditional expression at line 18. This approach leads the model checker to consider both branches of the conditional expression, whereas in reality only one of the branches is feasible. This results in infeasible counter-examples in the output of the model checker. Typically, feasibility analysis involves considering each counter-example to determine whether all the operations in the counter-example are consistent in the original source program. In contrast, we reduce the overheads of feasibility analysis by reducing (a) number of counter-examples to be checked and (b) number of operations to be checked for consistency.

These reductions are achieved by observing that given an FSS F comprising a feasible sequence of operations, there exists at least one feasible counter-example C with F as its subsequence. To check the feasibility of a counter-example, we therefore check the feasibility of the sequences of operations in the counter-example's FSS. Note that the length of a FSS is often less than that of the corresponding counter-example making feasibility checking of the former more efficient than the latter. Furthermore, if multiple counter-examples correspond to the same FSS, proving/disproving feasibility of all these counter-examples is performed by checking for feasibility of a single FSS.

Referring back to our example of Figure 4, the second FSS is infeasible due to the infeasibility of the operation at line 20 followed by the operation at line 18. The first FSS, however, is feasible. FSSs can therefore be used to both shorten counter-examples by eliminating unnecessary details and to effectively discard infeasible execution sequences.

3   Debugging Cimple Programs

3.1   Ranking the Counter-Examples

In many practical settings, a single error can force a program to behave erroneously in multiple ways leading to the generation of multiple counter-example sequences. For example, a single error in each of the programs of Figures 1 and 2 (missing initialization and incorrect assignment, respectively) generates more than one counter-example. While it is difficult, if not impossible, to localize the cause of multiple counter-examples to one single parameter in a program, it is possible develop techniques that will effectively guide the users toward making the correct choice in debugging programs. Ranking counter-examples on the basis of focus-statement sequences and their assumption sets is a methodology where error traces are sorted in terms of their complexity.

Definition 2 (Rank). *Given two FSSs F_1 and F_2, F_1 is said to be of higher rank than F_2, denoted by $F_1 \succeq F_2$, if:*

1. *the length of F_1 is less than that of F_2 or*
2. *the length of F_1 is equal to the length of F_2 and the number of variables in the assumptions of F_1 is less than number of variables in the assumptions of F_2.*

Definition 2 defines a partial order over FSSs. Higher ranked FSSs are more likely to be easier to parse and understand than the lower ranked ones. The rationale for selecting the two ranking criteria is based on the following observations. A user can potentially parse a smaller sequence of focus statements than a longer one. If two FSSs involve an identical number of statements, the one which requires assumptions over a fewer number of variables for its feasibility is potentially simpler to understand than the one requiring constraints over more variables. The involvement of a fewer number of variables in an assumption set means that a fewer number of program variables are affected by the assumptions and, therefore, the user will be required to concentrate on a fewer number of operations on variables in order to track down the error.

3.2   Localizing Program Errors Using Assumption Sets

In this section, we provide a methodology to further minimize the sequence of statements in each FSS that the user is required to inspect in order to find the potential cause of an error. Our objective is to localize the program error to a specific segment of an FSS. We show that in certain scenarios, our technique can identify the exact program statement that is the cause of the error, and provide useful feedback to the user about a possible remedy.

Our approach is based on algorithm Reduce given in Figure 5; it performs a reduction on a given set of FSS-assumption set pairs followed by a projection of the resulting assumption sets to their corresponding FSSs.

Input: A set S of FSSs $F_1, F_2, \ldots, F_n$ and their corresponding assumption sets $A_1, A_2, \ldots, A_n$. **Output:** Reduce(S).

1. Initially Reduce(S) $= S$. Repeat Steps 2 and 3 till no change in Reduce(S).
2. If there exits a constraint c in a unique A_i and its negation $\neg c$ in a unique A_j, $i \neq j$, then delete c from A_i and $\neg c$ from A_j. Iterate this step until no such c is found.
   (*reduction by eliminating complementary assumptions*)
3. If there exist in Reduce(S) identical FSSs F_i and F_j with identical assumption sets A_i and A_j, $i \neq j$, remove any one of these FSS-assumption set pairs from Reduce(S).
   (*reduction by eliminating identical FSS-assumption pairs*)
4. Project each A_i in Reduce(S) to its corresponding FSS F_i as follows.
5. Start with statement s_k, $k = 1$, the first statement in F_i and repeat the following cases.
   (a) s_k is a conditional statement with conditional expression c:
       i. if $c \notin A_i$ or $\neg c \notin A_i$ then mark all focus statements in the block containing s_k and go to step 4
       ii. else $k{+}{+}$
   (b) s_k is an assignment statement $x = y$ (*call statements are considered as assignments of actual parameters to the corresponding formal parameters*)
       i. if $\exists c \in A_i$ involving y then add the new constraint over x in A_i by replicating constraints over y and replacing y by x in the replication. $k{+}{+}$
       ii. if $\exists c \in A_i$ involving x then delete c from A_i. $k{+}{+}$
   (c) If s_k is the last statement of F_i, mark the entire F_i; go to step 4.

Fig. 5.   Algorithm Reduce

Definition 3 (Reduced Set of Focus Statement Sequences). *A set of focus-statement sequences* $\{F_1, F_2, \ldots, F_n\}$, *where each* F_i *is paired with assumption set* A_i, *is said to be* reduced *if the following conditions hold:*

1. *If* c *is a constraint in* A_i, *then* $\neg c$ *is either not present in any* A_j *or is present in at least two* A_j *($j \neq i$) (reduction of assumptions).*
2. $\forall i, j(i \neq j) \Rightarrow (F_i \neq F_j \vee A_i \neq A_j)$ *(reduction of FSSs).*
3. *A sequence of statements* $\langle s_{i_1}, s_{i_2}, \ldots, s_{i_n} \rangle$ *is* marked *in each FSS* F_i *such that the outer-most conditional expression[1] over input variables in* F_i *cannot be evaluated using the constraints present in* A_i *(Neighborhood of Error Statements).*

Eliminating Complementary Assumptions Recall that assumption sets represent the constraints on uninitialized or input variables necessary for the

---

[1] A conditional expression is outer-most in an FSS if it appears in the first conditional statement in the FSS

feasibility of a counter-example sequence. Specifically, assumptions represent the constraints necessary to validate the conditional expressions present in the counter-example. Our technique for eliminating complementary assumptions from a set of FSSs is based on the following observation:

> *If a constraint c and its negation ¬c appear in* exactly two *distinct assumption sets, then c and ¬c are most likely generated from the same conditional statement which has exactly one FSS for each of its branches.*

There are three possible ways in which the above observation holds:

(a) **Error statement followed by a conditional.** Consider first the case where an error in a program is caused by an incorrect assignment that is followed by a conditional block. If the assignment affects statements in both branches of the conditional block and if these statements affect the assertion violation, then two FSSs are generated. Each FSS is accompanied by an assumption set containing the constraint required to obtain the appropriate valuation of the conditional expression; i.e., a constraint and its negation appear in two different assumption sets.

(b) **Error in a conditional expression.** An error caused by an incorrect conditional expression also produces at least two FSSs. This is due to the fact that both branches in the conditional lead to the assertion violation. Thus, each branch leads to the generation of an FSS along with an assumption set containing the constraint required for the corresponding valuation of the conditional expression.

(c) **Errors in both branches of a conditional block.** This case corresponds to the situation where there are errors in both branches of a conditional block.

In all of the above cases, the pair under consideration (a constraint c and its negation $¬c$ appearing in two different assumption sets) can be safely classified as uninteresting constraints. The reason for this is that negating the conditional expression in the program that generated c and $¬c$ followed by reachability analysis of error state will generate the same set of FSSs. In case the pair of constraints is generated from two different conditional statements our method will localize the bug in an ancestor block of the block containing the error. This imprecision can be removed by associating program location with each assumption and eliminating complementary assumptions only if they are generated at the same program location.

Another important feature of the constraint pair is that they must appear in exactly two assumption sets. The requirement of exactly two instead of at least two assumption sets has its root in the following observation. Suppose there are two assumption sets containing constraint c and a single assumption set containing $¬c$; i.e., there are two FSSs corresponding to constraint c and one FSS corresponding to $¬c$. In this case, it is most likely there are errors present in both branches of a conditional block with conditional expression c (or $¬c$) (see item(c) above). Further, as there are multiple FSSs corresponding

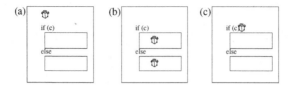

Fig. 6. NESTs are the focus statements in the outer and inner blocks for different bug positions

to c, the error is present in a block nested in the then-branch or else-branch of the conditional. Our aim is to localize the error in the block nested inside the conditional statement. As such we do not discard the constraints c and $\neg c$.

Removal of a constraint and its negation from two assumption sets might make these FSSs and their corresponding assumption sets identical; one of of these FSSs can be safely removed from further consideration. Reduction is therefore achieved in two different dimensions: the size of assumption sets and the number of FSSs. Steps 1–3 of algorithm Reduce (Figure 5) encode the reduction steps described in this section. The following section describes our technique for identifying erroneous program segments in each of the remaining FSSs.

Projecting Assumptions to Focus-Statement Sequences Our technique is based on projecting the assumptions (left after discarding complementary constraints) on the corresponding FSS. We refer to the resulting subsequence as the Neighborhood of Error STatements (NEST), the region in the FSS where the user must apply corrective measures to remedy the corresponding counterexample (steps 5(a), (b) and (c) in Figure 5).

Projection proceeds by forward analysis of the FSS. Each statement may or may not update the assumption set depending on whether or not it affects the constraints in the assumption set. Each statement is interpreted under the assumption set obtained after analyzing the statement preceding it in the FSS. The first statement is interpreted using the reduced assumption set of the FSS obtained by discarding complementary constraints in the assumption sets.

The terminating condition (5(a)i in Figure 5) implies that we have identified the outermost conditional statement whose condition has generated unimportant constraints (discarded in the previous steps of the algorithm). Next, we mark the NEST as all of the focus statements that belong to the same block [2] as the conditional statement (error localization). Note that the size of the NEST can be significantly smaller than the actual program block in which it belongs as only the statements responsible for the assertion violation (i.e., the subsequence of the FSS) are included in the NEST.

The NEST presents to the user a region which encompasses the error statement(s) present in the program (See figure 6). In the worst case (e.g., only one

---

[2] A block refers to all of the statements which are in the same or nested static scope.

FSS is generated due to the program error), the NEST encompasses the entire FSS, while in the best case, NEST identifies the exact statement which, if altered, will remove the program error.

Analyzing the Median Identification Program. We illustrate the effectiveness of algorithm Reduce using the program given in Figure 7. This program sorts five integers a1, a2, a3, a4, and a5, in only five comparisons given the partial order a1>a2, a3>a4, a1>a3. The output of the program is a sorted list of output variables o1, o2, o3, o4, o5 in descending order. The program is based on the algorithm for finding the median of a list of numbers in linear time [8].

The program proceeds by considering inequalities between pairs of inputs. Consider first the two cases when a3>a5 [lines 9-40] and a3≤a5 [lines 41-61]. In the former case, if a4>a5 is satisfied, the program proceeds to identify the correct position for a2 in the ordered list a3>a4>a5 [lines 12-24]. A similar technique is used for a4≤a5 when the ordering is a3>a5>a4 [lines 26-38]. In the latter case, i.e., when a3≤a5, the condition a2>a3 is used to find the correct position of a5 with respect to the ordering a1,a2,a3 [lines 42-50]; on the other hand, a2≤a3 implies that the sorted ordering is a1, a5, a3, a2, a4 [lines 52-61].

Consider now an error in the program caused by an artificially injected incorrect conditional expression at line 14: a2 < a3 instead of a2 > a3. In this case we will get two FSSs, $F_1 = \langle 4, 6, 9, 10, 11, 12, 13, 14, 15, 62, 63 \rangle$ with assumption set $A_1 = \{a1 > a2, a3 > a4, a1 > a3, a3 > a5, a4 > a5, a2 > a4, a2 > a3\}$ and $F_2 = \langle 4, 6, 9, 10, 11, 12, 13, 14, 17, 62, 63 \rangle$ with assumption set $A_2 = \{a1 > a2, a3 > a4, a1 > a3, a3 > a5, a4 > a5, a2 > a4, a2 \leq a3\}$. Step 2 of algorithm Reduce will delete the constraints a2 > a3, a2 ≤ a3 from assumption sets A_1 and A_2, respectively. In steps 4 and 5 of the algorithm we project the modified set A_1 on F_1 and modified set A_2 on F_2. NEST is identified as $\langle 13, 14, 15 \rangle$ for F_1 and $\langle 13, 14, 17 \rangle$ for F_2.

Introducing another bug at line 48 by copying line 46 to line 48 will generate three FSSs, two of which are the same as F_1 and F_2 described above. The third FSS F_3 comprises $(\langle 4, 6, 9, 40, 41, 42, 43, 44, 45, 48, 62, 63 \rangle)$ and its corresponding assumption set A_3 is $\{a3 \leq a5, a2 > a3, a5, > a2, a5 \leq a1\}$. In this case, step 2 of our algorithm will not delete the constraint a3 > a5 and a3 ≤ a5 from any assumption sets as a3 > a5 exists both in A_1 and A_2. This will led us to identify NESTs $\langle 3, 14, 15 \rangle$ and $\langle 13, 14, 17 \rangle$ as in the previous case. This justifies the deletion of a constraint and its negation only if they exist in exactly two distinct FSSs. In the present case, there exists only one FSS (F_3) that goes through the else-block of the condition at line 9. We cannot localize the error for F_3 since step 5 of algorithm Reduce is iteratively executed until we reach the last statement in F_3 and as such the entire F_3 is marked as a NEST.

3.3   Detecting Focus-Statement Sequence Modularly via Summarization

Model checking involves finding whether an error state in the system is reachable from its start state. Efficient reachability analysis [11, 21] of programs with

```
1: int main(){                22:       else              45:       if(a5 > a1)
2: int a1,a2,a3,a4,a5;         23:          o4=a5,o5=a5;   46:          o1=a5,o2=a1;
3: int o1,o2,o3,o4,o5;         24:       }                 47:       else
4: int error=0;                25:    else  /* line 11 */  48:          o1=a1,o2=a5;
5: // input a1, a2, a3, a4, a5; 26:      if(a2 > a5){     49:       }else
6: if(!((a1>a2)&&(a3>a4)       27:          o4=a5,o5=a4;   50:          o1=a1,o2=a2,o3=a5;
       &&(a1>a3))){            28:          if(a2 > a3)   51:       }else{
7:     exit(0);                29:             o2=a2,o3=a3; 52:          o3=a3;
8: }                           30:          else           53:          if(a1 > a5)
9:  if(a3 > a5){               31:             o2=a3,o3=a4; 54:             o1=a1,o2=a5;
10:    o1=a1;                  32:       }else{             55:          else
11:    if(a4 > a5)             33:          o2=a3,o3=a5;    56:             o1=a5,o2=a1;
12:      if(a2 > a4){          34:          if(a2 > a4)     57:          if(a2 > a4)
13:         o4=a4,o5=a5;       35:             o4=a2,o5=a4; 58:             o4=a2,o5=a4;
14:         if(a2 > a3)        36:          else            59:          else
15:           o2=a2,o3=a3;     37:             o4=a4,o5=a2; 60:             o4=a4,o5=a2;
16:         else               38:       }                  61:       }
17:           o2=a3,o3=a3;     39:    }                     62:    if((o1<o2)||(o2<o3)||
18:      }else{                40:    else                      (o3<o4)||(o4<o5)){
19:         o2=a3,o3=a4;       41:       if(a2 > a3){        63:       error=1;
20:      if(a2 > a5)           42:          o4=a3,o5=a4;    64:    }
21:         o4=a2,o5=a5;       43:          if(a5 > a2){
                              44:             o3=a2;
```

Fig. 7. Sorting five partially ordered numbers

recursions employs summarization of procedures with respect to the valuation of global variables. Intuitively, summarization represents the effect of a procedure and involves computing the relation between variable valuations at its start and exit points. The main advantage of this technique is modularity and efficiency; each procedure is analyzed in isolation and their summaries are used for forward reachability analysis. Observe that program behavior is classified using three types of transitions:

Statement	Transition	Stack depth	Global variable valuations
return:	$s, g \longrightarrow \epsilon, g'$	decreases by 1	g and g' respectively before and after executing s
call:	$s, g \longrightarrow s_1, g_1 : s_2, g_2$	increases by 1	g, g_1, g_2 at call statement s of callee, start statement s_1 of the called procedure and return location s_2 of the callee respectively
other:	$s, g \longrightarrow s', g'$	no change	g and g' respectively before and after executing s

Based on the above observations, the effect of a procedure on the global variables is the least fixed point of relation $\mathtt{fsum}(g, s, g')$, where s is the start state of the procedure and g and g' are the valuations of global variables at the entry and exit point of the procedure, respectively. It can be shown that the procedure with m transitions can be summarized in time $O(m \times g^3)$ [11].

$$\begin{aligned}
\mathtt{fsum}(g, s, g') &\Leftarrow & s, g \longrightarrow \epsilon, g' \\
\mathtt{fsum}(g, s, g') &\Leftarrow & s, g \longrightarrow s_1, g_1 : s_2, g_2 \wedge \mathtt{fsum}(g_1, s_1, g_2) \wedge \mathtt{fsum}(g_2, s_2, g') \\
\mathtt{fsum}(g, s, g') &\Leftarrow & s, g \longrightarrow s_1, g_1 \wedge \mathtt{fsum}(g_1, s_1, g')
\end{aligned}$$

To find a sequence of statements leading to violating state our FocusCheck model checker performs forward reachability analysis from the start state of the program. Each call site in the program is interpreted in terms of the effect of the called procedure on the global variables. In other words, if there are multiple calls (say k) to the same procedure, the called procedure is analyzed *once* to compute the fsum relation instead of analyzing it k times. Summarization, therefore, makes a significant contribution to the efficiency of model checker.

Summarizing Effects of Procedures Using Backward Reachability.
Focus statements are identified by backward reachability analysis of counter-examples (Section 2). The technique involves dynamically computing a set Error consisting of variables whose valuations directly or indirectly affect the variable valuation that caused assertion violation. As in forward reachability analysis, backward reachability is also performed efficiently using summarization of procedures. Given the set Error and the valuations of global variables at the exit point of a procedure, summarization involves computing the Error set, the valuation of global variables at the start location of the procedure, and the sequences of focus statements. The summary of a procedure computed via backward analysis is defined by the least model of the $\mathtt{bsum}(g, e, \mathtt{fss}, s, g', e', \mathtt{fss}')$ relation, where (a) s is the start location of the procedure, (b) $g', e', \mathtt{fss}'$ are the valuation of the global variables, the Error set, and the sequence of focus statements at the exit point of the procedure and (c) $g, e, \mathtt{fss}$ are the valuation of global variables, the Error set, and sequence of focus statements at the entry point.

$$\mathtt{bsum}(g, e, \mathtt{fss}, s, g', e', \mathtt{fss}') \Leftarrow s, g \longrightarrow \epsilon, g' \ \wedge \ \mathtt{update}(e, \mathtt{fss}, s, e', \mathtt{fss}')$$
$$\mathtt{bsum}(g, e, \mathtt{fss}, s, g', e', \mathtt{fss}') \Leftarrow s, g \longrightarrow s_1, g_1 : s_2, g_2 \ \wedge \ \mathtt{bsum}(g_2, e_2, \mathtt{fss}_2, s_2, g', e', \mathtt{fss}') \ \wedge$$
$$\mathtt{bsum}(g_1, e_1, \mathtt{fss}_1, s_1, g_2, e_2, \mathtt{fss}_2) \ \wedge \mathtt{update}(e, \mathtt{fss}, s, e_1, \mathtt{fss}_1)$$
$$\mathtt{bsum}(g, e, \mathtt{fss}, s, g', e', \mathtt{fss}') \Leftarrow s, g \longrightarrow s_1, g_1 \wedge \mathtt{bsum}(g_1, e_1, \mathtt{fss}_1, s_1, g', e', \mathtt{fss}') \ \wedge$$
$$\mathtt{update}(e, \mathtt{fss}, s, e', \mathtt{fss}')$$

$\mathtt{update}(e, \mathtt{fss}, s, e', \mathtt{fss}')$ checks whether the statement s affects the Error set (e'). $\mathtt{fss}'$ is the FSS identified up to the point statement s is visited in backward reachability analysis. In the event s is classified as a focus statement, fss is generated by pre-pending s to $\mathtt{fss}'$ while e' is appropriately updated to e.

The distinguishing feature between fsum and bsum relations, used for summarizing procedures during forward and backward reachability analysis respectively, is the order in which the transition between statements appearing in the execution sequence is analyzed. Consider the second rule in the definition of the relations fsum and bsum, the case where s corresponds to a call statement. The fsum relation proceeds by computing the fsum of the called procedure followed by the fsum of the callee starting from the return location. On the other hand, bsum first computes the bsum of the callee starting from the return location followed by the bsum of the called procedure.

However, the common aspect of fsum and bsum is that summarization makes forward and backward analysis of program traces efficient. Both relations once computed for each procedure are used multiple times if the same procedure is invoked multiple times in a program with the same input/output parameters (global valuations, Error sets, focus statements). To illustrate the impact of the bsum relation in finding FSSs, consider the following example. Assume procedure Q is invoked k times in the error trace in procedure P, and Q has m different paths from its start to exit point. Further assume that Q does not affect the counter-example sequence and as such does not contribute to set Error.

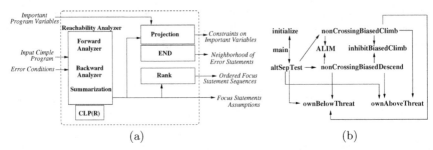

Fig. 8. (a) Architecture of the `FocusCheck` model checker. (b) Call graph for RA module

That is, statements in Q do not appear in the FSS. Naive backward reachability analysis from the error state will analyze Q by inlining the procedure at its call sites; i.e., the m different paths in Q will be analyzed k times. On the other hand, summarization will analyze the m different paths in Q only once and use the summary result at each of the call sites.

4 Tool Description

In this section, we describe the salient features of our `FocusCheck` model checker `FocusCheck`, in which we have implemented the techniques described in this paper.

Input Language Description. The `FocusCheck` model checker takes as input programs written in `Cimple`, an expressive subset of C. The basic building blocks of `Cimple` are integer, boolean and array data types, and assignment, conditional (`if`, `while` statements), call and return statements. Due to the absence of pointers and address reference mechanisms, array of size n is treated as n different variables identified by the name of the array appended to the index value of the element; e.g. the third element in an array `arr` is identified by the variable `arr3`. Calls to procedure are treated as call-by-value and returns from procedure are explicitly handled by assigning the return value to a pre-specified global variable.

Reachability Analyzer. The input to the reachability analyzer is a `Cimple` program and one or more error conditions. Forward reachability searches for all counter-examples in the program, and records the control and data dependencies at each statement present in the search path. Backward reachability analysis of counter-examples identifies the FSSs using dependency information. Operations of FSSs are checked for feasibility using CLP(R), a built-in constraint solver in the XSB tabled logic-programming environment [26]. The primary advantage of using logic programming to implement the reachability analyzer includes the direct implementation of least fixed-point summarization relations `fsum` and `bsum`.

Error Conditions	Assumptions	Simple Reachability (sec)	Reachability by Summarizing (sec)
altSep=UPWARD_RA	otherTrackedAlt>ownTrackedAlt upSeparation>downSeparation downSeparation<positiveRAAltThresh	8.76	4.23
altSep=DOWNWARD_RA	ownTrackedAlt>otherTrackedAlt upSeparation≤downSeparation upSeparation≥positiveRAAltThresh	7.44	3.98

Fig. 9. Results of model checking the RA module

The output of the reachability analyzer is a set of focus-statement sequences along with their assumption sets.

Components for Post-processing FSSs. Ranker orders FSS-assumption pairs and presents the ordered list to the user (Section 3.1). The user can also provide a subset of input variables that s/he considers as important and Projector identifies the constraints over these variables from the assumptions of each FSS. Finally, the Error Neighborhood Detector (END) employs the technique described in Section 3.2 to localize errors to specific segments in each FSS.

5   Verification of the TCAS Resolution Advisory Module

The *Traffic Alert and Collision Avoidance System* (TCAS) [23] issues commercial airline pilots traffic advisories when one or more aircrafts comes in close proximity (airspace) of the controlled aircraft. We concentrate here on the Resolution Advisory (RA) module of TCAS which is used to identify the safest maneuver for the controlled aircraft in the context of various parameters: relative position of the intruder aircraft, motion trajectory, minimum protected zone for the controlled aircraft, etc. The RA module sets a variable altsep to UPWARD_RA or DOWNWARD_RA depending on whether the preferred safety action of the controlled aircraft is to move to a higher or lower altitude.

We analyzed the RA module (174 lines of C source code[3] [15]) using our FocusCheck model checker, using different valuations of altsep as error conditions. The objective was to identify various preconditions on input variables necessary for specific valuation of altsep. The assumptions generated exactly match the preconditions and prove the correct behavior of the RA module (Table 9). Another important aspect of the RA module is its control structure (Figure 8(b)): a number of procedures are invoked multiple times from different procedures. Timing results reveal that reachability analysis using summarization outperforms naive reachability analysis based on inlining.

---

[3] Implementation of RA module only uses the C language constructs that can be handled by FocusCheck model checker and as such we are not required to perform any abstraction or transformation of the source code.

6   Related Work

A number of techniques have recently been proposed to provide users with minimal information required to explain counter-examples resulting from model checking. In [25], the authors introduce the notion of *neighborhood of counter-examples* which can be used to understand the cause of counter-examples. A different approach based on game-theoretic techniques is put forth in [20] where counter-examples are augmented into *free segments* (choices) and *fated segments* (unavoidable). Errors are most likely to be removed by careful selection of free segments.

In [1], errors in programs are localized by identifying the diverging point between a counter-example and a *positive* example; a positive example is a sequence of statements in programs that does not lead to a violation of the property of interest. A similar approach is presented in [14] where errors are localized to program statements absent in all positive examples and present in all counter-examples leading to the same error condition. Based on the idea of detecting the divergence as the cause of the counter-example, [13] has developed a technique that uses a distance matrix and constraint manipulations to pin-point the variable operations that led to the divergence. The technique, however, is applied to one counter-example in the program. In contrast, we present a hierarchy of error explanations by analyzing multiple counter-examples.

7   Conclusion

We have presented a methodology for helping users locate and debug program errors. The essence of our approach is to present the user with an ordered set of focus-statement sequences, obtained by variable dependency analysis of all counter-examples present in a program written in the `Cimple` programming language.

As future work, we intend to enrich the `Cimple` language with pointer constructs and dynamic memory allocation, and concomitantly apply subset-based, interprocedural, flow-sensitive pointer-analysis techniques. The `FocusCheck` model checker will be appropriately enhanced to handle these new constructs. We would also like to apply our approach to large code bases in order to understand various scalability issues. One approach we plan to pursue utilizes partial code coverage. Finally, extending our techniques to concurrent programs in order to verify temporal safety and liveness properties is another avenue of future research.

References

[1] T. Ball, M. Naik, and S. K. Rajamani. From symptom to cause: Localizing error in counterexample traces. In *Proceedings of POPL*, 2003. 95

[2] T. Ball, A. Podelski, and S. K. Rajamani. Relative completeness of abstraction refinement for software model checking. In *Proceedings of TACAS*, 2002. 79

[3] T. Ball and S. K. Rajamani. Bebop: A symbolic model checker for boolean programs. In *Proceedings of SPIN Workshop*, 2000. 79

[4] T. Ball and S. K. Rajamani. Slam, 2003. `http://research.microsoft.com/slam`. 79

[5] S. Basu, D. Saha, and S. A. Smolka. Getting to the root of the problem: Focus statements for the analysis of counter-examples. Technical report, SUNYSB, 2004. 80, 83

[6] BLAST. Berkeley lazy abstraction software verification tool, 2003. `http://www-cad.eecs.berkeley.edu/~rupak/blast/`. 79

[7] E. M. Clarke, E. A. Emerson, and A. P. Sistla. Automatic verification of finite-state concurrent systems using temporal logic specifications. *ACM TOPLAS*, 8(2), 1986. 79

[8] T. H. Corman, C. E. Leiserson, , and R. L. Rivest. *Introduction to Algorithm*. MIT Press, 1990. 90

[9] M. B. Dwyer and J. Hatcliff. Slicing software for model construction. In *Partial Evaluation and Semantic-Based Program Manipulation*, 1999. 84

[10] D. Engler and K. Ashcraft. RacerX: Effective, static detection of race conditions and deadlocks. In *Proceedings of SOSP*, 2003. 81

[11] J. Esparza and S. Schwoon. A BDD-based model checker for recursive programs. In *Proceedings of CAV*, 2001. 79, 90, 91

[12] P. Godefroid. Model checking for programming languages using verisoft. In *Proceedings of POPL*, 1997. 79

[13] A. Groce. Error explanation with distance metrics. In *Proceedings of TACAS*, 2004. 82, 95

[14] A. Groce and W. Visser. What went wrong: Explaining counterexamples. In *Proceedings of SPIN Workshop on Model Checking of Software*, 2003. 95

[15] Aristotle Research Group. Program analysis based software engineering, 2003. `http://www.cc.gatech.edu/aristotle/`. 94

[16] J. Hatcliff and M. Dwyer. Using the bandera tool set to model-check properties of concurrent Java software. *LNCS*, 2154:39–??, 2001. 79

[17] T. A. Henzinger, R. Jhala, R. Majumdar, and G. Sutre. Lazy abstraction. In *Proceedings of POPL*, 2002. 79, 80

[18] G. J. Holzmann and M. H. Smith. Software model checking: Extracting verification models from source code. In *Proceedings of FORTE*, 1999. 79

[19] S. Horwitz, T. Reps, and D. Binkley. Interprocedural slicing using dependence graphs. In *Proceedings of PLDI*, 1988. 84

[20] H. Jin, K. Ravi, and F. Somenzi. Fate and free will in error traces. In *Proceedings of TACAS*, 2002. 95

[21] MOPED. A model checker for pushdown systems, 2003. `http://www.fmi.uni-stuttgart.de/szs/tools/moped/`. 90

[22] J. P. Queille and J. Sifakis. Specification and verification of concurrent systems in Cesar. In *Proceedings of the ISP*, 1982. 79

[23] RTCA. Minimum operational performance stardards for traffic alert and collision aviodance system (TCAS) airborne equipment consolidated edition, 1990. 94

[24] A. Rybalchenko. *A Model Checker based on Abstraction Refinement*. PhD thesis, Universitt des Saarlandes, 2002. 79

[25] N. Sharygina and D. Peled. A combined testing and verification approach for software reliability. In *Proceedings of FME*, 2001. 95

[26] The XSB logic programming system, 2003. `http://xsb.sourceforge.net`. 93

Formal Verification
of a Practical Lock-Free Queue Algorithm

Simon Doherty[1], Lindsay Groves[1], Victor Luchangco[2], and Mark Moir[2]

[1] School of Mathematical and Computing Sciences
Victoria University of Wellington, New Zealand
[2] Sun Microsystems Laboratories, 1 Network Drive
Burlington, MA 01803, USA

Abstract. We describe a semi-automated verification of a slightly opti-
mised version of Michael and Scott's lock-free FIFO queue implementation. We verify the algorithm with a simulation proof consisting of two
stages: a forward simulation from an automaton modelling the algorithm
to an intermediate automaton, and a backward simulation from the intermediate automaton to an automaton that models the behaviour of
a FIFO queue. These automata are encoded in the input language of the
PVS proof system, and the properties needed to show that the algorithm
implements the specification are proved using PVS's theorem prover.

1 Introduction

Performance and software engineering problems resulting from the use of locks
have motivated researchers to develop *lock-free* algorithms to implement concurrent data structures. However, these algorithms are significantly more complicated than lock-based algorithms, and thus require careful proofs to ensure
their correctness. Such proofs typically involve long and tedious case analyses,
with few interesting cases. Thus, it is desirable to have a tool that generates and
checks all the cases, requiring human guidance only in the few interesting cases.

In this paper, we discuss the verification of a lock-free queue algorithm based
on the practical and widely used algorithm of Michael and Scott [1]. which to our
knowledge has not been formally verified before. We prove that the algorithm is
linearisable [2], using a *simulation proof*, which involves constructing a special
kind of relation, called a *simulation*, between the states of two automata modelling the algorithm and its specification. We use the PVS verification system [3]
to check the proof.

Our verification has three principal points of interest: First, unlike many
practical algorithms, which can be verified using only a *forward simulation*, this
algorithm also requires a *backward simulation*, which is trickier to verify. Second,
the way in which we model a dynamic heap, and use an existentially quantified
function to relate objects in the heap with abstract data, avoids many difficulties
associated with reasoning about dynamic data structures. Third, we developed
various techniques to help PVS automatically dispose of most of the cases in the

D. de Frutos-Escrig and M. Núñez (Eds.): FORTE 2004, LNCS 3235, pp. 97–114, 2004.

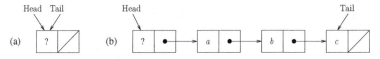

Fig. 1. Basic queue representation

structure pointer_t {*ptr*: **pointer to** node_t, *ver*: **unsigned integer**}
structure node_t   {*value*: data type, *next*: pointer_t}
structure queue_t   {*Head*: pointer_t, *Tail*: pointer_t}

INITIALISE(Q: **pointer to** queue_t)
    node = *new_node*(); node→*next.ptr* = *null*;
    Q→*Head* = Q→*Tail* = [node, 0];

Fig. 2. Global declarations and initialisation

simulation proofs. Using these techniques, we encountered few cases in which we needed to provide guidance to the prover.

We present the queue algorithm in Sect. 2. In Sect. 3, we introduce I/O automata and show how to model the queue specification and implementation. Sect. 4 describes our verification. Sect. 5 discusses our experience using PVS. We conclude in Sect. 6.

2   The Queue Implementation

Our algorithm implements a queue as a linked list of nodes, each having a *value* and a *next* field, along with *Head* and *Tail* pointers. *Head* points to the first node in the list, which is a dummy node; the remaining nodes contain the values in the queue. In quiescent states (i.e., when no operation is in progress), *Tail* points to the last node in the list. Fig. 1 shows an empty queue and a queue containing values *a*, *b* and *c*. The declarations and initialisation are shown in Fig. 2. Pseudocode for the ENQUEUE and DEQUEUE operations is given in Fig. 3.

Shared locations containing pointers (i.e., *Head*, *Tail* and *next*) are updated using *compare-and-swap* (CAS) operations.[1] CAS takes the address of a memory location, an "expected" value, and a "new" value. If the location contains the expected value, the CAS *succeeds*, atomically storing the new value into the location and returning *true*. Otherwise, the CAS *fails*, returning *false* and leaving the memory unchanged.

These shared locations also contain a *version number*, which is incremented atomically every time the location is written.[2] Thus, if such a location contains

---

[1] The one exception is in the initialisation of a new node (line E3), where a store is sufficient because no other process can access a node while it is being initialised.

[2] In this paper, we treat version numbers as unbounded naturals, so they never "wrap around". This simplification is reasonable as long as enough bits are used for the version number [4].

ENQUEUE(Q: **pointer to** queue_t,
             value: data type)
E1: $node = new\_node()$
E2: $node{\rightarrow}value = value$
E3: $node{\rightarrow}next.ptr = null$
E4:   **loop**
E5: $tail = Q{\rightarrow}Tail$
E6: $next = tail.ptr{\rightarrow}next$
E7:   **if** $tail == Q{\rightarrow}Tail$
E8:   **if** $next.ptr == null$
E9:   **if** CAS(&$tail.ptr{\rightarrow}next$, $next$,
                       [$node$, $next.ver+1$])
E10:   **break**
E11:   **endif**
E12:   **else**
E13:   CAS(&$Q{\rightarrow}Tail$, $tail$,
                       [$next.ptr$, $tail.ver+1$])
E14:   **endif**
E15:   **endif**
E16: **endloop**
E17: CAS(&$Q{\rightarrow}Tail$, $tail$,
          [$node$, $tail.ver+1$])

DEQUEUE(Q: **pointer to** queue_t,
             pvalue: **pointer to** data type): boolean
D1:   **loop**
D2: $head = Q{\rightarrow}Head$
D3: $next = head{\rightarrow}next$
D4:   **if** $head == Q{\rightarrow}Head$
D5:   **if** $next.ptr == null$
D6:   **return** *false*
D7:   **else**
D8:   *pvalue = $next.ptr{\rightarrow}value$
D9:   **if** CAS(&$Q{\rightarrow}Head$, $head$,
                       [$next.ptr$, $head.ver+1$])
D10: $tail = Q{\rightarrow}Tail$;
D11:   **if** ($head.ptr == tail.ptr$)
D12:   CAS(&$Q{\rightarrow}Tail$, $tail$,
                           [$next.ptr$, $tail.ver+1$]);
                      endif
                      break
D13:   **endif**
D14:   **endif**
D15:   **endif**
D16: **endloop**
D17: $free\_node(head.ptr)$
D18: **return** *true*

Fig. 3.   Queue operations

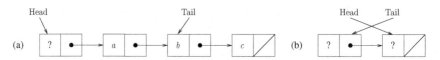

Fig. 4.   Queue representation variations

the same value at two different times, then the location had that value during
the entire interval.

A process p executing an ENQUEUE operation acquires and initialises a new
node (E1–E3), and appends the new node to the list by repeatedly determining
the last node in the list, i.e., the node whose *next.ptr* field is *null* (E5–E8, E13),
and attempting to make its *next.ptr* field point to the new node (E9). Then p
attempts to make *Tail* point to this node (E17).[3] Between p appending its new
node and *Tail* being updated, *Tail* *lags* behind the last node in the list (see
Fig. 4).

We cannot determine the last node in the list by just reading *Tail*, because
another enqueuing process q may cause *Tail* to lag. Since p cannot wait for q to
update *Tail*, p attempts to "help" q by doing the update (E13). Thus, *Tail* can
lag behind the end of the list by at most one node.

Also, another process may change *Tail* after p reads it at E5, but before p
dereferences (its local copy of) the pointer at E6. To ensure that the value read
at E6 is valid, p checks at E7 that *Tail* has not changed since p executed E5. If
the test at E8 shows that the node accessed at E6 had no successor at that time,

---

[3] The CAS at E17 can be deleted without affecting the correctness of the algorithm.
However, without this CAS, *Tail* would not point to the last node of the list in all
quiescent states.

then we know that the node was the last node in the list at that time. Similarly, a successful CAS at E9 guarantees that the *next* field of that node is unchanged in the interval between p's executions of E6 and E9.

A process p executing a DEQUEUE operation checks whether the dummy node has a successor (D2–D5). If not, then the queue was empty when p executed D3, so the operation returns *false* (D6). As in the ENQUEUE operation, *Head* is read twice to ensure that the node accessed at D3 was the dummy node at that time.

If the dummy node has a successor, then p reads the value in the successor node (D8), expecting that this node is the first non-dummy node in the list. Then p attempts to swing *Head* to point to the node whose value p read at D8 (D9). If the attempt succeeds, that node is the new dummy node; its value is removed from the queue by the successful CAS. If the attempt fails, p retries the operation from the beginning.

Once p has successfully executed the CAS at D9, it remains to allow the old dummy node to be reused. This node cannot be freed to the system because another process may be about to access it; instead, it is placed on a *freelist*, using the *free_node* operation (D17). The *new_node* operation (E1) returns a node from the freelist, if one is available; otherwise, it allocates and returns a new node.

Before passing the old dummy node to *free_node*, a dequeuing process checks for the special case shown in Fig. 4(b), where the *Head* and *Tail* have "crossed", because *Tail* points to the old dummy node (D10-D11). In this case, it attempts to update *Tail* (D12) before putting the old dummy node on the freelist.

Our algorithm differs from Michael and Scott's [1] in that we test whether *Tail* points to the dummy node only *after Head* has been updated, so a dequeuing process reads *Tail* only once. The DEQUEUE in [1] performs this test before checking whether the *next* pointer in the dummy node is *null*, so it reads *Tail* every time a dequeuing process loops. Under high load, when operations retry frequently, this change will reduce the number of accesses to shared memory.

3   Modelling the Queue Specification and Implementation

This section briefly introduces the *input/output automaton* (IOA) formalism [5], and shows how we use IOAs to model the queue specification and implementation.

An *input/output automaton* is a labelled transition system, along with a signature partitioning its actions into external and internal actions. Formally, an IOA consists of: a set *states*(A) of states; a nonempty set *start*(A) $\subseteq$ *states*(A) of start states; a set *acts*(A) of actions; a signature, *sig*(A) = (*external*(A), *internal*(A)), which partitions *acts*(A); and a transition relation, *trans*(A) $\subseteq$ *states*(A) $\times$ *acts*(A) $\times$ *states*(A).[4]

We describe the states by a collection of state variables, and the transition relation by specifying a *precondition* and *effect* for each action. A precondition

---

[4] The definition in [5] includes additional structure to support fairness and composition, which we do not require for this work.

is a predicate on states, and an effect is a set of assignments showing only those state variables that change, to be performed as a single atomic action. For states s and s' and action a with precondition pre_a and effect eff_a, the transition (s, a, s') is in $trans(A)$, written $s \xrightarrow{a} s'$, if and only if pre_a holds in s (the *pre-state*) and s' (the *post-state*) is the result of applying eff_a to s. We say that an action a is *enabled* in s if pre_a holds in s. These descriptions are parameterised by process and sometimes by other values, so they actually describe sets of transitions.

A *(finite) execution fragment* of A is a sequence of alternating states and actions of A, $\pi = s_0, a_1, s_1, \ldots s_n$, such that $(s_{k-1}, a_k, s_k) \in trans(A)$ for $k \in [1, n]$. An *execution* is an execution fragment with $s_0 \in start(A)$.[5] A *trace* is the sequence of external actions in some execution. We say that two executions (not necessarily of the same automaton) are *equivalent* if they have the same trace, and we write $traces(A)$ for the set of all traces of A. We also write $trace(\alpha)$ to denote the sequence of external actions in a sequence $\alpha \in acts(A)^*$, where $acts(A)^*$ is the set of finite sequences over $acts(A)$. For $\alpha \in acts(A)^*$, we write $s \xrightarrow{\alpha} s'$ to mean that there is an execution fragment beginning with s, ending with s', and containing exactly the actions of α.

I/O automata can be use to model both specifications and implementations; in both cases, the set of traces represents the possible external behaviours of the automaton. For an "abstract" automaton A, modelling a specification, and a "concrete" automaton C, modelling an implementation, we say that C *implements* A if $traces(C) \subseteq traces(A)$, that is, if all behaviours of the implementation are allowed by the specification.

3.1   The Abstract Automaton

The standard correctness condition for shared data structures is *linearisability* [2], which requires that every operation appears to take effect atomically at some point between its invocation and its response; this point is called the operation's *linearisation point*. We specify the acceptable behaviours for a set of concurrent processes operating on a shared queue, by defining an abstract automaton *AbsAut* which generates their linearizable traces. The transition relation for *AbsAut* is defined in Fig. 5.

AbsAut has external actions $enq\_inv_p(v)$ and deq_inv_p, representing operation invocations, and enq_resp_p, representing the response from an ENQUEUE, for all processes p and values v. For simplicity, we assume that queue values are pointers, and model DEQUEUE as always returning a pointer, which is *null* when the queue is empty. Thus, *AbsAut* has external actions $deq\_resp_p(r)$, where p is any process and r is any value (i.e., non-*null* pointer) or *null*. *AbsAut* also has internal actions do_enq_p and do_deq_p, for all processes p, representing the operations' linearisation points.

---

[5] The full theory of I/O automata also allows infinite executions, which are necessary to reason about liveness, which we do not consider in this paper.

$enq\_inv_p(v)$:
pre: $pc_p = idle$
eff: $pc_p := enq(v)$

do_enq_p:
pre: $pc_p = enq(v)$
eff: $pc_p := enq\_resp$
$\quad\quad Q := enq(Q, v)$

enq_resp:
pre: $pc_p = enq\_resp$
eff: $pc_p := idle$

deq_inv_p:
pre: $pc_p = idle$
eff: $pc_p := deq$

do_deq_p:
pre: $pc_p = deq$
eff: $pc_p := deq\_resp(deq(Q).v)$
$\quad\quad Q := deq(Q).q$

$deq\_resp_p(r)$:
pre: $pc_p = deq\_resp(r)$
eff: $pc_p := idle$

Fig. 5. Abstract transitions for process p; v may be any value, and r may be any value or *null*

Each process p has a "program counter" pc_p that controls the order in which actions can occur by determining which actions are enabled, and sometimes also encodes the value being enqueued or dequeued. For example, when p is not in the midst of any operation, $pc_p = idle$, so $enq\_inv_p(v)$ and deq_inv_p are both enabled; if an $enq\_inv_p(v)$ action occurs, pc_p is set to $enq(v)$, so then only do_enq_p is enabled.

AbsAut has a global variable Q, which holds the abstract queue. The abstract queue is modelled as a function *seq* from naturals to values, along with *Head* and *Tail* counters that delimit the range corresponding to queue elements. The queue consists of $seq(Head+1)$ through $seq(Tail)$, inclusive; it is empty if $Head = Tail$. The effects of do_enq_p and do_deq_p actions are defined in terms of functions *enq* and *deq*: $enq(Q, v)$ returns the queue obtained by incrementing $Q.Tail$ and placing v at the new *Tail* index. When Q is not empty, $deq(Q)$ returns a pair $(deq(Q).q, deq(Q).v)$ consisting of the queue obtained by incrementing $Q.Head$ and the element at the new *Head* index. When Q is empty, $deq(Q) = (Q, null)$.

Each process repeatedly performs either an ENQUEUE or DEQUEUE operation, and each such operation consists of an invocation, a single internal action that atomically updates the abstract queue, and a response. Thus, the trace of any execution of *AbsAut* is consistent with a set of processes operating on a linearisable queue.

3.2 The Concrete Automaton

The concrete automaton *ConcAut* models the queue implementation described in Sect. 2. *ConcAut* has the same external actions as *AbsAut*, and has one internal action for each line of code shown in Fig. 3 that contains a read or a write, and two internal actions for each line of code containing a conditional or a CAS. For example, action e_1_p models a process p executing line E1 of ENQUEUE, and $d\_4\_yes_p$ and $d\_4\_no_p$ model p executing D4 when the condition evaluates to *true* and *false*, respectively.

Each process p has a "program counter" pc_p, ranging over a type that contains one value for each line of code containing a read, write, conditional or

CAS, and special values *idle*, *enq_resp* and *deq_resp* that play the same roles as in *AbsAut*.

We model a heap in which every object is a node with two fields *value* and *next*, each of which contains a pointer/version-number pair, whose components are denoted by *pair.ptr* and *pair.ver*. We write $\mathcal{P}$ for the set of pointers, $\mathcal{H}$ for the set of heaps, and $\mathcal{F}$ for the set of field names (either *value* or *next*). A heap $h \in \mathcal{H}$ is a pair $(h.\textit{eval}, h.\textit{unalloc})$: the function $h.\textit{eval}: \mathcal{P} \times \mathcal{F} \to \mathcal{P} \times \mathbb{N}$ takes a pointer to a node and a field, and returns the pointer value and version number associated with that field of that node in h; and $h.\textit{unalloc}$ is the set of pointers that are not allocated in h. Generalising this model to allow multiple object types is straightforward, but this simple model suffices for our purposes.

ConcAut has variables $h \in \mathcal{H}$, *Head*, *Tail* $\in \mathcal{P} \times \mathbb{N}$, and *freelist* $\subseteq \mathcal{P}$, which model the heap, *Head*, *Tail* and the freelist. For each process p, there are variables $head_p, tail_p, next_p \in \mathcal{P} \times \mathbb{N}$, and $node_p \in \mathcal{P}$, which model the local variables in the code, and a local variable $result_p \in \mathcal{P}$ to hold the value that p returns from DEQUEUE.

An assignment $pt \to fd := (pt', i)$, which updates field fd in the node pointed to by pt, is modelled using a function $update: \mathcal{H} \times \mathcal{P} \times \mathcal{F} \times \mathcal{P} \times \mathbb{N} \to \mathcal{H}$ defined by:[6]

$$update(h, pt, fd, pt', i) = (h.\textit{eval} \oplus \{(pt, fd) \mapsto (pt', i)\}, h.\textit{unalloc})$$

Allocation of a new node is modelled with the function $new: \mathcal{H} \to \mathcal{H} \times \mathcal{P}$ satisfying the following properties:[7]

$$new(h) = (h', \textit{null}) \Rightarrow h.\textit{unalloc} = \varnothing \wedge h' = h$$
$$new(h) = (h', p) \wedge p \neq \textit{null} \Rightarrow$$
$$p \in h.\textit{unalloc} \wedge h'.\textit{eval} = h.\textit{eval} \wedge h'.\textit{unalloc} = h.\textit{unalloc} \setminus \{p\}$$

The preconditions and effects of some representative actions of the concrete automaton are shown in Fig. 6. Transitions for the other actions are defined similarly.

In subsequent sections, we write $pt \xrightarrow{cs} fd$ for $cs.h.\textit{eval}(pt, fd)$, and $cs.\textit{free?}(pt)$ for $pt \in cs.\textit{unalloc} \cup cs.\textit{freelist}$, where cs is a state of *ConcAut*.

4   Verification

To verify our queue implementation, we use a simulation proof [6], which shows how to construct, from any execution of the concrete automaton, an equivalent execution of the abstract automaton, proving that *ConcAut* implements *AbsAut*.

Simulation proofs can often be done using a *forward simulation* (see Fig. 7), in which the abstract execution is constructed by starting at the beginning of

---

[6] $f \oplus \{x \mapsto y\}$ yields a function $f^\blacksquare$ such that $f^\blacksquare(x) = y$ and $f^\blacksquare(z) = f(z)$, for $z \neq x$.

[7] Michael and Scott do not specify what happens if ENQUEUE is unable to allocate a new node. In our model, if *new* returns a *null* pointer, *ConcAut* loops until space becomes available. A practical implementation would trap this error.

e_3_p:
pre: $pc_p = e\_3$
eff: $node_p \rightarrow next.ptr := null$
    $pc_p := e\_5$

$e\_9\_yes_p$:
pre: $pc_p = e\_9 \wedge next_p = tail_p.ptr \rightarrow next$
eff: $tail_p.ptr \rightarrow next := (node_p, next_p.ver + 1)$
    $pc_p := e\_17$

d_2_p:
pre: $pc_p = d\_2$
eff: $head_p := Head$
    $pc_p := d\_3$

$e\_9\_no_p$:
pre: $pc_p = e\_9 \wedge next_p \neq tail_p.ptr \rightarrow next$
eff: $pc_p := e\_5$

Fig. 6. Part of the transition relation of *ConcAut*

the concrete execution and working forwards. However, forward simulation is not sufficient to prove that *ConcAut* implements *AbsAut*. The only point during a DEQUEUE operation at which the queue is guaranteed to be empty is when the operation executes D3, loading *null* into *next*. A forward simulation would need to determine at this point whether the operation will return *null*. This is not possible, however, since the operation will retry if *Head* is changed between the operation's execution of D2 and D4. Therefore, we need to use a *backward simulation* (see Fig. 8), showing how to construct an abstract execution by working from the last step of a concrete execution back to the beginning.

Since only this one aspect requires backward simulation, we define an intermediate automaton *IntAut*, which captures the behaviour of the implementation that defies forward simulation, namely the handling of DEQUEUE on an empty queue, and is otherwise identical to *AbsAut*. We then prove a backward simulation from *IntAut* to *AbsAut* (see Sect. 4.2), and a forward simulation from *ConcAut* to *IntAut* (see Sect. 4.3).

4.1   The Intermediate Automaton

The intermediate automaton *IntAut* is identical to the abstract automaton, except that in *IntAut*, a process executing a DEQUEUE operation may "observe" whether or not the queue is empty at any time before it decides what value to return. In addition to the queue and counter variables that are in *AbsAut*, each state of *IntAut* has a variable $empty\_ok_p$, to record whether p has observed an empty queue during the current DEQUEUE operation.

IntAut has the same external actions as *AbsAut*, and the same internal action do_enq_p; the only difference for these transitions is that deq_inv_p sets $empty\_ok_p$ to *false*. *IntAut* has a new internal action $observe\_empty_p$ that sets $empty\_ok_p$ to record whether or not the queue Q is empty, which p may perform whenever its program counter value is *deq*. Also, in place of the do_deq_p action in *AbsAut*, *IntAut* has two actions, deq_empty_p and $deq\_nonempty_p$, allowing these cases to be treated separately. The $deq\_nonempty_p$ action is the same as the abstract automaton's do_deq_p action except that its precondition additionally requires that the queue is nonempty. The deq_empty_p action simply changes p's program counter from *deq* to $deq\_resp(null)$. The precondition for this action requires that

$$(\forall cs_0 \bullet (\exists as_0 \bullet R(cs, as))) \qquad (1)$$

$$(\forall cs, cs^{\scriptscriptstyle\square}, as, a \bullet$$
$$R(cs, as) \wedge cs \xrightarrow{a} cs^{\scriptscriptstyle\square} \Rightarrow$$
$$(\exists as^{\scriptscriptstyle\square}, b \bullet$$
$$R(cs^{\scriptscriptstyle\square}, as^{\scriptscriptstyle\square}) \wedge as \xrightarrow{b} as^{\scriptscriptstyle\square} \wedge$$
$$trace(a) = trace(b))) \qquad (2)$$

$$(\forall cs \bullet (\exists as \bullet R(cs, as))) \qquad (3)$$

$$(\forall cs_0 : start(C), as \bullet R(cs, as) \Rightarrow$$
$$as \in start(A)) \qquad (4)$$

$$(\forall cs, cs^{\scriptscriptstyle\square}, as^{\scriptscriptstyle\square}, a \bullet$$
$$R(cs^{\scriptscriptstyle\square}, as^{\scriptscriptstyle\square}) \wedge cs \xrightarrow{a} cs^{\scriptscriptstyle\square} \Rightarrow$$
$$(\exists as, b \bullet$$
$$(cs, as) \wedge as \xrightarrow{b} as^{\scriptscriptstyle\square} \wedge$$
$$trace(a) = trace(b))) \qquad (5)$$

Fig. 7. A relation $R \subseteq states(C) \times states(A)$ is a *forward simulation* from C to A if C and A have the same external actions and these conditions hold, where $cs_0 : start(C)$, $as_0 : start(A)$ $cs, cs^{\scriptscriptstyle\square} : states(C)$, $as, as^{\scriptscriptstyle\square} : states(A)$, $a : acts(C)$, $b : acts(C)$

Fig. 8. A relation $R \subseteq states(C) \times states(A)$ is a *forward simulation* from C to A if C and A have the same external actions and these conditions hold

$empty\_ok_p$ is true, indicating that p has observed that the queue was empty at some point during its execution; the DEQUEUE operation is linearised to one such point.

Splitting DEQUEUE operations that return *null* into one or more observations that the queue is empty, followed by a decision to return *null* based on the knowledge that we have observed the queue to be empty at some point during the operation, makes it possible to prove a forward simulation from the concrete automaton to the intermediate one, as we show in Sect. 4.3.

It is easy to see that *IntAut* captures the behaviour of a set of processes accessing a linearisable FIFO queue; we describe a formal proof in the following section.

4.2   Backward Simulation Proof

In this section we define a relation *BSR* (see Fig. 9), and show that it is a backward simulation from *IntAut* to *AbsAut*. Given states *as* of *AbsAut* and *is* of *IntAut*, the third conjunct of *BSR* requires that the queues represented by the two states are the same. The first two conjuncts require that each process is roughly speaking "at the same stage" of the same operation in both states, or is not executing any operation in either state. For example, if p is idle in *is* (i.e., $is.pc_p = idle$) then p is also idle in *as*. The first conjunct (*basic_ok*) covers the simple cases; the second conjunct (*dequeuer_ok*) covers the only interesting case, in which a process can be at slightly different stages in the two automata because DEQUEUE operations can take two or more steps. Specifically, if in *is*, p has invoked DEQUEUE but has not yet executed either deq_empty_p or $deq\_nonempty_p$

$$BSR(as, is) \stackrel{def}{=} basic\_ok(as, is) \wedge dequeuer\_ok(as, is) \wedge is.Q = as.Q$$

$basic\_ok(is, as) \stackrel{def}{=}$
  $\forall p \bullet is.pc_p \neq deq \Rightarrow is.pc_p = as.pc_p$

$dequeuer\_ok(as, is) \stackrel{def}{=}$
  $\forall p \bullet is.pc_p = deq \Rightarrow (as.pc_p = deq \vee (as.pc_p = deq\_resp(null) \wedge is.empty\_ok_p))$

Fig. 9. The backward simulation relation BSR

(i.e., $is.pc_p = deq$), then in as, either pc_p is also deq, or $pc_p = deq\_resp(null)$, indicating that p has already executed deq_empty_p. In the latter case, $is.empty\_ok_p$ must also be true, showing that p has observed that the queue was empty at some point during its DEQUEUE operation.

Conditions (3) and (4) of Fig. 8 are trivial, because related states of $AbsAut$ and $IntAut$ are almost identical. Condition (5) requires that, for every transition $is \stackrel{a}{\longrightarrow} is'$ of $IntAut$, if $BSR(is', as')$ holds, then there is some abstract state as and some sequence b of abstract actions, containing exactly the same external actions as a, such that executing each action b, starting from as, takes the abstract automaton into state as'.

To aid in the automation of our proof, we define a function that calculates as given is, is', as' and a. Similarly, we define a *step-correspondence* function [7], that determines the action sequence to choose for the abstract automaton given an action of the intermediate automaton (in our proof, this sequence always consists of either zero or one action). Specifying these functions allows us to avoid manually instantiating the existentially quantified abstract state and abstract action required by the proof obligation: instead we simply use the two functions to calculate them directly.

These functions are defined as follows. For every intermediate action a except *observe_empty*, *deq_empty* and *deq_nonempty*, we choose the same action a for $AbsAut$; for *deq_nonempty*, we choose *do_deq*; and for *deq_empty*, we choose the empty action sequence. Recall that a DEQUEUE operation on an empty queue is linearised to a point at which it executes *observe_empty*, and not when it executes *deq_empty*. We reflect this choice of linearisation point by choosing *do_deq* for exactly one execution of *observe_empty* within that operation.

Given the abstract action chosen for a particular intermediate transition, it is generally easy to construct a pre-state as from the post-state as'. In many cases, we simply replace the program counter of the process p whose action is being executed in the intermediate transition with the value required by the precondition of the abstract action. The only nontrivial case arises for the *do_enq* action, because to construct the program counter before the action, we must determine what value the ENQUEUE operation is enqueuing. This is achieved by taking the value from the queue position that is updated by the *do_enq* action.

Having chosen an abstract action b, it is usually straightforward to prove $as \stackrel{b}{\longrightarrow} as'$, since the construction of as ensures that the precondition for b holds and applying the effect of b to as yields as'. It is slightly trickier in one case, where the intermediate transition is an *observe_empty* action. Not every execution of *observe_empty* corresponds to a linearisation point for a DEQUEUE operation that returns *null* (*IntAut* can execute *observe_empty* multiple times within a single DEQUEUE operation, while in *AbsAut* there is exactly one *do_deq* action per DEQUEUE operation). Therefore, for each DEQUEUE operation that returns *null*, we must choose *do_deq* for exactly one occurrence of *observe_empty*, and choose the empty action sequence for the others.

We can only linearise a DEQUEUE operation by process p to an execution of the *observe_empty*$_p$ action if the DEQUEUE operation returns *null*. This is true if pc_p in as' is *deq_resp(null)*, in which case we can infer that *empty_ok*$_p$ in is' is *true*, from the *dequeuer_ok* conjunct of *BSR*. Because *observe_empty*$_p$ sets *empty_ok*$_p$ to *true* if and only if the queue is empty in state is, and does not modify the queue, it follows that the queue is empty in state is', and therefore by *BSR*, the queue is empty in state as'. Therefore, we can construct the state as with an empty queue, which is needed to show that $as \xrightarrow{do\_deq_p} as'$ is a transition of the abstract automaton. Thus, we show that we can choose *do_deq*$_p$ when a is *observe_empty*$_p$ and $as'.pc_p$ is *deq_resp(null)*. In all other cases, we choose the empty sequence for the abstract automaton when a is *observe_empty*$_p$. It is easy to see that $BSR(is, as')$ holds in these cases because the only possible difference between states is and is' is that *empty_ok*$_p$ is true; the value of this variable affects the truth of $BSR(is, as')$ only if pc_p in as' is *deq_resp(null)*.

4.3   Forward Simulation Proof

In this section we describe a relation *FSR*, which is a forward simulation from *ConcAut* to *IntAut*. Because the concrete and intermediate automata are very different, the simulation relation and the proof are both substantially more complicated than the relation and proof described in Sect. 4.2. We do not have space here to describe the whole simulation relation or the whole proof; instead we present a detailed overview of the most interesting parts.

The forward simulation relation over intermediate state is and concrete state cs is

$$FSR(cs, is) \stackrel{def}{=} \exists f \colon rel(is, cs, f)$$

where f is a function from naturals to pointers called the *representation function*; we explain the purpose of f below. Fig. 10 defines *rel*. Fig. 11 defines *obj_ok*, and Fig. 12 defines some of the other predicates used in defining *rel*.

The most important part of *rel* is the predicate *obj_ok*, which expresses the relationship between the concrete data structure, represented by nodes and pointers in *ConcAut*, and the queue variable of *IntAut*. To express this relationship, *obj_ok* uses the representation function f as follows. Recall that a state is of *IntAut* contains a queue variable Q, represented by a sequence and *Head* and *Tail* variables indicating which indexes are relevant in the current queue state. If *obj_ok(is, cs, f)* holds, then f indicates which node corresponds to each relevant

$$rel(is, cs, f) \stackrel{def}{=} enqueue\_ok(is, cs, f) \wedge dequeue\_ok(is, cs, f) \wedge obj\_ok(is, cs, f) \wedge$$
$$nds\_ok(is, cs, f) \wedge distinctness\_ok(is, cs, f) \wedge procs\_ok(is, cs, f) \wedge$$
$$injective\_ok(is, cs, f) \wedge access\_safety\_ok(is, cs, f)$$

Fig. 10. The *rel* predicate

$obj\_ok(is, cs, f) \stackrel{def}{=}$

$$f(is.Q.Head) = cs.Head.ptr \wedge \tag{1}$$
$$f(is.Q.Tail) \stackrel{cs}{\rightarrow} next.ptr = null \wedge \tag{2}$$
$$(f(is.Q.Tail) = cs.Tail.ptr \vee \tag{3a}$$
$$\quad (f(is.Q.Tail) = cs.Tail.ptr \stackrel{cs}{\rightarrow} next.ptr \wedge \neg cs.free(cs.Tail.ptr) \wedge$$
$$\quad cs.Tail.ptr \neq null)) \wedge \tag{3b}$$
$$\forall i : \mathbb{N} \bullet is.Q.Head \leq i \leq is.Q.Tail \Rightarrow$$
$$\quad (i \neq is.Q.Tail \Rightarrow (f(i) \stackrel{cs}{\rightarrow} next).ptr = f(i+1)) \wedge \tag{4a}$$
$$\quad is.Q.seq(i) = (f(i) \stackrel{cs}{\rightarrow} val).ptr \wedge \tag{4b}$$
$$\quad \neg cs.free(f(i)) \wedge \tag{4c}$$
$$\quad f(i) \neq null \tag{4d}$$

Fig. 11. The *obj_ok* predicate

position in $is.Q.seq$; i.e., for each $i \in [is.Q.Head + 1 \cdots is.Q.Tail]$, $f(i)$ is the queue node in cs containing the value $is.Q.seq[i]$, and $f(is.Q.Head)$ indicates which queue node in cs is the dummy node pointed to by $cs.Head.ptr$. The latter is stated by Conjunct (1) of *obj_ok*. Conjunct (2) states that the last node in the queue has a *null* next pointer. Conjunct (3) captures the fact that *Tail* can "lag" behind the real tail of the queue: either *Tail* is accurate (3a), or *Tail.ptr* points to the next-to-last node in the queue, and several other properties that help the proof to go through hold (3b). Conjunct (4) expresses the properties of the nodes in the concrete queue: the pointer value of the *next* field of each node points to the node corresponding to the next index (4a); the value in each relevant node is the value in the corresponding position in $is.Q.seq$ (4b); none of the relevant nodes is unallocated or in the freelist (4c); and none of the relevant nodes is *null* (4d).

Predicates *enqueue_ok* and *dequeue_ok* (Fig. 12) play the same role as *basic_ok* and *dequeuer_ok* in the backward simulation. The other predicates capture properties needed to support the proof of the other properties. $nds\_ok(is, cs, f)$ expresses properties of a node as it gets initialised (Fig. 12). The *distinctness_ok* predicate expresses that various values are distinct, for example, that nodes being initialised by two different processes are different. The *procs_ok* predicate expresses several properties about the private variables of processes. Some of its subpredicates are shown in Fig. 12. For example, *procs_ok_15* says that if a process p is executing ENQUEUE and pc_p is e_9, then the pointer component of $next_p$ is *null*. The *injective_ok* predicate ensures that each node corresponds to only one index (in the relevant range), so that modifications to

$enqueue\_ok(is, cs, f) \overset{def}{=}$

$\quad \forall p \bullet (cs.pc_p = idle \Rightarrow is.pc_p = idle) \land$

$\qquad (pc\_e\_1\_9(cs, p) \lor cs.pc_p = e\_13 \Rightarrow is.pc_p = enqueuing(cs.value_p)) \land$

$\qquad (cs.pc_p = e\_17 \lor cs.pc_p = enq\_resp \Rightarrow is.pc_p = enq\_resp)$

$nds\_ok(is, cs, f) \overset{def}{=} \forall p \bullet (pc\_e\_2\_13(cs, p) \Rightarrow \neg cs.free?(cs.node_p) \land cs.node_p \neq null) \land$

$\qquad (pc\_e\_3\_13(cs, p) \Rightarrow cs.node_p \overset{cs}{\rightarrow} value.ptr = cs.value_p) \land$

$\qquad (pc\_e\_4\_13(cs, p) \Rightarrow cs.node_p \overset{cs}{\rightarrow} next.ptr = null)$

$procs\_ok\_5(is, cs, f) \overset{def}{=}$

$\quad \forall p \bullet pc\_e\_8\_9(cs, p) \land cs.next_p.ptr = null \Rightarrow$

$\qquad cs.next_p.ver < cs.tail_p.ptr \overset{cs}{\rightarrow} next.ver \lor (cs.next_p = cs.tail_p.ptr \overset{cs}{\rightarrow} next \land$

$\qquad cs.tail_p = cs.Tail \land cs.tail_p.ptr = f(is.Q.Tail))$

$procs\_ok\_15(is, cs, f) \overset{def}{=} \forall p \bullet cs.pc_p = e\_9 \Rightarrow cs.next_p.ptr = null$

$procs\_ok\_16(is, cs, f) \overset{def}{=} \forall p \bullet pc\_e\_6\_13(cs, p) \Rightarrow cs.node_p.ptr \neq cs.tail_p.ptr$

$injective\_ok(is, cs, f) \overset{def}{=}$

$\quad \forall i, j \bullet is.Tail \leq i \leq is.Head \land is.Tail \leq j \leq is.Head \land f(i) = f(j) \Rightarrow i = j$

Fig. 12. Some predicates used in *FSR*. A predicate of the form $pc\_e\_m\_n(cs, p)$, where m, n are integers, holds when $cs.pc_p = e\_i$ for some $i \in [m, n]$

a node corresponding to one index do not destroy properties required of nodes corresponding to other indexes. The *access_safety_ok* predicate says that the implementation never dereferences *null* or accesses a node that is in *unalloc*, which is important for correct interaction with a memory allocator.

As in the backward simulation proof, we use a step-correspondence function to determine the intermediate action sequence to choose given a particular transition of the concrete automaton. (Again, we always choose either a single action, or the empty action sequence.) As before, this function maps each external action to itself, and maps all internal actions to the empty action sequence, with the following exceptions: $e\_9\_yes_p$, which models a successful CAS at line E9, is mapped to do_enq_p; $d\_9\_yes_p$ is mapped to $deq\_nonempty_p$; d_3_p is mapped to $observe\_empty_p$; and $d\_5\_yes_p$ is mapped to deq_empty_p.

In contrast to the backward simulation, we do not need to specify a function to calculate the intermediate state, because this is uniquely determined by the intermediate pre-state and the action (if any) chosen. However, we specify a *witness function* that shows how to choose the new f so that *FSR* holds between the concrete and intermediate post-states. For a representation function f, concrete action a, concrete state cs and intermediate state is, the witness function returns the function $f' = f \oplus \{is.Q.Tail + 1 \mapsto cs.node_p\}$.

We now present a careful manual proof that *obj_ok* is preserved across transitions that represent the execution of line E9 by some process, where the CAS is successful. This is intended to illustrate the use of the representation function, and the style of reasoning we use to verify algorithms that employ dynamic memory.

Consider a concrete transition $cs \xrightarrow{a} cs'$, where $a = e\_9\_yes_p$ for some p, intermediate state is and representation function f, and let as' and f' be respectively the intermediate state and function determined by the step-correspondence and witness functions. When we say that part of the simulation relation *holds in the pre-state* (resp. *holds in the post-state*), we mean that it is true for cs, is and f (resp. cs', is', f').

The step-correspondence associates $e\_9\_yes_p$ with $do\_enq_p(cs.value_p)$, so we need to show that if the precondition of $e\_9\_yes_p$ holds in the pre-state (see Fig. 6) and $rel(is, cs, f)$ then $obj\_ok(is', cs', f')$.

First, we make some observations about the transition:

$$cs.Tail.ptr = cs.tail_p.ptr = f(is.Q.Tail) \tag{i}$$

$$f'(is'.Q.Tail) = cs.node_p \tag{ii}$$

Claim (i) is shown using $procs\_ok\_15$ to yield that $cs.next_p.ptr = null$, and then using $procs\_ok\_5$ to yield that $cs.Tail.ptr = cs.tail_p.ptr = f(is.Q.Tail)$. Claim (ii) follows immediately from the construction of f' and the effect of do_enq_p.

(1) of obj_ok is preserved because $is'.Q.Head = is.Q.Head$, but $is.Q.Head < is.Q.Tail + 1$ (this is a simple invariant of $IntAut$). Therefore $is'.Q.Head \neq is.Q.Tail + 1$, so by construction of f' and because obj_ok holds in the pre-state, $f'(as'.Q.Head) = f(is.Q.Head) = cs.Head.ptr = cs'.Head.ptr$.

For (2), by construction of f' and the effect of do_enq_p, $f'(is'.Q.Tail) = f'(is.Q.Tail + 1) = cs.node_p$. Moreover, by nds_ok, $cs.node_p \xrightarrow{cs} next.ptr = null$. By $procs\_ok\_16$, $cs.tail_p.ptr \neq cs.node_p$, so $cs.node_p \xrightarrow{cs'} next.ptr = null$, and thus $f'(is'.Q.Tail) \xrightarrow{cs'} next.ptr = cs.node_p \xrightarrow{cs'} next.ptr = null$.

We show that (3b) holds in the post-state, arguing each sub-conjunct in turn.

$$
\begin{aligned}
f^{\square}(is^{\square}.Q.Tail) &= cs.node_p & &\text{by (ii) above} \\
&= cs.tail_p.ptr \xrightarrow{cs'} next.ptr & &\text{by construction of } cs^{\square} \\
&= cs.Tail.ptr \xrightarrow{cs'} next.ptr & &\text{by (i) above} \\
&= cs^{\square}.Tail.ptr \xrightarrow{cs'} next.ptr & &\text{because } cs^{\square}.Tail = cs.Tail
\end{aligned}
$$

$$
\begin{aligned}
cs^{\square}.free?(cs^{\square}.Tail.ptr) &= cs.free?(cs^{\square}.Tail.ptr) & &\text{because } cs^{\square}.free? = cs.free? \\
&= cs.free?(cs.Tail.ptr) & &\text{because } cs^{\square}.Tail = cs.Tail \\
&= cs.free?(f(is.Q.Tail)) & &\text{by (i) above} \\
&= false & &\text{conjunct 4c with} \\
& & &i = is.Q.Tail
\end{aligned}
$$

Now by claim (i), $cs.Tail.ptr = f(is.Q.Tail)$, so by Conjunct (4d) applied to $is.Q.Tail$, $cs.Tail.ptr \neq null$. Therefore, $cs'.Tail.ptr \neq null$ by the effect of the e_9_yes transition, so the third conjunct is preserved. For the last conjunct of (3b) we have

$$f^{\square}(is^{\square}.Q.Tail) = cs.node_p \qquad \text{by (ii) above}$$
$$\neq cs.tail_p.ptr \qquad \text{by } procs\_ok\_16$$
$$= cs.Tail.ptr \qquad \text{by (i) above}$$
$$= cs^{\square}.Tail.ptr$$

We prove (4) by cases. For any i such that $is'.Q.Head \leq i \leq is'.Q.Tail$, either $i = is.Q.Tail + 1$ or $is.Q.Head \leq i \leq is.Q.Tail$. We treat the case in which $i = is.Q.Tail + 1$ first. $is.Q.Tail + 1 = is'.Q.Tail$ so there is nothing to prove for (4a). For (4b) we have

$$is^{\square}.Q.seq(i) = cs.value_p \qquad \text{by effect of } do\_enq_p$$
$$\text{and } enqueue\_ok$$
$$= cs.node_p \overset{cs}{\to} value.ptr \qquad \text{by } nds\_ok$$
$$= cs.node_p \overset{cs'}{\to} value.ptr \qquad \text{by effect of } e\_9\_yesw_p$$
$$= f^{\square}(i) \overset{cs'}{\to} value.ptr \qquad \text{by (ii) above}$$

4c and 4d follow from nds_ok and (ii) above.

It remains to consider the case in which $is.Q.Head \leq i \leq is.Q.Tail$. For 4a, we further distinguish the cases in which $i = is.Q.Tail$ and $is.Q.Head \leq i < is.Q.Tail$. For the first case, we have

$$f^{\square}(i) \overset{cs'}{\to} next.ptr = f(i) \overset{cs'}{\to} next.ptr \qquad \text{because } i \neq is.Q.Tail + 1$$
$$= cs.tail_p.ptr \overset{cs'}{\to} next.ptr \qquad \text{by (i) above}$$
$$= cs.node_p \qquad \text{by effect of } e\_9\_yes_p$$
$$= f^{\square}(is^{\square}.Q.Tail) \qquad \text{by (ii) above}$$
$$= f^{\square}(i + 1) \qquad \text{by effect of } do\_enq_p$$

If $is.Q.Head \leq i < is.Q.Tail$, (4a) follows directly if we can show that $f(i) \neq cs.tail_p.ptr$. This is because $i \neq is.Q.Tail$ and so (4a) holds for i in the pre-state and

$$(f(i) \overset{cs}{\to} next).ptr = f(i + 1) \Rightarrow (f(i) \overset{cs'}{\to} next).ptr = f(i + 1) \qquad \text{given}$$
$$f(i) \neq cs.tail_p.ptr$$
$$\Rightarrow (f^{\square}(i) \overset{cs'}{\to} next).ptr = f^{\square}(i + 1) \qquad i < is.Q.Tail \text{ so}$$
$$f^{\square}(i) = f(i)$$
$$\text{and}$$
$$f^{\square}(i + 1) = f(i + 1)$$

But if $f(i) = cs.tail_p.ptr$ then by $injective\_ok$ and (i) above, we have $i = is.Q.Tail$, contradicting the hypothesis that $i < is.Q.Tail$.

(4b), (4c) and (4d) all follow for i from the fact that these conjuncts held in the pre-state and that because $i \neq is.Q.Tail + 1$, $is'.Q.seq(i) = is.Q.seq(i)$ and $f'(i) = f(i)$. Moreover, no value fields, nor $free?$ are modified by the transition.

5   Experience with PVS

In this section we describe our experience using PVS to prove that the relations presented in the previous sections are in fact simulations. We focus on the forward simulation from *ConcAut* to *IntAut* because of its greater complexity. The techniques used to verify the backward simulation are similar.

The PVS system [3] provides a specification language, which we used to define the notions of backward and forward simulation. Using techniques adapted from [8], we also encoded the three automata, *AbsAut*, *IntAut* and *ConcAut*, as well as the simulation relations, *BSR* and *FSR*.

One of the goals of our verification effort was to construct the proof without requiring the human prover to attend to the tedious and uninformative aspects. We achieved this using two techniques: using the step-correspondence and witness functions, and dividing the forward simulation proof into many small, manageable parts. As noted in Sect. 4.2, using predefined functions to instantiate existentially quantified variables relieves the user of needing to manually instantiate these variables during proofs. Also, as described below, dividing the proof into many small parts allowed us to quickly isolate the parts of the proof that required human insight.

We divided the forward simulation verification condition into over 1000 lemmas. One lemma covers condition 1 of Fig. 7; for each concrete action associated by the step-correspondence with a nonempty intermediate action sequence, there is a lemma stating that if the concrete precondition holds, then the intermediate precondition holds in all related states; and finally, more than 900 *preservation lemmas*, each asserting that a part of the simulation relation is preserved across some transition. We used the mechanical proof facilities of PVS to prove a large proportion of these lemmas automatically.

Constructing proofs for the preservation lemmas constituted by far the bulk of the proof effort, and so we describe the techniques used to achieve this here. The conjuncts of the simulation relation can be divided into a small number of classes, depending on the presence and structure of the top level quantification: for example, *enqueue_ok* and all the subpredicates of *procs_ok* are universally quantified over a single process, so fall into the same class. For each of these classes, we developed a simple strategy that set up a proof, to be continued by a user or automated strategy. All these strategies begin by executing a strategy called **Begin-Simstep**, which evaluates the step-correspondence and witness functions, and expands the definition of *rel* and the definitions on which it depends, resulting in a set of subformulae each making assertions about *is*, *cs* and *f*. **Begin-SimStep** then labels each subformulae, allowing strategies applied later to refer to each subformula by name. Because *rel* is too complex to be analysed by PVS's automated strategies, **Begin-SimStep** *hides* the subformulae of *rel*. In PVS, each subgoal of a proof is associated with a set of formulae that are *hidden*; that is, they are not visible to any strategies, unless they are first *revealed*.

After **Begin-SimStep** has completed, one or more strategies are applied, each of which applies proof steps that are always needed to prove a conjunct of a particular form. For example, the `SimStep-obj-ok` strategy, which is applied at the beginning of preservation proofs involving *obj_ok* (which has no top-level quantifier), expands *obj_ok* in the consequent, and generates a set of new subgoals, where each conjunct must be shown to hold in the post-state. Once this strategy is completed, either an automatic strategy is applied to attempt to complete the proof without user intervention, if possible, or PVS waits for a command to be invoked interactively.

Now we have a situation in which the user is presented with a set of subgoals. Using primitive PVS proof commands and the labels defined by `Begin-SimStep`, the user reveals antecedent formulae that assert facts about the pre-state that are relevant to the subgoal at hand and instantiates any universally quantified variables. Once the relevant formulae have been revealed and instantiated, it remains to invoke the PVS automated strategies on the subgoal. These strategies apply boolean decision procedures, rewrite rules, and sometimes heuristic instantiations to attempt to complete the goal.

The limited form of interaction with the theorem prover not only reduces user-effort, but also improves the robustness of the proof. As the project progressed, we often made small modifications to the simulation relation and even the automata. Because we used proof commands that did not depend on fine aspects of the formulae being proved, we were able to successfully re-run most proofs after a modification, without changing the proofs themselves.

6   Concluding Remarks

We have presented a variation on the practical lock-free FIFO queue algorithm of Michael and Scott, and described a semi-automated proof of its linearisability we developed using the PVS system. The algorithm and specification are both modelled using I/O automata, and the proof is based on a combination of forward and backward simulation proofs. Our work illustrates some techniques for modelling and reasoning about dynamically allocated memory, and also some techniques for fully automating the easy parts of proofs, allowing the human prover to focus on aspects of the proof that require human insight. Future work includes refining our techniques to increase automation and applicability, as well as applying them to other problems. We expect that our efforts to automate the easy parts of the proof will enable us to tackle larger and more complicated problems in the future.

References

[1] Michael, M., Scott, M.: Nonblocking algorithms and preemption safe locking on multiprogrammed shared memory multiprocessors. Journal of Parallel and Distributed Computing **51** (1998) 1–26   97, 100
[2] Herlihy, M. P., Wing, J. M.: Linearizability: a correctness condition for concurrent objects. TOPLAS **12** (1990) 463–492   97, 101

[3] Crow, J., Owre, S., Rushby, J., Shankar, N., Srivas, M.: A tutorial introduction to PVS. In: Workshop on Industrial-Strength Formal Specification Techniques, Boca Raton, Florida (1995) 97, 112

[4] Moir, M.: Practical implementations of non-blocking synchronization primitives. In: Proceedings of the 15th Annual ACM Symposium on the Principles of Distributed Computing, Santa Barbara, CA. (1997) 98

[5] Lynch, N. A.: Distributed Algorithms. Morgan Kaufmann (1996) 100

[6] Lynch, N. A., Vaandrager, F. W.: Forward and backward simulations – Part I: Untimed systems. Information and Computation **121** (1995) 214–233 103

[7] Ramírez-Robredo, J. A.: Paired simulation of I/O automata. Master's thesis, Massachusetts Institute of Technology (2000) 106

[8] Devillers, M.: Translating IOA automata to PVS. Technical Report CSI-R9903, Computing Science Institute, University of Nijmegen, the Netherlands (1999) 112

Formal Verification of Web Applications Modeled by Communicating Automata

May Haydar[1,2], Alexandre Petrenko[1], and Houari Sahraoui[2]

[1] CRIM, Centre de recherche informatique de Montréal
550 Sherbrooke West, Suite 100, Montreal, Quebec, H3A 1B9, Canada
{mhaydar,petrenko}@crim.ca
[2] Département d'informatique et de recherche opérationnelle, Université de Montréal
CP 6128 succ. Centre-Ville, Montreal, Quebec, H3C 3J7, Canada
sahraouh@iro.umontreal.ca

Abstract. In this paper, we present an approach for modeling an existing web application using communicating finite automata model based on the user-defined properties to be validated. We elaborate a method for automatic generation of such a model from a recorded browsing session. The obtained model could then be used to verify properties with a model checker, as well as for regression testing and documentation. Unlike previous attempts, our approach is oriented towards complex multi-window/frame applications. We present an implementation of the approach that uses the model checker Spin and provide an example.

1 Introduction

The Internet has reshaped the way people deal with information. In particular, web applications have affected the daily life in many ways, where they are used in information management/gathering, e-commerce, software development, learning, education, entertainment, etc. With such pervasive and radical growth of web applications, correctness is a primary concern, especially that Web Applications (WA) interact with many components such as scripts (CGI, ASP, JSP, PHP, etc.), browsers, proxy servers, backend databases, etc. Unlike traditional software, WA have an extremely short development and evolution life cycle and often have a large number of untrained users that could experiment with the WA unpredictably. Therefore, thorough analysis and verification of WA is indispensable to assure the release of high quality applications. In recent years, software community started to acquire formal methods as a practical and reliable solution to analyze various applications. In this paper, we present a formal approach for modeling web applications using a communicating automata model. We observe the external behavior of an explored part of a web application using a monitoring tool. The observed behavior is then converted into communicating automata representing all windows, frames, and framesets of the application under test. The obtained model could then be used to verify user-defined properties of the application with a model checker. Our implementation of the approach uses the model checker Spin. In

D. de Frutos-Escrig and M. Núñez (Eds.): FORTE 2004, LNCS 3235, pp. 115-132, 2004.

Section 2, we present an overview of the main notions of the web. In Section 3, we discuss the related work on formal modeling and analysis of web applications. Section 4 introduces our approach. In Section 5, we suggest a method to model a browsing session of a single window application by a single automaton. Section 6 describes a method to partition a single browsing session into local sessions and to convert the local sessions into communicating automata. In Section 7, we present the implementation of the approach using Spin and provide a case study in Section 8. We conclude in Section 9.

2   Preliminaries

We present the main terminology encountered in studying web applications. Further information can be found in [1,2,3]. A web application is defined in [3] as "a software application that is accessible using a web browser or HTTP user agent. It typically consists of a thin-client tier (the web browser), a presentation tier (web servers), an application tier (application servers) and a database tier". We see a *web application* as an application providing interactive services by rendering web resources in the form of web pages (containing text and images, forms and etc.). A page can be static, residing on the server, or dynamic, resulting from the execution of a script at the server or the client side. A page is rendered by a browser to the user in windows. A *form* is a section of a web page that includes textual content, controls (buttons, checkboxes, etc.), optional labels, an action and a method. A frame element is an HTML tag that defines a frame. It includes a source *src* attribute specifying the URI of the source (initial) page loaded in the frame and an optional *name* attribute that assigns a name to the frame. A *frameset* element is an HTML tag that groups frame elements and possibly other frameset elements. The HTML document that describes the layout of frames is called the Frameset document having a frameset element that can be nested at any level. A Frameset document can be viewed as a *frame tree* whose leaves are frame elements and internal nodes are frameset elements. Detailed information on forms, frames, and HTTP protocol can be found in [1,3,20,21]. Note that we distinguish between two classes of WA: applications whose behavior is independent of its history and does not rely on the client's or the server's state. The second class represents WA whose behavior is determined by its history and thus affected by previous information kept at the client/server side (such as cookies). In this work, we consider the first class of WA where the same HTTP request always has the same response independently of past information in previous request/response pairs.

3   Related Work

Formal modeling of web applications is a relatively new research direction. Previous work on the topic includes modeling approaches that target the verification of such applications [25,26,27,28], testing [29,30,32,32], design and implementation [10,11,12,13,14]. In [25,26] an approach is presented where a web site is modeled as a directed graph. A node in the graph represents a web page and the edges represent links clicked. If the page contains frames the graph node is then a tree whose tree nodes are pages loaded in frames and tree edges are labeled by frame names. This model is used to verify properties of web sites with frames. However, only static pages are considered in this work, concurrent behavior of multiple windows is not modeled, and all the links whose targets could create new independent windows are treated as broken links. Besides, any frameset that could be present in the application is completely ignored. Also, in the model, a page loaded in an unnamed window (as a result of the predefined target "_blank" associated with a link) is represented as a graph node that replaces the existing node as if the page is loaded on top of page where the link was clicked; this incorrectness is due to the inadequacy of the proposed model to represent concurrent behavior of multiple windows. In [27,28] the authors present a model based on Petri nets to model check static hyperdocuments [27] and framed pages [28]. While Petri nets can express parallel and concurrent behavior, the authors build the overall state space as input of the model checker, which is a tedious and erroneous approach especially with large applications with several frames and windows. [25,26,27,28] do not tackle the modeling and verification of form-based pages that are dynamically generated by a server program, neither concurrent behavior of applications with multiple windows. The work in [29,30] focuses on inferring a UML model of web applications. This model, merely a class diagram, is mainly used for the static analysis of web applications: HTML code inspection and scanning, data flow analysis, and semi automatic test case generation. In [31], the above mentioned modeling technique is extended such that a web application is executed to extract models for dynamic web pages using server's access logs. These logs present limited information on the requests since only the request headers are logged. In case dynamic pages are generated based on POST method requests, the form data submitted is usually stored in the message body of the request; thus, making those pages requests undistinguishable and introduce unnecessary non-determinism into the resulting model. Besides, the approach is inadequate for modeling concurrent behavior of frames and multiple windows. In [32], a modeling technique for web applications is presented based on regular expressions. The focus is on modeling the behavior of web applications, consisting of merely dynamically generated pages, for the purpose of functional testing. Other approaches for modeling web applications are oriented towards the design rather than analysis of WA. These include object oriented based models [10] and statechart based models [11,12,13,14], that are tailored to forward engineering, logical and hierarchical representation of web applications. Such models are not available for analyzing existing WA developed without formal models. Each of the existing related work concentrates on some aspects of web applications leaving out other aspects that remain untouched, or unfeasible to model using the corresponding proposed approach. These attempts indicate that formal modeling of WA is still an open complex problem especially when it comes down to modeling multiple frames and windows, and properties which have to reflect various concerns of different stakeholders of WA.

In this paper, we attempt to develop a modeling approach that could produce a finite automaton model tuned to features of WA that have to be validated, while delegating the task of property verification to an existing model checker. We elaborate a black-box (dynamic) approach by executing the web application under test (WAUT) and analyzing only its external behavior without any access to server programs or databases. The observations are provided by a monitoring tool, a proxy server [5] or an off-the-shelf network monitoring tool [18], where HTTP requests and responses are logged. Our model is a system of communicating automata representing all windows, frames, and framesets of the application under test. The existence of frames, framesets, and windows reflects concurrent behavior of the WAUT, where these objects affect each other behaviors via links and forms with specified targets. Therefore, a suitable and natural modeling technique is communicating automata, where the burden of building a global state graph of the model is left to a model checker. As opposed to the existing approaches, we model not only static pages, but also dynamic pages with form filling (with GET and POST methods), frames and frameset behavior, multiple windows, and their concurrent behavior. Generally speaking, one could build a special web-oriented model checker, as in [26], to verify specific properties. This task requires the building of all the necessary algorithms from scratch. We opt to the use of an existing model checker, Spin, used in several industrial applications [22], such that we only have to describe our model in the model checker's input language.

4   Observing Web Application

To define a formal model of a web application in case when the code of the application is available, one may apply abstraction techniques developed in software reverse engineering following a *static* (white-box based) approach [7,8,9]. To build a formal model according to a *dynamic* (black-box based) approach, one executes a given application and uses only the observations of an external behavior of the application [15,16,17,31]. In case of web applications that rely on the HTTP protocol considered in this work, an "external" behavior consists of requests and responses. In our framework, we follow the dynamic approach and assume that the request/response traffic between a client side and a server in the WA under test is observable. One possible way of achieving this is to use a proxy server [5]. A proxy server monitors the traffic between the client and the server and records it in proxy logs. The proxy logs contain the requests for the pages and the responses to these requests.

With this approach, a behavior of a WAUT, we call it a *browsing session*, is interpreted as a possible sequence of web pages that have the same domain name intermittent with the corresponding requests. Note that a behavior of a WA is independent of the navigation aids provided by the browser (back button, forward button, etc.). In other words, we build a model that is independent of a browser. We assume that a next request is not submitted before the browser delivers a response to a previous request. If the user clicks a link, and that leads to a page with k frames then $k+1$ request/response pairs are observed. The first request/response pair corresponds to the link clicked and thus to the frameset document; and k requests, initiated by the browser, along with their responses, correspond to the URIs defined in the frameset document. Exhaustive exploration could hardly be achieved for non-trivial web applications with a database tier. This is why we have to build a model just for a part of the WAUT, which is explored in a browsing session. To generate sequences of requests, instead of the user, one may consider a crawler that automatically explores links in the WAUT [6], though in case of pages with forms to fill, the user actions would still be required. In the next section, we explain our approach for building a finite automaton that models a browsing session.

5 Modeling Single Window Web Applications

We first present our modeling approach for web applications whose web pages do not have frames and assume that the WAUT is browsed in a single browser window, in other words, that all the links have undefined target attributes. Later we provide extensions to more complex applications.

The purpose of building a formal model for a WAUT is to validate whether the application exhibits certain predefined properties. We assume that the properties to be specified in a temporal logic of a chosen model checker are composed of atomic propositions, and for each visited page the value of each proposition is uniquely determined by the content of the page, be it dynamic or static. These propositions refer to the page attributes that have to be checked (and reflected in a model). These attributes can be of various types, for instance: a numerical type to count the occurrence of a certain entity, a string type to denote the domain name of a page, or features of a page link, such as a hypertext associated with the link. However, there are cases when an attribute representing a certain feature of the visited page cannot be defined for another page. For instance, a Boolean attribute that indicates whether the menu is framed in a page that does not contain menus, or an attribute representing the percentage of the number of occurrences of a certain string with respect to the number of all the strings in a page that contains no text. In such cases, we assign to these attributes the value "not available". The atomic propositions that refer to such attributes are then false in the corresponding pages. In the following, we describe how to determine automata that model an observed behavior of a WAUT based on the information available in the corresponding browsing session. The session includes requests initiated by the user, namely links clicked and filled form submissions, as well as requests initiated by the browser, namely requests for URIs present in an HTTP-EQUIV tag [3,4]; for simplicity, we call those URIs *implicit* links.

5.1 Definitions

Each request is represented by a string l. In case the request method is Get or Head, l is the URI sent in the request. If the request is for a filled form then we represent it in the form $a?d$, where a is the form action and d is the form data set that corresponds to the data fields filled in the form; in case of the Get method, data set is a part of the URI sent in the request, while in case of Post method, data set is included in the message body as a data stream.

Each response corresponding to a visited page is abstracted by a tuple $<u, c, I, L, V>$, where u denotes the request l identifying the page; $c \in C$ represents the status code of the page, C is the set of valid status codes defined as integers ranging between 100 and 599 [20]; I is the set of URIs specified by the action attribute of each form in the page; L is the set of URIs associated with links, including the implicit links if any, in the page (L does not include links that cause the scrolling to sections in the same page); and V is a vector $<v_1, ..., v_k>$, where v_i is the valuation of the page attribute i and k is the number of all the page attributes over which the atomic propositions are defined. Pages with status code 3xx have their URL u different from the request l that triggered the response due to a redirection to another location of the pages. Pages with status code 4xx or 5xx may or may not have links leading back to the application.

A browsing session is a Request/Response Sequence RRS = $<u_0, c_0, I_0, L_0, V_0> l_1$ $<u_1, c_1, I_1, L_1, V_1> ... l_n <u_n, c_n, I_n, L_n, V_n>$, where $<u_0, c_0, I_0, L_0, V_0>$ is the default page displayed in the browser window from which the first request was triggered; this page is not observed in the browsing session, therefore, u_0 and c_0 are null, and I_0, L_0, and V_0 are empty sets; l_i is a request that is followed by the response page $<u_i, c_i, I_i, L_i, V_i>$; for all $i > 1$, $l_i \in L_{i-1}$ if l_i is a request corresponding to a clicked or implicit link, or if l_i is of the form $a_i?d_i$, then $a_i \in I_{i-1}$; and for all $i > 0$ $l_i = u_i$ if $c_i \neq$ 3xx; (otherwise, $l_i \neq u_i$); and n is the total number of requests in the browsing session, starting from the first request l_1 for the initial (home) page of the application. Page attributes or atomic propositions, along with u and c, are considered as state attributes and used for model checking in a way similar to Kripke structure [19].

We say that a link of the application under test is *explored* in a browsing session if it's URI is one of the requests in the browsing session; otherwise, we say that the link is *unexplored*. Similarly, we say that a form is explored if its action a appears in one of the requests $a?d$ in the browsing session; otherwise we say the form is unexplored.

Two pages $<u_i, c_i, I_i, L_i, V_i>$ and $<u_j, c_j, I_j, L_j, V_j>$ have a repeated (common) link if $L_i \cap L_j \neq \emptyset$; similarly, a repeated form exists if $I_i \cap I_j \neq \emptyset$.

5.2 Converting a Browsing Session into an Automaton

In this section, we provide a high-level description of our algorithm to convert *RRS* into an automaton, called a *session automaton*.

Algorithm 1. Given a browsing session RRS = $<u_0, c_0, I_0, L_0, V_0> l_1 <u_1, c_1, I_1, L_1, V_1> ... l_n <u_n, c_n, I_n, L_n, V_n>$, where n is the total number of observed responses:

1. The tuple $<u_0, c_0, I_0, L_0, V_0>$ is mapped into a designated state called *inactive*, denoted s_0, where u_0 and c_0 are null, and I_0, L_0, and V_0 are empty sets.

2. For all $i > 0$, a tuple $<u_i, c_i, I_i, L_i, V_i>$ corresponds to a state of the session automaton. Tuples $<u_i, c_i, I_i, L_i, V_i>$ and $<u_j, c_j, I_j, L_j, V_j>$, where $j > i$, are mapped into the same state if $c_i = c_j$, $I_i = I_j$, $L_i = L_j$, and $V_i = V_j$. Let S denote the set of thus defined states.

3. The set of events of the automaton is defined by the union of the sets Γ, Δ, *Req*. $\Gamma = \{l \mid l \in L_i, 1 \leq i \leq n\}$ is the set of all the URIs associated with links in the observed responses, $\Delta \subseteq \{a \mid a \in I_i, 1 \leq i \leq n\}$ is the set of all form actions that correspond to the unexplored forms in the observed responses, *Req* is the set of all the observed requests. Thus, $\Gamma \cup \Delta \cup$ *Req* is the alphabet of the automaton, denoted Σ.

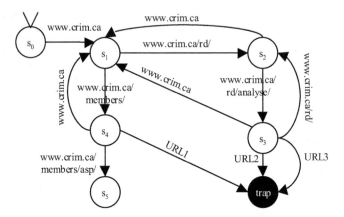

Fig.1. Example of a Session Automaton

4. Each triple ($<u_i, c_i, I_i, L_i, V_i>$, l_{i+1}, $<u_{i+1}, c_{i+1}, I_{i+1}, L_{i+1}, V_{i+1}>$) defines a transition ($s_i$, l_i, s_{i+1}), where s_i, s_{i+1} correspond to the pages $<u_i, c_i, I_i, L_i, V_i>$, $<u_{i+1}, c_{i+1}, I_{i+1}, L_{i+1}, V_{i+1}>$ respectively, and $l_{i+1} \in L_i$ if l_{i+1} is a request corresponding to a clicked or implicit link, or if l_{i+1} is of the form $a_{i+1}?d_{i+1}$, then $a_{i+1} \in I_i$; and $l_{i+1} = u_{i+1}$ if $c_{i+1} \neq 3xx$; (otherwise, $l_{i+1} \neq u_{i+1}$);
5. Each request corresponding to an explored repeated form or link defines a transition from the state where it occurs to the state that corresponds to the response of the submitted filled form or clicked link.
6. Each request corresponding to an unexplored link $l \in L_i$ or unexplored form $a \in I_i$ defines a transition from the state representing the page $<u_i, c_i, I_i, L_i, V_i>$ to a designated state, called a *trap* state that represents the unexplored part of the WAUT and whose attributes are undefined. Let T denote the set of thus defined transitions.
7. The session automaton is $A_{RRS} = <S \cup \{trap\}, s_0, \Sigma, T>$.

The automaton that models the whole WAUT could be built from an exhaustive browsing session obtained by exploring each link, and filling in every possible way and submitting each form, on every page of the application (which is usually unfeasible).

The following is a fragment of a browsing session representing five web pages, and Figure 1 shows the automaton that represents the browsing session, where state s_5 is a deadlock state representing an error page whose status code is 404. URL1, URL2, and URL3 (named as such for simplicity) represent few unexplored links that label transitions to the trap state.

```
GET http://www.crim.ca HTTP/1.0
Host: www.crim.ca
Accept: application/vnd.ms-excel, application/msword, application/vnd.ms-powerpoint, image/gif,
User-Agent: Mozilla/4.0 (compatible; MSIE 6.0; Windows NT 4.0)
Accept-Language: en-us
-----------------------END OF HTTP REQUEST----------------------------
```

```
HTTP/1.1 200 OK
Content-Type: text/html
Content-Length: 18316
Server: Apache/1.3.9 (Unix) mod_perl/1.21 mod_ssl/2.4.9 OpenSSL/0.9.4
Date: Wed, 10 Apr 2003 19:40:02 GMT
<HTML>
<HEAD> <LINK rel="stylesheet" href="/styles.css">
<TITLE> CRIM</TITLE></HEAD> ...
...<a href="/rd/"> recherche-développement </a> ...
</HTML>
------------------------END OF HTTP RESPONSE----------------------------------
```

6   Web Applications with Frames and Multiple Windows

In the previous section, we presented an automata model for single window web applications. However, web applications often use frames and multiple windows. These options allow rendering several pages at the same time, thus introducing concurrency in the behaviors of such web applications. Therefore, using a single automaton is insufficient to adequately model a concurrent behavior of web applications with several frames/windows. In this section, we extend our approach, using communicating finite automata, to model such web applications, which we call *multi-display WA* for simplicity. Before we introduce our extended approach, we define the elements of a browsing session of a multi-display WA.

6.1 Definitions

A response in a multi-display WA is defined as a tuple $<u, c, I, F, L, V>$, where u, c, and V are the same as in Section 5. I and L are extended to include for each action and link the corresponding target. Therefore, an element of L is a tuple $<l, t>$, where l is a URI associated with a link and t is the corresponding target or the empty string ε when no target is defined. Similarly, an element of I becomes a tuple $<a, t>$, where a denotes a form action and t its corresponding target. F is a frame tree defined in the page and whose leaves are frames and internal nodes are framesets. A frame is a tuple of the form $<f, b>$ where f is the URI defined by the value of the *src* attribute of the HTML frame element and b is the frame name. We denote by *leaves*(F) a function that returns the set of leaf nodes (frames) of the tree F.

We define a browsing session of a multi-display WA as a sequence of requests (along with their corresponding targets) and responses. For simplicity, we keep using the term Request/Response Sequence (RRS) to represent a browsing session.

A RRS = $<u_0, c_0, I_0, F_0, L_0, V_0>$ $<r_1, l_1, t_1>$ $<u_1, c_1, I_1, F_1, L_1, V_1>$ ... $<r_n, l_n, t_n>$ $<u_n, c_n, I_n, F_n, L_n, V_n>$, where n is the total number of requests in the browsing session starting from $<r_1, l_1, t_1>$. $<r_i, l_i, t_i>$ represents a request such that r_i is a string denoting the request header field, "referer", which is the URI of the page where the request was triggered; and $<l_i, t_i>$ is such that

- if the request is for a filled form then l_i is of the form $a_i?d_i$, where a_i forms with the target t_i a tuple $<a_i, t_i> \in I_j$ of the page $<u_j, c_j, I_j, F_j, L_j, V_j>$, where $u_j = r_i$,
- if the request is for a frame source page then $<l_i, t_i> \in$ *leaves*(F_j) of the page $<u_j, c_j, I_j, F_j, L_j, V_j>$, where $u_j = r_i$, or

- otherwise (if the request is for a link, clicked or implicit), then $<l_i, t_i> \in L_j$ of the page $<u_j, c_j, I_j, F_j, L_j, V_j>$, where $u_j = r_{i_i}$.

Notice that, similar to the case of a single window WA, $<u_0, c_0, I_0, F_0, L_0, V_0>$ corresponds to the initial default page displayed in the browser window such that u_0, c_0 are null, and I_0, F_0, L_0, V_0 are empty sets; $<r_1, l_1, t_1>$ includes the URI l_1 of the starting page, and r_1 and t_1 are the empty string ε. In addition, $l_i = u_i$ if $c_i \neq$ 3xx; otherwise, $l_i \neq u_i$ and $<u_i, c_i, I_i, F_i, L_i, V_i>$ immediately follows r_i in the RRS.

6.2 Basic Assumptions

Before we elaborate the model of a multi-display WA, we state basic assumptions about the observed browsing session of the application under test. As in Section 4, we assume that a request is not submitted before the browser delivers the responses to the requests for all frames source pages or for pages displayed in different windows. Also, the following assumptions are essential due to a limitation to directly determine from a request the window/frame from which it was triggered. An observed request/response pair does not include the name of the window/frame targeted by the corresponding URI. To determine the window/frame, we track the "referer" header field in the request which is the URI of the page, where the request is triggered. Thus the following assumptions must hold in the observed browsing session:

1. At each moment, different pages are displayed in frames/windows. If two pages have links to the same page, then only one request corresponding to one of the links is present in the session.
2. If a link is repeated in the same page with different targets and a request for that link is in the session, then this request corresponds to the first instance of that link appearing on the page.

These assumptions are not difficult to satisfy when the browsing session is created by the tester.

6.3 Communicating Finite Automata Model of Multi-display Web Applications

Here we describe how an observed browsing session can be modeled by a system of communicating automata. Given the browsing session, we first determine local browsing sessions that correspond to the behaviors of the entities in the browsed part of the WAUT, such as windows, frames, and framesets, each of which is modeled by an automaton. Then we explain how to convert the local browsing sessions into communicating automata and present the corresponding algorithm which is an extension of Algorithm 1 presented in Section 5.2.

Finite state automata communicate synchronously by rendezvous, executing common actions. Such communication is formalized by the parallel composition operator on automata. Formally, two communicating automata $A_1 = < S_1, s_{01}, \Sigma_1, T_1 >$ and $A_2 = < S_2, s_{02}, \Sigma_2, T_2 >$ are composed using the $\parallel$ operator. The resulting automaton, denoted $A_1 \parallel A_2$, is a tuple $< S, s_0, \Sigma, T >$, where $s_0 = (s_{01}, s_{02})$ and $s_0 \in S$; Σ

$= \Sigma_1 \cup \Sigma_2$; and $S \subseteq S_1 \times S_2$ and T are the smallest sets obtained by applying the following rules:

- If $(s_1, e, s'_1) \in T_1$, $e \notin \Sigma_2$, and $(s_1, s_2) \in S$, then $(s'_1, s_2) \in S$, and $((s_1, s_2), e, (s'_1, s_2)) \in T$.
- If $(s_2, e, s'_2) \in T_2$, $e \notin \Sigma_1$, and $(s_1, s_2) \in S$, then $(s_1, s'_2) \in S$, and $((s_1, s_2), e, (s_1, s'_2)) \in T$.
- If $(s_1, e, s'_1) \in T_1$, $(s_2, e, s'_2) \in T_2$, and $(s_1, s_2) \in S$, then $(s'_1, s'_2) \in S$, and $((s_1, s_2), e, (s'_1, s'_2)) \in T$.

The composition is associative and can be applied to finitely many automata.

6.3.1   Local Browsing Sessions

A browsing session represents the behavior of k communicating entities, namely, browser's main and independent windows, frames and framesets, denoted $o_1, o_2, \ldots, o_k$, where o_1 corresponds to the browser's main window. The entities corresponding to independent windows are determined by analyzing the targets present in the requests; if the target in a request is not an existing frame name, it corresponds to an independent window; for each request whose target is "_blank", a new entity is defined corresponding to a new unnamed independent window. The entities that correspond to frames are determined by the frame names indicated in the frame trees of the response pages; where each frame entity is uniquely identified by $<f, b>$ and the URI u of the frameset document where the corresponding frame tree is defined. The entities corresponding to framesets are identified by analyzing the internal nodes of the frame trees. The number of communicating entities k is then defined as follows. Given a browsing session, $<u_0, c_0, I_0, F_0, L_0, V_0>$ $<r_1, l_1, t_1>$ $<u_1, c_1, I_1, F_1, L_1, V_1>$ ... $<r_n, l_n, t_n>$ $<u_n, c_n, I_n, F_n, L_n, V_n>$, let $\{t_1, \ldots, t_q\}$, such that $q \le n$, be the set of all the distinct targets observed in the requests including window names, frame names, and predefined targets ("_parent", "_top", "_self", "_blank"). Let $\{b_1, \ldots, b_p\}$ be the set of all the frame names defined in all the responses, and m the number of all the framesets defined as well in all the responses. Then, $k = 1 + |\{t_1, \ldots, t_q\} \cup \{b_1, \ldots, b_p\} - \{t_i \mid t_i = $ "_top" or $t_i = $ "_parent" or $t_i = $ "_self" or $t_i = $ "_blank" or $t_i = \varepsilon\}| + |\{<r_j, l_j, t_j> \mid t_i = $ "_blank"\}| + m$. We further analyze the hierarchical relationship among the different entities of the application. We consider each window entity as a *window tree* whose root node represents the window itself. The first frame tree occurring in (frameset document loaded into) the window is appended to the root of the window tree. If a request's target is a frame name, such that the response is another frameset document (having a frame tree), in the window tree, the response's frame tree is appended to the node of the targeted frame. Similarly, if the target is a frame name, frameset, or the window itself, any subsequent children are removed from the node of the targeted entity and replaced by the response's frame tree if any.

The local browsing sessions $(RRS_1, \ldots, RRS_k)$ corresponding to the observed behavior of k entities of the application are determined as follows. A request/response pair $<r_j, l_j, t_j>$ $<u_j, c_j, I_j, F_j, L_j, V_j>$ belongs to a RRS_i if the target t_j refers to the entity o_i. Also, the RRS of each frame/frameset that could be a child of o_i contains the same request $<r_j, l_j, t_j>$ whose response is the inactive page. At the same time, the *RRS* of the (targeting) entity from which $<r_j, l_j, t_j>$ is triggered must contain $<r_j, l_j, t_j>$ itself with its response being the page where the request is initiated. This is explained by the fact that the targeting entity does not change its displayed page. However, if the target t_j is "_parent", "_top", or a parent entity name, then the response in the *RRS* of the targeting entity is the inactive page. Similarly, the *RRS* of each frame/frameset that is a child of the targeted entity contains the same request $<r_j, l_j, t_j>$ whose response is the inactive page. This means that those frames and framesets are deactivated and erased from the window. If the target attribute is absent or "_self" then $<r_j, l_j, t_j> <u_j, c_j, I_j, F_j, L_j, V_j>$ belongs to a RRS_i provided that the request is triggered from the last page displayed in the corresponding entity o_i. Following is a high-level description of the algorithm that determines the local sessions.

Algorithm 2. Sessions RRS_i, $i = 1, \ldots, k$, are formed using the following algorithm:

1. $RRS_1 := <u_0, c_0, I_0, F_0, L_0, V_0>$ corresponds to the inactive page of the *RRS* of the main window similar to the inactive page defined in Section 4. For $i > 1$, $RRS_i := <u_\Theta, c_\Theta, I_\Theta, F_\Theta, L_\Theta, V_\Theta>$, is defined similarly to $<u_0, c_0, I_0, F_0, L_0, V_0>$ which corresponds to the inactive page from which the local session starts.
2. The first request response pair $<r_1, l_1, t_1> <u_1, c_1, I_1, F_1, L_1, V_1>$ is appended to the session of the browser's main window, i.e., $RRS_1 := RRS_1 <r_1, l_1, t_1> <u_1, c_1, I_1, F_1, L_1, V_1>$.
3. For each request/response pair $<r_j, l_j, t_j> <u_j, c_j, I_j, F_j, L_j, V_j>, j > 1$,
   a. if the target t_j refers to entity o_i, $<r_j, l_j, t_j> <u_j, c_j, I_j, F_j, L_j, V_j>$ is appended to RRS_i i.e., $RRS_i := RRS_i <r_j, l_j, t_j> <u_j, c_j, I_j, F_j, L_j, V_j>$. At the same time, $<r_j, l_j, t_j> <u_\Theta, c_\Theta, I_\Theta, F_\Theta, L_\Theta, V_\Theta>$ is appended to the sessions of all the frames and framesets (if any) that are children of o_i.
   b. If the "referer" r_j is equal to the URI of the last response in RRS_i then,
      i. If the target t_j corresponds to a parent entity, the response corresponding to $<r_j, l_j, t_j>$ in RRS_i is the inactive page $<u_\Theta, c_\Theta, I_\Theta, F_\Theta, L_\Theta, V_\Theta>$. Thus, $RRS_i := RRS_i <r_j, l_j, t_j> <u_\Theta, c_\Theta, I_\Theta, F_\Theta, L_\Theta, V_\Theta>$. At the same time, $<r_j, l_j, t_j> <u_\Theta, c_\Theta, I_\Theta, F_\Theta, L_\Theta, V_\Theta>$ is also appended to the sessions of all the frames and framesets that are children of the targeted parent; otherwise,
      ii. the response to $<r_j, l_j, t_j>$ is a tuple $<u, c, I, F, L, V>$ such that $r_j = u$. Thus, $RRS_i := RRS_i <r_j, l_j, t_j> <u, c, I, F, L, V>$.
   c. If the target $t_j = $ "_self" or $t_j = \varepsilon$ and r_j is the URI of the last page displayed in RRS_i, then $RRS_i := RRS_i <r_j, l_j, t_j> <u_j, c_j, I_j, F_j, L_j, V_j>$.

6.3.2   Communicating Finite Automata Model

To build an automata model of a browsing session of a multi-display WA, we convert each local browsing session $RRS_i = <u_{i\Theta}, c_{i\Theta}, I_{i\Theta}, F_{i\Theta}, L_{i\Theta}, V_{i\Theta}> <r_{i1}, l_{i1}, t_{i1}> <u_{i1}, c_{i1}, I_{i1}, F_{i1}, L_{i1}, V_{i1}> \ldots <r_{im}, l_{im}, t_{im}> <u_{im}, c_{im}, I_{im}, F_{im}, L_{im}, V_{im}>$ into an automaton A_i, called the *local session automaton*, by extending Algorithm 1 of Section 5.2.

The set of events Σ_i of the automaton A_i is defined by the union of the following four sets Γ_i, Δ_i, Req_i, and Φ_i. Similar to what is previously defined, $\Gamma_i = \{<l_i, t_i> \mid <l_i,$

$t_i> \in L_{iw}$, $1 \leq w \leq m\}$ is the set of all the URIs associated with links in the observed responses, $\Delta_i \subseteq \{<a_i, t_i> \mid <a_i, t_i> \in I_{iw}, 1 \leq w \leq m\}$ is the set of all form actions that correspond to the unexplored forms in the observed responses, and Req_i is the set of all the observed requests. $\Phi_i = \{<f_i, b_i> \mid <f_i, b_i> \in leaves(F_{iw}), 1 \leq w \leq m\}$ is the set of URIs corresponding to the source pages loaded in the frames.

Algorithm 3. Given an entity o_i and its local browsing session RRS_i, we extend Algorithm 1 to convert RRS_i into a local session automaton A_i as follows.

1. Algorithm 1 is used to convert RRS_i into A_i.
2. The set of events Σ_i is extended to include the set Φ_i of URIs corresponding to the source pages loaded in the frames; thus, $\Sigma_i := \Sigma_i \cup \Phi_i$.
3. Each triple ($<u_{ij}, c_{ij}, I_{ij}, F_{ij}, L_{ij}, V_{ij}> <r_{ij}, l_{ij}, t_{ij}> <u_{i\theta}, c_{i\theta}, I_{i\theta}, F_{i\theta}, L_{i\theta}, V_{i\theta}>$) defines a transition ($s_{ij}, <r_{ij}, l_{ij}, t_{ij}>, s_{i0}$), where s_{ij}, s_{i0} correspond to the pages $<u_{ij}, c_{ij}, I_{ij}, F_{ij}, L_{ij}, V_{ij}>$, $<u_{i\theta}, c_{i\theta}, I_{i\theta}, F_{i\theta}, L_{i\theta}, V_{i\theta}>$, respectively;
4. Each triple ($<u_{ij}, c_{ij}, I_{ij}, F_{ij}, L_{ij}, V_{ij}> <r_{ij}, l_{ij}, t_{ij}> <u_{ij+1}, c_{ij+1}, I_{ij+1}, F_{ij+1}, L_{ij+1}, V_{ij+1}>$) such that $<u_{ij}, c_{ij}, I_{ij}, F_{ij}, L_{ij}, V_{ij}> = <u_{ij+1}, c_{ij+1}, I_{ij+1}, F_{ij+1}, L_{ij+1}, V_{ij+1}>$, defines a transition ($s_{ij}, <r_{ij}, l_{ij}, t_{ij}>, s_{ij}$), where s_{ij} correspond to $<u_{ij}, c_{ij}, I_{ij}, F_{ij}, L_{ij}, V_{ij}>$;
5. Every event corresponding to a request targeting o_i itself labels a transition from every state of the automaton to the state of the corresponding response page.

The last three steps of the algorithm define the transitions labeled by the events shared by different automata. Step 3 of the algorithm defines transitions labeled by a request initiated by o_i or one of its siblings/children, and whose target is a parent entity. Then, o_i is deactivated and A_i is in the inactive state s_{i0}. Step 4 defines transitions labeled by a request initiated by o_i targeting another entity which is not a parent of o_i. In this case, o_i does not change its displayed page and A_i remains in the current state. The last step of the algorithm states that a shared event targeting o_i is not under the control of A_i and thus should label transitions from every state of A_i to the corresponding state. Thus, in case of an ill-designed application or unreasonable user behavior, where multiple instances of a same window created using the predefined target "_blank", are all treated as a single entity, avoiding state explosion.

Note that there are cases where a frameset in a web application is merely used to group nested frames/framesets within a certain layout without having any behavior itself (it is not the target of any of its children's links). As a result, the corresponding automaton has a single state s_0 (inactive). Therefore, to simplify the model, we discard every automaton that models a frameset entity without any behavior. An automaton for a frameset has more than one state in the case when a request, initiated from a child frame of the frameset and whose target is "_parent", exists in the observed browsing session. As described in Section 6.3.1, in the frameset automaton (initially in state s_0), a transition labeled by the event that corresponds to the request exists from s_0 to the state corresponding to the page displayed in the frameset. At the same time, this event labels transitions in the automaton of each child entity of the frameset from every state to its inactive state. This behavior of framesets in a WA is not modeled in any previous work that we know about.

Let $A_1, \ldots, A_z$ ($k\text{-}m \leq z \leq k$, m is the total number of framesets, k is the total number of existing entities in the application) be the automata that model z windows, frames, and possibly framesets. The composition automata A is $A_1 \| \ldots \| A_z$, such that $A = <S \cup \{trap\}, s_0, \Sigma, T>$. The initial state of A is $s_0 = (s_{01}, \ldots, s_{0z})$; the set of events Σ of A is the union of all Σ_i; the set of states S and the transition relation T of A are defined according to the semantics of the composition operator $\|$. The trap state of A is $trap = (trap_1, \ldots, trap_z)$.

7   Implementing the Approach

In this section we describe the framework and the tool that implement our approach for modeling a browsing session recorded when a WAUT is navigated.

7.1 Framework

Our approach is implemented following the framework illustrated in Figure 2:

- The user/tester starts by selecting the web application to test and defining some desired attributes. These attributes, which are defined prior to the analysis process, are used in formulating the properties to verify on the application.
- A monitoring tool intercepts HTTP requests and responses during the navigation of the WAUT performed by the user.
- The intercepted data is fed to an analysis tool that continuously analyzes the data in real time (online mode), incrementally builds an internal data structure of the automata model of the browsing session, and translates it into XML-Promela. The XML-Promela file is then imported to Promela using a functionality of aSpin [23], an extension of Spin model checker [22] that includes the feature of importing a XML-Promela file to Promela language and exporting a Promela file to XML-Promela. The specification of XML-Promela syntax is defined in the Document Type Definition (DTD) file provided with aSpin.

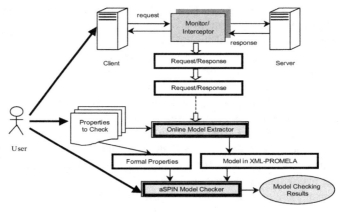

Fig.2. Framework

- aSpin verifies the properties against the model and generates a counter example if a property is not satisfied.

7.2 Online Model Extractor

The Online Model Extractor is implemented in Java as an experimental multithreaded tool that has the following components:

1. A graphical user interface where a range of web related attributes that characterize web applications is provided, and a window showing the progress of the analysis performed during the browsing session.
2. An HTTP Reader that continuously reads intercepted data in an online mode by a monitoring tool, HTTP proxy [5] in our case.
3. A Web Modeler that parses and analyzes the request/response pairs. This module incrementally builds an internal data structure representing the automata model of the WAUT.
4. An XML-Creator that reads the internal data structure and translates it into an XML-Promela based tree which is continuously updated.

8 Case Study

In this section, we illustrate the applicability of our approach using a browsing session of the web application of the Eclipse Consortium, www.eclipse.org. The corresponding web site uses framed pages and multiple windows. The first step in modeling the WAUT is to specify the desired attributes. This is done using the interface of the Model Extractor.

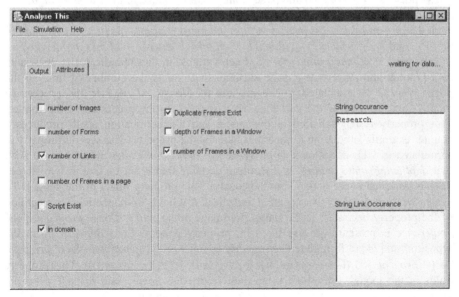

Fig.3. Attribute input window

Fig. 3 shows the attribute input window in the tool. Next, we navigate the application while the request/response pairs are intercepted by the proxy server. The intercepted pairs are fed into the Model Extractor/Manipulator, which produces the model of the application in XML Promela. The resulting XML file is imported into aSpin. The extracted model consists of ten processes reflecting the fact that the application includes seven frames and two windows in which 26 distinct web pages were visited. The frames are within the main browser's window and the second independent window has no frames within it. The global state graph corresponding to our model consists of 847 states and 9652 transitions (stored + matched). In order to prove the validity of our modeling approach, we verified various properties on the model of the application. These properties include reachability properties, and the checking for frame errors such as depth of frames does not exceed a user defined threshold, frames having same name are not active simultaneously, and pages displayed in frames are within the domain name of the application. As an example, we explain the verification of three properties. The first property requires that in the window *mainW*, and thus the frames within it, and the window *blank0*, the number of links in the displayed pages should be balanced, i.e., the difference between the number of links in the displayed pages in the two windows should not exceed a certain number which we fix to 15. This global property requires the exploration of all possible executions of the transitions of the automata of the main window *mainW*, the frames displayed with it, and the independent window *blank0*. The second property requires the absence of a frames error where frames having same names are not active simultaneously. The third property is a reachability property that requires that given three web pages, *program*, *conference*, and *home_main*, there exists at least a path where page *program* is reachable from page *home_main* without going through page *conference*. Note that pages *program* and *conference* are loaded in the independent window *blank0* and page *home_main* is loaded in the frame *main_0*. The first property is formulated in LTL as follows: $[] \ (p \ || \ q)$, where p and q are predicates such that $p = nLinks2 - (nLinks1 + nLinks\_banner0 + nLinks\_nav0 + nLinks\_main0)$ $<= 15$, and $q = nLinks2 - (nLinks1 + nLinks\_banner5 + nLinks\_home\_nav5 + nLinks\_nav5 + nLinks\_main5) <= 15$. Each variable in these predicates is associated to a process and represents a page attribute that counts the number of links in the page. *nLinks2* is associated to the process of *blank0*, *nLinks1* to the process of *mainW*, and the rest of the variables are associated to the processes of the frames. This property is not satisfied in the model and the verification result produces a counter example simulating a trace that violates the property. The second property is formulated in LTL as follows: $[] \ p$, where $p = duplicateFrames\_mainW == 0$ such that *duplicateFrames_mainW* is a Boolean variable that is set to True if two frames having same name are active simultaneously. This property holds in our model. To verify the third property, we negate it and check if it holds in the model. The negation of the property becomes: on all paths from page *home_main* to page *program*, page *conference* is present. We use the LTL property pattern, *Exist Between*, from the repository in [24] to formulate this property as follows: $[] \ (home\_main \ \&\& \ ! \ program$ $\rightarrow ((! \ program) \ U \ ((\ conference \ \&\& \ ! \ program) \ || \ [] \ (! \ program))))$. This property holds in the model, thus there is no path from page *home_main* to page *program* where page *conference* is absent. Thus, the original property does not hold in model.

9   Conclusion

In this paper, we presented an approach to formally model web applications for the purpose of verification and validation using model checking. We used the dynamic (black-box based) approach by executing the application under test (navigation and form filling), and observing the external behavior of the application by intercepting HTTP requests and responses using a proxy server. We devised algorithms to convert the observed behavior, which we call a browsing session, into an automata based model. In case of applications with frames and multiple windows that exhibit concurrent behavior, the browsing session is partitioned into local browsing sessions, each corresponding to the frame/window/frameset entities in the application under test. These local sessions are then converted into communicating automata. We also presented the framework and tools that implemented the proposed approach, and demonstrated the approach by applying it to a real web application. The constructed models can also be used for other purposes such as documenting, testing, and maintenance of web applications. Currently, we are experimenting with the tool using several types of web applications that reflect both good and bad practices in the development of WA. Our approach is based on the assumption that we observe behavior of WA which is independent of its history. As a future extension, we intend to treat WA behavior that is based on the observation of cookies in requests and responses.

Acknowledgements

We would like to thank Serge Boroday and Andreas Ulrich for the fruitful discussions and their feedback and insights on this work. We also acknowledge students support in the implementation process.

References

[1]   "Online Dictionary and Search Engine for Computer and Internet Technology", http://www.pcwebopedia.com/.
[2]   "A glossary of World Wide Web Terminology", http://www-personal.umich.edu/~zoe/Glossary.html.
[3]   "W3C World Wide Web Consortium", http://www.w3.org.
[4]   S. Graham, "HTML Sourcebook, A Complete Guide to HTML 3.0", John Wiley & Sons, Inc., 1996.
[5]   "HTTP Proxy Server 1.0", http://www.reitshamer.com/source/httpproxy.html.
[6]   "HTTrack Website Copier", http://www.httrack.com/index.php.
[7]   J. C. Corbett, M. B. Dwyer, J. Hatcliff, S. Laubach, C. S. Pasareanu, Robby, H. Zheng, "Bandera: Extracting Finite-state Models from Java Source Code", *In Proc. International Conference on Software Engineering*, 2000.
[8]   J. C. Corbett, M. B. Dwyer, J. Hatcliff, and Robby, "A, Language Framework For Expressing Checkable Properties of Dynamic Software", *In Proc. of the SPIN Software Model Checking Workshop*, LNCS, Springer-Verlag, Aug, 2000.

[9]   S. A. Becker, A. R. Hevner, "A White Box Analysis of Concurrent System Designs", *In Proc. of the 10th Annual International Phoenix Conference on Computers and Communications*, 1991, Scottsdale, AZ, USA, p. 332-338.

[10] J. Conallen, "Modeling Web Application Architectures, with UML", *In Proc. of Communications of the ACM*, October 1999, vol. 2, No. 10.

[11] M.C.F. de Oliveira, P.C. Masiero, "A Statechart-Based Model for Hypermedia Applications", *ACM Transactions on Information Systems*, Vol. 19, No. 1, 28-52, January 2001.

[12] F.B. Paulo, P.C. Masiero, M.C.F. de Olivieira, "Hypercharts: Extended Statecharts to Support Hypermedia Specification", *IEEE Transactions on Software Engineering*, Vol. 25, No. 1, Jan. 1999.

[13] F.B. Paulo, M.A.S. Turine, M.C.F. de Olivieira, "XHMBS: a Formal Model to Support Hypermedia Specification", *In Proc. of the 9th ACM Conference on Hypertext*, United Kingdom, June 1998.

[14] K.R.P.H. Leung, L.C.K. Hui, S.M. Yui, R.W.M. Tang, "Modeling Web Navigation by Statechart", *In Proc. of the 24th IEEE Annual International Computer Software and Applications Conference*, Taipei, Taiwan, October 2000.

[15] IEEE Computer Society, "Software Reengineering Bibliography", http://www.informatik.uni-stuttgart.de/ifi/ps/reengineering, October 28, 2002.

[16] T. Systä, "Static and Dynamic Reverse Engineering Techniques for Java Software Systems", Ph.D. dissertation, Dept. of Computer and Information Sciences, University of Tampere, 2000.

[17] Mansurov N., Probert R., "Dynamic Scenario-Based Approach to Re-Engineering of Legacy Telecommunication Systems", *In Proc. of the 9th SDL Forum (SDL1999)*, pp. 325–341, Montreal, 21–25 June 1999.

[18] "Ethereal, Network Protocol Analyzer", http://www.ethereal.com/.

[19] E. M. Clarke, O. Grumberg, D. A. Peled, "Model Checking", MIT Press, 2000.

[20] Luotonen, "Web Proxy Servers", Prentice Hall PTR, 1998.

[21] Krishnamurthy, J. Rexford, "Web Protocols and Practice: HTTP/1.1, Networking Protocols, Caching, and Traffic Measurement", Addison-Wesley, 2001.

[22] G.J. Holzmann, "The Spin Model Checker, Primer and Reference Manual", Addison-Wesley, 2003.

[23] "aSpin Model Checker", http://polaris.lcc.uma.es/~gisum/fmse/tools/mainframe.html.

[24] "Repository of Property Specification Patterns",http://patterns.projects.cis.ksu.edu/.

[25] L. de Alfaro, "Model Checking the World Wide Web", *In Proc. of the 13th International Conference on Computer Aided Verification*, Paris, France, July 2001.

[26] L. de Alfaro, T.A. Henziger, F.Y.C. Mang, "MCWEB: A Model-Checking Tool for Web Site Debugging", *Poster, 10th WWW Conference*, Hong Kong, 2001.

[27] P.D. Stotts, C.R. Cabarrus, "Hyperdocuments as Automata: Verification of Trace-Based Browsing Properties by Model Checking", *ACM Transactions on Information Systems*, Vol.16, No. 1, January 1998, 1-30.

[28] P.D. Stotts, J. Navon, "Model Checking CobWeb Protocols for Verification of HTML Frames Behavior", *In Proc. of the 11th WWW Conference*, Hawai, U.S.A., May 2002.

[29] F. Ricca, P. Tonella, "Web Site Analysis: Structure and Evolution", *In Proc. of International Conference on Software Maintenance (ICSM'2000)*, pp. 76-86, San Jose, California, USA, October 11-14, 2000.

[30] F. Ricca and P. Tonella, "Analysis and Testing of Web Applications", *In Proc. of the International Conference on Software Engineering (ICSE'2001)*, pp. 25-34, Toronto, Ontario, Canada, May 12-19, 2001.

[31] P. Tonella and F. Ricca, "Dynamic Model Extraction and Statistical Analysis of Web Applications", *In Proc. of International Workshop on Web Site Evolution (WSE 2002)*, pp. 43-52, Montreal, Canada, October 2, 2002.

[32] Y. Wu, J. Offutt, "Modeling and Testing Web-based Applications", GMU ISE Technical ISE-TR-02-08, November 2002.

Towards Design Recovery from Observations

Hasan Ural[1] and Hüsnü Yenigün[2]

[1] School of Information Technology and Engineering (SITE)
University of Ottawa, 800 King Edward Avenue
Ottawa, Ontario, Canada, K1N 6N5
[2] Faculty of Engineering and Natural Sciences
Sabancı University, Tuzla, Istanbul, Turkey 34956

Abstract. This paper proposes an algorithm for the construction of an MSC graph from a given set of actual behaviors of an existing concurrent system which has repetitive subfunctions. Such a graph can then be checked for safe realizability and be used as input to existing synthesis techniques.

1 Introduction

A concurrent system consists of two or more processes communicating among themselves via message exchanges. Each individual functionality (i.e., intended or actual behavior) of such a system can be viewed as a sequence of subfunctions. Often, depictions of individual intended behaviors of a concurrent system are given by designers as Message Sequence Charts (MSCs) [1, 2]. An individual MSC is a visual description of a series of message exchanges among communicating processes in a concurrent system where the local view of the message exchanges is a total order with respect to each process but the global view is a partial order. A tuple consisting of a local view for each process of the message exchanges depicted in an MSC uniquely determines that MSC. Thus, an MSC represents a partial order execution of a concurrent system which stands for a set of linearizations (total order executions of the system) determined by considering all possible interleavings of concurrent message exchanges implied by the partial order.

Formal semantics associated with MSCs provides a basis for their analysis such as detecting timing conflicts and race conditions [3], non–local choices [4], model checking [5], and checking safe realizability [6] (revised version appeared as [7]). Safe realizability is a property that characterizes whether behaviors represented by a given set of MSCs can be realizable by some deadlock-free implementation of communicating processes. [7] shows that if the given set of MSCs is safely realizable then an approach similar to existing synthesis algorithms can be used to synthesize a deadlock-free design. If it is not, then unspecified (and possibly unwanted) MSCs that are implied can be detected and fed back to the design process. While checking for safe realizability of a given set of MSCs that does not imply any repetitive system subfunctions can be done in polynomial

D. de Frutos-Escrig and M. Núñez (Eds.): FORTE 2004, LNCS 3235, pp. 133–149, 2004.

time [7], that of a given bounded MSC graph is in EXPSPACE [8], which is later
shown to be EXPSPACE–complete [9].

Design representations are helpful not only for implementing software systems, but also for software maintenance, e.g. to detect and eliminate errors in
a system, to extend the capability of a system, or to adapt a system to different operating environments. Further, the developers of a new software system
whose functionality contains some of the functionality of an existing system can
benefit by using the related part of the design of the existing system. However,
up-to-date or complete designs of many existing systems may not always be
available.

One of the aims of the reverse engineering [10, 11] is to recover the design of an
existing system from the run time behavior of its implementation. In this paper,
we consider the reverse engineering of designs of existing concurrent systems
from given sets of observations of their implementations. Here, a given set of
observations consists of individual linearizations of a set of MSCs that is not
given. We propose an algorithm for constructing an MSC graph from a given
set of observations of an existing concurrent system as a representation of the
system's design.

We assume that every repetitive subfunction of the system (if any) is represented in the given set of observations at least twice: once with no occurrence
or one occurrence, and once with two or more consecutive occurrences. This assumption stems from the fact that some repetitive subfunctions can be skipped
during executions, whereas others cannot.

When the resulting graph is acyclic, it is guaranteed that the system's functionality is free from repetitive subfunctions. Otherwise, the resulting MSC graph
is cyclic due to the existence of repetitive subfunctions in system's behavior. In
either case, the resulting MSC graph may then be checked for safe realizability
and, when found safely realizable, can be used directly as input to the existing
automated synthesis techniques.

The rest of the paper is organized as follows: Section 2 introduces the terminology and notation used throughout the paper. Section 3 gives the formal
definition of the problem. Section 4 presents the construction of an MSC graph
from a given set of observations. Section 5 discusses some open problems and
gives the concluding remarks.

2   Preliminaries

The notation we will be using is directly adopted from [7]. A concurrent system
$\mathcal{P}$ is a set of processes $\mathcal{P} = \{P_1, P_2, \ldots, P_n\}$, communicating with each other by
passing messages from an alphabet Σ, over infinite slot (not necessarily FIFO)
buffers. An event labeled as $snd(i, j, a)$ denotes the transmission of a message $a \in$
Σ by the process P_i to the process P_j. Similarly, an event labeled as $rcv(j, i, a)$
denotes the reception of a message a by the process P_j, which must have been
sent by P_i.

We use $[n]$ to denote the set $\{1, 2, \ldots, n\}$. Let $\hat{\Sigma}_i^s = \{snd(i, j, a) | j \in [n], a \in \Sigma\}$, $\hat{\Sigma}_i^r = \{rcv(i, j, a) | j \in [n], a \in \Sigma\}$, and $\hat{\Sigma}_i = \hat{\Sigma}_i^s \cup \hat{\Sigma}_i^r$ be the set of send event labels, the set of receive event labels, and the set of event labels of the process P_i, respectively. Then we define, $\hat{\Sigma}^s = \cup_{i \in [n]} \hat{\Sigma}_i^s$, $\hat{\Sigma}^r = \cup_{i \in [n]} \hat{\Sigma}_i^r$, and $\hat{\Sigma} = \hat{\Sigma}^s \cup \hat{\Sigma}^r$, as the set of send event labels, set of receive event labels, and the set of event labels, respectively.

A *word* w over an alphabet $\hat{\Sigma}$ is a finite sequence of elements from that alphabet. For two words w and w', juxtaposition of the two words, ww', denotes the concatenation of w and w'. w' is said to be a *prefix* of w, if there exists w'' such that $w = w'w''$. For an integer $k \geq 0$, $w^{(k)}$ denotes the concatenation of k copies of w, where $w^{(0)}$ is defined to be the empty word. We will use the notation $w^\star$ to denote concatenation of 0 or more copies, and w^+ to denote concatenation of 1 or more copies of the word w.

Given a word w over $\hat{\Sigma}$ and an event label $\alpha \in \hat{\Sigma}$, let $\#(w, \alpha)$ be the number of occurrences of α in w. w is said to be *well–formed* if $\forall$prefix w' of w, $\forall i, j \in [n]$ and $\forall a \in \Sigma$, $\#(w', snd(i, j, a)) - \#(w', rcv(j, i, a)) \geq 0$. In other words, every receive event must be preceded by a matching send event. w is said to be *complete* if $\forall i, j \in [n]$ and $\forall a \in \Sigma$, $\#(w, snd(i, j, a)) = \#(w, rcv(j, i, a))$. That is, every message a sent by P_i to P_j must be received by P_j, within the word.

Given a word w and a set K, we use $w|_K$ (projection onto K) to denote the word that is derived by removing all the elements in w that are not in K. We use the same notation to denote the restriction of the domain of a binary relation R onto a set K. That is, $R|_K$ is the projection of R onto K.

Again, we directly adopt the formal definition of an MSC as introduced in [7]. A Σ–labeled MSC M for a concurrent system $\mathcal{P}$ is composed of the following components[1]:

(i) A finite set S of send events and a finite set R of receive events. Let $E = S \cup R$.

(ii) A mapping $l : E \to \hat{\Sigma}$ that maps each event to a label such that $l(S) \subseteq \hat{\Sigma}^S$ and $l(R) \subseteq \hat{\Sigma}^R$.

(iii) A bijection $f : S \to R$ mapping each send event e with its matching receive event such that if $l(e) = snd(i, j, a)$ then $l(f(e)) = rcv(j, i, a)$.

(iv) A mapping $p : E \to [n]$ such that if $l(e) = snd(i, j, a)$ then $p(e) = i$, and if $l(e) = rcv(i, j, a)$ then $p(e) = i$. p simply gives the process on which e occurs. Let $E_i = \{e \in E | p(e) = i\}$ be set of events of P_i for $i \in [n]$.

(v) For each $i \in [n]$, a total order $\leq_i$ on E_i, such that when the relation $\leq$ is defined to be

$$\leq \triangleq \cup_{i \in [n]} \leq_i \cup \{(s, f(s)) | s \in S\}$$

the transitive closure $\leq^\star$ of $\leq$ is a partial order on E.

The total order $\leq_i$ on E_i gives a strict execution order of the events of P_i as seen on the vertical process lines of P_i in the visual representation of the MSC.

---

[1] Note that, this definition of MSCs does not include the notion of *co–region* (the region on a process line in which the events of the processes are not ordered) in MSCs which is also omitted in this paper.

The pairs $(s, f(s)) \in \leq$ correspond, in the visual representation, to the message passing arrows from the process line of $p(s)$ to the process line of $p(f(s))$.

Throughout the paper, Σ and $\mathcal{P}$ are assumed to be fixed and all the MSCs mentioned will be Σ–labeled and defined on $\mathcal{P}$. Let $\mathbb{M}$ denote the set of all Σ–labeled MSCs for $\mathcal{P}$.

Let $|E|$ denote the cardinality of the set E. A permutation of the events E of an MSC as $e_1 e_2 \ldots e_{|E|}$ is *valid* when $\forall i, j \in [|E|]$, $e_i \leq^* e_j$ implies $i \leq j$. In other words, the total order induced by the given permutation on E is consistent with the partial order $\leq^*$. A word w on $\hat{\Sigma}$ is a linearization of an MSC M if there exists a valid permutation $e_1 e_2 \ldots e_{|E|}$ of M such that $w = l(e_1) l(e_2) \ldots l(e_{|E|})$. The language of an MSC M, denoted by $L(M)$, is the set of all linearizations of M. Two MSCs M and M' are considered to be equal, $M = M'$, iff $L(M) = L(M')$.

Note that, by definition, if $w \in L(M)$, then w is well–formed and complete. Further note that, $\forall w, w' \in L(M)$, $w|_{\Sigma_i} = w'|_{\Sigma_i}$. In other words, the projections of the words in $L(M)$ onto the event labels of a process is unique. This follows from the fact that all the valid permutations of M must respect the total order $\leq_i$ which is included in $\leq^*$. In fact, this unique word, which will be denoted by $M|_i$, is the concatenation of the labels of the events that appear on the vertical line of P_i in the visual representation of M. Therefore, as shown in [7], given a well–formed and complete word w, there exists a unique MSC M, such that $w \in L(M)$, under a non–degeneracy assumption (that there is no message overtaking between same labeled events) which we also adopt in this paper. We will denote this unique MSC by $msc(w)$. We also let $\overline{w} = L(msc(w))$.

Due to this fact, an MSC can be characterized by the sequence of sequences of the event labels that appear on the processes, i.e. $M = \langle M|_i \mid i \in [n] \rangle$. Given such a sequence, the actual MSC can be constructed easily as explained in [7]. Roughly, the procedure is to scan each $M|_i$ starting from the beginning. During this scanning, a send event with a label $snd(i, j, a)$ is matched with the first not–yet–matched receive event with a label $rcv(j, i, a)$ in $M|_j$.

Proposition 1. *Let M and M' be two MSCs. $M = M'$ iff for each process P_i, $M|_i = M'|_i$.*

Proof. The proof follows from the fact that MSCs are fully characterized by their projections onto the event labels in the processes as explained above.   □

Consider the visual representation of an MSC M and imagine that we draw a line through M by crossing each process line exactly once, and without crossing any message arrows. Such a line divides M into two parts M_p (the part above the cutting line) and M_s (the part below the cutting line). M_p and M_s can be shown to be MSCs again. In fact, M_p and M_s are, what we are going to call below, a prefix of M and a suffix of M, respectively.

Formally, given two MSCs M and M', with the set of events respectively E and E', M' is said to be a *prefix* (resp. *suffix*) of M, iff:

(i) $E' \subseteq E$.

(ii) $e \in E'$ implies $\forall e' \in E$, if $e' \leq^* e$ then $e' \in E'$ (resp. $e \in E'$ implies $\forall e' \in E$, if $e \leq^* e'$ then $e' \in E'$)

(iii) $e \in E' \cap S$ implies $f(e) \in E'$ (resp. $e \in E' \cap R$ implies $f^{-1}(e) \in E'$, where f^{-1} is the inverse of the bijection f)

(iv) $S' = S \cap E'$, $R' = R \cap E'$, $l' = l|_{E'}$, $f' = f|_{E'}$, $p' = p|_{E'}$, and $\forall i \in [n]$, $\leq'_i = \leq_i |_{E'}$.

The imaginary cutting line mentioned in the intuitive explanation above is the one that crosses P_i's line right below (resp. right above) the largest (resp. the smallest) event $e \in E'_i$ with respect to the total order $\leq_i$.

Let M, M_p and M_s be MSCs with the corresponding set of events E, E_p and E_s such that M_p is a prefix of M, M_s is a suffix of M, $E_p \cap E_s = \emptyset$ and $E = E_p \cup E_s$. Then, M is said to be the *sequential composition* of M_p and M_s, denoted by the juxtaposition of M_p and M_s as $M_p M_s$. Given two MSCs M' and M'', $L(M'M'') = \{w | w \in \overline{w'w''}, w' \in L(M'), w'' \in L(M'')\}$.

For an integer $k \geq 0$, $M^{(k)}$ denotes the sequential composition of k copies of M, where $M^{(0)}$ is defined to be the empty MSC, i.e. an MSC with the empty set of events. We will use the notation M^* to denote sequential composition of 0 or more copies, and M^+ to denote sequential composition of 1 or more copies of the MSC M.

While describing the scenarios that a concurrent system must perform, a set of MSCs can be used. However, when this set gets large, it is usually presented in a more structured way by using High Level MSCs, or HMSCs, which is formally equivalent to an MSC graph given below. An MSC graph is a labeled transition system $G = (V, v_0, v_f, T)$, where V is a finite set of nodes, $v_0, v_f \in V$ are the entry and exit nodes (respectively). The relation $T \subseteq V \times \mathbb{M} \times V$ gives the edges between the nodes with the labels from $\mathbb{M}$. A *path* in G is a sequence of edges

$$(v_1, M_1, v_2)(v_2, M_2, v_3)(v_3, M_3, v_4) \cdots (v_m, M_m, v_{m+1})$$

Such a path is said to start at node v_1 and end at node v_{m+1}. The language of a path is given by the concatenation of the language of the MSCs that appear on the edges, $L(M_1)L(M_2) \cdots L(M_m)$. Given an ordered pair of nodes (v, v'), the language of the pair (v, v'), denoted by $L(v, v')$, is the union of the languages of all the paths that start at v and end at v'. The language of a node v, denoted by $L(v)$, is $L(v, v_f)$. The language of an MSC graph G is defined as $L(G) = L(v_0)$. We will use the notation $v \xrightarrow{M} v'$ to denote $(v, M, v') \in T$.

3   Problem Definition

Each function implemented by a concurrent system can be viewed as a combination of some subfunctions. For example, in a file transfer function of a communication protocol, we may have connection establishment (CE), data transfer

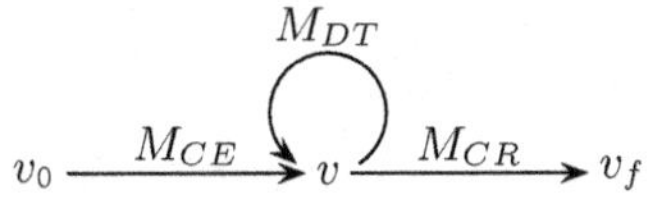

Fig. 1. An example MSC Graph

(DT), connection release (CR) subfunctions. If one could identify the subfunctions as they are being executed, then a typical execution would consist of the following steps:

$$CE, DT, DT, ..., DT, CR \qquad (1)$$

Based on the size of the data being transferred, the subfunction DT would be executed repeatedly, as many times it is required to transfer the amount of data at hand. If we consider how one would start describing such a function at an abstract level when the system was first built, it is not unreasonable to imagine that an MSC graph similar to the one given Figure 1 had been used.

In the context of reverse engineering, several attempts appeared in the literature to recover the design of an implementation from a given set of observations [12, 13, 14, 15, 16, 17]. However, if the sequence given in (1) is reverse engineered with the current techniques, the existence of repetitions of DT will cause problems. In general, it is not possible to decide if the repetitions of DT in (1) are due to a loop or due to the sequential appearance of DT in the design. Current techniques favor the latter and therefore, do not attempt to recover a design with the loops. In this paper, we will introduce a method that will help recover designs *with* loops.

As observations, we consider the execution logs (logs of message transmissions and receptions of the processes) of an implementation Imp of a concurrent system. In other words, if Σ is the set of messages used for the communication between the processes of Imp, then an observation is a well–formed and complete word over $\hat{\Sigma}$. We assume that an observation $w \in \hat{\Sigma}^\star$ corresponds to a complete execution of a single function of Imp, and the functions are assumed to start from the initial system state, and end back at the initial system state, without going through the initial system state. That is, if w is an observation and the system is at the initial state, then after performing the message exchanges given in w (in the order they appear in w), the system goes back to the initial state right after the last member of w (which must be a reception since w is complete) is realized. Furthermore, at no point in w, the system must be in the initial system state, since otherwise the prefix of w up to that point would be considered as a separate observation.

Suppose that we are given a set of observations O. In Section 2, it is shown that a well–formed and complete word corresponds to a unique MSC. Consider the MSC $msc(w)$ corresponding to an observation $w \in O$, and a word $w' \in L(msc(w))$ but $w' \notin O$. Since the individual processes are behaving, from their local point of view, exactly in the same way for both w and w', although not given as an observation, w' must also be an observation of Imp. Only the interleaving preferences between the processes change from w to w'. Therefore, the given set of observations O, together with these implied observations, actually corresponds to a wider set which is:

$$\overline{O} = \bigcup_{w \in O} \overline{w} = \bigcup_{w \in O} L(msc(w))$$

Since each given observation in $w \in O$ actually corresponds to an MSC $msc(w)$, we consider our input to be the set of MSCs $\mathcal{M} = \{msc(w) \mid w \in O\}$, and we will consider an observation to be an MSC from now on unless stated otherwise.

In our view of a function being composed of subfunctions, we also consider a subfunction to be specified by an MSC. This can be justified by considering that all the messages sent within a subfunction will be consumed within the same subfunction. In an observation M, which is given as a single MSC, the MSCs corresponding to the subfunctions are not apparent. However, our purpose is not to identify the MSCs of all the subfunctions one by one, but rather to identify those MSCs that correspond to repetitive subfunctions.

Note that, if there are any loops in the design of Imp, and if an observation $M \in \mathcal{M}$ is generated by more than one iteration of some loop, then there must be some repeated pattern in M where the pattern being repeated is generated by the iterations of the loop. However, the converse is not correct in general, i.e., a repeated pattern seen in an observation is not necessarily due to a loop.

To be able to infer a loop in the design by looking at observations, we demand some evidence. We do not readily accept that a repeated pattern seen in a single observation is due to a loop. However, if the same pattern is seen different number of repetitions *within the same context*, then we assume this is a sufficient evidence for the existence a loop. Below is the formal definition of the notion of this evidence.

Definition 1. *An MSC M is said to be* the basic repetitive MSC *of MSC M' if $M' = M^{(k)}$ for some $k \geq 2$ and there does not exist a basic repetitive MSC of M.*

Definition 2. *Two MSCs M_1 and M_2 are said to infer M to be repetitive within the context M_p–M_s if all the following are satisfied:*

  (i) M does not have a basic repetitive MSC;
  (ii) $M_1 = M_p M^{(k)} M_s$ for some $k \geq 2$;
  (iii) M is not a suffix of M_p;
  (iv) M is not a prefix of M_s;
  (v) either $M_2 = M_p M_s$ (in which case M is said to be while–repetitive*) or $M_2 = M_p M M_s$ (in which case M is said to be* repeat–repetitive*).*

Note that Definition 2 captures the essence of two different repetitive subfunctions, one which can be skipped, whereas the other cannot be skipped during the execution of the system. In order to differentiate these two different types, we call them as *while* and *repeat* repetitive respectively, by using an analogy to standard programming loop types.

What we require in observations to infer a loop is that, there must be an observation in which the loop is iterated $k \geq 2$ times, and there must also be another observation in which the same loop iterated the least possible number of times (which is 0 for a while loop, and 1 for a repeat loop). Furthermore, these two observations must have exactly the same prefix before the iterations of M, and exactly the same suffix after the iterations of M, that is they must appear within the same context. Under such an evidence, M will be assumed to be generated by a loop in the design, or more precisely, by the matching loops (sending and receiving matching messages) in the processes.

Suppose that M is found to be while–repetitive under the evidence of two observations M_1 and M_2 with the prefix M_p and suffix M_s, and suppose that M is indeed generated by a loop in the design. Then the state right before the execution of M, and right after the execution of M are the same. Hence, any MSC in the form $M_p M^\star M_s$ must be realizable by Imp. A similar argument can be applied to show that when M is found to be repeat-repetitive, any MSC in the form $M_p M^+ M_s$ must be realizable by Imp.

Since we assume that Imp does not go through the initial system state during the execution of an observation, M_p and M_s in Definition 2 must not be empty. This can be justified by the following observation. If M is repetitive, then the state just before and just after an iteration of M are the same. If M_p is empty, then M starts its execution from the initial state, since the observations start from the initial state. After the first iteration of M, the system will again be at the initial state. However, this is the definition of a function in our setting, hence M and M_s must be given as separate observations. Similarly, if M_s is empty, then the state after an iteration, hence before an iteration of M is the initial state, since observations are assumed to end at this state. In this case, M_p and M must be given as separate observations.

It is also important to note that, an iteration of a loop in an observation is allowed only to provide the required evidence to infer a loop. Further, each repetitive subfunction is inferred only once using the given observations. Moreover, in order to establish the relative ordering of two or more loops $l_1, l_2, \ldots, l_n$ in an MSC graph, $k \geq 2$ iterations of at least two loops l_i and l_j need to be given in the same observation such that the relative ordering of a pair of loops l_i and l_k can be determined from the relative ordering of two pairs of loops l_i and l_j, and l_j and l_k, $1 \leq i, j, k \leq n$, and by transitivity.

4   Problem Solution

When a pair of MSCs M_1 and M_2 is identified within the given set $\mathcal{M}$, such that M_1 and M_2 infers M to be repetitive within the context M_p–M_s, then M_1 and M_2 will be represented in the output MSC graph by using either one of the following templates, depending on whether it is while–repetitive (left) or repeat–repetitive (right).

$$v_0 \xrightarrow{\ M_p\ } v \xrightarrow{\ M_s\ } v_f \qquad\qquad v_0 \xrightarrow{\ M_p\ } v \xrightarrow{\ M\ } v' \xrightarrow{\ M_s\ } v_f$$

An algorithm that will find such pairs of MSCs, must identify the context part, i.e. common prefix M_p and the common suffix M_s, and must also check if the part remaining in the middle has a basic repetitive MSC. Before presenting such an algorithm, we need to introduce the following notions on MSCs. A *common prefix* of two MSCs M_1 and M_2, is an MSC M, such that M is a prefix of both M_1 and M_2. The *maximal common prefix* of M_1 and M_2 is a common prefix M of M_1 and M_2 with the largest number of events. Similarly, M is said to be a *common suffix* of M_1 and M_2 if it is a suffix of both M_1 and M_2. The common suffix of M_1 and M_2 with largest number of elements is called the *maximal common suffix* of M_1 and M_2.

Suppose that $M = M_p M_s$. Given M and M_p, it is trivial to find M_s, by simply removing all the events in M_p from the first part of M. Similarly, when we are given M and M_s, removing all the events in M_s starting from the last part of M will give M_p. In both of these algorithms, we need to match the labels of the events. Let us assume that these algorithms are called as "remove_prefix" and "remove_suffix", respectively.

We can now present an algorithm that can check if two given MSCs identify a repetitive MSC. Without loss of generality, we assume that M_1 has more events than M_2.

Recall that, in order to infer M to be repetitive from M_1 and M_2, we must have $M_1 = M_p M^{(k)} M_s$ and either $M_2 = M_p M_s$ or $M_2 = M_p M M_s$. The maximal common prefix of M_1 and M_2 will be consisting of M_p, followed by an optional single occurrence of M. In either case, however, M_2'' in Algorithm 1 given in Figure 2 must be empty (line 7). At line 10 and 11, we check if M_1'' has a basic repetitive MSC, by using the algorithm "basic_repetitive_MSC", which is explained in Section 4.1. For the time being, assume that it returns the basic repetitive MSC of its input MSC, if there exists one, or returns the empty MSC otherwise. If such an M does not exist, we may still infer a repetitive MSC. This corresponds to the case where $M_1 = M_p M^{(2)} M_s$ and $M_2 = M_p M M_s$. In this specific case, the maximal common prefix M_{mp} would be $M_p M$. Line 12 checks this singularity, and the correct left context is calculated at line 13.

However, if M_1'' has a basic repetitive MSC M, then we decide if it is while–repetitive or repeat–repetitive, between the lines 18–23. Note that when M is found to be repeat–repetitive (line 19-20), M will be a common suffix of the maximal common prefix of M_1 and M_2. In order to find the correct left context, line 19 extracts this common suffix from M_{mp}.

Note that, there may be multiple ways for dividing M_1 and M_2 to identify M_p, M and M_s. For example, let $M_1 = M_a M_b M_c M_b M_c M_b M_d$ and let $M_2 = M_a M_b M_d$. In this case, it is possible to infer $M_b M_c$ as while–repetitive within the context M_a– $M_b M_d$. However, it is also possible to infer $M_c M_b$ as

```
 1:  M_mp = maximal_common_prefix(M_1, M_2);
 2:  M_1^◘ = remove_prefix(M_mp, M_1);
 3:  M_2^◘ = remove_prefix(M_mp, M_2);
 4:  M_s = maximal_common_suffix(M_1^◘, M_2^◘);
 5:  M_1^◙ = remove_suffix(M_s, M_1^◘);
 6:  M_2^◙ = remove_suffix(M_s, M_2^◘);
 7:  if M_2^◙ is not empty or M_mp is empty or M_s is empty then
 8:      M_1 and M_2 do not infer a repetitive MSC
 9:  else
10:      M = basic_repetitive_MSC(M_1^◙);
11:      if M is empty then
12:          if M_1^◙ is a suffix of M_mp then
13:              M_p = remove_suffix(M_mp, M_1^◙);
14:              M_1 and M_2 infer M_1^◙ to be repeat–repetitive within the context M_p–M_s
15:          else
16:              M_1 and M_2 do not infer a repetitive MSC
17:          end if
18:      else if M is a suffix of M_mp then
19:          M_p = remove_suffix(M_mp, M);
20:          M_1 and M_2 infer M to be repeat–repetitive within the context M_p–M_s
21:      else
22:          M_1 and M_2 infer M to be while–repetitive within the context M_mp–M_s
23:      end if
24:  end if
```

Fig. 2. Algorithm 1 – Checking if M_1 and M_2 infers an MSC M to be repetitive

while–repetitive within the context $M_a M_b$–M_d. By convention, we prefer to keep preamble of the loop as long as possible, hence use the latter alternative. Note that, this is only a convention as both $M_a M_b (M_c M_b)^\star M_d$ and $M_a (M_b M_c)^\star M_b M_d$ have the same language. Algorithm 1 implements this convention by extracting the maximal common prefix of M_1 and M_2 at line 1.

We explain four elementary functions and the algorithm basic_repetitive_MSC referenced in Algorithm 1 in the following subsections.

4.1   Finding the Basic Repetitive MSC

In this subsection, we explain how to check the existence of and find the basic repetitive MSC M of a given MSC M'.

Recall that $M|_i$ denotes the sequence of event labels of process P_i in the MSC M. If $M' = M^{(k)}$, it is obvious that for each process P_i, we have

$$M'|_i = \underbrace{M|_i M|_i \cdots M|_i}_{k \text{ times}}$$

In other words, we must see these repeating patterns in the events of the processes as well. Checking if a word w' consists of repetitions of another word w

is a well–known and well–studied problem (e.g. see [18]) in pattern matching and text processing. If $w' = w^{(r)}$, then r is called *the power of w in w'* (we are only interested in integer powers, although the general theory of repetitions in words considers rational powers as well), and w is called a *root* of w'. If w cannot be written as a repetition of another word, then it is called as *primitive*. Linear time algorithms exist to find the primitive root of a word. Note that a word is always a root of itself with power 1.

Proposition 2. *Given an MSC M', let r_i be the power of the primitive root of $M'|_i$, where $i \in [n]$, and let $r = gcd(r_1, r_2, \ldots, r_n)$. M' has a basic repetitive MSC iff $r \geq 2$.*

Proof. Assume that M' has a basic repetitive MSC, i.e. $M' = M^{(k)}$ for some M and $k \geq 2$. Since the projections onto the processes must be the same, $M'|_i = M|_i^{(k)}$. Therefore, $r_i = kr_i'$ where r_i' is the power of the primitive root of $M|_i$ (note that $M|_i$ is not necessarily primitive). Therefore k is a common divisor of $r_1, r_2, \ldots, r_n$, and hence $r = gcd(r_1, r_2, \ldots, r_n) \geq k \geq 2$.

For the proof of the reverse direction, assume that $r \geq 2$. Consider an MSC M, where $M|_i$ is the first $|E_i'|/r$ event labels in $M'|_i$. Note that $M' = M^{(r)}$, since process wise projections are the same. It remains to show that M does not have a basic repetitive MSC. In fact this must be true, since if $M = M''^{(r')}$ for some $r' \geq 2$, then we must have $M' = M''^{(rr')}$. However in this case, rr', which is strictly greater than r would be a common divisor of $r_1, r_2, \ldots, r_n$, contradicting with the fact that $r = gcd(r_1, r_2, \ldots, r_n)$. □

4.2 Functions on Maximal Common Prefix–Suffix, and Prefix–Suffix Removal

Finding the maximal common prefix of two words is trivial, and based on scanning and comparing the elements of the words starting from the beginning and stopping when a difference is seen.

Finding the maximal common prefix of two MSCs is not as trivial as the case of words, since we require the prefix to be an MSC as well. Let M' and M'' be two MSCs. Consider again the sequence of event labels $M'|_i$ and $M''|_i$ of process P_i on M' and M''. Note that $M'|_i$ and $M''|_i$ are words. Let w_i be the maximal common prefix of the words $M'|_i$ and $M''|_i$. Note that the sequence of event labels $\langle w_i \mid i \in [n] \rangle$ does not necessarily characterize an MSC. However, this problem can be solved by removing some of the suffixes of w_i's. Recall the procedure explained shortly in Section 2, for building an MSC based on a sequence of sequence of event labels. This procedure can be adapted to eliminate the problematic suffixes in w_i's while finding the maximal common prefix in the following way. Initially, all the event labels in w_i's are unmarked. Then perform a scan on each w_i starting from the beginning. For each send event label of the form $snd(i, j, a)$ in w_i, find the first unmarked event label of the form $rcv(j, i, a)$ in w_j. If such an unmarked event could be found in w_j, mark both $snd(i, j, a)$ and $rcv(j, i, a)$ instances under consideration, and proceed to the next send event in w_i. When we mark two such events, they are called as marking pairs. It is necessary to remember this association since, if and when one of them is removed, the other will also be removed in the second phase of this procedure. If no such an unmarked event could be found in w_j, then leave $snd(i, j, a)$ and all the remaining events in w_i as unmarked. After this marking phase, we have an iterative suffix removal phase. For each w_i, the suffix of w_i that starts with the first unmarked event label is removed. Note that, some of the event labels in such a suffix may be marked. While removing such a marked event label, the mark of its marking pair (which must also be present in some w_j as marked) is removed. This iteration continues until all the event labels in all the w_i's are marked. The remaining event labels characterize an MSC which is the maximal common prefix. Finding the maximal common suffix of two MSCs can be performed in a similar way, by adapting the approach in the procedure explained above.

Given an MSC M and a prefix M' of M, removing the prefix M' can be performed by removing the event label sequence $M'|_i$ from the first part of $M|_i$ for each process P_i. Similarly, the removal of a suffix M' of M would be performed by removing the event label sequence $M'|_i$ from the last part of $M|_i$ for each process P_i.

4.3   Forming the Final MSC Graph

Algorithm 2 given in Figure 4 is used to produce an MSC graph based on a given set of MSCs $\mathcal{M}$. It has two phases. The first phase considers every pair of MSCs M_1 and M_2 in $\mathcal{M}$ and checks whether M_1 and M_2 infer a repetitive MSC. The output of the first phase is an MSC graph with a special structure. For each pair of MSCs that infer a repetitive MSC, a separate subgraph, that is disjoint with the rest of the graph except at v_0 and v_f, is created. Such a subgraph has a different structure depending on whether the inferred MSC is while— or repeat–repetitive, which are shown in Figure 3 at the top and in the middle, respectively. If an MSC M does not infer a repetitive MSC by pairing with another MSC, then a subgraph which consists of only (v_0, M, v_f) is created, as shown at the bottom in Figure 3. We will call these subgraphs as paths below. These paths will be referenced using the labels of the edges. The loops in the labels of the paths will be represented by using $\star$. The second column of Figure 3 gives the label template associated with each path type.

As an example for the execution of the first phase, let us suppose that initially we have three MSCs

$$M_a = M_1 M_2 M_2 M_3 M_4 M_5,$$
$$M_b = M_1 M_2 M_2 M_3 M_4 M_4 M_5,$$
$$M_c = M_1 M_3 M_4 M_5.$$

M_a and M_b infer M_4 to be repeat–repetitive within the context $M_1 M_2^{(2)} M_3{-}M_5$. Hence

$$M_d = M_1 M_2^{(2)} M_3 M_4 M_4^\star M_5$$

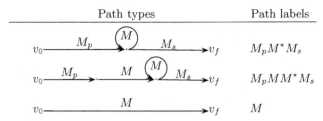

Path types   Path labels

$M_p M^\star M_s$

$M_p M M^\star M_s$

M

Fig. 3. Three different path types

is inferred as a path in G. Similarly, M_a and M_c infer M_2 to be a while-repetitive within the context of M_1–$M_3 M_4 M_5$. So

$$M_e = M_1 M_2^\star M_3 M_4 M_5$$

is inferred as a path in G.

Note that the subgraph generated from M_1 and M_2 is guaranteed to represent both M_1 and M_2, i.e. the language of M_1 and M_2 are included in the language of the generated subgraph. Thus, M_1 and M_2 are marked for deletion since we generated a new path from them. However, if for an MSC M_1, there does not exist an MSC M_2 which infers a repetitive MSC, then M_1 will simply be put into G and left unmarked. At the end of the first phase, there is no other loop left to be inferred. However, all possible relative positions of these loops must be represented in the final MSC graph G' which is constructed in the second phase of Algorithm 2.

The MSC graph G constructed by the first phase can be nondeterministic. In other words, there may be two different paths with a nonempty common prefix. In general, there is no guarantee that the system state is the same after the execution of the same prefix along these different paths, since the observations only give the message exchanges, and the local actions within the processes are hidden from the observer. There needs to be some evidence in the observations that allow some paths to be merged. Especially when a given observation M is used in the generation of two different paths p_1 and p_2 with labels M_1 and M_2 respectively, the execution of p_1 and p_2 also corresponds to the execution of M. Hence the system state along p_1 and p_2 that correspond to the execution of M must be same, and therefore p_1 and p_2 need to be merged.

The second phase of Algorithm 2 performs the merging of paths using Algorithm 3 given in Figure 5. Since we need to know the actual observations from which a path p is generated, the first phase of the algorithm associates this information to the generated path p by $src(p)$.

In the example above, after the first phase, MSCs M_a, M_b and M_c are marked and thus removed, and we have the paths corresponding to M_d and M_e added to G. In the second phase, there are two paths M_d and M_e in G. Since the sources of these two paths have a nonempty intersection, they will be in the same partition, which is actually the only partition of paths in this example.

1: /* phase 1: infer loops and form G^* */
2: initially all the MSCs in $\mathcal{M}$ are unmarked
3: generate the initial and the final nodes v_0 and v_f in G
4: **for** each pair $M_1, M_2 \in \mathcal{M}$ **do**
5:    **if** M_1 and M_2 infers an MSC M to be repetitive within a context M_p–M_s **then**
6:       mark both M_1 and M_2
7:       **if** M is while–repetitive **then**
8:          generate a new path p in G given below, where v is a new node
          $p = \{(v_0, M_p, v), (v, M, v), (v, M_s, v_f)\}$
9:       **else**
10:          generate a new path p in G given below, where v and $v^{\square}$ are new nodes
          $p = \{(v_0, M_p, v), (v, M, v^{\square}), (v^{\square}, M, v^{\square}), (v^{\square}, M_s, v_f)\}$
11:       **end if**
12:       let $src(p) = \{M_1, M_2\}$
13:    **end if**
14: **end for**
15: **for** each unmarked MSC M **do**
16:    generate a new path $p = \{(v_0, M, v_f)\}$
17:    let $src(p) = \{M\}$
18: **end for**
19: /* phase 2: merge paths and form $G^{\square}$ */
20: let $G^{\square}$ be an empty graph
21: obtain a partition Π of the set of paths such that two paths $p, p^{\square}$ are in the same
    subset P of Π iff $\exists$ a sequence of paths $p_1, p_2, \ldots, p_k$ where $p_j \in P$, $1 \le j \le k$,
    $p = p_1$, $p^{\square} = p_k$, and for $1 \le i < k$, $src(p_i) \cap src(p_{i+1}) \ne \emptyset$
22: **for** all $P \in \Pi$ **do**
23:    insert $merge(P)$ into $G^{\square}$
24: **end for**

Fig. 4. Algorithm 2 – Building the MSC graph based on a set of MSCs $\mathcal{M}$

Hence, the for loop at lines 22–24 in Algorithm 2 will iterate only once, and will insert the merging of M_d and M_e into G'.

In Algorithm 3, we consider every path as a set of three edges : (v_0, M_p, v_1), (v_1, M, v_1) and (v_1, M_s, v_f). M_p, M and M_s will be referred to as the prefix, loop and the suffix labels of the path, respectively. Note that, if the path is generated for a repeat repetitive subfunctionality, then we consider the first iteration of the loop as embedded in the prefix label.

Note that, G' produced by the second phase will effectively have the loops in G placed in their relative order, which also includes placing a loop into another, i.e. nesting of the loops. Deciding the relative orders of the loops in different paths in the merged path is based on having a common observation used in the generation of these paths. For instance, see the example given above.

Note that, Algorithm 3 depends on tracing $M_p M_s$ on the path p_m (which is actually an MSC graph) accumulated so far. Given an MSC M and an MSC graph G, it is known that deciding if $M \in L(G)$ is NP–complete [8, 19]. For-

1: let p be a path in P whose prefix label is the shortest among other paths in P
2: let $p_m = p$
3: let $src(p_m) = src(p)$
4: let $P = P - \{p\}$
5: **while** P is not empty **do**
6:     let p be a path in P such that $src(p) \cap src(p_m) \neq \emptyset$ and the prefix label of p is the shortest among other such paths in P.
7:     $src(p_m) = src(p_m) \cup src(p)$
8:     $P = P - \{p\}$
9:     trace the concatenation of the prefix label M_p and the suffix label M_s of p in p_m (by skipping ε edges)
10:     **if** during this trace M_p ends in the middle of an edge in p_m **then**
11:         insert a new node v in the middle of that edge in p_m
12:         insert a new edge (v, M, v) in p_m where M is the loop label of p
13:     **else**
14:         let v be the node at which the trace of M_p has ended
15:         **if** during the trace of M_p, v is visited exactly once **then**
16:             insert a new edge (v, M, v) in p_m where M is the loop label of p
17:         **else**
18:             let $(v, M^{\blacksquare}, v^{\blacksquare})$ be the edge which is not used during the trace of M_p
19:             remove the edge $(v, M^{\blacksquare}, v^{\blacksquare})$
20:             insert a new node $v^{\boxplus}$ in p_m
21:             insert a new edge $(v^{\boxplus}, M^{\blacksquare}, v^{\blacksquare})$
22:             insert a new edge $(v, \varepsilon, v^{\boxplus})$
23:             insert a new edge $(v^{\boxplus}, M, v^{\boxplus})$
24:         **end if**
25:     **end if**
26: **end while**
27: return (p_m)

Fig. 5. Algorithm 3 – Merging paths in a partition P

tunately, in principle, tracing of $M_p M_s$ on p_m corresponds to the case given in Theorem 6 of [8] with a time complexity of $O(|p_m| \times |M_p M_s|)$.

5 Conclusion

We have presented an algorithm to derive an MSC graph G' from a given set of observations of an existing implementation of a concurrent system. This algorithm is based on inferring repetitive subfunctions from a given set of observations. The language of the MSC graph G' derived consists of all the given observations and the inferred observations, in which the loops and their relative positions are all explored. And thus, the language of the MSC graph G' is a design representation of the existing system.

An interesting problem that remains open is the following. When the evidences of some loops are missing in the given set of observations, generated subgraphs may provide these missing evidences. For example, assume that initially we have three MSCs $M_a = M_1 M_2^{(2)} M_3 M_5$, $M_b = M_1 M_2^{(2)} M_3 M_4^{(2)} M_5$, and $M_c = M_1 M_3 M_4^{(3)} M_5$. M_a and M_b infers M_4 to be while–repetitive within the context $M_1 M_2^{(2)} M_3 - M_5$. Hence $M_d = M_1 M_2^{(2)} M_3 M_4^\star M_5$ is generated. Although M_c does not infer any repetitive subfunctionality with M_a or M_b, it infers M_2 to be while–repetitive within the context $M_1 - M_3 M_4^{(3)} M_5$ when it is considered together with $M_e = M_1 M_2^{(2)} M_3 M_4^{(3)} M_5$ which is obtained by instantiating $\star$ by 3 in M_d. However, these new repetitive subfunctions must be confirmed by the observer. Hence the question is, can and how an MSC graph, which is a design representation of the existing system, be generated under such missing evidences.

It will also be interesting to consider the effects of a) the number of occurrences of repetitive subfunctions in the given set of observations to be a fixed value, and b) some apriori knowledge of the structure of the communicating processes on the derivation of an MSC graph.

Acknowledgement

The authors wish to acknowledge many useful discussions with Jessica Chen. This work was supported in part by the Natural Sciences and Engineering Research Council of Canada, under grant OGP 976.

References

[1] ITU-T Recommendation Z.120. Message Sequence Charts (MSC96) (1996) 133
[2] Rudolph, E., Graubmann, P., Gabowski, J.: Tutorial on message sequence charts. Computer Networks and ISDN Systems–SDL and MSC **28** (1996) 133
[3] Alur, R., Holzmann, G. J., Peled, D.: An analyzer for message sequence charts. Software Concepts and Tools **17** (1996) 70–77 133
[4] Ben-Abdallah, H., Leue, S.: Syntactic detection of progress divergence and non–local choice in message sequence charts. In: 2nd TACAS. (1997) 259–274 133
[5] Alur, R., Yannakakis, M.: Model checking of message sequence charts. In: 10th International Conference on Concurrency Theory, Springer Verlag (1999) 114–129 133
[6] Alur, R., Etessami, K., Yannakakis, M.: Inference of message sequence charts. In: 22nd International Conference on Software Engineering. (2000) 304–313 133
[7] Alur, R., Etessami, K., Yannakakis, M.: Inference of message sequence charts. IEEE Transactions on Software Engineering **29** (2003) 623–633 133, 134, 135, 136
[8] Alur, R., Etessami, K., Yannakakis, M.: Realizability and verification of MSC graphs. In: Automata, Languages and Programming, 28th International Colloquium, ICALP, LNCS 2076. (2001) 134, 146, 147
[9] Lohrey, M.: Safe realizability of high–level message sequence charts. In: 13th International Conference in Concurrency Theory, CONCUR 2002. (2002) 177–192 134
[10] Chikofsky, E., Cross, J.: Reverse engineering and design recovery. IEEE Software **7** (1990) 13–17 134

[11] Lee, D., Sabnani, K.: Reverse engineering of communication protocols. (In: IEEE ICNP'93) 208–216   134

[12] Koskimies, K., Makinen, E.: Automatic synthesis of state machines from trace diagrams. Software–Practice & Experience **24** (1994) 643–658   138

[13] Rajagopal, M., Miller, R. E.: Synthesizing a protocol converter from executable protocol traces. IEEE Transactions on Computers **40** (1991) 487–499   138

[14] Zafiropulo, P., West, C., Rudin, H., Cowan, D. D., Brand, D.: Towards analyzing and synthesizing protocols. IEEE Transactions on Communications **28** (1980) 651–660   138

[15] Saleh, K., Boujarwah, A.: Communications software reverse engineering: A semi–automatic approach. Information & Software Technology **38** (1996) 379–390   138

[16] Saleh, K., Probert, R. L., Manonmani, I.: Recovery of communication protocol design from protocol execution traces. (In: IEEE ICECCS'96) 265–272   138

[17] Chen, X. J., Ural, H.: Construction of deadlock–free designs of communication protocols from observations. The Computer Journal **45** (2002) 162–173   138

[18] Crochemore, M., Rytter, W.: Text Algorithms. Oxford University Press (1994) 143

[19] Muscholl, A., Peled, D., Su, Z.: Deciding properties of message sequence charts. In: Foundations of Software Science and Computation Structures. (1998)   146

Network Protocol System Passive Testing for Fault Management: A Backward Checking Approach

Baptiste Alcalde[1], Ana Cavalli[1], Dongluo Chen[2], Davy Khuu[1], and David Lee[3]

[1] Institut National des Télécommunications GET-INT, Evry, France
{baptiste.alcalde,ana.cavalli,davy.khuu}@int-evry.fr
[2] Department of Computer Science, Tsinghua University, Beijing, China
chdl@csnet1.cs.tsinghua.edu.cn
[3] Bell Labs Research, Lucent Technologies lee@research.bell-labs.com

Abstract. Passive testing has proved to be a powerful technique for protocol system fault detection by observing its input/output behaviors yet without interrupting its normal operations. To improve the fault detection capabilities we propose a backward checking method that analyzes in a backward fashion the input/output trace from passive testing and its past. It effectively checks both the control and data portion of a protocol system, compliments the forward checking approaches, and detects more errors. We present our algorithm, study its termination and complexity, and report experiment results on the protocol SCP.

1 Introduction

Passive testing is an activity of detecting faults in a system under test by observing its input/output behaviors without interfering its normal operations. The usual approach of passive testing consists in recording the trace produced by the implementation under test and trying to find a fault by comparing this trace with the specification ([4], [6], [7]). Other approaches explore relevant properties required for a correct implementation, and then check on the implementation traces of the systems under test ([1], [2]). Most of the work on passive testing are based on finite state machines (FSMs) and they are focused on the control part of the tested systems without taking into account data parts. To cope with protocol data portions, Extended Finite State Machines (EFSMs) are used to model the systems, which include parameters and variables to encode data. In [7] a first approach to perform passive testing on EFSMs was proposed. An algorithm based on constraints on variables was developed and applied to GSM-MAP protocol. However, this algorithm cannot detect transfer errors. In [5], an algorithm based on variable determination with the constraints on variables was presented. This algorithm allows to trace the variables values as well as the system state, however, every transfer errors still cannot be detected.

To overcome this limitation, we propose a new approach based on backward tracing. This algorithm is strongly inspired by this presented in [5], but processes

D. de Frutos-Escrig and M. Núñez (Eds.): FORTE 2004, LNCS 3235, pp. 150–166, 2004.

the trace backward in order to further narrow down the possible configurations for the beginning of the trace and to continue the exploration in the past of the trace with the help of the specification. This algorithm contains two phases. It first follows a given trace backward, from the current configuration to a set of starting ones, according to the specification. The goal is to find the possible starting configurations of the trace, which leads to the current configuration. Then it analyses the past of this set of starting configurations, also in a backward manner, seeking for end configurations, that is to say configurations in which the variables are determined. When such configurations are reached, we can take a decision on the validity of the studied path.

This new algorithm is applied to Simple Connection Protocol (SCP) that allows to connect two entities after a negotiation of the quality of service required for the connection. Even it is a simple protocol it presents a number of key characteristics of real communication protocols. The testing results are compared to the passive testing algorithm in [5].

The rest of the paper is organized as follows. Section 2 describes the basic concepts used in the paper. Section 3 contains preliminary algorithms for processing transition back tracing. The section 4 presents the main backward tracing algorithm. In section 5 the issues related to the termination and complexity of the main algorithms are discussed. Section 6 reports the experiments of the algorithm on the Simple Connection Protocol.

2 Preliminaries

We first introduce basic concepts needed and then present an overview of our algorithm.

2.1 Extended Finite State Machine

We use Extended Finite State Machine (EFSM) to model the protocol systems.

Definition 1. *An Extended Finite State Machine M is a 6-tuple $M = <S, s_0, I, O, x, T>$ where S is a finite set of states, s_0 is the initial state, I is a finite set of input symbols (eventually with parameters), O is a finite set of output symbols (eventually with parameters), x is a vector denoting a finite set of variables, and T is a finite set of transitions. A transition t is a 6-tuple $t = <s_i, s_f, i, o, P, A>$ where s_i and s_f are the initial and final state of the transition, i and o are the input and the output, P is the predicate (a boolean expression), and A is the ordered set (sequence) of actions.*

Definition 2. *An events trace is a sequence of I/O pairs.*

In this paper we consider that the traces can start at any moment of the implementation execution.

Given a trace from the implementation under test and a specification, the algorithm will detect the three types of error that can occur in an EFSM.

Fig. 1.   Output(1), transfer(2), and mixed(3) errors

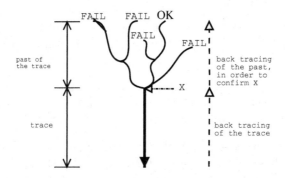

Fig. 2.   Overview of Backward Checking

Definition 3. *The three types of error are:*

1. **the output errors**: *when the output of a transition in the implementation differs from the output of the corresponding transition in the specification.*
2. **the transfer errors**: *when the ending state of a transition in the implementation differs from the ending state of the corresponding transition in the specification.*
3. **the mixed errors**: *a mix between the two errors defined above.*

2.2   Candidate Configuration Set

The backward checking algorithm processes in two phases as shown in figure 2. The first step consists in following the trace w backward, from the end to the beginning, according to the specification. The goal is to arrive to the set X of possible start configurations of w. In order to keep information we use configurations named Candidate Configuration Set (CCS) inspired from [5].

Definition 4. *Let M be an EFSM. A Candidate Configuration Set (CCS), is a 3-tuple $(e, R, Assert)$ where e is a state of M, R is an environment (that is to say that each variable v has a constraint $R(v)$), and Assert is an assertion (Boolean expression).*

The second step is the backward checking of the trace past. This step consists in confirming at least one of the departure configurations extracted from the back tracing of a trace. It means we must verify that the variable values or constraints are compliant with the specification. We need to trace the transitions from their end states to their start states until we reach a validation criteria. We need to confirm the variables ranges. However, often there is only a subset of variables that we can confirm, and we call these variables determinant of a trace.

Definition 5. *A variable v is a determinant of a trace t if v must be necessarily validated before validating t.*

In order to keep information about determinants, we define a new structure for the past of the trace: the Extended Candidate Configuration Set (also called Extended Configuration).

Definition 6. *Let M be an EFSM. An Extended Candidate Configuration Set (ECCS) is a 4-tuple $(e, R, Assert, D)$, where e is a state of M, R is an environment, Assert is an assertion, and D is a set of determinant variables.*

Between the two steps we check the determinant variable set as follows: every variable whose interval in a configuration of X - the set of possible start configurations of the trace that is included in its specified domain - must be added to the determinant variables set to be checked.

3   Preliminary Algorithms

In the following section, we present the preliminary algorithms that will be used in the main algorithm. We begin with the inverse actions algorithm, and then consistency checking and the transition back tracing algorithms.
What we do is checking backward the trace and then exploring its past as shown in Fig 2, determining the variables. In order to perform this checking on the whole trace and its past we need a process that checks a transition backward. The algorithms presented in this section make it possible.

3.1   The Inversed Actions

A main difficulty is the application of the inverse action A^{-1}. The inverse actions will be processed in a reversed order. Hence the following normal ordered actions $\{a_1, \ldots, a_n\}$ will be processed in an order: $\{a_n, \ldots, a_1\}$.
Each inverse action depends on the type of the corresponding normal action. There are three types of actions:

1. $w \longleftarrow constant$
2. $w \longleftarrow f(u, v, \ldots)$ where w is not a variable of f
3. $w \longleftarrow f(w, u, v, \ldots)$ where w is also a variable of f

These three types of actions are assignations: they overwrite the value of the left variable w with the value of the right component. We note that the value of w is modified by an action, but the other variables after action keep the value they had before the action and that only the value of the variable w will be modified by back tracing a transition. Except for this, every type of action must be inverted:

1. Action of type 1. The value of w after the action is a *constant*. This gives us a first occasion of detecting an error. If the *constant* does not conform the current constraint then we are on an invalid path. Otherwise, we replace every occurrence of w with the *constant* and refine the constraints of other variables. However, it is impossible to know the value of w before the action; indeed, actions simply overwrite the former value of w. After the action back tracing the value of w is UNDEFINED;

2. Action of type 2. We could take that $R(w)$ is equal to $R(f(u, v, \ldots))$ but we can be more precise: it is $R(w) \cap R(f(u, v, \ldots))$. In order to keep as much information as possible, every occurrence of w will be replaced by $f(u, v, \ldots)$. However, the value of w before action remains UNDEFINED;

3. Action type 3. This action brings no new constraint refinement on the variable w (on the left side of the assignment) after the action (left member) but it gives a constraint on the variable w (on the right side of the assignment) before the action. Consequently, every occurrence of w will be replaced by $f^{-1}(w)$.

3.2   Final Checking Phase

The check_consistency process is from [5] and is able to detect inconsistency in the definition of the variables by refining the intervals of variables and its constraints.

There are no big differences between the transition back tracing algorithms for the trace and for its past, and we ignore in the trace algorithm what can happen to the set of determinants before the action. Indeed, in the trace we do not determine variables; we can only refine their values, and we invalid the trace if the constraints are not consistent. For the trace we must check the output before processing the inverse actions. After processing every action we can determine the variables involved in the input if its constraint is consistent with what we found. Otherwise, we invalid the transition.

On the other hand, we must check that the variable values that we found are consistent with the predicates. Otherwise, the path is invalid. Therefore, in the checking we must determine if a transition is valid or not. We need a process called check_pred for the past of the trace to modify the set of determinants. In the case of back tracing, we just need to add the predicates to the set of assertions and process check_consistency - no specific operations are needed.

The pseudo code for back tracing of the trace and of its past, followed by the check_pred and check_consistency algorithms are presented in the appendix.

3.3 Example

We show now an example of this process. Consider the common steps of the trace and past cases, a transition without input/output, and we include the variable set D into parentheses.

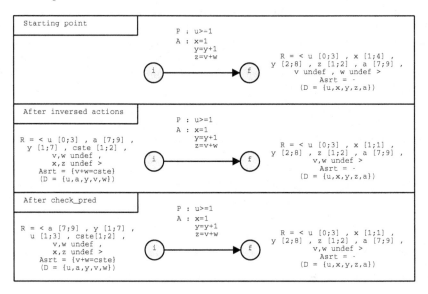

4   Main Algorithms

We are ready to present our main algorithm of backward checking.

4.1 Backward Checking of a Trace

The backward checking for a whole trace can be derived from the algorithm for back tracing a transition (Back_trace_transition):

- *trace*: The observed trace. *gettail*(*trace*) removes and returns the last *i/o* pair from *trace*.
- X: Set of starting extended configurations from back trace of an event trace. Each configuration is a 4-tuple $(e, R, Assert, D)$
- X': Current set of extended configurations
- V: Set of known extended configurations
- c': A new configuration
- : Returns TRUE if the sequence is correct, and FALSE otherwise

1. $V \longleftarrow X$	6. . .
2. **while**	.$c^\blacksquare \longleftarrow$ **Back_trace_transition**(t, c)
$X \neq \emptyset$ & $i/o := gettail(trace)$ **do**	7. . . .$X^\blacksquare \longleftarrow X^\blacksquare \cup \{c^\blacksquare\}$
3. $.X^\blacksquare \longleftarrow \emptyset$	
4. .**for** each configuration $c \in X$ **do**	8. . . .$V \longleftarrow V \cup X^\blacksquare$
5. . .**for** each transition t where	9. .$X \longleftarrow X^\blacksquare$
$t.end\_state = c.state$ and	
$t.i/o = i/o$ **do**	10. **return** FALSE

4.2 Backward Checking of the Past of an Event Trace

The backward checking algorithm applied to the past of a trace consists of a breadth-first search in the past of the configurations, which are extracted from the back tracing of a trace due to the fact that one cannot use a variable value before it is assigned. In order to validate a trace, we only need to find a path binding a set of assignments or predicates to one of the configurations extracted from back tracing. We now proceed to the main algorithm. We first define the operations $\sqcap$ and $\setminus$ on the Extended Candidate Configuration Sets (ECCS) that will be used for pruning the exploration tree of the past. Then we study the path convergence and discuss the algorithm termination, the correctness and the complexity.

The $\sqcap$ Operation. It is an intersection between two configurations:

Definition 7. *Let be three configurations* $c_1 = (e, R_1, Assert_1, D)$, $c_2 = (e, R_2, Assert_2, D)$, *and* $c = (e, R, Assert, D)$. *We define the intersection operator* $\sqcap$ *as follows. If* $c = c_1 \sqcap c_2$, *then:*

1. *for each variable* v, $R(v) = R_1(v) \cap R_2(v)$ *where* $\cap$ *is the intervals intersection operator*
2. $Assert = Assert_1 \wedge Assert_2$ *where* $\wedge$ *is the boolean "and" operator*

   Remark on $\sqcap$. The configuration states and the variable sets, which are not validated yet, are the same. If they are not, the "intersection" equals to NULL.

The $\setminus$ Operation. It is a privation. Given two configurations c_1 and c_2, the result of $c_1 \setminus c_2$ is a couple (c_a, c_b). We obtain c_a by removing c_2 from c_1, but only in case of each variable is restricted to the intersection of the intervals c_1 and c_2, respectively. c_b is the rest of c_1.

Definition 8. *Given four configurations* $c_1 = (e, R_1, Assert_1, D)$, $c_2 = (e, R_2, Assert_2, D)$, $c_a = (e, R_a, Assert_a, D)$ *and* $c_b = (e, R_b, Assert_b, D)$, *we define the privation operator* $\setminus$ *as follows. If* $(c_a, c_b) = c_1 \setminus c_2$, *then:*

1. *for* c_a:
   (a) *for each variable* v, *we have got:* $R_a(v) = R_1(v) \cap R_2(v)$ *where* $\cap$ *is the intervals intersection operator*

   (b) $Assert_a = Assert_1 \wedge \overline{Assert_2}$, where $\wedge$ is the boolean "and" operator
2. for c_b:
   (a) $R_b = R_1$
   (b) $Assert_b = Assert_1 \wedge (\bigvee\limits_{i=0}^{|V|-1} (v_i \notin R_2(v_i)))$ where $\wedge$ is the boolean "and"
      operator, and $\vee$ is the boolean "or" operator (be careful of priorities of
      parenthesis)

   Remark on \. If $Assert_2$ equals to $\emptyset$, then c_a equals to NULL. Indeed $Assert_2$
means we have to keep all of the values that R_2 allows, yet on the contrary
$\overline{Assert_2}$ implies that we must delete all of them.

   General remark. The operations $\sqcap$ and \ may return configurations, which are
inconsistent. For example, the result of $c_1 \backslash c_1$ is not consistent. Moreover, some
results may need to be refined. Indeed when two assertions are concatenated
the constraints intervals of each variable may have to be changed. So we should
use the **Check_consistency** procedure that has already been presented. For
now, we consider that the results of $\sqcap$ and \ are automatically checked and
transformed by **Check_consistency**.

Examples. Consider the configurations $c_1 = (e, < x = [0; 5], y = [0; 3] >, \_, \{x\})$
(where $\_$ means no assertion) and $c_2 = (e, < x = [0; 2], y = [-1; 1] >, \{x > y\}, \{x\})$, and three configurations c_i, c_a and c_b, which are defined as following:

  – $c_i = c_1 \sqcap c_2$
  – $(c_a, c_b) = c_1 \backslash c_2$

   We first determinate c_i. R_i is defined as the intersection of R_1 and R_2, and
$Assert_i$ is $Assert_1 \wedge Assert_2$. Then we have:
$c_i = (e, < x = [0; 2], y = [0; 1], \{x > y\}, \{x\})$.

   Determinating c_a and c_b is a little bit more complicated. R_a is the intersection of R_1 and R_2, and $Assert_a$ is $Assert_1 \wedge \overline{Assert_2}$. Then we have:
$c_a = (e, < x = [0; 2], y = [0; 1] >, \{x \leq y\}, \{x\})$.

   At last for c_b, we have the following properties. R_b equals R_1, and we must
add $x < 0 \vee x > 2$ and $y < 0 \vee y > 1$ to $Assert_b$. Then we have:
$c_b = (e, < x = [0; 5], y = [0; 3] >, \{(x < 0 \vee x > 2) \wedge (y < 0 \vee y > 1)\}, \{x\})$.

   Note that the two last configurations c_a and c_b are not refined as it was defined in [5]. If we apply the **Check_consistency** procedure, we obtain:
$c_a = (e, < x = [0; 1], y = [0; 1] >, \{x \leq y\}, \{x\})$ and $c_b = (e, < x = [3; 5], y = [2; 3] >, \_, \{x\})$.

Path Convergence. Consider a step r of our algorithm. If we find a configuration c that we have already found earlier, in a previous step or earlier in the
step r, we have got a "path convergence" phenomena.

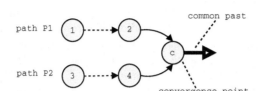

Fig. 3.   Example of Path Convergence

Definition 9. *Two paths P_1 and P_2 are convergent (in the past!) if they lead to the same configuration c.*

Consequently both P_1 and P_2 have the same past. So we will obtain the same information if we explore the common past from P_1 or from P_2. Consider that we have first followed P_1. When we find that P_2 converges toward c, we do not continue the exploration: we prune P_2 at c. The pruning enables us to deal with the infinite exploration paths.

Unfortunately extended configurations make convergences hard to be detected; they are non-empty intersections of configurations. We proceed as follows. Given three configurations c, c_1 and c_2, let c be equal to $c_1 \sqcap c_2$. Suppose that c_2 has been found before c_1. Then we have the following:

- c =NULL. c_1 and c_2 are independent and the respective pasts of c_1 and c_2 must be explored;
- $(c \neq \text{NULL}) \wedge (c = c_1)$. c_1 is included in c_2 and we must delete c_1;
- $(c \neq \text{NULL}) \wedge (c \neq c_1)$. c_2 is included in c_1 and we must substitute c_1 by $c_1 \backslash c_2$.

The algorithm **Check_redundancy**, that will be described later, deals with the convergence cases.

Algorithm of Backward Checking of the Past of a Trace. The Backward_checking_past algorithm backward traces the past of a trace in order to validate it. The input is the set of starting extended configurations, which we extracted from the trace back tracing.

Note that if the start configuration is invalid (not reachable from the initial configuration set) then we have to explore backward all the configurations to tell whether there is no valid path from the initial configuration set. However, if it is indeed valid, finding a valid path is enough. In most cases of passive testing, the traces do not contain faults and it is desirable to use a heuristic method to find a valid path. We now present such a procedure.

In order to guide the heuristic search, we have figure out the end configurations. A configuration set c is an end configuration set if it satisfies one of the following conditions:

1. $c \cap c\_init \neq \emptyset$ where c_init is the initial configuration set of the machine
2. $c.D = \emptyset$
3. c is contained in another configuration set that has been explored

The second criteria is valid, since $c.state$ is reachable from the initial state of the machine, and there must be a valid path from the initial configuration.

We now present a heuristic search. We assign a weight for each configuration-transition pair $< c, t >$. Since we want to trace back to the initial configuration or reduce $c.D$, we increase the weight of such pairs. A priority queue Q contains all the configuration-transition pairs to be explored, sorted by their weights. The pair with the highest weight is placed in the head of Q and will be selected first.

The weight wgt of a configuration-transition pair $< c, t >$ with an initial value 0 can be incremented by the following rules:

1. if $t.start\_state = c\_init.state$, $wgt += w1$
2. if $t.start\_state$ has not been explored, $wgt += w2$
3. if $t.action$ defines k variables in $c.D$, $wgt += w3 * k$

The first two rules guide the search towards the initial state of the specification while the third one is to reduce the set of determinants. It is important to remark that we don't need to reach the initial state itself, and that a transition determining every variables left in the set of determinants is enough to conclude on the correctness of the explored path. This explains the importance of the third rule (we can note that the initial state is a particular case of it as it is supposed to determine every variables).

The values of $w1, w2$, and $w3$ can be given after practical usage.

The following is the procedure where

 - Q: Set of configuration-transition pairs to be explored
 - V: Set of already-explored Extended Configurations
 - : Returns TRUE if the trace is correct, and FALSE otherwise.

1. initialize Q, V	9. $c^{\square}$=**Check_redundancy**$(c^{\square}, V)$
2. **while** $Q \neq \emptyset$ **do**	10. .If $c^{\square} \neq \emptyset$ **do**
3. .take the first item $< c, t >$ from Q	11. . $.V \longleftarrow V \cup c^{\square}$
4. .build a new configuration $c^{\square}$: $c^{\square} \longleftarrow$ **Back_past_transition**(t, c)	12. . .for each transition t where $t.end\_state = c^{\square}.state$ **do**
5. .if $c^{\square} == NULL$	13. . . .calculate the weight of $< c^{\square}, t >$
6. . .goto 2	14. . . .insert $< c^{\square}, t >$ into Q by its weight
7. .if $c^{\square}.D = \emptyset$ **do**	15. **return** FALSE
8. . .**return** TRUE	

In the worst case, this algorithm will explore backward all the possible configurations. When Q becomes empty no valid path is possible from the trace information from the passive testing and "FALSE" is returned - there are faults in the protocol system under test.

5   Algorithm Termination and Complexity

In the first part of the algorithm (backtracking of the trace) there is no problem of termination because we follow the trace, so this step finishes when the trace finishes. The problem we had and we solved is in the second part of the algorithm (in the past of the trace). We present these problems in the following subsection.

5.1   Loop Termination

There are two problems that we must solve: infinite paths, and infinite number of paths. These problems are often caused by loops.

A first infinite path case occurs when a path infinitely often reachs a configuration. This problem is solved thanks to the detection of path convergence (see 4.2), and ECCS operations that prevents exploring more than once in a configuration. A second case occurs when a variable is infinitely increased or decreased. In this case the loop is limited by the upper or lower bound of the interval of definition of the variable.

There are two cases when we have an infinite number of paths. First, a configuration has an infinite number of parents. Secondly there is an infinite path from which several paths start. But if the configurations number is finite, then a configuration can not have an infinite number of parents.

We proved the termination of the algorithm, and we present in the next subsection a study of the algorithm complexity.

5.2   Complexity

In the first part of the algorithm (trace) the complexity depends on the trace. We have:

Proposition 1. Suppose that the observed event trace is of length l, then the complexity of the first part of the presented algorithm is proportional to l.

For the second part (past of the trace) the complexity depends on the number of possible configurations. A configuration includes a state number, interval of definition of variables, and a list of determinant variables. The complexity of the second part of the algorithm is:

Proposition 2. Let n_s be the number of states in the EFSM of the specification, $|R(x_i)|$ the number of values the variable x_i can take (in the interval of definition), and n the number of variables, then there is in $O(n_s(\prod_i |R(x_i)|)(2^n - 1))$ possible configurations.

We must balance this complexity with the power of the algorithm. The worst case of this algorithm is the case where there is an error because we must check every path of the past. When there is no error our algorithm gives a sure answer (in constrast with former algorithms) at the first correct path we meet (that is supposed to be fast using the heuristic). Anyway, the backward checking - if we

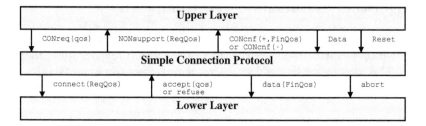

Fig. 4. Simple Connection Protocol: Layers

consider only the trace analysis - is an improvement of former algorithm, and has the same complexity.

6   Experiments on SCP Protocol

We now report the application of our algorithms on the Simple Connection Protocol (SCP). SCP is a very interesting protocol for test purpose because it includes most possible difficulties for passive testing in a small specification. Therefore, it can show the efficiency of the algorithm on bigger real protocols. We first describe this protocol and then report the experiments of the algorithm from [5] and our new algorithm.

6.1   The Simple Connection Protocol

SCP allows us to connect an entity called *upper layer* to an entity called *lower layer* (Fig 4). The upper layer performs a dialogue with SCP to fix the quality of service desirable for the future connection. Once this negotiation finished, SCP dialogues with the lower layer to ask for the establishment of a connection satisfying the quality of service previously negotiated. The lower layer accepts or refuses this connection request. If it accepts the connection, SCP informs the upper layer that connection was established and the upper layer can start to transit data towards the lower layer via SCP. Once the transmission of the data finished, the upper layer sends a message to close the connection. On the other hand, if the lower layer refuses the connection, the system allows SCP to make three requests before informing the upper layer that the connection attempts all failed. If the upper layer wishes again to be connected to the lower layer, it is necessary to restart the QoS negotiation with SCP from beginning. Every variable is defined in the interval $[0; 3]$. An EFSM specification of SCP is in the figure 5.

6.2   Experiments of the Two Algorithms

Consider a false implementation of SCP, that has been used in [2]: the predicate of the transition $s_3 \longrightarrow s_1$ is replaced by $TryCount = 0$. The figures 6, 7 and 8 show the executions of the first algorithm and of the backward

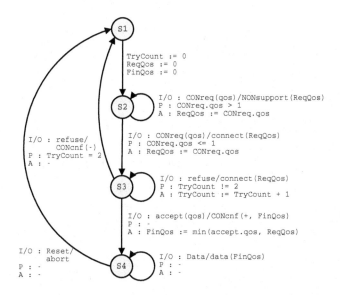

Fig. 5. Simple Connection Protocol: EFMS specification

checking algorithm (trace and past) on the trace **CONreq(1)/ connect(1), refuse/CONcnf(-)**.

The figure 6 shows that the error is not detected by the algorithm presented in [5]. The trace is left "possible" for it.

The figure 8 shows the execution of backward checking algorithm in the past. We obtain the configuration $(S2, < TryCount = 2; ReqQos = 1; FinQos = [0; 3]; CONreq.qos = 1 >, \_, \{TryCount; ReqQos; CONreq.qos\})$ from the back tracing of the trace (Fig. 7) and we continue in the past. After the first step of the while loop, X is empty because the transition ⓢ₂⟶ⓢ₂ leads to a contradiction between $CONreq.qos$ value (=1) and the predicate $CONreq.qos > 1$, and the transition ⓢ₁⟶ⓢ₂ is also invalid due to a contradiction between $ReqQos$ value (=1) and the action $ReqQos = 0$. Then there is no more configuration to backtrack and the algorithm terminates, returning FALSE - there are faults in the protocol implementation.

7   Conclusion

Apparently, passive testing is a promising method for protocol fault management, as it allows to test without disturbing the normal operation of a protocol system or service. In this paper, we present a new backward checking algorithm. It detects output and transfer errors in an implementation by observing and analyzing its event traces. A major difficulty of passive testing is its analysis for faults. Our approach provides a backward trace analysis that is efficient and also a compliment to the forward analysis in [5], and can uncover more faults.

step	event	configurations
0	-	$(S_i; < TC = [0;3], RQ = [0;3], FQ = [0;3], Crq.qos = [0;3], acc.qos = [0;3] >, \_)$ (for each i state number)
1	CONreq(1) / connect(1)	$(S_3; < TC = [0;3], RQ = 1, FQ = [0;3], Crq.qos = 1, acc.qos = [0;3] >, \_)$
2	refuse / CONcnf(-)	$(S_1; < TC = 2, RQ = 1, FQ = [0;3], Crq.qos = 1, acc.qos = [0;3] >, \_)$

Fig. 6. Execution of the First Algorithm

step	event	configurations
0	-	$(S_i; < TC = [0;3], RQ = [0;3], FQ = [0;3], Crq.qos = [0;3], acc.qos = [0;3] >, \_)$ (for each i state number)
1	refuse / CONcnf(-)	$(S_3; < TC = 2, RQ = [0;3], FQ = [0;3], Crq.qos = [0;3], acc.qos = [0;3] >, \_)$
2	CONreq(1) / connect(1)	$(S_2; < TC = 2, RQ = 1, FQ = [0;3], Crq.qos = 1, acc.qos = [0;3] >, \_)$

Fig. 7. Back Tracing the Trace

step				
0	current conf.	$(S_2, < TC = 2; RQ = 1; FQ = [0;3]; Crq.qos = 1 >, \_, \{TC;RQ; Crq.qos\})$		
	seen conf.	$(S_2, < TC = 2; RQ = 1; FQ = [0;3]; Crq.qos = 1 >, \_, \{TC;RQ; Crq.qos\})$		
	transition $S_2 \longleftarrow S_2$	back tracing	next config.	$\emptyset$
	transition $S_2 \longleftarrow S_1$	back tracing	next config.	$\emptyset$
	validation	there is no more configuration: return FALSE		

Fig. 8. Back Tracing the Past of the Trace

Passive testing is a formal approach for network protocol system monitoring and measurement where Internet protocols such as OSPF and BGP were monitored for fault detection [3]. Formal method will continue to exhibit its power in network protocol system fault management in a wider range of applications and protocol layers.

8 Appendix

Back_trace_transition(t,c) Algorithm
This algorithm is used for backtracing a transition during the trace processing.

– : returns c' if $c' \xrightarrow{t} c$ is possible, NULL if not.

1. **if** $(output.v \notin c.R(v))$ **do**	16. . .replace every occurrence of w by
2. .**return** NULL	$f(x)$ in $c^{\square}.Asrt$
3. **else**	17. . .**if** $w \in x$ **then**
4. .$c^{\square} = clone(c)$	18. . . .$c^{\square}.R(w) = R(f^{\square^{-1}}(x))$
5. .$c^{\square}.R(v) = Def(v)$	19. . .**else**
6. .replace every occurrence of v in $c^{\square}.Asrt$ by	20. . . .$c^{\square}.Asrt = c^{\square}.Asrt\wedge$ $(\underline{w} \leq f(x) \leq \overline{w})$
$output.v$	21. . . .$c^{\square}.R(w) = Def(w)$
7. inverse list of actions	22. **foreach** predicate p **do**
8. **foreach** action a **do**	23. .normalize p
9. .**if** action a is: $w \longleftarrow constante$ **then**	24. .$c^{\square}.Asrt = c^{\square}.Asrt \wedge p$
10. . .**if** $c^{\square}.R(w) \cap constante = \emptyset$ **then**	25. **if** $(input.v \notin c^{\square}.R(v))$ **do**
11. . . .**return** incorrect trace	26. .**return** NULL
12. . .**else**	27. **else**
13. . . .$c^{\square}.R(w) = Def(w)$	28. .$c^{\square}.R(v) = Def(v)$
14. . . .replace every occurrence of w in $c^{\square}.Asrt$ by $constante$	29. .replace every occurrence of v by $input.v$ in $c^{\square}.Asrt$
15. .**if** action a is: $w \longleftarrow f(x)$ **then**	30. check_consistency$(c^{\square})$
	31. **return** $c^{\square}$

Back_past_transition(t,c) Algorithm

This algorithm is used for backtracing a transition during the past trace processing.

1. $c^{\square} = clone(c)$	12. . .replace every occurrence of w by
2. inverse list of actions	$f(x)$ in $c^{\square}.Asrt$
3. **foreach** action a **do**	13. . .**if** $w \in x$ **then**
4. .**if** action a is: $w \longleftarrow constante$ **then**	14. . . .$c^{\square}.R(w) = R(f^{\square^{-1}}(x))$
5. . .**if** $c^{\square}.R(w) \cap constante = \emptyset$ **then**	15. . .**else**
6. . . .**return** incorrect trace	16. . . .$D = D - w$
7. . .**else**	17. . . .$c^{\square}.Asrt = c^{\square}.Asrt\wedge$ $(\underline{w} - cst \leq f(x) \leq \overline{w} - cst)$
8. . . .$c^{\square}.R(w) = Def(w)$	18. . . .$c^{\square}.R(w) = Def(w)$
9. . . .replace every occurrence of w in $c^{\square}.Asrt$ by $constante$	19. . .$D = D \cup y$
10. . . .$D = D - w$ //w is validated	20. check_consistency(c')
11. .**if** action a is: $w \longleftarrow f(x)$ **then**	21. check_pred(p,c')
	22. **return** $c^{\square}$

Check_pred(P, c) Algorithm

1. **for each** predicate $v = f(x) \in P$ **do**	3. . .$c.D = c.D - v$ // v is validated
	4. . .$c.R(v) = c.R(v) \cap c.R(f(x))$
2. .**if** $(c.R(v) \cap c.R(f(x)) \subseteq c.R(v))$ **then**	5. .**else return** FALSE
	6. **return** TRUE

Check_consistency(c) Algorithm

The following algorithm derives from the one presented in [5]. It tests configurations consistency, refines their constraints and delete all unused assertions. It returns the processed configuration if the initial one is consistent, or NULL if it is not.

Variable assignment Rule (**R**): for each variable range if we have a set of non empty intervals from the processing of the conjunctive terms then the new variable range consists of an interval whose lower (upper) bound is the minimum (maximum) of all the interval lower (upper) bounds.

- c: configuration that must be refined
- c': copy of c. Note $c' = (e, R, Assert, D)$
- return the refinment of c, or NULL
- S: a new set of intervals
- At: a new assertion

1. $c^\square \longleftarrow c$	21. . . .
2. transform $c^\square.Assert$ in DNF	$.R_l^\square(x_j) \longleftarrow \dfrac{R(\square\ Z)\square \sum_{i \neq j}(a_i R(x_i))}{a_j}$
3. $S \longleftarrow \emptyset$	$\cap R_l(x_j)$
4. $At \longleftarrow \emptyset$	22. . . . .if $R_l^\square(x_j) = $ NULL do
5. **for each** conjunctive term D_t of $c^\square.Assert$ **do**	23. . . . . .$dt\_true \longleftarrow$ FALSE
6. .$dt\_true \longleftarrow$ TRUE	24. . . . . .**go to** 35
7. .$refine \longleftarrow$ TRUE	25. . . . .if $R_l^\square(x_j) \subset R_l(x_j)$ **do**
8. **.while** $refine = $ TRUE **do**	26. . . . . .$refine \longleftarrow$ TRUE
9. . .$refine \longleftarrow$ FALSE	27. . . . . .$R_l(x_j) \longleftarrow R_l^\square(x_j)$
10. . .$R_l \longleftarrow c^\square.R$	28. .if $dt_true = $ FALSE **then**
11. . .$R_l^\square \longleftarrow \emptyset$	29. . .remove D_t from $c^\square.Assert$
12. . .**for each** predicate p of D_t **do**	30. .**else**
13. . . .normalize p	31. . .**for each** variable v **do**
14. . . .**if** $\sum_i(a_i R_l(x_i)) \subseteq R(\sim Z)$ **do**	32. . . .$At \longleftarrow At \wedge (v \in R_l(v))$
	33. . . .$S(v) \longleftarrow$ combination of $S(v)$ and
/*p is TRUE*/	$R_l(v),$
15. . . . .remove p from D_t	according to **R**
16. . . . .**go to** 12	34. **if** $|S| = 0$ **do**
17. . . .**if** $\sum_i(a_i R_l(x_i)) \cap R(\sim Z) = \emptyset$ **then**	35. .**return** NULL
18. . . . .$dt\_true \longleftarrow$ FALSE	36. **else**
19. . . . .**go to** 28	37. .$c^\square.R \longleftarrow S$
20. . . .**for each** $x_j,\ j = 1, \ldots, k$ **do**	38. .$c^\square.Assert \longleftarrow c^\square.Assert \wedge At$
	39. .**return** $c^\square$

Check_redundancy(c, V) Algorithm

The following algorithm aims to deal with convergence cases, in order to solve the infinite loops problem.

- c: configuration to be checked
- V: set of already-seen configurations
- X: set of configurations from redundancy check
- X': intermediate set of configurations

1. $X \longleftarrow \{c\}$	10. . . .goto 4
2. **for** each configuration $c_V \in V$ **do**	11. . .**else if** $(c_i^\square \neq \text{NULL}) \& (c_i^\square \neq c_i)$
3. .$X^\square \longleftarrow \emptyset$	**do**
4. .**for** each configuration $c_i \in X$ **do**	12. . . .$(c_i^a, c_i^b) \longleftarrow c_i \backslash c_i^\square$
5. . .$c_i^\square \longleftarrow c_i \sqcap c_V$	13. . . .**if** $c_i^a \neq \text{NULL}$ **do**
6. . .**if** $c_i^\square = \text{NULL}$ **do**	14. . . . .$X^\square \longleftarrow X^\square \cup \{c_i^a\}$
7. . .$X^\square \longleftarrow X^\square \cup \{c_i\}$	15. . . .**if** $c_i^b \neq \text{NULL}$ **do**
8. . . .goto 4	16. . . . .$X^\square \longleftarrow X^\square \cup \{c_i^b\}$
9. . .**else if** $(c_i^\square \neq \text{NULL}) \& (c_i^\square = c_i)$	17. .$X \longleftarrow X^\square$
do	18. **return** X

References

[1] J. A. Arnedo, A. Cavalli, M. Núñez, *Fast Testing of Critical Properties through Passive Testing*, Lecture Notes on Computer Science, vol. 2644/2003, pages 295-310, Springer, 2003. 150

[2] A. Cavalli, C. Gervy, S. Prokopenko, *New approaches for passive testing using an Extended Finite State Machine specification*, in Information and Software Technology 45(12) (15 sept. 2003), pages 837-852, Elsevier. 150, 161

[3] R. Hao, D. Lee, and J. Ma, *Fault Management for Networks with Link-State Routing Protocols* Proceedings of the IEEE/IFIP Network Operations and Management Symposium (NOMS), April 2004. 163

[4] D. Lee, A. N. Netravali, K. Sabnani, B. Sugla, A. John, *Passive testing and applications to network management*, IEEE International Conference on Network Protocols, ICNP'97, pages 113-122. IEEE Computer Society Press, 1997. 150

[5] D. Lee, D. Chen, R. Hao, R. E. Miller, J. Wu and X. Yin, *A formal approach for passive testing of protocol data portions*, Proceedings of the IEEE International Conference on Network Protocols, ICNP'02, 2002. 150, 151, 152, 154, 157, 161, 162, 165

[6] R. E. Miller, and K. A. Arisha, *On fault location in networks by passive testing*, Technical Report #4044, Departement of Computer Science, University of Maryland, College Park, August 1999. 150

[7] M. Tabourier and A. Cavalli, *Passive testing and application to the GSM-MAP protocol*, in Information and Software Technology 41(11) (15 sept. 1999), pages 813-821, Elsevier, 1999. 150

Connectivity Testing Through Model-Checking

Jens Chr. Godskesen[1,2], Brian Nielsen[1], and Arne Skou[1]

[1] Center of Embedded Software Systems, Aalborg University,
Fredrik Bajersvej 7B, DK-9220 Aalborg, Denmark
{jcg,bnielsen,ask}@cs.auc.dk
[2] IT-University of Copenhagen
Glentevej 67, DK-2400 Copenhagen NV., Denmark

Abstract. In this paper we show how to automatically generate test sequences that are aimed at testing the interconnections of embedded and communicating systems. Our proposal is based on the *connectivity fault model* proposed by [8], where faults may occur in the interface between the software and its environment rather than in the software implementation.
We show that the test generation task can be carried out by solving a reachability problem in a system consisting essentially of a specification of the communicating system and its fault model. Our technique can be applied using most off-the-shelf model-checking tools to synthesize minimal test sequences, and we demonstrate it using the UppAal real-time model-checker.
We present two algorithms for generating minimal tests: one for single faults and one for multiple faults. Moreover, we demonstrate how to exploit the unique time- and cost-planning- facilities of UppAal to derive cheapest possible test suites for restricted types of timed systems.

1 Introduction

Testing modern embedded and communicating systems is a very challenging and difficult task. In part, this is due to their complex communication patterns and by their reduced controllability and observability caused by the embedding and close integration with hardware. Although testing is the primary validation technique used by industry today, it remains quite ad hoc and error prone. Therefore there is a high demand for systematic and theoretically well founded techniques that work in practice and that can be supported by automated test tools.

A promising approach to improve the effectiveness of testing is to base test generation on an abstract formal model of the system under test (SUT) and use a test generation tool to (automatically or user guided) generate and execute test cases. A main problem is to automatically generate and *select* a reasonably small number of effective test cases that can be executed within the time allocated to testing.

This paper presents a technique for (formal) model-based (extended-finite state machines) black-box behavioral testing of embedded systems where a particular fault model, *connectivity faults*, is used to select test cases. Moreover, we

D. de Frutos-Escrig and M. Núñez (Eds.): FORTE 2004, LNCS 3235, pp. 167–184, 2004.
© IFIP International Federation for Information Processing 2004

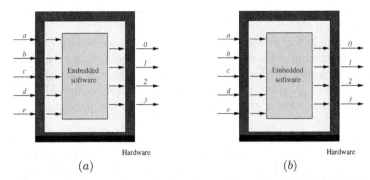

Fig. 1. An idealized view on embedded systems (a) and faulty embedded systems (b)

demonstrate how such test cases can be generated using the diagnostic trace facility of a standard, unmodified, model checking tool using standard reachability analysis.

1.1 Connectivity Testing

An embedded system may as presented in [8] idealistically be regarded as consisting of embedded software encapsulated by hardware, like depicted in Figure $1(a)$, where all communications to and from the software pass through the hardware. This is visualized by letting the inputs from the system environment to the software (a, b, c, d, e) pass through the hardware towards the software via *connections* (the unlabeled arrows). Likewise the outputs $(0, 1, 2, 3)$ generated by the software have to pass via connections through the hardware in order to emerge at the system environment.

A connection is by assumption related to exactly one input or output. This assumption implicitly implies that there is a one to one correspondence between external inputs to the system and the inputs to the embedded software, likewise there is a one to one correspondence between the outputs from the software and the outputs from the system.

Ideally it should be ascertained that the specification of the software component is correct. For instance, it may have been verified by some FSM verification technique. Then exploiting the ability to automatically generate executable code from specifications and assuming a careful construction of such compilers it would be reasonable to expect the generated code to be correct with respect to the specification, that is the two perform the same FSM behaviour.

In the composition of the two system components it then follows that the hardware (and probably drivers managing the interaction between the hardware and the software or malfunctioning sensors and actuators) may be the only error prone part. Therefore, in order to manage the multitude of potential errors we shall make an abstraction and regard the hardware (and the drivers, sensors, and actuators) as a black box interfacing the embedded software through the connections. As a consequence system errors may now only be referred to in terms of the connections.

In the system in Figure 1(a) a fault could for instance be that one of the input connections is missing as shown in Figure 1(b), where the b-input is *disconnected*. In the physical world, say for a mobile phone for instance, this may correspond to the situation where some button of the phone is not connected such that the software will never receive the input, and therefore the pressing of the button will cause no effect.

To ensure that the faults are testable they are assumed to be *permanent*. Testing in order to detect the kind of faults addressed in this paper is a matter of providing sequences of inputs that will reveal the missing connections. If say the b-input connection in Figure 1(a) is missing this may be revealed by an input sequence containing b and where eventually an expected output event is not produced or (in case the system is not input enabled) an expected input is not allowed.

We require that test generation is sound and complete, but from a practical perspective the generated suite should also be cost effective, e.g., in terms of test execution time. Thus, the suite should be minimized in the number of tests and length.

1.2   Contributions

We provide algorithms for generating tests for embedded systems with respect to fault models for input connectivity errors where for the system under test, it is assumed that the embedded software behaves as an FSM. By exploiting a real-time model-checker like UppAal [13] we are able to generate timed test sequences. However, to ease presentation we define our algorithms in the untimed setting of I/O deterministic EFSM (previous work [8] defined connectivity errors in term of Mealy machines). We prove that a *minimal* length sound and complete test (with respect to single connectivity faults) can be found via a reachability question of a composition of the system model, its fault model, and a simple environment model. We extend the basic algorithm to generate a *minimal* length test for *multiple* connectivity faults, and we prove its soundness and completeness.

Previous work [8] provided *dedicated, heuristic* polynomial time reduction algorithms; ours always produce the minimal (at the expense of increased complexity). Our algorithms can be implemented in most model-checking tools, but are additionally valid for a particular class of timed automatons using a real-time model-checker like UppAal. It symbolically solves clock constraints to perform reachability analysis on a network of timed automata, and produces a timed diagnostic trace (an alternating sequence of discrete transitions and time delays) to explain how the property is (is not) satisfied. We demonstrate the applicability of the algorithms on a medium size example (a cruise controller) – both in an untimed and a timed version, and indicate how the unique time- and cost-optimizing features of UppAal can be used to generate optimal tests.

The paper is organized as follows: Section 2 formally presents I/O EFSM's and tests. Section 3 presents the modelling of connectivity faults and illustrates how to test for such faults. Section 4 and Section 5 respectively present the algorithm for single and multiple faults. Section 6 presents the case study, and Section 7 elaborate on generation of time- and cost- optimal tests using UppAal's unique diagnostic trace features. Section 8 concludes and outlines future work.

1.3   Related Work

The use of diagnostic traces produced by model-checkers as test sequences has been proposed by many others [2, 3, 5, 6, 7, 10, 11, 15, 9]. A simple approach is based on manually stated test purposes, (i.e specific observation objectives to be made on the system under test) such as observing a given output, or bringing the SUT to a given state or mode, see e.g.,[6]. The test purpose is then formalized and translated to a logical (reachability) property to be analyzed by a model-checker. The resulting diagnostic trace is interpreted as a test case for that test purpose.

Another common approach is based on producing test suites that satisfy some coverage criteria of the specification, e.g. state- or transition- coverage, def-use pair coverage, MC/DC coverage etc. The simplest way of realizing e.g.,transition coverage is to formulate a property for each transition separately and use the model checker to produce a test case for each transition. More advanced techniques will naturally try to reduce the size of the test suite by removing redundant prefix-traces [15] or composing test cases by generating (minimal [9]) transition tours, [11, 9].

In [2] mutation testing is considered although in another setting than ours (they consider software testing). Mutations are used for generating tests to implementations of FSM's using model checking. Given is an FSM, M, and a constraining temporal logic formula, ϕ. A mutation may be either a change of a transition in M, or a change of ϕ. For each mutation a test is generated as a counter example as to why $M \not\models \phi$ (if $M \not\models \phi$). Duplicates and test being prefixes of other tests are removed, hence they do not as in our case generate a smallest possible test suite.

2   I/O EFSM

In this section we define input/output extended finite state automata (I/O EFSM) and their semantics.

Definition 1. *An* I/O EFSM *is a tuple*

$$M = (S, I, O, X, s_0, \longrightarrow)$$

where S is a finite set of states, $s_0 \in S$ is the initial state, I and O are finite disjoint sets of input and output labels respectively, X is a finite set of integer variables, and $\longrightarrow \subseteq S \times G_X \times (I \cup O) \times A_X \times S$ is a transition relation, G_X is a set of guards, over the variables in X, and A_X is a set of finite sequences (possibly the empty sequence ϵ) of assignments to variables in X. Each guard is a boolean *expression over integer constants and variables in X, and each assignment is on the form $x := e$ where $x \in X$ and $e \in E_X$ is a arithmetical expression over the variables in X and integer constants.*

Whenever $(s, g, \alpha, a, s') \in \longrightarrow$ we write $s \xrightarrow{g,\alpha,a} s'$. We write $s \xrightarrow{g,\alpha} s'$ ($s \xrightarrow{\alpha,a} s'$) instead of $s \xrightarrow{g,\alpha,\epsilon} s'$ ($s \xrightarrow{true,\alpha,a} s'$). We write $s \xrightarrow{\alpha} s'$ instead of $s \xrightarrow{\alpha,\epsilon} s'$. Often we write $\alpha!$ ($\alpha?$) whenever α is an output (input) symbol. Note that, for reasons of clarity and ease of presentation, we have omitted internal τ actions; our algorithms can easily be adapted to handle these as well.

2.1   Semantics

The semantics of an I/O EFSM M is a labelled transition system defined wrt. a *valuation function* assigning values to the variables of M and used to evaluate the guards on transitions.

Definition 2. *A valuation v for a set of integer variables X is a function $v : X \rightarrow \mathbf{N}$. We let V_X denote the set of all valuations for X. $\bar{0}_X \in V_X$ is the valuation where $\bar{0}_X(x) = 0$ for all $x \in X$. For $n \in \mathbf{N}$, $v[x \mapsto n]$ evaluates all variables y to $v(y)$ except x that is evaluated to n.*

Given a valuation $v \in V_X$, the value of a guard $g \in G_X$ with respect to v, denoted by $v(g)$, is the obvious evaluation of the boolean expression g relative to v. Moreover, for a sequence of assignments $a \in A_X$, $v(a) \in V_X$ is defined inductively by $v(\epsilon) = v$ and $v(x := e, a) = v[x \mapsto n](a)$ where n is the value obtained by evaluating expression e using the valuation v.

The semantics of an I/O EFSM is defined as a labelled transition system.

Definition 3. *Let $M = (S, I, O, X, s_0, \longrightarrow_M)$. The labelled transition system induced by M is*

$$T_M = (S \times V_X, I \cup O, (s_0, \bar{0}_X), \longrightarrow)$$

where $(s_0, \bar{0}_X) \in S \times V_X$ is the initial state. The labelled transition relation $\longrightarrow \subseteq (S \times V_X) \times (I \cup O) \times (S \times V_X)$ is the least relation satisfying:

$$\frac{s \xrightarrow{g,\alpha,a}_M s'}{(s, v) \xrightarrow{\alpha} (s', v(a))} \quad v(g) \text{ is true}$$

Whenever $(s, v) \xrightarrow{\alpha} (s', v')$ we write $(s, v) \xrightarrow{\alpha?} (s', v')$ if $\alpha \in I$, otherwise if $\alpha \in O$ we write $(s, v) \xrightarrow{\alpha!} (s', v')$.

We say that a transition system is *I/O deterministic* if for any state there are at most one output transition and at most one input transition for any input. M is I/O deterministic if its induced transition system T_M is I/O deterministic.

Two automatons M and M' are equivalent, $M \sim M'$, if the initial states in T_M and $T_{M'}$ are trace equivalent.

We only consider the parallel composition of I/O EFSM's at the semantic level. By convenience, and without loss of generality, we assume all machines have the same variables. It follows from the definition that output actions are broadcasted.

Definition 4. *Let* $T_i = (S_i \times V_X, L_i, (s_0^i, \bar{0}_X), \longrightarrow_i)$, $i = 1, \ldots, k$ *be I/O EFSM induced labelled transition systems. The parallel composition* $\Pi_{i=1}^k T_i$ *is defined by*

$$\Pi_{i=1}^k T_i = ((S_1 \times \ldots \times S_k) \times V_X, L, ((s_0^1, \ldots, s_0^k), \bar{0}_X), \longrightarrow)$$

where $L = \cup_{i=1}^k L_i$, *and* $\longrightarrow$ *is the least relation satisfying*

$$\frac{(s_i, v) \xrightarrow{\alpha!}_i (s_i', v_i') \quad \forall j \neq i. \ (s_j, v_j) \xmapsto{\alpha?}_j (s_j', v_j')}{((s_1, \ldots, s_k), v) \xrightarrow{\alpha} ((s_1', \ldots, s_k'), v')}$$

where $(s, v) \xmapsto{\alpha?}_n (s', v')$ *if* $(s, v) \xrightarrow{\alpha?}_n (s', v')$ *and* $(s, v) \xmapsto{\alpha?}_n (s, v)$ *if* $(s, v) \xrightarrow{\alpha?}_n$ *and* v' *is a valuation accumulating all the updates* $v_1', \ldots, v_k'$.[1]

2.2   Tests

In our setting a *test* is an I/O EFSM except that each state is annotated by either the verdict *pass* or *fail*.

Definition 5. *Let* I *and* O *be finite disjoint sets of input and output symbols respectively. Let* $\alpha_1 \ldots \alpha_n \in (I \cup O)^+$. *Define the test*

$$M_{\alpha_1 \ldots \alpha_n}^{pass}(I, O) = (\{s_0, \ldots, s_n\}, I, O, s_0, \longrightarrow)$$

such that $\longrightarrow$ *is the least relation where*

$$s_0 \xrightarrow{\alpha_1} s_1 \xrightarrow{\alpha_2} \ldots \xrightarrow{\alpha_n} s_n$$

and where s_n *is annotated by pass and all* $s_0, \ldots, s_{n-1}$ *are annotated by fail. Define* $M_{\alpha_1 \ldots \alpha_n}^{fail}(I, O)$ *as* $M_{\alpha_1 \ldots \alpha_n}^{pass}(I, O)$ *except that the state* s_{n-1} *is annotated by pass and the remaining states by fail.*

If in every complete run of $T_M \parallel T_{M_t^v(I,O)}$ the component $T_{M_t^v(I,O)}$ terminates in the state *pass* (*fail*) we say that M passes (fails) the test $M_t^v(I, O)$; otherwise I/O deterministic $T_M \parallel T_{M_t^v(I,O)}$ has precisely one complete run.

---

[1] We leave out the formal definition of $v^\square$. Our algorithms make use of shared variables between automatons but carefully ensure that simultaneous updates cause no problems.

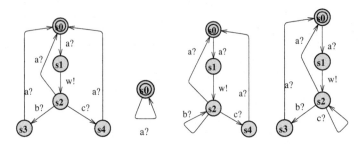

Fig. 2. A simple model M and its mutants $M[a]$, $M[b]$, $M[c]$. The initial location is doubly encircled

3   Modelling and Testing Connectivity Faults

As mentioned previously, a connection is assumed to be related to exactly one input[2]. That is, when the connection related to a given input (say α) is faulty, the software will not receive any α-input, i.e. the state of the software will remain unchanged, whenever the environment makes an input to the system via α. We can therefore model a connectivity fault as a so-called *mutation* $M[\alpha]$ of a correct model M by changing all α-transitions so that the state is not changed. This is made precise in the following definition:

Definition 6. *Let* $M = (S, I, O, X, s_0, \longrightarrow)$ *and* $\alpha \in I$*. Define*

$$M[\alpha] = (S, I, O, X, s_0, \longrightarrow_1)$$

where $\longrightarrow_1$ *is* $\longrightarrow$ *except that all transitions* $s \xrightarrow{g, \alpha, a} s'$ *are replaced by* $s \xrightarrow{g, \alpha}_1 s$*.*

Figure 2 shows a simple model with 3 inputs (a,b,c) and the mutants $M[a], M[b], M[c]$. An α-connectivity fault may be found by applying a test that distinguish M from $M[\alpha]$. For the mutants $M[a]$, $M[b]$, and $M[c]$ in Figure 2, we may construct the tests $M^{pass}_{aw}(I, O)$, $M^{fail}_{awbc}(I, O)$, and $M^{fail}_{awcb}(I, O)$ respectively where $I = \{w\}$ and $O = \{a, b, c\}$. Clearly, the tests are minimal (in terms of the number of synchronizations between the tester and the system) and $M^{fail}_{awbc}(I, O)$ and $M^{fail}_{awcb}(I, O)$ are sufficient to distinguish M from all three mutations. There exists no single test distinguishing M from all the mutations.

4   The Test Generation Algorithm

In this section we present an algorithm for generating a test that distinguish an I/O EFSM from a single mutation (if they are distinguishable). In the algorithm

---

[2] We restrict ourselves to input faults. However, the extension to output faults is straightforward.

we use the following two operators: $M?$ is M where outputs become inputs and $M(x := e)$ is M where on any transition x is updated by e. Formally we have

Definition 7. Let $M = (S, I, O, X, s_0, \longrightarrow)$ then $M? = (S, I \cup O, \emptyset, X, s_0, \longrightarrow)$.

Definition 8. Let $M = (S, I, O, X, s_0, \longrightarrow)$. Then for any x and $e \in E_{X \cup \{x\}}$

$$M(x := e) = (S, I, O, X \cup \{x\}, s_0, \longrightarrow_1)$$

where $\longrightarrow_1$ is $\longrightarrow$ except that for every $\alpha \in I \cup O$, any $s \xrightarrow{g, \alpha, a} s'$ is replaced by $s \xrightarrow{g, \alpha, a'}_1 s'$ where a' is $a, x := e$.

We let $M(x_1, \ldots, x_k := e_1, \ldots, e_k)$ be $M(x_1 := e_1) \ldots (x_k := e_k)$ whenever $e_i \in E_{X \cup \{x_i\}}$, $i = 1, \ldots, n$.

4.1   The Algorithm

The problem we want the algorithm to solve is the following:

Given an I/O deterministic EFSM M and one of its input symbols α, if $M \not\sim M[\alpha]$ then find a test M' with fewest possible states such that M and $M[\alpha]$ respectively passes and fails M'.

Intuitively, the idea behind the algorithm is to put M and its mutation together in parallel with a third machine, the environment E. Only E is allowed to submit actions, the other machines are modified to contain solely input actions. The role of E is to broadcast actions such that whenever the two other machines do not agree on receiving an action (recall they are I/O deterministic) a fault has been detected. The algorithm searches for a shortest possible trace of actions broadcast by E leading to a fault.

Pseudo Code

1. Let x, y and z be disjoint variables none of which belong to X.
2. Let $E = (\{s\}, \emptyset, I \cup O, X \cup \{x, y, z\}, s, \{(s, \beta, s) \mid \beta \in I \cup O\})$.
3. Let c_1 and c_2 be distinct constants and let $M_1 = M?(x, y, z := (x + 1)\%2, y, c_1)$ and $M_2 = M[\alpha]?(x, y, z := x, (y + 1)\%2, c_2)$.
4. Construct $T_E \parallel T_{M_1} \parallel T_{M_2}$ with initial state s_T.
5. Let t, if it exists, be a minimal trace such that $s_T \xrightarrow{t} (s_t, v_t)$ with v_t satisfying $x \neq y$. If t doesn't exists return false.
6. If $v_t(z) = c_1$ return $M_t^{pass}(O, I)$, otherwise return $M_t^{fail}(O, I)$.

The only technicality of the algorithm is the use of the variables x, y, and z. The role of x and y is to count (modulo 2) whenever $M?$ and $M[\alpha]?$ respectively have synchronized with E. Hence, whenever $x \neq y$ a fault have been detected. The role of z is to register which of $M?$ and $M[\alpha]?$ engaged in a synchronization with E, this is important as to wheter the returned test should be a test with verdict *pass* or *fail*.

The correctness of the construction of the test automaton follows from the theorem below.

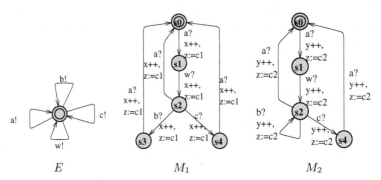

Fig. 3.   Annotated automata

Theorem 1. *If the algorithm on input M and α returns false then $M \sim M[\alpha]$, otherwise it returns a test M' with fewest possible states such that M passes M' and $M[\alpha]$ fails M'.*

4.2   Example

If we apply the algorithm on input M (Figure 3) and action b then the three machines put in parallel, M_1, M_2, and E, are as devised in Figure 3. For illustrative clarity $x++$ is taken to mean x incremented modolus 2.

The test $M_{awbc}^{fail}(\{w\}, \{a, b, c\})$ is a minimal length test that may be constructed by the algorithm. Clearly, $awbc$ is a shortest possible sequence leading to a state in $T_E \parallel T_{M_1} \parallel T_{M_2}$ where $x \neq y$, and since only M_2 can engage in the last event c the value of z is c_2.

5   The Generalized Algorithm

Next, we generalize the algorithm above such that a whole suite of test automatons are generated for a set of mutations (if all mutations are distinguishable from M).

5.1   The Algorithm

The problem the algorithm solves is

Given $M = (S, I, O, X, s_0, \rightarrow)$, an I/O deterministic automaton, and a set of input symbols $\mathcal{A} \subseteq I$, if $M \not\sim M[\alpha]$ for all $\alpha \in \mathcal{A}$, find a minimal test suite $\mathcal{M}$ such that 1) M passes all automatons in $\mathcal{M}$, and 2) for all $\alpha \in \mathcal{A}$, $M[\alpha]$ fails M', for some $M' \in \mathcal{M}$.

Notice, that a minimal test suite $\mathcal{M}$ satisfies that for all $M' \in \mathcal{M}$ there exists $\alpha \in \mathcal{A}$ such that $M[\alpha]$ fails M' and $M[\alpha]$ passes all other test automatons in $\mathcal{M}$, i.e. all tests returned by the algorithm are indeed needed and cannot be removed from the suite if all connectivity faults are to be revealed.

The main idea is to extend the previous algorithm by running *all* mutants concurrently, but tightly synchronized, with the unmutated automaton M. Whenever the unmutated machine M cannot match a transition by one of its mutations a connectivity error has been detected, and M needs to be reset (and only then) to extend the sequence to kill more mutants.

Pseudo Code

1. Let $\{x, x_\alpha, y_\alpha, z \mid \alpha \in \mathcal{A}\}$ be fresh variables disjoint from X. Extend M to contain the variables $Y = X \cup \{x, x_\alpha, y_\alpha, z \mid \alpha \in \mathcal{A}\}$.
2. Let $M' = M?(x := (x + 1)\%2)$ and let for all $\alpha \in \mathcal{A}$, $M_\alpha = M[\alpha]?(x_\alpha := (x_\alpha + 1)\%2)$
3. Let go and $reset$ be two new fresh actions not in $I \cup O$. Add $\{go, reset\}$ to the set of output labels for M'. Let M'' be M' with any transition $s \xrightarrow{g,\alpha,a} s'$ where $\alpha \in I \cup O$, replaced by $s \xrightarrow{g,\alpha,a} s'' \xrightarrow{go} s' \xrightarrow{reset} s_0$ where for each replacement s'' is a new fresh state.
4. For each $\alpha \in \mathcal{A}$, add $\{reset\}$ to the set of input labels for M_α and add a reset transition, $s \xrightarrow{reset} s_0$, for any state s in M_α to its initial state s_0.
5. Let $E = (\{s_0, s_1\}, \{go, reset\}, I \cup O, Y, s_0, \longrightarrow)$ where

$$\longrightarrow = \{(s_0, (\alpha, z := 0), s_1) \mid \alpha \in I \cup O\} \cup \{s_1 \xrightarrow{go, z:=1} s_0, s_1 \xrightarrow{reset, z:=1} s_0\}$$

6. Construct $M'_\alpha = (\{s_0, s_1\}, \emptyset, \emptyset, Y, s_0, \longrightarrow)$ for all $\alpha \in \mathcal{A}$ where $s_0 \xrightarrow{g,\tau,a} s_1$ with $a = (y_\alpha := 1)$ and $g = (x \neq x_\alpha)$.
7. Construct $T_E \parallel T_{M''} \parallel \Pi_{\alpha \in \mathcal{A}} T_{M_\alpha} \parallel \Pi_{\alpha \in \mathcal{A}} T_{M'_\alpha}$ with initial state s_T.
8. Let P be $z \neq 0 \wedge \forall \alpha \in \mathcal{A}. \ y_\alpha \neq 0$.
9. Let $t = t'\beta$, if it exists, be a minimal trace such that $s_T \xrightarrow{t} (s_t, v_t)$ with v_t satisfying P. If t doesn't exists return false.
10. Let $t_1, \ldots, t_k$ be such that $u = t_1 \ reset \ t_2 \ldots reset \ t_k$ where u is t' with all go and τ's removed.
11. Return $\mathcal{M} = \{M_{t_1}^{fail}(O, I), \ldots, M_{t_{k-1}}^{fail}(O, I), M_{t_k}^v(O, I)\}$ where v is *fail* if $\beta = reset$, otherwise if $\beta = go$ then v is *pass*.

To control when M has to be reset every α transition by M is now followed by a new output action called go which intuitively acknowledge to the environment E that M could match α. After having ouput an action, E waits for this acknowledgement before it sends a new action. If the acknowledge does not arrive E knows that M could not perform the action, implying that a test has been found for at least one of the mutations. In that case the only possible synchronization is a *reset* between M and the environment automaton.

In order to detect when a connectivity error has been identified we introduce an observation automaton M'_α for each mutation α. It consists of two states and

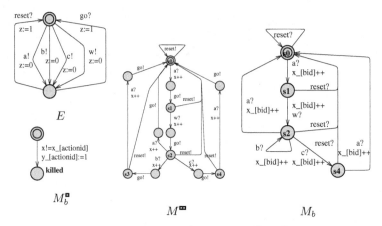

Fig. 4. The annotated automata (M_a, M_c, $M_a^\square$, $M_c^\square$, omitted). The notation $v[i]$ is UppAal notation for indexing array v at position i. bid is the position for action b

one transition that fires when M and $M[\alpha]$ does not agree on some input or output transition, i.e. when $x \neq x_\alpha$. All mutations have been revealed when all observation automata has fired, i.e, when all $y_\alpha = 1$.

Based upon the trace $t = t'\beta$ found (if a trace is found) a set of test automatons are constructed. First all go's and τ's are removed from t'. Then t' is split in the parts $t_1, \ldots, t_k$ separated by $reset$ labels. For all t_i, but t_k, $fail$ test automations, $M_{t_i}^{fail}(O, I)$ are created, since M clearly cannot perform those traces—that was the sole reason why M was reset. To be able to tell whether the final part, t_k, should give rise to a fail or pass test automaton we force the trace to always end with either $reset$ or go. This is done by introducing a variable z in the environment automaton that is set to 0 on transitions with labels in $I \cup O$ and to 1 when a go or $reset$ is performed. Then searching for t we require z is not zero. Clearly, if the last event in t, i.e. β, is a go then $M_{t_k}^{pass}(O, I)$ is created, otherwise if it is $reset$ then $M_{t_k}^{fail}(O, I)$ is created.

Notice, that a test automaton $M_{t_i}^v(O, I)$ may detect several mutations.

Theorem 2. *If the algorithm on input M and $\mathcal{A}$ returns false then $M \sim M[\alpha]$ for some $\alpha \in \mathcal{A}$, otherwise it returns some $\mathcal{M}$ satisfying the properties in Section 5.1.*

5.2 Example

Given the I/O EFSM M in Figure 2 the algorithm produces the sequence $awbb.reset.awcb.reset$, resulting in the two tests $M_{awbb}^{fail}(\{w\}, \{a, b, c\})$ and $M_{awcb}^{fail}(\{w\}, \{a, b, c\})$. Both tests for connectivity of a. The used annotated models are depicted in Figure 4.

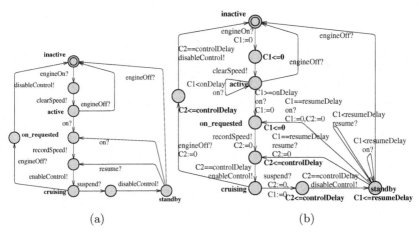

Fig. 5.   User Interface Automaton (*a*) Timed user interface (*b*)

6   Cruise Controller Example

In this section we exemplify and benchmark our technique on a medium sized cruise controller example. The cruise controller is commonly studied and found in many variations in the literature, and thus serves as an illustrative example, see e.g., [14, 2].

6.1   The Cruise Controller

The model consists of two automatons. The *user interface* controls the different modes of operation according to the various user inputs, whereas the *speed control* keeps the actual speed close to a given desired speed by affecting the throttle of the engine.

The *user interface* (Figure 5(*a*)) basically has four modes, i.e. *inactive* when the engine is turned off, *active* when the engine is turned on, *cruising* when the speed control is enabled, and *standby* when the speed control is temporarily suspended. When the engine is turned on, the desired speed is cleared, and when cruise mode is entered, the actual speed is recorded and set as the desired speed. The cruise mode may be reentered from standby mode.

The *speed control* (Figure 6) switches between its two operational modes *disabled* and *enabled* according to enable and disable control signals from the user interface. In disabled mode, it sets the desired speed to zero or to the sampled actual speed when commanded by the user interface. In enabled mode, it samples the actual speed and based on the difference between actual and desired speed (represented by variables cSpeed, dSpeed), it stops acceleration of the engine (output *inc0*), or commands the engine to do medium (output *inc1*) or high (output *inc2*) acceleration. Further, in enabled mode, the user can manually increase or decrease the desired speed.

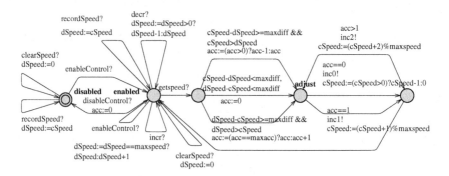

Fig. 6.   Speed Control Automaton

The actions of the user interface are $I_u = \{engineOn, engineOff, on, suspend\}$, $O_u = \{clearSpeed, recordSpeed, enableControl, disableControl\}$. The actions of the speed ontroller are $I_s = O_u \cup \{incr, decr, getspeed, \}, O_s = \{inc0, inc1, inc2\}$. For the system composed of the user interface and speed controller synchronizing internally[3] on actions $O_u \cap I_s$, the actions are $I_c = I_u \cup I_s \setminus O_u$, $O_c = O_s$.

6.2   Generated Test Sequences

Unless the length of the test suite is important, the normal and computationally most efficient method is to generate a separate test sequence for each mutant. Our experimental results show that a sequence could be successfully generated for each mutant; also the sequences are quite short. The test suites generated for the cruise interface, the speed controller and the composed system contain respectively 5 (16), 7 (31), 8 (34) test cases (total steps). All were generated on a standard PC in less than one second. Table 1 lists some examples.

These results indicate that our technique may be feasible for much larger systems, both in terms of test suite size and model size (number of inputs and state space). Since the algorithm generates the minimal sequences, some of them are quite surprising and would not likely be found by hand, e.g., the test for *engineOn*. Observe especially that it is not obvious how the desired and current speed should be set to distinguish the mutants of the speed controller. For instance, it would be incorrect to use the intuitive test $M^{pass}_{enableControl.incr.getspeed.inc0}(O_s, I_s)$ to check for connectivity of *incr* because *inc0* would also be output if *incr* was disconnected (given that $maxDiff = 2$, *dSpeed* and *cSpeed* initially equals 0, *acc* becomes 0 in both cases). Hence at least two increments are needed.

Also note that—because our algorithms does not require the specification or implementation to be input enabled—not all sequences end with an output,

---

[3] Recall that our technique can be adapted to handle these. The semantics of the input fault mutations in a composed system is as if they were made to their (synchronous) product I/O EFSM, hiding internal communication channels.

Table 1.   Selection of Generated Tests (if v =P then $M_t^{pass}(O, I)$; if v =F then $M_t^{fail}(O, I)$)

Mutant	v	Generated Event Sequence t
		User Interface
engineOff	P	engineOn.clearSpeed.engineOff.engineOn
suspend	P	engineOn.clearSpeed.on.recordSpeed.enableControl.suspend.disableControl
resume	F	engineOn.clearSpeed.on.recordSpeed.enableControl.suspend.- disableControl.resume.engineOff
		Speed Controller
incr	P	enableControl.incr.incr.getspeed.inc1
decr	P	enableControl.incr.incr.decr.getspeed.inc0
clearSpeed	P	enableControl.incr.incr.clearSpeed.getspeed.inc0
		Cruise Controller System
engineOn	F	engineOn.engineOn
resume	F	engineOn.on.suspend.resume.resume
incr	P	engineOn.on.incr.incr.getSpeed.inc1

meaning that if the last input can be performed by the tester, the test will pass (or fail, depending on the verdict). If this is felt to be unnatural for some applications, it is very easy to force our algorithms to produce tests that ends with an output. The generated test for *engineOff* is then

$$M_{engineOn.clearSpeed.engineOff.engineOn.clearspeed}^{pass}(O_u, I_u).$$

6.3   Multi-fault Test Sequences

In some cases it is important to produce a smallest test suite with as few and short tests as possible. A simple reduction technique like prefix elimination does not work well for connectivity testing (see sequences presented in Section 6.2). Our generalized algorithm from Section 5 is therefore more involved and guarantees that the minimal length test suite is computed, although at the expense of computational complexity (the problem is NP-hard [8]). It involves analyzing a system consisting of all mutants running concurrently in a synchronized step-lock fashion. Thus, state space explosion theoretically limits how many mutants can be composed, and it should be examined where this limit occur in practice. The following experiments are run on a 8x900 MHZ Sun Sparc Fire v880R workstation with 32 GB memory running Sun Solaris 9 (SunOS 5.9). However, UppAal only exploits one CPU and addresses at most 4 GB of memory. The results are tabulated in Table 2.

For the user interface, it turns out that it is possible to compute (using only a few seconds and megabytes of memory) a single test of 11 steps that detects all input faults $M_t^{pass}(O_u, O_u)$ where $t =$ *engineOn.clearSpeed.on.recordSpeed.enableControl.suspend.disableControl.-resume.enableControl.engineOff.disableControl*, giving a reduction of 31% (11 versus 16 steps).

The speed controller and the composed system have much larger state spaces and are more challenging. Still, all mutants but two could be composed in both cases. The multiple-fault test suite (up to and including the *incr* mu-

Table 2.   Performance of multi-fault algorithm

Speed Control			Cruise System		
Mutant(s)	CPU-time(s)	Memory (KB)	Mutant(s)	CPU-time(s)	Memory (KB)
enableControl	0.21	3704	*engineOn*	0.16	5232
+*disableControl*	0.37	5672	+*engineOff*	0.29	5584
+*clearSpeed*	10.98	29008	+*resume*	27.51	97608
+*recordSpeed*	152.77	281072	+*on*	39.01	100208
+*incr*	1917.02	2128824	+*suspend*	50.60	131192
+*decr*	-	-	+*incr*	874.00	1516800
+*getspeed*	-	-	+*decr*	-	-
			+*getspeed*	-	-

tant) for the speed control consists of two tests: $M_{t_1}^{fail}(O_s, I_s)$ and $M_{t_2}^{fail}(O_s, I_s)$ where $t_1=$ *enableControl.incr.incr.getspeed.inc1.recordSpeed.incr.getspeed.inc0.-clearspeed.getspeed.inc1*, $t_2=$ *enableControl.disableControl.incr*, giving a reduction of 25% compared to detecting the same faults using seperate sequences. In addition many system resets are avoided. The cruise system (up to *incr*) requires only one test: $M_t^{fail}(O_c, I_c)$ where $t=$ *engineOn.engineOff.engineOn.-on.suspend.resume.incr.incr.getspeed.inc0*, giving a reduction of 40%. The order of addition of mutants was arbitrary. Even if the test suite is generated by more rounds composing only some of the mutants each time, the reduction in test suite size is significant.

7   Timed Test Generation

We next demonstrate how connectivity tests for a class of timed systems can be generated. The tester now needs to be time aware to reveal them. This result requires no change to the basic algorithm if a real-time model-checker like UppAal is used.

Informally, a timed automaton [1] is an I/O EFSM equipped with a set of non-negative real-valued variables called *clocks* that may be used in guards, and may be set to zero on transition assignments. In addition, *location invariants* forces the automaton to take a transition before it becomes false. The semantics of a timed automaton is defined in terms of an infinite timed transition system consisting of both discrete transitions and time delay transitions. To ensure testability we impose similar semantic restrictions as in [16]: Our model, called DOUTA, are deterministic, output urgent (an output or τ occurs as soon as it is enbled) timed automata. DOUTA is formally defined in [9].

Consider the following real-time requirements for the user-interface automaton in Figure 5(a). 1) For safety reasons, the engine must be on for at least *onDelay* before cruise control may be switched on. Earlier requests must be ignored. 2) When cruise mode is suspended, at least *resumeDelay* must elapse before reengagement to avoid too rapid enabling and disabling of the speed controller. 3) It takes *controlDelay* to enable or disable the speed controller (involves external communication), whereas the speed can be set or cleared with a zero delay (assumed internal communication). These requirements are satisfied by the

DOUTA in Figure 5(*b*). Boldfaced clock constraints below locations are location invariants.

Given this specification (*onDelay*=5000, *controlDelay*=3000, *controlDelay*=200) UppAal produces the following timed test $M_t^{fail}(O_u, I_u)$ to reveal disconnection of the *resume* action, where *t*= *0.engineOn.0.clearSpeed.5000.-on.0.recordSpeed.200.enableControl.0.suspend.200.disableControl.2800.resume.-0.engineOff* . Note that the delays are not a trivial insertion of the delay constants occurring in the model (e.g the 2800 ms between *disableControl* and *resume*). It is usually infeasible to compute these by hand because it involves solving a large set of inequations on clock variables. The zero delays in the above sequence can be avoided by replacing the universal environment E by a more accurate (and slower) environment model timed automaton E' which restricts the choices of the tester.

UppAal also has efficient facilities for generation of time- and cost- optimal diagnostic traces [4, 12]. In fact, the above test is not only of minimal length, but also the fastest (minimal accumulated time delay). To avoid expensive operations, e.g., resets, UppAal can be used to generate suites with the fewest such operations. As a simple example, the generated multi-fault test presented in Section 6.3 for the speed controller required two tests, and thus one reset. Searching for a test with fewer resets UppAal found one (only two communication events longer that the minimal length test suite): $M_t^{pass}(O_u, I_u)$ where *t*= *enableControl.incr.clearSpeed.incr.getspeed.inc0.incr.getspeed.inc1.-disableControl.enableControl.clearSpeed.recordSpeed.incr.incr.getspeed.inc1*. It is also possible to take the actual time/cost for a reset into account.

8   Conclusions and Future Work

This paper describes two sound and complete algorithms that generate minimal test cases and test suites respectively for input connectivity faults. The algorithms are based on reachability analysis and may thus be implemented in most model-checkers. Based on experiments with a concrete model-checker, UppAal, and a medium sized example, we conclude that our techniques are feasible, and for the simple algorithm appear to scale to larger systems. For the generalized algorithm the number of simultaneous mutants that can be handled is limited due to state space explosion (recall that the problem is NP hard). Finally, we show how timed connectivity and examples of cost optimized test suites can be generated by the same algorithms.

We only looked at input connectivity faults, however it is trivial to generate test sequences for output connectivity faults, since this amounts to finding a sequence that visits a transition where the output is produced, hence making it observable.

As future work we plan to examine other more involved fault models, e.g. models where connections may be whole protocols. Since our algorithms are based on finding a trace that can be performed by the original automaton and not its mutant, or vice versa, our algorithms appear to be so general that many other fault models can be supported. In particular we plan to investigate how to test wrongly interconnected communicating (distributed) components that have been tested or verified in isolation. Also, we plan to investigate a timed connectivity fault model where disconnects are not permanent and we intend to do practical application and further experiments with time-and cost-optimal test suite generation.

References

[1] R. Alur and D. L. Dill. A Theory of Timed Automata. *Theoretical Computer Science*, 126(2):183–235, April 1994. 181

[2] P. Ammann, P. E. Black, and W. Majurski. Using model checking to generate tests from specifications. In *ICFEM*, page 46, 1998. 170, 178

[3] P. Ammann, W. Ding, and D. Xu. Using a model checker to test safety properties. 170

[4] G. Behrmann, A. Fehnker, T. Hune, K. G. Larsen, P. Pettersson, and J. Romijn. Efficient Guiding Towards Cost-Optimality in UPPAAL. In T. Margaria and W. Yi, editors, *TACAS 2001*, number 2031 in LNCS, pages 174–188. Springer–Verlag, 2001. 182

[5] J. Callahan, F. Schneider, and S. Easterbrook. Automated software testing using modelchecking. In *1996 SPIN Workshop*, August 1996. Also WVU Report NASA-IVV-96-022. 170

[6] A. Engels, L. Feijs, and S. Mauw:. Test generation for intelligent networks using model checking. In Ed Brinksma, editor, *Tools and Algorithms for the Construction and Analysis of Systems. TACAS'97*, number 1217 in LNCS, 1997. 170

[7] A. Gargantini and C. L. Heitmeyer. Using model checking to generate tests from requirements specifications. In *ESEC / SIGSOFT FSE*, pages 146–162, 1999. 170

[8] Jens Chr. Godskesen. Complexity issues in connectivity testing. In Ed Brinksma and Jan Tretmans, editors, *Proceedings of the Workshop on Formal Approaches to Testing of Software, FATES '01, (Aalborg, Denmark, August 25, 2001)*, 2001. 167, 168, 169, 180

[9] A. Hessel, K. G. Larsen, B. Nielsen, P. Pettersson, and A. Skou. Time-Optimal Test Cases for Real-Time Systems. In *3rd Intl. Workshop on Formal Approaches to Testing of Software (FATES 2003)*, Montréal, Québec, Canada, October 2003. 170, 181

[10] H. Hong, I. Lee, O. Sokolsky, and S. Cha. Automatic test generation from statecharts using model checking. In Ed Brinksma and Jan Tretmans, editors, *Workshop on Formal Approaches to Testing of Software, FATES '01, (Aalborg, Denmark, August 25, 2001)*, 2001. 170

[11] H. S. Hong, I. Lee, O. Sokolsky, and H. Ural. A Temporal Logic Based Theory of Test Coverage and Generation. In J.-P. Katoen and P. Stevens, editors, *TACAS 2002*, pages 327–341. Kluwer Academic Publishers, April 2002. 170

[12] K. G. Larsen, G. Behrmann, E. Brinksma, A. Fehnker, T. Hune, P. Pettersson, and J. Romijn. As cheap as possible: Efficient cost-optimal reachability for priced timed automat. In G. Berry, H. Comon, and A. Finkel, editors, *Proc. of CAV 2001*, number 2102 in LNSC, pages 493–505. Springer–Verlag, 2001. 182

[13] K. G. Larsen, P. Pettersson, and W. Yi. UppAal in a Nutshell. *International Journal on Software Tools for Technology Transfer*, 1(1):134–152, 1997. 169

[14] Magee and Kramer. *Concurrency: State Models and Java Programs*. Wiley, 2002. 178

[15] M. P. E. Heimdahl and S. Rayadurgam and W. Visser and G. Devaraj and J. Gao. Auto-generating Test Sequences Using Model Checkers: A Case Study. In A. Petrenko and A. Ulrich, editors, *3rd Intl. Workshop on Formal Approaches to Testing of Software, FATES 2003*, volume 2931 of *LNCS*, pages 42–59, Montréal, Québec, CA, 2004. 170

[16] J. G. Springintveld, F. W. Vaandrager, and P. R. D'Argenio. Testing timed automata. *Theoretical Computer Science*, 254(1-2), March 2001. 181

Fault Propagation by Equation Solving

Khaled El-Fakih[1] and Nina Yevtushenko[2]

[1] American University of Sharjah, PO Box 26666, Sharjah, UAE
kelfakih@aus.ac.ae
[2] Tomsk State University, 36 Lenin str., Tomsk, 634050, Russia
yevtushenko@elefot.tsu.ru

Abstract. In this paper we use equation solving for translating internal tests derived for a component embedded within a composite system into external tests defined over the external alphabets of the system. The composite system is represented as two communicating finite state machines (FSMs), an embedded component FSM, and a context FSM that models the remaining part of the system and which is assumed to be correctly implemented. Application example is given to demonstrate the steps of the method. The method can be adapted for test derivation for a system of two or more communicating FSMs.

1 Introduction

Several methods have been developed for testing a component embedded within a composite system [12]. Usually the composite system is represented as two communicating machines, an embedded component machine, and a context machine that models the remaining part of the system and that is assumed to be correctly implemented.

A number of test derivation methods have been proposed for testing in context when the system components are modeled as Finite State Machines (FSMs). Some of these methods [4, 15] return test suites that satisfy appropriate test purposes. However, these test suites are not complete, i.e. they do not detect all possible faulty implementations of the embedded component. Other methods [for example, 14] return complete but redundant test suites since they consider fault domains that include infeasible implementations that do not correspond to any possible implementation of the embedded FSM. Accordingly, in order to alleviate the problem of infeasible machines, tests can be derived directly from the embedded component machine as proposed in [18, 20]. In this case, a test suite is derived based on the largest set of permissible behaviors of the embedded component FSM that is a largest solution to an appropriate FSM equation. Usually, a largest solution is a nondeterministic FSM, and a test suite is derived w.r.t. the reduction relation. Hence the methods presented in [11, 19, 22] can be used for deriving corresponding test suites. However, tests generated by all of the above methods are given in the form of input/output sequences defined over the input/output alphabets of the embedded machine, i.e. over internal alphabets. These tests are then translated, using adhoc methods, into external tests defined over the external observable input alphabets of the system. The problem of translating internal tests into external ones is called the *fault propagation problem* and is known to have exponential complexity

D. de Frutos-Escrig and M. Núñez (Eds.): FORTE 2004, LNCS 3235, pp. 185-198, 2004.
© IFIP International Federation for Information Processing 2004

In this paper we present an equation solving based approach for solving the fault propagation problem. The *equation solving* problem is to describe a behavior of a component of a system knowing the specifications of the other components and the specification of the whole system. In 1980, a first paper [2] (see also [16]) gives a solution to the problem for the case where the system behavior is described in terms of labeled transition systems (LTS). This work was later extended to the cases where the behavior of the components is described in CCS or CSP [17], by FSM [21, 26] or input/output automata [6, 13, 23]. Moreover, the applications of the equation solving problem were first considered in the context of the design of communication protocols [16]. Later it was recognized that equation solving this method could also be useful for the design of protocol converters in communication gateways [10, 13, 24], and for the selection of test cases for testing a module in a context [20]. Another application area of equation solving is the design of controllers for discrete event systems [1, 27].

We solve the fault propagation problem using equation solving as follows: Given the specifications of the context and embedded components, first, we derive the largest set of permissible behaviors of the embedded component FSM as the largest solution to an appropriate FSM equation. The FSM equation is solved using the automata based equation solving method presented in [3]. Then, we derive, using the method proposed in [19], from the largest FSM solution, internal tests for the embedded component FSM. These tests are derived w.r.t. the reduction relation since the largest solution is generally non-deterministic. The internal tests are then represented by an appropriate automaton. This automaton is used with the automaton that represents the context to solve an appropriate automata equation. External tests are then derived from the solution to the latter equation.

This paper is organized as follows. Section 2 includes necessary FSM and automata definitions and an overview of testing in context. Section 3 includes our method for translating internal tests by equation solving with a related application example. Section 4 concludes the paper.

2   Preliminaries

2.1 Finite State Machine

A *finite state machine*, often simply called a *machine*, is a quintuple $A = \langle S, I, O, T_A, s_0 \rangle$, where S is a finite nonempty set of states with the initial state s_0, I and O are input and output alphabets, and $T_A \subseteq S \times I \times O \times S$ is a transition relation. We say that there is a transition from a state $s \in S$ to a state $s' \in S$ labeled with an I/O pair i/o, if and only if the 4-tuple (s, i, o, s') is in the transition relation T_A. FSM A is *observable* if for each triple $(i, s, o) \in I \times S \times O$ there exists at most one state $n \in S$ such that $(i, s, n, o) \in T_A$. An FSM A is called *deterministic*, if for each state $s \in S$ and each input $i \in I$ there exist at most one pair of output o and state s', such that $(s, i, o, s') \in T_A$. If A is not deterministic, then it is called *non-deterministic*. FSM $B = (S_B, I, O_B, T_B, s_0)$, where $S_B \subseteq S_A$ and $O_B \subseteq O_A$, is a *submachine* of FSM $A = \langle S_A, I, O_A, T_A, s_0 \rangle$, if $\forall (s', i) \in S_B \times I (T_B \subseteq T_A)$.

As usual, the transition relation T_A of the FSM A can be extended to sequences over the alphabet I. The extended relation is also denoted by T_A and is a subset of $S \times I^* \times O^* \times S$. By definition, for each state $s \in S$ of the FSM A the tuple $(s, \varepsilon, \varepsilon, s')$ is in the relation T_A. Given a tuple $(s, \alpha, \beta, s') \in T_A$, $\alpha \in I^*$, $\beta \in O^*$, and an input $i \in I$ and an output $o \in O$, the tuple $(s, \alpha i, \beta o, s'') \in T_A$, if and only if $(s', i, o, s'') \in T_A$. Given state s, an I/O sequence $i_1 o_1 ... i_k o_k$, $i_1 ... i_k \in I^*$, $o_1 ... o_k \in I^*$, such that $(s, i_1 ... i_k, o_1 ... o_k, s') \in T_A$ is called a *trace* of A at state s. The set of all traces at state s is denoted $Tr_A(s)$. We denote Tr_A the set of traces at the initial state s_0, i.e. the set of traces of the FSM A, for short. As usual, to represent the set of traces of an FSM we use the notion of a finite automaton.

A *finite state automaton*, often called an *automaton* throughout the paper, is a quintuple $P = \langle S, V, \delta_P, s_0, F_P \rangle$, where S is a finite nonempty set of states with the initial state s_0 and a subset F_P of *final* (or *accepting*) states, V is an alphabet of actions, and $\delta_P \subseteq S \times V \times S$ is a transition relation. We say that there is a transition from a state s to a state s' labeled with an action v, if and only if the triple (s, v, s') is in the transition relation δ_P. The automaton P is called *deterministic*, if for each state $s \in S$ and any action $v \in V$ there exists at most one state s', such that $(s, v, s') \in \delta_P$. If P is not deterministic, then it is called *nondeterministic*. As usual, the transition relation δ_P of the automaton P is extended to sequences over the alphabet V. These sequences are usually called *traces* of the automaton P. Given a state s of the automaton P, the set of traces $L_P(s) = \{ \alpha \in V^* | \exists s' \in F_P ((s, \alpha, s') \in \delta_P) \}$ is cal led the language *generated at the state* s. The language, generated by the automaton P at the initial state, is called the *language generated by the automaton P* and is denoted by L_P, for short.

Given an FSM $A = \langle S, I, O, T_A, s_0 \rangle$, we derive the automaton $Aut(A) = \langle S \cup (S \times I), I \cup O, \delta_P, s_0, F_P = S \rangle$ [26] with the language that coincides with the set of all traces of the FSM. Each transition (s_i, i, o, s_j) in T_A is represented by the two consecutive transitions $(s_i, i, (s_i, i))$ and $((s_i, i), o, s_j)$ in P. That is the automaton is obtained from the original FSM by replacing each edge labeled by i/o with an edge labeled by i, followed by a new non-accepting state, followed by an edge labeled by o. All original states are accepting. If the FSM A is observable then the automaton $Aut(A)$ is known to be deterministic.

Let $A = \langle S, I, O, T_A, s_0 \rangle$ and $B = \langle Q, I, O, T_B, q_0 \rangle$ be two FSMs, state q of FSM B is said to be a *reduction* of state s of FSM $A = \langle S, I, O, T_A, s_0 \rangle$ (written $q \leq s$), if $Tr_B(q) \subseteq Tr_A(s)$. States q and s is said to be *equivalent* (written $q \cong s$) if $q \leq s$ and $s \leq q$; otherwise, states q and s are not equivalent. Moreover, B is a *reduction* of FSM A, if $Tr_B \subseteq Tr_A$. If $Tr_B = Tr_A$ then FSMs A and B are *equivalent*, written as $A \cong B$. For complete deterministic FSMs the reduction and the equivalence relations coincide.

A non-deterministic automaton can be converted into a deterministic automaton with the same language [9]. For this reason, we consider only observable FSMs. If an FSM is non-observable then it can be transformed into an equivalent observable FSM by determinizing the corresponding automaton. Given a deterministic automaton $P = \langle R, I \cup O, \delta_P, r_0, F_P \rangle$ with the set of traces that is a subset of $(IO)^*$, P can be converted into an observable FSM $FSM(P)$ over input alphabet I and O if for each trace $\alpha i o \in Tr_P$ the prefix α also is a trace of the automaton P. States of the $FSM(P)$ are the initial state and all accepting states of the automaton P. Let $P = \langle R, V, \delta_P, r_0, F_P \rangle$ and $R = \langle Q, W, \delta_R, q_0, F_R \rangle$ be two automata. We further describe some operations over finite automata that will be used throughout the paper.

Intersection. If alphabets V and W intersect then the *intersection* $P \cap R$ of automata P and R is the largest connected sub-machine of the automaton $\langle S \times Q, V \cap W, \delta, $

$(s_0, q_0), F_P \times F_R\rangle$. Given an action $a \in V \cap W$ and a state (r, q), there is a transition at the state (r, q) labeled with a, if and only if there are transitions at states s and q labeled with a, i.e. $\delta = \{(r, q), a, (r', q')) \mid (r, a, r') \in \delta_P \wedge (q, a, q') \in \delta_R\}$ The set of traces of the automaton $P \cap R$ accepts the intersection of the sets Tr_P and Tr_R. If V and W are disjoint then intersection of P and R is not defined, since the alphabet of an automaton cannot be empty.

Restriction. Given a sequence α over alphabet V and an alphabet U, the U-*restriction* of α is obtained by deleting from α all symbols that are not in U. If there are no symbols from U in α then the U-restriction of α is equal to the empty sequence ε. Given an automaton P and an alphabet U, the U-*restriction* of P is the deterministic automaton $P_{\downarrow U}$ that is equivalent to the automaton $\langle S, U, \delta, s_0, F_P\rangle$, where $\delta = \{(r, u, r') \mid \exists \alpha \in V^* \ (\exists (r, \alpha, r') \in \delta_P \ \& \ (\alpha_{\downarrow U} = u))\}$ The set of traces of the automaton $P_{\downarrow U}$ is the set of U-restrictions of all traces of the automaton P, i.e. is the set $\{\alpha \in U^* \mid \exists \beta \in L(P) \ (\alpha = \beta_{\downarrow U})\}$

Expansion. Given an alphabet U, the U-*expansion* of P is the automaton $P_{\uparrow U} = \langle R, V \cup U, \delta, r_0, F_P\rangle$, where $\delta = \delta_P \cup \{(r, u, r) \mid r \in R \ \& \ u \in U \setminus V\}$ The automaton $P_{\uparrow U}$ is obtained from P by adding at each state a loop transition labeled with each action of the alphabet $U \setminus V$. If U is a subset of V then the automaton $P_{\uparrow U}$ coincides with the automaton P. Automaton $P_{\uparrow U}$ has the set of traces $\{\alpha \in (V \cup U)^* \mid \exists \beta \in Tr_P \ (\alpha_{\downarrow V} = \beta)\}$

2.2 Parallel Composition of FSMs

We consider a system of two Communicating FSMs of the context FSM $Context = \langle S, I \cup V, O \cup U, T_A, s_0\rangle$ and of the embedded FSM $Emb = \langle T, U, V, T_B, t_0\rangle$, as shown in Fig. 1. above. The alphabets I and O represent the *external* inputs and outputs of the system, while the alphabets V and U represent the *internal* interactions between the two machines. As usual, for the sake of simplicity, we assume that the sets I, O, V, U are pair-wise disjoint. The system produces an output in response to each input. We assume that the system at hand has at most one message in transit, i.e. the next external input is submitted to the system only after it produces an external output to the previous input. Under these assumptions, the collective behavior of the two communicating FSMs *Context* and *Emb* can be described by an FSM as follows [26]:

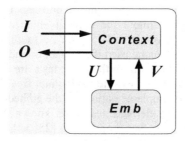

Fig. 1. Parallel Composition of two FSMs

First, we transform the two FSMs *Context* and *Emb* into the corresponding automata *Aut(Context)* and *Aut(Emb)*. Then, we derive the automaton $Aut(Context) \lozenge Aut(Emb) = (Aut(Context) \cap Aut(Emb)_{\uparrow I \cup O}) \downarrow_{I \cup O}$. Then, we intersect $Aut(A) \lozenge Aut(B)$ with the automaton of the chaos FSM defined over the alphabet $I \cup O$. The obtained automaton is shown to have an FSM language over the alphabets I and O [26]. The FSM corresponding to the obtained automaton is called the *parallel composition* of FSMs *Context* and *Emb*, and is written as $Context \lozenge Emb$. In this paper, the context and the embedded FSMs are assumed to be complete and deterministic.

As an example, consider the two FSMs shown in Figures 4.1 and 7, respectively. The set of external inputs is $I = \{x_1, x_2\}$ t he set of external outputs is $O = \{o_1, o_2, o_3\}$ the sets of internal interactions are $V = \{v_1, v_2\}$ and $U = \{u_1, u_2\}$ Th e corresponding composed FSM is shown as the specification FSM *Spec* in Fig 3.1.

2.3 Testing in Context

Testing in context deals with the generation of tests for implementations of the embedded machine *Emb* assuming that the implementation of the context machine is fault free [20, 18]. Moreover, usually it is assumed that the implementation system has been tested w.r.t. livelocks, for example, as proposed in [7], and found to be livelock free; thus, the system under test $Context \lozenge Imp$, where *Imp* is a complete deterministic implementation of *Emb*, is assumed to be complete and deterministic. Under these assumptions embedded implementations are tested w.r.t. external equivalence or equivalence in context.

Given complete deterministic FSMs $Context = \langle S, I \cup V, O \cup U, T_A, s_0 \rangle$ and embedded FSM $Emb = \langle T, U, V, T_B, t_0 \rangle$, let the composed FSM $Context \lozenge Emb$ be also deterministic and complete. FSM $Imp = \langle Q, U, V, T_B, q_0 \rangle$ is said to be *externally equivalent* (or *equivalent in the context*) to the embedded FSM *Emb* if the FSMs $Context \lozenge Emb \cong Context \lozenge Imp$ are equivalent, i.e. $Context \lozenge Emb \cong Context \lozenge Imp$.

A test suite *TS* w.r.t. external equivalence is a set of external input sequences defined over the alphabet I. Given a set $\mathfrak{R}$ of possible implementations of the embedded machine *Emb*, called the *fault domain* of *Emb*, a test suite *TS* is said to be *complete* w.r.t. the fault domain $\mathfrak{R}$ if and only if for each FSM *Imp* of $\mathfrak{R}$ such that $Context \lozenge Imp$ is not equivalent to $Context \lozenge Emb$, there exists a test case in *TS* that eliminates *Imp*.

Several fault models have been proposed for testing an embedded FSM w.r.t. external equivalence [18]. For example, one can explicitly enumerate all possible implementations of the embedded component if the number of these implementations is not huge. When the fault domain is huge, one can use for test derivation the methods that generate tests without the explicit enumeration of the fault domain machines. For instance, the W-method [5] and its modifications, namely the Wp, UIOv, and the HIS methods, can be used if an upper bound on the number of states of an implementation system is known. In this case, tests are derived without taking into account the fact that the context is assumed to be fault free. Thus, the considered fault domain includes all possible implementations of the embedded and context machines. Therefore, in this case, the derived tests are known to be redundant and an optimization procedure such as that proposed in [25] is needed to reduce redundant tests. As an alternative approach, one can consider as a fault domain for the embedded machine, the set of all submachines of an appropriate nondeterministic FSM. This non-deterministic FSM is combined with the context machine and a test suite is then derived from the obtained Mutation Machine (MM) [28]. However, a mutation machine is known to have infeasible machines that do not correspond to any possible implementation system. The number of these machines can still be large even if we decrease their number by using several mutation machines as done in [8, 7]. In order to avoid fault domains with infeasible machines, one can use as a fault domain for the embedded machine the largest solution M to the equation $Context \lozenge X \cong Context \lozenge Emb$. A complete deterministic implementation FSM Imp is not externally equivalent to the specification embedded machine Emb if and only if Imp is not a reduction of M [20]. Therefore, we can derive a complete test suite from a largest solution M w.r.t. the fault domain $\mathfrak{R}$ and the reduction relation. However, in this case, the sequences of an obtained test suite are defined over the internal alphabets U and V and thus, have to be translated to tests defined over the external input alphabets (i.e. external tests). In [20] some adhoc recommendations for such translation have been proposed. In the following sections, we propose a rigorous equation solving based approach for translating internal tests to external ones.

3   Translating Internal Tests by Equation Solving

In this section we use equation solving for translating internal tests of an embedded machine into external ones defined over the external input alphabets of the system. First, in subsection 3.1, we present a method for solving an FSM equation [3, 21], assuming that the internal interactions between the system components are unobservable, then, in subsection 3.2, we propose a method for translating internal tests by solving an appropriate automata equation.

3.1 Solving an FSM Equation

We consider the equation $Context \lozenge X \cong Spec$, where $Spec = Context \lozenge Emb$. We recall that this equation has a largest solution M that contains all possible implementations that are externally equivalent to the embedded component Emb.

An FSM B over the alphabets U and V is called a *solution* to the equation $Context \lozenge X \cong Spec$ if $Context \lozenge B \cong Spec$. A complete solution M is called *largest* if it includes as its reductions all complete solutions to the equation $Context \lozenge X \cong Spec$, i.e. each solution to the equation is a reduction of the largest solution. In order to derive M, we use the methods proposed in [3, 21].

We replace the FSMs $Context$ and $Spec$ with the corresponding automata $Aut(Context)$ and $Aut(Spec)$ and solve the automata equation $Aut(Context) \lozenge X \cong Aut(Spec)$. Since we are interested in an FSM solution, we derive the largest automaton with the set of traces that is a subset of $(UV)^*$. Thus, we derive as a largest solution the largest reduction of the automaton $Aut(Chaos\text{-}UV)$, where $Chaos\text{-}UV = \langle R, U, V, T_{Ch}, r_0 \rangle$ is the chaos FSM over the alphabets U and V.

Similar to [3] we first derive the automaton Λ $(Aut(Context), Aut(Chaos\text{-}UV), Aut(Spec)) = Aut(Context) \cap Aut(Chaos\text{-}UV)_{\uparrow I \cup O} \cap Aut(Spec)_{\uparrow U \cup V}$. A state (s,r,q) of the automaton is called *forbidden* if the external restriction of the language generated at state (s,r,q) is not equal to the language generated at state q of the specification

Spec. We restrict the automaton to the alphabets U and V of the embedded FSM, replace each subset that has a forbidden state with the designated state '*FAIL*', and then convert the obtained automaton into an FSM defined over the alphabets U and V. Each undefined transition in the obtained FSM is specified as a transition to the DNC (don't care or chaos) state, and the '*FAIL*' state and its incoming and outgoing transitions are deleted. The DNC state accepts all input/output sequences of the set $(UV)^*$. The largest complete submachine of the obtained FSM (if it exists) is the largest complete solution M to the FSM equation *Context* $\Diamond X \cong Spec$. In our case, M always exists since the equation has a solution, in particular the embedded component FSM *Emb* is a solution to the equation. In the following subsection we illustrate the above steps through an application example.

3.2 Translating Internal Tests

Given the largest complete solution M to the equation *Context* $\Diamond X \cong Spec$, consider a complete test suite *TS* derived from M w.r.t. the fault domain $\Re$ and the reduction relation. The sequences of *TS* are defined over the internal alphabet U. A test suite *TS* is said to be *complete* if for each implementation FSM *Imp* $\in \Re$ that is not a reduction of M, there exists a test case $\alpha \in TS$ s.t. the set of output responses of the FSM *Imp* to α is not a subset of the set of output responses of M to α. Since the FSM *Imp* is deterministic, the latter means that if the implementation FSM *Imp* is not a reduction of M, then there exists an input sequence $\alpha \in TS$ s.t. the trace of FSM *Imp* with the U-restriction α does not intersect the set of traces of M with the U-restriction α. Based on the complete test suite *TS*, we derive the set $\widehat{TS}$ of input/output sequences of the set $(UV)^*$ such that the set $\widehat{TS}$ intersects the set of traces of each possible implementation *Imp* $\in \Re$ that is not a reduction of M. For each non-empty prefix u_1v_1 ... u_kv_k of each trace of the set $\{\beta : \beta \in \text{Traces of } M \,\&\, \beta_{\downarrow U} \in TS\}$ we include into the set $\widehat{TS}$ the set of sequences $\{u_1v_1 \ldots u_kv : u_1v_1 \ldots u_kv \notin \text{Traces of } M\}$ (if it exists).

Proposition 1. Given a largest solution M to the equation *Context* $\Diamond X \cong Spec$. An implementation FSM *Imp* $\in \Re$ is not a reduction of M if and only if the set of traces of *Imp* intersects the set $\widehat{TS}$.

According to the above proposition, if an implementation FSM *Imp* $\in \Re$ has a trace of the set $\widehat{TS}$ then *Imp* is not externally equivalent to the embedded machine *Emb*. The traces of the set $\widehat{TS}$ can be represented as traces of an automaton *Aut*$\widehat{TS}$, where each trace of $\widehat{TS}$ leads to the designated *Trap* state of *Aut*$\widehat{TS}$. The state *Trap* is the only accepting state of the automaton and the language generated at the state *Trap* is the set $(UV)^*$. We obtain a test generator that generates all sequences over $(IO)^*$ such that for each *Imp* $\in \Re$ that is not externally equivalent to *Emb*, the generator induces in *Imp* at least one trace of the set $\widehat{TS}$ in order to detect that *Imp* is not a reduction (i.e. *Imp* is a nonconforming implementation of *Emb*) of M,. Due to the test architecture shown in Figure 2, the generator is obtained by solving the equation $Aut(Context) \lozenge X \cong Aut\widehat{TS}$.

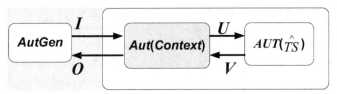

Fig. 2. Test Architecture

As an application example, consider the specification FSM *Spec*, shown in Fig 3.1, defined over the inputs $I = \{x_1, x_2\}$an d outputs $O = \{o_1, o_2, o_3\}$ The c orresponding automaton *Aut(Spec)* is shown in Fig 3.2. Moreover, consider the context FSM *Context*, shown in Figures 4.1, defined over the external inputs $I = \{x_1, x_2\}$ external outputs $O = \{o_1, o_2, o_3\}$ in ternal inputs $V=\{v_1, v_2\}$and i nternal outputs $U=\{u_1, u_2\}$ The automaton *Aut(Context)* that corresponds to *Context* is shown in Fig 4.2. Accepting states of both automata are shown by double lines. We are required to solve the FSM equation *Context* $\lozenge X \cong Spec$ and obtain its largest solution M. This solution is defined over FSMs, thus it is a submachine of automaton *Chaos-UV* shown in Fig. 5. In order to solve the equation, we combine the automata *Aut(Spec)* and *Aut(Context)* with *Aut(Chaos-UV)* and obtain the automaton $\Lambda(Aut(Context)$, $Aut(Spec), Aut(Chaos-UV))$ shown in Fig. 6. Each state (s, j, Q) where the external restriction of the set of traces at the state does not coincide with the set of traces at state j of the specification, i.e. states h3A, m4A, n3A, c2A, and g4A are declared as the designated state '*FAIL*'. We restrict the automaton onto the alphabet $\{u_1, u_2, v_1,$ $v_2\}$of the solution. Each subset of states of the restricted automaton that includes the '*FAIL*' state is designated as the '*FAIL*' state. We add the DNC state for the transitions (f4A, u_1) and (f3A, u_1) since there are no transitions from these states under the input u_1, delete the '*FAIL*' state with its incoming transitions and obtain the largest FSM solution M shown in Fig 7. Then, we derive from M the complete internal test suite TS $= \{u_1 u_2 u_2, u_2 u_2\}$w.r.t . all FSMs with at most two states using the HIS method [19]. The set of all traces of the FSM M with the U-restriction in the set TS is $\{u_1/v_1 u_2/v_2$ $u_2/v_1, u_2/v_1 u_2/v_1\}$ Accord ing to Proposition 1, if an implementation of the embedded

component has one of the sequences of the set $\widehat{TS} = \{u_1/v_2; u_1/v_1 u_2/v_1; u_1/v_1 u_2/v_2$ $u_2/v_2; u_2/v_2; u_2/v_1 u_2/v_2\}$th en this implementation is not externally equivalent to the

specification of the embedded component FSM. We represent the sequences of $\widehat{TS}$ as the finite automaton $Aut\widehat{TS}$ shown in Fig 8 and solve the equation $Aut(Context) \lozenge$ $X \cong Aut\widehat{TS}$.

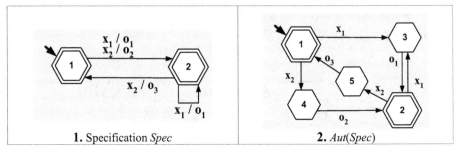

1. Specification *Spec*   **2.** *Aut(Spec)*

Fig. 3. Specification

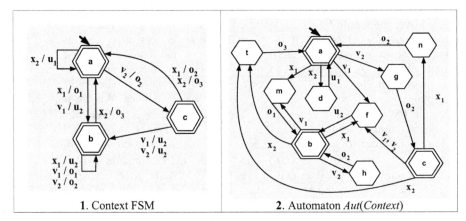

1. Context FSM   2. Automaton *Aut(Context)*

Fig. 4. Context FSM and Automaton *Aut(Context)*

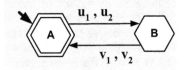

Fig. 5. Automaton *Aut(Chaos-UV)*

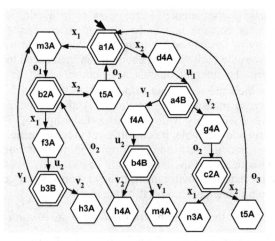

Fig. 6. Automaton $\Lambda(Aut(Context),\ Aut(Spec), Aut(Chaos\text{-}UV))$

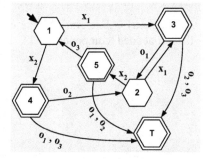

Fig. 7. Largest FSM Solution

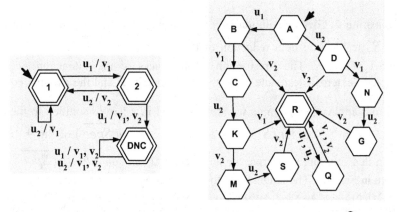

Fig. 8. Automaton $Aut\ \widehat{TS}$

Fig. 9. $Aut(\overline{Spec})$

When no access to the internal interactions is available, some faults of the embedded component become latent. To illustrate latent faults consider a faulty implementation *Imp* of the embedded component that has the trace u_1v_2 instead of u_1v_1. The trace u_1v_2 in the faulty implementation can be induced by the external input x_2. However, when the internal outputs are unobservable, the composed system *Context* ◊ *Imp* has the expected output response o_2 to the input x_2. In order to detect that *Imp* has the wrong trace u_1v_2, we have to apply after x_2 the input x_1. In this case the composed system will reply with the unexpected output o_2. Therefore, since the internal channels are unobservable, it is insufficient to have a generator that induces at least one forbidden trace of each non-conforming implementation of the embedded machine. The consequences of the fault have to be externally observable, i.e. have to be propagated to the external environment. In other words, a test generator has to be a reduction of the complement of the specification machine.

Thus, when solving the equation $Aut(Context) \, ◊ \, X \cong Aut\widehat{TS}$ we look for a solution that is a reduction of the complement of the specification machine $\overline{Spec}$. This is done since an internal fault is detected if and only if an unexpected output is produced to some external test case. The following statement holds.

Proposition 2. Given a solution *Gen* to the automaton equation $Aut(Context) \, ◊ \, X \cong Aut\widehat{TS}$, let *AutGen* be a reduction of the automaton $Aut(\overline{Spec})$ and have a finite number of traces. The *I*-restriction of the traces of the automaton *AutGen* is a complete (external) test suite w.r.t. the fault domain $\Re$ and the external equivalence relation.

In our application example we are interested in a largest solution to the equation $Aut(Context) \, ◊ \, X \cong Aut\widehat{TS}$ that is a reduction of $Aut(\overline{Spec})$ of Fig 9. In order to obtain this solution, we derive the automaton $\Lambda(Aut(Context), Aut(\overline{Spec}), Aut\widehat{TS})$ shown in Fig. 10. The language of the *I*-restriction of the obtained largest solution is $x_1(x_2x_1)^*x_1x_1$, $(x_1(x_2x_1)^*x_1(x_2x_1)^*$, $x_2x_2(x_1x_2)^*x_1$, x_2x_1, $x_2x_2x_2^*(x_1x_2)^*$, and correspondingly a reduction of this largest solution that has the sequences $TS = \{_1x_1x_1, x_2x_2x_1, x_2x_1, x_2x_2x_2\}$ (these sequences are the labels of all simple paths from the initial state of the reduction to a final state that includes the trap state R) is also a solution to the equation $Aut(Context) \, ◊ \, X \cong Aut\widehat{TS}$. The external test suite *TS* is a complete test suite for the embedded component w.r.t. the external equivalence relation.

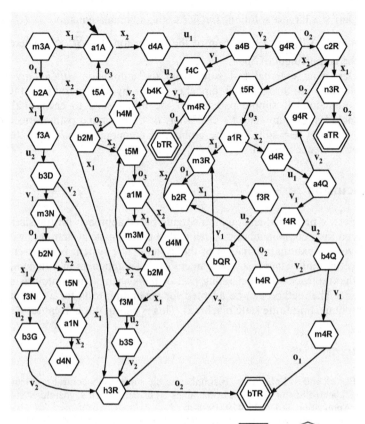

Fig. 10. Automaton $\Lambda(Aut(Context), Aut(\overline{Spec}), Aut\widehat{TS})$

A Summary of the Fault Propagation Approach:

Input: A deterministic $Context=\langle S, I\cup V, O\cup U, T_A, s_0\rangle$, a deterministic embedded component $Emb=\langle T, U, V, T_B, t_0\rangle$, and a deterministic specification $Spec =\langle Q, I, O, T_{Spec}, q_0\rangle = Context \lozenge Emb$, and the fault domain $\mathfrak{R}$ of the embedded component Emb.

Output: A complete external test suite defined over the external alphabet I for testing the embedded component Emb. The test suite is complete w.r.t. the fault model $<Context \lozenge Emb, \cong, Context \lozenge \mathfrak{R}>$

Step 1: Derive a largest FSM solution M to the equation $Context \lozenge X = Spec$.

Step 2: Derive a complete test suite TS w.r.t. the fault model $<M, \leq, \mathfrak{R}>$ Then, derive from TS the set of sequences $\widehat{TS}$, over the alphabet $(UV)^*$, that intersects the set of traces of each possible implementation Imp in $\mathfrak{R}$ that is not a reduction of M. Represent the sequences of $\widehat{TS}$ by the automaton $Aut\widehat{TS}$.

Step 3: Derive a largest solution *AutGen* to the automata equation *Aut*(*Context*) ◊ *X* = *Aut* $\widehat{TS}$ that is a reduction of the automaton *Aut*($\overline{Spec}$), where $\overline{Spec}$ is the complement of *Spec*.

Step 4: Derive an external test suite from the automaton *AutGen* by projecting *AutGen* on the external alphabet *I* and by considering in the obtained automaton all simple paths from the initial state to each final state that includes the trap state *R*. The labels of these simple paths form a complete (external) test suite for the embedded component *Emb* w.r.t. the external equivalence relation.

4   Conclusion

In this paper we presented an equation solving based approach for translating internal tests derived for a component embedded within a composite system into external tests defined over the external alphabets of the system. The system is represented as two communicating finite state machines, an embedded component machine and a context machine that represents the remaining part of the system. The context is assumed to be fault free. The method can be adapted for generating tests for a system of two or more communicating finite state machines. This is part of our current research work.

References

[1]   G. Barrett and S. Lafortune, "Bisimulation, the supervisory control problem, and strong model matching for finite ftate machines", Discrete Event Dynamic Systems: Theory and Application, 8(4), 377-429, 1998.

[2]   G. v. Bochmann and P. M. Merlin, "On the construction of communication protocols". ICCC (1980) 371-378, reprinted in "Communication Protocol Modeling", edited by C. Sunshine, Artech House Publ. (1981).

[3]   S. Buffalov, K. El-Fakih, N. Yevtushenko, & G.v. Bochmann, "Progressive solutions to a parallel automata equation". In Proc. of the IFIP 23rd International Conference on Formal Techniques for Networked and Distributed Systems (FORTE 2003), Berlin, Germany, Published as LNCS 2767, pp.367-382, 2003.

[4]   Cavalli, , D. Lee, D., C. Rinderknecht, , and F. Zaidi, "Hit-or-Ju mp: An algorithm for embedded testing with applications to IN services". Proceedings of Joint Inter. Conf. FORTE/PSTV99, pp: 41-58, 1999.

[5]   T. S. Chow, "Test design modeled by finite-state machines," IEEE Trans. SE, vol. 4, no.3, pp. 178-187, 1978.

[6]   J. Drissi and G. v. Bochmann, Submodule Construction for systems of I/O Automata. Technical Report #133, DIRO,   Universite' de Montreal, Canada, 1999.

[7]   K. El-Fakih, V. Trenkaev, N. Spitsyna, N. Yevtushenko, "FSM Based Interoperability Testing Methods", in Proc. of the IFIP 16th International Conference on Testing of Communicating Systems, Oxford, U.K., Published as LNCS 2978, pp. 60-75, 2004.

[8]   K. El-Fakih, S. Prokopenko, N. Yevtushenko, and G. v. Bochmann, "Fault diagnosis in extended finite state machines", in Proc. of the IFIP 15th International Conference on Testing of Communicating Systems, France, published as LCNC 2644, pp. 197-210, 2003.

[9]   J. E. Hopcroft, and J. D. Ullman, Introduction to automata theory, languages, and computation, Addison-Wesley, N.Y., 1979.

[10] S. G. H. Kelekar, Synthesis of protocols and protocol converters using the submodule construction approach. In. A. Danthine et al, editors, Protocol Specification, Testing, and Verification- PSTV XIII, 1994.

[11] R. Hierons and H. Ural, "Concerning the ordering of adaptive test sequences", In Proc. of the IFIP 23rd International Conference on Formal Techniques for Networked and Distributed Systems (FORTE 2003), Berlin, Germany, Published as LNCS 2767, pp.289-302, 2003.

[12] Information technology. "Open systems interaction. Conformance testing methodology and framework". International standard IS-9646, 1991.

[13] R. Kumar, S. Nelvagal, and S. I. Marcus. "A discrete event systems approach for protocol conversion", Discrete Event Dynamical Systems: Theory and Applications, 7(3) 295-315, 1997.

[14] L. P Lima, , and A. R. Cavalli, "A pragmatic approach to generating test sequences for embedded systems". Proceedings of 10th IWTCS, pp: 125-140, 1997.

[15] D. Lee, K. Sabnani, D. M. Kristol, and S. Paul, "Conformance testing of protocols specified as communicating finite state machines - a guided random walk based approach". IEEE Transactions on Communications, 44(5): 631-640, 1996.

[16] P. Merlin and G. v. Bochman. On the construction of submodule specifications and communication protocols, ACM Trans. On Programming Languages and Systems. 5(1) 1-25, 1983.

[17] J. Parrow, Submodule construction as equation solving in CCS, Theoretical Computer Science, 68, 1989.

[18] Petrenko, N. Yevtushenko, G. v. Bochmann. "Fault models for testing in context", FORTE 96.

[19] Petrenko, N. Yevtushenko, and G. v. Bochmann. "Testing deterministic implementations from their nondeterministic specifications". Proceedings of the IFIP 9th International Workshop on Testing of Communicating Systems, Germany, pp. 125-140, 1996.

[20] Petrenko, N. Yevtushenko, G. v. Bochmann, and R. Dssouli, "Testing in context: framework and test derivation", Computer communications, Vol. 19, pp. 1236-1249, 1996.

[21] Petrenko and N. Yevtushenko, Solving asynchronous equations. In S. Bukowski, A. Cavalli, and E. Najm, editors, Formal Description Techniques and Protocol Specification, Testing, and Verification- FORTE XI/PSTVXVIII 98, Chapman-Hall, 231-247, 1998.

[22] Petrenko, N. Yevtushenko, A. Lebedev, and A. Das, "Nondeterministic State Machines in Protocol Conformance Testing," Proc. of the IFIP 6th IWPTS, France, pp. 363-378, 1993.

[23] H. Qin and P. Lewis, Factorisation of finite state machines under strong and observational equivalences, Journal of Formal Aspects of Computing, 3, 284- 307, 1991.

[24] Z Tao, G. v. Bochmann and R. Dssouli, A formal method for synthesizing optimized protocol converters and its application to mobile data networks. Mobile Networks & Applications, 2(3) 259-69, 1997.

[25] N. Yevtushenko, A. R. Cavalli, and L.P. Lima, "Test minimization for testing in context". Proceedings of the 11th IWTCS, pp: 127-145, 1998.

[26] N. Yevtushenko, T. Villa. R. K. Brayton, A. Petrenko, A. Sangiovanni-Vincentelli. Solution of parallel language equations for logic synthesis. In Proc. of the International Conference on Computer-Aided Design, 103-110, 2001.

[27] W. M. Wonham and P. J. Ramadge, On the supremal controllable sublanguage of a given language. SIAM J. Control. Optimization. 25(3) (1987) 637-659.

[28] K. El-Fakih, N. Yevtushenko, and G. v. Bochmann,"Diagnosing multiple faults in communicating finite state machines", In Proc. of the IFIP 21st International Conference on Formal Techniques for Networked and Distributed Systems (FORTE 2001), Cheju Island, Korea), pp. 85-100, 2001.

Automatic Generation of Run-Time Test Oracles for Distributed Real-Time Systems [*]

Xin Wang, Ji Wang, and Zhi-Chang Qi

National Laboratory for Parallel and Distributed Processing
300 Lichen Rd., Changsha, 410073 China
xinwang76@yahoo.com.cn, ji.wang@263.net

Abstract. Distributed real-time systems are of one important type of real-time systems. They are usually characterized by both reactive and real-time factors and it has long been recognized that how to automatically check such systems' correctness at run time is still an unaddressed problem. As one of the main solutions, test oracle is a method usually used to check whether the system under test has behaved correctly on a particular execution. Test oracle is not only the indispensable stage of software testing, but also the weak link of the software testing research. In this paper, real-time specifications are adopted to describe the properties of distributed real-time systems and a real-time specification-based method for automatic run-time test oracles generating is proposed. The method proposed here is based on tableau construction theory of real-time model checking, automatically generates timed automata as test oracles, which can automatically check system behaviors' correctness from real-time specifications written in $MITL_{[0,d]}$.

1 Introduction

With the development of the network, distributed computing has become the mainstream of the computing technology undoubtedly. As a special kind of real-time systems, Distributed Real-Time Systems (DRTS) built on network environment have been applied widely in industry, military and commercial high-tech areas, especially in power engineering, aviation, real-time control systems, flexible manufacturing system, vision systems, etc [1]. Most of DRTS require high safety and strict time constraints, though the complexity of DRTS spans the gamut from very simple control of laboratory experiment, to very complicated projects such as the fighter avionic. So they are new challenge to the software testing methods during the software development.

Test oracle is a method for checking whether the system under test has behaved correctly on a particular execution [2]. It is the indispensable stage of software testing and also the weak link of the software testing research. The

---

[*] This work is supported by the National Natural Science Foundation of China under Grant No. 60233020 and No. 90104007; the National High Technology Development 863 Program of China under Grant No. 2001AA113202.

D. de Frutos-Escrig and M. Núñez (Eds.): FORTE 2004, LNCS 3235, pp. 199–212, 2004.

correctness of DRTS depends not only on the logical result of the computation, but also on the time when the results are produced [3]. Using run-time test oracles can not only check whether the system run is correct, but also improve the efficiency of software testing, set free testers from heavy work of checking system results.

DRTS are usually command-control systems, so their primary characteristics are event-triggered, complex event sequences, and real-time, precise time constraints. Temporal logic is the most important formal specification that describes distributed event-triggered, real-time systems' properties, and is used widely during software development. Using test oracles generated from temporal logic can reduce the costs of rewriting specifications greatly. The properties about time constraints of DRTS that described by real-time temporal logic are called real-time specifications. Test oracles generated from real-time specifications can automatically check if the run sequences of tested systems satisfy their specifications, if not, they can report corresponding error information.

The method proposed here is based on tableau construction theory of real-time model checking [4], automatically generates timed automata as test oracles, which can automatically check system behaviors' correctness, from real-time specifications written in $MITL_{[0,d]}$. The remainder of this paper is organized as follows. Section 2 describes relevant methods of automatically generating test oracles for reactive, real-time systems and their relative merits. Section 3 introduces the logic and timed automata that we use. Section 4 gives two approaches to acquire the traces of distributed real-time systems as input of test oracles. The work presented in core section 5 represents the method of automatically generating test oracles and case study. Section 6 concludes this paper and points out future work.

2   Related Work

Based on the generic tableau algorithm that generates specification automata for model checking, Dillon and Yu have proposed an automata-based method that can translate a temporal logic formula into a finite state machine as a test oracle [5, 6]. Once an execution sequence of a program is put into the finite state machine, the finite state machine can check if this execution sequence satisfies its specification. Proposition temporal logic can be applied only to describe the properties of reactive systems, but not real-time systems, because it doesn't support time quantifier. Therefore, this method can only be applied to reactive systems.

Method proposed by Geilen [7] also comes from the idea of model checking, which is very similar with the algorithm proposed by Kupferman and Vardi. This method has on-the-fly feature and has the same applicability as Dillon and Yu's.

Temporal assertions are proposed by Doron Drusinsky of Time-Rover Press [8]. The main idea is that temporal logic formulas are translated into some special kind of assertions (i.e. temporal assertions) as test oracles. Assertions are inserted into a tested program manually in order that they can automatically check the program's correctness at run time. Assertion preprocessor must insert sub-assertions (assertions get by decomposing temporal assertions) into all related positions and maintain the relationship among them at run time. The costs of assertion maintenance will seriously influence the run of real-time systems and lend to the violation of time constraints, thus this method is more perfect for reactive systems or real-time simulators that amplify the absolute time than real-time systems.

John Håkansson has given an on-line test oracle generation method that is the only one that can check the correctness of real-time systems at run time [9]. Based on the rewriting rules of safety properties of real-time systems, this method discretizes the continuous time and automatically generates test oracles to monitor systems' behaviors externally. The test oracles fetch system data through sampling corresponding signals externally and compute the state-of-the-art pattern of systems at every end of the cycles, and in this way this method can support relatively strict time constraints. Because time is discretized, some system behaviors may be lost or some wrong behaviors may not be checked out if the time constraints in specifications are not integral multiple of read cycle.

3   Preliminaries

This section introduces the propaedeutics about logic and automata that we will use when automatically generating test oracles from real-time specifications.

3.1   Timed State Sequences

Let time domain be the non-negative real number set $R_{\geq 0}$. An interval I is a convex subset of $R_{\geq 0}$, which has the form $[a, b)$ where $a, b \in R_{\geq 0}$ and $a \leq b$. For a finite interval I, let $l(I)$ and $r(I)$ denote the left and right end of I respectively, and $|I|$ denote the length of I. Two intervals I, I' are adjacent if and only if $r(I) = l(I)$. We use $t + I$ to denote the interval $\{t + t' | t' \in I\}$. Let P be a finite proposition set and state s be a subset of P. If $s \subseteq P$ and $p \in s$ is a proposition in s, s is called p-state, denoting as $s \models p$.

Definition 1. *[10] A state sequence $\bar{s} = s_0 s_1 s_2 \ldots$ is an infinite sequence of states $s_i \subseteq P$. An interval sequence $\bar{I} = I_0 I_1 I_2 \ldots$ is an infinite sequence of timed interval such that*
   [Initiality] I_0 is left-closed and $l(I_0) = 0$;
   [Adjacency] for all $i \geq 0$, the intervals I_i and I_{i+1} are adjacent;
   [progress] every time $t \in R_{\geq 0}$ belongs to some interval I_i.

A timed state sequence $\tau = (\bar{s}, \bar{I})$ is a pair that consists of a state sequence $\bar{s}$ and an interval sequence $\bar{I}$.

3.2 Real-Time Logic $MITL_{[0,d]}$

$MITL$ is a kind of linear temporal logic that is interpreted over timed state sequence [10]. In this paper, we only consider the real-time specifications written in $MITL_{[0,d]}(d \in R_{\geq 0})$, a restrict version of $MITL$.

Definition 2. *The formulas of $MITL_{[0,d]}$ can be inductively defined as follows:*
$$\phi ::= true|\ p\ |\ \neg\phi\ |\ \phi_1 \wedge \phi_2\ |\ \phi_1 U_{[0,d]}\phi_2$$

The semantics of $MITL_{[0,d]}$ is presented in [10].

We also use dual operators "$\vee$" and "V" to define $\phi_1 \vee \phi_2 \triangleq \neg(\neg\phi_1 \wedge \neg\phi_2)$ and $\phi_1 V_{[0,d]}\phi_2 \triangleq \neg(\neg\phi_1 U_{[0,d]}\neg\phi_2)$. Similar with the "Always ('$\square$')" and "Sometime ('$\Diamond$')" operators in LTL(Linear Temporal Logic), we use operators "Always in the interval [0,d] ('$\square_{[0,d]}$')" and "Sometime in the interval [0,d] ('$\Diamond_{[0,d]}$')" to define $\square_{[0,d]}\phi \triangleq false V_{[0,d]}\phi$ and $\Diamond_{[0,d]}\phi \triangleq true U_{[0,d]}\phi$.

Definition 3. *[10] Let ϕ be a formula of $MITL_{[0,d]}$. We call interval sequence $\bar{I}$ is ϕ-fine if for every sub-formula ψ of ϕ, every $k \geq 0$ and every $t_1, t_2 \in \bar{I}(k)$, $\tau^{t_1} \models \psi$ if and only if $\tau^{t_2} \models \psi$. We call a timed state sequence $\tau = (\bar{s}, \bar{I})$ is ϕ-fine if the $\bar{I}$ in $(\bar{s}, \bar{I})$ is ϕ-fine.*

In [11], Lemma 4.11 is shown that the intervals of any timed state sequence can always be refined to be fine for any $MITL$ formula. It holds for the subset of $MITL$, $MITL_{[0,d]}$ too.

The tableau construction theory of real-time model checking requires that the truth value of the formulas interpreted over the time state sequence $(\bar{s}, \bar{I})$ can't change during a single interval of $\bar{I}$, i.e. the timed state sequence $(\bar{s}, \bar{I})$ must be ϕ-fine.

3.3 Timed Automata

The test oracles studied here are a variant of timed automata originally proposed by Alur and Dill [11] to serve as our test oracles. Timed automata use clocks whose values are positive real number to record the points when real-time specifications become true and when states change. Give a clock set C, clock interpretation function $v \in CInt(C)$ and clock setting function $CS \in Cset(C)$ are partial mappings from C to $R_{\geq 0}$. For some $d \in R_{\geq 0}$ and every $x \in dom(v)$, $v+d$ denotes the clock interpretation that assigns $v(x) + d$ to any clock x in the domain of v, and $CS(v)$ denotes that $CS(x)$(if defined)or $v(x)$ is assigned to $CS(v)(x)$. For a subset γ of C, we use $CS[\gamma := n]$ to denote the clock setting that maps all clocks in γ to n and keeps other clocks unchanged. Clock condition set $CCond(C)$ over clock set C is $\{x := t, x \geq d, 0 \leq t < d, x \leq t < d + x, y := t - x \mid x, y, t \in C\}$.

Definition 4. *Let P be a priority function. For a set $I = \{c_1, c_2, \ldots c_n\}$ ($i \in N$, $c_i \in CCond(C)$) and the natural number set N, we define:*

- *sorting function $o : I \mapsto <c_{i_1}, c_{i_2}, \ldots c_{i_n}>$ for $i_r \in \{1, 2, \ldots .n\}$ such that for every $1 \leq i_r \leq i_s \leq n$, $P(c_{i_r}) < P(c_{i_s})$ holds or their is no comparability between c_{i_r} and c_{i_s};*

- o's inverse function $o^{-1} : \{c_1, c_2, \ldots c_n\} \mapsto I$ such that $o^{-1} \circ o(I) = I$.

Definition 5. Let P be a set of proposition constraints. A finite-input timed automaton $< S, S_0, C, Q, CC, OCC, Tran, s_e >$ over P is defined as follow:

- S is a finite set of states;
- C is a finite set of clocks;
- S_0 is a finite set of initial extended states, $(s_0, v_0) \in S_0 \subseteq S \times CInt(C)$;
- $Q : S \to 2^P$ is a state labelling function which maps a state to a proposition constraint subset, i.e. $Q(s) \subseteq 2^P$;
- $CC : S \to 2^{CCond(C)}$ is also a state labelling function which maps a state to a clock condition subset;
- $OCC : S \to o(2^{CCond(C)})$ is an another kind of state labelling which maps a state to an ordered clock condition subset;
- $Tran \subseteq S \times CSet(C) \times S$ is a set of transitions, each of which labels with a clock setting function;
- $S_e \in S$ is a set of finite states.

Definition 6. A run of a finite-input timed automaton $< S, S_0, C, Q, CC, OCC, Tran, S_e >$ is a finite sequence $\overset{v_0}{\underset{\gamma_0}{\to}}(s_0, t_0)\overset{v_1}{\underset{\gamma_1}{\to}}(s_1, t_1)\overset{v_2}{\underset{\gamma_2}{\to}}\cdots\overset{v_r}{\underset{\gamma_r}{\to}}(s_r, t_r)\overset{v_{r+1}}{\underset{\gamma_{r+1}}{\to}}\cdots\overset{v_n}{\underset{\gamma_n}{\to}}(s_n, t_n)$ of states $s_i \in S$ $(0 \le i \le n)$, clock $t \in C$, clock sets $\gamma_i \subseteq C$ and a sequence of clock interpretation function $\bar{v} = (v_0, v_1, \ldots, v_{n-1})$ satisfying the following constraints:

- $(s_0, v_0) \in S_0$, $s_n \in S_e$;
- For every $0 \le k < n$, there exists some (s_k, CS_{k+1}, s_{k+1}) such that for every $c \in C$,

$$
v_{k+1}(c) = \begin{cases} t_{k+1} & c = t \\ CS_{k+1}[\gamma_{k+1} := 0](c) & c \ne t \text{ and } CS(c) \text{ is defined} \\ v_k(c) & \text{otherwise} \end{cases} ;
$$

- For every $0 \le k < n$, every $c \in C$, $v_k(c)$ satisfies $CC_k(s_k)$ and $OCC_k(s_k)$.

Definition 7. Let $\tau = (\bar{s}, \bar{I})$ be a timed state sequence and be ϕ-fine, A is a finite-input timed automaton $< S, S_0, C, Q, CC, OCC, Tran, S_e >$. We say that $\tau = (\bar{s}, \bar{I})$ can be accepted by A, if:

- for $\varepsilon \to 0+$ there is some $r \in N$ such that $\overset{v_0}{\underset{C}{\to}}(s_0, r(I_0) - \varepsilon)\overset{v_1}{\underset{\gamma_1}{\to}}(s_1, r(I_1) - \varepsilon)\overset{v_2}{\underset{\gamma_2}{\to}}\cdots\overset{v_r}{\underset{\gamma_r}{\to}}(s_r, r(I_r) - \varepsilon)$ is a run of A;
- for every $k \in Z^+$, we have $\bar{s}_k \subseteq Q(u(k))$ if $u(k)$ is a state of A which corresponds to the k-th position of the above run.

In fact, the acceptable input of a timed automaton is not timed sequences, but the sequences of state-time pairs like $(s_0 s_1 \ldots s_n, t_0 t_1 \ldots t_n)$. Thereby, we must translate the timed state sequences into the above format. With this end of view, we introduce $\varepsilon(\varepsilon \to 0+)$ and use $r(I_i) - \varepsilon$ to replace the right end of the interval I_i. In the field of real number, it is not holds to treat $r(I_i) - \varepsilon$ as the right end of I_i, because no matter how close ε approximates to zero, $\varepsilon/2 < \varepsilon$ always holds. But from the fact that the run of computers is step by step, i.e. the time is discrete, the interval $(r(I_i) - \varepsilon, r(I_i))$ doesn't exist if the value of ε is small enough, such as let ε equal to or smaller than the minimal click of the clock in a real-time system.

4   Traces Acquisition from DRTS

The behaviors that we want to acquire from DRTS are decided by the atomic formulas of real-time specifications. There are only two methods that can acquire the behaviors of DRTS and their occurring time; one is acquiring traces from outside of DRTS, another is acquiring traces from inside.

If all system behaviors involved by real-time specifications can be detected from outside of the DRTS, the first method can be used. Some kind of program module serves as monitor, detecting observable signals from outside of systems periodically and sending them to test oracles. The point when the output signals change is the left end of interval, and the point when the output signals change next time is the right end of interval; the interval is left-closed and right-open.

If real-time specifications involve internal states of systems, the second method must be used, i.e. some kind of assertions are inserted into proper positions (such as where the related states maybe change) of DRTS; assertions will send the information on which states change and when they change as soon as the true value of assertions change to test oracles. The point when the output signals change is the left end of interval, and the point when the output signals change next time is the right end of interval; the interval is left-closed and right-open.

Example: We consider the Carrier Sense, Multiple Access with Collision Detection protocol, or CSMA/CD for short [12, 13] which is widely used on LANs in the MAC sublayer. One safety property of CSMA/CD can be described as $\Box_{[0,\infty]}((Trans1 \wedge Trans2) \Rightarrow \Diamond_{[0,\sigma]}coll)$ written in MITL that means whenever both senders begin transmitting, a collision is inevitably detected within σ. The value of varies with the network on which the protocol runs. For instance, for a 10 Mbps Ethernet with a typical worst case round trip propagation delay of $51.2\mu s$, we set σ to be $25.6\mu s$. We can get three system events from the above property: $Trans1$, $Trans2$ and $coll$.

Fig.1 is the oscillogram of $Trans1$, $Trans2$ and $coll$. While the three traces come to test oracles, one part of test oracles must arrange them into one trace according to the time they happen and assure the trace is ϕ-fine. Suppose that the vertical dash lines denote the right end of the refined intervals, we can get following timed state sequence from Fig. 1:

$$(\{\neg Trans1, \neg Trans2, \neg coll\}[0, t_1))\ (\{\neg Trans1, \neg Trans2, \neg coll\}[t_1, t_2))$$
$$(\{Trans1, \neg Trans2, \neg coll\}[t_2, t_3))\ (\{Trans1, Trans2, \neg coll\}[t_3, t_4))$$

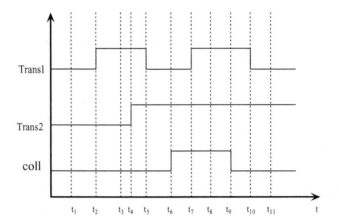

Fig. 1. The oscillogram of events $Trans1$, $Trans2$ and $coll$

$(\{Trans1, Trans2, \neg coll\}[t_4, t_5))$ $(\{\neg Trans1, Trans2, \neg coll\}[t_5, t_6))$
$(\{\neg Trans1, Trans2, coll\}[t_6, t_7))$ $(\{Trans1, Trans2, coll\}[t_7, t_8))$
$(\{Trans1, Trans2, coll\}[t_8, t_9))$ $(\{Trans1, Trans2, \neg coll\}[t_9, t_{10}))$
$(\{\neg Trans1, Trans2, \neg coll\}[t_{10}, t_{11})) \ldots$

The refinement procedure is done from the inner sub-formulas to outer sub-formulas, which give in [10]. In out example, as long as we get an event, we should refine the interval of $coll$ first, then refine the interval of $Trans1 \wedge Trans2$ and the refined interval of $coll$. In this way, one interval may be cut into several smaller intervals which act as the actual input of the test oracles.

In this example, there must be three assertions corresponding to the three events. The assertions should be put on the neck of the statements that can cause the event status to change, such as *readin, assignment, output* statement and etc. In each of the assertions, there must be two variables to record the value before the current point and at the current point respectively. When the values of the two variables don't equal, the assertions should output the current values of the events and the time acquired from the system clock or specific external clock.

5   Automatic Generation of Run-Time Test Oracles

Generating run-time test oracles automatically is to construct timed automata based on real-time specifications written in $MITL_{[0,d]}$. Differing from specification automata in real-time model checking, the automata constructed for software testing need only accept finite state sequences. We say that a timed state sequence satisfies its specifications if this timed state sequence can reach the final states of automata constructed based on its specifications, i.e. it can

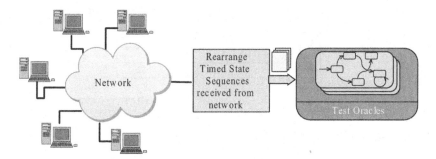

Fig. 2. The role of test oracle in software testing

pass through test oracles. The role of test oracles generated by our method in software testing is represented in Fig.2.

5.1   Rewrite Rules

The procedure that generates automata automatically from logic formulas often has to use rewrite rules. Based on rewrite rules, a logic formula can be equivalently decomposed tow parts: constraints that can be computed in current state and constraints that will be computed in subsequent states. Rewrite rules usually use "$\bigcirc$" operator to denote the constraints that will be computed in the subsequent states. In order to express the constraints that will be computed after some time point in $MITL_{[0,d]}$, we define similarly operator "$\bigcirc$" and extend the syntax of $MITL_{[0,d]}$.

Extended $MITL_{[0,d]}$ In order to rewrite the formulas of $MITL_{[0,d]}$, we use "$\bigcirc$" operator, clocks, clock conditions and clock interpretation function to extend the syntax and semantics of basic $MITL_{[0,d]}$.

Definition 8. *Based on the formulas of basic $MITL_{[0,d]}$, the formulas of $EMITL_{[0,d]}$ can be defined inductively as follows, where ϕ, ϕ_1 and ϕ_2 are formulas of $MITL_{[0,d]}$, x and t are clocks, $d \in R_{\geq 0}$:*
$$\varphi ::= \phi \mid \varphi_1 \vee \varphi_2 \mid \varphi_1 \wedge \varphi_2 \mid CS.\varphi \mid x \geq d \mid 0 \leq t \leq d \mid x \leq t \leq x + d \mid x := t \mid y := t - x \mid \phi_1 U_{[0,d]_x} \phi_2 \mid \phi_1 V_{[0,d]_x} \phi_2 \mid \phi_1 V_{[x,d]} \phi_2 \mid \phi_1 V_{[y,d]_x} \phi_2 \mid \bigcirc \varphi$$

Definition 9. *The satisfiability relationship $\tau \models_v \phi$ denotes that the timed state sequence τ satisfies ϕ in context of the clock interpretation v. The semantics of $EMITL_{[0,d]}$ is extended as follows:*

- $\tau \models_v \phi$ *iff* $\tau \models \phi$;
- $\tau \models_v \varphi_1 \vee \varphi_2$ *iff* $\tau \models_v \varphi_1$ *or* $\tau \models_v \varphi_2$;
- $\tau \models_v \varphi_1 \wedge \varphi_2$ *iff* $\tau \models_v \varphi_1$ *and* $\tau \models_v \varphi_2$;
- $\tau \models_v CS.\varphi$ *iff* $\tau \models_{CS(v)} \varphi$;
- $\tau \models_v x \geq d$ *iff* $v(x) \geq d$;

Table 1. Rules for decomposing a basic $MITL_{[0,d]}$ formula ϕ

$\phi =$	$\Phi \cup \{\phi\}$ reduces to
$\phi_1 \Xi \phi_2$	$\Phi \cup \{\phi\}$
$\phi_1 \Delta \phi_2$	$\Phi \cup \{\phi_1, \phi_2\}$

- $\tau \models_v 0 \leq t \leq d$ *iff* $0 \leq v(t) \leq d$;
- $\tau \models_v x \leq t \leq x + d$ *iff* $v(x) \leq v(t) \leq v(x) + d$;
- $\tau \models_v x := t$ *iff* $v(x) := v(t)$;
- $\tau \models_v y := t - x$ *iff* $v(y) := v(t) - v(x)$;
- $\tau \models_v \phi_1 U_{[0,d]_x} \phi_2$ *iff there is some* $d_1 \in [v(x), v(x) + d]$, *such that* $\tau^{d_1} \models_{v+d_1}$ ϕ_2 *and for every* $d_2 \in [v(x), d_1]$, $\tau^{d_2} \models_{v+d_2} \phi_1$;
- $\tau \models_v \phi_1 V_{[x,d]} \phi_2$ *iff for every* $d_1 \in [v(x), d]$, $\tau^{d_1} \models_{v+d_1} \phi_2$, *or there is some* $d_2 \in [v(x), d_1]$, *such that* $\tau^{d_2} \models_{v+d_2} \phi_1$;
- $\tau \models_v \phi_1 V_{[0,d]_x} \phi_2$ *iff for every* $d_1 \in [v(x), v(x) + d]$, $\tau^{d_1} \models_{v+d_1} \phi_2$, *or there is some* $d_2 \in [v(x), d_1]$, *such that* $\tau^{d_2} \models_{v+d_2} \phi_1$;
- $\tau \models_v \phi_1 V_{[y,d]_x} \phi_2$ *iff for every* $d_1 \in [v(x) + v(y), v(x) + d]$, $\tau^{d_1} \models_{v+d_1} \phi_2$, *or there is some* $d_2 \in [v(x) + v(y), d_1]$, *such that* $\tau^{d_2} \models_{v+d_2} \phi_1$;
- $\tau \models_v \bigcirc \varphi$ *iff* $(\bar{s}^1, \bar{I}^1) \models_{v+|I_0|} \varphi$.

For a basic formula of $MITL_{[0,d]}$, we use operator "$\vee$" and "$V_{[0,d]}$" to push all negations inward until they reach atomic propositions. When mentioning the basic formulas of $MITL_{[0,d]}$ in rest of this paper, we mean the formulas of $MITL_{[0,d]}$ whose negations have been pushed inward.

Then we must define the clocks for the temporal operators in basic $MITL_{[0,d]}$ formulas. The decomposition rules is presented in Table 1 for a basic $MITL_{[0,d]}$ formula ϕ, $\Xi \in \{U_{[0,d]}, V_{[0,d]}\}$ and $\Delta \in \{\wedge, \vee\}$.

Definition 10. *Let ϕ be a basic $MITL_{[0,d]}$ formula. The set of the clocks of the temporal operators in ϕ can be defined recursively using following steps:*

1. *Let $\Phi_0 = \{\phi\}$. As long as one of the rule in Table 1 can be applied to any terms in Φ_n, then apply one to a term to obtain Φ_{n+1}. When no more rules can be applied, we get a set of sub-formulas of ϕ. In this set, each element either is a proposition, or has a temporal operator as outermost operator.*
2. *For each element whose outermost operator is a temporal operator, we define a clock x for the outermost temporal operator and an null ancestor set $AncSet_x$ for every clock.*
3. *For each element φ in Φ_{n+1}, let $\Phi_0 = \{\varphi_1, \varphi_2\}$ and repeat step 1 if its form is $\varphi_1 \Xi \varphi_2$. As a result, we will get a set similar to the one in step 1. For each element which has an outermost temporal operator, the clock of its outermost temporal operator is $y \mid_x$ if the clock of the operator Ξ is x, i.e. a clock y whose value is relative to clock x, the ancestor set of the clock $AncSet_y$ equals $\{x\} \cup AncSet_x$.*
4. *Repeat step 3 until all elements of all sets generated by these steps are propositions.*

Rewrite rules The aim of using rewrite rules is to transform a basic $MITL_{[0,d]}$ formula ϕ into normal form: $\phi = \bigvee_i CS_i.(cc_i \wedge \phi_i \wedge \bigcirc \varphi_i)$, where CS_i denotes that current clocks are set by clock setting function, cc_i are conjunctions and "ordered conjunctions" of clock conditions, ϕ_i are conjunctions of atomic propositions, and φ_i are subsequent formulas, i.e. conjunctions of $EMITL_{[0,d]}$.

While constructing timed automaton, we use triple $< CS, Now, Next >$ to denote $\phi = \bigvee_i CS_i.(cc_i \wedge \phi_i \wedge \bigcirc \varphi_i)$, where CS denotes the labels of transitions, Now includes clock conditions and propositional ϕ_i that must be satisfied in current state, and $Next$ includes subsequent formulas that will be satisfied. The data structure of Now is the same as the labels of the states of the timed automata, i.e. $Now =< D, E >$, where D is a set of clock conditions and propositions, E is an order set of clock conditions. Thereby, we must define the priorities for the clock conditions.

Definition 11. *A priority function $P : CCond(C) \times CCond(C) \rightarrow \{>\}$ is defined as follows:*

- *if $x \in C$ and $x := t, x \geq d \in CCond(C)$, $P(x := t) > P(x \geq d)$;*
- *if $x, y \in C$ and $x := t, y := t - x \in CCond(C)$, $P(y := t - x) > P(x := t)$;*

Definition 12. *Based on the sorting function o, its inverse function o^{-1} from Definition 4, we define operations $\oplus : Now \times Now \mapsto Now$ and $\ominus : Now \times Now \mapsto Now$ as follows, where $Prop \in 2^P$ is a proposition constraint subset, $CCS, \{e_1, e_2, \ldots, e_n\} \subseteq CCond(C)$:*

- $Now \oplus < Prop \cup CCS, o(\{e_1, e_2, \ldots, e_n\}) >=$
  $< Now.D \cup Prop \cup CCS, o(o^{-1}(Now.E) \cup \{e_1, e_2, \ldots, e_n\}) >;$
- $Now \ominus < Prop \cup CCS, o(\{e_1, e_2, \ldots, e_n\}) >=$
  $< Now.D \setminus (Prop \cup CCS), o(o^{-1}(Now.E) \setminus \{e_1, e_2, \ldots, e_n\}) >.$

Definition 13. *For the clock x of a temporal operator, we define an assignment set $AssSet_x = \{y := t, y := t - z \mid y, z \in AncSet_x \text{ and } z \in AncSet_y\}$.*

5.2   Algorithm of Constructing Timed Automaton

Definition 14. *If Ψ is a set of $MITL_{[0,d]}$ formulas, the normal form $NF(\Psi)$ of Ψ is computed with the following procedure. Let $P_0 = \{< \varnothing, < \{\phi\}, \varnothing >, \varnothing >\}$. As long as one of the rewrite rules in Table 2 [1] can be applied to any of the terms in $Now.D$ of P_n, then apply one to a term to obtain P_{n+1}. The normal form $NF(\Psi)$ is obtained from P_n when no more rules can be applied.*

Lemma 1. *The equivalences between the basic $MITL_{[0,d]}$ formulas and their rewritten forms hold and the value of clocks is the time when the truth values of the sub-formulas within their domains are true until now.*

---

[1] The clocks mentioned in this table is the clocks binding with its temporal operators defined in Definition 10.

Table 2. Rewrite rules

$\phi =$	Conditions	$\Phi \cup \{< CS, Now \oplus < \{\phi\}, \varnothing >, Next >\}$ reduces to
$true$		$\Phi \cup \{< CS, Now, Next >\}$
$false$		Φ
$\phi_1 \vee \phi_2$		$\Phi \cup \{< CS, Now \oplus < \{\phi_1\}, \varnothing >, Next >,$ $< CS, Now \oplus < \{\phi_2\}, \varnothing >, Next >\}$
$\phi_1 \wedge \phi_2$		$\Phi \cup \{< CS, Now \oplus < \{\phi_1, \phi_2\}, \varnothing >, Next >\}$
$\phi_1 V_{[0,d]} \phi_2$		$\Phi \cup \{< CS[x := 0], Now \oplus < \{\phi_1 V_{[x,d]} \phi_2\} >\}, \varnothing >, Next >$
$\phi_1 V_{[x,d]} \phi_2$		$\Phi \cup \{< CS, Now \oplus < \{\phi_1, \phi_2\}, < x := t >>, Next >,$ $< CS, Now \oplus < \{\phi_2\}, < x := t >>, Next \cup \{\phi_1 V_{[x,d]} \phi_2\} >,$ $< CS, Now \oplus < \{\phi_2\}, < x := t, x \geq d >>, Next >\}$
$\phi_1 V_{[0,d]_x} \phi_2$		$\Phi \cup \{< CS[y := 0], Now \oplus < \{\phi_1 V_{[y,d]_x} \phi_2\} >, \varnothing >, Next >>\}$
$\phi_1 V_{[y,d]_x} \phi_2$		$\Phi \cup \{< CS, Now \oplus < \{\phi_1, \phi_2\}, < y := t - x >>, Next >,$ $< CS, Now \ominus < \varnothing, o(AssSet_y) > \oplus < \{\phi_2\},$ $< y := t - x >>, Next \cup \{\phi_1 V_{[y,d]_x} \phi\} >, < CS, Now \oplus$ $< \{\phi_2\}, < y := t - x, y \geq d >>, Next >\}$
$\phi_1 U_{[0,d]} \phi_2$	$\phi_2 \in Now.D$	$\Phi \cup \{< CS, Now, Next >\}$
	$\phi_2 \notin Now.D$	$\Phi \cup \{< CS, Now \oplus < \{\phi_2\}, < x := t >>, Next >,$ $< CS, Now \oplus < \{\phi_1, 0 \leq t < d\}, < x := t >>,$ $Next \cup \{\phi_1 U_{[0,d]} \phi_2\} >\}$
$\phi_1 U_{[0,d]_x} \phi_2$	$\phi_2 \in Now.D$	$\Phi \cup \{< CS, Now, Next >\}$
	$\phi_2 \notin Now.D$	$\Phi \cup \{< CS, Now \oplus < \{\phi_2\}, < y := t - x >>, Next >,$ $< CS, Now \ominus < \varnothing, o(AssSet_y) > \oplus < \{\phi_1, x \leq t < x + d\},$ $< y := t - x >>, Next \cup \{\phi_1 U_{[0,d]} \phi_2\} >\}$

Definition 15. Let ϕ be a basic $MITL_{[0,d]}$ formula, P be the set of propositions that occur in ϕ. The tableau automaton A_ϕ is the finite-input timed automaton $< S, S_0, C, Q, CC, OCC, Tran, S_e >$ over 2^P, where

- C is the set of all clocks computed by Definition 10;
- $S, S_0, Tran$ and S_e can be computed by the procedure depicted in Fig. 3.
- $Q(s) = \{\phi \in 2^P \mid \forall_{p \in P} p \in Now.D \Rightarrow p \in \phi, \neg p \in Now.D \Rightarrow p \notin \phi\}$
- $CC(s) = \{\eta \in CCond(C) \mid \eta \in Now.D\}$
- $OCC(s) = o\{\eta \in CCond(C) \mid \eta \in Now.E\}$

The algorithm presented above is correct and it can be stated by the following theorem.

Theorem 1. Let ϕ be an $MITL_{[0,d]}$ formula and timed automaton A_ϕ be the corresponding tableau automaton, then for every timed state sequence τ, A_ϕ accepts τ iff $\tau \models \phi$.

Case Study We consider the CSMA/CD protocol in section 4 again. While testing, we need presuppose the max testing time, such as $10^{10} \mu s$. So above property can be rewritten as $\Box_{[0,10^{10}]}((Trans1 \wedge Trans2) \rightarrow \Diamond_{[0,60]} coll)$ in $MITL_{[0,d]}$. Using our method, we can get the tableau automaton for the above property, which consists of 18 states and 70 transitions. But the state and transition amount of the resulting automaton can be decreased to 12 and 35 ulteriorly, if we treat the sub-formula $Trans1 \wedge Trans2$ from the example of CSMA/CD protocol as an atomic formula. And what we must modify is the component of rearrangement. For clarity we only draw the smaller automaton as Fig. 4, in which the round-corner rectangles denote states, the arrowed lines denote transitions. Every state

$$S_0 := \{(Now, Next) | < Now, Next > \in NF(\phi)\};$$
$$S_{New} := \{(Now, Next) | (Now, Next) \in S_0\};$$
$$S := \varnothing, Tran := \varnothing;$$
while $S_{New} \neq \varnothing$ do
{
    Let $(Now, Next) \in S_{New}$;
    $S_{New} := S_{New} \setminus \{(Now, Next)\};$
    $S := S \cup \{(Now, Next)\};$
    for every $(Now', Next') \in NF(Next)$ do
    {
        if $(Now', Next') = (\varnothing, \varnothing, \varnothing)$ then
            $S_e := S_e \cup (Now, Next);$
        $Tran := Tran \cup \{((Now, Next), (Now', Next'))\};$
        if $(Now', Next') \notin S$ then $S := S \cup \{(Now', Next')\};$
    }
}

Fig. 3. Algorithm for constructing the states and transitions of the tableau automaton

is divided into two parts, the upper of which denotes $Now.D$, and the lower of which denotes $Now.E$. In order to simplifying the representation, only the formulas in Now have been depicted. The initial extended states are represented by an arrow not originating form any state, and the finite states are denoted by a filled circle inside a slightly larger unfilled circle put in the lower part of the states.

6 Conclusions and Future Work

This paper presents a new method that can automatically generate run-time test oracles for DRTS. Test oracles can check whether a distributed real-time system's traces are correct, based on real-time specifications written in $MITL_{[0,d]}$ formulas. If the test oracles can accept the timed event sequences, we can say that the runs are correct, i.e. the system runs correctly. Otherwise, if all current states can't accept any subsequence timed events that violate state or time constraints, or the tail of some trace does not arrive at final state, we say the system has some errors or some real-time specifications errors exist.

Compared with [9], whose computation is done at each end of cycles, our method does computation only if necessary (i.e. when system states change) so as to save precious computing time. Assertions inserted into the different parts of DRTS not only can obtain the inner events of DRTS, send out the values of states only when they change, but also can get the precise occurrence time of events.

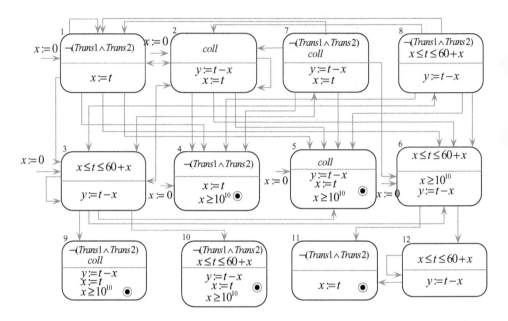

Fig. 4. The Optimized tableau automata of $\Box_{[0,10^{10}]}((Trans1 \wedge Trans2) \rightarrow \Diamond_{[0,60]} coll)$

The ongoing works include:

1. The method of automatic test oracles generating needs to be optimized in order to reduce the complexity of tableau automata and checking costs. This can be done by optimizing rewrite rules and timed automata.

2. The real-time specifications used in this paper is the restrict version of MITL, $MITL_{[0,d]}$, that limits the ability of logic expression for properties of DRTS. For example, $\Box_{[0,100]}(\Diamond_{[10,20]}p)$ can not be transformed into a test oracle. So how to extend the detection capability of test oracles is the main problem of future work.

3. DRTS are running on networked environments, so we must consider the delay of network transmission while acquiring the system traces. When the events and their timestamps reach the test oracle, there must be a special part to arrange them so that the whole timed sequence is reordered by time and are ϕ-fine.

4. We must evaluate the computing costs of assertions inserted into the DRTS so as to assure that assertions will not influence the normal running of DRTS. The computing costs of assertions are decided by the amount and the data structures of assertions. And the next works must include it.

5. Finally, more experiments in real environments are required.

References

[1] (http://www.ii.uj.edu.pl/progroz/dishard/home.html)   199
[2] Baresi, L., Young, M.: Test Oracles. Technical Report, CIS-TR01-02, Dept. of Computer and Information Science, Univ. of Oregon (Aug.2001)   199
[3] J. A.Stankovic: Misconceptions about real-time computing - a serious problem for next generation systems, IEEE Computer (1998)   200
[4] Geilen, M.: Formal Techniques for Verification of Complex Real-Time Systems. PhD thesis, Eindhoven University of Technology (2002)   200
[5] Dillon, L., Yu, Q.: Oracles for checking temporal properties of concurrent systems. In: Proceedings of the ACM SIGSOFT '94 Symposium on the Foundations of Software Engineering. (1994)   200
[6] Dillon, L., Ramakrishna, Y.: Generating oracles from your favorite temporal logic specifications. In: Proceedings of the Fourth ACM SIGSOFT Symposium on the Foundations of Software Engineering. (1996)   200
[7] Geilen, M.: On the construction of monitors for temporal logic properties. In: K. Havelund and G. Rosu, editors, Proceedings of RV'01 - FirstWorkshop on Runtime Verification. Satellite Workshop of CAV'01, Electronic Notes in Theoretical Computer Science 55(2), Amsterdam, 2001. Elsevier Science, Paris, France (2001)   200
[8] Drusinsky, D.: The temporal rover and the atg rover. In: SPIN Model Checking and Software Verification, Proc, 7th SPIN Workshop, 1885 of Springer-Verlag Lecture Notes in Computer Science, Springer Verlag, Stanford, California (2000)   200
[9] Håkansson, J.: Automated generation of test scripts from temporal logic specification. Master's thesis, Uppsala University (2000)   201, 210
[10] R. Alur, T. F., Henzinger, T.: The benefits of relaxing punctuality. Journal of the ACM **43** (January 1996) 116–146   201, 202, 205
[11] Alur, R.: Techniques of Automatic Verification of Real-Time Systems. PhD thesis, Stanford University (1991)   202
[12] IEEE: ANSI/IEEE 802.3, ISO/DIS 8802/3. IEEE Computer Society Press (1985)   204
[13] Tanenbaum, A. S.: Computer Networks. Prentice-Hall, Englewood Cliffs, second edition (1989)   204

Formal Composition of Distributed Scenarios

Aziz Salah[1], Rabeb Mizouni[2], Rachida Dssouli[3], and Benoît Parreaux[4]

[1] Department of C.S., University of Quebec at Montreal
salah.aziz@uqam.ca
[2] Electrical & Computer Engineering, Concordia University
mizouni@ece.concordia.ca
[3] Institute For Information System Engineering, Concordia University
dssouli@ciise.concordia.ca
[4] France Telecom R&D, Lannion, France
benoit.parreaux@rd.francetelecom.com

Abstract. Eliciting, modeling, and analyzing the requirements are the main challenges to face up when you want to produce a formal specification for distributed systems. The distribution and the race conditions between events make it difficult to include all the possible scenario combinations and thus to get a complete specification. Most research about formal methods dealt with languages and neglected the process of how getting a formal specification. This paper describes a scenario-based process to synthesize a formal specification in the case of a distributed system. The requirements are represented by a set of use cases where each one is composed of a collection of distributed scenarios. The architectural assumptions about the communication between the objects of the distributed system imply some completions and reorganizations in the use cases. Then, the latter are composed into a global finite state machine (FSM) from which we derive a communicating FSM per object in the distributed system.

Keywords: Use case, Scenario-based approach, Scenario composition, Formal specification, Distributed systems, FSM

1 Introduction

The computer science community agrees that the requirement elicitation and analysis is a crucial step in the development process. Nevertheless, most research about formal methods dealt with languages and neglected the process of how getting a formal specification. Consequently, there is gap that makes difficult moving from requirements towards a formal specification. Developers avoid this phase by passing directly from informal requirements to implementation. Unspecified reception, service denial, and deadlock are common bugs that may have uncontrolled consequences in the case of distributed systems. Detecting such bugs during the validation stage becomes difficult, reducing thus the reliability of the system and increasing the development costs.

Scenario approaches have been emerged to fill the gap and facilitate the construction of a formal specification by promoting a "Divide and Conquer" strategy. A distributed scenario is a sequence of actions representing an execution trace

D. de Frutos-Escrig and M. Núñez (Eds.): FORTE 2004, LNCS 3235, pp. 213-228, 2004.
© IFIP International Federation for Information Processing 2004

describing a partial behavior, and providing a system level functionality. The actions represent concurrent interactions between different system objects. The different scenarios have to be composed in order to provide a formal specification of the system.

The requirements are widely represented by use cases where each one depicts a collection of scenarios. A scenario can be described by a message sequence chart (MSC), which emphasizes the interactions among objects. Our objective is to synthesize finite state machines (FSMs) from a set of use cases. Constructing communicating FSMs from MSCs is a very hard problem because MSCs may represent incomplete and inconsistent requirements. Combinatorial complexity makes it difficult to express MSCs for all of the possible scenario combination in the system behavior. Furthermore, systems may have many infinite traces, which cannot be easily captured by having only the MSC model. As a result, during the synthesis of FSMs, the analyst uses ad hoc methods based on his creativity and his expertness to fill the gaps.

MSCs and FSMs share some information, but emphasize two different views of the system behavior. First, MSCs represent the specification that the system should respect while FSMs are a model of the specification. Second, an MSC describes a story in which only some objects participate. Hence, it provides an inter-object view which makes it suitable for test and validation activities, but not for the implementation. In contrast, an FSM shows an intra-objects view where all the stories are about the same object [7] and may reflect their implementation.

Assuming that the system is composed of a set of objects, we aim at automating the synthesis of FSMs from use cases. We propose a two-phase method. The first phase consists of generating MSCs from use cases for completing them with missing scenarios. The intended communicating FSMs should allow infinite runs but use cases describe only finite traces about the behavior. Therefore, the second phase consists of enriching the use cases with some information that captures loops in the behavior and allows a system state characterization used for the automatic synthesis of a communicating FSM per object.

The paper is structured as follows: in Section 2, we give an overview of the notation we are using. Section 3 presents the formalization of use cases and scenarios using the tree presentation as well as the derivation of their MSCs. In Section 4 and 5 respectively, we describe the approach we are proposing for decorating use cases and synthesizing the communicating FSMs. Discussions on some related work are given in Section 6. Finally, Section 7 closes the paper with conclusions and future work.

2   Preliminaries, Definitions and Formal Semantics

Let $\Omega = \{O_1, O_2, ..., O_n\}$ be the set of objects in the targeted distributed system, *Env* its environment, and $A_{O_i} = (S_{O_i}, S_{O_i init}, T_{O_i})$ the FSM of object $O_i \in \Omega$. S_{O_i} is the set of states of O_i, $S_{O_i init}$ is the set of initial states of O_i, and $T_{O_i} \subset S_{O_i} \times \Sigma_{O_i} \times S_{O_i}$ is the set of transitions where Σ_{O_i} is set of labels in the form (O_i, O_j, m) or (O_j, O_i, m). The FSM has a powerful capability of abstraction needed during first stages of the development process.

In this work, the FSMs of objects are assumed to be communicating FSMs according to the semantics of input/output automata defined in [12]. Each FSM object is autonomous and can communicate with other FSMs by means of message exchange. When an FSM object sends a message to another FSM, the latter is assumed to be ready to receive this message; otherwise there is an unspecified reception fault. The communication between FSMs is modeled by their parallel composition FSM denoted by $\Pi A_{O_i}=(S,S_{init},T)$. It is defined as the connected components of the composition FSM of $A_{O_1},A_{O_2},\ldots$ and A_{O_n}, which contains a state from S_{init}, where $S=S_1\times S_2\times\ldots\times S_n$, and $S_{init}=S_{O_1 init}\times S_{O_2 init}\times\ldots\times S_{O_n init}$. $T\subset S\times\Sigma\times S$ is the set of transitions of ΠA_{O_i} defined by the following rules:

- Rule 1: $(s_i,a,s_i')\in T_{O_i}$ _and_ $(a=(O,O_i.m)$ _or_ $a=(O_i,O.m))$ _and_ $O \in \{O_i, Env\}$ _**implies**_ $((s_1,..,s_{i-1},s_i,s_{i+1}..,s_n),a, (s_1,..,s_{i-1},s_i', s_{i+1},..,s_n)) \in T$
- Rule 2: _let_ $O_i,O_j \in\Omega$ _and_ $i<j$
  $(s_i,a,s_i')\in T_{Oi}$ _and_ $(s_j,a,s_j')\in T_{Oj}$ _and_ $(a=(O_i,O_j.m)$ _or_ $a=(O_i,O_j.m))$ _**implies**_ $((s_1,..,s_i,..,s_j, ..,s_n),a, (s_1,..,s_i',..,s_j',..,s_n)) \in T$

Rule 1 treats internal actions or communication with the environment while Rule2 treats communication among two different objects O_i and O_j.

Message sequence charts (MSCs) [9] are a commonly used visual representation of scenarios expressing the interactions among objects, components or processes. An MSC focuses on message exchange and shows a partial order of events. A message represents an interaction between two objects, a sender and a receiver. MSCs may display an order of events which is not always the only case supported by the implementation of MSCs. The formalization of MSCs allows the definition of the real partial order according to particular architectural communication assumptions. The formalization of MSC was traited by many reseachers [3,4], and we propose a similar approach.

We formalize an MSC as a structure $(I, SE, RE, r, L, p, <_D , <_m)$ where

- $I \subset \Omega\cup\{Env\}$ _is a set of objects_
- _SE is the set of sending events and RE the set of receiving events. We denote by SE_O (respectively RE_O) the set of sending events (respectively the set of receiving events) in object O_
- $r : SE \rightarrow RE$ _maps a sending event to its receiving event. r is a bijection._
- _L is a set of labels of the messages in the MSC_
- $p : SE\cup RE\rightarrow I$ _maps a sending event or receiving event to an object from I_
- $<_D= \cup_{O\in I} <_O$ _where_ $<_O \subset SE_O\cup RE_O \times SE_O\cup RE_O$ _is a total order between the local events in object O according to the visual order as displayed in the MSC._
- $<_m = \{(s, r(s)) \mid s \in SE\}$ _is an ordering relation which means that a message cannot be received before it is sent._

The previous definition is very general and does not include any assumption about the communication architecture in the system. As the behavior described by MSCs will be translated into a set of communicating FSMs, their respective semantics should be compatible. Since the communication between FSMs, as defined in this paper, has no buffering facility, we assume that the FIFO order is preserved when an object receives two or more messages from the same object. Thus, the events should fulfill the partial ordering relation $<_{FIFO} = \{(r(s),r(s')) \mid (s,s') \in <_D$ and $p(s)=p(s')$ and $p(r(s))=p(r(s'))$ and $s \in SE$ and $s' \in SE \}$. Furthermore, FSMs are modeling autonomous objects. Consequently, an object has the control over its sending events. Hence, its scheduling of sending events is granted according to the visual order $<_D$. We also grant the local visual order between a receiving event and the next sending events in an object. Those facts are expressed by the following control ordering relation: $<_C = \{(e,s) \mid e \in SE \cup RE, s \in SE$ and $(e,s) \in <_O$ and $O \in I\}$. Finally, the interpretation of an MSC is given by the partial order relation $<$ defined as the transitive closure of the combination of the three partial ordering $<_C$, $<_m$ and $<_{FIFO}$:

$$< = (<_C \cup <_m \cup <_{FIFO})^*$$

3   Formalization of Use Cases and Scenarios

A use case is used to describe a distributed functionality of the system as seen by actors (external users). The analyst usually builds use case diagrams, which emphasize the relationships between use cases. Then, she or he provides a textual description of the possible scenarios of each use case. This informal description is hard to be used in automatic processing of scenarios. Consequently, we conceived a formal model, which describes a use case by a tree of actions. The analyst constructs the tree of a use case by using either a depth-first or a breadth-first strategy in order to get a complete description according to the current requirements. As the use case tree paths are the scenarios of running the use case, the depth-first strategy is more convenient from a user point of view. However, the breath-first strategy is suitable to check that all of the possible scenarios have already been included in the use case tree since after each action all the possible afterward actions are checked. Actions (also called messages) are labels like $(O_i, O_j.m)$ where O_i and O_j are objects of the system. $(O_i, O_j.m)$ means that message m is sent from O_i to O_j.

We will be using a basic telephone system to illustrate our work. Fig. 1 shows use case "Make a call" that describes the behavior of the system when a *user A* calls a *user B*. We will assume that Ω for the telephone system is composed of the following objects: *A*, *B* and a switch S. Let's now present the formal definition of our use case model:

Definition: A use case Γ is a tree $\Gamma=<Id,M,M_{start},Parent>$ where:

-     $\Gamma.Id$ is the id of the use case,
-     $\Gamma.M \subset (\Omega \cup \{Env\}) \times (\Omega \cup \{Env\}.Label)$ *is the set of messages in the form* $(O,O'.m)$,
-     $\Gamma.M_{start} \subset \Gamma.M$ *is the set of starting messages,*
-     $\Gamma.Parent$ *is a function that associates to a message the index of its parent message. Function* $\Gamma.Parent$ *is not defined for starting messages.*

The scenarios of a use case are complete paths starting from a *start message* and ending at one of the tree leaves. From each use case scenario, an MSC is generated. The generation of MSCs is only based on the syntax of messages and their order in the use case tree paths. The syntax of message label identifies the sender and the receiver objects. The use case tree of Fig.1 contains three scenarios. We have drawn in Fig. 2 the MSCs generated from use case "Make a call".

MSCs are less intuitive than expected. Their visual order does not always represent all their possible executions as only a partial order of events is garanted according to a particular adopted semantics of MSCs. For this reason, researchers defined the notion of MSC linearizations [2] [15] to represent the possible executions of an MSC.

In this work, the linearization of an MSC is a total order relation which is consistent with its partial order relation <. If an MSC has many linearizations, some of them may not be included in the use case tree since they may have escaped to the user requirements. Thus, the partial order of an MSC helps the analyst to detect and possibly complete the use case tree by adding those absent linearizations after the user validation as illustrated in Fig. 3. If the user refuted one of the linearizations of an MSC, it means that the use case tree should be modified so that its generated MSCs accept no more the refuted linearization.

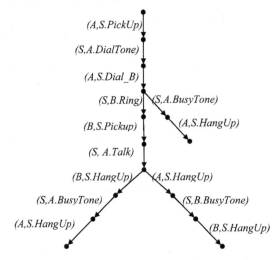

Fig. 1. The tree of use case "Make a call"

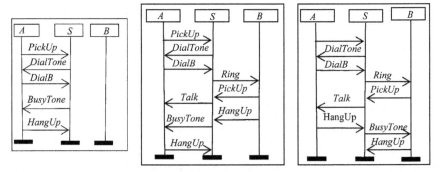

Fig. 2. The MSCs generated from the use case in Fig. 1

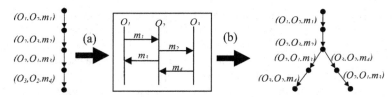

Fig. 3. Use case completion by adding absent linearizations; step (a): the MSC generation; step (b): adding a missing linearization to the use case

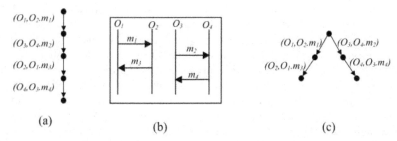

Fig. 4. Use case reorganization process: (a) Original use case tree. (b) Its generated MSC. (c) The proposed reorganized use case tree

The user may sometimes be confused and does not realize that his use case is composed of a combination of independent traces. To formally define what independent traces means, let first define the set of minimum event *Min* of an MSC:

$$Min=\{e \in SE \mid \forall e' \in SE \cup RE . (e',e) \notin <\}$$

Min denotes the set of sending events where each one may initiate a sequence of events, called independent trace. If *Min* is not a singleton, the partial order of an MSC may be used to find out independent traces.

If the generated MSCs of a use case include many independent traces as shown in Fig.4 (b), the computation of the set *Min* allows a reorganization of the use case so that the causality relationship between the independent traces becomes explicit as illustrated in Fig.4 (c). However, if the user refuted the proposed reorganization of the use case, it may mean that there are parts of the use case that are missing and should establish the causality relationship he intended.

4   Decorating Use Cases with a State Characterization

The compatibility of use cases and their generated MSCs is reached when both of them accept the same scenarios. Our goal is to synthesize FSMs from use cases. As known, it is possible to generate FSMs from a set of traces. However, the behavior provided by use cases is partial since they don't include infinite traces or repetitive behaviors. High-level MSCs (HMSCs) are MSC-graphs where each node is an MSC [9]. They provide a mean to define how MSCs can be combined and they can express infinite traces of the system behavior. However, HMSCs specify an explicit combination of MSCs, available only in an advanced stage during system requirement analysis. Therefore, we adopted an alternative strategy that consists of decorating use cases with a state characterization. The latter allows not only capturing infinite traces, but also recognizing shared states in different scenarios and thus determining their relationships as well as the relationship between their respective use cases.

Decorating use cases gives the analysts the opportunity to add their interpretations regarding the state of the system when an action is performed. It consists of specifying for each message (action) of the use case partial pre and partial post conditions expressed by state variable constraints. Those conditions are qualified to be partial because they have to be completed by the fact that this action takes place before and after specific actions in the use case. State variables are defined by the analyst and their values represent the state of the system. As the latter is composed of a set of objects, the state of the system is also composed of the states of its objects. Subsequently, the state of an object can be derived from the global system state.

In practice, state variables have symbolic names. However, we will use here a vector-based notation because it is more convenient to present the general case. The state of the system is represented by a state vector $V=(v_1,v_2,..,v_k)$ where v_i is the *value* of state variable $V[i]$ and k is the number of state variables. We write $dom(V[i])$ the finite domain of possible values of state variable $V[i]$. A state variable may also be instantiated with a special value, denoted by *nil*, which means that its current value is not fixed yet in that state. Hence, the space of state vectors is the product set $DOM=(dom(V[1])\cup\{nil\})\times(dom(V[2])\cup\{nil\})\times... \times(dom(V[k])\cup\{nil\})$.

Table 1. Decoration of use case "*Make a call*". The state vector is composed of the values of four variables *SigA*, *StaA*, *SigB* and *StaB*. *SigA* describes signals of *terminal A, and Dom(SigA)={N,DT,D,BT,T}* where *N* means *no signal*, *DT dial tone signal*, *D* dialing *signal*, *BT busy tone signal* and *T talking signal*. *StaA* describes the status of *terminal A and Dom(StaA)={I,B}* where *B* stands for *busy* and *I* for *idle*. Variables *SigB* and *StaB* describe respectively the signals and the status of *terminal B. Dom(SigB)={N,BT,R,T}* where R stands for ring signal and the other values are the same like in *Dom(SigA). Dom(StaB)={B,I}*. We have also decided that *EP* is set to *False* for all messages in this use case tree

Index (msg)	Parent (msg)	msg	ppre(msg)	ppost(msg)
0	-	(A,S.PickUp)	SigA=N and StaA=I and SigB=nil and StaB=nil	StaA'=B
1	0	(S,A.DialTone)	True	SigA'=DT
2	1	(A,S.DialB)	True	SigA'=D
3	2	(S,A.BusyTone)	StaB=B	SigA'=BT
4	3	(A,S.HangUp)	True	SigA'=N and StaA'=I and SigB'=nil and StaB'=nil
5	2	(S,B.Ring)	SigB=N and StaB=I	SigB'=R and StaB'=B
6	5	(B,S.PickUp)	True	SigB'=T
7	6	(S,A.Talk)	True	SigA'=T
8	7	(B,S.HangUp)	True	SigB'=nil and StaB'=nil
9	8	(S,A.BusyTone)	True	SigA'=BT
10	9	(A,S.HangUp)	True	SigA'=N and StaA'=I
11	7	(A,S.HangUp)	True	SigA'=N and StaA'=I
12	11	(S,B.BusyTone)	True	SigB'=BT
13	12	(B,S.HangUp)	True	SigB'=nil and StaB'=nil

The decoration of a use case consists of specifying for each message three declarative attributes: a partial pre-condition, a partial post-condition, and an extension point. The partial pre and post-conditions of a message m are denoted by $ppre(m)$ and $ppost(m)$ respectively. The state variables must fulfill the constraints $ppre(m)$ before sending message m and $ppost(m)$ after its reception. $ppre(m)$ is a conjunction of elementary constraints in the form $(V[i]=v)$ where v is a constant of $dom(V[i])$. In contrast, $ppost(m)$ constraints the relation between the vector state V before m and V' the state after m. Thus, $ppost(m)$ is a conjunction where elementary constraints are either $(V'[i]=v)$, $V'[i]= V[i]$ op $v)$, or $(V'[i]= V[I])$, and where op is an operator defined on the variables domain.

By default, a non-instantiated variable will be initially set to *nil*. Afterwards, we adopt the STRIPS [5] strategy to deal with the frame problem and assume all that is not explicitly changed by an action remains unchanged. Furthermore, whenever we have a conjunction[1] in the form $(V[i]=v$ and $V[i]=nil)$ the latter is unified to $(V[i]=v)$. This unification is needed later on in the computation of the canonical form of the use case.

Finally, the third element of the decoration is the extension point. Since the analyst has to compose many use cases to construct the overall system behavior model, we associate to each message m a predicate denoted by $EP(m)$ which stands for extension point, similar to use case *extension point* in UML [16]. EP provides to the analyst a mean by which she or he can control how parts of FSMs coming from different use cases can be connected. By default, for a message m that it is not a leaf, the value of $EP(m)$ is *"False"* in order to prevent overlapping use case traces. In contrast, the analyst decides which value should be assigned to predicate EP for other messages. If the EP is "*True*", it means that the execution of the system continues in the current use case. Otherwise, it indicates that the system may exit the current use case and continues its execution in another one. In this case, it represents the concatenation of use case traces. The decoration use case "Make a call" is presented in Table 1.

5   Synthesis of Communicating FSMs

Synthesizing communicating FSMs from decorated use case trees takes three steps: (1) transforming use cases into a canonical form, (2) synthesizing a global finite state machine (GFSM) from the canonical form of all use cases, (3) deriving from the GFSM a communicating FSM for each object in the system.

Step (1): Canonical Representation of Use Case Trees

The requirements of a system are composed of a number of use cases. Their overall behavior can be implemented by synthesizing communicating FSMs. For this end, we need a representation of use cases that not only captures their behavior, but also facilitates their merge into a global state model. We adopt thus a canonical representation of use cases in the form of a flat set of m-rules. An m-rule is an atomic

---

[1]   This conjunction differs from the ordinary logical AND since it provides a rewriting rule when a formula contains "$V[i]=nil$".

message rule, which describes the states of the system before a message is sent and after it is received. Formally, an m-rule is a 3-tuple *mr=(LHS,RHS,lab)* where *mr.LHS* is the left hand side of the rule and represents the pre-condition part, *mr.RHS* is the right hand side which is the post-condition part, and *mr.lab* is the message synchronization label of the m-rule. We recall that *mr.lab* is in the form *(Oi,Oj.m)*.

In order to tag the states and the transitions in the targeted FSMs with the use case id from which they come, we extend the set of state variables with a new variable called *uc*. Tagging the FSMs is not only used for traceability reasons, but also to implement information given by predicate *EP* related to the extension points of a use case. From now and on, the state vector is composed of all state variable values and the value of the recently introduced variable *uc*. The domain of variable *uc* is the set of use case ids plus a special value denoted by *noUc* that tags the state vectors that may be shared by a certain number of use cases.

```
Input      <Γ,pre,post,EP> where Γ=<Id,M,M_init,Parent>
is a decorated tree with ppre, ppost, and EP
Output     <R,R_init>
(1)  R:=∅;  R_init:=∅
(2)  For each msg ∈ Γ.M do
(3)           mr.lab:=msg
(4)           If msg∈ Γ.M_init then
(5)             mr.LHS:= ( ppre(msg) and  uc= noUc)
(6)           Else mr.LHS:=(ppre(msg)and
              ppost(parent(msg)
                      and uc=Γ.Id )
(7)           For each msg'∈ Γ.M | msg=parent(msg') do
(8)            If EP(msg)=False then
(9)               mr.RHS:= ( ppost(msg) and ppre(msg')
                     and  uc=Γ.Id )
(10)           Else mr.RHS:= (ppost(msg) and ppre(msg')
                     and uc=noUc)
(11)           R:=R∪{mr} /*mr is added to R unless
                      mr∉R*/
(12)          If msg ∈ Γ.M_init then R_init:=R_init∪{mr}
(13)         Done
(14) Done
```

Fig. 5. Computing the canonical form of a use case

We define the canonical representation of a use case as a pair of m-rule sets denoted by *<R,R_start>* and derived from the use case. The algorithm at Fig.5 describes how *<R,R_start>* is computed from a use case. As shown in lines (8) to (11) in this algorithm, the same message may be duplicated into several m-rules such that each one would have an *RHS* that conforms the pre-condition in one of its next messages in the use case. Each extracted m-rule is tagged with the use case id by constraining its *LHS* and *LRS* with either the constraint *(uc=Γ.Id)* or the constraint *(uc=noUc)* according to the value of the predicate *EP* in its message. Hence, state vectors satisfying *(uc=Γ.Id)* are specific to use case *Γ*. In contrast, state vectors where we have *(uc=noUc)* shared by the use cases where the other state vector components coincide. Consequently, use cases having such state vectors may have their respective FSMs connected to each other by those shared state vectors. A conflict is reported to the designer whenever there is any m-rule from a use case that has false in either its *LHS* or *RHS* constraints.

Step (2): Synthesizing a Global Finite State Machine from Decorated Use Case Trees

The global finite state machine (GFSM) is an FSM constructed from all use cases. Assuming that we have a communicating FSM for each object, the GFSM should represent the FSM of their parallel composition. The GFSM accepts at least all the complete paths of the use case trees.

In practice, we directly derive the GFSM of a use case from its canonical representation. Let $<S, S_{init}, T>$ be the GFSM of a use case for which the canonical representation is $<R, R_{init}>$. Let *[r.LHS]* be the set of state vectors which verify the constraint *r.LHS* and *[r.RHS]* the set of pairs of state vectors that verify the constraint *r.RHS*. We define the GFSM $<S, S_{init}, T>$ by the following:

$$T = \{(V, l, V') \mid \exists r \in R . V \in [r.LHS]$$
$$\text{and } (V, V') \in [r.RHS] \text{ and } l = r.lab\}$$
$$S = \{V \in DOM \mid (V, \_, \_) \in T \quad \text{or} \quad (\_, \_, V) \in T\}$$
$$S_{init} = \bigcup_{r \in R_{start}} [r.LHS]$$

S is the set of states of the GFSM and composed of state vectors, which satisfy either the *LHS* or the *RHS* of an m-rule. *T* is the set of transitions. Each one comes from an m-rule. We point out that the GFSM can be non deterministic. The GFSM of use case "Make a call" is drawn in Fig.6, and its state vectors are described in Table 2.

We have so far treated the construction of the GFSM of one use case. The generalization to the case of two or more use cases consists of synthesizing the GFSM derived from the union of those use cases canonical representation. We define the union of two canonical representations $<R, R_{init}>$ and $<R', R_{init}'>$ as $<R \cup R', R_{init} \cup R_{init}'>$.

Table 2. State vectors of GFSM of use case "Make a call"

	1	2	3	4	5	6	7	8	9	10	11	12
SigA	*N*	*N*	*DT*	*D*	*BT*	*D*	*D*	*D*	*T*	*T*	*N*	*N*
StaA	*I*	*B*	*B*	*B*	*B*	*B*	*B*	*B*	*B*	*B*	*I*	*I*
SigB	*nil*	*nil*	*nil*	*nil*	*nil*	*N*	*R*	*T*	*T*	*Nil*	*T*	*BT*
StatB	*nil*	*nil*	*nil*	*B*	*B*	*I*	*B*	*B*	*B*	*Nil*	*B*	*B*
uc	*noUc*	*1*	*1*	*1*	*1*	*1*	*1*	*1*	*1*	*1*	*1*	*1*

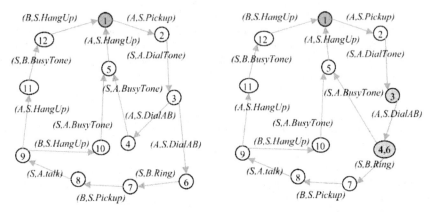

Fig. 6. GFSM of use case "Make a call"   **Fig. 7.** DGFSM of use case "Make a call"

```
Inputs:
        - DGFSM <S,S_init,T>, { S_init is a singleton }
        - O an object in Ω
Output:
        -<S_O,S_Oinit, T_O>, the FSM of object O

T_O:=∅; S_O:=∅; S_Oinit:=∅
/*Clustering states */
For each (V,(O_i,O_j.m),V') in T do
        If (O_i≠O and O_j≠O) then
            S_O:=Cluster(V,V',S_O)
        Else
            S_O:=Cluster(V,V,S_O)
            S_O:=Cluster(V',V',S_O)
        fi
done
T_O:={(C,msg,C') | (V,msg,V') ∈ T and V∈C
                    and V'∈C'}
S_Oinit:= {C | C∈S_O and ∃ V∈S_init . V∈C}
Return(S_O,S_Oinit,T_O)

Where  Cluster(V,V',CS):
        If (∃ CE ∈ CS such that V∈ CE ) then C:=CE
        Else C:= ∅
        If (∃ CE' ∈ CS' such that V'∈ CE' ) then C':=CE'
        Else C:= ∅
        Return(CS\{C,C'}∪{C∪C'∪{V,V'}})
```

Fig. 8. Construction of the FSM of an Object

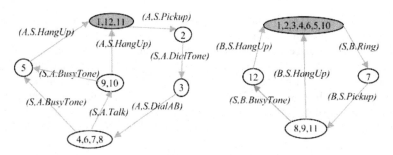

Fig. 9. The FSM of Terminal A (left side) and the FSM of the Terminal B (right side)

Step (3): Deriving Communicating FSM for Each Object

The derivation of an FSM for an object consists of clustering some states and removing some transitions from the deterministic FSM (DGFSM) which correspond to the GSFM of all use cases. The DGFSM can be obtained from the GFSM by using the algorithm given in [1]. We assume that the state of an object is supposed unchanged if no action occurs in that object according to the GFSM. Consequently, the FSM states of an object O are obtained by clustering into the same state all the states of the GFSM that are connected with a transition in which object O does not participate. The transitions of the FSM of an object O are only those transitions of the GFSM representing messages or actions in which the object O participates. This algorithm is presented in Fig.8. The FSM of an object implements all the parts of use cases in which that object participates. Consequently, the FSM of an object implements the object behavior.

We have constructed from the DGFSM (c.f. Fig.7) the FSMs of objects "*Terminal A*", "*Terminal B*", and "*Switch*". The FSM of object "*Switch S*" resulting from that algorithm is exactly the entire FSM in Fig.7. However, The FSMs of objects "*Terminal A*" and "*Terminal B*" respectively are drawn in Fig.9.

The FSM of an object represents its behavior as described by the input decorated use cases and it is not error free. The FSMs can be inspected for some patterns and may reflect some errors. For example, the states in the FSM of an object should not have any self-loop transition. The latter shows that the object accomplishes an action, but its state does not change, a contradictory fact to use case decoration assumptions. With the use case id in the state vector we can trace back exactly where the analyst should intervene to correct the anomaly.

6   Related Work and Discussion

Researchers have intensively investigated the transformation of scenarios into transition-based system model during the last ten years. To deal with these topics, the key idea is how to identify states at the scenario level such that those states can be recognized in different scenarios and then integrated in the target global model. There are two kinds of state characterization: trace-based [8,10,11,13], and variable (or label) state-based characterization [17,18,19]. In this paper we adopted the second approach to identify the states of the system.

Harel et al. [8] tackled the problem of synthesizing statecharts from LSCs (Live sequence charts), an extended form of MSCs which support liveness by specifying universal and existential scenarios. Their approach consists of synthesizing global automaton with accepting states from LSCs using trace-based state characterization. The global automaton can be decomposed into an automaton per object. The latter constitutes the overall statechart. Since we focus on first stages of requirement analysis, we believe that MSCs are easier to use with decoration and to validate. Moreover, practicing decoration is not compatible with LSCs because it may threaten their notion of universal scenarios.

The closest approaches, in terms of state characterization, to our are [17,18,20]. In the first one, Whittle et al. [20] captured domain information by specifying for each message type a pre and a post-condition once for all. Contrarily to what we propose, sequence diagrams SDs (a variant of MSCs) are transformed into an FSM per object and per SD using a state-variable unification and propagation procedure. However, the state unification definition does not consider the causality relation between the unified states. The FSMs of an object are then merged into a single FSM based on defined state similarities. The authors introduced hierarchy into FSMs based on state variable ordering, class diagrams and generalization of transitions. Moreover, message passing is assumed to be hand shacking. Thus, the SDs would have only a single linearization.

The work presented in [17,18] shows techniques for synthesizing timed automata from scenarios with respect to time constraints. Timed automata allow the description of the behavior of real time reactive systems. The scenarios can be seen as an enriched form of MSCs. The state characterization is very similar to the one we have presented in this paper. In contrast, the state vectors as defined in this paper are global, so they capture simultaneously the states of all objects. Giese [6] presented too an approach towards the synthesis of parametric timed automata from scenarios. Un-timed scenario are first derived according to existing approach like the one of Uchitel et al. [19], then the timing constraints are added in an incremental manner as time boundaries. The approach detects all the timing conflicts that can occur when integrating different scenarios, and hence can be adjusted. Contrarily to the approach in [18], Giese is synthesizing more than one automaton in the same time.

In most cases, the composition of scenarios ends up with the creation of unexpected implied scenarios. The latter could stress incompleteness in the specification so it is useful to add them to the use case, or they express undesired behaviors that have to be removed from the targeted model. Many researchers have tackled the problem of detection and elimination of implied scenarios [2,13,14,19]. Alur et al. [2] have developed an algorithm to transform a set of MSCs into communicating state machines. Their approach has the potential of detecting all the implied scenarios from a set of MSCs. However, they consider only the case of finite traces. Uchitel *et al* [19] added the HMSCs to the specification so that they introduce the infinite execution aspects. Their approach consists of first constructing the labeled transition system of each object after what they compose them to obtain the overall implementation of the system. Our approach, however, uses the concept of decoration to detect loops and hence introducing the infinite behavior aspect in the specification.

An important issue is whether or not all implied scenario have to be eliminated. Some researchers make the choice to produce a specification that is the closest possible to the original use cases. Thus, they conduct their approaches in such a way they detect implied scenarios and eliminate them [14,19]. Such decision has the advantage to be automatic. However, others [13] make the choice to return back to the user to accept or refute a detected implied behavior. The advantage here is the enhancement done to the original use case. We opted for the second alternative because we believe it has the potential to complete the system behavior.

Our approach differs substantially from the earlier presented work by the following points. We introduced an intermediate level of granularity, which is the level of use cases. Use cases themselves include a finer level of granularity represented by scenarios.

Furthermore, from the described behavior in the user case and using its generated MSCs, we detect the other unexpected scenarios due to race conditions in a distributed system. Those implied scenarios are detected by enumerating all the linearizations of the MSCs the use case does not accept. This procedure offers the opportunity to remove in an early stage the undesired behaviors and allows the user to complete his current use case. In addition, the decoration of a use case by state characterization is easier than the decoration of an isolated MSC because a use case provides a broader view that shows the relationships between its scenarios. Moreover, a message which belongs to several scenarios will be decorated only once in the use case.

Our approach distinguishes between two classes of implied scenarios: the intra-use case implied scenarios and the inter-use case implied scenarios. We define the former as a trace that the GFSM of a use case accepts but not its tree. This trace is the direct result of the use case decoration for which the role is to make possible such traces. The use case decoration configures the set of accepted traces to fit the user expectations. An inter-use-case implied scenario could be defined as a trace, which cannot be completed to correspond to a concatenation of complete path from different use cases. By construction, we can claim that there are no such implied scenarios in the GFSM of the system because of tagging private states in the use cases with their respective ids.

7   Conclusion

We have so far presented a method for constructing a communicating FSM from use cases expressed in the form of trees. MSCs are generated from use case trees and validated by users. The validation process consists of inviting the user to decide about accepting or not each one of the MSC linearizations missing in the use cases. Moreover, the user can also be prompted how to reorganize a use case in order to move forward a more structured specification. At the end of this stage, the original use cases may be modified to reflect more a desired and realizable system behavior. Use cases are then decorated for detecting repetitive behaviors and constructing their GFSM. Afterward, the latter is decomposed to derive a communicating FSM for each object.

The decoration of the use case trees seems difficult at first time, but with practice, analysts will develop skills to perform appropriate declarative decoration. Moreover, practicing decoration is very helpful for a well understanding of the requirements, especially in the case of distributed systems. Besides, even not explicitly shown, our approach preserves the traceability between use cases and the FSMs of objects. Hence, for any element (either a state or a transition) in the FSMs, we can retrieve the use case it is related to. So, when errors are detected in the FSM level, the analyst will be able to trace them back and correct them in the use case level. Our approach would be more efficient when implemented as a computer aided design tool with a graphical interface, which is under development.

Ackowledgements

This work has been supported France Telecom R&D through a contract between France Telecom and Concordia University. Aziz Salah is also supported by an NSERC grant.

References

[1]   A. V. Aho, R. Sethi, and J. D. Ullman, *Compilers: principles, techniques, and tools*. Reading, Mass.: Addison Wesley, 1986.

[2]   R. Alur, K. Etessami, and M. Yannakakis, "Inference of message sequence charts," presented at 22nd International Conference on Software Engineering, 2000.

[3]   R. Alur, G. Holzmann, and D. Peled, "An Analyzer for Message Sequence Charts," *Software: Concepts and Tools*, vol. 17, pp. 70-77, 1996.

[4]   H. Ben-Abdallah and S. Leue, "Syntactic Detection of Process Divergence and Non-local Choice inMessage Sequence Charts," in *TACAS*, 1997, pp. 259-274.

[5]   R. Fikes and N. J. Nilsson, "STRIPS: A New Approach to the Application of Theorem Proving to Problem Solving," *Artif. Intell.*, vol. 2, pp. 189-208, 1971.

[6]   H. Giese, "Towards Scenario-Based Synthesis for Parametric Timed Automata," presented at the 2nd International Workshop on Scenarios and State Machines: Models, Algorithms, and Tools, ICSE, Portland, USA, 2003.

[7]   D. Harel, "From Play-In Scenarios To Code: An Achievable Dream," *IEEE Computer*, vol. 34, pp. 53-60, 2001.

[8]   D. Harel and H. Kugler, "Synthesizing State-Based Object Systems from LSC Specifications," *Int. J. of Foundations of Computer Science*, vol. 13, pp. 5-51, 2002.

[9]   ITU, *Recommendation Z.120: Message Sequence Chart (MSC)*, 1999,.

[10]   K. Koskimies and E. Mäkinen, "Automatic Synthesis of State Machines from Trace Diagrams," *Software-Practice and Experience*, vol. 24, pp. 643-658, 1994.

[11]   I. Krüger, R. Grosu, P. Scholz, and M. Broy, "From MSCs to Statecharts," presented at Distributed and Parallel Embedded Systems, 1998.

[12]   N. Lynch, "I/O Automata: A model for discrete event systems," presented at 22nd Annual Conference on Information Sciences and Systems, Princeton University, Princeton, N.J., 1988.

[13]   E. Mäkinen and T. Systä, "MAS – An Interactive Synthesizer to Support Behavioral Modeling in UML," presented at ICSE 2001, Toronto, Canada, 2001.

[14]   H. Muccini, "Detecting Implied Scenarios analyzing non-local Branching Choices," presented at Conf. on Fundamental Approaches to Software Engineering (FASE 2003), ETAPS2003, Warsaw, Poland, 2003.

[15]   M. Mukund, K. N. Kumar, and M. A. Sohoni, "Synthesizing distributed finite-state systems from MSCs," presented at Proc. CONCUR '00, 2000.

[16]   OMG, "Unified Modeling Language (UML) specification v1.5," OMG document ad/2003-03-01, March 2003.

[17]   A. Salah, R. Dssouli, and G. Lapalme, "Compiling real-time scenarios into a Timed Automaton," presented at FORTE XIV/PSTV XXI, 2001.

[18]   S. Somé, R. Dssouli, and J. Vaucher, "Toward an Automation of Requirements Engineering using Scenarios," *Journal of Computing and Information*, vol. 2, pp. 1110-1132, 1996.

[19]   S. Uchitel, J. Kramer, and J. Magee, "Synthesis of behavioral models from scenarios," *IEEE Transactions on Software Engineering*, vol. 29, pp. 99-115, 2003.

[20]   J. Whittle and J. Schumann, "Generating statechart designs from scenarios," presented at 22nd International Conference on Software, 2000.

Conditions for Resolving Observability Problems in Distributed Testing

Jessica Chen[1], Robert M. Hierons[2], and Hasan Ural[3]

[1] School of Computer Science, University of Windsor
Windsor, Ontario, Canada N9B 3P4
`xjchen@uwindsor.ca`
[2] Department of Information Systems and Computing, Brunel University
Uxbridge, Middlesex, UB8 3PH United Kingdom
`rob.hierons@brunel.ac.uk`
[3] School of Information Technology and Engineering, University of Ottawa
Ottawa, Ontario, Canada K1N 6N5
`ural@site.ottawa.ca`

Abstract. Controllability and observability problems may manifest themselves during the application of a test or checking sequence in a test architecture where there are multiple remote testers. These problems often require the use of external coordination message exchanges among testers during testing. It is desired to construct a test or checking sequence from the specification of the system under test such that it will be free from these problems without requiring the use of external coordination messages. This paper investigates conditions that allow us to construct such a test or checking sequence. For specifications satisfying these conditions, procedures for constructing subsequences that eliminate the need for using external coordination messages are given.

1   Introduction

Testing an implementation of a system is often carried out by constructing an input sequence from the specification of the system, applying the input sequence in a test architecture, and analyzing the resulting output sequence to determine whether the implementation conforms to the specification on this input sequence. In distributed testing, a *distributed test architecture* is used where a tester is placed at each port of the *system under test* (SUT) N and an input sequence constructed from the specification M modeling the externally observable behaviour of N is applied. Such an input sequence is called a *test sequence* [11, 12] or *checking sequence* [4, 6] and is constructed from M to determine whether N is a correct or faulty implementation of M.

During the application of a test or checking sequence to N in a distributed test architecture, the existence of multiple testers brings out the possibility of coordination problems among remote testers known as *controllability* and *observability* problems. These problems occur if a tester cannot determine either when to apply a particular input to an SUT, or whether a particular output

D. de Frutos-Escrig and M. Núñez (Eds.): FORTE 2004, LNCS 3235, pp. 229–242, 2004.
© IFIP International Federation for Information Processing 2004

from an SUT is generated in response to a specific input, respectively. Without loss of generality, let us consider a distributed architecture where there are two testers called, for instance, the lower tester (L) and the upper tester (U). In this architecture, U and L are two remote testers that are required to coordinate the application of a test or checking sequence. The controllability (synchronization) problem manifests itself when L (or U) is expected to send an input to N after N responds to an input from U (or L) with an output to U (or L), but L (or U) is unable to determine whether N sent that output. It is therefore important to construct a synchronizable test or checking sequence that causes no controllability problems during its application in the distributed test architecture. For some specifications, an input sequence can be constructed such that no two consecutive inputs will cause a controllability problem, and hence the coordination among testers is achieved indirectly through their interactions with N [12]. However, for some other specifications, there may not exist an input sequence in which the testers can coordinate solely via their interactions with N [1]. In this case it is necessary for testers to communicate directly by exchanging external coordination messages among themselves over a dedicated channel during the application of the input sequence [2].

During the application of even a synchronizable input sequence in a distributed test architecture, the observability problem manifests itself when L (or U) is expected to receive an output from N in response to either the previous input or the current input and because L (or U) is not the one to send the current input, L (or U) is unable to determine when to start and stop waiting. Such observability problems hamper the detectability of *output shift faults* in N i.e., an output associated with the current input is generated by N in response to either the previous input or the next input. To ensure the detectability of potential output shift faults in N the test or checking sequence needs to be augmented either by additional input subsequences selected from the specification M [10] or by external coordination message exchanges between testers [2] such that during the application of the input sequence testers can determine whether the output observed is received in response to the correct input as specified in M. Again, for some specifications, an input sequence can be constructed without using external coordination messages among testers such that no potential output shift faults will remain undetected, and hence the coordination among testers is achieved indirectly through their interactions with N. However, for some other specifications, there may not exist an input sequence in which observability problems can be resolved without using direct external coordination message exchanges among testers.

Both controllability problems and observability problems may be overcome through the use of external coordination messages. However, there is often a cost associated with the use of such messages. This cost includes the expense of implementing the infrastructure required in order to allow the messages to be sent and may also include a cost of a delay introduced by the sending of each message. It is thus desirable to construct a test or checking sequence from the specification of the system under test such that it will be free of controllability and observability problems without requiring the use of external coordination message exchanges. Previous authors have investigated the problem of producing a test or checking sequence that either has no controllability problems or no controllability and observability problems and that either uses no external coordination message exchanges or uses a minimum number of external coordination message exchanges (see, for example, [1, 3, 5, 7, 8, 9, 13, 14, 15, 16]).

This paper investigates conditions that allow us to construct a test or checking sequence without encountering controllability and observability problems and without using external coordination messages among testers. The rest of the paper is organized as follows: Section 2 introduces the terminology. Section 3 gives a formal definition of the problem and identifies the conditions that the specification of the system under test is checked against. Section 4 presents new procedures for constructing subsequences that eliminate the need for using external coordination messages: for a transition t and port p we produce a subsequence that does not allow a fault in the output of t at p to be masked by an output shift fault. Section 5 gives the concluding remarks.

2   Preliminaries

2.1   FSM and Its Graphical Representation

An *n-port Finite State Machine* M (simply called FSM M below) is defined as $M = (S, I, O, \delta, \lambda, s_0)$ where

- S is a finite set of states of M;
- $s_0 \in S$ is the initial state of M;
- $I = \bigcup_{i=1}^{n} I_i$, where I_i is the input alphabet of port i, and $I_i \cap I_j = \emptyset$ for $i, j \in [1, n]$, $i \neq j$;
- $O = \prod_{i=1}^{n}(O_i \cup \{-\})$, where O_i is the output alphabet of port i, and $-$ means null output;
- δ is the transition function that maps $S \times I$ to S, i.e., $\delta : S \times I \to S$;
- λ is the output function that maps $S \times I$ to O, i.e., $\lambda : S \times I \to O$.

Note that each $y \in O$ is a *vector of outputs*, i.e., $y = <o_1, o_2, ..., o_n>$ where $o_i \in O_i \cup \{-\}$ for $i \in [1, n]$. We will use $*$ to denote any possible output, including $-$, at a port. We also use $*$ to denote any possible input or any possible vector of outputs of a transition. In the following, $p \in [1, n]$ is a port, $x \in I$ is a general input, and $x^p \in I_p$ is an input at specific port p. We use $y[p, c]$ to denote the output vector y of a transition whose output at port p is c. Alternatively, we use $y \mid_p$ to denote the output at port p in y.

A *transition* of an FSM M is a triple $t = (s_1, s_2, x/y)$, where $s_1, s_2 \in S$, $x \in I$, and $y \in O$ such that $\delta(s_1, x) = s_2$, $\lambda(s_1, x) = y$. s_1 and s_2 are called the *starting state* and the *ending state* of t respectively. The *input/output pair* x/y is called the *label* of the transition. A transition $(s_1, s_2, x/y)$ will also be denoted as $s_1 \xrightarrow{x/y} s_2$.

A *path* $\rho = t_1\, t_2\, \ldots\, t_k$ $(k \geq 0)$ is a finite sequence of transitions such that for $k \geq 2$, the ending state of t_i is the starting state of t_{i+1} for all $i \in [1, k-1]$. When the ending state of the last transition of path ρ_1 is the starting state of the first transition of path ρ_2, we use $\rho_1 @ \rho_2$ to denote the *concatenation* of paths ρ_1 and ρ_2. The *label* of a path $(s_1, s_2, x_1/y_1)\, (s_2, s_3, x_2/y_2) \ldots (s_k, s_{k+1}, x_k/y_k)$ $(k \geq 1)$ is the sequence of input/output pairs $x_1/y_1\, x_2/y_2 \ldots x_k/y_k$ which is called an *input/output sequence*. We will consider FSMs that are free from *same-port-output-cycles* and *isolated-port-cycles*. A same-port-output-cycle in an FSM is a path $(s_1, s_2, x_1/y_1)\, (s_2, s_3, x_2/y_2) \ldots (s_k, s_{k+1}, x_k/y_k)$ $(k \geq 2)$ such that $s_1 = s_{k+1}$, $s_i \neq s_{i+1}$ for $i \in [1, k]$, and there exists a port p with $y_i \mid_p \neq\, -$ and $x_i \notin I_p$ for all $i \in [1, k]$. An isolated-port-cycle in an FSM is a path $(s_1, s_2, x_1/y_1)$ $(s_2, s_3, x_2/y_2) \ldots (s_k, s_{k+1}, x_k/y_k)$ $(k \geq 2)$ such that $s_1 = s_{k+1}$, $s_i \neq s_{i+1}$ for $i \in [1, k]$, and there exists a port p with $y_i \mid_p =\, -$ and $x_i \notin I_p$ for all $i \in [1, k]$.

We will use 2-port FSMs to show some examples. In a 2-port FSM, we will denote the ports U and L to stand for the upper interface and the lower interface of the FSM. We use u, u_1, u_2, ... to denote inputs at port U, and l, l_1, l_2, ... to denote the inputs at port L. The output vector $y = \langle o_1, o_2 \rangle$ on the label of a transition of the 2-port FSM are pairs of output $o_1 \in O_1$ at port U and output $o_2 \in O_2$ at port L.

2.2   Controllability (Synchronization) Problem

Given an FSM M and an input/output sequence $x_1/y_1\, x_2/y_2 \ldots x_k/y_k$ of M, where $x_i \in I$ and $y_i \in O$, $i \in [1, k]$, a *controllability (synchronization) problem* occurs when, in the labels x_i/y_i and x_{i+1}/y_{i+1} of any two consecutive transitions, $\exists p \in [1, n]$ such that $x_{i+1} \in I_p$, $x_i \notin I_p$, $y_i \mid_p =\, -$ $(i \in [1, k-1])$. Two consecutive transitions t_i and t_{i+1} whose labels are x_i/y_i and x_{i+1}/y_{i+1}, form a *synchronizable pair* of transitions if t_{i+1} can follow t_i without causing a synchronization problem. Any (sub)sequence of transitions in which every pair of transitions is synchronizable is called a *synchronizable transition (sub)sequence*. An input/output sequence is said to be *synchronizable* if it is the label of a synchronizable transition sequence.

2.3   Observability Problem

Suppose we are given an FSM M and an input/output sequence $x_1/y_1\, x_2/y_2$ $\ldots x_k/y_k$ of M, where $x_i \in I$ and $y_i \in O$, $i \in [1, k]$. A *1-shift output fault* in an implementation N of M exists when, in the labels x_i/y_i and x_{i+1}/y_{i+1} of any two consecutive transitions, one of the following holds:

1. There exists $o \in O_p$ and $p \in [1, n]$ such that $y_i \mid_p =\, o$, $y_{i+1} \mid_p =\, -$, N produces output $-$ at p in response to x_i after $x_1 \ldots x_{i-1}$, and N produces output o at p in response to x_{i+1} after $x_1 \ldots x_i$.
2. There exists $o \in O_p$ and $p \in [1, n]$ such that $y_i \mid_p =\, -$, $y_{i+1} \mid_p =\, o$, N produces output o at p in response to x_i after $x_1 \ldots x_{i-1}$, and N produces output $-$ at p in response to x_{i+1} after $x_1 \ldots x_i$.

An instance of the observability problem manifests itself as a *potentially undetectable 1-shift output fault* if there is a 1-shift output fault related to $o \in O_p$ in any two consecutive transitions whose labels are x_i/y_i and x_{i+1}/y_{i+1}, such that $x_{i+1} \notin I_p$. In this case, we say that the tester at port p is *involved* in the shift, and would not be able to detect it.

3   Problem Definition and Conditions

3.1   Problem Definition

Suppose that a specification of the system under test is given as an n-port FSM. Each potential undetectable 1-shift output fault in the given FSM is related to a pair of transitions t_1 and t_2 adjacent at a state of the FSM. Clearly, one can identify all potential undetectable 1-shift output faults in the given FSM using the definition in Section 2.3, and form a set of pairs of transitions where each pair of transitions t_1 and t_2 is related to a potential undetectable shift of an output at a specific port p. Note that, if there exists a potential undetectable forward shift of output d at port p from transition t_1 to transition t_2, then, this potential shift may be realized in an implementation, by a missing output d at port p in t_1 and an extra output d at port p in t_2. Similarly, if there exists a potential undetectable backward shift of output d at port p from transition t_2 to transition t_1, then, this potential shift may be realized in an implementation, by an extra output d at port p in t_1 and a missing output d at port p in t_2.

Therefore, one has to determine, for each pair of transitions t_1 and t_2 related to a potential undetectable shift of an output at a specific port p, whether there exists a missing/extra output at port p of transition t, for each transition t in $t_1 t_2$. In order to do this without using external coordination messages among testers, one has to determine whether there is a subsequence of transitions in the given FSM that will detect a missing/extra output at port p of transition t and then construct such a subsequence. Clearly, we also need to check whether every incoming transition of each state of the FSM forms a synchronizable pair of transitions with at least one of the outgoing transitions of that state and every outgoing transition of each state of the FSM forms a synchronizable pair of transitions with at least one of the incoming transitions of that state. If this condition does not hold, then the FSM is called *intrinsically non-synchronizable*. In this paper, we consider FSMs that are not intrinsically non-synchronizable.

Hence, the problem we consider is the following: for each transition t in each pair of transitions t_1 and t_2 of the FSM related to a potential undetectable shift of an output at a specific port p, we wish to produce a single subsequence $\rho_1 @ t @ \rho_2$ that checks whether the output produced by t at p represents a missing/extra output at port p. In addition, the subsequence $\rho_1 @ t @ \rho_2$ must have the following properties: it must be synchronized and it cannot contain an undetectable output shift fault involving t at port p. This places conditions on ρ_1 (called the leading path) and ρ_2 (called the trailing path). We give conditions under which such ρ_1 and ρ_2 exists. We also give algorithms that, when these conditions hold, generate ρ_1 and ρ_2 for given t and p. Where such subsequences exist for *both* t_1 and t_2

we say that they *resolve* the potential undetectable shift of the output at port p in $t_1 t_2$. In the rest of the paper, we will not qualify a subsequence or sequence as "synchronizable" as only synchronizable sequences and subsequences will be considered.

3.2   Conditions

Suppose that two transitions in the given FSM may be sequenced in a manner that gives a potential undetectable shift of an output at port p. The following gives conditions under which these two transitions may be checked separately for a missing/extra output at p, without using external coordination messages, in a manner that does not allow them to be involved in an undetectable shift of an output at p. Further, it will transpire that under these conditions, this may be achieved for *every* pair $t_1 t_2$ of transitions from the FSM. In Section 5 we will discuss how these conditions may be weakened when we are considering a given test or checking sequence derived from the given FSM.

Given an FSM with no same-port-output-cycles or isolated-port-cycles, we can resolve all of its potential undetectable 1-shift output faults without using external coordination messages if and only if for any pair of transitions $s_1 \xrightarrow{*/*} s$ and $s \xrightarrow{*/*} t_1$ in the FSM,

a *if there exists a potential undetectable forward shift of an output at port p, then there exists at least one transition to s with a null output at port p, and at least one transition from s with either an input or a non-empty output at port p.*

b *if there exists a potential undetectable backward shift of an output at port p, then there exists at least one transition to s with a non-empty output at port p, and at least one transition from s with either an input or a null output at port p.*

Below we show that the condition for the case of potential undetectable *forward* shift (i.e. part a.) is *necessary*. The necessity of the condition for the case of potential undetectable *backward* shift is analogous. In Section 4 we will show how, under these conditions, the potential undetectable output shift faults may be resolved without the use of external coordination messages and thus that these conditions are *sufficient* conditions.

Suppose we have transitions $t_1 = s_1 \xrightarrow{*/y_1[p,d]} s$ and $t_2 = s \xrightarrow{x/y_2[p,-]} r_1$ in the FSM of the specification where $x \notin I_p$. Thus, there is a potential undetectable forward shift of output d from t_1 to t_2.

- Suppose that the condition does not hold, and $\forall s'$ such that $s' \xrightarrow{x'/y'} s$, we have $y' \mid_p \neq -$. In this situation, the output at port p on any transition leading to s may be shifted to transition t_2, and these potential shifts are undetectable. So we have no way to check that transition t_2 has null output at port p in the implementation, because no matter how we get to state s,

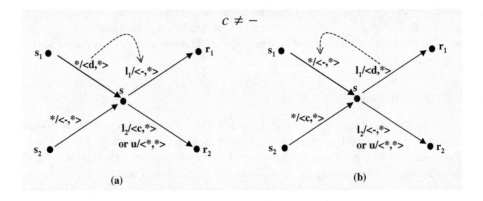

Fig. 1. illustration of the condition

there is always a possibility of an undetectable forward output shift at port p to t_2.

– Suppose that the condition does not hold, and $\forall s'$ such that $s \xrightarrow{x'/y'} s'$, we have $x' \notin I_p$ and $y' \mid_p = -$. In this situation, the output d on transition t_1 may be shifted to any transition starting from s, and these potential shifts are undetectable. So we have no way to check that transition t_1 has output d at port p in the implementation, because no matter how we continue from state s, there is always a possibility of an undetectable forward shift of output d from t_1.

Figure 1 illustrates an example of a 2-port FSM where the condition is satisfied. In this figure, we have potential undetectable forward output shift fault in (a) and potential undetectable backward output shift fault in (b), as the dashed arrows show. For such potential faults, we have transition from s_2 to s and transition from s to r_2, so the condition holds. In fact, in (a), transition from s to r_2 will be used to check if there is a missing output d in transition $s_1 \xrightarrow{*/<d,*>} s$, as a result of a forward output shift. The transition from s_2 to s will be used to check if there is an extra output in transition $s \xrightarrow{l_1/<-,*>} r_1$ as a result of a forward output shift. The transitions from s_2 to s and from s to r_2 in (b) will be used analogously.

Note that

– In $s_1 \xrightarrow{*/y_1[p,d]} s \xrightarrow{x/y_2[p,-]} r_1$ ($x \notin I_p$), having checked that the first transition does not have a missing output d at port p cannot guarantee that the second transition does not have an extra output at port p. In Figure 2 (a), suppose that using $s_2 \xrightarrow{*/<-,*>} s \xrightarrow{l_1/<-,*>} r_1$ we know that in transition $s \xrightarrow{l_1/<-,*>} r_1$ there is no extra output. However, we cannot jump to the conclusion that in $s_1 \xrightarrow{*/<d,*>} s$ there is no missing output d,

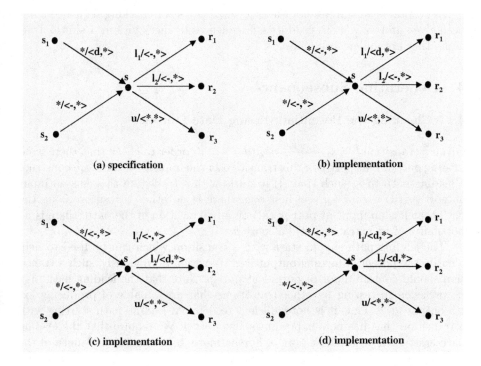

Fig. 2. An example to show possible undetectable 1-shift output faults

because Figure 2 (c) can be an implementation: Thus, we need to check both transition $s_1 \xrightarrow{*/<d,*>} s$ for possible missing output d, and transition $s \xrightarrow{l_1/<-,*>} r_1$ for possible extra output.

- The potential undetectable output shift faults may not be paired. In Figure 2, (a) may be implemented as in (d). Thus, we need to check transition $s_1 \xrightarrow{*/<d,*>} s$ for possible missing output d, and check both transitions $s \xrightarrow{l_1/<-,*>} r_1$ and $s \xrightarrow{l_2/<-,*>} r_2$ for possible extra output.

When the above condition holds, given a transition t, we show below how to check if there is a missing output or an extra output at a specific port on this transition in the implementation. To do so, we construct a *leading path* ρ_1 that leads to the starting state of t and a *trailing path* ρ_2 that starts from the ending state of t so that by applying subsequence $\rho_1@t@\rho_2$ to the implementation, we can detect if there is a missing/extra output at a specific port in transition t.

Note that we consider FSM with no same-port-output-cycles and no isolated-port-cycles. In this setting, our procedures to construct the leading paths and trailing paths will always terminate with subsequences that are adequate.

In Section 5 we will discuss the case where a test or checking sequence ρ has been given and we wish to produce subsequences to check for any 1-shift output faults that are undetectable in ρ.

4   Generating Subsequences

4.1   Checking the Potential Missing Data Output

Given a transition $t = s_1 \xrightarrow{*/y[p,d]} s_2$ ($d \neq -$), in order to check that there is no missing output d at port p in this transition in the implementation, we construct a leading path to s_1 such that (i) it starts with a transition that has an input at port p; (ii) except for the first one, there is no other transition along the path that has an input at port p; (iii) on any transition of the path, there is no possibility of an extra output d at port p.

The leading path should start with a transition which can be used to help identify the potential missing output d in transition t. Obviously, such a transition should contain input or output at port p. Note that the leading path may be preceded in testing by other transitions that are capable of producing extra output at p. Thus it is not sufficient to define a leading path starting with a transition that has non-empty output at port p: We require that the leading path start with an *input* at port p. Furthermore, to minimize the length of the leading path, we require that the input at port p at the beginning is the only input at port p in the leading path. We require that along the leading path there is no possibility of an extra output d at port p, because the occurrence of such an extra output d will prevent us from detecting the missing output d at port p in transition t.

The following procedure constructs the leading path ρ_1.

 i Let $\rho_1 = \varepsilon$
 ii If the transition t has input $x^p \in I_p$, terminate as no leading path is required.
 iii Let $v = s_1$
 iv If $\exists v'. \ v' \xrightarrow{x^p/y'[p,c]} v$ and $c \neq -$, then $\rho_1 = (v', v; x^p/y'[p, c])@\rho_1$, terminate.

  Otherwise, let v' be a state such that $v' \xrightarrow{x/y'[p,c]} v$ and $c \neq -$. Let $\rho_1 = (v', v; x/y'[p, c])@\rho_1$, $v = v'$, repeat iv.

For the first time in step (iv), if $\exists v''. \ v'' \xrightarrow{*/y'[p,-]} s_1$, then there exists a potential undetectable backward shift of output d between $v'' \xrightarrow{*/y'[p,-]} s_1$ and $s_1 \xrightarrow{*/y[p,d]} s_2$. According to our condition b., $\exists v'. \ v' \xrightarrow{*/y'[p,c]} s_1$ and $c \neq -$. The same argument holds for the repeated step (iv). Thus, in (iv), the existence of v' is guaranteed. Termination, with an adequate leading path, is guaranteed because M must be free from same-port-output-cycles. Further, since M has no same-port-output-cycles this procedure cannot repeat a state of M and thus, if M has m states, the leading path can have length at most $m - 1$.

At the end of the procedure, we have a leading path that, if it is non-empty, starts from a transition with an input at port p, followed by transitions with non-empty outputs at port p. Any of these outputs at p can be missing, but there is *no possibility* of an extra output at p.

Note that these outputs at port p can be d, and so, although there is no possibility of an extra d at port p, there exists possibility of a *missing* d in the leading path. So if a missing d at port p is detected, we may not be able to tell which d is missing: from a transition in the leading path or from transition $s_1 \xrightarrow{*/y[p,d]} s_2$. Additional conditions might be added to avoid this from happening. An example of such a condition is: *no two consecutive transitions have the same output data at the same port.*

The construction of the trailing path is quite similar: Given transition $s_1 \xrightarrow{*/y[p,d]} s_2$ ($d \neq -$), in order to check that there is no missing d in this transition in the implementation, we construct a trailing path starting from s_2 such that (i) it ends with a transition that has an input at port p; (ii) except for the last one, there is no other transition along the path that has an input at port p; (iii) on any transition of the path, there is no possibility of an extra output d at port p.

The following procedure constructs the trailing path ρ_2.

i Let $\rho_2 = \varepsilon$, $v = s_2$

ii If $\exists v'$. $v \xrightarrow{x^p/y'} v'$ for some input $x_p \in I_p$, then $\rho_2 = \rho_2@(v, v'; x^p/y')$, terminate.

Otherwise, let v' be a state such that $v \xrightarrow{x/y'[p,c]} v'$ and $c \neq -$. Let $\rho_2 = \rho_2@(v, v'; x/y'[p, c])$, $v = v'$, repeat ii.

Again, this must terminate, with an adequate trailing path of length at most $m - 1$.

4.2   Checking the Potential Extra Data Output

Given transition $s_1 \xrightarrow{*/y[p,-]} s_2$, in order to check that there is no extra output at port p in this transition in the implementation, we construct a leading path to s_1 such that (i) it starts from a transition with an input at port p; (ii) except for the first one, there is no other transition along the path that has an input at port p; (iii) on any transition of the path, there is no possibility of a missing output at port p.

The following procedure constructs the leading path ρ_1.

i Let $\rho_1 = \varepsilon$

ii If the transition t has input $x^p \in I_p$, terminate as no leading path is required.

iii Let $v = s_1$

iv If $\exists v'$. $v' \xrightarrow{x^p/y'[p,-]} v$, let $\rho_1 = (v', v; x^p/y'[p, -])@\rho_1$, terminate.

Otherwise, let v' be a state s.t. $v' \xrightarrow{x/y'[p,-]} v$. Let $\rho_1 = (v', v; x/y'[p, -])@\rho_1$, $v = v'$, repeat iv.

For the first time in step (iv), if $\exists v''$. $v'' \xrightarrow{*/y'[p,c]} s_1$ where $c \neq -$, then there exists potential undetectable forward shift of output c between $v'' \xrightarrow{*/y'[p,c]} s_1$ and $s_1 \xrightarrow{*/y[p,-]} s_2$. According to our condition a., $\exists v'$. $v' \xrightarrow{*/y'[p,-]} s_1$. The same argument holds for the repeated step (iv). Thus, in (iv), the existence of v' is guaranteed. Termination , with an adequate leading path of length at most $m-1$, is guaranteed because M must be free from isolated-port-cycles.

The leading path, if it is non-empty, starts from a transition with an input at port p, followed by a sequence of transitions with empty output at port p, and so there is no possibility of missing output at port p along the leading path.

The construction of the trailing path is similar: Given transition $s_1 \xrightarrow{*/y[p,-]} s_2$, in order to check that there is no extra output at port p in this transition in the implementation, we construct a trailing path from s_2 such that (i) it ends with a transition with an input at port p; (ii) except for the last one, there is no other transition along the path that has an input at port p; (iii) on any transition of the path, there is no possibility of a missing output at port p.

The following procedure constructs the trailing path ρ_2.

i Let $\rho_2 = \varepsilon$, $v = s_2$

ii If $\exists v'$. $v \xrightarrow{x^p/y'} v'$ for some $x^p \in I_p$, let $\rho_2 = \rho_2@(v, v'; x^p/y')$, terminate.

   Otherwise, let v' be a state s.t. $v \xrightarrow{x/y'[p,-]} v'$. Let $\rho_2 = \rho_2@(v, v'; x/y'[p, -])$, $v = v'$, repeat ii.

Clearly, this must terminate, with an adequate trailing path of length at most $m - 1$.

5   Concluding Remarks

Where a test architecture has remote testers it is necessary to consider controllability and observability issues. These problems often require the use of external coordination message exchanges among testers during testing. However, there is often a cost associated with the use of such messages: the cost of implementing the infrastructure required in order to allow the messages to be sent and possibly also a cost (or delay) due to the sending of each message. It is thus desirable to construct a test or checking sequence from the specification of the system under test such that it will be free of controllability and observability problems without requiring the use of external coordination message exchanges.

This paper investigates conditions that must be satisfied by the specification of the system under test for us to be able to produce a test for each transitions such that the test is free from controllability and observability problems. This problem is represented in the following way.

For each potential undetectable 1-shift output fault in the FSM, we have a pair of transitions $t_1 t_2$. For each transition t in $t_1 t_2$, we wish to produce a single subsequence $\rho_1@t@\rho_2$ that checks the output produced by transition t at port p. It is necessary to precede t by some appropriate sequence as the starting state of t must be reached in order to execute t and the sequence used to reach this state must not be able to lead to a potentially undetectable shift of the same output involving t. It is necessary to follow t with some appropriate sequence since we must ensure that the sequence following t does not allow a potentially undetectable shift of the same output involving t^1. The effectiveness of the subsequence $\rho_1@t@\rho_2$, at checking the output of t at p, must not be affected by controllability and observability problems. This paper gives necessary and sufficient conditions for there to be such a subsequence for each t in a pair of transitions t_1t_2 representing a potential undetectable output shift fault related to an output at port p. Further, given a transition t and port p, we have given algorithms that (if these conditions hold) produce a subsequence that checks the output of t at p without suffering from controllability and observability problems.

In practice, weaker conditions than those given in this paper will often suffice since:

i it may not be necessary to consider all pairs of transitions; and
ii it may be possible to use more than one subsequence to check a transition t.

We will now briefly discuss these factors. First, we may be concerned with potential observability problems in a *given* test or checking sequence ρ. Since some transition pairs representing potentially undetectable output shift faults may not be in ρ and since the paths leading to and trailing from those t_1t_2 pairs in ρ representing potential undetectable output shift faults are already determined in ρ, weaker conditions may suffice.

Suppose that ρ contains the subsequence t_1t_2 for transitions t_1 and t_2 and that these can participate in a potentially undetectable 1-shift output fault at port p. Sometimes we can eliminate this potentially undetectable 1-shift output fault by using a subsequence that checks the output of t_1 at p *or* a subsequence that checks the output of t_2 at p but not both. We now explain why this is the case. Suppose that we test the output of t_1 at p and find this to be correct; the case where we have checked the output of t_2 at p is similar. If we know that the subsequence t_1t_2 produces the (overall) correct output at p then we also know that t_2 produces the expected output at p. Naturally, further conditions must be placed on ρ in order for it to determine the overall output of t_1t_2 at p in the SUT.

This paper has investigated conditions under which it is possible to resolve potentially undetectable output shift faults. However, a number of questions remain. As already noted, weaker conditions sometimes suffice - the challenge is to produce general necessary and sufficient conditions. Suppose we produce a subsequence for each transition/port combination and generate a single sequence ρ that contains each of these subsequences. Then ρ is guaranteed to determine

---

[1] Sometimes it is possible to separate several test or checking sequences using a reset. Where this is the case, under certain conditions it is possible to replace ρ_2 with a reset.

correctness under the fault model in which only output faults are possible. However, this need not be an efficient sequence for this fault model. There is also the problem of producing an efficient test or checking sequence, from an FSM, that is guaranteed to determine correctness for more general fault models.

Acknowledgements

This work was supported in part by Natural Sciences and Engineering Research Council (NSERC) of Canada under grants OGP 976 and 209774, Leverhulme Trust grant number F/00275/D, Testing State Based Systems, and Engineering and Physical Sciences Research Council grant number GR/R43150, Formal Methods and Testing (FORTEST).

References

[1] S. Boyd and H. Ural. The synchronization problem in protocol testing and its complexity. *Information Processing Letters*, 40:131–136, 1991. 230, 231

[2] L. Cacciari and O. Rafiq. Controllability and observability in distributed testing. *Information and Software Technology*, 41:767–780, 1999. 230

[3] W. Chen and H. Ural. Synchronizable checking sequences based on multiple UIO sequences. *IEEE/ACM Transactions on Networking*, 3:152–157, 1995. 231

[4] A. Gill. *Introduction to the Theory of Finite-State Machines*. New York: McGraw-Hill, 1962. 229

[5] S. Guyot and H. Ural. Synchronizable checking sequences based on UIO sequences. In *Proc. of IFIP IWPTS'95*, pages 395–407, Evry, France, September 1995. 231

[6] F. Hennie. Fault detecting experiments for sequential circuits. In *Proc. of Fifth Ann. Symp. Switching Circuit Theory and Logical Design*, pages 95–110, Princeton, N. J., 1964. 229

[7] R. M. Hierons. Testing a distributed system: generating minimal synchronised test sequences that detect output-shifting faults. *Information and Software Technology*, 43(9):551–560, 2001. 231

[8] R. M. Hierons and H. Ural. UIO sequence based checking sequences for distributed test architectures. *Information and Software Technology*, 45(12):793–803, 2003. 231

[9] G. Luo, R. Dssouli, and G. v. Bochmann. Generating synchronizable test sequences based on finite state machine with distributed ports. In *The 6th IFIP Workshop on Protocol Test Systems*, pages 139–153. Elsevier (North-Holland), 1993. 231

[10] G. Luo, R. Dssouli, G. v. Bochmann, P. Venkataram, and A. Ghedamsi. Test generation with respect to distributed interfaces. *Computer Standards and Interfaces*, 16:119–132, 1994. 230

[11] K. Sabnani and A. Dahbura. A protocol test generation procedure. *Computer Networks*, 15:285–297, 1988. 229

[12] B. Sarikaya and G. v. Bochmann. Synchronization and specification issues in protocol testing. *IEEE Transactions on Communications*, 32:389–395, April 1984. 229, 230

[13] K. Tai and Y. Young. Synchronizable test sequences of finite state machines. *Computer Networks*, 13:1111–1134, 1998. 231

[14] H. Ural and Z. Wang. Synchronizable test sequence generation using UIO sequences. *Computer Communications*, 16:653–661, 1993. 231

[15] D. Whittier. Solutions to controllability and observability problems in distributed testing. Master's thesis, University of Ottawa, Canada, 2001. 231

[16] Y. Young and K. Tai. Observation inaccuracy in conformance testing with multiple testers. In *Proc. of IEEE WASET*, pages 80–85, 1998. 231

Integrating Formal Verification with Murφ of Distributed Cache Coherence Protocols in FAME Multiprocessor System Design

Ghassan Chehaibar

BULL, Platforms Hardware R&D
Rue Jean Jaurès, F-78340 Les Clayes Sous Bois, France
ghassan.chehaibar@bull.net

Abstract. Flexible Architecture for Multiple Environments (FAME) is Bull architecture for large symmetrical multiprocessors based on Intel's Itanium® 2 family, which is used in Bull NovaScale® servers series. A key point in the development of this distributed shared memory architecture is the definition of its cache coherence protocol. This paper reports experiences and results of integrating formal verification of FAME cache coherence protocol, on 4 successive versions of this architecture. The goal is to find protocol definition bugs (not implementation) in the early phases of the design, focusing on: cache coherency, data integrity and deadlock-freeness properties. We have performed modeling and verification using Murφ tool and language, because of its easiness of use and its efficient state reduction techniques. The analysis of the results shows that this approach is cost-effective, and in spite of the state explosion problem, it has helped us in finding hard-to-simulate protocol bugs, before the implementation is far ahead.

1 Introduction

Design and verification of complex systems are an outstanding application domain of formal methods. Cache coherence protocol of symmetric multiprocessor (SMP) over a distributed architecture is indeed a very complex system, where concurrency of transactions issued by different agents and the resulting conflicts are very difficult to master and verify without the help of rigorous analysis. Such help is provided by formal methods that allow to describe behaviors in a precise unambiguous language and to automatically prove properties of these descriptions.

Flexible Architecture for Multiple Environments (FAME) is Bull architecture to design large SMPs that can include up to 32 processors [4]. It is based on Intel Itanium®2 family and commercialized in the Bull NovaScale® server series [1]. This non-uniform access memory (NUMA) distributed shared memory multiprocessor is organized in modules managed by a key component, the FAME Scalability Switch (FSS). A FAME machine is obtained by connecting up to 4 modules, through an interconnection network that links the FSSs (Fig. 1 shows the module structure).

From the very beginning of this project we have applied formal protocol verification to the cache coherence protocol of 4 successive versions of this

D. de Frutos-Escrig and M. Núñez (Eds.): FORTE 2004, LNCS 3235, pp. 243–258, 2004.

architecture. (Formal verification results of the first version are partially mentioned in [15].)

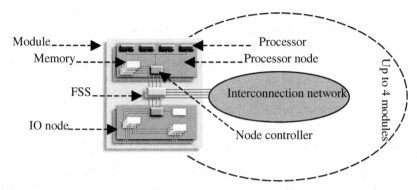

Fig. 1. FAME module architecture. Each *module* contains processor *nodes* and IO nodes that are connected by a switch called FAME Scalability Switch *(FSS)*. Here a module contains 2 processor nodes and two IO nodes, a processor node contains four processors and a memory subsystem

Our goal is to apply formal verification as a design aid [3], in order to find protocol definition bugs (not implementation) in the early phases of its specification and to increase confidence in its correctness. Protocol specification verification differs from other formal verification activities that address hardware implementation correctness. like formal verification of properties of the register-transfer level (RTL) descriptions, or equivalence checking between RTL and gate levels. Starting from a reference specification we build an abstracted, simplified and downsized model of the protocol and check that it verifies some properties. As we will see, this approach is cost-effective and allows finding hard-to-simulate protocol bugs before the implementation is far ahead, in spite of state explosion problem.

Among all requirements that must be implemented by FSS, we focus on the essential function of keeping memory coherent, which is ensured by the cache coherence protocol. Thus, formal modeling and verification address this protocol, focusing on coherence handling aspects, abstracting anything else, like routing, networking and resource management.

In order to show the complexity of the problem addressed, Section 2 gives an overview of a distributed cache coherence protocol like FAME's one, highlighting the main issues (conflict handling, race conditions and data integrity) and defining the properties we aim to check. Based on these properties, Section 3 states and informally justifies the protocol abstractions done in the modeling process: event aggregations and resource simplifications. Then in Section 4, we summarize the features of Murφ language and tool, which have made us choose it to model and verify our cache coherence protocol: amenity of the language, shortest explicit error traces, efficient state reduction techniques (symmetry and hash compaction) and asynchronous semantics. In Section 5, we analyze the results obtained in the modeling and verification of the four versions, from two viewpoints: the incremental modeling and verification process, and the cost-benefit Figures. Finally we draw our conclusions from this experience, summing up the benefits of this approach.

2   FAME Cache Coherence Protocols Issues

In order to give insights of the complexity of the addressed problem, we describe the features of cache coherence protocols in distributed shared-memory architecture [7]. We give some information on FAME protocol specifically, *without disclosing the details of this proprietary protocol.*

2.1 Distributed Cache Coherence Protocol

A private cache is associated to a processor in order to reduce the effects of memory access latency and contention. In shared-memory multiprocessor, a memory location can be present in several caches, thus introducing a *consistency* problem. A *cache coherence protocol* ensures that memory is kept coherent, that is, any change made to a memory location is made visible to all other processors. A common solution is to associate to each cache *line* (transfer unit between memory and caches) a state and associated access rights. When a processor initiates an access compatible with the line state, it is performed in the cache (it is a *hit*); otherwise it issues a transaction on the bus (it is a *miss*).

In *writeback* caching policy, all processor loads and stores are performed in the cache: thus even when a processor needs to write a location, first it fetches in its cache the memory line that contains this location, invalidating all the other caches (*read with invalidation* request). *Replacement* occurs when a processor needs to put a new line in its cache, and all the entries that it can fit in (depending on the organization of the cache) contain valid lines: then a replacement algorithm selects a line to be evicted from the cache: if it is not modified, this can be done silently; otherwise, a *memory update* request is sent to memory.

FAME protocol is based on the classical 4-state protocol called MESI [12] (acronym formed by the state initials): M (modified line, this cache owns the only valid copy of the system, and any access by its processor is a hit; this cache is responsible of providing data to other caches), E (exclusive, this cache is the only one to hold a copy, but it is the same as in memory; any access is a hit and a store will change it to M), S (shared line, it can be present in other caches, and data value is the same as in memory; a load causes a hit, but a store causes a miss), I (invalid line: not present or present but stale; any access is a miss). (Sometimes, M state is called *dirty* in the literature).

A cache coherence protocol defines the rules of handling the requests issued on a miss: how to get information on all cache states, cache state transition rules, where and how to send requests, where to find data, collision handling (concurrent requests to the same line). There are two basic kinds of protocols: snoopy-based and directory-based protocols.

In a snoopy-based protocol, any request is snooped by all processors and memory, and their responses are also snooped in a synchronous way: thus memory and cache controllers have all needed information in a synchronous way and can take appropriate actions. This protocol is suitable for a bus-based architecture and does not scale to distributed systems.

In a directory-based protocol, the original idea is a directory that indicates for any line contained in a processor cache, its state and the list of caches that contain it. In distributed shared-memory architecture, where there is a virtual unique global memory address space but memory is physically distributed, each memory piece has its associated directory. Then on a miss, a request to a line mapped in a memory slice (called the *home* memory of the line) is sent to its attached directory, which forwards request to the concerned caches, instead of the bus-broadcast scheme in snoopy-based case. Actually these directories can be distributed in various ways including grouping some of them in one directory or defining directory hierarchy.

As in caches, there are also replacements in directories: when a an entry holding the state of a line has to be evicted out of the directory, then the directory sends invalidation requests to all the caches that hold a copy of this line.

Often in actual implementation of distributed shared memory architecture, both kinds of cache coherence protocol are combined. In FAME, within a processor node, there is a bus-based snoopy-protocol that interacts with a directory based protocol at the module level. All directories are grouped in FSS.

2.2 Cache Coherence Correctness Properties

A cache coherence protocol aims to keep *memory coherent* not to implement some *memory consistency model*, like sequential or processor or weak or release consistency. Any memory model assumes basic memory coherency that is: all writes to the *same memory location* are seen in the same order by all processors [6] (otherwise, you cannot even implement a lock; notice the difference with sequential consistency for instance, where the set of accesses to *all memory locations* is seen in the same order by all processors).

Therefore, the properties to verify are:

1. Cache and directory state coherency, following the definition of the MESI states: for instance, when a line is E/M in some cache, it is I elsewhere. Since directories contain information about caches, there are inclusion relations between cache state and directories. When there is directory hierarchy, there are inclusion relations between directories.

2. Data integrity: a processor does not read stale data and no data modification is lost. This requirement is not implied by cache state coherency. For instance, as said above, a memory update is performed when a cache evicts a line in M state. After the eviction all caches are I (so the states are coherent), but there is an ongoing memory update. If a read request issued by a processor can get to memory before the update (race condition between read and write), it will get stale data.

3. Deadlock-freeness: actually, a lot of deadlock and starvation issues are related to resource management and so are implementation-dependent. Still, at the protocol level, we have an abstract view of outstanding resources that are used to handle coherency like directories and buffers that track request progression.

Besides, deadlock issues rise in coherence conflict resolution policies, where a colliding request can be held-off or retried.

2.3 Cache Coherence Issues

The main behavior issues of a cache coherence protocol, which we derive from the properties to verify, can be summarized as follows:

1. **Basic transaction handling**. What are the transactions of the protocol, how is memory updated, where to find up-to-date data? As hinted above, there are several types of transactions: read, read with invalidation, invalidation, memory update, etc., and each type has a particular cache and directory state transition rule. In FAME we have up to 10 transaction types.
2. **Conflict resolution rules**, which should ensure coherence without deadlock. A key issue of distributed directory-based cache coherence protocols is *conflict resolution*. Two concurrent requests issued by two processors are said to be in conflict (or to collide) if they are to the same address. In a snoopy-based protocol, the bus grant serializes accesses in an atomic way thus resolving conflicts: request *emission is serialized*; requests and responses are snooped *synchronously* by all the caches. But in distributed protocols, requests are issued *concurrently*, there are *multiple conflict points* (where conflicting requests meet) and various *race conditions* arise between requests or between requests and responses. For instance in FAME, within a module, a processor node can send requests to FSS and vice-versa, and there are requests between FSSs of different modules: then conflict points are in processor nodes and in FSS (where there are several types of conflicts depending on the request source). Thus, two concurrent conflicting requests that are issued by nodes in different modules can collide in either requesting node or in either FSS of both modules. Conflict resolution is complicated by race conditions: request and response channels are independent, so a request can overtake a response and vice-versa. For instance, if a node controller sends a request Rq1 to FSS, then FSS sends its corresponding response Rs1 followed by a request Rq2: the node controller may receive Rq2 before Rs1, without knowing whether its request has been acknowledged or not. There are similar race conditions in transfers between modules.
3. **Directory replacement handling**, in relation with conflicts and deadlocks. For instance, if a request on address A is received by a directory and it needs to cause a replacement in order to complete, if B is the line that is chosen to be evicted (and so invalidated) it may run into a coherence conflict with a pending request to B. Thus, the replacement triggering creates a connection between two requests on different addresses through resource (directory) and coherence conflict, which may cause deadlocks.

3   Protocol Behavior and Property Modeling

We aim to build a reduced model at the "right" abstraction level, trying to find a compromise between what is tractable and what is needed to verify cache coherence properties. The behavior details which are not related to the cache coherence protocol issues and properties brought out above are dropped.

3.1 Behavior Modeling

There are mainly two kinds of simplifications that are combined in modeling:

1. Aggregating a sequence of events in one atomic event. This means that the intermediate states between the aggregated events are not observable and some orderings are not possible in the model.
2. Reducing the resources of the system. This involves reducing the elements of the system: determining the number of processors, nodes, modules, memory addresses, choosing which tables or queues are to be modeled, and what information they contain is needed to model the behavior we want to verify.

Event Collapsing

As said above, the main issue of a cache coherence protocol is conflict resolution, and conflicts results from the concurrent behavior of the different agents of the protocol and race conditions between request/response transfers. So the abstraction, particularly the event collapsing one, should capture this concurrency, so that all kinds of conflict be possible in the model.

This is the general event aggregation scheme: a transaction goes through different phases incurring treatment in each agent (processor, node controller, FSS) and transfers between agents. We consider that there are three "treatment centers": the processor bus including the caches within the node, the node controller, and FSS. We can collapse several steps as long as there is no more than one transfer involved between these centers. There are 3 kinds of transfers: between the processor caches and the node controller, between the node controller and the FSS buffers and between two FSS buffers. A typical case is collapsing emission or reception of a transaction with its handling. An agent receives a transaction, then handles it (performing some treatment), then sends a result. We can collapse receiving the transaction and handling it in one event, or handling the transaction and sending the result. If we collapse the three events we could miss conflicts between several transactions received, or we miss some orderings like: a transaction T1 is received before T2, but the results of T2 is sent before that of T1.

Thus, considering that transfers between the agents are atomic and point-to-point, discarding the interconnection network and routing functions, does not miss the requests and responses concurrency from the coherence protocol viewpoint. This assumes we use a formalism based on *asynchronous interleaving semantics*.

So, in our models, events will be either internal events to caches or FSSs, or request/responses transfers with the associated treatment at the reception point.

Resource Reduction

The objects that are modeled are: caches (state and data), memory, node controller and FSS directories. Within nodes and modules, we represent the buffers that keep track of requests, sometimes collapsing several buffers in one.

Concerning, the number of memory line addresses, since the aim of a cache coherence protocol is memory coherency and not some consistency model, it is enough to perform verification with only one address [8]. This remains true for directory replacements, if they are modeled as non-deterministic events, as long as only coherence aspects are considered. However, we aim to capture some deadlock issues related to the resources present in the model, and as pointed above, coherence and resource conflict meet in directory replacements. Therefore, we set the number of addresses to 2 when we want to take replacements into account; otherwise we set it to 1. An additional reason, for using 2 addresses in replacements, is to model conflict rules specified by the protocol as they are without introducing modeling bias. (In our models, when there are 2 addresses they are mapped to the same home memory).

Beside varying the number of addresses, in order to perform incremental verification and be able to vary the configuration of the model in facing state explosion, we need facilities to set these parameters (a home node or module, is the one that contains the home memory):

- Number of processor nodes in a module, number of caches per node.
- Number of memory line addresses in the system.
- Sizes of the different buffers.
- Number of active nodes in home/non-home module: so that we can set a model where one node is active in home module and 2 nodes in non-home module, for instance.
- Option to prevent nodes in home or non-home module from issuing requests.
- For each kind of transaction, a switch to enable it or not (as said above, there is up to 10 kinds of transactions in FAME).

Caches, controllers, FSSs, modules, addresses, buffer index are all *symmetrical* types. Even if some node is home and the others not, we define the fact of being home as a boolean attached to a node, then this boolean can be set non-deterministically at the initial state. Then, in order to take advantage of these symmetries that allow reducing the state space, we need a tool that implements symmetry reduction techniques.

3.2 Property Modeling

Cache Coherence Properties
Cache coherence properties are typically *state invariants*. The fact that there may be transient states where a directory is not accessible and coherence is not maintained is included in the property. Such transient state could be, for instance, that a transaction is ongoing in some buffer. Then the cache coherence property is: we are in a transient state OR the coherence relation is true. An example of coherence relation: if one directory state is E, then all other directories states are I.

Valid Data Properties
In order to verify that a processor does not get stale data and that no data modifications are lost, we use a data model (borrowed from [13]) that avoids manipulating data values.

Data are modeled with two values: valid and invalid. When a processor writes a line, this copy takes the value "valid" and all other copies of the same address in the system become "invalid". These copies are in memory, caches, and buffers that keep track of requests and hold responses. *This implies the ability to manipulate global variables.* Then, to verify data integrity, we add these state invariants:

- If a cache is not I, it contains valid data.
- When there are no modified data in a cache, data in memory are valid.

Deadlock-Freeness

The actual deadlock-freeness property one expects from a real system is: "a transaction will always inevitably complete (within a bounded time)". But since we deal with abstract models that do not describe arbitration and starvation prevention mechanisms, and we use asynchronous modeling where it is possible to indefinitely delay the firing of a transition, the general property we would like to verify is: "always, whatever the point it has reached, a request can be completed". The different cases of request non-termination are: it has gone into a livelock, or it is stopped somewhere.

4   Murφ Language and Tool

Choosing a notation and its associated tool depends on the goal and the application domain. A comprehensive survey on verification methods for cache coherence protocols is given in [14]. Since we deal with complex specification of cache coherence protocol in distributed shared-memory architectures, and we focus on mastering the specification and finding bugs rather quickly, methods based on *explicit state enumeration* are more suitable: because, verification is fully automatic, and *error traces* can be minimal and explicit, giving a scenario showing the error origin. Efficient state reduction techniques are indispensable to take into account the minimal concurrency we need to verify conflict issues. These considerations have led us to choose to use the Murφ language and tool developed by the Hardware Verification Group of Stanford University [9].

Amenity of the Language and Specification Style

Murφ provides familiar data structures and programming constructs. For instance, there are types such as record and arrays that can be indexed over an enumerated type, imperative programming constructs such as if-then-else, switch, for, while… Besides, it is possible in Murφ to define constants that are parameters of the system: number of addresses, of processors, etc… So, we can change the configuration of the model by changing these constants and recompiling.

Building a model consists in defining a collection of global variables, which represent the system resources states and a collection of transitions rules. Each rule has an enabling condition, which is a boolean expression on the state variables, and an action, which is a sequence of statements that modify the values of the state variables, generating a new state: **rule** condition ➜ action_statements **endrule**. A rule is symbolically defined with parameters: it represents a set of instantiated rules. In a rule we can access any global variable.

If the global variable concept does not seem suitable to an architecture reference specification, it is an important mean of *abstraction* and *state reduction* in a model intended to verify the main points of a protocol. We use this global variable access feature in the verification of valid data property (Section 3.2): if caches, node controllers and modules were modeled as processes with local variables that are not accessible globally, we would not be able to simply model this property.

State Reduction Techniques

Murφ provides several state reduction techniques:

The `undefine` statement allows to give a nil value to a variable thus identifying irrelevant values at some point. This reduces the number of states since it avoids having two states that differ in non-relevant parts. In one of our verification tasks, forgetting to `undefine` a variable at some point has multiplied the state count by 10.

The *symmetry reduction* [11]: a special type constructor, `scalarset`, can be used to define a set of symmetrical identifiers (so it is user-provided symmetries). For instance, we declare the types of processor identifiers as `scalarset`. Then, in the state enumeration process, if a state can be obtained from another one by permuting the values of `scalarset` types, then both states are considered equal. As the complexity of trying all possible permutations may become exponential, there are options to limit the number of permutation trial or to use fast heuristic normalization algorithms.

Bit-compaction consists in compacting the state descriptor into a bit-string without loss of information. This reduces the state space but increases computing time. Generally, this reduction is not enough for complex configurations and we rather use the hash-compaction option detailed in the next point.

Probabilistic verification or hash compaction: instead of storing the whole state descriptor, a hash compacted descriptor is stored (typically on 40 bits). Thus, different states could be considered equal. In the verification status, the verifier prints the probabilities of having missed one state or one error [16].

Asynchronous Behavior

The Murφ language is asynchronous without a clock and without event duration. Its fundamental semantics is that of a transition system: there are events (transitions) that can occur when some enabling condition is true, and one event occurs at a time (no simultaneous events). The occurring of an event leads the system from a state to another one. This is insufficient if we want to describe and analyze the low-level design of a hardware piece (RTL level). But it is necessary abstraction means to describe system level protocol transactions, where we need an abstract way to describe all possible interleavings of events due to variable delays and different paths without describing the implementation details.

Verification and Error Diagnosis

The semantic of the model is the reachability graph of the transition system. A state is an assignment of the global variables. A rule is an atomic event. The graph is produced by an explicit state enumeration: beginning with an initial state, all the enabled rules in this state are executed yielding the successors states of the initial one. And this process continues with the generated new states, etc.

The properties to verify are expressed as boolean expressions and incorporated in the model:

- State invariants: boolean expression on global variables that should be satisfied by all the reachable states.
- "Assert" instructions: boolean expressions that should be true in some point during the execution of a rule.

Murφ compiler transforms a model into a C++ program, the verifier that explores the state graph. When an error is found, the verifier halts and prints an error trace. There are 4 kinds of errors:

- A reachable state that violates an invariant.
- An assert instruction result is false during the execution of a rule.
- An undefined variable is accessed during the execution of a rule: this could indicate an uncovered case in the protocol definition.
- A deadlock is reached: a state that has no successors (no rule is enabled).

Since we always use *breadth-first search* option, the error trace is a *minimal* one, producing a *scenario* leading from the initial state to the state exhibiting the problem. So, errors can be found quickly without the need to totally explore the state graph: this moderates state explosion problem consequences on finding errors.

Murφ Choice Motivation Discussion

Among all Murφ advantages listed above, the determining choice factors are symmetry and hash-compaction reductions, which have allowed us to verify fairly huge models (see Section 5.1, particularly Table 2 and its comment). Then the drawback is that liveness property verification is not supported with symmetry reduction.

In [5], a similar protocol to ours is model-checked using Cospan, SPIN and Murφ: the results demonstrate also the benefits to exploiting symmetries with Murφ.

However, even if we cannot verify deadlock-freeness properties like "always a transaction can complete" (Section 3.2), we can verify that there is no total system deadlock (a state where no event can occur). This is a sub-case of the liveness property we aim to, but *benefits outweigh this disadvantage* since we mainly focus on coherence properties and at least sink states can be detected (the limited resources of the model often make a blocked request result into a total deadlock).

(In a previous experiment, we had other property constraints and it was suitable to use LOTOS [2].)

5   Verification and Modeling Outcome

We have applied protocol formal verification to four versions of the FAME cache coherence protocol, which we call: FV1 to FV4. In FV1, modeling started at the very beginning of the cache protocol definition when it was still early thoughts, and went along its specification process. FV2 was a major revision, impacting transaction and conflict handling: in this case, formal modeling and verification started when the protocol definition was fairly mature but not finalized yet. FV3 has kept basic transaction handling but introduced a significant modification in conflict handling. FV4 had no significant impact on coherence protocol, but the evolutions were related to routing and system scaling: new protocol cases were added by this change but the transaction and conflict handling is the same.

In order to assess this experience, we examine two aspects: the modeling and verification process and the cost-benefit analysis.

5.1 Incremental Modeling and Verification

FAME Murφ models conform to the principles stated in Section 3. The global variables are: modules, each module contains FSS and processor nodes, FSS contains directories and buffers for ongoing transactions. A processor node contains memory, caches and input/output buffers of node controller. The cache states, data values, request and responses types are defined as enumerated types. The structures are defined as records and arrays. Identifiers of caches, nodes, addresses, and buffer index are defined as `scalarset` (symmetrical types). Replacements in caches are non-deterministic, but directory replacements occur only when needed and in models with 2 memory line addresses.

The model can be parameterized in order to define the configuration to be verified: the parameters are those listed in Section 3.1. There are 13 rules corresponding to: internal processor events, bus events within a processor node, transfers within a module, internal FSS events and transfers between two modules. The properties of interest (data integrity and cache coherence) are modeled as described in Section 3.2: there are 5 state invariants about directory coherence.

The process interleaves modeling and verification. From the protocol definition specification, we build a first incomplete model and run verification. If an error is found, it can be a modeling bug or a protocol bug. So we are concurrently debugging our model and verifying the protocol definition. Then we make corrections or add new features to the model. Even if we know that a configuration is tractable by the verification tool, we should begin verification with the smallest model and increase sizes of the different parameters in stages: because the same error is longer to detect on a larger configuration than on a smaller one.

Table 1 shows for each protocol major revision (FV1 to FV4), the number of Murφ model versions and the corresponding number of lines of code (LOC). For each case, there is a new model version at three points: model bug detection, protocol bug detection or new feature introduction in the incremental modeling process. So it is related to modeling effort and to issue finding. This explains why there are so many versions in FV1, where modeling started on early protocol definition and a lot of issues were detected, and why so few ones in FV4, where there are no protocol significant modifications and no error detected (see next subsection). The model sizes are similar and tantamount to a few thousands lines.

Table 2 shows the largest graphs that could be reached by the verification without state explosion. For each case we give the figures for the largest configuration with 1 memory address (so without directory replacement) in the model and the largest one with 2 addresses (with directory replacement). In FV1 case, we were using a machine with a 256MB memory, so it was not possible to go very far, while in the other experiments, the machines used had 1 GB of memory. Therefore FV1 largest graphs are not comparable to the other graphs and are not reported here.

Table 1. Incremental modeling effort

Case	Model versions count	LOC (smallest → biggest)
FV 1	41	920 → 3820
FV 2	36	1700 → 2750
FV 3	15	2643 → 3266
FV 4	4	3322 → 3459

The features of the verifications shown in Table 2 are: FV2a: 1 module, 4 processor nodes, 1 cache per node, 1 address, 6 transaction types. FV2b: 1 module, 3 processor nodes, 1 cache per node, 2 addresses, 5 transaction types. FV3a: 2 modules, 2 nodes/module but only 3 modules active in the system, 1 cache/node, 1 address, 7 kinds of transactions. FV3b: 2 modules, 1 node/module, 1 cache/node, 2 addresses, 7 kinds of transactions. FV4a: 3 modules, 1 node/module, 1 cache/node, 1 address, 7 kinds of transactions. FV4b: 3 modules, 1 node/module, 1 cache/node, 2 addresses, 4 kinds of transactions. Even when there are 2 addresses, a node can have at most one pending request. FSS buffer sizes are set, so that it can receives all node requests concurrently. Obviously, increasing the number of request sources (caches, nodes) has more impact than increasing the number of transaction types or addresses, since it increases concurrency in the system.

Notice that these are the states explored taken into account symmetries, so they are not all the states of the underlying graph explored. The graph diameter is a hint about the longest transaction path. The CPU time may be different even for similar counts of states for the same model, because with different parameters configurations, the non-compacted state sizes are different. Generally, enough early in the process, we have to use Murφ hash compaction to avoid state explosion and so perform probabilistic verification (actually we combine bit-compaction and hash compaction).

Table 2. Largest graphs. All this information is provided by Murφ. The "States" column gives the number of states explored. "Rules": number of rules fired. Bounds of omission probabilities induced by hash compaction: P1 is probability of "even one omitted state"; P2 of "even one undetected error". P<=0.000000 does not mean P=0, but that the bound of P, when rounded to 6 digits, gives 0. Diameter is the one of the reachability graph. CPU time is expressed in days

Case	States	Rules	Probabilities bounds	Diameter	CPU (d)
FV 2a	54,842,173	316,784,167	P1<=0.000024 P2<=0.000000	114	3.1
FV 2b	59,069,095	367,365,869	P1<=0.000029 P2<=0.000000	91	1.5
FV 3a	12,732,647	55,006,883	P1<=0.000001 P2<=0.000000	76	0.4

FV 3b	53,908,283	319,449,256	P1<=0.000013 P2<=0.000000	91	1.5
FV 4a	23,203,144	100,615,496	P1<=0.000006 P2<=0.000000	82	2.3
FV 4b	48,418,599	301,928,790	P1<=0.000025 P2<=0.000000	89	7.5

These reduction techniques (symmetry and hash compaction) are indispensable to extend the limit where state explosion occurs and has allowed us to obtain the results we analyze in next subsection.

5.2 Cost-Benefit Analysis

Since our goal is to find protocol definition issues, the benefits can be measured by the number of issues raised by modeling/verification activity. The cost is measured by the number of person.week needed to perform this task (actually the work was achieved by one person, the author). *A protocol issue can be found either by the verifier or as a result of the modeling and abstraction activity.* Modeling induces a thorough analysis of the protocol definition that can lead to finding issues, helping in clarifying, completing and mastering its specification.

When we run verification, there are 3 possible outcomes:

- It is complete with no error found: then we go into another modeling/verifying cycle by adding features to the model or rerun the same model by changing the configuration parameters.
- An error is found and a trace error is produced: then we check whether it is a protocol error or a model error. In order to get shortest error traces, we always use breadth-first search.
- The graph exploration cannot be complete due to memory lack (state explosion): then we use probabilistic verification, we try other configurations by tuning the model parameters, or we give up if we have already tried this.

We classify the issues following 2 criteria, its category and finding origin [10]:

1. Category of the issue: there are three kinds of issues:

- Uncovered or undefined case: the specification does not define the behavior of the protocol in this case.
- Ambiguous specification: several interpretations of the specification are possible. One of these leads to an error.
- Behavioral error: the behavior defined by the protocol specification leads to an error like reading stale data, coherency paradox or deadlock.

2. Origin of the issue detection: an issue can be found: by modeling (during the manual analysis of the protocol in order to model it); or by verification (by running the verification).

Table 3 shows cost, issue count (with their classification), along with the total CPU time consumed. This last figure is given as a hint and is not a rigorous comparison factor, because we have not used the same machines with the same processors in all cases. In FV1, we used 1 machine with small memory size (256 MB); in the other cases we had several machines with 1 GB of memory: we were able to launch up to 3 verifications in parallel. The usage distribution of this CPU time is more meaningful and is given by Table 4.

Table 3. Cost-benefits analysis. The categorization of issues read: A=Ambiguity, U=Uncovered, E=Error (coherence paradox or deadlock). Finding origin is M=Modeling or V=Verification. So EM means an error found by modeling

Case	Cost (p.w)	CPU (days)	Benefits (protocol issues raised)
FV 1	33	13	24 issues (1 AM, 9 UM, 2 EM, 1 AV, 4 UV, 7 EV)
FV 2	17	42	15 issues (5 AM, 3 UM, 4 EM, 3 EV)
FV 3	7	13	9 issues (1 AM, 1 UM, 2 UV, 5 EV)
FV 4	6	46	No issue raised

FV1 is the most costly one and also the one that raised the biggest number of issues, half of them by modeling. This is due to the following reasons: it is our first experience with Murφ and the modeling-verification process started at the very beginning of the protocol definition, when it was still early thoughts. This explains the preponderance of ambiguity and uncovered case issues. Half of the CPU time is wasted on verifications that did not complete, because of the small memory size.

In FV2 case, the protocol definition was mature enough (but not finalized) when the formal modeling started. We were already familiar with Murφ and a small part of the first model could be reused, so productivity increases and benefits are still important. Most of the issues are raised by modeling and are either uncovered or ambiguity issues. Since in this case we had up to 3 machines with more memory, we have tried to make use of it, and verify large configurations (with all kinds of transaction, for instance) which ended with state explosion: this explains the important CPU time consumed.

In FV3, the protocol is a fairly important extension of FV2 but with the basic transaction handling remaining the same (conflict handling is modified and directories distribution is modified). The productivity is further increased, there are more errors found by verification than by modeling. In this case, based on previous experience, we have found the configuration sizes that are manageable without state explosion. So, we have not tried to check larger ones, but instead, we have tried several combinations of up to 3 nodes in the system distributed over 2 modules. This explains that in this case the verification that ended with state explosion are not dominant.

The last case FV4 is a non-significant extension of FV3 from protocol viewpoint: the important modifications are at the routing level and increasing the number of supported modules, while we focus on cache coherence protocol. So, to follow this architecture extension, we tried to verify larger model configurations (up to 3 modules) to check new concurrency cases: this naturally increased again the effort spent on launching verifications that ended with state explosion. However, significant configurations were successfully verified and, as expected, no new issue was detected, increasing confidence in the protocol definition correctness.

Table 4. CPU time distribution. % of CPU time consumed in verifications that detected protocol issues, model bugs, were error-free (terminated with "no error" message), ran out of memory. These are rounded figures: 0% = 0, ~0% = a non-null negligible percentage

Case	Protocol Issues	Model bugs	Error-free	State explosion
FV 1	~0%	3%	46%	51%
FV 2	~0%	1%	30%	69%
FV 3	7%	7%	71%	15%
FV 4	0%	1%	38%	61%

Protocol issues found by verification are usually detected very quickly, since generally it happens on the first models and state graph exploration stops as soon as it detects an error. The time range for finding an error is between less than 1 minute and a few hours. The time consumed on debugging is not very significant either.

Finally, this approach was very fruitful and cost-effective, since it helped finding hard-to-simulate bugs, generally involving tricky conflict cases, in the early development stages. Moreover, these are protocol specification errors, not implementation errors, which are much more costly to detect in later development stages.

6   Conclusion

A distributed directory-based cache coherence protocol is a complex system to design, where the conflict resolution rules are a key issue, difficult to apprehend, because of concurrency and race conditions. Therefore, it is an outstanding domain of application of formal techniques, which provide rigorous analysis and verification methods. We have applied formal verification to FAME cache coherence protocol, aiming at finding protocol errors with abstracted simplified models.

Actually, even abstracted and simplified models of such a protocol, which focus on these coherence aspects, produce huge state spaces. Due to the Murφ reduction techniques (symmetry, hash-compaction), specification style and explicit state enumeration technique, this obstacle is overcome: the errors found by verification are detected very quickly at the beginning of the incremental modeling-verification process and are not impacted by state explosion that comes later. Error traces are minimal and exhibit a scenario explaining the error origin.

The experiments show that verifying an abstracted model is sufficient to find important protocol bugs: these are most of the time very hard-to-simulate errors that involve intricate conflict situations.

Besides, even if state-of-the-art tools were able to handle larger models, we think that building a complete protocol model instead of an abstracted protocol model would not be cost-effective in the beginning of the life-cycle of the development.

A simplified abstracted model is easier to build than a complete model and allows mastering more quickly the protocol specification complexity: then in the early phases of the development process, it helps in finding issues and improves the understanding of the system, as it is shown by the issues found by modeling, which are most of the time protocol specification "holes".

The method of protocol verification aimed at finding bugs and increasing confidence in protocol specification correctness proved to be an efficient protocol design aid. The benefits of this approach are to detect protocol specification errors not implementation ones, and to do it in the early development phases. Since the first experiment on FAME, it was considered fruitful and it was carried on to next versions; now it is a well-established practice in our protocol development process.

References

[1]   Bull NovaScale® servers. //www.bull.com/novascale/index.html
[2]   Chehaibar, G., Garavel, H., Mounier, L., Tawbi, N., Zulian, F.: Specification and Verification of the PowerScale Bus Arbitration Protocol: An Industrial Experiment with LOTOS. In Proc. of FORTE/PSTV'96 (1996) 435-450
[3]   Dill, D.L., Drexler, A.J., Hu, A.J., Yang, C.H.: Protocol Verification as a Hardware Design Aid. IEEE International Conference on Computer Design: VLSI in Computers and Processors, IEEE Computer Society (1992) 522-525
[4]   FAME Architecture, Statement of Direction
        www.bull.com/download/whitepapers/fame.pdf
[5]   Fisler, K., Girault, C.: Modelling and Model Checking a Distributed Shared Memory Consistency Protocol. Proc. 18th International Conference on Applications and Theory of Petri Nets, LNCS 1420, Springer Verlag (1998) pp 84-103
[6]   Gharachorloo, K., Lenoski, D., Laudon, J., Gibbons, P., Gupta, A., Hennessy, J.: Memory Consistency and Event Ordering in Scalable Shared-Memory Multiprocessors. In Proc. of the 17th Annual International Symposium on Computer Architecture (1990) 15-26
[7]   Hennessy, J., Heinrich, M., Gupta, A.: Cache-Coherent Distributed Shared Memory: Perspectives on Its Development and Future Challenges. In Proc. of the IEEE 87(3) (1999) 418-429 (Special issue on Distributed Shared Memory)
[8]   McMillan, K.L., Schwalbe, J.: Formal Verification of the Gigamax Cache Consistency Protocol. Proc. ISSM Int'l Conf. Parallel and Distributed Computing (1991)
[9]   Murφ description language and verifier: http://sprout.stanford.edu/dill/murphi.html
[10]   10.NASA Formal Methods Guidebook. Formal Methods, Specification and Verification Guidebook for Software and Computer Systems. Volume I: Planning and Technology Insertion. Release 2.0, [NASA/TP-98-208193] (1998) 88 pages
[11]   Norris Ip, C., Dill, D.L.: Better Verification through Symmetry. Formal Methods in System Design, Volume 9, Numbers 1/2 (1996) 41-75
[12]   Paramarcos, M., Patel, J.: A Low-Overhead Coherence Solution for Multiprocessors with Private Cache Memories. Proc. of 11th Int'l Symp. Computer Architecture, (1984) 348-354
[13]   Pong, F., Dubois, M.: A New Approach for the Verification of Cache Coherence Protocols. IEEE Transactions on Parallel and Distributed Systems, 6(8) (1995) 773-787
[14]   Pong, F., Dubois, M.: Verification Techniques for Cache Coherence Protocols. ACM Computing Surveys, Vol.29, 1, (1997) 82-126
[15]   Roucairol, G.: Using Formal Verification Methods in an Industrial Environment for a Decade, Conclusions and Perspectives. Keynote at FLOC99, Trento (1999)
[16]   Stern, U., Dill, D.L: A New Scheme for Memory-Efficient Probabilistic Verification. In Proc. of FORTE/PSTV'96, (1996) 333-348

Witness and Counterexample Automata for ACTL

Robert Meolic[1], Alessandro Fantechi[2], and Stefania Gnesi[3]

[1] Faculty of Electrical Engineering and Computer Science
University of Maribor, Maribor, Slovenia
meolic@uni-mb.si
[2] Dipartimento di Sistemi e Informatica
Università degli Studi di Firenze, Firenze, Italy
fantechi@dsi.unifi.it
[3] ISTI-CNR, Pisa, Italy
gnesi@isti.cnr.it

Abstract. Witnesses and counterexamples produced by model checkers provide a very useful source of diagnostic information. They are usually returned in the form of a single computation path along the model of the system. However, a single computation path is not enough to explain all reasons of a validity or a failure. Our work in this area is motivated by the application of action-based model checking algorithms to the test case generation for models formally specified with a CCS-like process algebra. There, only linear and finite witnesses and counterexamples are useful and for the given formula and model an efficient representation of the set of witnesses (counterexamples) explaining all reasons of validity (failure) is needed. This paper identifies a fragment of action computation tree logic (ACTL) that can be handled in this way. Moreover, a suitable form of witnesses and counterexamples is proposed and *witness* and *counterexample automata* are introduced, which are finite automata recognizing them. An algorithm for generating such automata is given.

1 Introduction

Witnesses that show why a formula is satisfied and (more often) counterexamples that show why it is not satisfied over a model have been used as useful diagnostic information since the first applications of model checking technology. They are usually returned by model checkers in the form of a computation path. However, only for certain kinds of formulae a computation path is able to explain completely the reason of satisfaction or missed satisfaction. Only recently, a greater interest was raised on the study of the relations between the formulae and their counterexamples, on one side looking for richer forms, such as tree-like counterexamples [4] or proof-like counterexamples [10], on the other side establishing the subsets of the logics whose formulae guarantee linear computation paths as counterexamples which completely explain the failure [1, 12].

Our work in this field has been motivated by another trend that has consolidated in the recent years, that is the usage of counterexamples as an help

D. de Frutos-Escrig and M. Núñez (Eds.): FORTE 2004, LNCS 3235, pp. 259–275, 2004.
© IFIP International Federation for Information Processing 2004

to generate test cases [6, 7, 8, 11, 14, 15]. When testing or simulation does not reach an adequate level of coverage (defined by some code coverage metrics, such as statement coverage and branch coverage) new test cases have to be defined, but the process of manually producing test cases for "corner-case" scenarios is time consuming and error prone. Model checking and counterexamples can help: if we have a model of the system, and we model-check on it a formula expressing "there is no uncovered point", a counterexample returns a computation path with enough information to generate the proper test case. In [7] it is shown that in the adoption of this principle with a "conquer and divide" approach in order to attack the typical state space explosion problem, a more effective option is to have the model checker generating not a single counterexample, but all the counterexamples for the given formula. We refer to [7] for more details, while here we focus on the problem of the efficient representation and generation of the set of counterexamples of a given formula.

Action computation tree logic (ACTL[1]) [13] is an action-based version of the branching time temporal logic CTL [3]. ACTL is suitable to express properties of reactive systems whose behaviour is characterized by the actions they perform and whose semantics is defined by means of LTS's. ACTL is adequate with respect to strong bisimulation equivalence, this means that if $p \sim q$, then p and q satisfy the same set of ACTL formulae. To define ACTL an auxiliary logic of actions is introduced. We limit our study to a subset of ACTL that guarantees linear witnesses and counterexamples; we address both witnesses and counterexamples, since one can switch between them using negated formulae. Moreover, we observe that for the purpose of practical applications (e.g. test case discovery) only finite linear witnesses and counterexamples are interesting. Further, we prove that the set of the desired finite linear witnesses and finite linear counterexamples forms a regular language and therefore they can be represented as automata, that will be called *witness automaton* and *counterexample automaton*, respectively.

Formal definitions are given in Section 2. In Section 3, we introduce a *viable* classes of witnesses and counterexamples for application in the field of test case generation and define witness and counterexample automata, such that the sets of witnesses and counterexamples recognized by them form such a viable class. In Section 4 an algorithm to generate witness and counterexample automata is reported and comprehensively explained on examples. Section 5 discusses complexity, implementation, and several directions of possible extension of our work. In Appendix, we show some additional examples of generated automata.

2   Definitions

Definition 1. (*Labelled transition system*)
A *labelled transition system* (LTS) is a quadruple $\mathcal{M} = (S, Act, D, s_0)$, where S

---

[1] The acronym ACTL is also used to denote the universal fragment of the CTL, whose original name used in [2] was ∀CTL, later its name has changed for easiness of writing, but generating a conflict with the already used name for Action CTL.

is a set of states, Act is a set of observable actions (an unobservable action τ is not in Act), $D \subseteq S \times Act \cup \{\tau\} \times S$ is the transition relation, and $s_0 \in S$ is the initial state.

For $A \subseteq Act$, we let $D_A(s)$ denote the set of successors of the state s reachable by an action from the set A. Moreover, we let $D_A^\tau(s)$ denote $D_{A \cup \{\tau\}}(s)$. If π is a computation path in an LTS, then $\pi(0)$ is the first state on π and $\pi(i+1)$ is the state on the path π immediately after the state $\pi(i)$.

Definition 2. (*Action formulae*)
The syntax of action formulae over Act is defined by the following grammar where χ, χ', range over action formulae, and $a \in Act$:

$$\chi ::= a \mid \neg\chi \mid \chi \wedge \chi$$

The satisfaction of an action formula χ by an action a, $a \models \chi$, is inductively defined as follows:

$$
\begin{aligned}
a &\models b && \text{iff } a = b; \\
a &\models \neg\chi && \text{iff } a \not\models \chi; \\
a &\models \chi \wedge \chi' && \text{iff } a \models \chi \text{ and } a \models \chi'
\end{aligned}
$$

We write false for $\alpha \wedge \neg\alpha$, where α is some arbitrarily chosen action, and true stands for $\neg$false. Moreover, we will write $\chi \vee \chi'$ for $\neg(\neg\chi \wedge \neg\chi')$. An action formula permits the expression of constraints on the actions that can be observed (along a path or after next step); for instance, $a \vee b$ says that the only possible observations are a or b, while true stands for "all actions are allowed" and false for "no actions can be observed", that is only silent actions can be performed.

Definition 3. (*Action computation tree logic*)
The syntax of ACTL is defined by the following grammar, where χ, χ' range over action formulae, $\exists, \forall$ are path quantifiers, and $\mathbf{X}, \mathbf{U}$ are *next* and *until* operators, respectively:

$$
\begin{aligned}
\varphi &::= \text{true} \mid \neg\varphi \mid \varphi \wedge \varphi \mid \exists\gamma \mid \forall\gamma \\
\gamma &::= \mathbf{X}_\chi \varphi \mid \mathbf{X}_\tau \varphi \mid \varphi \, \mathbf{U}_\chi \varphi \mid \varphi \, {}_\chi\mathbf{U}_{\chi'} \varphi
\end{aligned}
$$

Let $\kappa(\chi) = \{a \mid a \models \chi\}$. Being interpreted over an LTS $\mathcal{M} = (S, Act, D, s_0)$ with total transition relation the satisfaction of a state formula φ by a state s, $s \models_\mathcal{M} \varphi$, and path formula γ by a path π, $\pi \models_\mathcal{M} \gamma$, is inductively defined by:

$s \models_\mathcal{M}$ true   always;
$s \models_\mathcal{M} \neg\varphi$ iff $s \not\models_\mathcal{M} \varphi$;
$s \models_\mathcal{M} \varphi \wedge \varphi^{\scriptscriptstyle\blacksquare}$ iff $s \models_\mathcal{M} \varphi$ and $s \models_\mathcal{M} \varphi^{\scriptscriptstyle\blacksquare}$;
$s \models_\mathcal{M} \exists\gamma$ iff there exists a path π such that $\pi(0) = s$ and $\pi \models_\mathcal{M} \gamma$;
$s \models_\mathcal{M} \forall\gamma$ iff for all paths π such that $\pi(0) = s$, $\pi \models_\mathcal{M} \gamma$;
$\pi \models_\mathcal{M} \mathbf{X}_\chi \varphi$ iff there exists $\pi(1)$ such that $\pi(1) \in D_{\kappa(\chi)}(\pi(0))$ and $\pi(1) \models_\mathcal{M} \varphi$;
$\pi \models_\mathcal{M} \mathbf{X}_\tau \varphi$ iff there exists $\pi(1)$ such that $\pi(1) \in D_{(\tau)}(\pi(0))$ and $\pi(1) \models_\mathcal{M} \varphi$;

$\pi \models_M \varphi_\chi \mathbf{U} \varphi^\square$ iff there exists $i \geq 0$ such that $\pi(i) \models_M \varphi^\square$,

and for all $0 \leq j \leq i-1 \colon \pi(j) \models_M \varphi$ and $\pi(j+1) \in D^\tau_{\kappa(\chi)}(\pi(j))$;

$\pi \models_M \varphi_\chi \mathbf{U}_{\chi'} \varphi^\square$ iff there exists $i \geq 1$ such that

$\pi(0) \models_M \varphi$, $\pi(i) \models_M \varphi^\square$, $\pi(i) \in D_{\kappa(\chi')}(\pi(i-1))$, and for all $1 \leq j \leq i-1 \colon$
$\pi(j) \models_M \varphi$ and $\pi(j) \in D^\tau_{\kappa(\chi)}(\pi(j-1))$.

We write false for $\neg$true and $\varphi \vee \varphi'$ for $\neg(\neg\varphi \wedge \neg\varphi')$. When the transition system is clear from the context, we write $s \models \varphi$ instead of $s \models_M \varphi$. If $a \models \chi$ and $t \models \varphi$ then transition (s, a, t) is called a (χ, φ)-transition. Transitions, which are not (χ, φ)-transitions, are called $\neg(\chi, \varphi)$-transitions. If $s \models \varphi$ we say that φ holds in state s. An ACTL formula φ is satisfied over a given LTS M ($M \models \varphi$) iff φ holds in the initial state of M. The satisfaction of ACTL formulae over LTS M_f having a not total transition relation (i.e. M_f contains deadlocked states) is given as follows: let φ be an ACTL formula and M'_f be an LTS obtained from M_f by adding τ-loops in all its deadlocked-states; then $M_f \models \varphi$ if $M'_f \models \varphi$.

Several useful modalities can be defined, starting from the basic ones:

- $\exists \mathbf{F} \varphi$ for $\exists(\text{true}_{\text{true}} \mathbf{U} \varphi)$, and $\forall \mathbf{F} \varphi$ for $\forall(\text{true}_{\text{true}} \mathbf{U} \varphi)$ (*eventually* operators);
- $<\chi> \varphi$ for $\exists \mathbf{X}_\chi \varphi$, and $[\chi] \varphi$ for $\neg \exists \mathbf{X}_\chi \neg\varphi$ (Hennessy-Milner modalities[2]);
- $\exists \mathbf{G} \varphi$ for $\neg \forall \mathbf{F} \neg\varphi$, and $\forall \mathbf{G} \varphi$ for $\neg \exists \mathbf{F} \neg\varphi$ (*always* operators).

Given a model M and a formula φ such that $M \models \varphi$ ($M \not\models \varphi$), a witness (counterexample) is a structure R, in relation with M, that completely shows one of the possible reasons why $M \models \varphi$ ($M \not\models \varphi$). A reason why $M \models \varphi$ will be called *a reason of validity* and a reason why $M \not\models \varphi$ will be called *a reason of failure*. The type of the relation between R and M determines the nature of the witnesses and countererexamples. Linear witnesses and counterexamples are finite or infinite computation paths over M. More complex forms of witnesses and counterexamples [4, 10] are defined as non-linear structures related to the original model M. In our approach, M is an LTS and φ is an ACTL formula. Further, we formally define linear witnesses and counterexamples for an ACTL formula over an LTS; richer forms of witnesses and counterexamples are not directly addressed in this paper.

Definition 4. (*Linear witness and counterexample for ACTL formula over LTS*) Given an LTS M and an ACTL formula φ such that $M \models \varphi$ ($M \not\models \varphi$), a linear witness (counterexample) for φ over M is a sequence of actions that completely shows one of the possible reasons why $M \models \varphi$ ($M \not\models \varphi$).

3   Witness and Counterexample Automata

In [4], it has been recognized that for practical end-applications not all witnesses and counterexamples are usable. For example, the whole LTS is always a witness or a counterexample. Following the interpretation of [4], a *viable* class of witnesses (counterexamples) V meets the criteria of:

---

[2] In [13], $<\chi> \varphi$ and $[\chi] \varphi$ are defined and used instead as the weak version of the diamond and box operators of Hennessy-Milner logic.

- **Completeness**. Every reason of validity (failure), which is important for end-application, can be explained by a witness (counterexample) in $\mathcal{V}$.
- **Intelligibility**. Witnesses (counterexamples) in $\mathcal{V}$ are specific enough to suit the end-application (e.g. simple enough to be analysed by engineers).
- **Effectiveness**. There exist effective algorithms for generating and manipulating witnesses (counterexamples) in $\mathcal{V}$.

Note, that these criteria need to be adapted to the end-application. The test case generation approach in [7] is based on finite linear counterexamples, which are *no longer than necessary*, i.e. they contain only transitions, which contribute to the explanation of a particular reason of failure. Thus, we formally define the viability criteria in the field of test case generation as follows.

Definition 5. (*Viability criteria in the field of test case generation*)
The class of witnesses (counterexamples) $\mathcal{V}$ is a viable class for application in the field of test case generation iff for the given ACTL formula φ and LTS $\mathcal{M}$ there exists a suitable witness (counterexample) in $\mathcal{V}$, which

1. explains all reasons of validity (failure) of φ over $\mathcal{M}$ explainable by finite linear witnesses (counterexamples),
2. is as small as possible, and
3. is computable by an effective algorithm.

Let $\mathcal{M}$ be an LTS. In general, all reasons of validity (failure) of an arbitrary ACTL formula φ over $\mathcal{M}$ cannot be explained with finite linear witnesses (counterexamples). We avoid the problem of completeness by restricting the approach to the ACTL formulae which guarantee linearity and finiteness, i.e. for which all reasons of validity (failure) can be explained with finite linear witnesses (counterexamples) over **all** models.

Theorem 1. ACTL formulae of kind φ (ψ) as given by the grammar, when satisfied (not satisfied) over an LTS, guarantee linear witnesses (counterexamples):

$$\varphi ::= \text{true} \mid \neg\psi \mid \varphi \vee \varphi \mid \exists(\text{true}\,_\chi\mathbf{U}\,\varphi) \mid \exists(\text{true}\,_\chi\mathbf{U}_\chi\,\varphi) \mid \exists\mathbf{X}_\chi\,\varphi \mid \exists\mathbf{X}_\tau\,\varphi$$
$$\psi ::= \text{false} \mid \neg\varphi \mid \psi \wedge \psi \mid \forall(\psi\,_\chi\mathbf{U}\,\text{true}) \mid \forall(\psi\,_\chi\mathbf{U}_\chi\,\text{true}) \mid \forall\mathbf{X}_\chi\,\psi \mid \forall\mathbf{X}_\tau\,\psi$$

Proof. Theorem 1 can be proved by induction on subformulae. The basic cases are formulae true and false, and every path contains sufficient information for explaining them. Due to a short space, we give a proof only for ACTL formulae of kind $\exists(\text{true}\,_\chi\mathbf{U}_\chi\varphi)$. Let $\mathcal{M}$ be an LTS, $\gamma = \text{true}\,_\chi\mathbf{U}_{\chi'}\,\varphi'$, $\varphi = \exists\gamma$, and $\mathcal{M} \models \varphi$. According to Definition 3, the reason of validity is the existence of paths starting in the initial state of $\mathcal{M}$, which satisfy path formula γ. Thus, a witness is a proof that a particular path π satisfies path formula γ. If the path π itself contains sufficient information to show why $\pi \models \gamma$ then π is a linear witness. According to Definition 3 again, for each $\pi \models \gamma$ there exists $i \geq 1$ such that $\pi(i) \models \varphi'$ and $\pi(i) \in D_{\kappa(\chi')}(\pi(i-1))$, and for all $0 \leq j \leq i-1 \colon \pi(j) \in D_{\kappa(\chi)}^\tau(\pi(j-1))$. Now, the path from the first state until state $\pi(i)$ needs no additional explanation. We must only show $\pi(i) \models \varphi'$. But, due to the induction hypothesis, subformula φ' guarantees linear witnesses and therefore the suffix of the path from state $\pi(i)$

contains sufficient information for explaining $\pi(i) \models \varphi'$. Hence, any path π such that $\pi \models \gamma$ is a linear witness.

Some formulae with derived modalities can also be used in the presented approach. Indeed, formulae $\exists \mathbf{F}\, \varphi$ and $<\chi>\varphi$ guarantee linear witnesses, while formulae $\forall \mathbf{G}\, \psi$ and $[\chi]\psi$ guarantee linear counterexamples.

Theorem 1 assures linearity but not finiteness. In fact, all ACTL formulae of the given sublogic, except those of kind $\forall(\psi_\chi \mathbf{U}_\chi \text{ true})$, guarantee also finiteness. Therefore, we exclude formulae of this kind from this approach. We also exclude ACTL formulae of kind $\forall(\psi_\chi \mathbf{U} \text{ true})$, as they always hold and have no linear witnesses and no linear counterexamples. For all other kind of formuale of the given sublogic and an LTS $\mathcal{M}$ with total transition relation, we define in a constructive way $\mathcal{V}$-witnesses and $\mathcal{V}$-counterexamples, respectively.

Definition 6. (*$\mathcal{V}$-witness and $\mathcal{V}$-counterexample*)

(a) A $\mathcal{V}$-witness for ACTL formula true is a path consisting of only one state and no transitions.

(b) A path π in $\mathcal{M}$ is a $\mathcal{V}$-witness for ACTL formula $\varphi = \neg\psi$ iff π is a $\mathcal{V}$-counterexample for ACTL formula ψ.

(c) A path π in $\mathcal{M}$ is a $\mathcal{V}$-witness for ACTL formula $\varphi = \varphi_1 \vee \varphi_2$ iff π is a $\mathcal{V}$-witness for φ_1 (φ_2) and no proper prefix of π is a $\mathcal{V}$-witness for φ_2 (resp. φ_1).

(d) A path π in $\mathcal{M}$ is a $\mathcal{V}$-witness for ACTL formula $\varphi = \exists(\text{true}\,_\chi \mathbf{U}\, \varphi')$ iff there exists $i \geq 0$ such that suffix of π starting in $\pi(i)$ is a $\mathcal{V}$-witness for ACTL formula φ', and for all $0 \leq j \leq i-1$: $\pi(j+1) \in D^\tau_{\kappa(\chi)}(\pi(j))$ and $\pi(j) \not\models_\mathcal{M} \varphi'$.

(e) A path π in $\mathcal{M}$ is a $\mathcal{V}$-witness for ACTL formula $\varphi = \exists(\text{true}\,_\chi \mathbf{U}_{\chi'}\, \varphi')$ iff there exists $i \geq 1$ such that $\pi(i) \in D_{\kappa(\chi')}(\pi(i-1))$ and suffix of π starting in $\pi(i)$ is a $\mathcal{V}$-witness for ACTL formula φ', and for all $0 \leq j \leq i-1$: $\pi(j) \in D^\tau_{\kappa(\chi)}(\pi(j-1))$, and also $\pi(j) \notin D_{\kappa(\chi')}(\pi(j-1))$ or $\pi(j) \not\models_\mathcal{M} \varphi'$.

(f) A path π in $\mathcal{M}$ is a $\mathcal{V}$-witness for ACTL formula $\varphi = \exists\mathbf{X}_\chi\, \varphi'$ iff $\pi(1) \in D_{\kappa(\chi)}(\pi(0))$ and suffix of π starting in $\pi(1)$ is a $\mathcal{V}$-witness for ACTL formula φ'.

(g) A path π in $\mathcal{M}$ is a $\mathcal{V}$-witness for ACTL formula $\varphi = \exists\mathbf{X}_\tau\, \varphi'$ iff $\pi(1) \in D_{\{\tau\}}(\pi(0))$ and suffix of π starting in $\pi(1)$ is a $\mathcal{V}$-witness for ACTL formula φ'.

(h) A $\mathcal{V}$-counterexample for ACTL formula false is a path consisting of only one state and no transitions.

(i) A path π in $\mathcal{M}$ is a $\mathcal{V}$-counterexample for ACTL formula $\psi = \neg\varphi$ iff π is a $\mathcal{V}$-witness for ACTL formula φ.

(j) A path π in $\mathcal{M}$ is a $\mathcal{V}$-counterexample for ACTL formula $\psi = \psi_1 \wedge \psi_2$ iff π is a $\mathcal{V}$-counterexample for ψ_1 (ψ_2) and no proper prefix of π is a $\mathcal{V}$-counterexample for ψ_2 (resp. ψ_1).

(k) A path π in $\mathcal{M}$ is a $\mathcal{V}$-counterexample for ACTL formula $\psi = \forall\mathbf{X}_\chi\, \psi'$ iff $\pi(1) \notin D_{\kappa(\chi)}(\pi(0))$ and π contains only two states, or $\pi(1) \in D_{\kappa(\chi)}(\pi(0))$ and suffix of π starting in $\pi(1)$ is a $\mathcal{V}$-counterexample for ACTL formula φ'.

(1) A path π in $\mathcal{M}$ is a $\mathcal{V}$-counterexample for ACTL formula $\psi = \forall \mathbf{X}_\tau \, \psi'$ iff $\pi(1) \notin D_{\{\tau\}}(\pi(0))$ and π contains only two states, or $\pi(1) \in D_{\{\tau\}}(\pi(0))$ and suffix of π starting in $\pi(1)$ is a $\mathcal{V}$-counterexample for ACTL formula φ'.

It is straightforward to show that all $\mathcal{V}$-witnesses ($\mathcal{V}$-counterexamples) are finite linear witnesses (counterexamples). The following theorem shows that they are suitable for our approach.

Theorem 2. Let π be a finite linear witness (counterexample) explaining a reason of validity (failure) of an ACTL formula φ (ψ) over an LTS $\mathcal{M}$. Then, there exists $\mathcal{V}$-witness ($\mathcal{V}$-counterexample), which shows that $\mathcal{M} \models \varphi$ ($\mathcal{M} \not\models \psi$).

Proof. We claim, that the smallest (not necessary proper and therefore always existing) prefix of π, which shows that $\mathcal{M} \models \varphi$ ($\mathcal{M} \not\models \psi$) is a $\mathcal{V}$-witness ($\mathcal{V}$-counterexample). To show this, we observe finite linear witnesses (counterexamples), which are not $\mathcal{V}$-witnesses ($\mathcal{V}$-counterexamples) and prove, that a proper prefix of them exists, which explain $\mathcal{M} \models \varphi$ ($\mathcal{M} \not\models \psi$). We omit the details of the proof due to the lack of space.

Further, we show that we can characterize not only a single $\mathcal{V}$-witness and $\mathcal{V}$-counterexample, but also the set of *all* the possible ones. Actually, the number of the possible $\mathcal{V}$-witnesses and $\mathcal{V}$-counterexamples may be infinite and we are interested to a finite representation of them all.

Theorem 3. Let $\mathcal{M}$ be a finite state LTS and φ (ψ) an ACTL formula such that $\mathcal{M} \models \varphi$ ($\mathcal{M} \not\models \psi$). Then, there exists a finite-state automaton which recognizes all $\mathcal{V}$-witnesses ($\mathcal{V}$-counterexamples) for formula φ (ψ) over $\mathcal{M}$.

Proof. In order to check whether a path is a $\mathcal{V}$-witness ($\mathcal{V}$-counterexample), we just need to see whether it is a path over $\mathcal{M}$ and if it has the form given in Definition 6. Since the characterizations given in Definition 6 are given with a single right recursion, they can be expressed as a regular grammar. The language of $\mathcal{V}$-witnesses ($\mathcal{V}$-counterexamples) is the intersection of the regular language recognized by this grammar and the regular language of the finite paths over $\mathcal{M}$. Hence, it is a regular language and can be recognized by a finite state automaton.

Definition 7. (*Witness and counterexample automata*)
A witness (counterexample) automaton for an LTS $\mathcal{M}$ and an ACTL formula φ is an automaton which recognizes the language of all $\mathcal{V}$-witnesses ($\mathcal{V}$-counter-examples) of φ over $\mathcal{M}$.

Now, only an effective algorithm for generation of witness and counterexample automata is missing to fit the viability criteria in Definition 5.

4   Implementation

We present here an elegant recursive algorithm that, given a LTS and a formula φ from the subset of ACTL given in Theorem 1, generates the witness or counterexample automaton WCA for the formula φ over the given LTS. If the formula φ holds in the initial state of LTS, the generated WCA is a witness automaton, otherwise, it is a counterexample automaton. The algorithm is

```
WCAgenerator (LTS, φ) {
    forall subformulae φ' of formula φ {
        create subset of LTS states S_φ' in which formula φ' holds;
        create empty relation R_φ';
    }
    let s be the initial state of LTS;
    create empty automaton WCA;
    create the initial state t in WCA;
    if (s ∈ S_φ) generate (LTS, φ, s, t, witness);
        else generate (LTS, φ, s, t, counterexample);
}

generate (LTS, φ, s, t, type) {
    if (type == null) {
        add t to the set of WCA final states;
    } else {
        add the pair (t, s) to R_φ ;
        if (type == witness) WAgen (LTS, φ, s, t);
        if (type == counterexample) CAgen (LTS, φ, s, t);
    }
}

conbuild (LTS, φ, a, s', t, type) {
    if ((type == null) || (there is no state related to state s' in R_φ)) {
        create a new state t' in WCA;
        if not exists, add the transition (t, a, t') to WCA;
        generate (LTS, φ, s', t', type);
    } else {
        let t' be a state in WCA related to state s' in R_φ;
        if not exists, add the transition (t, a, t') to WCA;
    }
}
```

Fig. 1. Main function and two auxiliary functions of the algorithm

a direct implementation of the definitions of $\mathcal{V}$-witnesses and $\mathcal{V}$-counterexamples and it is given in a C-like pseudocode. It consists of the main function *WCA-generator*, two auxiliary functions *generate* and *conbuild* (Fig. 1), and functions processing ACTL formulae (Fig.2, 3). For the purpose of further work, the part for generation of counterexample automata is extended with formulae of type $\forall(\psi_\chi \mathbf{U}_\chi \text{true})$. For them, $\mathcal{V}$-counterexamples have not been defined. Computation paths recognized by the obtained automaton for this kind of ACTL formulae explain only those reasons of failure which can be explained with finite linear counterexamples. Due to the lack of space, we are not able to discuss details of this feature.

```
WAgen (LTS, φ, s, t) {
    case φ == true:
        generate (LTS, φ, s, t, null);
        break;
    case φ == ¬φ':
        generate (LTS, φ', s, t, counterexample);
        break;
    case φ == φ₁ ∨ φ₂:
        if (s ∈ S_{φ₁}) generate (LTS, φ₁, s, t, witness);
        if (s ∈ S_{φ₂}) generate (LTS, φ₂, s, t, witness);
        break;
    case φ == ∃X_χ φ':
        WAbuild (LTS, φ, s, t, false, false, χ, φ');
        break;
    case φ == ∃X_τ φ':
        if (s is a deadlocked state) generate (LTS, φ', s, t, witness);
            else WAbuild (LTS, φ, s, t, false, false, τ, φ');
        break;
    case φ == ∃(true _χ U φ'):
        if (s ∈ S_{φ'}) generate (LTS, φ', s, t, witness);
        WAbuild (LTS, φ, s, t, (χ ∨ τ), true, (χ ∨ τ), φ');
        break;
    case φ == ∃(true _χ U_{χ'} φ'):
        WAbuild (LTS, φ, s, t, (χ ∨ τ), true, χ', φ');
        break;
}

WAbuild (LTS, φ, s, t, χ₁, φ₁, χ₂, φ₂) {
    let δ₁ be the set of ¬(χ₂, φ₂)-trans. from s which are (χ₁, φ₁)-trans.;
    forall transitions (s, a, s') ∈ δ₁ {
        if (s' ∈ S_φ) conbuild (LTS, φ, a, s', t, witness);
    }
    let δ₂ be the set of (χ₂, φ₂)-transitions from s;
    forall transitions (s, a, s') ∈ δ₂ {
        conbuild (LTS, φ₂, a, s', t, witness);
    }
}
```

Fig. 2. The part of the algorithm, which generates witness automaton

The algorithm proceeds by visiting a portion of the state space of LTS. The visit is guided by the structural analysis of the formula itself, hence it is terminated when the leaves of the formula are reached. In ACTL, leaves can only be the formula true or the formula false. LTS is unfolded if a sequence of subformulae of φ matches with a loop in it. The visit is implemented by a depth-first search by recursion, and hence it has to be remembered which states of LTS have already been visited with a particular subformula of φ. Unfortunately, the resulting au-

```
CAgen (LTS, φ, s, t) {
    case φ == false:
        generate (LTS, φ, s, t, null);
        break;
    case φ == ¬φ′:
        generate (LTS, φ′, s, t, witness);
        break;
    case φ == φ₁ ∧ φ₂:
        if (s ∉ S_{φ₁}) generate (LTS, φ₁, s, t, counterexample);
        if (s ∉ S_{φ₂}) generate (LTS, φ₂, s, t, counterexample);
        break;
    case φ == ∀X_χ φ′:
        if (s is a deadlocked state) generate (LTS, φ, s, t, null);
            else CAbuild (LTS, φ, s, t, false, false, χ, φ′);
        break;
    case φ == ∀X_τ φ′:
        if (s is a deadlocked state) generate (LTS, φ′, s, t, counterexample);
            else CAbuild (LTS, φ, s, t, false, false, τ, φ′);
        break;
    case φ == ∀(φ′ _χ U_{χ′} true):
        if (s is a deadlocked state) generate (LTS, φ, s, t, null);
        if (s ∉ S_{φ′}) generate (LTS, φ′, s, t, counterexample);
        CAbuild (LTS, φ, s, t, (χ ∨ τ), φ′, χ′, true);
        break;
}

CAbuild (LTS, φ, s, t, χ₁, φ₁, χ₂, φ₂) {
    let δ₁ be the set of ¬(χ₂, φ₂)-trans. from s which are (χ₁, φ₁)-trans.;
    forall transitions (s, a, s′) ∈ δ₁ do {
        if (s′ ∉ S_φ) conbuild (LTS, φ, a, s′, t, counterexample);
    }
    let δ₂ be the set of ¬(χ₂, φ₂)-trans. from s which are ¬(χ₁, φ₁)-trans.;
    forall transitions (s, a, s′) ∈ δ₂ {
        if (a ⊭ χ₁ ∧ a ⊭ χ₂) conbuild (LTS, φ, a, s′, t, null);
        if (a ⊨ χ₁) conbuild (LTS, φ₁, a, s′, t, counterexample);
        if (a ⊨ χ₂) conbuild (LTS, φ₂, a, s′, t, counterexample);
    }
}
```

Fig. 3. The part of the algorithm, which generates counterexample automaton

tomaton can be slightly incorrect. It may recognize some paths, which are finite linear witnesses (counterexamples) but not $\mathcal{V}$-witnesses ($\mathcal{V}$-counterexamples). However, it can always be minimized to fit Definition 7. We will discuss about this in the next section.

The algorithm is further explained in details using a simple LTS and two simple ACTL formulae (Fig. 4). It starts in function *WCAgenerator*. The first

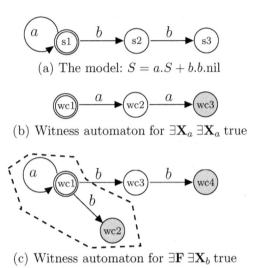

(a) The model: $S = a.S + b.b.\text{nil}$

(b) Witness automaton for $\exists \mathbf{X}_a \, \exists \mathbf{X}_a$ true

(c) Witness automaton for $\exists \mathbf{F} \, \exists \mathbf{X}_b$ true

Fig. 4. Two examples of generated witness automata. For the second ACTL formula, the resulting automaton must be properly minimized to obtain the correct witness automaton indicated by a dashed polygon

action is actually a call to a model checker, which computes S and initializes R for all subformulae of φ. S contains for each subformula the subset of states that satisfy the subformula. Thus, the algorithm takes for granted the information about validity of the subformulae on each state. R is a relation implemented as a set of pairs, where for each state of the LTS visited with a particular subformula the related state in WCA is stored. Variables WCA, S, and R are global, all others are local. Here is a program trace for the example in Fig. 4b.

```
ACTL model checking on S
EX{a} EX{a} true ==> TRUE
@@ WCAgenerator: created empty witness automaton WC1S
@@ WCAgenerator: created initial state wc1
@@ generate: starting formula 'EX{a} EX{a} true' for (s=s1, t=wc1)
@@    generate: added pair (wc1,s1) to R for the current formula
@@    WAbuild: chosen transition s1-a->s1 from delta2
@@    conbuild: created state wc2, created transition wc1-a->wc2
@@    generate: starting formula 'EX{a} true' for (s=s1, t=wc2)
@@       generate: added pair (wc2,s1) to R for the current formula
@@       WAbuild: chosen transition s1-a->s1 from delta2
@@       conbuild: created state wc3, created transition wc2-a->wc3
@@       generate: starting formula 'true' for (s=s1, t=wc3)
@@          generate: added pair (wc3,s1) to R for the current formula
@@          generate: state wc3 marked as final
@@ Witness automaton has been constructed.
```

After an ACTL model checker determines that formula $\exists\mathbf{X}_a\,\exists\mathbf{X}_a$ true holds in the initial state s1 of S, a generation of the witness automaton is started. A new automaton WC1S and its initial state wc1 are created. Function *generate* makes initial states of S and WC1S to be related for the formula $\exists\mathbf{X}_a\,\exists\mathbf{X}_a$ true. Then, function *WAgen* is started. The outermost operator is $\exists\mathbf{X}_a$ and therefore function *WAbuild* is called with parameters $\chi_1 = $ false, $\varphi_1 = $ false, $\chi_2 = a$, and $\varphi_2 = \exists\mathbf{X}_a$ true. Set δ_1 is empty, because there is no (χ_1, φ_1)-transition. Set δ_2 contains only the transition (s1, a, s1). State s1 has not been visited with formula $\exists\mathbf{X}_a$ true, yet, and therefore there is no state in WC1S related to it. Function *conbuild* creates a new state wc2 and the transition (wc1, a, wc2) in WC1S. Then, function *generate* is recursively called for the formula $\exists\mathbf{X}_a$ true. In this call, subformula $\varphi_2 = $ true. Again, set δ_1 is empty, while set δ_2 contains the transition (s1, a, s1). Because state s1 has not been visited with formula true, yet, function *conbuild* creates a new state wc3 and transition (wc2, a, wc3). Further, state wc3 is marked as final and the recursive calls end.

The usage of relation R is better shown on a program trace for ACTL formula $\exists\mathbf{F}\,\exists\mathbf{X}_b$ true. Actually, this is an abbreviation of formula $\exists(\text{true}_{\text{true}}\mathbf{U}\,\exists\mathbf{X}_b\text{true})$.

```
ACTL model checking on S
EF EX{b} true ==> TRUE
@@ WCAgenerator: created empty witness automaton WC2S
@@ WCAgenerator: created initial state wc1
@@ generate: starting formula 'EF EX{b} true' for (s=s1, t=wc1)
@@    generate: added pair (wc1,s1) to R for the current formula
@@    generate: starting formula 'EX{b} true' for (s=s1, t=wc1)
@@      generate: added pair (wc1,s1) to R for the current formula
@@      WAbuild: chosen transition s1-b->s2 from delta2
@@      conbuild: created state wc2, created transition wc1-b->wc2
@@      generate: starting formula 'true' for (s=s2, t=wc2)
@@        generate: added pair (wc2,s2) to R for the current formula
@@        generate: state wc2 marked as final
@@    WAbuild: chosen transition s1-b->s2 from delta2
@@    conbuild: created state wc3, created transition wc1-b->wc3
@@    generate: starting formula 'EX{b} true' for (s=s2, t=wc3)
@@      generate: added pair (wc3,s2) to R for the current formula
@@      WAbuild: chosen transition s2-b->s3 from delta2
@@      conbuild: created state wc4, created transition wc3-b->wc4
@@      generate: starting formula 'true' for (s=s3, t=wc4)
@@        generate: added pair (wc4,s3) to R for the current formula
@@        generate: state wc4 marked as final
@@    WAbuild: chosen transition s1-a->s1 from delta2
@@    conbuild: created transition wc1-a->wc1
@@ Witness automaton has been constructed.
```

Because subformula $\exists\mathbf{X}_b$ true holds in the initial state of S, first a $\mathcal{V}$-witness for it is generated. State wc2 and transition (wc1, b, wc2) are created. Then, function *WAgen* continues and calls function *WAbuild* with parameters $\chi_1 = $ true, $\varphi_1 = $ true, $\chi_2 = $ true, and $\varphi_2 = \exists\mathbf{X}_b$ true. Set δ_1 is empty, while set δ_2 contains transitions (s1, a, s1) and (s1, b, s2). The transition with action b is chosen first. Formula $\exists \mathbf{X}_b$ true has been already visited in state s1, but not in state s2. Therefore, state wc3 and transition (wc1, b, wc3) are created. Afterwards, the algorithm continues in the state s2. State wc4 and transition (wc3, b, wc4) are created. Because subformula true has been reached, state wc4 is marked as final and the path is finished. Now, function *WAbuild* must also process transition (s1, a, s1) from δ_2. State s1 has been visited with formula $\exists \mathbf{F}\ \exists \mathbf{X}_b$ true before, thus a new state is not created. State s1 is related to state wc1 in relation $R_{\exists \mathbf{F}\ \exists \mathbf{X}_b\ \text{true}}$, therefore transition (wc1, a, wc1) is created without further recursive calls.

5   Discussion

The algorithm for witness and counterexample automata generation basically works by following the given LTS and using unfolding when necessary, with an unfolding depth of at most the length of the formula. Therefore, the complexity is not higher than the size of the LTS (states and transitions) times the length of the formula. This is exactly the same complexity of an explicit model checking algorithm which has to be employed to compute the labeling of the LTS.

We have implemented the algorithm as an extension of a BDD-based ACTL model checker. Although LTSs are represented by BDDs and BDD-based functions are used for navigating the LTS, the algorithm indirectly still involves an implicit enumeration in functions *WAbuild* and *CAbuild*, where transitions are chosen from δ_1 and δ_2 one by one and then for each next state on the path a new recursive call is made. An open question remains whether a more efficient symbolic algorithm exists.

The last example in the previous section and some of the examples given in Appendix clearly show that the resulting automata may contain redundancy. In fact, there are two different kinds of redundancy. At first, some equal paths may be presented more than once. This is not very disturbing and among other reasons it appears because the program does not identify two semantic equal subformulae as the same one. For example, in the witness automaton generated for the ACTL formula $(\exists \mathbf{X}_\chi \varphi) \vee (\exists \mathbf{X}_\chi \varphi)$, all paths are doubled. The second type of redundancy is much more problematic as it leads to the incorrect result. It appears due to the fact, that during the generation of the automaton the algorithm does not check, whether one of the created paths explaining one reason of validity (failure) is a proper prefix of another created paths explaining another reason of validity (failure). In such case, only the shorter path is a $\mathcal{V}$-witness ($\mathcal{V}$-counterexample) and thus the generated automaton should recognize only the shorter one and not both. The ACTL formulae, which are subject to this kind of redundancy are all those which contain Boolean operator $\vee$ or $\wedge$, explicitly or implicitly as, for example, formula $\exists(\text{true}\ _\chi \mathbf{U}\ \varphi')$ and derived formula $\exists \mathbf{F}\ \varphi$. To obtain the correct automaton, all extra paths must be later eliminated by a proper minimization.

A result which is related to our work is the definition of more expressive *tree-like* counterexamples for Kripke Structures and CTL; such counterexamples are used as a support to guide a refinement technique [4]. The main difference with respect to our approach is that a tree-like counterexample is in its entirety a proof that the formula is not satisfied. Our counterexample automaton gives instead the set of linear counterexamples, each of which can be taken separately as a traditional counterexample. An evolution of tree-like counterexamples is represented by *proof-like* counterexamples [10], used to extract proofs for the non satisfiability of a formula over a model. Closer to our approach is the multiple counterexamples generation of [5, 9], which generates all the counterexamples up to a given length, expressed as a single counterexample trace annotated with possible values of binary variables.

There are some possible directions for further work. We have considered only finite witnesses and counterexamples, which are the ones suitable to be used as actual test cases (see [7]). Having more rich notions of acceptance than linear languages could provide the possibility of characterizing sets of more informative witnesses and counterexamples. In order to deal with infinite counterexamples and witnesses the same approach can be followed, for example, using Büchi automata for recognizing a language of infinite words. In this way, if the transition relation is total and if witnesses and counterexamples are extended to become infinite paths, our work becomes adequate to the work presented for CTL in [1].

An interesting extension of the given algorithm would be a generation of non-linear forms of witnesses and counterexamples. The core of the algorithm are functions *WAbuild* and *CAbuild*. We implemented them in a more general form w.r.t. what needed in this approach. For example, function *WAbuild* will also process ACTL formula $\exists(\varphi_1\ {}_\chi\mathbf{U}_{\chi'}\ \varphi_2)$, where parameter φ_1 is not just a simple formula true or false, although a witness for this formula is not always a linear computation path. The algorithm will produce an automaton recognizing linear witnesses and the main paths (sometimes referred as backbones) of non-linear witnesses. There will be no extra information given about which recognized witness completely explains the validity and which one is only a main path of a non-linear witness. Such general implementation allows extensions. If parameter φ_1 is not a simple formula true or false and if an explanation of validity is added to all states on the main path, we get richer non-linear forms of witnesses. Thus, the given algorithm can serve also as a basis for generation of tree-like witnesses and counterexamples. Note that for the formulae which guarantee linearity and finiteness of witnesses (counterexamples) the presented witness and counterexample automata explain all reasons of validity (failure) over a given model and thus they are equivalent to the tree-like witnesses and counterexamples, respectively.

6   Conclusions

We have defined witness and counterexample automata, which are intended to be used in the field of test case generation. These automata recognize $\mathcal{V}$-witnesses and $\mathcal{V}$-counterexamples which are finite linear witnesses and counterexamples for a given formula over a given LTS. The main result of the paper is the algorithm for generating witness and counterexample automata for a given LTS and a given ACTL formula from a subset of ACTL formulae which guarantee finite linear witnesses and counterexamples. The algorithm has been implemented and a stand-alone demo application has been made available online on http://fmt.isti.cnr.it/WCA/.

It seems reasonable that the given approach works as well with a state based formalism (such as Kripke structures) and a state based temporal logic (such as CTL). This needs to be verified: the very definition of witnesses, counterexamples, and automata recognizing them is actually highly sensitive to the logic used and to the assumptions on the models.

Acknowledgements

This work has been partially supported by Italian MIUR PRIN 2002 COVER project. The first author has been partially supported by a grant from Government of Italy through Italian Cultural Institute in Slovenia. We wish to thank Gianluca Trentanni for his help in the realization of the on-line demo application.

References

[1] F. Buccafurri, T. Eiter, G. Gottlob, N. Leone. On ACTL formulas having linear counterexamples. Journal of computer and syst. sciences, 62(3), 2001, pp. 463–515. 259, 272

[2] E. M. Clarke, O. Grumberg, D. E. Long. Model Checking and Abstraction ACM Transaction on Programming Languages and Systems, (16)5, 1994, pp. 1512-1542. 260

[3] E. M. Clarke, E. A. Emerson, A. P. Sistla. Automatic Verification of Finite State Concurrent Systems using Temporal Logic Specifications. ACM Transaction on Programming Languages and Systems, 8(2), 1986, pp. 244–263. 260

[4] E. M. Clarke, S. Jha, Y. Lu, H. Veith. Tree-like Counterexamples in Model Checking. In 17th IEEE Symp. on Logic in Computer Science (LICS), 2002, pp. 19–29. 259, 262, 272

[5] F. Copty, A. Irron, O. Weissberg, N. Kropp, G. Kamhi. Efficient Debugging in a Formal Verification Environment. In Conf. On Correct Hardware Design and Verification Methods (CHARME), LNCS 2144, 2001, pp. 275–292. 272

[6] A. Časar, Z. Brezočnik, T. Kapus. Exploiting Symbolic Model Checking for Sensing Stuck-at Faults in Digital Circuits. Informacije MIDEM, 32(3), 2002, pp. 171–180. 260

[7] A. Fantechi, S. Gnesi, A. Maggiore. Enhancing test coverage by back-tracing model-checker counterexamples. In Int. Workshop on Test and Analysis of Component Based Syst. (TACOS), 2004, to appear in Electronic Notes in Theoretical Computer Science. 260, 263, 272

[8] D. Geist, M. Farkas, A. Landver, Y. Lichenstein, S. Ur, Y. Wolfsthal. Coverage-Directed Test Generation Using Symbolic Techniques. In First Int. Conf. on Formal Method in Computer-Aided Design (FMCAD), LNCS 1166, 1996, pp. 143-158. 260

[9] M. Glusman, G. Kamhi, S. Mador-Heim, R. Fraer, M. Vardi. Multiple-Counter-example Guided Iterative Abstraction Refinement: An Industrial Evaluation. In *Tools and Algorithms for the construction and analysis of syst. (TACAS)*, LNCS 2619, 2003, pp. 176-191. 272

[10] A. Gurfinkel, M. Chechik. Proof-Like Counter-Examples. In *Tools and Algorithms for the construction and analysis of syst. (TACAS)*, LNCS 2619, 2003, pp. 160-175. 259, 262, 272

[11] P. H. Ho, T. Shiple, K. Harer, J. Kukula, R. Damiano, V. Bertacco, J. Taylor, J. Long. Smart Simulation Using Collaborative Formal and Simulation Engines. In *Int. Conf. on Computer Aided Design (ICCAD)*, 2000. 260

[12] M. Maidl. The Common Fragment of CTL and LTL. In *Proc. 41th Symp. on Foundations of Computer Science (FOCS)*, pp. 643-652, 2000. 259

[13] R. De Nicola, F. W. Vaandrager. Actions versus State Based Logics for Transition Systems. Proc. Ecole de Printemps on Semantics of Concurrency, Lecture Notes in Computer Science, vol. 469, 1990, pp. 407-419. 260, 262

[14] G. Ratzaby, S. Ur, Y. Wolfsthal, Coverability Analysis Using Symbolic Model Checking. In *Conf. On Correct Hardware Design and Verification Methods (CHARME)*, LNCS 2144, 2001. 260

[15] G. Ratsaby, B. Sterin, S. Ur. Improvements in Coverabiliy Analysis. In *Int. Symp. of Formal Methods Europe (FME)*, LNCS 2391, 2002. 260

Appendix

NOTE: Automata in dashed polygon are obtained by a minimization.

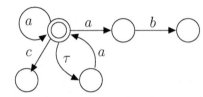

(a) The model: $S = a.S + \tau.a.S + a.b.\text{nil} + c.\text{nil}$

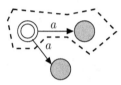

(b) Witness automaton for $\exists \mathbf{X}_a$ true

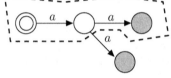

(c) Witness automaton for $\exists \mathbf{X}_a \exists \mathbf{X}_a$ true

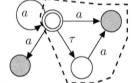

(d) Witness automaton for
$\exists \mathbf{F} \exists \mathbf{X}_a$ true

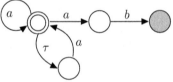

(e) Witness automaton for
$\exists(\text{true} \,_a\mathbf{U}_b \text{ true})$

(f) Counterexample automaton for
$\forall \mathbf{X}_a$ true

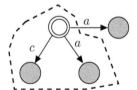

(g) Counterexample automaton for
$\forall \mathbf{X}_\tau \forall \mathbf{X}_a$ true

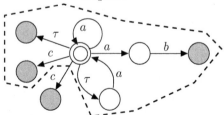

(h) Counterexample automaton for
$\forall \mathbf{G} \forall \mathbf{X}_a$ true

(i) An automaton generated for
$\forall(\text{true} \,_a\mathbf{U}_b \text{ true})$

A Symbolic Symbolic State Space Representation

Yann Thierry-Mieg, Jean-Michel Ilié, and Denis Poitrenaud

SRC - LIP6 - UMR 7606, Université Paris 6
4, Place Jussieu, 75252 Paris cedex 05
(firstname.lastname@lip6.fr)

Abstract. Symmetry based approaches are known to attack the state space explosion problem encountered during the analysis of distributed systems. In another way, BDD-like encodings enable the management of huge data sets. In this paper, we show how to benefit from both approaches automatically. Hence, a quotient set is built from a coloured Petri net description modeling the system. The reachability set is managed under some explicit symbolic operations. Also, data representations are managed symbolically based on a recently introduced data structure, called Data Decisions Diagrams, that allow flexible definition of application specific operators. Performances yielded by our prototype are reported in the paper.

Keywords: Decision Diagrams, Symbolic Model-checking, Symbolic Reachability Graph, Well-Formed Petri Nets, Symmetry Detection

1 Introduction

In this paper, we exploit both data symmetries to construct a set of reachable equivalence classes of states, and a symbolic coding of these classes and of the transition relation using a BDD-like representation. The construction of this reachability set is the basis for model-checking, verification of safety constraints, deadlock detection, etc.

Roughly speaking, model checking of symmetrical systems exploits the fact that many synchronization and communication protocols, involving parallel composition of n processes differing only by their identity, often exhibit considerable symmetries. This can be viewed as a redundancy of information in the state graph, as states identical up to a permutation can be aggregated into equivalence classes, yielding a possibly exponentially smaller quotient state space. The efficiency of this type of approach is demonstrated by tools like GreatSPN, SMC, Mur-φ, which offer mechanisms to define the symmetries allowed by the model (for instance the Mur-φ scalarset).

The core of the problem consists in determining whether two states are equivalent; one approach found in literature is to define a canonization operation that yields a unique representative for each equivalence class, thus only representatives need to be stored. However it has been proved that the BDD coding the orbit relation required to find a unique representative of an equivalence class would need an exponential number of nodes [3]. The approach used here is based on the work of [1] which uses dedicated data-structures to represent equivalence classes, termed Symbolic Markings (*SM*), instead of concrete states designated as representatives. In practice, such a direct coding

D. de Frutos-Escrig and M. Núñez (Eds.): FORTE 2004, LNCS 3235, pp. 276–291, 2004.
© IFIP International Federation for Information Processing 2004

of the equivalence classes can speed up the computation of the quotient graph. In the literature, one can find other codings which use close concepts [8].

Furthermore, the symmetries exploited to construct an SM are computed automatically through a structural exploration of a model. This procedure uses the algorithm described in [10] and assumes a modeling in a coloured Petri net to produce a Well-Formed net. It is fully automatic and has a polynomial complexity over the size of the model. The symbolic reachability set (SRS) is then built by means of a symbolic firing rule, that does not require the actual concrete states to be explored. The steps required for this construction are: from a set of SM, a symbolic firing rule is applied yielding a new set of (intermediate) symbolic states. These last SMs are then canonized yielding a set of canonical representatives, which can be compared to already obtained canonical SMs.

The challenge we address here is to define these operations on a BDD-like representation, although the structures used to describe equivalence classes of states are calculated dynamically, use *a priori* unbounded integer domains, have a variable domain size according to the dynamically grouped elements, and require quite complex data-structures to represent them. We show how the specific dag library called *Data Decision Diagrams* (DDD), that allows flexible operation definition possibilities through inductive homomorphisms, meets our needs. Application of DDD to uncoloured "extended Petri nets" [4] has shown their expression power and dynamic capabilities. We make full use of available DDD features: variable repeats, variable length vectors, and we rely on hierarchical computations to maximize cache hit ratio.

This paper is organized as follows: section 2 presents a brief overview of DDD capabilities and introduces the Well-Formed nets (*WN*) formalism; section 3 gives the principles used in the coding of a state; section 4 presents the main symbolic firing operation and section 5 the minimization and canonization procedures; section 6 describes the state space construction procedure; finally, section 7 reports the performances of the tool implementing this technique on a few classical examples.

2 Context

2.1 DDD Basic Concepts and Inductive Homomorphism

Data Decision Diagrams (DDD) are a data structure for representing finite sets of assignments sequences of the form $(x_1 := v_1) \cdot (x_2 := v_2) \cdots (x_n := v_n)$ where x_i are variables and v_i are the assigned integer values. When an ordering on the variables is fixed and the values are booleans, DDD coincides with the well-known Binary Decision Diagram. When the ordering on the variables is the only assumption, DDDs correspond to the specialized version of the Multi-valued Decision Diagrams representing characteristic function of sets [2]. However DDDs assume no variable ordering and, even more, the same variable may occur many times in a same assignment sequence. Moreover, variables are not assumed to be part of all paths. Therefore, the maximal length of a sequence is not fixed, and sequences of different lengths can coexist in a DDD. This feature is very useful when dealing with dynamic structures like queues.

DDDs have three terminals : 1, 0 and $\top$. As usual for decision diagram, 1-leaves stand for accepting terminators and 0-leaves for non-accepting ones. Since there is no assumption on the variable domains, the non-accepted sequences are suppressed from the structure. 0 is considered as the default value and is only used to denote the empty set of sequence. This characteristic of DDDs is important as it allows the use of variables of finite domain with *a priori* unknown bounds. The $\top$ terminal is introduced to resolve conflicts introduced by the fact that no variable ordering is required and that a same variable can appear several times in a same sequence.

In the following, X denotes a set of variables, and for any x in X, $Dom(x)$ represents the domain of x.

Definition 1 (Data Decision Diagram). *The set $\mathbb{D}$ of DDDs is defined by $d \in \mathbb{D}$ if:*

- $d \in \{0, 1, \top\}$ *or*
- $d = \langle x, \alpha \rangle$ *with:*
  - $x \in X$
  - $\alpha : Dom(x) \rightarrow \mathbb{D}$, *such that $\{v \in Dom(x) \mid \alpha(v) \neq 0\}$ is finite.*

We denote $x \xrightarrow{a} d$, the DDD (x, α) with $\alpha(a) = d$ and for all $v \neq a$, $\alpha(v) = 0$.

As usual, DDDs are encoded as (shared) decision trees. Hence, a DDD of the form $\langle x, \alpha \rangle$ is encoded by a node labeled x and for each $v \in Dom(x)$ such that $\alpha(v) \neq 0$, there is an arc from this node to the root of $\alpha(v)$. By the definition 1, from a node $\langle x, \alpha \rangle$ there can be at most one arc labeled by $v \in Dom(x)$ and leading to $\alpha(v)$. This may cause conflicts when computing the union (noted $+$) of two DDDs. Consider for instance $d = (a \xrightarrow{1} b \xrightarrow{2} 1) + (a \xrightarrow{1} a \xrightarrow{3} 1) = a \xrightarrow{1} (b \xrightarrow{2} 1 + a \xrightarrow{3} 1)$. We need to compute $(b \xrightarrow{2} 1 + a \xrightarrow{3} 1)$. If $a = b$, this can be resolved by creating a node of variable a having two arcs to the terminal 1 labeled with values 2 and 3. However if $a \neq b$ we cannot decide what variable the resulting node should bear. The result is therefore undefined, and is noted as such by the terminal $\top$. Thus d will evaluate to $d = a \xrightarrow{1} \top$. More formally, $\top$ represents *any* set of finite assignment sequences, therefore $\top$ is the worst approximation of a finite set of assignment sequences. When $\top$ does not appear in a DDD d, d represents a unique finite set of assignment sequences. Such DDDs are said *well-defined*. We require that the DDDs we manipulate be well-defined, and we will detail in section 3.1 how we ensure this property. For a complete definition of DDDs and particulary of their operations, please refer to [4].

DDDs are equipped with the classical set-theoretic operations. They also offer a concatenation operation $d_1 \cdot d_2$ which replaces 1 terminals of d_1 by d_2. Applied to well-defined DDDs, it corresponds to a cartesian product. In addition, homomorphisms are defined to allow flexibility in the definition of application specific operations.

A basic homomorphism is a mapping Φ from $\mathbb{D}$ to $\mathbb{D}$ such that $\Phi(0) = 0$ and $\Phi(d + d') = \Phi(d) + \Phi(d'), \forall d, d' \in \mathbb{D}$. The sum and the composition of two homomorphisms are homomorphisms. Some basic homomorphisms are hard-coded. For instance, the homomorphism $d * Id$ where $d \in \mathbb{D}$, $*$ stands for the intersection and Id for the identity, allows to select the sequences belonging to d. The homomorphisms $d \cdot Id$ and $Id \cdot d$ permit to left or right concatenate sequences. We widely use the simpler left concatenation that adds a single assignment $(x := v)$, noted $x \xrightarrow{v} Id$.

Furthermore, application-specific mappings can be defined by *inductive* homomorphisms. An inductive homomorphism Φ is defined by its evaluation on the 1 terminal

$\Phi(1) \in \mathrm{ID}$, and its evaluation $\Phi' = \Phi(x\xrightarrow{v}d)$ for any $x\xrightarrow{v}d$. Φ' is itself a (possibly inductive) homomorphism, that will be applied on the successor node d. The result of $\Phi(\langle x, \alpha\rangle)$ is then defined as $\sum_{v\in Dom(x)} \Phi(x\xrightarrow{v}\alpha(v))$.

Inductive Homomorphism Examples: $inc(x_1)$ increments the value of the first occurrence of the variable x_1. It returns $\top$ if x_1 is not part of the sequence. $setCst(x_1,v_1,v_2)$ assigns to each occurrence of x_1 the values in the range $[v_1,v_2]$. The application of $setCst$ to a simple DDD is shown below.

$$inc(x_1)(x,v) =$$
$$\begin{cases} x\xrightarrow{v+1}Id & \text{if } x = x_1 \\ x\xrightarrow{v}inc(x_1) & \text{otherwise} \end{cases}$$
$$inc(x_1)(1) = 1$$

$$setCst(x_1,v_1,v_2)(x,v) =$$
$$\begin{cases} \sum_{v'\in[v_1,v_2]}x\xrightarrow{v'}setCst(x_1,v_1,v_2) & \text{if } x = x_1 \\ x\xrightarrow{v}setCst(x_1,v_1,v_2) & \text{otherwise} \end{cases}$$
$$setCst(x_1,v_1,v_2)(1) = 1$$

$$setCst(a,1,2)(a\xrightarrow{1}b\xrightarrow{2}a\xrightarrow{3}1) =$$
$$a\xrightarrow{1}setCst(a,1,2)(b\xrightarrow{2}a\xrightarrow{3}1) + a\xrightarrow{2}setCst(a,1,2)(b\xrightarrow{2}a\xrightarrow{3}1)$$
$$= a\xrightarrow{1}b\xrightarrow{2}setCst(a,1,2)(a\xrightarrow{3}1) + a\xrightarrow{2}b\xrightarrow{2}setCst(a,1,2)(a\xrightarrow{3}1)$$
$$= a\xrightarrow{1}b\xrightarrow{2}\left(\begin{array}{l} a\xrightarrow{1}setCst(a,1,2)(1) + \\ a\xrightarrow{2}setCst(a,1,2)(1) \end{array}\right) + a\xrightarrow{2}b\xrightarrow{2}\left(\begin{array}{l} a\xrightarrow{1}setCst(a,1,2)(1) + \\ a\xrightarrow{2}setCst(a,1,2)(1) \end{array}\right)$$
$$= a\xrightarrow{1}b\xrightarrow{2}a\xrightarrow{1}1 + a\xrightarrow{1}b\xrightarrow{2}a\xrightarrow{2}1 + a\xrightarrow{2}b\xrightarrow{2}a\xrightarrow{1}1 + a\xrightarrow{2}b\xrightarrow{2}a\xrightarrow{2}1$$

Like in BDD packages, a hash table is used to ensure the unicity of DDD nodes. Moreover, a cache is maintained by the library to store the result of the application of a homomorphism to a DDD. Thus, although the expression $setCst(a,1,2)(b\xrightarrow{2}a\xrightarrow{3}1)$ needs to be evaluated twice, the second evaluation will constitute a constant time cache hit.

2.2   Well-Formed Net and Symbolic Reachability Set (SRS)

Symbolic markings (SM) are equivalence classes of states constructed using symmetries that are computed before starting to explore the state space. The tokens which have structurally similar behaviour, i.e. that can be exchanged at any point in the evolution of the system with no impact on the sequences of fireable transitions, are grouped into "static subclasses" (slow and fast processors for instance), which are not modified during the construction. In contrast "dynamic subclasses" are introduced to represent sets of tokens that have the same *distribution* throughout the places of the model. Although the number and cardinality of these dynamic subclasses evolve during the SRS construction, dynamic subclasses always constitute a partition of static subclasses (the slow processors that are waiting and those that are at rest for instance). Thus dynamic subclasses concisely represent the permutations that are permitted on an SM without modifying future sequences of fireable transitions.

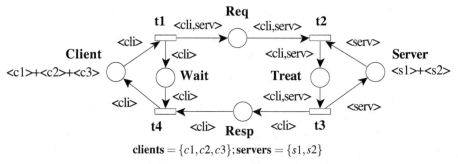

clients $= \{c1,c2,c3\}$; servers $= \{s1,s2\}$

Fig. 1. Client Server Protocol

We now informally explain the SRS construction through a simple example. A coding of SM is also introduced, and will be reused in section 3 in our DDD representation. For a more formal description of SRS algorithms, please refer to [1].

Figure 1 represents a simple client server protocol. The system is composed of **clients**, initially positioned in place *Client* and of **servers** initially in place *Server*. At some point, a client can emit a request for treatment by firing transition t_1, thus generating a request in *Req* for an arbitrary server *serv* (the parameter *serv* is "free" and may be bound to any server). The client then waits for a response from the server in place *Wait*. When the chosen server is available, it will fire t_2, consuming the request and placing the server in place *Treat*. When treatment is finished, the server generates a response in *Resp* for the client and returns to place *Server* by firing t_3. Finally the client can acknowledge the reply by t_4, and return to its initial state.

It can be noticed that whatever their numbers, all clients and respectively servers, have a symmetric role. The structural symmetry analysis module therefore places all clients in a single static subclass C and all servers in a static subclass S (here, there is no need of further refinements into static subclasses). As they are equal, we will not distinguish C from **clients** and S from **servers**. The initial symbolic marking S_0 is expressed symbolically by the expression $S_0 = Client(Z_{C0}) + Server(Z_{S0}), |Z_{C0}| = 3, |Z_{S0}| = 2$; this SM corresponds to the concrete initial marking: $Client(c_1 + c_2 + c_3) + Server(s_1 + s_2)$. Z_{C0} and Z_{S0} are the dynamic subclasses which respectively represent the **clients** in place *Client* and the **servers** in place *Server*. As we can see, permuting elements within a Z_i does not modify the marking, as all elements within a Z_i have the same distribution over all places.

From the concrete initial marking, 6 firings of t_1 are possible, since *cli* may be bound to any c_1, c_2, c_3 and independently *serv* can be bound to s_1 or s_2. However, since all elements within a dynamic subclass Z_i are fully equivalent, there is only one way to bind a variable to any Z_i, whatever it's cardinality. Hence, a single symbolic binding is possible from the SM S_0, *cli* is bound to (a value in) Z_{C0} and *serv* to (a value in) Z_{S0}. To compute the firing, we first isolate Z_{C1} as the value bound to *cli* and Z_{S1} as the value bound to *serv*. We can then modify the distribution of these new dynamic subclasses, by applying pre and post arc functions of t_1. We obtain the SM $S_1 = Client(Z_{C0}) + Server(Z_{S0} + Z_{S1}) + Wait(Z_{C1}) + Req(\langle Z_{C1}, Z_{S1} \rangle), |Z_{C0}| = 2, |Z_{C1}| = 1, |Z_{S0}| = |Z_{S1}| = 1$.

This distribution of **clients** into Z_{Ci} can be encoded by **clients**$= \begin{pmatrix} 2 & 1 \end{pmatrix}$ specifying the cardinalities of the Z_{Ci}, and similarly **servers** $= \begin{pmatrix} 1 & 1 \end{pmatrix}$. The place markings can be coded by: *Client* $= \begin{pmatrix} 1 & 0 \end{pmatrix}$; *Server* $= \begin{pmatrix} 1 & 1 \end{pmatrix}$; *Wait* $= \begin{pmatrix} 0 & 1 \end{pmatrix}$, indicating that place *Client* contains $1 * Z_{C0} + 0 * Z_{C1}$, etc... The marking of place *Req* is defined over the colour domain **clients** $\times$ **servers** and can be represented by a matrix $Req = \begin{pmatrix} 0 & 0 \\ 0 & 1 \end{pmatrix}$, indicating it contains $0 * \langle Z_{C0}, Z_{S0} \rangle + 0 * \langle Z_{C0}, Z_{S1} \rangle + 0 * \langle Z_{C1}, Z_{S0} \rangle + 1 * \langle Z_{C1}, Z_{S1} \rangle$.

We have shown how firing may split dynamic subclasses ; to exhibit the grouping of dynamic subclasses, let us fire t_1 again. *cli* must be bound to a token present in *Client*, therefore must be bound to Z_{C0}, but *serv* may be bound either to Z_{S1} or Z_{S2}. This yields two possible symbolic firings of t_1, instead of the 24 concrete possible firings.

Let us detail the firing $cli \in Z_{C0}, serv \in Z_{S0}$: the second request is addressed to the same server as the first one. Again we split Z_{C0} to distinguish Z_{C2}, the value *cli* is bound to. The marking obtained is $Client(Z_{C0}) + Server(Z_{S0} + Z_{S1}) + Wait(Z_{C1} + Z_{C2}) + Req(\langle Z_{C1}, Z_{S0} \rangle + \langle Z_{C2}, Z_{S0} \rangle), |Z_{C0}| = |Z_{C1}| = |Z_{C2}| = 1$ and $|Z_{S0}| = |Z_{S1}| = 1$. This SM can be coded by the tensors: **clients** $= \begin{pmatrix} 1 & 1 & 1 \end{pmatrix}$ and **servers** $= \begin{pmatrix} 1 & 1 \end{pmatrix}$ giving the Z_i and

$$Server = \begin{pmatrix} 1 & 1 \end{pmatrix}, Client = \begin{pmatrix} 1 & 0 & 0 \end{pmatrix}, Wait = \begin{pmatrix} 0 & 1 & 1 \end{pmatrix} \text{ and } Req = \begin{pmatrix} 0 & 0 \\ 1 & 0 \\ 1 & 0 \end{pmatrix}.$$

We can observe that Z_{C1} and Z_{C2} have the same distribution in all places in this configuration. Indeed for any place P of domain **clients**, $P[1] = P[2]$ and for place *Req*, the second and third *lines* are equal. We therefore group them in a single subclass of cardinality 2. The resulting SM S_3 is: **clients** $= \begin{pmatrix} 2 & 1 \end{pmatrix}$, **servers** $= \begin{pmatrix} 1 & 1 \end{pmatrix}$ giving the Z_i and $Server = \begin{pmatrix} 1 & 1 \end{pmatrix}, Client = \begin{pmatrix} 0 & 1 \end{pmatrix}, Wait = \begin{pmatrix} 1 & 0 \end{pmatrix}$ and $Req = \begin{pmatrix} 1 & 0 \\ 0 & 0 \end{pmatrix}$. It should be noted that the Z_{Ci} dynamic subclasses have been reindexed, in order to have $|Z_{C0}| > |Z_{C1}|$; this reordering is necessary to ensure the unicity of representation of the SM, and will be discussed in detail within Section 5.2.

3   State Encoding

3.1   Tensor Coding

As our example in section 2.2 has shown, the data that need to be stored are expressed in terms of variable length vectors, matrices or more generally tensors. The mechanism used to store a vector of size n is simply to repeat a same variable V n times. Moreover, a vector is always terminated by an *End* marker, represented by an occurrence of $V \xrightarrow{\sharp}$. Although the number of repeats of V may vary along paths within our DDD, the variables always occur in the same order, thus the $V \xrightarrow{\sharp}$ always leads to the same variable. This ensures that our structures can be safely united, intersected, etc without risk of creating $\top$ terminals.

As we have seen, the marking of a place P of arbitrary domain $D = C_{k_1} \times \cdots C_{k_n}$ can be stored as an n-tensor, n being the number of classes composing D. We therefore need a representation of an n-tensor over what is basically a linear coding, as a DDD stores a sequence of variable/value pairs. Furthermore the operations we need to define manipulate $(n-1)$-tensors extracted from an n-tensor, such as lines of a matrix, or faces of a cubic 3-tensor, so we need to easily determine where to find the elements of an $(n-1)$-tensor. We have chosen a lexicographic coding, which meets our requirements, and is a generalization of the coding used for simple vectors.

Let t be an n-tensor of dimensions $d_0 \times \cdots \times d_{n-1}$. Let $a_{i_0,i_1,\cdots i_{n-1}}$ be an element of the tensor. The elements of the tensor t are encountered in lexicographic order: $a_{0,\cdots 0,0} \rightarrow a_{0,\cdots 0,1} \rightarrow \cdots \rightarrow a_{0,\cdots 0,(d_{n-1}-1)} \rightarrow a_{0,\cdots 1,0} \rightarrow \cdots \rightarrow a_{(d_1-1),\cdots (d_{n-2}-1),(d_{n-1}-1)}$. We are trying to characterize the elements of a target $(n-1)$-tensor. For instance $\forall i \in [0 \cdots d_1 - 1], a_{3,i}$ would give the elements of line 3 of a matrix. Let d_k be the target dimension, and v the target index along this dimension. In our example, $k = 0$ and $v = 3$.

Property 1. Let $\pi = \prod_{j>k} d_j$ and $\mu = \prod_{j \geq k} d_j$; the indexes i of the elements of the vth (n-1)-tensor along dimension k satisfy:

$$v \cdot \pi \leq i < (v+1) \cdot \pi \quad mod(\mu).$$

Where the whole inequation is evaluated modulus μ. The proof of this property is straightforward and is omitted here.

Let us apply this property to an example 2-tensor (a matrix) of dimension 3×4 :

$$\begin{pmatrix} 0 & 1 & 2 & 3 \\ 4 & 5 & 6 & 7 \\ 8 & 9 & 10 & 11 \end{pmatrix}$$

The indexes i of the second line are given by $k = 0; v = 1; \pi = d_1 = 4; \mu = d_0 \cdot d_1 = 12$; thus $4 \leq i < 8 \quad mod(12)$.
In the same way the third column is found at indexes i computed by: $k = 1; v = 2; \pi = 1; \mu = d_1 = 4$; thus $2 \leq i < 3 \quad mod(4)$.

Generally the indexes of the elements of a (n-1)-tensor are not contiguous within the structure, however operations don't need to read all the values to begin processing the operation. For instance, an operation comparing the second and third columns, needs only to store the value at index 2, to compare it to value at index 3 when it is reached, then if they are not equal the result can directly be given, else values 2 and 3 are "dropped" and the process will be iterated for the next element of index i meeting the $2 \leq i < 3 \quad mod(4)$ criterion.

3.2   States and Motifs

In this section, we present our coding of symbolic states (SM). This coding was developed with two preoccupations: allow the definition of the symbolic firing relation and of the canonization operation with algorithms that only need to perform a unique traversal of the structure to determine their results. This means that the decision of what must be done on a node n only depends on the path traversed from the root to n and not on what may follow. In effect an algorithm that respects this constraint is at most of polynomial complexity over the size in number of nodes of the DDD. The second preoccupation is to obtain a high level of sharing within the representation.

The data stored for each state is organized in motifs. Two primary motifs are distinguished: the class motif corresponding to the definition of the partition of a static subclass C_i into dynamic subclasses Z_i (C motif) and the motif corresponding to the marking of a place (M motif).

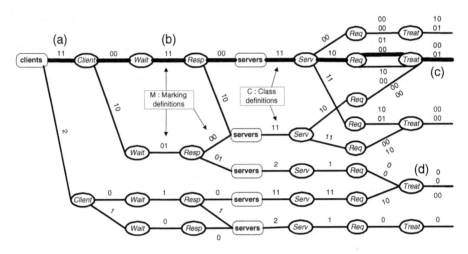

(a) A sample C motif: $Z \xrightarrow{1} Z \xrightarrow{1} Z \xrightarrow{\sharp}$

(b) A sample M motif: $M \xrightarrow{1} M \xrightarrow{1} M \xrightarrow{\sharp}$

(c) A matrix M motif: $M \xrightarrow{0} M \xrightarrow{0} M \xrightarrow{0} M \xrightarrow{1} M \xrightarrow{\sharp}$

(d) Place *Treat* is marked by: $M \xrightarrow{0} M \xrightarrow{0} M \xrightarrow{\sharp}$ that is interpreted as a 2×1 matrix if coming from the top branch or as a 1×2 matrix if coming from the bottom branch.

Fig. 2. Client Server Protocol, 2 clients, 2 servers: 12 symbolic states

C motif, or class definition motif: The current distribution of each class or static subclass C_i into $Z_{C_{ij}}$ subclasses. As we have seen in section 2.2 this can be coded as a variable length vector of integers. As the marking evolves, the number, cardinality and order of these subclasses is modified, subclasses being split up whenever a particular token is extracted, and merged whenever they have the same distribution.

M motif, or marking motif: Given a partition into dynamic subclasses, a marking of a place is expressed as the number of times m each subclass or combination of subclasses (i.e. $m* < Z_{C_11}, Z_{C_20} >$) is present in the place. We represent the marking of a place of domain $C_0 \times \cdots C_{n-1}$ by an n-tensor, of dimensions $d_{C_0} \times \cdots d_{C_{n-1}}$ where d_{C_i} is the current number of dynamic subclasses in C_i.

Figure 2 depicts the state space for our client server protocol with 2 clients and 2 servers. The figure reads from left to right, the root of our DDD being the colour domain definition of **clients**, and the last place described is *Treat*, which leads to the 1 terminal node not represented here. This diagram is an abstraction of the real DDD, as we have directly labeled arcs with tensors (vectors, matrices), instead of repeating the variable and representing the $V \xrightarrow{\sharp} End$ marker. Furthermore, we have named the variables to allow correspondence with the model, but all M motifs use the same variable M, and all C motifs use the same variable Z. Some sharing amongst paths of our representation is obvious here. As the size of the example increases, so does sharing, as we will discuss in section 7.

The state shown in bold corresponds to a state where **clients** are distributed into two dynamic subclasses Z_{C0} and Z_{C1} both of cardinality one, the place *Client* is empty, the place *wait* contains $Z_{C0} + Z_{C1}$, place *Resp* is empty, the **servers** are distributed into two dynamic subclasses Z_{S0} and Z_{S1} both of cardinality one, place *Server* contains one server Z_{S0}, place *Req* contains one request $\langle Z_{C0}, Z_{S1} \rangle$, and *Treat* contains $\langle Z_{C1}, Z_{S1} \rangle$. Thus in english, both clients are waiting for a reply and their requests target the same server Z_{S1}, one request is being treated and the other has not yet been received. The state that differs only by the marking of *Req* corresponds an analogous state except the client's requests are not for the same server.

3.3   Operation Framework

Our prototype is developed in C++, and takes full advantage of both inheritance and template arguments to provide an open framework in which to code operations over these motifs. Thus an abstract operation class provides the functionality required to keep track of the current position within the motif and the concrete operations inherit this behaviour.

When exploring the DDD seen as a tree, this generic operation stores the tensors encountered; upon reaching an $\sharp$ *End* marker, the tensor that has been stored is passed to the concrete operation being run for evaluation. Thus our generic operation reads the tensor values represented on the arcs of Figure 2 into a DDD $\mathcal{M}$, evaluates a concrete operation on the extracted tensors $\mathcal{M}' = op(args)(\mathcal{M})$, and continues evaluation based on the value of $\mathcal{M}'$.

This means that each place marking is isolated before running an operation on it, and since the number of possible place markings (actual different matrices on the arcs of figure 2) is low with respect to the combinations of place markings, sharing is high on the actual operations performed on tensors, although the storage phase has a higher complexity due to lower sharing. Furthermore, except for the transition firing operation, operations are evaluated independently of the actual place being considered, thus the concrete operation run on the extracted tensors have less arguments. In effect it means tensor operations are independent of the position of the tensor within the full state motif, thus operations on different place marking matrices can be shared, increasing the cache hit ratio.

4   Symbolic Firing Operation

As we have seen in section 2.2, there is only one way to bind a variable to any Z_i, whatever it's cardinality. However, if the dynamic subclass Z_i a variable X is being bound to has a cardinality $c > 1$, a new dynamic subclass Z_X of cardinality 1 must be created to isolate the value X is bound to. With Z_X isolated, one can test if a place contains X by using the number of occurrences of Z_X in P, or add X in P by incrementing the number of occurrences of Z_X in P. An operation "add dim" is defined to create these new dynamic subclasses as needed. This operation simply copies the $(n-1)$-tensor corresponding to Z_i in position $i+1$, prior to evaluating the inhibitor, pre, and post functions for the considered place. On the other hand, if X is bound to a class Z_i of cardinality one, no new subclass need be created, we can use $Z_X = Z_i$.

The transition relation is defined as operating over a set of SM represented by a DDD. But since it is implemented by an inductive homomorphism, we describe the behaviour of the transition as a visit of the word constituting a single SM S. A transition thus has the following behaviour:

1. When encountering a colour domain definition C, all the possible variable bindings are constructed. A variable binding $(vars, adim)$ is composed of the correspondence variable to dynamic subclass index $vars$, and of the associated "add dim" operation $adim$ that should be applied prior to evaluating the arc functions. Illegal variable bindings with respect to the guard of the transition are filtered out in this phase. Then a composite operation defined as a sum of all possible bindings is returned for evaluation on the rest of the SM.
2. When encountering a place marking $\mathcal{M}$, the $adim$ operation corresponding to the current variable bindings is first applied. Then the colour functions associated to the current place are evaluated. If a pre or inhibitor function returns the 0 terminal, the transition stops evaluation and it's homomorphism returns 0 thus pruning the partially constructed resulting marking from the DDD. Otherwise the newly obtained marking is inserted and the operation continues.
3. If a transition reaches the 1 terminal the transition has been successfully fired with the current variable bindings.

Colour functions are compositions of the three basic colour functions: diffusion noted S, identity represented by a formal parameter X, and only for ordered colour domains the successor operation $X++$. These colour functions may have a multiplicative factor associated. For instance $2 \cdot <X> + <Y>$, or $<S,X> + 2 \cdot <X,Y>$ are possible colour functions labeling an arc to or from a place of domain respectively C and $C \times C$.

Given the definition of a place's colour domain, the number of dynamic subclasses in each of the C_i that form the domain, and the bindings of all variables or formal parameters to their Z_i, we compute the indexes in the M motif that are targeted by a colour function, and the multiplicative factor m associated to these indexes. This computation is common to all types of arcs; given this list of target indexes and multiplicities, a homomorphism specific to the type of arc is applied for each target index i. These homomorphisms are defined by (inhibitor not represented) :

$$\mathcal{W}^-(i,m)(x,v) =$$
$$\begin{cases} \text{if} \quad i \neq 0 & \Rightarrow x \xrightarrow{v} \mathcal{W}^-(i-1,m) \\ \text{else if } v \geq m \Rightarrow x \xrightarrow{v-m} Id \\ \quad \text{else} \quad \Rightarrow 0 \end{cases}$$
$$\mathcal{W}^-(1) = \top$$

$$\mathcal{W}^+(i,m)(x,v) =$$
$$\begin{cases} \text{if} \quad i \neq 0 \Rightarrow x \xrightarrow{v} \mathcal{W}^+(i-1,m) \\ \text{else} \quad \Rightarrow x \xrightarrow{v+m} Id \end{cases}$$
$$\mathcal{W}^+(1) = \top$$

Where $\mathcal{W}^-, \mathcal{W}^+$ are respectively the pre and post arc operations. None of these operations should ever encounter the 1 terminal as the index i that is targeted will be reached before, and reaching i terminates the operation.

5   Canonization Algorithms

This section presents the operations that we have defined to implement the canonization algorithms. The construction of the SRS is based on the notion of canonic representation for an equivalence class of states. From a symbolic state S, a transition is fired yielding a new symbolic state S_1. S_1 is then minimized by groupings of dynamic Z_i subclasses and canonized to ensure the unicity of its representation.

As we have seen, the firing of a transition is liable to create new dynamic subclasses bound to the different formal parameters of the transition, and changes the distribution of dynamic subclasses within an SM. The goal of the minimization operation is to group dynamic subclasses that have the same distribution in all places, yielding a reduced expression of place markings. This can be accomplished by testing for any two dynamic subclasses Z_i and Z_j whether the $(n-1)$-tensor corresponding to them are equal in all M motifs of the SM. Once all possible groupings have been accomplished, we must ensure that a state has a unique representation by finding an indexation of dynamic subclasses that yields a "minimal" or canonic representant for a state. To this end, we define a total order on SMs that are equivalent up to a permutation of Z_i, and use the smallest according to this order as canonic representative. This stage is called the canonization phase.

5.1   Minimization

The group operation consists in testing for all target colour classes C of index tC, whether any two dynamic subclasses Z_i and Z_j can be grouped into a single dynamic subclass such that $|Z_k| = |Z_i| + |Z_j|$. This is possible iff all places have the same marking with respect to Z_i and Z_j.

The group operation follows the generic schema described in section 3. Its specific operation arguments are i, j the indexes of the subclasses to be grouped if possible within the target class tC. The operation is initially created with the values $tC = i = j = -1$ meaning that none of these values are bound yet. A group operation $group(tC, i, j)(S)$ thus has the following behaviour:

1. Upon encountering a new colour domain C_k, if tC is yet unbound the operation binds to C_k and lets run the operation with tC unbound by returning $group(-1, -1, -1) + group(k, -1, -1)$. If tC is already bound the operation follows its course normally.
2. When traversing its definition in terms of Z and their cardinality, all possible bindings of i and j are constructed and summed.
3. Upon reaching the end of an M motif $\mathcal{M}$, a first operation *groupable* is run on $\mathcal{M}$ to test whether the group operation is possible with the currently values of i and j. This operation tests the equality of lines i and j of $\mathcal{M}$ and breaks by returning the 0 terminal at the first difference. If $\mathcal{M}$ allows grouping, a second operation is run that deletes the values of line j from $\mathcal{M}$. If groupable returns 0, the global operation also returns 0, pruning the state being constructed from the full DDD.

It should be noted that the group operation thus defined prunes any state that does not allow any grouping. Moreover, whenever two (or more) groupings are possible on an SM, a single call of the group operation will create two partially grouped SMs. Given the DDD of the newly reached markings, the group operation is therefore called iteratively to stability as in:

$group\_iter\,(S)$:
while groupable $(S) \neq 0$ **do**
    $S \leftarrow S-$ groupable $(S)+$ group(S)
end while

5.2   Canonization

In order to obtain a canonic representative of a state, we need to select one of the permutations of dynamic subclass indexes as the canonic one. This is done by *sorting* our DDD. Any ordering criterion is appropriate, as long as it defines a total order over permutations of the Z_is. But to keep the complexity of our operation reasonable, it is essential to define a criterion that can be evaluated as we travel from the root of our DDD to the terminals.

Our sort is thus based on two levels of sort:

- The first level of sort is cardinality based: we require that dynamic subclasses Z_i be encountered in decreasing order of size. This can be evaluated as soon as a C motif definition is encountered.
- Then for two Z_i, Z_j of equal cardinality, we use a lexical sort that defines a total order over tensors of same size.

We define a swap operation that swaps two adjacent Z_i and Z_{i+1} through a whole SM. The behaviour of our sort homomorphism is defined by:

1. Within a C motif, when comparing $|Z_i|$ to $|Z_{i+1}|$, three cases are possible:
    (a) $|Z_i| > |Z_{i+1}|$: The order is already correct, iterate over the next Z_{i+1}, Z_{i+2}
    (b) $|Z_i| < |Z_{i+1}|$: The order is wrong, the procedure swaps Z_i and Z_{i+1} over the rest of the state
    (c) $|Z_i| = |Z_{i+1}|$: Apply a lexical sort on lines i and $i+1$ then continue over the next Z_{i+1}, Z_{i+2}
2. Upon reading a place marking tensor $\mathcal{M}$ for place P, which will only happen if the cardinality sort failed ($|Z_i| = |Z_{i+1}|$), we compute $\mathcal{M}' \leftarrow$ swap$(i, i+1)(\mathcal{M})$ and compare $\mathcal{M}$ to $\mathcal{M}'$ lexicographically.
    (a) If $\mathcal{M} = \mathcal{M}'$, $\mathcal{M}$ is put back as marking of P and the lexical sort operation continues downwards,
    (b) if $\mathcal{M} < \mathcal{M}'$ then $\mathcal{M}'$ replaces the previous $\mathcal{M}$ as marking of P and a swap operation is applied downwards,
    (c) if $\mathcal{M} > \mathcal{M}'$ then the DDD is already sorted, $\mathcal{M}$ is put back and the identity homomorphism is returned.

As a single application of the sort operation may not be enough to fully sort a set of states, a sort_iter procedure is defined, that simply iteratively calls the sort homomorphism to stability. When stability is reached, we are ensured that all the SMs of the DDD are fully canonic.

6 Building the State Space

We have defined the following operations in the previous sections, all applicable to a set of states S:

- $fire(S,t)$: fires the transition t for all possible variable bindings over a set of states S(section 4). The states returned are not canonical however.
- $group\_iter(S)$: Groups the Z_i that are groupable of a set of states S(section 5.1).
- $sort\_iter(S)$: Sorts the states of a set S (section 5.2).

The canonized successors of a set of states S by symbolic firing of a transition t, for all possible bindings of t's variables, is obtained by:

> $succ\ (S,t)$:
> $S \leftarrow fire(S,t)$ {Obtain successors (non-canonic)}
> $S \leftarrow sort\_iter(S)$ {Apply a canonization (sort)}
> $S \leftarrow group\_iter(S)$ {Apply minimization (group)}
> $S \leftarrow sort\_iter(S)$ {Canonize the result (sort)}

Let us note that $sort$ is applied twice in the $succ$ operation, which may seem counter-productive. Indeed, the group operation will operate correctly whether the Z_i are sorted or not. But in fact this accelerates the procedure because the first $sort$ may reduce the number of states in S, as it only keeps one "version" of states identical up to a permutation of Z_i. Furthermore the cache for the $group$ operation is used more efficiently as the input S for the $group$ operation is always sorted, and the number of sorted SMs (canonic representatives) is very small w.r.t. the number of unsorted SMs. Finally the second $sort$ comes at a very low cost, as the result of the first $sort$ is still in cache. Thus the full $sort$ operation is only fully evaluated on the newly grouped SMs (this last assertion is only mostly true, since it assumes that most of the nodes in $group\_iter(S)$ already existed in S).

Given this $succ$ operation, the state space reached from a set of initial states S by firing a set of transitions T is computed by the following algorithm :

$srs\ (S,T)$:	**With:**
$S_1 \leftarrow S$	$saturate\ (S,t)$:
repeat	$S_1 \leftarrow S$
$\quad S \leftarrow S_1$	$S_2 \leftarrow S$
$\quad$ **for all** $t \in T$ **do**	**repeat**
$\qquad S_1 \leftarrow saturate(S_1,t)$	$\quad S \leftarrow S_2$
$\qquad$ *do garbage collection*	$\quad S_1 \leftarrow succ(S_1,t)$
$\quad$ **end for**	$\quad S_2 \leftarrow S_2 + S_1$
until $S_1 = S$	**until** $S_2 = S$

We initiate a construction of the full SRS by invoking $srs(S_0, T_{all})$ where S_0 is the initial state and T_{all} is the set of all transitions of the model. Thus the algorithm is based on two fixpoint computations: the first fires a transition until it is no longer fireable (*saturate*), the second saturates the firings of each transition successively until no new states are reached (our main *srs*). This double fixpoint method heuristically gives good results, because the cache doesn't need to be cleared within *saturate* (though in truth, we do garbage collection whenever memory consumption exceeds reasonable limits). The cache doesn't overfill as the operations are exactly the same in each loop of saturate, whereas we cannot hope to store all the intermediate results constructed during a loop of *srs*.

It also tends to saturate place markings, thus increasing sharing: when all the possible markings of a place have been reached, sharing between states and operations increases. This can be understood by considering a system composed of two unrelated places P_1 and P_2; if P_1 has n possible markings and P_2 has m possible markings; when adding newly reached states sharing in the structure will be poor at first, until enough states have been added to allow sharing, and ultimately we will only require two nodes $P_1 \xrightarrow{all\ n\ values} P_2 \xrightarrow{all\ m\ values} 1$. It also favours cache hit, as a transition that only touches P_1 will return Id upon reaching P_2, thus all reached markings of P_2 will be concatenated to the new value of P_1.

The evaluation order of transitions also plays an important role on the number of iterations required to reach the fixpoint. The heuristic used to order transitions is to follow approximate flows: we start by evaluating transitions which have all their input places initially marked (whatever their marking thus the approximation); all output places of these transitions are then noted as marked, and the next transitions to be evaluated are again those that have all their input places marked, etc . . . Although very simple, this heuristic has given good results over the models tested (2 or 3 iterations).

7   Implementation and Results

The table below gives an overview of the performances of our prototype over a few examples taken from literature. The models presented are:

- Peterson's mutual exclusion algorithm for n processes [5]. This protocol is not strongly symmetric: although the process identities (*pid*) can be abstracted away, one must keep track of the level of each process.
- A critical section(CS) protocol with waves ensuring fairness [6]. Processes constitute a wave, then the wave is locked: idle processes can no longer enter the wave until the whole wave has passed into CS. Furthermore, processes within a wave are let through into CS in a static order specified by their *pid*. Although this protocol may seem asymmetric, it functions by taking the process with highest *pid* from a set (the wave) and allowing it into CS. If no other transition of the model distinguishes processes by their identities, we can consider all *pids* equivalent: indeed in any case one of the processes *will* be let through. The performances reported isolate the process of lowest pid 1 in a static subclass. Thus the SRS generated could allow verification of properties such as: the process of $pid = 1$ is always last of his wave to be let into CS.
- A distributed database protocol [7]. This model exhibits considerable symmetry, and allows a high level of sharing within the DDD representation.
- The client server protocol presented in section 1. The performances over this model are parameterized by the number of clients (first column) and the number of servers (second column).

For each model, the number of concrete states is given (this in an over-approximation for the CS Wave protocol), the number of SMs, the number of nodes in the full SRS, the average share (80% share means the reduced DDD representation is 20% of the size of the decision tree with no sharing), the average length of the paths of the resulting DDD in number of nodes (DDDs of SMs have variable length path as we have seen), and the time to compute the SRS are given.

Model	N (#)	States (#)	SM (#)	final nodes (#)	Avg share (%)	Avg SM len (# nodes)	SRS time (sec)
peterson	7	692777	320	6159	65.3 %	55.5	15.7
	10	$3.46 \cdot 10^9$	3328	42442	85.1%	85.9	247.0
	11	$7.19 \cdot 10^{10}$	7168	74039	89.4 %	97.3	545.4
	12	$1.62 \cdot 10^{12}$	15360	126807	92.4%	109.6	1946.4
CS Wave	40	$1.74 \cdot 10^{20}$	5620	831	99.3%	23.8	14.83
	100	$1.76 \cdot 10^{49}$	35050	1011	99.8%	24.0	127.88
	200	$1.79 \cdot 10^{97}$	140100	1313	99.9%	24.07	1041.75
	300	$1.02 \cdot 10^{371}$	315150	1600	99.98 %	24.09	3h20
dist. DB	40	$1.77 \cdot 10^{97}$	20101	725	99.8%	27.6	56.95
	300	$5.39 \cdot 10^{370}$	45151	875	99.93%	27.6	205.45
	500	$4.01 \cdot 10^{622}$	125251	1175	99.96%	27.6	1841.68
	700	$4.89 \cdot 10^{623}$	245351	1482	99.97%	27.6	8 hours
Cli. Serv.	5 2	5484	82	884	67.1 %	32.7	3
	10 2	$1.35 \cdot 10^7$	476	2419	86.3 %	37.11	28.56
	20 2	$4.17 \cdot 10^{13}$	3201	2914	97.7 %	40.4	116.92
	6 6	$2.44 \cdot 10^7$	281	4091	72.5 %	53.1	21.2
	8 8	$1.12 \cdot 10^{11}$	964	13123	80.5 %	69.8	170.4
	9 9	$1.05 \cdot 10^{13}$	1698	22016	83.5 %	78.8	450.5

We can observe that the representation is extremely dense, with as many as $4.8 \cdot 10^{623}$ concrete states represented by only 1500 nodes. This is mainly due to the low number of SMs representing such a state space, only 245,000 in this instance. The average length of an SM, which corresponds to the average number of dynamic sub-classes in a static subclass, asymptotically tends toward a structural limit imposed by the P-invariants of the models studied, thus does not follow the evolution of N. For the client/server however, we have worst case SMs with M tensors of size N^2.

Unfortunately computation time does not directly follow the number of nodes. Indeed, the number of SMs is a clear component of the time complexity. This is partly due to the fact that the complexity of evaluating an operation on a node is necessarily linear to the number of sons, as the inductive homomorphism is applied to each son. Our compact encoding generates nodes with a very high number of sons, particularly when the P-invariant bounds have been reached, and only the cardinalities of the Z_i change from one SM to another. We also attribute this in part to the fact that the DDD library is still at a prototype stage, and that caching policies in particular are inefficient. This could certainly be improved by integrating into the DDD library caching and accelerated access algorithms developed for other variants of BDDs [11].

8 Conclusion

We have shown in this paper how the algorithms for SRG construction [1] can be implemented over a DDD [4] representation. The key idea is to exploit both explicitly expressed symmetries by building equivalence classes of states (SMs), and implicit symmetry through the similarities in the representation of these SM. The flexibility offered by DDDs and inductive homomorphisms allows to both represent and operate over complex and dynamic structures, such as the tensors representing place markings in an SM. The prototype developed shows that extremely compact encodings of a state space can be obtained, allowing storage of $4.8 \cdot 10^{623}$ states on 1,500 nodes. Memory consumption is thus very low, however time complexity remains high.

Further directions include improving the DDD library core, with respect to our specific needs, and developing a full LTL model checker using the symbolic observation graph method [9]. We are also interested in developing extensions of the SRG construction, such as the ESRG construction [6] that captures partial symmetries, using our symbolic symbolic framework.

References

[1] G. Chiola, C. Dutheillet, G. Franceschinis, and S. Haddad. Stochastic well-formed colored nets and symmetric modeling applications. *IEEE Transactions on Computers*, 42(11):1343–1360, 1993. 276, 280, 291

[2] G. Ciardo, G. Lüttgen, and R. Siminiceanu. Efficient symbolic state-space construction for asynchronous systems. In *Proc. of ICATPN'2000*, volume 1825 of *Lecture Notes in Computer Science*, pages 103–122. Springer Verlag, June 2000. 277

[3] E. M. Clarke, R. Enders, T. Filkorn, and S. Jha. Exploiting symmetry in temporal logic model checking. *Formal Methods in System Design*, 9(1-2):77–104, 1996. 276

[4] J.-M. Couvreur, E. Encrenaz, E. Paviot-Adet, D. Poitrenaud, and P.-A. Wacrenier. Data decision diagrams for Petri net analysis. In *Proc. of ICATPN'2002*, volume 2360 of *Lecture Notes in Computer Science*, pages 101–120. Springer Verlag, June 2002. 277, 278, 291

[5] J.-M. Couvreur and E. Paviot-Adet. New structural invariant for Petri net analysis. In *Proc. of ICATPN'1994*, volume 815 of *Lecture Notes in Computer Science*, pages 199–218. Springer Verlag, June 1994. 289

[6] S. Haddad, J.-M. Ilié, and K. Ajami. A model checking method for partially symmetric systems. In *Proc. of FORTE/PSTV'2000*, pages 121–136. Kluwer, 2000. 289, 291

[7] K. Jensen. Coloured Petri nets. In *Petri Nets: Central Model and their Properties, Advances in Petri Nets 86*, volume 254 of *Lecture Notes in Computer Science*, pages 248–299. Springer Verlag, September 1986. 289

[8] T. Junttila. New canonical representative marking algorithms for place/transition-nets. In *Proc. of ICATPN'2004*, Lecture Notes in Computer Science. Springer Verlag, June 2004. 277

[9] K. Klai. *Réseaux de Petri : Vérification Symbolique et Modulaire (chapter 3)*. PhD thesis, Laboratoire d'Informatique de Paris 6, December 2003. 291

[10] Y. Thierry-Mieg, C. Dutheillet, and I. Mounier. Automatic symmetry detection in well-formed nets. In *Proc. of ICATPN'2003*, volume 2679 of *Lecture Notes in Computer Science*, pages 82–101. Springer Verlag, June 2003. 277

[11] B. Yang, R. E. Bryant, D. R. O'Hallaron, A. Biere, O. Coudert, G. Janssen, R. K. Ranjan, and F. Somenzi. A performance study of BDD-based model checking. In *Proc. of FMCAD'98*, pages 255–289, 1998. 290

Introducing the Iteration in sPBC[*]

Hermenegilda Maciá, Valentín Valero, Diego Cazorla, and Fernando Cuartero

Escuela Politécnica Superior de Albacete
Universidad de Castilla-La Mancha, 02071 Albacete, Spain
{hermenegilda.macia,valentin.valero,diego.cazorla}@uclm.es
fernando.cuartero@uclm.es

Abstract. The main goal of this paper is to extend sPBC with the iteration operator, providing an operational semantics for the language, as well as a denotational semantics, which is based on stochastic Petri nets. With this new operator we can model some repetitive behaviours, and then we obtain a formal method that can be easily used for the design of communication protocols and distributed systems.

Keywords: Stochastic Petri Nets, Stochastic Process Algebra, Performance Evaluation, Petri Box Calculus

1 Introduction

Petri Box Calculus (PBC) [4, 3, 5, 6, 7] is an algebraic model for the specification of concurrent systems which has a natural and compositional translation into a special kind of labelled Petri nets, called *boxes*. The description of a wider class of systems, such as real-time systems and fault-tolerance systems, is the goal of two timed extensions of PBC that we may find in the literature, namely tPBC [11] and TPBC [15], both of them considering a deterministic model of time. In the same line we presented sPBC in [14, 13], which is a Markovian extension of PBC.

In sPBC we consider that each multiaction has associated a delay which follows a Markovian distribution, as the transition delays of stochastic Petri Nets (SPNs) [1]. Thus, a stochastic multiaction of sPBC is represented by a pair $< \alpha, r >$, where α represents a (classical) multiaction of PBC, and $r \in \mathbb{R}^+$ is the parameter of the associated exponential distribution. Moreover, as in SPNs, the *race policy* governs the dynamic behaviour.

In the literature we may find some different approaches that deal with stochastic extensions of process algebras such as PEPA [10], TIPP [8] and EMPA [2]. There are some important differences with respect to them. In sPBC we allow multiactions (multisets of actions), we consider a synchronization operator totally independent from the parallel operator (as in PBC) and, finally,

---

[*] This work has been supported by the MCyT project "Description and Performance of Distributed Systems and Application to Multimedia Systems, Ref. TIC2003-07848-c02-02".

D. de Frutos-Escrig and M. Núñez (Eds.): FORTE 2004, LNCS 3235, pp. 292–309, 2004.

we obtain the parameter of the new multiaction generated after synchronization following a different technique (see [9] for a complete discussion about all the different alternatives for that).

The technique that we use is based on *conflict rates*, which are inspired in the *apparent rates* of PEPA [10]. Nevertheless, in our approach we can find an important advantage: we have been able to obtain a static translation into stochastic Petri nets, while in PEPA rates of transitions are in some cases marking dependent [17].

In our two previous works we only considered finite sPBC [14, 13]. Then the aim of this paper is twofold: including in the syntax the iteration operator and proving that the operational and the denotational semantics (the latter based on a special kind of labelled SPNs, called *s-boxes*) are fully abstract. The iteration operator allows us to describe infinite behaviours and, therefore, it is a powerful tool to describe the behaviour of concurrent systems. Then, with this formalism we can deal with the design of communication protocols and distributed systems with a Markov time, but joining in a single model both the advantages of process algebras and Petri nets.

This paper tries to be, as far as possible, self-contained, so we will first review the syntax, the operational semantics and the denotational semantics of the finite operators. For further details the reader is referred to the previous works of the authors [14, 13]. The paper is structured as follows: in Section 2 we present an overview of the syntax. The operational and the denotational semantics can be found in Sections 3 and 4, respectively. Section 5 contains an example, and finally, Section 6 contains some conclusions and our plans for future work.

2   Syntax of Stochastic Petri Box Calculus

In this section we present some notations and the syntax of sPBC, with an informal interpretation of the operators. In this paper we do not consider the recursion operator because it requires a more sophisticated treatment, as it occurs in plain PBC. Nevertheless, with the iteration operator we are expanding the power of description of sPBC significantly, and in fact some potentially infinite behaviours can be described with it.

2.1   Notation

From now onwards we will use the following notation: $\mathcal{A}$ will be a countable set of action names, $\forall a \in \mathcal{A}$, $\exists \widehat{a} \in \mathcal{A}$, such that $a \neq \widehat{a}$ and $\widehat{\widehat{a}} = a$, as in CCS [16]. Letters $a, b, \widehat{a}, ...$ will be used to denote the elements of $\mathcal{A}$; $\mathcal{L} = \mathcal{B}(\mathcal{A})$, will represent the set of finite multisets of elements in $\mathcal{A}$ (*multiactions*). We will consider relabelling functions $f : \mathcal{A} \to \mathcal{A}$, which are functions that preserve conjugates, i.e.: $\forall a \in \mathcal{A}$, $f(\widehat{a}) = \widehat{f(a)}$. We will only consider bijective relabelling functions. We define the alphabet of $\alpha \in \mathcal{L}$ by: $A(\alpha) = \{a \in \mathcal{A} \,|\, \alpha(a) > 0\}$, and the set of stochastic multiactions by $\mathcal{SL} = \{<\alpha, r> \,|\, \alpha \in \mathcal{L}, r \in \mathbb{R}^+\}$. We allow the same multiaction $\alpha \in \mathcal{L}$ to have different stochastic rates in the same specification. Finally, we define the synchronization of multiactions: $\alpha \oplus_a \beta =_{def}$ γ, where:

$$\gamma(b) = \begin{cases} \alpha(b) + \beta(b) - 1 & \text{if } b = a \vee b = \widehat{a} \\ \alpha(b) + \beta(b) & \text{otherwise} \end{cases}$$

which is only applicable when either $a \in A(\alpha)$ and $\widehat{a} \in A(\beta)$, or $\widehat{a} \in A(\alpha)$ and $a \in A(\beta)$.

2.2   Syntax

As in plain PBC, static s-expressions are used to describe the structure of a concurrent system, while dynamic s-expressions describe the current state of a system (they correspond to unmarked and marked Petri nets, respectively). As a system evolves by executing multiactions, the dynamic s-expression describing its current state changes; this is captured by means of both overbars and underbars that decorate the static s-expression. Static s-expressions of sPBC are those defined by the following BNF expression:

$$E ::= <\alpha, r> \mid E; E \mid E \square E \mid E \parallel E \mid E[f] \mid E \, sy \, a \mid E \, rs \, a \mid [a : E] \mid [E * E * E]$$

where $< \alpha, r > \in \mathcal{SL}$ stands for the *basic multiaction*, which corresponds to the simultaneous execution of all the actions in α, after a delay that follows a negative exponential distribution with parameter r. $E_1 \, ; \, E_2$ stands for the sequential execution of E_1 and E_2, while $E_1 \square E_2$ is the choice between its arguments, $E[f]$ is the relabelling operator, and $E \, rs \, a$ denotes the restriction over the single action a (this process cannot execute any stochastic multiactions $< \alpha, r >$ with either $a \in A(\alpha)$ or $\hat{a} \in A(\alpha)$). The parallel operator, $\parallel$, represents the (independent) parallel execution of both components, where there is no any synchronization embedded in the operator (as in PBC). Synchronization is introduced by the operator sy, thus the process $E \, sy \, a$ behaves in the same way as E, but it can also execute those new multiactions generated by the synchronization of a pair of actions $(a, \hat{a})$. $[a : E]$ is the derived operator *scoping* defined by $[a : E] = (E \, sy \, a) \, rs \, a$. Finally, the iteration operator $[E_1 * E_2 * E_3]$ represents the process that performs E_1, then executes several (possibly 0) times E_2, and finishes after performing E_3. We can obtain infinite behaviours by adequately combining both the iteration and the restriction operators; for instance, $[< \{a\}, r_1 > * < \{b\}, r_2 > * < \{c\}, r_3 >] \, rs \, c$, represents the process that performs $< \{a\}, r_1 >$ once, and then it executes $< \{b\}, r_2 >$ infinitely many times.

However, we need to restrict the syntax of sPBC to those terms for which no parallel behaviour appears at the highest level in a choice or in the two last arguments of an iteration. In principle, with this restriction we slightly reduce the expressiveness of the language, although we could prefix parallel operators appearing at the highest level of a choice or in one argument of an iteration by an empty multiaction, whose rate could be adequately selected in order to preserve the probability of execution of the multiactions involved in the choice or in the iteration. Terms fulfilling this restriction will be called *regular terms*, and the operational semantics will be only defined for them. This restriction is introduced in order to guarantee that the moment in which the rule for the synchronization is applied does not affect the value that we obtain for the rate of the stochastic multiaction obtained as result of a synchronization (this will be illustrated in Example 1).

More exactly, regular static s-expressions E are those static s-expressions of sPBC fulfilling:

$$D ::= <\alpha, r> \mid D; E \mid D \, sy \, a \mid D \, rs \, a \mid D[f] \mid [a:D] \mid D \,\square\, D \mid [D * D * D]$$
$$E ::= <\alpha, r> \mid E; E \mid E \, sy \, a \mid E \, rs \, a \mid E[f] \mid [a:E] \mid E \parallel E \mid D \,\square\, D \mid [E * D * D]$$

The operational semantics of sPBC is defined on dynamic s-expressions G, which derive from the static s-expressions, annotating them with either upper or lower bars, which indicate the *active components* at the current instant of time. Thus, we have:

$$G ::= \overline{E} \mid \underline{E} \mid G; E \mid E; G \mid G \,\square\, E \mid E \,\square\, G \mid G \parallel G \mid G[f] \mid G \, sy \, a \mid G \, rs \, a \mid$$
$$[a:G] \mid [G * E * E] \mid [E * G * E] \mid [E * E * G]$$

where $\overline{E}$ denotes the initial state of E, and $\underline{E}$ its final state. We will say that a dynamic s-expression is regular if the underlying static s-expression is regular. The set of regular dynamic s-expressions will be denoted by *ReDynExpr*.

3   Operational Semantics

We have two kind of transitions: inaction transitions, annotated with $\emptyset$, which just denote a rewriting of a term by redistributing its bars, in order to prepare the term to apply new transitions; and stochastic transitions, which correspond to the execution of a stochastic multiaction. Therefore, inaction rules define in fact an equivalence between regular dynamic s-expressions as defined in Def. 2. Inaction rules for sPBC are those presented in Tables 1 and 2.

Definition 1. *We say that a regular dynamic s-expression G is operative if it is not possible to apply any inaction rule from it. We will denote the set of all the operative regular dynamic s-expressions by OpReDynExpr.*   □

Definition 2. *We define the structural equivalence relation for regular dynamic s-expressions by:*

$$\equiv \; =_{def} \; (\xrightarrow{\emptyset} \cup \xleftarrow{\emptyset})^*$$

As usual, we denote the class of G with respect to $\equiv$ by $[G]_\equiv$.   □

Rules defining the stochastic transitions are those presented in Table 3, together with those corresponding to the synchronization operator, which will be described in detail later. We assume that all dynamic s-expressions that appear on the left-hand sides of each transition in the rules are regular and operative.

Table 1. Inaction rules (I)

$$\overline{E};F \xrightarrow{\square} \overline{E};F \qquad \underline{E};F \xrightarrow{\square} E;\overline{F} \qquad E;\underline{F} \xrightarrow{\square} E;F$$

$$\overline{E}\square F \xrightarrow{\square} \overline{E}\square F \qquad \overline{E\square F} \xrightarrow{\square} E\square\overline{F} \qquad \underline{E}\square F \xrightarrow{\square} \underline{E}\square F$$

$$E\square\underline{F} \xrightarrow{\square} \underline{E}\square F \qquad \overline{E\|F} \xrightarrow{\square} \overline{E}\|\overline{F} \qquad \underline{E}\|\underline{F} \xrightarrow{\square} E\|F$$

$$\overline{E[f]} \xrightarrow{\square} \overline{E}[f] \qquad \underline{E}[f] \xrightarrow{\square} E[f] \qquad \overline{E\,sy\,a} \xrightarrow{\square} \overline{E}\,sy\,a$$

$$\underline{E}\,sy\,a \xrightarrow{\square} E\,sy\,a \qquad \overline{E\,rs\,a} \xrightarrow{\square} \overline{E}\,rs\,a \qquad \underline{E}\,rs\,a \xrightarrow{\square} E\,rs\,a$$

$$\dfrac{\forall op \in \{;,\square\},\ G \xrightarrow{\square} G^{\square}}{G\,op\,E \xrightarrow{\square} G^{\square}\,op\,E} \qquad \dfrac{\forall op \in \{;,\square\},\ G \xrightarrow{\square} G^{\square}}{E\,op\,G \xrightarrow{\square} E\,op\,G^{\square}} \qquad \dfrac{G \xrightarrow{\square} G^{\square}}{G[f] \xrightarrow{\square} G^{\square}[f]}$$

$$\dfrac{G_1 \xrightarrow{\square} G_1^{\square}}{G1\,\|\,G_2 \xrightarrow{\square} G_1^{\square}\,\|\,G_2} \qquad \dfrac{G_2 \xrightarrow{\square} G_2^{\square}}{G1\,\|\,G_2 \xrightarrow{\square} G_1\,\|\,G_2^{\square}} \qquad \dfrac{\forall op \in \{sy,\,rs\},\ G \xrightarrow{\square} G^{\square}}{G\,op\,a \xrightarrow{\square} G^{\square}\,op\,a}$$

Table 2. Inaction rules (II)

$$\overline{[E*F*E^{\square}]} \xrightarrow{\square} [\overline{E}*F*E^{\square}] \qquad [\underline{E}*F*E^{\square}] \xrightarrow{\square} [E*\overline{F}*E^{\square}]$$

$$[E*\underline{F}*E^{\square}] \xrightarrow{\square} [E*\overline{F}*E^{\square}] \qquad [E*\underline{F}*E^{\square}] \xrightarrow{\square} [E*F*\overline{E^{\square}}]$$

$$[E*F*\underline{E^{\square}}] \xrightarrow{\square} [E*F*E^{\square}] \qquad \dfrac{G \xrightarrow{\square} G^{\square}}{[G*E*F] \xrightarrow{\square} [G^{\square}*E*F]}$$

$$\dfrac{G \xrightarrow{\square} G^{\square}}{[E*G*F] \xrightarrow{\square} [E*G^{\square}*F]} \qquad \dfrac{G \xrightarrow{\square} G^{\square}}{[E*F*G] \xrightarrow{\square} [E*F*G^{\square}]}$$

Rules in Table 3 define a total order semantics, in the sense that it is not contemplated the possibility of executing two multiactions at the same time. Then, in order to define the semantics of the synchronization operator, we need to calculate all the possible sets of bags of stochastic multiactions that could be executed concurrently as result of one or several synchronizations over each operative regular dynamic s-expression.

Definition 3. *We define* $BC : OpReDynExpr \longrightarrow \mathcal{P}(\mathcal{B}(SL))$, *as follows:*

- *If* $G \in OpReDynExpr$ *is final, i.e.* $G=\underline{E}$, *we take* $BC(G) = \emptyset$.
- *If* $G \in OpReDynExpr$ *is not final, we distinguish the following cases:*
  - $BC(\overline{<\alpha,r>}) = \{\{<\alpha,r>\}\}$
  - *If* $\gamma \in BC(G)$, *then:* $\gamma \in BC(G;E)$, $\gamma \in BC(E;G)$, $\gamma \in BC(E\square G)$, $\gamma \in BC(G\square E)$, $\gamma \in BC(G\,rs\,a)$ *(when* $a,\widehat{a} \notin A(\gamma)$*)*, $\gamma \in BC(G\,sy\,a)$, $f(\gamma) \in BC(G[f])$, $\gamma \in BC([G*E*F])$, $\gamma \in BC([E*G*F])$, $\gamma \in BC([E*F*G])$.
  - *If* $\gamma_1 \in BC(G)$, $\gamma_2 \in BC(H)$, *then* $\gamma_1 \in BC(G\|H)$, $\gamma_2 \in BC(G\|H)$, *and* $\gamma_1 + \gamma_2 \in BC(G\|H)$.

Table 3. Rules defining the stochastic transitions (I)

(B) $\dfrac{}{<\alpha,r> \xrightarrow{<\alpha,r>} <\alpha,r>}$	**(S1)** $\dfrac{G \xrightarrow{<\alpha,r>} G^\blacksquare}{G;F \xrightarrow{<\alpha,r>} G^\blacksquare;F}$
(S2) $\dfrac{H \xrightarrow{<\alpha,r>} H^\blacksquare}{E;H \xrightarrow{<\alpha,r>} E;H^\blacksquare}$	**(Rs)** $\dfrac{G \xrightarrow{<\alpha,r>} G^\blacksquare}{G\,rs\,a \xrightarrow{<\alpha,r>} G^\blacksquare\,rs\,a}\; a,\hat a \notin A(\alpha)$
(Re) $\dfrac{G \xrightarrow{<\alpha,r>} G^\blacksquare}{G[f] \xrightarrow{<f(\alpha),r>} G^\blacksquare[f]}$	**(E1)** $\dfrac{G \xrightarrow{<\alpha,r>} G^\blacksquare}{G\Box F \xrightarrow{<\alpha,r>} G^\blacksquare\Box F}$
(E2) $\dfrac{H \xrightarrow{<\alpha,r>} H^\blacksquare}{E\Box H \xrightarrow{<\alpha,r>} E\Box H^\blacksquare}$	**(C1)** $\dfrac{G \xrightarrow{<\alpha,r>} G^\blacksquare}{G\|H \xrightarrow{<\alpha,r>} G^\blacksquare\|H}$
(C2) $\dfrac{H \xrightarrow{<\alpha,r>} H^\blacksquare}{G\|H \xrightarrow{<\alpha,r>} G\|H^\blacksquare}$	**(It1)** $\dfrac{G \xrightarrow{<\alpha,r>} G^\blacksquare}{[\,G*E*F\,] \xrightarrow{<\alpha,r>} [\,G^\blacksquare*E*F\,]}$
(It2) $\dfrac{G \xrightarrow{<\alpha,r>} G^\blacksquare}{[\,E*G*F\,] \xrightarrow{<\alpha,r>} [\,E*G^\blacksquare*F\,]}$	**(It3)** $\dfrac{G \xrightarrow{<\alpha,r>} G^\blacksquare}{[\,E*F*G\,] \xrightarrow{<\alpha,r>} [\,E*F*G^\blacksquare\,]}$

- $\gamma \in BC(G\,sy\,a)$, and $<\alpha,r_1>, <\beta,r_2> \in \gamma$, (with either $<\alpha,r_1> \neq <\beta,r_2>$ or they are two different instances of the same stochastic multiaction in γ), with $a \in A(\alpha)$, and $\hat a \in A(\beta)$, then: $\gamma' \in BC(G\,sy\,a)$, where: $\gamma' = (\gamma + \{<\alpha \oplus_a \beta, R>\}) \setminus \{<\alpha,r_1>, <\beta,r_2>\}$ and R is the rate of the new stochastic multiaction, to be later defined (see rule Sy2 in Table 4).

$\square$

In order to define the rates for the stochastic multiactions generated by a synchronization we need to identify the situations of conflict. Concretely, for each operative regular dynamic s-expression G we define the multiset of associated conflicts for every instance of a stochastic multiaction $<\alpha,r>_i$ executable from G, which we will denote by $Conflict(G, <\alpha,r>_i)$, but we will only take those stochastic multiactions with exactly the same multiaction α. We will denote this multiset of conflicts by $Conflict(G, <\alpha,r>_i)$, although we will omit the subindex i if it is clear which instance of $<\alpha,r>$ we are considering [1].

Definition 4. *We define the following partial function:*

$$Conflict : OpReDynExpr \times \mathcal{SL} \longrightarrow \mathcal{B}(\mathcal{SL})$$

which for each instance i of the stochastic multiaction $<\alpha,r>$ executable from G gives us the multiset of stochastic multiactions $<\alpha,r'>$ in conflict with it. We define the function in a structural way:

---

[1] To avoid a more sophisticated formal definition, we have preferred to omit the indices in the definition.

1. $Conflict\,(\overline{<\alpha,r>},<\alpha,r>)=\{<\alpha,r>\}$
2. If $<\alpha,r>$ is executable from G, and $C=Conflict\,(G,<\alpha,r>)$, then:
   (a) $Conflict\,(G;E,<\alpha,r>)=Conflict\,(E;G,<\alpha,r>)=C$,
   (b) $Conflict\,(G\|H,<\alpha,r>)=Conflict\,(H\|G,<\alpha,r>)=C$,
   (c) If $a,\hat{a}\notin A(\alpha)$, then $Conflict\,(G\,rs\,a,<\alpha,r>)=C$,
   (d) For any bijective function f, $Conflict\,(G[f],<f(\alpha),r>)=f(C)$,
   (e) For the choice operator we need to distinguish the following two cases:
   - If $G\not\equiv\overline{E}$: $Conflict\,(G\,\square\,F,<\alpha,r>)=Conflict\,(F\,\square\,G,<\alpha,r>)=C$
   - If $G\equiv\overline{E}$: $Conflict\,(G\,\square\,F,<\alpha,r>)=Conflict\,(F\,\square\,G,<\alpha,r>)=$
     $C+\{<\alpha,r_j>\,|\,\exists\,H_i\in OpReDynExpr\,,\ H_i\equiv\overline{F}\ and\ H_i\overset{<\alpha,r_j>}{\longrightarrow}H_i'\}$
   (f) For the iteration operator we have:
   - $Conflict(\,[\,G*E*F\,],<\alpha,r>)=C$
   - For the two last arguments of an iteration we have:
     - If $G\not\equiv\overline{E'}$: $Conflict\,(\,[\,E*G*F\,],<\alpha,r>)=$
       $Conflict\,(\,[\,E*F*G\,],<\alpha,r>)=C$
     - If $G\equiv\overline{E'}$: $Conflict\,(\,[\,E*G*F\,],<\alpha,r>)=$
       $Conflict\,(\,[\,E*F*G\,],<\alpha,r>)=C+$
       $\{<\alpha,r_j>\,|\,\exists\,H_i\in OpReDynExpr\,,\ H_i\equiv\overline{F}\ and\ H_i\overset{<\alpha,r_j>}{\longrightarrow}H_i'\}$
   (g) $Conflict\,(G\,sy\,a,<\alpha,r>)=C$,
3. Let $\{<\alpha_1,r_1>,\,<\alpha_2,r_2>\}\in BC\,(G\,sy\,a)$, $a\in A(\alpha_1)$, $\hat{a}\in A(\alpha_2)$ and
   $G\,sy\,a\overset{<\alpha_1\oplus_a\alpha_2,R_{12}>}{\longrightarrow}G'\,sy\,a$ obtained by applying rule $Sy2$. Then:
   $Conflict\,(G\,sy\,a,<\alpha_1\oplus_a\alpha_2\,,\,R_{12}>)=$
   $\{\,<\alpha_1\oplus_a\alpha_2,\,R_{ij}>\,|\,<\alpha_1,r_i>\in C_1,\,<\alpha_2,r_j>\in C_2,$ where
   $R_{ij}=\dfrac{r_i}{cr(Gsy\,a,<\alpha_1,r_1>)}\dfrac{r_j}{cr(Gsy\,a,<\alpha_2,r_2>)}\cdot\underset{i=1,2}{min}\{cr(G\,sy\,a,<\alpha_i,r_i>)\}\,\}$
   taking: $C_i=Conflict(G\,sy\,a,<\alpha_i,r_i>)$, $i=1,2$, and $cr(\,G,<\alpha,r>_i)$ is
   the so called conflict rate for G and $<\alpha,r>_i$, defined by:

   $$cr(\,G,<\alpha,r>_i)=\sum_{<\alpha,r_j>\,\in Conflict\,(G,<\alpha,r>_i)}r_j\cdot n_j$$

   where n_j is the number of instances of $<\alpha,r_j>$ in $Conflict(G,<\alpha,r>_i)$.

   $\square$

Rules for the synchronization operator are shown in Table 4. Observe that we take as rate of the generated stochastic multiaction the minimum of the conflict rates of $<\alpha_1,r_1>$, $<\alpha_2,r_2>$, weighted by a factor, which is introduced in order to guarantee that an equivalence relation defined in [12] is in fact a congruence. For short, we will denote the stochastic multiaction obtained by synchronization of the stochastic multiactions $<\alpha_1,r_1>$ and $<\alpha_2,r_2>$ by $<\alpha_1,r_1>\oplus_a<\alpha_2,r_2>$.

Definition 5. For each $G\in ReDynExpr$ we define the set of the dynamic s-expressions that can be derived from $[G]_{\equiv}$ by:

Table 4. Rules for the synchronization operator

$$
\textbf{(Sy1)} \quad \frac{G \xrightarrow{<\alpha,r>} H}{G \; sy \; a \xrightarrow{<\alpha,r>} H \; sy \; a}
$$

(Sy2) Let $\{<\alpha_1, r_1>, <\alpha_2, r_2>\} \in BC(G \; sy \; a)$, $a \in A(\alpha_1)$, $\hat{a} \in A(\alpha_2)$, then

$$
\frac{G \; sy \; a \xrightarrow{<\alpha_1,r_1>} G_1 \; sy \; a \; (\xrightarrow{\blacksquare})^\blacksquare \; G_1^\blacksquare \; sy \; a \xrightarrow{<\alpha_2,r_2>} G_{12} \; sy \; a}{G \; sy \; a \xrightarrow{<\alpha_1 \blacksquare_a \alpha_2, \; R>} G_{12} \; sy \; a}
$$

$$
R = \frac{r_1}{cr(G \; sy \; a, <\alpha_1,r_1>)} \frac{r_2}{cr(G \; sy \; a, <\alpha_2,r_2>)} \cdot \min_{i=1,2} \{cr(G \; sy \; a, <\alpha_i, r_i>)\}
$$

$$
[G\rangle = \{G' \mid G' \in [G]_\equiv\} \cup \{H' \in ReDynExpr \mid \exists <\alpha_1, r_1>, \dots, <\alpha_n, r_n> \in \mathcal{SL}
$$
$$
\text{with } G \equiv G' \xrightarrow{<\alpha_1,r_1>} G_1 \equiv G_1' \xrightarrow{<\alpha_2,r_2>} \dots G_{n-1} \equiv G_{n-1}' \xrightarrow{<\alpha_n,r_n>} H \equiv H'\}
$$

$\square$

In [13] we proved for finite sPBC (without iteration) that for any bag γ of stochastic multiactions executable from a regular dynamic s-expression G, any serialization of γ can be executed from G, and the multiset of conflicts for any stochastic multiaction in γ is preserved along the serialized execution of γ. This result can be easily extended to sPBC with iteration, and we can use it in order to compute the rate of the stochastic multiactions obtained after a number of synchronizations.

Proposition 1. *Let G be a regular operative dynamic s-expression, $\gamma = \{<\alpha_1, r_1>, <\alpha_2, r_2>, \dots, <\alpha_n, r_n>\} \in BC(G)$, and a serialization of γ, for which we may apply $n-1$ times rule Sy2:*

$$
G \xrightarrow{<\alpha_1,r_1>} G_1(\xrightarrow{\emptyset})^* G_1^* \xrightarrow{<\alpha_2,r_2>} \dots \xrightarrow{<\alpha_n,r_n>} G_n
$$

to obtain a single transition $G \xrightarrow{<\beta,R>} G_n$.

Then we have:

$$
R = (\prod_{k=1}^{n} \frac{r_k}{cr(G, <\alpha_k, r_k>)}) \cdot \min_{k=1,\dots,n} \{cr(G, <\alpha_k, r_k>)\}
$$
$$
cr(G, <\beta, R>) = \min_{k=1,\dots,n} \{cr(G, <\alpha_k, r_k>)\}
$$

Proof. It can be found in [12]. $\square$

Consequently, for all the possible transition sequences obtained by a serialization of γ, if we can apply rule $Sy2$ a number of times to reach a single stochastic multiaction, then we have that it does not matter the order in which rule $Sy2$ has been applied, neither the transition sequence used, i.e., we will always obtain the same stochastic multiaction.

Corollary 1. *Let G be a regular operative dynamic s-expression, $\gamma = \{< \alpha_1, r_1 >, < \alpha_2, r_2 >, \ldots, < \alpha_n, r_n >\} \in BC(G)$, and two permutations of the set $\{1, \cdots, n\} : \{i_1, \cdots, i_n\}$ and $\{j_1, \cdots, j_n\}$. Assuming that there are two serializations:*

$$G \xrightarrow{<\alpha_{i_1}, r_{i_1}>} G_1(\xrightarrow{\emptyset})^* G_1^* \xrightarrow{<\alpha_{i_2}, r_{i_2}>} \cdots \xrightarrow{<\alpha_{i_n}, r_{i_n}>} G_n$$
$$G \xrightarrow{<\alpha_{j_1}, r_{j_1}>} G_1'(\xrightarrow{\emptyset})^* G_1'^* \xrightarrow{<\alpha_{j_2}, r_{j_2}>} \cdots \xrightarrow{<\alpha_{j_n}, r_{j_n}>} G_n'$$

from which we may apply $n-1$ times rule Sy2 (for the same actions $a_1, \ldots, a_{n-1}$, possibly repeated, but the same number of times in both cases), to obtain a single transition $G \xrightarrow{<\beta_i, R_i>} G_n$ and $G \xrightarrow{<\beta_j, R_j>} G_n'$, respectively, then we have: $G_n \equiv G_n'$ and $< \beta_i, R_i > = < \beta_j, R_j >$. □

Now we show an example that motivates the need for the syntactical restriction introduced, specifically in the case of iteration. With this example we will raise the problem that appears when we consider a parallel behaviour in the highest level in the body of an iteration.

Example 1. Let G be the following non-regular operative dynamic s-expression:

$$G = ([< \{a\}, r_1 > *(\overline{< \{b\}, r_2 > \| < \{b\}, r_3 > \| < \{\hat{b}, \hat{b}\}, r_4 >})* < \{b\}, r_5 >]) \, sy \, a$$

It follows that $\gamma = \{< \{b\}, r_2 >, < \{b\}, r_3 > < \{\hat{b}, \hat{b}\}, r_4 >\} \in BC(G)$. Then, according to the definition of BC, we also have $\gamma_1 = \{< \{b\}, r_2 >, < \{\hat{b}\}, R_{34} >\} \in BC(G)$, with

$$R_{34} = \frac{r_3}{r_3 + r_5} \cdot min\{r_3 + r_5, r_4\}$$

However, not every serialization of γ_1 is possible from G, because $< \{\hat{b}\}, R_{34} >$ cannot be executed from G_1, where $G \xrightarrow{<\{b\}, r_2>} G_1$ and

$$G_1 = ([< \{a\}, r_1 > *(\underline{< \{b\}, r_2 >} \| \overline{< \{b\}, r_3 >} \| \overline{< \{\hat{b}, \hat{b}\}, r_4 >})* < \{b\}, r_5 >]) \, sy \, a$$

Actually, we can execute $< \{\hat{b}\}, R'_{34} >$ from G_1, with $R'_{34} = min\{r_3, r_4\}$, and in general we have $R_{34} \neq R'_{34}$. □

Definition 6. *We define the labelled (multi)transition system of any regular dynamic s-expression G, $ts(G) = (V, A, v_0)$, where:*

- $V = \{[H]_\equiv \mid H \in [G)\}$ *is the set of states.*
- $v_0 = [G]_\equiv$ *is the initial state.*
- A *is the multiset of transitions, given by:*

$$A = \{ ([H]_\equiv, < \alpha, r >, [J]_\equiv) \mid H \in [G) \land H \xrightarrow{<\alpha, r>} J \}$$

In order to compute the number of different instances of each transition $([H]_\equiv, <\alpha, r>, [J]_\equiv)$ *in A, we consider equivalent all the different ways to derive the same stochastic transition by considering the different serializations of the same* γ *(Corollary 1). Therefore, for each equivalence class, we will only consider one of its representatives, which can be chosen imposing that the stochastic multiactions in each* $\gamma \in BC(G)$ *will be executed in the same order as they appear in the syntax of the s-expression G, i.e., we enumerate the stochastic multiactions from left to right in the syntax of the s-expression, and then, when we apply rule Sy2, the generated stochastic multiaction can be annotated with the concatenation of the numbering of the corresponding stochastic multiactions involved in the synchronization, so that when we detect that a permutation of the numbering has been already obtained, by a previous application of the rule, then that new stochastic transition will not be considered (see [14] for more details).* □

The *race policy* will govern the dynamic behaviour of the system when two or more stochastic multiactions are simultaneously enabled (i.e., when several stochastic multiactions are possible, the fastest one will win the race). Then, as we are using exponential distributions, the stochastic process associated with the evolution of every regular dynamic s-expression $\overline{E}$ is a Continuous Time Markov Chain (CTMC), which can be easily obtained from $ts(\overline{E})$ in the same way as we showed in [14]: we modify the multigraph $ts(\overline{E})$ by combining into a single edge all the edges connecting the same pair of nodes. These new edges will be labelled by the sum of the rates of the combined edges.

4   Denotational Semantics

We now present a denotational semantics for s-expressions, which is obtained taking stochastic Petri nets as plain boxes. Therefore, the semantic objects that we use will be called stochastic Petri boxes or just *s-boxes*. Thus, these *s-boxes* are essentially SPNs, but they have the same structure as Petri boxes of PBC. These boxes of PBC are labelled Petri nets fulfilling some restrictions. Concretely, they are labelled Petri nets $\Sigma = (S, T, W, \lambda)$, where (S, T, W) is a Petri net, and λ is a labelling function, which labels places with values from $\{e, i, x\}$, representing *entry places*, *internal places*, and *exit places* respectively; and transitions with elements in $\mathcal{B}(\mathcal{L}) \times \mathcal{L}$; i.e., $\lambda(t)$ is a relation which associates elements of $\mathcal{L}$ to bags of multiactions. By convention, $^\circ\Sigma$ and Σ° will denote the set of *e-labelled* places and the set of *x-labelled* places, respectively. Given a place $s \in S$, we will denote by $^\bullet s$ ($s^\bullet$) the set of input (output) transitions of s (called preconditions and postconditions of s, respectively). A similar notation is used for preconditions and postconditions of transitions. Both can be easily extended to sets of places and sets of transitions. Then, our boxes are defined to be labelled simple nets such that the following conditions hold: $^\circ\Sigma \neq \emptyset \neq \Sigma^\circ$, $^\bullet(^\circ\Sigma) = \emptyset = (\Sigma^\circ)^\bullet$ and $\forall t \in T : {}^\bullet t \neq \emptyset \neq t^\bullet$. A box is said to be *plain* when for every $t \in T$, $\lambda(t)$ is a constant relation, i.e., an element of $\mathcal{L}$.

Definition 7. *A plain stochastic Petri box (or just* plain s-box*) is a tuple* $\Sigma = (S, T, W, \lambda, \mu)$, *where* (S, T, W, λ) *is a plain box, and* $\mu : T \longrightarrow \mathbb{R}^+$ *is a stochastic function, which associates a rate to every transition.*   □

A plain s-box can be either marked or not [2]. We will denote by M_e the marking in which only *entry* places are marked (each one with a single token); on the other hand, M_x will denote the marking in which only *exit* places are marked, each one with a single token. We say that a marking M is k-safe if for all $s \in S$, $M(s) \leq k$, and we say that M is clean if it is not a proper super-multiset of $°\Sigma$ nor $\Sigma°$. Then, a marked plain s-box is k-safe if all its reachable markings are k-safe, safe if all its its reachable markings are 1-safe, and clean if all its reachable markings are clean.

4.1   Algebra of S-Boxes

For each transition that we can obtain compositionally we need to know which transitions are in conflict with it, in order to compute its *conflict rates*. Thus, we enumerate stochastic multiactions appearing from left to right in the syntax of regular static s-expressions, and we preserve this enumeration in the corresponding transitions of the stochastic Petri net. Only with the synchronization operator we can obtain some new transitions, which will be annotated with the concatenation of the numeration of the transitions involved.

Another decision that we must take is the selection of the operator box that we will use for the iteration, since we have two proposals in plain PBC for that [5]; one of them provides us with a 1-safe version (with six transitions in the operator box), but there is also a simpler version, which has only three transitions in the operator box. In general, in PBC, with the latter version we may generate 2-safe nets, which only occurs when a parallel behaviour appears at the highest level of the body of the iteration. Nevertheless, in our case, and due to the syntactical restriction introduced, this particular case cannot occur, so that the net obtained will be always 1-safe.

In order to define the semantic function that associates a plain s-box with every regular term of sPBC, we need to consider the following functions:

$$\eta : T \longrightarrow \mathbb{N}^* \quad \text{and} \kappa : T \longrightarrow \mathcal{P}(\mathbb{N}^*)$$

where $\eta(t)$ stands for the numeration of t according to our criterion (enumeration from left to right, and concatenation in case of synchronization), and $\kappa(t)$ identifies the set of transitions in conflict with t. These functions will be defined in a structural way, as we construct the corresponding plain s-box.

For each transition $t \in T$, we also define its corresponding *conflict rate*, and we will denote it by $cr(t)$:

$$cr(t) = \sum_{\eta(t_j) \in \kappa(t)} \mu(t_j)$$

---

[2] A marked plain s-box is essentially a kind of marked labelled stochastic Petri net, whose behaviour follows the classical *firing rule* of SPNs.

Then, the structure of the net is obtained as in PBC, combining both refinement and relabelling. Consequently, the s-boxes thus obtained will be safe and clean. Therefore, the denotational semantics for regular static s-expressions can be formally defined by the following homomorphism:

$$Box_s(<\alpha, r>_i) = N_{<\alpha,r>_i}$$
$$Box_s(op(E_1,\ldots,E_n)) = \Omega_{op}(Box_s(E_1),\ldots,Box_s(E_n))$$

As previously mentioned, we have to define η, κ for every operator of sPBC.

- $Box_s(<\alpha, r>_i) = N_{<\alpha,r>_i} =$

taking $\eta(t_i) = i$ and $\kappa(t_i) = \{i\}$.

For the remaining operators of sPBC the corresponding operator s-boxes are shown in Fig. 1, where the relabelling functions $\rho_{op} \subseteq \mathcal{B}(\mathcal{SL}) \times \mathcal{SL}$ that appear in that Figure are defined as follows:[3]

- $\rho_{id} = \{(\{<\alpha,r>\}, <\alpha,r>) \mid <\alpha,r> \in \mathcal{SL}\}$
- $\rho_{[f]} = \{(\{<\alpha,r>\}, <f(\alpha),r>) \mid <\alpha,r> \in \mathcal{SL}\}$
- $\rho_{rs\,a} = \{(\{<\alpha,r>\}, <\alpha,r>) \mid <\alpha,r> \in \mathcal{SL} \wedge a,\widehat{a} \notin A(\alpha)\}$

Thus, the corresponding semantic functions are defined as follows, where $Box_s(E_i) = (S_i, T_i, W_i, \lambda_i, \mu_i)$ is the plain s-box corresponding to E_i, and η_i, κ_i are the enumeration and conflict functions for T_i, $i = 1, 2, 3$.

- $Box_s(E_1\,;\,E_2) = \Omega_;(Box_s(E_1), Box_s(E_2))$. Then, we take:

$$\eta(t) = \begin{cases} \eta_1(t) & \text{if } t \in T_1 \\ \eta_2(t) & \text{if } t \in T_2 \end{cases} \qquad \kappa(t) = \begin{cases} \kappa_1(t) & \text{if } t \in T_1 \\ \kappa_2(t) & \text{if } t \in T_2 \end{cases}$$

- $Box_s(E_1 \parallel E_2) = \Omega_\parallel(Box_s(E_1), Box_s(E_2))$. η and κ are defined in exactly the same way as in the previous case.
- $Box_s(E_1[f]) = \Omega_{[f]}(Box_s(E_1))$.

$$\eta(t) = \eta_1(t), \quad t \in T_1 \quad \text{and} \quad \kappa(t) = \kappa_1(t), \quad t \in T_1$$

- $Box_s(E_1 \,\square\, E_2) = \Omega_\square(Box_s(E_1), Box_s(E_2))$.

$$\eta(t) = \begin{cases} \eta_1(t) & \text{if } t \in T_1 \\ \eta_2(t) & \text{if } t \in T_2 \end{cases}$$

$$\kappa(t) = \begin{cases} \kappa_1(t) \cup \kappa_2(t') & \text{if } t \in T_1, \;{}^\bullet t \in {}^\circ Box_s(E_1), \exists\, t' \in T_2, \;{}^\bullet t' \in {}^\circ Box_s(E_2), \lambda(t) = \lambda(t') \\ \kappa_1(t) & \text{if } t \in T_1, \;{}^\bullet t \in {}^\circ Box_s(E_1), \not\exists\, t' \in T_2, \;{}^\bullet t' \in {}^\circ Box_s(E_2), \lambda(t) = \lambda(t') \\ \kappa_1(t) & \text{if } t \in T_1, \;{}^\bullet t \notin {}^\circ Box_s(E_1) \\ \kappa_2(t) \cup \kappa_1(t') & \text{if } t \in T_2, \;{}^\bullet t \in {}^\circ Box_s(E_2), \exists\, t' \in T_1, \;{}^\bullet t' \in {}^\circ Box_s(E_1), \lambda(t) = \lambda(t') \\ \kappa_2(t) & \text{if } t \in T_2, \;{}^\bullet t \in {}^\circ Box_s(E_2), \not\exists\, t' \in T_1, \;{}^\bullet t' \in {}^\circ Box_s(E_1), \lambda(t) = \lambda(t') \\ \kappa_2(t) & \text{if } t \in T_2, \;{}^\bullet t \notin {}^\circ Box_s(E_2) \end{cases}$$

---

[3] We separate the definition of $\rho_{sy\,a}$, which will be presented later, when we formally define $Box_s(E_1\,sy\,a)$.

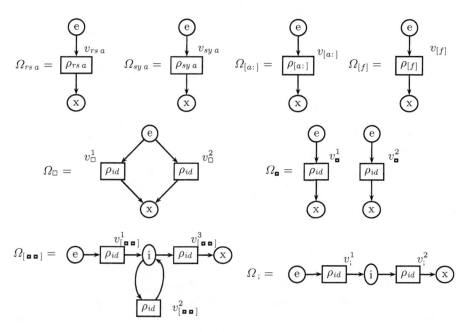

Fig. 1. The operator s-boxes for sPBC

- $Box_s([E_1 * E_2 * E_3]) = \Omega_{[**]}(Box_s(E_1), Box_s(E_2), Box_s(E_3))$. No new transitions are introduced with this operator, so the numeration of transitions is preserved. However, it is clear that this operator will introduce some new conflicts. Specifically, those transitions in T_2 having their preconditions in $^\circ Box_s(E_2)$ are in conflict with those transitions in T_3 with preconditions in $^\circ Box_s(E_3)$, if they have the same associated multiaction (the same label). Notice that since we are working with regular terms, $Box_s(E_2)$ and $Box_s(E_3)$ will have a single entry place. Formally:

$$\eta(t) = \begin{cases} \eta_1(t) & \text{if } t \in T_1 \\ \eta_2(t) & \text{if } t \in T_2 \\ \eta_3(t) & \text{if } t \in T_3 \end{cases}$$

$$\kappa(t) = \begin{cases} \kappa_1(t) & \text{if } t \in T_1 \\ \kappa_2(t) \cup \kappa_3(t') & \text{if } t \in T_2, \ ^\bullet t \in {}^\circ Box_s(E_2), \ \exists t' \in T_3, \ ^\bullet t' \in {}^\circ Box_s(E_3), \ \lambda(t) = \lambda(t') \\ \kappa_2(t) & \text{if } t \in T_2, \ ^\bullet t \in {}^\circ Box_s(E_2), \ \not\exists t' \in T_3, \ ^\bullet t' \in {}^\circ Box_s(E_3), \ \lambda(t) = \lambda(t') \\ \kappa_2(t) & \text{if } t \in T_2, \ ^\bullet t \notin {}^\circ Box_s(E_2) \\ \kappa_3(t) \cup \kappa_2(t') & \text{if } t \in T_3, \ ^\bullet t \in {}^\circ Box_s(E_3), \ \exists t' \in T_2, \ ^\bullet t' \in {}^\circ Box_s(E_2), \ \lambda(t) = \lambda(t') \\ \kappa_3(t) & \text{if } t \in T_3, \ ^\bullet t \in {}^\circ Box_s(E_3), \ \not\exists t' \in T_2, \ ^\bullet t' \in {}^\circ Box_s(E_2), \ \lambda(t) = \lambda(t') \\ \kappa_3(t) & \text{if } t \in T_3, \ ^\bullet t \notin {}^\circ Box_s(E_3) \end{cases}$$

Notice that $\kappa(t)$ is well defined for the second and fifth cases, because $\kappa_3(t')$ coincides for every $t' \in T_3$, $^\bullet t' \in {}^\circ Box_s(E_3)$, $\lambda(t) = \lambda(t')$, and respectively for the other case.

- $Box_s(E_1 \ rs \ a) = \Omega_{rs\,a}(Box_s(E_1))$.

$$\eta(t) = \eta_1(t), \ t \in T_1, \ a, \hat{a} \notin \lambda(t) \quad \text{and} \quad \kappa(t) = \kappa_1(t), \ t \in T_1, \ a, \hat{a} \notin \lambda(t)$$

– $Box_s(E_1 \, sy \, a) = \Omega_{sy\,a}(Box_s(E_1))$.   We take the following relation for the synchronization: $\rho_{sy\,a} \subseteq \mathcal{B}(\mathcal{SL}) \times \mathcal{SL}$, as the least relabelling relation containing ρ_{id}, and fulfilling:

$$(\Gamma, \alpha + \{a\}) \in \rho_{sy\,a} \quad \wedge \quad (\Delta, \beta + \{\hat{a}\}) \in \rho_{sy\,a} \text{ then } (\Gamma + \Delta, \alpha + \beta) \in \rho_{sy\,a}$$

Thus, $\rho_{sy\,a}$ allows us to obtain the net structure, as well as the multiactions labelling the transitions. Now, for every $t_1, t_2 \in T_1$, $\lambda(t_1) = \alpha + \{a\}$, $\lambda(t_2) = \beta + \{\hat{a}\}$, a new transition t is generated by the synchronization, whose label is $\alpha + \beta$, and its rate is computed as follows:

$$\frac{\mu_1(t_1)}{cr(t_1)} \cdot \frac{\mu(t_2)}{cr(t_2)} \cdot min(cr(t_1), cr(t_2))$$

Moreover,

$$\eta(t) = \eta_1(t_1) \cdot \eta_1(t_2)$$
$$\kappa(t) = \kappa_1(t_1) \otimes \kappa_1(t_2) = \{n_1 \cdot n_2 \mid n_1 \in \kappa_1(t_1), \, n_2 \in \kappa_2(t_2)\}$$

Notice that in order not to introduce redundant transitions, we only consider in the plain s-box a single one of the possible transitions that we can obtain by synchronizing (in different order) the same set of transitions. Furthermore, those transitions that were in T_1 have the same label, rate, numeration and conflict as they had in $Box_s(E_1)$. On the other hand, with this construction we can obtain in principle infinite nets, as it occurs in PBC, but, taking into account that the obtained nets are safe, the arcs having non-unitary weight will not enable the corresponding transitions, and thus, these transitions and arcs can be removed from the net structure, without affecting its behaviour.

Finally, we show that given a regular static s-expression E, the operational semantics of $\overline{E}$ and the semantics of the corresponding plain s-box are isomorphic.

Theorem 1. *For any regular static s-expression E, the transition system $ts(\overline{E})$ associated with $\overline{E}$, and the reachability graph of the marked SPN $(Box_s(E), M_e)$ are isomorphic.*

Proof. It is clear that at the functional level we have the same isomorphism as in PBC, because we take a total order semantics both in the algebra and in s-boxes. Furthermore, the stochastic multiactions obtained in the algebra and the corresponding transitions in the plain s-box are labelled with the same rate; thus, the transition system $ts(\overline{E})$ and the reachability graph of the marked SPN $(Box_s(E), M_e)$ behave in exactly the same way. □

5   A Simple Example: The Producer/Consumer System

In this section we consider the classical *Producer/Consumer* system, firstly considering a buffer with capacity 1, and afterwards we will see how to extend the specification to a more general case (buffer with capacity n).

Each multiaction α in the specification has associated a delay that follows a negative exponential distribution with rate r_α. There are three different components: P (Producer), C (Consumer) and B (Buffer). The three components work in parallel, but they have to synchronize in a set of actions: i (for *initiating* the process), f (for *finishing* it), s (for *storing* an item into the buffer) and g (for *getting* an item from the buffer). The specification of every component is as follows.

Producer: At the beginning, it is ready to initiate the process: $< \{i\}, r_{i_P} >$. Then, it starts a cyclic behaviour consisting of producing an item $< \{p\}, r_p >$, followed by storing the item into the buffer $< \{s\}, r_s >$. Finally, it ends its execution $(< \{f\}, r_{f_P} >)$. This behaviour can be modelled by:

$$Producer = [< \{i\}, r_{i_P} > * (< \{p\}, r_p >; < \{s\}, r_s >) * < \{f\}, r_{f_P} >]$$

Consumer: At the beginning, it is ready to initiate the process: $< \{i\}, r_{i_C} >$. Then, it starts a cyclic behaviour consisting of getting an item from the buffer $< \{g\}, r_g >$, followed by consuming the item $< \{c\}, r_c >$. Finally, it ends its execution $(< \{f\}, r_{f_C} >)$. The corresponding specification in sPBC follows:

$$Consumer = [< \{i\}, r_{i_C} > * (< \{g\}, r_g >; < \{c\}, r_c >) * < \{f\}, r_{f_C} >]$$

The corresponding plain s-boxes are:

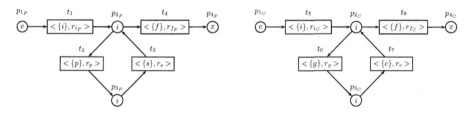

Buffer₁ : we first consider a buffer with capacity 1; the corresponding specification in sPBC is:

$$Buffer_1 = [< \{\hat{i}, \hat{i}\}, r_{i_B} > * (< \hat{s}, r_{\hat{s}} > ; < \hat{g}, r_{\hat{g}} >) * < \{\hat{f}, \hat{f}\}, r_{f_B} >]$$

Finally, the complete specification of the System is:

$$System = [A : (Producer \parallel Consumer \parallel Buffer_1)]$$

where $A = \{i, f, s, g\}$.

The generalization to a buffer of capacity n $(n \geq 2)$ is straightforward, we just need to change the specification of the buffer as follows:

$$I_1 = (< \hat{s}, r_{\hat{s}} >; < \hat{g}, r_{\hat{g}} >)$$
$$I_n = [< \hat{s}, r_{\hat{s}} > * I_{n-1} * < \hat{g}, r_{\hat{g}} >], \quad n \geq 2$$
$$Buffer_n = [< \{\hat{i}, \hat{i}\}, r_{i_B} > * I_n * < \{\hat{f}, \hat{f}\}, r_{f_B} >]$$

The corresponding plain s-box for *Buffer_n* is shown in Fig. 2.

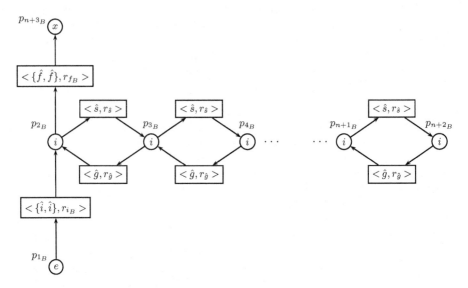

Fig. 2. Plain s-box of *Buffer$_n$*

In this case:

$$System_n = [\, A \,:\, (\, Producer \,\|\, Consumer \,\|\, Buffer_n \,)\,]$$

where $A = \{i, f, s, g\}$.

6   Conclusions and Future Work

sPBC is a Markovian extension of PBC which preserves the main features of that model. Thus, the syntax of sPBC is a natural stochastic extension of PBC, by annotating the multiactions with rates, which represent the parameter of an exponential distribution.

In this paper we have extended the operational and the denotational semantics that we presented in [14] for finite sPBC, by including the iteration operator, and considering the new version for the semantics of the synchronization operator, which is inspired in that one presented in [13].

The denotational semantics of sPBC is defined using as semantic objects a special kind of labelled stochastic Petri nets, called *s-boxes*. This will be a static translation in the sense that the rates of the transitions of the corresponding SPNs will not be marking dependent.

Our work in progress is focused to the definition of a stochastic bisimulation, which will capture more precisely those processes that can be considered equivalent taking into account the stochastic information. Our plans for future work include the treatment of the recursion operator, and the inclusion of some additional features in the language, such as immediate multiactions.

References

[1] M. Ajmone Marsan, G. Balbo, G. Conte, S. Donatelli, and G. Franceschinis. *Modelling with Generalized Stochastic Petri Nets*. Wiley, 1995. 292

[2] M. Bernando and R. Gorrieri. A Tutorial on EMPA : A Theory of Concurrent Process with Nondeterminism, Priorities, Probabilities and Time. *Theorical Computer Science, 202:1-54*, 1998. 292

[3] E. Best, R. Devillers, and M. Koutny. Petri Nets, Process Algebras and Programming Languages. In *Lectures on Petri Nets II: Applications,* W. Reisig and Rozenberg (eds.), Advances in Petri Nets, Volume 1492, Springer-Verlag, pp. 1-84,, 1998. 292

[4] E. Best, R. Devillers, and M. Koutny. A Consistent Model for Nets and Process Algebras. In the book *The Handbook on Process Algebras,* J. A. Bergstra, A. Ponse and S. S. Smolka (Eds.), North Holland, Chapter 14, pages 873-944, 2001. 292

[5] E. Best, R. Devillers, and M. Koutny. *Petri Net Algebra*. EATC, Springer, 2001. 292, 302

[6] E. Best, R. Devilllers, and J. Hall. The Box Calculus: A New Causal Algebra with Multi-label Communication. In *Advances in Petri Nets,* G. Rozenberg (Eds.), LNCS 609, Springer, pages 21-69, 1992. 292

[7] E. Best and M. Koutny. A Refined View of the Box Algebra. In *Proc. Application and Theory of Petri Nets.* LNCS 935, Springer, pp. 1-20, 1995. 292

[8] H. Hermanns and M. Rettelbach. Syntax, Semantics, Equivalences and Axioms for MTIPP. In *Proc. of the 2nd Workshop on Process Algebra and Performance Modelling,* U. Herzog and M. Rettelbach, (Eds.) Regensberg/Erlangen, pp.71-88, 1994. 292

[9] J. Hillston. The nature of the synchronization. In *Int. Workshop on Process Algebra and Performance Modelling,* 1994. 293

[10] J. Hillston. *A Compositional Approach to Performance Modelling*. Cambridge University Press, 1996. 292, 293

[11] M. Koutny. A Compositional Model of Time Petri Nets. *International Conference on Theory and Application of Petri Nets, 2000, LNCS 1825,* pp. 303-322, Springer, 2000. 292

[12] H. Macià. *sPBC: Una Extensión Markoviana del Petri Box Calculus.* PhD thesis, Departamento de Informática, Universidad de Castilla-La Mancha (in spanish), 2003. 298, 299

[13] H. Macià, V. Valero, F. Cuartero, and F. L. Pelayo. A new proposal for the synchronization in sPBC. In *Proc. Third IEEE Int. Conference on Application of Concurrent to System Design (ACSD'03),* pp. 216-225, IEEE Computer Society Press, 2003. 292, 293, 299, 307

[14] H. Macià, V. Valero, and D. de Frutos. sPBC: A Markovian Extension of Finite Petri Box Calculus. In *Proc. 9th IEEE Int. Workshop on Petri Nets and Performance Models (PNPM'01),* pp. 207-216. IEEE Computer Society Press, 2001. 292, 293, 301, 307

[15] O. Marroquín and D. de Frutos. Extending the Petri Box Calculus with Time. In *Proc. Int. Conf. on Theory and Application of Petri Nets 2001. LNCS 2075, Springer,* pp. 195-207, 2001. 292

[16] R. Milner. *Communication and Concurrency*. Prentice-Hall International, 1989. 293

[17] M. Ribaudo. Stochastic Petri Net Semantics for Stochastic Process Algebra. In *Proc. 6th Int. Workshop on Petri Nets and Performance Models, (PNPM'95),* Durham, 1995. 293

Petri Net Semantics of the Finite π-Calculus

Raymond Devillers[1], Hanna Klaudel[2], and Maciej Koutny[3]

[1] Université Libre de Bruxelles, B-1050 Bruxelles, Belgium
rdevil @ ulb.ac.be
[2] Université d'Évry, LaMI, 91000 Évry, France
klaudel @ lami.univ-evry.fr
[3] University of Newcastle, NE1 7RU, U.K.
maciej.koutny @ ncl.ac.uk

Abstract. In this paper we propose a translation into high level Petri nets of a finite fragment of the π-calculus. Our construction renders in a compositional way the control flow aspects present in π-calculus process expressions, by adapting the existing graph-theoretic net composition operators. Those aspects which are related to term rewriting, as well as name binding, are handled through special inscription of places, transitions and arcs, together with a suitable choice of the initial marking for a compositionally derived high level Petri net.

1 Introduction

In recent years, mobility has emerged as a key feature of many complex real life computing systems. In order to be able to model such a feature, dedicated process algebras have been designed, among which a central role is occupied by the π-calculus [13]. Within such a formalism, it is possible, for example, to model an interaction between a name server and a client willing to access a mobile provider known to the server (but not to the client), through which the physical address of the provider is acquired enabling a direct access to the provider by the client. The basic mechanism facilitating such a dynamic change is the ability to pass a *reference* (or a *channel*) through a communication on a previously known channel, allowing the recipient to use the new channel in future interactions.

The standard presentations of the π-calculus are based heavily on term rewriting and, as a result, tend to be difficult to translate into automata-based formalisms, such as Petri nets, which allow one to specify and reason about the causality and concurrency exhibited by a system. The main problem is that the standard term rewriting rules change the structure of an expression modelling the system, whereas an automata-based representation retains its structure over possible evolutions, and the changes of the state are represented explicitly (e.g., as net markings).

In this paper, we outline a compositional translation from the π-calculus to high-level Petri nets coping with this fundamental problem. Although, for brevity, we shall restrict ourselves to the finite fragment of the π-calculus without

D. de Frutos-Escrig and M. Núñez (Eds.): FORTE 2004, LNCS 3235, pp. 309–325, 2004.
© IFIP International Federation for Information Processing 2004

the match and mismatch constructs, the resulting theory is still rich enough to allow the description of non-trivial systems.

2   Finite π-Calculus

We start by briefly recalling the syntax and operational semantics of the π-calculus [13, 15], assuming that $\mathbb{C} \overset{\text{df}}{=} \{a, b, c, \ldots\}$ is a countably infinite set of channels. The concrete syntax of the *finite* π-calculus we use is given below, where P denotes an arbitrary agent (or π-expression).

output/input/internal Prefixes $\quad \ell \quad ::= \quad \bar{a}b \ \mid \ ac \ \mid \ \tau$

Agents $\quad P \quad ::= \quad 0 \ \mid \ \ell.P \ \mid \ P + P \ \mid \ P|P \ \mid \ (\nu c)P$

The constructs $ac.P$ (input) and $(\nu c)P$ (restriction) bind the channel c in P, and by $fn(P)$ we will denote the free channels of P. Agents are defined up to the *alpha-conversion* of bound channels, implying that the latter may be *coherently* replaced by *new* channels provided that name clashes are avoided. It is always possible to alpha-convert any agent in such a way that each bound channel only generates a single binding, and no channel is both free and bound; for instance, $ab.bb.ba.\bar{a}b.0$ can be rewritten as $ab.bc.cd.\bar{d}c.0$.

We will denote by $\{b/c\}P$ the agent obtained from P by replacing all the free occurrences of c by b, possibly after alpha-converting P in order to avoid channel clashes; for instance, $\{b/c\}\bar{a}c.cd.0 = \bar{a}b.bd.0$ and $\{b/c\}ab.\bar{d}b.\bar{d}c.0 = ae.\bar{d}e.\bar{d}b.0$.

Operational Semantics. There are several variants of the operational semantics of the π-calculus (see [15]), mainly due to different treatments of the restriction operator, which is generally considered to be the most intricate feature of the whole theory. Basically, it is possible to 'send to the outside world' a restricted channel c through a known channel a, but if c is captured by a receiving process then both the sender and receiver become part of an encompassing restriction (see the Com rule in table 1). To handle this situation correctly, one needs to know which channels are presently 'known' to the external environment, and which ones are migrating restricted channels. Unfortunately, this may not be determined just by looking at a sub-expression without considering its surrounding 'context'. As a result, we have found it advantageous to use the semantical presentation expounded in [6, 7], where the usual transition steps are augmented with an explicit information about unrestricted channels. More precisely, we use transitions of the form

$$A \vdash P \overset{\ell}{\longrightarrow} B \vdash Q ,$$

where ℓ is a prefix and $A, B \subset \mathbb{C}$ are finite sets of *indexing* channels. Its intuitive meaning (see [7]) is that 'in a state where the channels A may be known by agent P and by its environment, P can do ℓ to become agent Q and the channels B may be known to Q and its environment'. As a result, Q may know more channels than P as an input $\ell = ab$ adds b provided that $b \notin A$ (intuitively,

Table 1. Operational semantics of π-expressions, where: $ns(\tau) \overset{\mathrm{df}}{=} \emptyset$; $ns(ab) = ns(\bar{a}b) \overset{\mathrm{df}}{=} \{a, b\}$; the notation A, c stands for the disjoint union $A \uplus \{c\}$; and $(\nu c \setminus A)P$ is P if $c \in A$ and $(\nu c)P$ otherwise. Symmetric versions of Sum, Par and Com are omitted

$$\text{Tau} \quad \frac{\rule{3cm}{0.4pt}}{A \vdash \tau.P \overset{\tau}{\longrightarrow} A \vdash P} \qquad\qquad \frac{\rule{5cm}{0.4pt}}{A \vdash ac.P \overset{ab}{\longrightarrow} A \cup \{b\} \vdash \{b/c\}P} \quad \text{In}$$

$$\text{Out} \quad \frac{\rule{3cm}{0.4pt}}{A \vdash \bar{a}b.P \overset{\bar{a}b}{\longrightarrow} A \vdash P} \qquad\qquad \frac{A, c \vdash P \overset{\bar{a}c}{\longrightarrow} A, c \vdash P' \wedge a \neq c}{A \vdash (\nu c)P \overset{\bar{a}c}{\longrightarrow} A \cup \{c\} \vdash P'} \quad \text{Open}$$

$$\text{Par} \quad \frac{A \vdash P \overset{\ell}{\longrightarrow} A' \vdash P'}{A \vdash P|Q \overset{\ell}{\longrightarrow} A' \vdash P'|Q} \qquad\qquad \frac{A, c \vdash P \overset{\ell}{\longrightarrow} A', c \vdash P' \wedge c \notin ns(\ell)}{A \vdash (\nu c)P \overset{\ell}{\longrightarrow} A' \vdash (\nu c)P'} \quad \text{Res}$$

$$\text{Sum} \quad \frac{A \vdash P \overset{\ell}{\longrightarrow} A' \vdash P'}{A \vdash P+Q \overset{\ell}{\longrightarrow} A' \vdash P'} \qquad \frac{A \vdash P \overset{\bar{a}c}{\longrightarrow} A' \vdash P' \wedge A \vdash Q \overset{ac}{\longrightarrow} A'' \vdash Q'}{A \vdash P|Q \overset{\tau}{\longrightarrow} A \vdash (\nu c \setminus A)(P'|Q')} \quad \text{Com}$$

such a b is a new channel communicated by the outside world – see the In rule in table 1), and an output $\ell = \bar{a}\, b$ adds b provided $b \notin A$ (intuitively, such a b is a channel restricted in P which becomes a new known channel in Q – see the Open rule in table 1). We call $A \vdash P$ a *valid* indexed π-expression if P is a π-expression and $fn(P) \subseteq A$. Similarly as P, the indexed π-expression $A \vdash P$ will also be defined up to alpha-conversion (affecting P but not A). Hence we may assume that no bound channel of P is present in A, and that each bound channel only generates a single binding; in such a case, a valid indexed π-expression will be called *well-formed*. In order to simplify the presentation, we shall often omit the trailing 0's in (indexed) π-expressions.

The operational semantics of indexed π-expressions is given in table 1 (in [6, 7], the '$B \vdash$' parts of the rules are implicit). It preserves the validity of expressions and, in combination with renaming and alpha-conversion, also their well-formedness. As usual, a complete behaviour of a valid indexed π-expression $\mathcal{P} = A \vdash P$ (defined up to alpha-conversion) can be represented by a labelled transition system (or lts) derived using the rules in table 1 and denoted $\mathsf{lts}_{\mathcal{P}}$.

In order to achieve a closer correspondence with the Petri net semantics, we slightly modify the Sum rule (as well as its symmetric version) into

$$\text{Sum}' \quad \frac{A \vdash P \overset{\ell}{\longrightarrow} A' \vdash P'}{A \vdash P+Q \overset{\ell}{\longrightarrow} A' \vdash P'+0}$$

This has the advantage of better keeping track of the origin of the move. Indeed, if $Q = P$ then a move $A \vdash P+Q \overset{\ell}{\longrightarrow} A' \vdash P'$ could well have been derived from an application of Sum as well as of its symmetric counterpart. On the other hand, a move $P+Q \overset{\ell}{\longrightarrow} A' \vdash P'+0$ clearly arises from Sum', and $A \vdash P+Q \overset{\ell}{\longrightarrow} A' \vdash 0+P'$ from its symmetric counterpart. We shall need this distinction since, in the Petri net translation of $A \vdash P{+}P$, one gets different (though in some sense equivalent) markings depending on which of the two translations of P has evolved. The above modification is harmless anyway, since we still have in the modified setup the standard π-calculus rules $P + 0 \equiv P \equiv 0 + P$.

A Running Example. We consider a system DBASE modelling a simple database composed of a manager $\text{MANAGER} \stackrel{\text{df}}{=} ab.(\bar{f}g + \bar{b}c)$, a file compressing process (zipper) $\text{GZIP} \stackrel{\text{df}}{=} gd.\bar{a}d$, and a memory location $\text{STORE} \stackrel{\text{df}}{=} (\boldsymbol{\nu}h)(fe.\bar{e}h)$. Informally, the manager receives a request for a file on a visible channel a. If the file is not available, a negative response is sent back (using a newly acquired channel represented by b). Otherwise, the manager initiates a sequence of actions, the first being a sending on f to the store of a channel g (previously restricted to the manager and zipper processes) allowing a direct access to the zipper process. Upon receiving this message, the store uses the now available channel g to send a private (signified by the restriction $(\boldsymbol{\nu}h)$) file h to the zipper process. The file is then compressed and forwarded outside on channel a.

The database system is obtained by putting the three constituent processes in parallel as well as restricting the channel g connecting the manager with the zipper:

$$\text{DBASE} \stackrel{\text{df}}{=} (\boldsymbol{\nu}g)(\text{MANAGER} \mid \text{GZIP}) \mid \text{STORE} .$$

In concrete terms, the above scenario consists of the following four stages:

– The manager receives a request an for a data file from the external environment carrying a channel n which could be used for a negative response:

$$\{a, c, f\} \vdash \text{DBASE} \xrightarrow{\ an\ } \atop \{a, c, f, n\} \vdash (\boldsymbol{\nu}g)(\bar{f}g + \bar{n}c \mid gd.\bar{a}d) \mid (\boldsymbol{\nu}h)(fe.\bar{e}h) . \tag{1}$$

This move has been obtained using the following sequence of rules in table 1: In (where a previously unknown channel n is added to the indexing set), Par, Res and Par. Notice that the rule In could have been applied with b being substituted by any channel from the original indexing set; in such a case, the latter would have remained unchanged, e.g., $\ldots \xrightarrow{\ ac\ } \{a, c, f\} \vdash \ldots$.

– The manager can now either reply that the requested data is not available (using the $\bar{n}c$ branch) which is an option our scenario ignores, or initiate a positive response (using the other branch), as shown below:

$$\xrightarrow{\ \tau\ } \{a, c, f, n\} \vdash (\boldsymbol{\nu}m)(0 + 0 \mid md.\bar{a}d \mid (\boldsymbol{\nu}h)(\bar{m}h)) . \tag{2}$$

The above move is more complicated and it is built upon two sub-derivations. First, using the rules Out (after alpha-converting the bound channel g to a fresh channel m), Sum$'$, Par and Open, we get:

$$\{a, c, f, n\} \vdash (\boldsymbol{\nu}g)((\bar{f}g + \bar{n}c) \mid gd.\bar{a}d) \xrightarrow{\ \bar{f}m\ } \{a, c, f, n, m\} \vdash 0 + 0 \mid md.\bar{a}d .$$

Second, using the rule In followed by Res, we get:

$$\{a, c, f, n\} \vdash (\nu h)(fe.\bar{e}h) \xrightarrow{fm} \{a, c, f, n, m\} \vdash (\nu h)(\bar{m}h) .$$

The two derivations are then combined together using the Com rule. This exemplifies the *scope extrusion* which is a key concept of the π-calculus.

- Using the newly acquired restricted channel m, the store transfers the file h it held to the zipper:

$$\xrightarrow{\tau} \{a, c, f, n\} \vdash (\nu m)(0 + 0 \mid (\nu h)(\bar{a}h \mid 0)) . \tag{3}$$

This is another example of scope extrusion (for the restriction on h) and at the same time communication over the restricted channel m.

- The scenario concludes when the zipper sends off the compressed file to the external environment:

$$\xrightarrow{\bar{a}r} \{a, c, f, n, r\} \vdash (\nu m)(0 + 0 \mid 0 \mid 0) . \tag{4}$$

This step removes the restriction on h and adds r to the indexing set.

A Context-Based Representation of Indexed π-Terms. The original syntactic definition of the π-calculus in table 1 is ill-suited for a compositional translation into the domain of Petri nets. For example, the scope of the restriction of a channel can change dynamically as a result of an application of the Open rule, and channels bound by input or restriction can be substituted by fresh ones. We address these problems by introducing an auxiliary representation in the form of indexed π-terms based on the separation of their static features (related to control flow) and dynamic features (related to channel substitution and channel binding).

The signature over which the context based representation is based is slightly richer than that of the original syntax. We assume that there are countably infinite disjoint sets of:

- *potentially known channels* $\mathbb{C}$ (as in the definition of the π-calculus, ranged over by the lower case letters, except u and v);
- *potentially restricted channels* $\mathbb{R}$ (ranged over by the upper case Greek letters);
- *channel holders* $\mathbb{H}$ (ranged over by the lower case Greek letters, except ς).

We then represent a well-formed indexed π-expression like $\{b, d\} \vdash ba.(\nu c)\bar{a}c.\bar{c}b.0$ as a context based expression $\mathcal{C} \stackrel{\mathrm{df}}{=} \mathcal{H}{:}\varsigma$, where $\mathcal{H} \stackrel{\mathrm{df}}{=} \beta\alpha.\bar{a}\gamma.\bar{\gamma}\beta.0$ is a restriction-free agent based solely on channel holders (the identity of the channel holders is irrelevant) and $\varsigma \stackrel{\mathrm{df}}{=} [\beta \mapsto b, \delta \mapsto d, \gamma \mapsto \Delta]$ is a context allowing one to correctly interpret the channel holders. From the example ς, we may read that: α is presently a channel holder bound by an input (since α is not in the domain of the context mapping though is present in the expression $\mathcal{H}$); β and δ correspond respectively to the known channels b and d; and γ is a channel holder corresponding to the restricted channel Δ (again, the identity of this restricted channel is irrelevant).

In general, a *context* is a partial mapping $\varsigma : \mathbb{H} \to \mathbb{C} \cup \mathbb{R}$ with a finite domain. For each ς, we define:

$$
\begin{aligned}
known(\varsigma) &\overset{\mathrm{df}}{=} \varsigma(\mathbb{H}) \cap \mathbb{C} && \text{(known channels)} \\
new(\varsigma) &\overset{\mathrm{df}}{=} \mathbb{C} \setminus known(\varsigma) && \text{(potentially known channels)} \\
rstr(\varsigma) &\overset{\mathrm{df}}{=} \varsigma(\mathbb{H}) \cap \mathbb{R} && \text{(restricted channels).}
\end{aligned}
$$

And the syntax of the context based notation is defined as follows:

$$
\begin{aligned}
\text{Prefixes} \quad && p \quad &::= \quad \bar{\alpha}\beta \ \mid \ \alpha\beta \ \mid \ \tau \\
\text{Agents} \quad && \mathcal{H} \quad &::= \quad 0 \ \mid \ p.\mathcal{H} \ \mid \ \mathcal{H} + \mathcal{H} \ \mid \ \mathcal{H}|\mathcal{H} \\
\text{Expressions} \quad && \mathcal{C} \quad &::= \quad \mathcal{H}{:}\varsigma
\end{aligned}
$$

A channel holder is *bound input* if it occurs in the second position of an input prefix. A context based expression $\mathcal{H}{:}\varsigma$ is *well-formed* if we have that: all the channel holders in $\mathcal{H}$ are uniquely used (no channel holder may be bound by more than one input prefix, and then its other usages are in the suffix of this prefix); and no bound input channel holder belongs to $dom(\varsigma)$ while all the remaining channel holders used in the expression do belong to $dom(\varsigma)$. In the following, we shall only consider well-formed expressions.

It is straightforward to translate a well-formed indexed π-expression $\mathcal{P} = A \vdash P$ into a corresponding context based one, $\mathcal{C} = \mathcal{H}{:}\varsigma$. First, for each channel c occurring in P and A, we introduce a unique channel holder α_c. Then we replace each occurrence of c within P by α_c, and delete all occurrences of the hiding operator, resulting in $\mathcal{H}$. The context mapping has as the domain all channel holders α_c such that c was not input bound in P, and is given by $\varsigma(\alpha_c) = c$ if c was not restricted, and $\varsigma(\alpha_c) = \Delta_c$ otherwise (we assume that $\Delta_c \neq \Delta_d$ for $c \neq d$). E.g., our running example can be rendered in the context-based representation as:

$$\text{DBASE}' \overset{\mathrm{df}}{=} (\text{MANAGER}' \mid \text{GZIP}' \mid \text{STORE}') : \varsigma$$

where $\text{MANAGER}' \overset{\mathrm{df}}{=} \alpha\beta.(\bar{\gamma}\delta + \bar{\beta}\eta)$, $\text{GZIP}' \overset{\mathrm{df}}{=} \delta\phi.\bar{\alpha}\phi$ and $\text{STORE}' \overset{\mathrm{df}}{=} \gamma\kappa.\bar{\kappa}\psi$ are the three processes expressed in the channel holder notation, and the context mapping is given by:

$$\varsigma \overset{\mathrm{df}}{=} [\alpha \mapsto a \ , \ \gamma \mapsto f \ , \ \delta \mapsto \Delta \ , \ \eta \mapsto c \ , \ \psi \mapsto \Omega] \ .$$

From the above we can read off the *known* (indexing) channels, $known(\varsigma) = \varsigma(\mathbb{H}) \cap \mathbb{C} = \{a, f, c\}$, and the *restricted* channels, $rstr(\varsigma) = \varsigma(\mathbb{H}) \cap \mathbb{R} = \{\Delta, \Omega\}$. Note that there is now no need to represent channel restriction within an expression, as in the original syntax, since the relevant information is conveyed by the context mapping.

Later on, we will see how the structure of a holder-based term yields a Petri net (with each channel holder being translated into a corresponding place), and how the initial marking of these places is derived using the context mapping.

3   An Algebra of Nets

Our target Petri net model, called *p-nets*, is inspired by the box algebra [2, 3, 11], designed with the aim of providing a compositional Petri net semantics of concurrent programming languages. In this paper, we shall modify the original model and, in particular, use coloured tokens together with suitably labelled transitions, arcs and read-arcs. The latter are a Petri net specific device allowing an arbitrary number of transitions to simultaneously check for the presence of a resource stored in a place [8].

Transitions in p-nets have three different kinds of labels:

- UV, Uv and $\bar{U}V$ to specify communication with the external environment;
- τ to represent an invisible action;
- uv and $\bar{u}v$ to effect synchronous interprocess interactions.

Places are also labelled in ways reflecting their intended role. Those used to model control flow are labelled by their status symbols (*internal* places by i, and *interface* places by e and x, for entry and exit, respectively); the tokens they hold are the standard 'black' ones. *Holder* places carry coloured tokens representing channels; in the diagrams, their borders are thick, and they are labelled by the elements of $\mathbb{H}$. (A third kind of places will be introduced later on.)

Referring to figure 1, a holder place can be accessed by directed arcs, which can deposit or remove tokens, as well as by read arcs (drawn as thick undirected edges), which test for the presence of specific tokens. For example, N_{out} and N_{in} may be seen as preliminary translations of two context-based expressions, $\bar{\alpha}\beta : \varsigma$ and $\alpha\gamma : \varsigma$, where $\varsigma \stackrel{df}{=} [\alpha \mapsto a, \beta \mapsto b]$ (note also that N_{out} and N_{in} correspond to the output and input prefixes, $\bar{a}b$ and ac, of the π-calculus). Furthermore, N_{com} represents the translation of $\bar{\alpha}\beta|\alpha\gamma : \varsigma$ (or $\bar{a}b|ac$ in the π-calculus syntax). The idea here is to represent a π-calculus channel a by a holder place labelled α, marked by a token coloured by the actual channel name replacing a. Initially, if a is known then the place will contain a single a-token; otherwise it will be empty (like the γ-labelled place) until a communication or an input prefix inserts a channel into it.[1]

In order to observe these mechanisms at work, consider the nets N_{out} and N_{in} in figure 1, each consisting of one transition, two interface places, and two holder places. Interface places are connected using the standard Petri net arcs, while holder places are connected using directed arcs and read arcs labelled with *channel variables*, u, U, v and V (note that, due to a strict naming discipline, no other channel variables will ever be needed). The initial marking on the holder places

---

[1]   It is worth emphasising the importance of using read arcs in the proposed translation. In the interleaving semantics, each read arc in nets N_{out} and N_{in} could simply be replaced by a side loop (two arcs to and from the connected place and transition, with the same inscription). However, the transition in N_{com} coming from the synchronisation of N_{out} and N_{in}, would then not be executable because it would require *two* tokens a in the α-labelled place (whereas at most one is available).

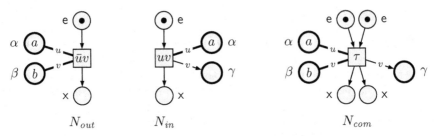

Fig. 1. Holder places and read arcs

is derived from the context ς which associates, in particular, a and b to the α-labelled and β-labelled holder places, respectively. (For control flow places, the default initial marking inserts a single black token into each entry place.)

The annotation of the various arcs by channel variables establishes a *binding* $\flat : \{u, U, v, V\} \to \mathbb{C}$ for the channels transferred/tested along arcs adjacent to a given transition. The transition of N_{in} is enabled if the entry place is non-empty and there exists a binding $\flat$ such that the α-labelled place contains at least one channel $\flat(u)$ (in our case, a). The execution of the transition transforms the marking in the following way: the black token is removed from the entry place and deposited in the exit one; the channel in the α-labelled place is left unchanged; and the channel $\flat(v)$ (e.g., channel e or channel b) is put into the γ-labelled holder place. With such a binding $\flat$, the firing generates a visible action $\flat(u)\flat(v)$ (e.g., ae or ab). Similarly, the firing of the transition in N_{out} generates the action $\bar{a}b$ (notice that no other visible action is possible for N_{out} as any binding enabling its only transition must satisfy $\flat(u) =$ and $\flat(v) = b$). Now, if we look at the firing of the τ-labelled transition in N_{com}, which corresponds to the fusion of the two transitions considered previously, the binding with $\flat(v) = e$ is inconsistent with the only binding option for v in N_{out} (i.e., $\flat(v) = b$), and so the internal communication is effected through which the γ-labelled holder place acquires the channel b.

The third, and last, kind of node in a p-net is a special holder place, called the *tag-place*, which is always present (though it may well be disjoint from the rest of the net) and is indicated in the diagrams by a double border. The tokens stored in this place are coloured and structured by being *tagged* with a member of the set $\mathbb{T} \stackrel{\mathrm{df}}{=} \{\mathsf{K}, \mathsf{N}, \mathsf{R}\}$; the place itself is $\mathbb{T}$-labelled. The first tag, K, will be used to indicate the channels in $known(\varsigma)$. The second tag, N, will be used to indicated the new (unknown) channels in $new(\varsigma)$. And the third tag, R, will be used to indicate the restricted channels in $rstr(\varsigma)$. The first case is slightly more complicated than the remaining two. For a restricted channel, say Δ, may be present in various holder places, due to synchronisation with various input prefixes. Then, if the restricted channel is *opened* (Δ becomes a newly known channel c), it is not possible to replace Δ by c in all the relevant holder places without some global transformation of the net. Instead, we shall indicate this fact by inserting a token $c.\Delta.\mathsf{K}$ in the tag-place, and then consulting it whenever

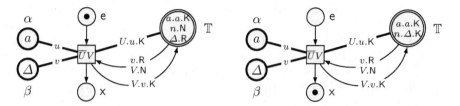

Fig. 2. Example of the usage of the tag-place in the net N_{res}

necessary (i.e., whenever we need to establish whether a restricted channel has been opened and what is the corresponding known value). In order to make the notation uniform, we shall use tokens $a.a.\mathsf{K}$ to denote all those known channels which were never restricted. To summarise, a token in the tag-place may be of the form:

- $a.\mathsf{N}$ meaning that a is a new channel;
- $\Delta.\mathsf{R}$ meaning that Δ is a restricted channel;
- $a.a.\mathsf{K}$ meaning that a is a known channel (either a has always been known or a was initially new and then became known);
- $a.\Delta.\mathsf{K}$ meaning that the restricted channel Δ has become known as a.

The arcs adjacent to the tag-place (both directed and read ones) are labelled with annotations of the form $U.u.\mathsf{K}$, $v.v.\mathsf{K}$, $V.v.\mathsf{K}$, $V.\mathsf{N}$, $v.\mathsf{N}$ or $v.\mathsf{R}$. For a given binding $\flat$, such annotations evaluate respectively to $\flat(U).\flat(u).\mathsf{K}$, $\flat(v).\flat(v).\mathsf{K}$, $\flat(V).\flat(v).\mathsf{K}$, $\flat(V).\mathsf{N}$, $\flat(v).\mathsf{N}$ and $\flat(v).\mathsf{R}$. Notice that the channel variables (U, V, u and v) will also be used in transition labels.

Consider the p-net N_{res} on the left in figure 2 (only some tokens in the tag-place are shown). Such a net gives a translation of a context based expression $\bar{\alpha}\beta$, assuming that $\alpha \mapsto a$ and $\beta \mapsto \Delta$ (in other words, of the π-calculus prefix $\bar{a}d$ when d is a restricted channel). The marking in the tag-place indicates that Δ is a restricted channel, n is an unknown channel and a a known one. The transition is enabled with the binding $\flat$ such that $\flat(u) = \flat(U) = a$, $\flat(v) = \Delta$ and $\flat(V) = n$. Its execution produces the visible action $\flat(\bar{U}V) = \bar{a}n$ and leads to the marking exhibited in the net on the right. This execution illustrates how a restricted channel becomes known (which is represented by the insertion of the token $n.\Delta.\mathsf{K}$ in the tag-place), and corresponds to the Open rule in table 1.

The p-net composition operators that we need are *prefixing*, $N.N'$, *choice* $N + N'$, and *parallel composition*, $N|N'$. All three operators merge the tag-places, as well as the corresponding holder places (i.e., labelled by the same channel holder). This corresponds to the asynchronous links used in [11], and will allow one to mimic the rewriting mechanism of the standard π-calculus. For two operand nets, their transitions and control flow places are made disjoint before applying a composition operator in order to allow to properly handle the cases when, for example, $N = N'$.

In the choice composition, the entry places of N and N' are combined, and so are their exit places. For example, 'combining' the entry places means performing a cartesian product of these two sets, and connecting a new entry place (s, s') to a transition t from N (or from N') in the same way as it was connected to s in N (resp. s' in N'). This corresponds to the choice operation in the box algebra [3] and has the following effect: if we start from the initial marking (i.e., one black token is inserted into each entry place), then either N or N' can be executed, mimicking the Sum (or Sum') rule and its symmetric counterpart.

When applying the prefixing operator, there is only one exit place in N which is combined with the entry places of N', all the resulting places becoming internal. This corresponds to the sequence operator in the box algebra, and the effect is that the execution of N after reaching the terminal marking, where the only exit place is marked, is followed by that of N'. Such a behaviour mimics the Tau, In and Out rules.

Finally, when composing N and N' in parallel, the p-nets are placed side by side and the pairs of transitions labelled uv and $\bar{u}v$ (one coming from N and the other from N') are synchronised, resulting in τ-labelled transitions. E.g., in figure 1, the net N_{com} can be derived as the parallel composition N_{out} and N_{in}, and the τ-labelled transition results from synchronisation of the two transitions labelled by uv and $\bar{u}v$ (which will be wiped out at the end of the translation). This, in particular, corresponds to the synchronisation operation in the M-net theory [2]. Putting the nets side by side allows to execute both parts in parallel, as in the Par rule and its symmetric counterpart, and the synchronisation of transition has effect similar to that of the Com rule.

4   Translating Context-Based Expressions into p-Nets

Given a context-based expression $\mathcal{C} \stackrel{\text{df}}{=} \mathcal{H} : \varsigma$, our translation into p-nets is done in two phases. First, we compositionally translate $\mathcal{H}$ into an unmarked p-net $\mathbb{K}(\mathcal{H})$ and then, using the context ς, we fill holder places with appropriate channels, set the default initial marking on the control flow places, and delete some transitions which are no longer needed. This results in the target p-net denoted by $\mathbb{PN}(\mathcal{C})$.

Phase I The translation $\mathbb{K}(\mathcal{H})$, guided by the syntax tree of $\mathcal{H}$, consists in first giving the translation for the basic sub-terms (i.e., 0 and the internal, input and output prefixes) shown in figure 3, and then applying p-net operators.

The basic process 0 is translated into a net consisting of a single entry place, a single exit place, and a single tag-place. As a result, we shall have up to isomorphism that $\mathbb{K}(N + 0) = \mathbb{K}(N) = \mathbb{K}(0 + N)$, and that $\mathbb{K}(N|0) = \mathbb{K}(0|N)$ only differ from $\mathbb{K}(N)$ by two isolated places and so have identical behaviours. Hence the standard π-calculus rules $N \equiv N + 0 \equiv 0 + N \equiv N|0 \equiv 0|N$ are also observed in the net model.

The translation of the internal prefix τ is very simple as it does not involve any manipulation on channels.

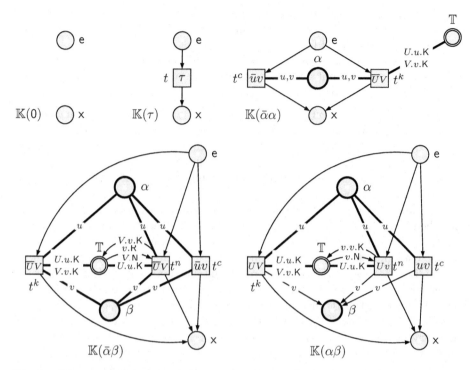

Fig. 3. The unmarked p-nets for 0 and the three kinds of prefixes (the tag-place is omitted when disconnected)

Each output prefix $\bar{\alpha}\beta$, when $\alpha \neq \beta$, is translated into the p-net $\mathbb{K}(\bar{\alpha}\beta)$ which may exhibit three kinds of behaviours, corresponding to the firing of three specific transitions:

- t^k: known output. A known channel (matching) V is sent through a channel (matching) U. The actual values of U and V are provided by the tokens present in the tag-place matching those in the holder places α and β, accessed through u and v. This corresponds to the Out rule. That the channels matching U and V are known is determined by the presence in the tag-place of tokens tagged with K. Notice that even if the entry place is marked, it may happen that this transition is not enabled; this may happen if α (and/or β) is unmarked (it is bound input and the binding prefix has not been executed yet), or it is marked by a restricted channel which has not been opened (yet).
- t^n: new output. A new channel V is sent through a known channel U. That the channels v and V are respectively restricted and new is determined by the presence in the tag-place of a channel tagged with R for v, and a channel tagged with N for V. After the execution of this transition, the restricted channel represented by v becomes known as the channel value of V; this is indicated by a token of the form $V.v.\mathsf{K}$ inserted into the tag-place to replace $v.\mathsf{R}$ and $V.\mathsf{N}$. This corresponds to the Open rule. Again, this transition may

be blocked (possibly temporarily), if α or β is unmarked, or if α is marked by a restricted and unopened channel, or if β is marked by a known or previously restricted but now opened channel.

- t^c: communicating output. It is intended to synchronize with a corresponding communication input in order to provide the transfer of a channel v through the channel u, be it known or restricted.

The special case of the output prefix $\bar{a}a$ has a simpler translation, since α may not be both known and restricted, so that t^n is unnecessary. Even though the α-labelled holder place will never contain more than one token, it is not a problem to have two variables on the arcs adjacent to it since these are read arcs, and so transitions will be enabled by simply identifying u and v with the same token in the α-labelled place.

For an input prefix $\alpha\beta$, when $\alpha \neq \beta$, the translation is broadly the same as for the output prefix. In particular, the known, new and communicating inputs should be interpreted in a similar way. Simply, v is now put into β instead of being read (checked), t^k corresponds to the rule In when b is already known (including the case of a previously restricted channel), and t^n to the same rule when b is new (it may not be restricted here). In the latter case, the variable V is not involved, and the transition is labelled Uv rather than UV. Notice also that, for t^k, while v is known as V, it is the possibly restricted original value v which is written into β, and not the corresponding known value V. This is important in order to allow subsequent synchronisations between uv with the u coming from this place and $\bar{u}v$ with the u coming from another holder place and containing a copy of the original token. Finally, prefixes of the form $\alpha\alpha$ are excluded by the well-formedness assumption (no channel holder can be both known and bound input).

For the compound sub-terms, we proceed compositionally:

$$\mathbb{K}(p.\mathcal{H}) \overset{\mathrm{df}}{=} \mathbb{K}(p).\mathbb{K}(\mathcal{H})$$
$$\mathbb{K}(\mathcal{H} + \mathcal{H}') \overset{\mathrm{df}}{=} \mathbb{K}(\mathcal{H}) + \mathbb{K}(\mathcal{H}')$$
$$\mathbb{K}(\mathcal{H} \mid \mathcal{H}') \overset{\mathrm{df}}{=} \mathbb{K}(\mathcal{H}) \mid \mathbb{K}(\mathcal{H}').$$

As an illustration of this phase of translation, we show in figure 4 the p-net obtained for STORE$'$. It is composed of the upper and lower parts corresponding respectively to the p-nets for input and output prefixes $\gamma.\kappa$ and $\kappa.\psi$ (the concatenation with the implicit trailing 0 has been omitted for simplicity without changing the essence of the overall picture). These parts have been composed using the prefixing operation which merged the exit place of the first p-net with the entry place of the second p-net (leading to an internal place), the holder places labelled κ from the first and second p-nets as well as their tag-places. The transitions labelled uv and $\bar{u}v$ are intended for synchronisation during subsequent parallel compositions and will be deleted in phase II.

Phase II Having derived $\mathbb{K}(\mathcal{H})$, we construct the target p-net by first removing all the transitions labelled by uv and $\bar{u}v$, and then inserting one black token into each entry place as well as the following channels into holder places:

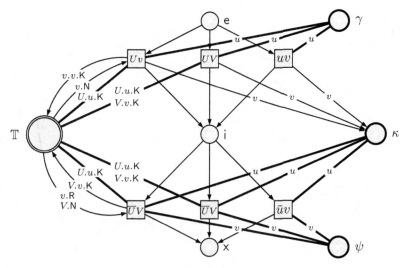

Fig. 4. The p-net resulting from phase I for STORE' $\stackrel{\mathrm{df}}{=} \gamma\kappa.\bar{\kappa}\psi$

- $\varsigma(\alpha)$ into each α-labelled holder place such that $\alpha \in dom(\varsigma)$.
- $a.a.\mathsf{K}$ into the tag-place for each $a \in known(\varsigma)$.
- $n.\mathsf{N}$ into the tag-place for each $n \in \mathbb{C} \setminus known(\varsigma)$.
- $\Delta.\mathsf{R}$ into the tag-place for each $\Delta \in rstr(\varsigma)$.

Phase II is illustrated in figure 5 which shows the part of p-net for the context-based expression DBASE' : ς corresponding to the scenario used in our running example (still omitting the trailing 0's). The control-flow places form three vertical lines respectively corresponding to the control-flow places of the sub-expressions MANAGER' (on the left), STORE' (in the middle) and GZIP' (on the right). The τ-labelled transitions come from the parallel composition (which includes synchronisation) between MANAGER' and STORE' (the upper one) and between STORE' and GZIP' (the lower one). All the entry places are marked, the tag-place and the holder places corresponding to the known or restricted channels are marked accordingly to the context ς.

At the initial marking, the Uv-labelled transition may be fired under a binding satisfying $\flat(u) = \flat(U) = a$ and $\flat(v) = n$ since:

- a is present in α-labelled holder place and $a.a.\mathsf{K}$ is present in the tag-place (which means that a is a known channel);
- $n.\mathsf{N}$ is present in the tag-place, which means that n is an unknown (fresh) channel.

The firing of this transition:

- consumes $\bullet$ from the input entry place and $n.\mathsf{N}$ from the tag-place;
- generates the visible action an;

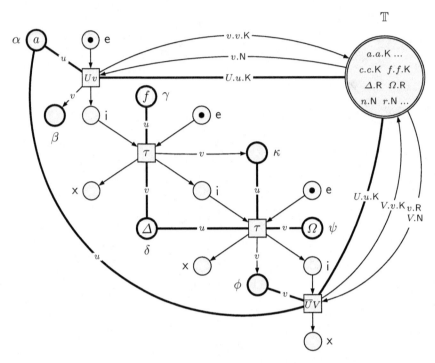

Fig. 5. The relevant fragment of the p-net resulting from phase II for the running example

- produces a black token in the internal output place, n in the β-labelled holder place and $n.n.\mathsf{K}$ in the tag-place (which means that n is now a known channel).

Next, the firing of the first τ-labelled transition is possible. It produces, in particular, the restricted Δ in the κ-labelled holder place which implements the scope extrusion of the π-calculus.

After that the second τ-labelled transition can be fired. It represents the transfer of the restricted channel Ω between STORE$'$ and GZIP$'$ through the private (restricted) channel Δ. It results, in particular, in putting Ω in the ϕ-labelled holder place.

At this stage, the firing of the last transition is possible with a binding satisfying $\flat'(u) = \flat'(U) = a$, $\flat'(v) = \Omega$ and $\flat'(V) = r$. It generates the visible action $\bar{a}r$, and replaces $\Omega.\mathsf{R}$ and $r.\mathsf{N}$ with $r.\Omega.\mathsf{K}$ inside the tag-place. This means that Ω is not longer restricted and that r has became known.

Main Result. It turns out that the proposed translation is sound, in a rather strict sense, which is expressed by the following theorem, the proof of which may be found in the technical report version of this paper [9].

Theorem. *For every indexed π-expression $\mathcal{P}$, its labelled transition system* $\mathsf{lts}_{\mathcal{P}}$ *(considered up to alpha-conversion) is isomorphic to the labelled transition system* $\mathsf{lts}_{\mathbb{PN}(\mathcal{C})}$ *of the p-net $\mathbb{PN}(\mathcal{C})$, where $\mathcal{C}$ is any well-formed context based expression corresponding to $\mathcal{P}$.*

5 Related Work

A first paper dedicated to giving a Petri net semantics for the π-calculus appears to be [10]. However, it only considers the so-called 'small' π-calculus (without the choice composition) provided with the reduction semantics (addressing only the communications between parallel components). Due to these limited aims, the problem is greatly simplified as restrictions may be managed syntactically (in fact, eliminated by renaming the restricted channels by fresh ones).

While not based on nets, [4] already considers the causality structures of the π-calculus, and distinguishes structural and link dependencies (the former mainly due to prefixing and communications, and the latter due to extrusion). However, the authors only capture the first kind of causality in their semantic model, while we taken both of them into account.

A graph-rewriting system is proposed in [14] as a semantic model for a rather restricted fragment of the π-calculus. This approach mainly addresses the concurrency feature of systems whereas we concentrated here on their interleaving semantics, since our aim was to show that our translation leads to nets with the same sequential behaviour as that defined by the standard interleaving semantics of the π-calculus. One of our immediate goal is to look at concurrency issues, and in this respect we may notice a fundamental discrepancy between our approach and [14] in the handling of restriction. More precisely, [14] allows parallel opening for expressions like $(\nu y)(\bar{x}y|P|\bar{z}y)$ by letting the actions $\bar{x}y$ and $\bar{z}y$ to occur independently (in parallel), while in our approach they must in some sense agree on their common exportation, so that only one of them (chosen arbitrarily) is in fact an opening, the other one accepting the choice already made.

The most frequently cited translation of π-terms into Petri nets is probably [5], which uses (low-level) labelled Petri nets extended with inhibitor arcs, while we use high-level nets with read-arcs. Moreover, the way compositionality is obtained is different from that used in our approach. Indeed, the approach from [5] proceeds by first establishing a general infrastructure, with places corresponding to all the possible sequential π-terms decorated with some conflicting set, and to all possible restrictions and conflicts, with all possible transitions between those places. It then defines compositionally the initial marking corresponding to each π-term (here, guarded recursions are allowed). As a consequence, even for a very simple process expression $\tau.0$, this leads to a net with infinitely many places and transitions (but only a single token in a single place).

6   Conclusions

In this paper, we outlined a Petri net based translation of the finite π-calculus, as well as an intermediate process algebra. Both approaches are based on the notions of a channel holder and context. Our development has been motivated by a desire to provide a compositional translation of the original π-calculus to the domain of automata-based models of computation (in particular, Petri nets). We therefore needed to address problems relating to the fact that a number of fundamental features of the former are based on purely language theoretic concepts (such as alpha-conversion and channel restriction). One of possible practical applications of our translation will be in making it possible to use Petri net based verification techniques to prove properties of mobility systems.

We now plan to investigate the extension of the theory to infinite behaviours through replication or recursion, as in the full π-calculus, or through iteration, as in the box algebra.

Acknowledgement

We would like to thank the anonymous referees for their helpful comments.

References

[1] E.Best and R.Devillers: Sequential and Concurrent Behaviour in Petri Net Theory. *Theoretical Computer Science* 55 (1988) 87–136.

[2] E.Best, W.Frączak, R.P.Hopkins, H.Klaudel and E.Pelz: M-nets: an Algebra of High Level Petri Nets, with an Application to the Semantics of Concurrent Programming Languages. *Acta Informatica* 35 (1998) 813–857. 315, 318

[3] E.Best, R.Devillers and M.Koutny: *Petri Net Algebra*. EATCS Monographs on TCS, Springer (2001). 315, 318

[4] M.Boreale and D.Sangiorgi: A Fully Abstract Semantics for Causality in the π-calculus. Proc. of *STACS'95*, Springer, LNCS 900 (1995) 243–254. 323

[5] N.Busi and R.Gorrieri: A Petri net Semantics for π-calculus. Proc. of *Concur'95*, LNCS 962 (1995) 145–159. 323

[6] G.L.Cattani and P.Sewell: Models for Name-Passing Processes: Interleaving and Causal. Proc. of *LICS'2000*, IEEE CS Press (2000) 322–333. 310, 311

[7] G.L.Cattani and P.Sewell: Models for Name-Passing Processes: Interleaving and Causal. Technical Report TR-505, University of Cambridge (2000). 310, 311

[8] S.Christensen and N.D.Hansen: Coloured Petri Nets Extended with Place Capacities, Test Arcs and Inhibitor Arcs. Proc. of *ICATPN'93*, Springer, LNCS 691 (1993) 186–205. 315

[9] R.Devillers, H.Klaudel and M.Koutny: Petri net semantics of the finite π-calculus CS-TR-846 University of Newcastle 2004 322

[10] J.Engelfriet: A Multiset Semantics for the π-calculus with Replication. *Theoretical Computer Science* 153 (1996) 65–94. 323

[11] H.Klaudel and F.Pommereau: Asynchronous links in the PBC and M-nets. Proc. of *ASIAN'99*, Springer, LNCS 1742 (1999) 190–200. 315, 317

[12] R.Milner: *Communication and Concurrency*. Prentice Hall (1989).

[13] R.Milner, J.Parrow and D.Walker: A Calculus of Mobile Processes. *Information and Computation* 100 (1992) 1–77. 309, 310

[14] U.Montanari and M.Pistore: Concurrent Semantics for the π-calculus. Proc. of *MFPS'95*, Elsevier (1995) Electronic Notes in Computer Science 1. 323

[15] J.Parrow: An Introduction to the π-calculus. In: *Handbook of Process Algebra*, Bergstra, Ponse, Smolka (Eds.). Elsevier (2001) 479–543. 310

[16] G. D.Plotkin: A Structural Approach to Operational Semantics. Technical Report FN-19, Computer Science Department, University of Aarhus (1981).

[17] W.Vogler: Partial Order Semantics and Read Arcs. Proc. of *MFCS'97*, Springer, LNCS 1295 (1997) 508–517.

Symbolic Diagnosis of Partially Observable Concurrent Systems*

Thomas Chatain and Claude Jard

IRISA/ENS Cachan-Bretagne
Campus de Beaulieu, F-35042 Rennes cedex, France
{thomas.chatain,claude.jard}@irisa.fr

Abstract. Monitoring large distributed concurrent systems is a challenging task. In this paper we formulate (model-based) diagnosis by means of hidden state history reconstruction, from event (e.g. alarm) observations. We follow a so-called true concurrency approach: the model defines explicitly the causal and concurrency relations between the observable events, produced by the system under supervision on different points of observation. The problem is to compute on-the-fly the different partial order histories, which are the possible explanations of the observable events. In this paper we extend our first method based on Petri nets unfolding to high-level parameterized Petri nets. This allows the designer to model data aspects (even on infinite domains) and non deterministic actions. The observation of such an action gives only partial information and the supervisor has to introduce parameters to represent the hidden aspects of the reached state. This supposes that the possible values for the parameters are symbolically computed and refined during supervision. In practice, non deterministic actions can also be used as an approximation to deal with incomplete information about the system. In this case the refinement of the parameters during supervision improves the knowledge of the model.

1 Introduction

Concurrent and distributed systems have been at the heart of computer science and engineering for decades. Formal models and mathematical theories of concurrent systems have been essential to the development of languages, formalisms, and validation techniques that are needed for a correct design of large distributed applications.

In this paper, we consider another instance of the use of formal models to master the complexity of distributed applications, namely the problem of inferring, from measurements, the hidden internal state of a distributed and asynchronous system. An important application is *distributed alarm correlation and fault diagnosis* in telecommunications networks, which motivated this work.

---

* This work was supported by the French RNRT project SWAN, funded by the Ministère de la Recherche; partners of the project are Inria, France Telecom R&D, Alcatel, QosMetrics, and Paris-Nord University.

D. de Frutos-Escrig and M. Núñez (Eds.): FORTE 2004, LNCS 3235, pp. 326–342, 2004.

The problem of recovering state histories from observations is pervasive throughout the general area of information technologies. For instance, estimating the state trajectory from noisy measurements is central in control engineering, with the Kalman filter as its most popular instance [8]; the same problem is considered in the area of pattern recognition, for stochastic finite state automata, in the theory of Hidden Markov Models [13]. For both cases, however, no extension exists to handle distributed systems. Finally, fault diagnosis in discrete event systems (e.g., automata) has been extensively studied [2, 15], but the problem of dealing with concurrent model is just starting.

We follow a so-called true concurrency approach: the model defines explicitly the causal and concurrency relations between the observable events, produced by the system under supervision on different points of observation. The problem is to compute on-the-fly the different partial order histories, which are the possible explanations of the observable events. A natural candidate to formalize the approach are 1-safe Petri nets with branching processes and unfoldings. The previous work of our group used this framework to define the histories and a distributed algorithm to build them as a collection of consistent local views [1].

In this paper we extend our method to *high-level parameterized Petri nets*. This allows the designer to model data aspects (even on infinite domains) and non deterministic actions. The observation of such an action gives only partial information and the supervisor has to introduce parameters to represent the hidden aspects of the reached state. This supposes that the possible values for the parameters are symbolically computed and refined during supervision. In practice, non deterministic actions can also be used as an approximation to deal with incomplete information about the system. In this case the refinement of the parameters during supervision improves the knowledge of the model. We think this symbolic approach will be able to deal with more complex distributed systems. At the heart of our scientific contribution is the definition of a symbolic unfolding for high-level Petri nets, which combines the traditional unfolding [10, 11] with a kind of α-conversion (λ-calculus) to deal with parameters. Up to our knowledge, this is original. The idea of using an unknown symbolic initial marking has already been addressed in [16], but restricted to the framework of simple Petri nets and their marking graphs.

This paper is organized as follows. We first begin in Section 2 by an informal presentation of the problem on a toy example, illustrating the high-level Petri net model we use, its unfolding and the trajectories we want to compute with respect to a given partially ordered observation. The mathematical background is recalled in Section 3, following the usual notation for Petri nets, as used for instance in [10]. In Section 4, we present an original algorithm to compute a symbolic unfolding. This allows us to formally express the diagnosis problem, which is done in Section 5 using a composition between the observation and the model, which can be then symbolically unfolded. We also show that unfolding can be performed on-the-fly, observable event by observable event. We conclude in Section 6 by presenting different perspectives on the use of the approach to monitor real distributed systems.

2   An Example of Diagnosis Under Partial Observation

2.1   The Parameterized Concurrent Model

Our parameterized concurrent model is based on the standard high-level Petri net introduced in [9] and augmented with free variables. It is exemplified in Figure 1, which shows two interacting components, named A and B. Component A may fail (observed as α) with a given non observable severity level (parameter l). To be completely repaired, component A must execute a local action (observed as ρ, and possible only if the severity level is less than 10), and wait for the completion of the recovery procedure of component B, which has been informed of the failure. To recover from a failure of severity l, component B must execute l repairs, observed as γ. But, at any time, component B may also fail and stop (observed as β). The initial transition $\perp$ starts the system in feeding the places 1 and 2 with black tokens (transported by the local variable m). Component A has two private states: safe, represented by place 1, and faulty, represented by place 3. Upon entering its faulty state, component A emits an alarm α. The failure of component A causes repairing actions in component B. This causality is modeled by the shared place 4. The monitoring system of component B (sensor B) only detects that component B provides an elementary action of repairing (observed as γ). The last action recovers the fail by putting the system again in state 2, shared with component A. This action is not observable.

All the observable events are also called *alarms* in the sequel, and represented by a grek letter on the figures. The fact that a transition is not observable is shown by writing ϵ instead of an alarm. It is to be noticed that the exact severity level of the fail l is not observable, and will be inferred during supervision using a kind of symbolic execution of the model.

In order to define the dynamics of such network, we consider that each place can be fed by a multiset of values (often called "colors"). These values are tested and forwarded by the transitions. As we can see, each transition associates a label $(\alpha, \beta, \gamma, \rho, \epsilon)$ and a predicate (printed near the transition in a curly brace, as a conjunction of expressions), called the *guard*. Furthermore, each incident edge is labeled by a local variable. The transition guard is composed with these local free variables. Informally, a transition is fireable if its guard is satisfiable. This means there exist some values to the variables for which the guard is true. One can thus select an instance of these values, which are unified (matched) to the variables. It is required that the values unified to the input arcs variables are present in the input places. The firing of the transition removes these values from the input places. The output places are then filled by the values unified to the output arc variables. In our example, the firing of the transition $\perp$ puts one token in places 1 and 2. The transition labeled by α becomes fireable. When it fires, it removes the tokens from 1 and 2 and puts a token in place 3 and an arbitrary integer l (provided $l \geq 0$) in place 4. The dynamics is formally defined in Section 3.

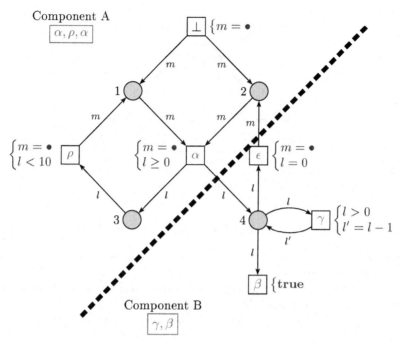

Fig. 1. A concurrent machine with two components, which may fail with an unknown severity level and can be repaired accordingly

2.2   Supervision Architecture

We consider the following setup for diagnosis, assuming that messages are not lost. Each sensor records its local alarms in sequence, while respecting causality (i.e. the observed sequence cannot contradict the causalities defined in the model). The different sensors perform independently and asynchronously, and a single supervisor collects the records from the different sensors. Thus any interleaving of the records from different sensors is possible, and causalities among alarms from different sensors are lost. This architecture is illustrated in Figure 2.

For the development of the example, we consider that the system under supervision produces the sequences $\alpha\rho\alpha$ on sensor A, and $\gamma\beta$ on sensor B.

We think such an architecture is the first important step towards a distributed supervision, in which the monitoring is itself distributed, with different supervisors cooperating asynchronously. Each supervisor is attached to a sensor (i.e. a component of the model), records its local alarms in sequence, and can exchange supervision messages with the other supervisors, asynchronously. This aspect is deferred to a subsequent paper.

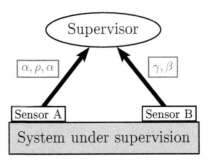

Fig. 2. The considered supervision architecture, composed of several sensors that report alarms asynchronously to a unique diagnoser

2.3 Unfoldings: An Efficient Data Structure to Represent All Runs

The construction of the runs of the high-level parameterized Petri net of Figure 1 is illustrated in Figure 3.

The algorithm is to consider all the transitions of the original Petri net, and to place them, one at a time, if they are possible. Let us start by placing the initial transition $\bot$. Once placed, a transition becomes a unique event (denoted by $\bot$, a_1, e_1 etc.) in the graph. The local variables acquire then the status of global variables and for this purpose are renamed (actually indexed by the event name). An event e, instance of a transition t, is placed only if its preset (the input places) is present in the graph and if the following enabling condition is satisfiable. The enabling condition is formed by the conjunction of the local conditions of the events located in the causal past of e (see below the definition of causality) and of its local condition. The local condition is the guard of the transition t (in which the local variables have been renamed by their global names), augmented with the constraint that the variables of the input arcs have the same values that the variables of the output arcs of the input event of the input places, in order to capture the causal relation. To keep track of this condition, we associate a new predicate with the new event. In the graph of Figure 3, the local condition of each event is printed in a curly brace. This graph is usually infinite. We have drawn only a prefix of it. In the formal description of Section 4, the local condition is the predicate $loc\_pred(e)$ and the enabling condition is the predicate $pred(e)$.

Two events linked by a path of the graph are *causally* related, since there exists a flow of values between them. Two events are *concurrent* if they are causally related and if they are not in *conflict* (i.e. cannot belong to a same run). There are two causes of conflict. The first one, called *structural conflict* is that they have been separated by a choice in the system, represented in the graph by a branching from an ancestor place of these events. The second possibility is specific to the parameterized model: two events are also in conflict (called *non-structural conflict*) if their predicates are not simultaneously satisfiable. We thus show that the symbolic unfolding is an interesting structure to represent the different runs, in which causality and concurrency are explicitly given. The different runs are superimposed in the graph and separated by the notion of conflict. In Figure 3, the event r is a cause of event a'_2; the event e_1 is concurrent with event r; event a_2 is structurally in conflict with event e'_1. A non-structural conflict is also possible between the event r and an event labeled by γ reachable after more than 10 consecutive repairs on component B (not represented in the prefix chosen in the figure).

2.4 Asynchronous Diagnosis

Figure 3 showed different runs of the system, represented in a single graph. The question now is to select the runs that are compatible with the observations. In

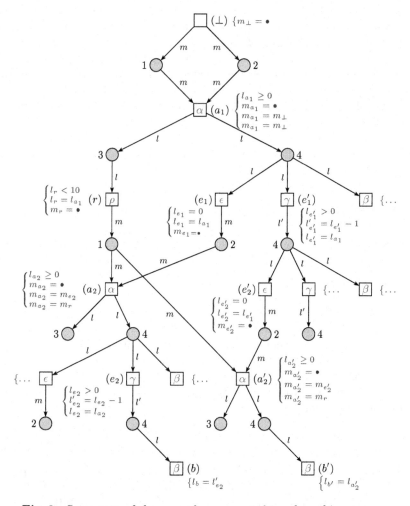

Fig. 3. Some runs of the example represented in a branching process

Figure 4, we have projected the graph of Figure 3 by considering that some events are not compatible with the actual observation. This is the case for instance for the first β transitions, which cannot be considered since γ have to be explained before and that the occurrence of β stops the production of γ in the model. The resulting graph shows two possible explanations: the first corresponds to the left part of the graph with the following partial order $\alpha.(\rho \parallel \epsilon).\alpha.\gamma.\beta$; the second is the right part of the graph: $\alpha.(\rho \parallel (\gamma.\epsilon)).\alpha.\beta$. We see that these two possible explanations share a same prefix $\alpha.\rho$ in the graph. Another interesting fact is the refinement of constraints on variables during the unfolding: for instance, at the end of the first explanation, we can infer that the severity level of the first fail α was 0, because of the conjunction of the predicates of the events a_1 and e_1.

In practice, the desired projection is obtained by synchronizing the system model with the observations. This augmented model is then unfolded. The last phase is to keep only the system part of the unfolding to present the explanations to the user. Figure 5 shows our original model, constrained with the considered observations. The sequencing of local observations are represented as the linear nets at the left and right parts of the figure. The observations constrain the execution of the original model since the treatment of the next local observation requires that a transition with the same label in the model has been fired. This is the role of places A, B, and their complements $\overline{A}$ and $\overline{B}$ in the figure.

The rest of the paper defines mathematically these different objects and operations. The final contribution is an on-the-fly algorithm, which builds the different possible explanations in the form of an unfolding, increasing step by step at each observation.

3 Mathematical Background: High-Level Petri Nets

Basic references are [2, 4, 14]. We use the standard notations, adopted from [10].

3.1 Notations

We recall the notations:

- $f : A \longmapsto B$ denotes a mapping f from A to B;
- $A \uplus B$ denotes the disjoint union of the sets A and B;
- $e[n \leftarrow n']$ is the expression e in which all the occurrences of the name n have been replaced by the expression n'.
  $e[n \leftarrow f(n)]_{n \in N}$ is the result of the parallel replacement of each name $n \in N$ by the expression $f(n)$.

A *multiset* over a set X is a mapping $\mu : X \longmapsto \mathbb{N}$. We denote $x \in \mu$ if $\mu(x) > 0$. We define the empty multiset $\emptyset$ as $\emptyset(x) \stackrel{\text{def}}{=} 0$ for all $x \in X$. We define the union of two multisets μ_1 and μ_2 over X as $(\mu_1 + \mu_2)(x) \stackrel{\text{def}}{=} \mu_1(x) + \mu_2(x)$ for all $x \in X$. For two multisets μ and μ' over X, we write $\mu \leq \mu'$ if for all $x \in X$, $\mu(x) \leq \mu'(x)$. A multiset μ is finite if $\{x \in X \mid x \in \mu\}$ is finite. In this case we can represent it with $\{\!| \ldots |\!\}$ delimiters. For example $\{\!| a, a, b |\!\}$ will denote the multiset μ defined by $\mu(a) = 2$, $\mu(b) = 1$ and $\mu(x) = 0$ for all $x \in X \setminus \{a, b\}$. For a mapping $h : X \longmapsto Y$, we denote $\{h(x) \mid x \in \mu\}$ or $h(\mu)$ the multiset μ' over Y such that for all $y \in Y$, $\mu'(y) \stackrel{\text{def}}{=} \sum_{x \in X \wedge h(x) = y} \mu(x)$.

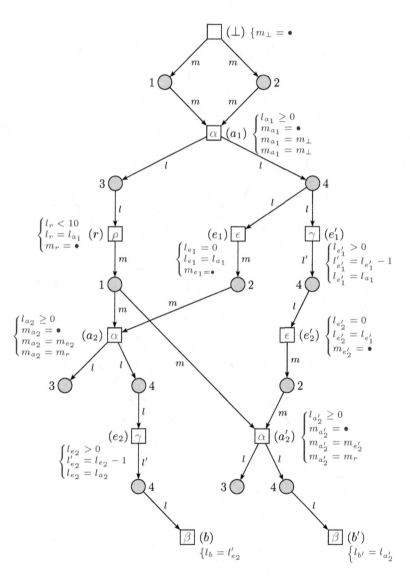

Fig. 4. The causal graph resulting of our diagnosis algorithm

3.2 High-Level Petri Nets

In this section we present the formal model we use to represent the system we work on and its behavior. The example of Figure 1 illustrates this model.

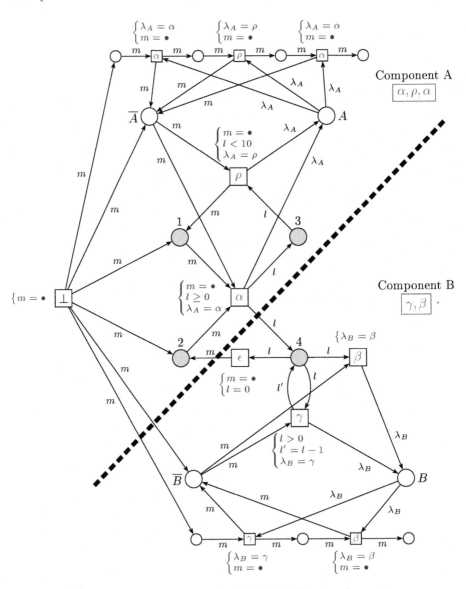

Fig. 5. The model of Figure 1, constrained by the observation

It is assumed that there exists a (finite or infinite) set *Tok* of elements (or 'colors') [1] and a set *VAR* of variable names, such that $Tok \cap VAR = \emptyset$.

A *high-level Petri net* is a quadruple $N \stackrel{\text{def}}{=} (P, T, W, \iota)$ such that:

- P and T are disjoint sets of *places* and *transitions* respectively;
- W is a multiset over $(P \times VAR \times T) \cup (T \times VAR \times P)$ of arcs;
- ι maps each $t \in T$ to a predicate $\iota(t)$ on $VAR(t)$, where $VAR(t) \stackrel{\text{def}}{=} \{v \mid (p, v, t) \in W \vee (t, v, p) \in W\}$. For every $t \in T$, $\iota(t)$ is called the *guard* of t.

For two nodes $y, y' \in P \cup T$, we denote $y \to y'$ if there exists a variable v such that $(y, v, y') \in W$. The reflexive and irreflexive transitive closures of $\to$ are denoted respectively by $\preceq$ and $\prec$. For a transition $t \in T$, let ${}^\bullet t \stackrel{\text{def}}{=} \{|(p, v) \mid (p, v, t) \in W|\}$, $t^\bullet \stackrel{\text{def}}{=} \{|(p, v) \mid (t, v, p) \in W|\}$.

In figures, places are usually represented by circles and transitions by squares. Labeled arrows between places and transitions represent the arcs. The guards of the transitions are printed in a curly brace.

A *homomorphism* from a high-level Petri net $N = (P, T, W, \iota)$ to a high-level Petri net $N' = (P', T', W', \iota')$ is a mapping $h : P \cup T \longmapsto P' \cup T'$ such that:

- $h(P) \subseteq P'$ and $h(T) \subseteq T'$;
- for all $t \in T$, $\begin{cases} {}^\bullet h(t) = \{|(h(p), v) \mid (p, v) \in {}^\bullet t|\} \\ h(t)^\bullet = \{|(h(p), v) \mid (p, v) \in t^\bullet|\} \\ \iota'(h(t)) = \iota(t) \end{cases}$

A *firing mode* of a transition t is a mapping $\sigma : VAR(t) \longmapsto Tok$ such that $\iota(t)$ evaluates to **true** under the substitution given by σ. We denote ${}^\bullet(t, \sigma) \stackrel{\text{def}}{=} \{|(p, \sigma(v)) \mid (p, v) \in {}^\bullet t|\}$ and $(t, \sigma)^\bullet \stackrel{\text{def}}{=} \{|(p, \sigma(v)) \mid (p, v) \in t^\bullet|\}$.

A *marking* of a net N is a multiset over $P \times Tok$. A transition t is *enabled* at marking M with firing mode σ if ${}^\bullet(t, \sigma) \leq M$. Such a transition can *fire*, leading to a new marking $M' \stackrel{\text{def}}{=} M - {}^\bullet(t, \sigma) + (t, \sigma)^\bullet$.

A *high-level Petri net system* is a high-level Petri net $\Upsilon \stackrel{\text{def}}{=} (P, T, W, \iota)$, which has a unique initial transition called $\bot$ such that ${}^\bullet \bot = \emptyset$. In the sequel we assume that $\iota(\bot)$ is satisfiable, i.e. $\bot$ has at least one firing mode. $\bot$ fires only once, at the empty marking, to start the system.

Remark: low-level Petri nets can be seen as particular high-level Petri nets, in which all the arcs use the same variable m, and all the guards are $(m = \bullet)$. The drawback with low-level Petri nets is the lack of manipulations of data. In practice, the data aspects have to be enumerated, and thus explode and are limited to finite domains for variables. This is why we consider the extension to the so-called high-level Petri nets.

---

[1] We do not mention any type conditions on the colors because this is not essential for our application. Adding types would only be a refinement of the firing conditions of the transitions.

4   Symbolic Unfolding

This section formally defines the structure we use to represent the different runs of a system. Figure 3 shows a symbolic branching process of the system of Figure 1. For each event e, the predicate $loc\_pred(e)$ is printed near the event.

4.1   High-Level Occurrence Nets

The net $N \stackrel{\text{def}}{=} (P, T, W, \iota)$ is called *ordinary* if for each pair y, y' of nodes of N, there exists at most one arc connecting y and y' ($\sum_{v \in VAR} W((y, v, y')) \leq 1$).

Two nodes (places or transitions), y and y', of an ordinary net $N \stackrel{\text{def}}{=} (P, T, W, \iota)$ are in *structural conflict*, denoted by $y \# y'$, if there exist distinct transitions $t, t' \in T$ and a place $p \in P$ such that $p \to t$, $p \to t'$, $t \preceq y$ and $t' \preceq y'$. A node y is in *structural self-conflict* if $y \# y$.

A *high-level occurrence net* is an ordinary net system $ON \stackrel{\text{def}}{=} (B, E, G, \iota)$, where B is a set of *conditions* (places), E is a set of *events* (transitions) and G is a flow relation, satisfying the following conditions:

- for every $b \in B$, there exists a unique pair (e, v) called $^\bullet b$ such that $(e, v, b) \in G$;

- for every $y \in B \cup E$, $\begin{cases} \neg(y \# y) \\ \neg(y \prec y) \\ \bot \preceq y \\ \text{there are finitely many } y' \text{ such that } y' \prec y. \end{cases}$

$\prec$ is called the *causality relation*. We say that node y is *causally related* to node y' if $y \prec y'$.

For all $e \in E$ we denote $\lceil e \rceil \stackrel{\text{def}}{=} \{f \in E \mid f \preceq e\}$. For all $F \subseteq E$ we denote $\lceil F \rceil \stackrel{\text{def}}{=} \bigcup_{f \in F} \lceil f \rceil$.

For a high-level occurrence net $ON \stackrel{\text{def}}{=} (B, E, G, \iota)$ we define the mappings loc_pred and $pred$ which map each $e \in E$ to the predicates

$$loc\_pred(e) \stackrel{\text{def}}{=} \iota(e)[v \leftarrow v_e]_{v \in VAR(e)}$$
$$\wedge \bigwedge_{(b,v) \in {}^\bullet e} (v_e = v'_{e'}) \quad \text{with } {}^\bullet b = (e', v')$$

$$pred(e) \stackrel{\text{def}}{=} \bigwedge_{f \preceq e} loc\_pred(f)$$

4.2   Symbolic Branching Processes

A *symbolic branching process* of Υ is a pair $\pi \stackrel{\text{def}}{=} (ON, h)$ such that:

- ON is a high-level occurrence net such that for all $e \in E$, $pred(e)$ is satisfiable;
- h is a homomorphism from ON to Υ;
- $h(\bot) = \bot$;
- for all $e, f \in E$, if $h(e) = h(f)$ and $^\bullet e = {}^\bullet f$, then $e = f$.

4.3 Non Structural Conflict, Concurrency

In branching processes of high-level Petri nets, the causality relation is the same as in branching processes of low-level Petri nets. But there are two different causes of conflict. The *structural conflict* is the equivalent of the conflict relation in branching processes of low-level Petri nets; and we define a *non structural conflict*, that restricts the concurrency relation. This notion of non structural conflict is due to the existence of symbolic parameters.

The events of the set $F \subseteq E$ are in *non structural conflict* if $\bigwedge_{f \in F} pred(f)$ is not satisfiable. We note that for all F in non structural conflict and $F' \subseteq E$, if $\lceil F \rceil \subsetneqq \lceil F' \rceil$ then F' is also in non structural conflict.

The events of F are in *minimal non structural conflict* if there does not exist any $F' \subseteq E$ such that $\lceil F' \rceil \subsetneqq \lceil F \rceil$ and the events of F' are in non structural conflict.

The events of the set $F \subseteq E$ are *concurrent* if they are not in non structural conflict, and for each $e, e' \in F$, neither $e \prec e'$, nor $e' \prec e$, nor $e \# e'$ holds. We extend the notion of concurrency to conditions: a set C of conditions are concurrent if the events of the set $\{e \in E \mid \exists b \in C \quad e \to b\}$ are concurrent.

A *co-set* is a set of concurrent conditions. A *configuration* is a set of events $F \subseteq E$ whose elements are not in non structural conflict, and which is conflict-free (for all $e, f \in F$, $\neg(e \# f)$) and causally closed (for all $f \in F$ and $e \in E$, $e \prec f$ implies $e \in F$).

4.4 Symbolic Unfolding

The set of all symbolic branching processes of a high-level Petri net system is uniquely defined, up to an isomorphism (i.e. a renaming of the conditions and events), and we shall not distinguish isomorphic branching processes. For π, π' two symbolic branching processes, π' is a prefix of π, written $\pi' \sqsubseteq \pi$, if there exists an injective homomorphism ϕ from π' into π, such that $\phi(\bot) = \bot$, and the composition $h \circ \phi$ coincides with h', where $\circ$ denotes the composition of maps.

Thus, the notion of unfolding of a Petri net as the unique maximum branching process up to isomorphism, proved in theorem 23 of [3], can be adapted to symbolic branching processes of high-level Petri nets to define the *symbolic unfolding* $\mathcal{U}_\Upsilon$ of a high-level Petri net system Υ.

Branching processes of a (high-level) Petri net represent the different runs. The interest is that the causalities and the concurrency between the transitions figuring in the run are explicitly represented in a graph. This is why, this kind of behavioral semantics for Petri nets is called "true concurrency semantics", and fits particularly well with the kind of trajectories we want to produce as the monitoring activity.

Some applications use the notion of finite complete prefix defined on low-level Petri nets. We do not need this notion in the area of diagnosis because the unfoldings we generate are finite, as the model is constrained by the observation. Furthermore we think that it would not be obvious to define a notion of finite complete prefix for symbolic unfoldings of high-level Petri nets, because of the theoretical power of the model.

4.5   Algorithm

We propose an algorithm to compute the symbolic unfolding of a high-level Petri net. This algorithm needs to decide if the predicates $pred(e)$ are satisfiable. This is possible if the guards of the transitions are expressed in some weak enough language. One possible framework is the use of Presburger arithmetics [12] (arithmetics without multiplication).

The algorithm consists in a non deterministic iteration, after the placement of the initial event $\perp$. In each iteration we choose a transition t and a co-set C to create a new event e. The predicate $pred(e)$ is memorized for each event. The minimal non structural conflicts are memorized in the variable *conflict*, which is used to find the co-sets.

Initialization

1. initialize the sets B, E, G to $\emptyset$, h and $pred$ to the empty mapping and *conflict* to $\emptyset$;
2. add the event $\perp$ to E, and update h with $h(\perp) = \perp$;
3. for each $(p, v) \in \perp^{\bullet}$, add a new condition b to B, add $(\perp, v, b)$ to G and update h with $h(b) = p$;
4. extend $pred$ with $pred(\perp) = \iota(\perp)[v \leftarrow v_{\perp}]_{v \in VAR(\perp)}$;

Non deterministic iteration

Repeat until no transition can be chosen:

1. choose nondeterministically a transition $t \in T \setminus \{\perp\}$ such that there exist a co-set C and a bijection pin from ${}^{\bullet}t$ to C, satisfying:
   - for all $(p, v) \in {}^{\bullet}t$, $h(pin((p, v))) = p$;
   - the predicate $pred\_e \overset{\text{def}}{=} loc\_pred \wedge \bigwedge_{b \in C} pred(b)$ is satisfiable, where:
     - $pred(b) \overset{\text{def}}{=} pred(e')$ with ${}^{\bullet}b = (e', v')$
     - $loc\_pred \overset{\text{def}}{=} \iota(t)[v \leftarrow v_e]_{v \in VAR(t)}$
       $$\wedge \bigwedge_{(p,v) \in {}^{\bullet}t} (v_e = v'_{e'}) \quad \text{with } {}^{\bullet}pin((p, v)) = (e', v')$$
     - e is a new event.
2. add the event e to E, and update h with $h(e) = t$;
3. for each $(p, v) \in {}^{\bullet}t$, add $(pin((p, v)), v, e)$ to G;
4. for each $(p, v) \in t^{\bullet}$, add a new condition b to B, add (e, v, b) to G and update h with $h(b) = p$;
5. extend $pred$ with $pred(e) = pred\_e$;
6. extend *conflict* with the newly created minimal non structural conflicts, if any.

In the area of diagnosis, the net is constrained by the observation as we will see in Section 5. Thus its unfolding is finite and the algorithm terminates, if we except models that contain loops of non observable transitions. But in the general case the unfolding may be infinite, and precautions have to be taken to ensure that all the events of the unfolding are computed. One method is to use the *causal depth* of the events defined as follows: the *causal depth* of an event $e \in E$ is the number of events on the longest path from $\bot$ to e. For all integer n, the number of events at depth n is finite. If the algorithm is forced to compute all the events at depth n before those at depth $n+1$, then all the events will be computed.

5   Symbolic Diagnosis: Formal Problem Setting

5.1   Observations

Observations and their impact on the original system model are represented by adding new places and transitions in the high-level Petri net.

A *sensor* is a place s of a high-level Petri net that has no output arc and at most one input arc from each transition $t \in T$. To simplify the notations, we assume that the variable associated with this arc is always λ_s. When a transition $t \in T$ fires, the value taken by λ_s is called the alarm.

A *local observation sequence* from the sensor s is a finite sequence of alarms $(\lambda_{s,1}, \ldots, \lambda_{s,n_s})$. A *global observation* from a set S of sensors is a mapping A from sensors $s \in S$ to observation sequences $(\lambda_{s,1}, \ldots, \lambda_{s,n_s})$. Consider two observations A and A', which associate with each sensor $s \in S$, the observation sequences $(\lambda_{s,1}, \ldots, \lambda_{s,n_s})$ and $(\lambda'_{s,1}, \ldots, \lambda'_{s,n'_s})$ respectively. We say that A is a *prefix* of A', written $A \leq A'$, if for all $s \in S$, $n_s \leq n'_s$ and $(\lambda_{s,1}, \ldots, \lambda_{s,n_s}) = (\lambda'_{s,1}, \ldots, \lambda'_{s,n_s})$.

5.2   Diagnosis Net $\mathcal{D}(N, A)$

In this section we show how to build a net $\mathcal{D}(N, A)$ from a net N modeling a system and an observation A of this system. The idea is to constrain the model so that each transition of the model that sends an alarm to a sensor s is not allowed to fire until all the previous alarms sent to s have been treated. To achieve this we create a new place $\bar{s}$, add an arc from $\bar{s}$ to each transition that sends an alarm to s, and ensure that s contains a token if and only if all the alarms sent to s have been treated. The treatment of the alarms received by sensor s is modeled by a set of new transitions $t_{s,i}$, $i = 1, \ldots, n_s$ (one for each observation). Transition $t_{s,i}$ guarantees that the ith alarm received by s matches the observation $\lambda_{s,i}$. Once the alarm is treated, $t_{s,i}$ puts a token in the place $\bar{s}$, which allows the transitions of the model to emit new alarms. The formal definition of $\mathcal{D}(N, A)$ follows.

For a net $N \stackrel{\text{def}}{=} (P_N, T_N, W_N, \iota_N)$ and an observation A from a set S of sensors of N, we define the net $\mathcal{D}(N, A) \stackrel{\text{def}}{=} (P, T, W, \iota)$, called *net N observed as A*, as follows (we assume that m is a fresh variable name):

- $P \stackrel{\text{def}}{=} P_N \uplus \{\bar{s} \mid s \in S\} \uplus \{p_{s,i} \mid s \in S, \ i = 0, \ldots, n_s\}$
- $T \stackrel{\text{def}}{=} T_N \uplus \{t_{s,i} \mid s \in S, \ i = 1, \ldots, n_s\}$

$$- W \stackrel{\text{def}}{=} W_N + \{\!\!|(\bot, m, \bar{s}), (\bot, m, p_{s,0}) \mid s \in S|\!\!\}$$
$$+ \{\!\!|(\bar{s}, m, t) \mid s \in S \wedge (t, \lambda_s, s) \in W_N|\!\!\}$$
$$+ \{\!\!|(s, \lambda_s, t_{s,i}), (t_{s,i}, m, \bar{s}) \mid s \in S, \ i = 1, \ldots, n_s|\!\!\}$$
$$+ \{\!\!|(p_{s,i-1}, m, t_{s,i}), (t_{s,i}, m, p_{s,i}) \mid s \in S, \ i = 1, \ldots, n_s|\!\!\}$$

$$- \iota(t) \quad \stackrel{\text{def}}{=} \iota_N(t) \wedge (m = \bullet) \qquad \text{if } t \in T_N$$
$$\iota(t_{s,i}) \stackrel{\text{def}}{=} (\lambda_s = \lambda_{s,i}) \wedge (m = \bullet) \text{ for all } s \in S, \ i = 1, \ldots, n_s$$

Figure 5 shows the net of Figure 3 observed as α, ρ, α from sensor A and γ, β from sensor B.

Remark. For two observations A and A' such that $A \leq A'$, $\mathcal{D}(N, A)$ is a subnet of $\mathcal{D}(N, A')$. Indeed $\mathcal{D}(N, A')$ can be built from $\mathcal{D}(N, A)$ by adding the places and transitions required by the new alarms, and arcs connecting the new transitions. No new arc is added to the old transitions. That is why every execution of the net $\mathcal{D}(N, A)$ is also a valid execution of $\mathcal{D}(N, A')$.

5.3   Global Diagnosis

We call *diagnosis of observation A on net N* the symbolic unfolding $\mathcal{U}_{\mathcal{D}(N,A)}$ of the net N observed as A. For each set $F \subseteq E$ of concurrent events such that the restriction of h to F is a bijection from F to $\{t_{s,n_s} \mid s \in S\}$, the configuration $\lceil F \rceil$ explains the observation A.

We may want to get rid of the causalities due to the observation. For this purpose, we remove all the events and conditions corresponding to the sensors or to the observation. This operation, called projection on N removes the causalities due to the observation. But we must keep the information of the (structural and non structural) conflicts due to the observation, that do not appear any more in the projected net.

Figure 4 shows all the possible explanations of the example of Figure 3.

On-the-Fly Computation. The unfolding of $\mathcal{D}(N, A)$ can be computed by the algorithm of Section 4.5. Moreover, we can adapt this algorithm in order to compute on-the-fly the partial order histories that explain the observed alarms. Indeed, if A and A' are two observations such that A is a prefix of A', then, consecutively to the final remark of Section 5.2, each branching process of $\mathcal{D}(N, A)$ is also a branching process of $\mathcal{D}(N, A')$. Then we can compute on-the-fly the explanations by updating $\mathcal{D}(N, A)$ each time a new alarm is observed. After this modification is done, the algorithm will continue and compute the explanations of the new observation.

6   Conclusion

We have presented a possible approach to the supervision/diagnosis of distributed systems, in which the explanations are given by a family of partial orders on the observable events, represented by an unfolding graph. The main contribution of the paper is to consider parameters in the model. These parameters are used to model incomplete information on the system under supervision (i.e. partially observed). We think it is an important aspect to deal with real contexts. We have different perspectives. From the practical point of view, we are starting the implementation of the algorithm. The main extension we plan is to deal with a distributed supervision architecture; that is extend the approach presented in [7] to the symbolic framework we consider. An other work in progress is to study time Petri nets as a particular case of our parameterized model. The variables of the model are used to model the different instant of transition firings. This will define a new notion of unfolding for time Petri nets, which keeps concurrency. More generally, because of the "local" property of the unfolding algorithm, we think our approach could be extended to deal with dynamic systems, in which the model can evolve during observation.

References

[1] Benveniste, A., Fabre, E., Jard, C., Haar, S.: Diagnosis of asynchronous discrete event systems, a net unfolding approach. IEEE Trans. on Automatic Control **48(5)** (2003) 714-727   327

[2] Cassandras, C., Lafortune, S.: Introduction to discrete event systems. Kluwer Academic Publishers (1999)   327, 332

[3] Engelfriet, J.: Branching processes of Petri nets. Acta Informatica **28** (1991) 575–591   337

[4] Desel, J., and Esparza, J.: Free choice Petri nets. Cambridge University Press (1995)   332

[5] Esparza, J., Römer, S., Vogler, W.: An improvement of McMillan's unfolding algorithm. In: Proc. of International Conference on Tools and Algorithms for the Construction and Analysis of Systems (TACAS'1996) T. Margaria and B. Steffen (Eds.), Springer-Verlag, Lecture Notes in Computer Science **1664** (1999) 2–20

[6] Esparza, J., Römer, S.: An unfolding algorithm for synchronous products of transition systems. In: Proc. of CONCUR'99, Springer-Verlag, Lecture Notes in Computer Science **1664** (1999)

[7] Fabre, E.: Monitoring distributed systems with distributed algorithms. In: Proc. of the 2002 IEEE Conf. on Decision and Control (2002) 411–416   341

[8] Goodwin, G. C., Sin, K. S.: Adaptive filtering, prediction, and control. Prentice-Hall, Upper Sadle River, N. J. (1984)   327

[9] Jensen, K.: Coloured Petri nets. Basic concepts, analysis methods and practical use. EATCS Monographs on Theoretical Computer Science, Springer-Verlag (1992)   328

[10] Khomenko, V., Koutny, M.: Branching processes of high-level Petri nets. In: Proc. of International Conference on Tools and Algorithms for the Construction and Analysis of Systems (TACAS'2003), H. Garavel and J. Hatcliff (Eds.), Springer-Verlag, Lecture Notes in Computer Science (2003)   327, 332

[11] Kozura, V. E.: Unfolding of coloured Petri nets. Technical Report 80, A. P. Ershov Institute of Informatics Systems (2000)   327

[12] Presburger, M.: Über die Vollständigkeit eines gewissen Systems der Arithmetik ganzer Zahlen, in welchem die Addition als einzige Operation hervortritt. Comptes

Rendus du Premier Congrès des Mathématiciens des Pays Slaves **395** (1927) 92–101 338

[13] Rabiner, L. R., Juang, B. H.: An introduction to hidden Markov models. IEEE ASSP magazine **3** (1986) 4–16 327

[14] Reisig, W.: Petri Net: an introduction. ETACS Monographs on Theoretical Computer Science, Springer-Verlag **4** (1985) 332

[15] Sampath, M., Sengupta, R., Sinnamohideen, K., Lafortune, S., Teneketzis, D.: Failure diagnosis using discrete event models. IEEE Trans. on Systems Technology **4(2)** (1996) 105–124 327

[16] Vernier, I. Symbolic executions of symmetrical parallel programs. In: Proc. of 4th Euromicro Workshop on Parallel and Distributed Processing, Braga, Portugal (1996) 327–334 327

Automatized Verification
of Ad Hoc Routing Protocols

Oskar Wibling, Joachim Parrow, and Arnold Pears

Department of Information Technology, Uppsala University
Box 337, SE-751 05 Uppsala, Sweden
{oskarw,joachim,arnoldp}@it.uu.se

Abstract. Numerous specialized ad hoc routing protocols are currently proposed for use, or being implemented. Few of them have been subjected to formal verification. This paper evaluates two model checking tools, SPIN and UPPAAL, using the verification of the Lightweight Underlay Network Ad hoc Routing protocol (LUNAR) as a case study. Insights are reported in terms of identifying important modeling considerations and the types of ad hoc protocol properties that can realistically be verified.

Keywords: Mobile ad hoc networks, routing protocols, formal verification, model checking, SPIN, UPPAAL, LUNAR

1 Introduction

Mobile ad hoc networks (MANETS) require efficient and correct routing protocols. So far they have mainly been evaluated by simulation and live testing, and most of the formal verifications have involved a significant amount of user intervention. We here consider a completely automatic verification strategy where the user specifies the protocol in a high level formalism and provides some general properties. These are given to a tool which will output a pass or fail answer to questions regarding key protocol properties, without involving the user in additional interaction. Compared to interactive methods much is gained in ease of use for non experts. With this intent we evaluate two model checking tools, SPIN and UPPAAL. This enables us to analyze the modeling constraints that have to be imposed, and also to provide a comparison of the tools and their suitability for the verification of ad hoc routing protocols. The evaluation additionally provides a good starting point for further work on infinite-state verification.

A MANET (Figure 1), is a spontaneous network of computers which communicate over a wireless medium. Nodes can join or leave at any time and are free to move around as they desire. There is no centralized infrastructure and so all participating nodes need to function both as end nodes and routers. Because the radio transmission range is limited, packets to distant recipients have to be routed over some intermediate node(s) in order to reach nodes outside direct transmission range. If one node has a path to another node, packets are expected to be routed there correctly.

D. de Frutos-Escrig and M. Núñez (Eds.): FORTE 2004, LNCS 3235, pp. 343–358, 2004.
© IFIP International Federation for Information Processing 2004

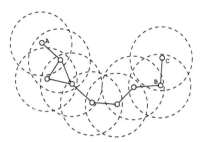

Fig. 1. A mobile ad hoc network

The situations in which ad hoc networks can or will be applied are still a topic of discussion, but scenarios such as search-and-rescue operations and sensor networks have been suggested [11, 16]. An ad hoc network needs a specifically designed routing protocol. There is ideally no pre-configuration in such a network and the network structure is expected to change constantly over time. Therefore, the nodes do not know beforehand or even during a session exactly which nodes are currently their direct neighbors. Consequently, most ad hoc routing protocols are based on broadcasting as a way to detect and map the current surroundings. There have been numerous ad hoc routing protocol proposals [28]. Currently, four of these are being considered for standardization by the Internet Engineering Task Force (IETF) MANET group [9]. They are AODV [20], DSR [12], OLSR [4] and TBRPF [19]. Very few attempts have so far been made to formally verify their operation.

As in most other computer networking areas, simulations and live testing [16] are most often employed to verify new protocols. The "Network Simulator - ns2" [10] is commonly used for simulation studies, and for real-world comparisons an assisting tool such as the "Ad hoc Protocol Evaluation (APE) testbed" [17] can be utilized. Testing and simulation are not sufficient to verify that there are no subtle errors or design flaws left in a protocol. If this goal is to be achieved approaches based on formal methods will be needed. Our emphasis is deliberately on automatic tools, since they are easier to use for non experts.

As a case study, the Lightweight Underlay Network Ad hoc Routing protocol (LUNAR) [23] has been used. LUNAR has relatively low complexity compared to many other ad hoc routing protocols and is intended as a platform to explore novel ad hoc routing strategies. Even so, it has been shown to compete well with more complex protocols such as OLSR and AODV [23]. The simplicity of the core functionality in LUNAR enables us to more clearly study the modeling of properties which are not tied to the protocol itself, such as connectivity, dynamics and broadcasting. This way we can identify key considerations that apply to the modeling of any ad hoc routing protocol.

The remainder of the paper is organized as follows. Section 2 describes ad hoc routing protocols, problems that can occur in their operation, as well as a definition of what we mean by correct operation. This section also introduces the LUNAR protocol. Section 3 describes the verification that has been performed.

Pros and cons of the different tools are discussed and lessons learned from applying them to LUNAR are presented. Section 4 covers relevant related work and finally Section 5 provides conclusions and directions for future research.

2   Ad Hoc Routing Protocols

2.1   Correct Operation

The most fundamental error in routing protocol operation (ad hoc or otherwise) is failure to route correctly. In addition to this, there are timing considerations to be taken into account, since a protocol of this kind needs to be able to react swiftly to topology changes.

In the following, when we say that a path exists between two nodes, we mean that the path is valid for some time longer than what is required to complete the route formation process. A route formation process is the process at the end of which a particular routing protocol has managed to set up a route from a source node to a destination node, possibly traversing one or more intermediate nodes. The route can thereafter be used to send packets from source to destination until the path becomes invalid as the result of a link breakage. This can occur because a node moves out of range or because the protocol itself proactively dismantles routes after a given time interval. For simplicity intermittent transmission errors at the link/physical layer are treated as link breakages in our model.

A *routing loop* in a protocol is a situation in which, somewhere along the path from the source to its destination a packet can enter a forwarding circle. This is very undesirable since there appears to be a valid path, but in reality it cannot be used to forward packets to the intended destination. As a practical example consider the description of routing loop formation in the original formulation of AODV [21] as described by Obradovic [18] (see Example 1).

Example 1. Looping behavior in AODV. The situation is depicted in Figure 2 and a brief explanation of the scenario is the following:

1. Node A initially has a route to node C through node B. The link between B and C then suddenly goes down.

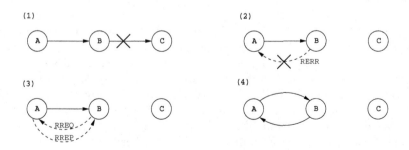

Fig. 2. Example AODV looping scenario

2. The RERR message (an inherent part of the AODV protocol) from node B to node A is lost and hence node A is not notified that the route to C has become invalid.
3. Node B then sends out a route request for node C. Node A, still thinking that it has a valid route responds that packets for C can therefore be sent to it.
4. The result is a routing loop in which A will send packets for C to node B. B on the other hand will send packets for C to node A.

These types of errors can be very subtle, and even expert designers may not be capable of detecting flaws in new protocol specifications.

To assist us in determining the correctness of a particular protocol we provide the following definition.

Definition 1. Correct operation of an ad hoc routing protocol
If there at one point in time exists a path between two nodes, then the protocol must be able to find some path between the nodes. When a path has been found, and for the time it stays valid, it shall be possible to send packets along the path from the source node to the destination node.

The definition says nothing about the behavior of the protocol when there are no paths between the nodes, but note that it excludes the possibility of loops when valid paths are available. Consider the scenario above in situation 4. If the link between nodes B and C goes up again then there is a valid path between A and C, but the protocol will keep using the loop between A and B, thus breaking the definition of correctness.

2.2   LUNAR – A Protocol Overview

Lightweight Underlay Network Ad hoc Routing (LUNAR) [23] is a reactive ad hoc routing protocol. The term "reactive" is used to denote that the protocol discovers paths only when required. However, route maintenance is proactive meaning that LUNAR rebuilds active paths from scratch every three seconds.

LUNAR creates an Internet Protocol (IP) subnet illusion by placing itself below the IP layer and above the link layer, i.e. at "layer 2.5". The IP layer of the platform on which LUNAR is running is not aware of the presence of LUNAR. Outgoing Address Resolution Protocol (ARP) solicit requests are trapped by LUNAR at which point its own multi-hop route request procedure is initiated. When a route reply has been received, the ARP table of the host is manipulated to contain an IP→selector mapping instead of an IP→Medium Access Control (MAC) address mapping. Selectors are addressing units analogous to the notion of a port and are used by LUNAR to determine the correct operation to perform on a given packet. Hence, when an outgoing IP packet is trapped, LUNAR uses the selector to determine the path for the packet. The packet is thereafter wrapped in a so called SAPF (Simple Active Packet Format) packet and delivered to its destination. When a SAPF packet is received by a node, the selector value which it contains is used to determine if it has reached its final destination, in

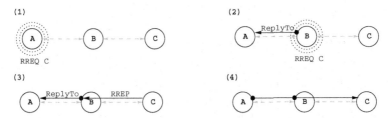

Fig. 3. LUNAR route formation overview

which case it is delivered up the IP stack. If this is not its final destination, it is forwarded along the next hop.

Broadcast dampening is an important part of the protocol and makes sure that packets are not rebroadcast more than once, thus avoiding broadcast storms. Typical usage areas for LUNAR are spontaneous ad hoc networks and wireless ad hoc Internet access links. Example 2 gives a short informal explanation of the route formation process in order to facilitate the understanding of the algorithm. Note that the simultaneous back path creation has here been omitted as a modeling simplification.

Example 2. LUNAR route formation. The situation is depicted in Figure 3. In the figure grey, dashed, bidirectional arrows indicate connectivity. The black, solid, unidirectional arrows indicate paths that have been set up in the network. An overview of the route formation process is as follows.

1. Node A wants to set up a route to node C and therefore broadcasts a LUNAR route request (RREQ).
2. The RREQ is only received by node B who concludes that it is not the node sought and therefore rebroadcasts the request. Before doing so, however, it connects the new request to a back path back to the originally requesting node (which is A).
3. The RREQ is now received by both A and C. A, through the use of the dampening mechanism concludes that the request originates from itself and drops it. C on the other hand, receives and handles the request. Since it is itself the requested node it sets up a "port" for later reception of IP packets, after which it generates a route reply (RREP) destined for B. When B receives this RREP it notes that it is a response to an original request from A, therefore it forwards the response to A. Before doing so, however, it sets up a relay so that packages received for C are forwarded to the port set up there.
4. When A receives the RREP it constructs an outgoing port to which IP packets destined for C are to be sent. This port is connected to the relay at B which is in turn connected to the port at C.

3 Case Study: Verification of LUNAR

3.1 The Model and Its Limitations

We have used a somewhat simplified version of LUNAR for our verification [27].
Apart from the simultaneous back path creation, features [23] such as automatic
address configuration and forced route rediscovery, etc. are missing in our description. The same goes for the RREQ Time To Live (TTL) field since the
diameters of the networks studied are small enough that we do not need to limit
them explicitly.

3.2 Central Modeling Issues

When modeling an ad hoc network protocol, apart from the usual considerations
regarding limiting the resulting state space, the following questions are central:

- How do we model broadcast?
- How do we model connectivity? This influences the handling of broadcast.
- How do we model topology changes (dynamics)? This directly influences the
  connectivity graph.

In the two sections that follow, besides giving our model checking results, we
describe our solutions to each of the above issues.

3.3 Verification Using SPIN

SPIN [7] is a model checking tool that can be used for formal verification of
distributed software systems. System descriptions are given in the high level
language PROMELA (PROcess MEta LAnguage) and requirements to be verified can either be given as assertions directly in the code and/or by specifying
correctness properties as Linear Temporal Logic (LTL) formulae. SPIN works
on-the-fly, i.e. does not need to construct the complete state space prior to verification, instead this is done dynamically during processing. Furthermore, as
a measure to cope with the state space explosion problem, SPIN includes a partial order reduction algorithm [8]. The state space explosion problem refers to
the situation in which the state space generated by the model because of paral-
lelism becomes so large that all the visited states cannot be stored. In the worst
case the state space grows exponentially with the length of the program.

We use SPIN because of its relatively low learning threshold and powerful
model checking capabilities. A PROMELA model of LUNAR has thus been constructed. The model consists of about 250 lines of code excluding comments. Our
initial approach, and the one described in this work, has been to naively model
the complete system and model check it as a whole. We feel that demonstrating
that this is possible will lower the resistance to using these tools and increase
the chances of more people verifying their protocols.

Connectivity and Dynamics. The communication "ports" where each node can be reached are modeled using PROMELA channels stored in an array indexed by node id. Node id and MAC address are used interchangeably in our model, which provides a straightforward addressing of nodes. To model connectivity a symmetric, two dimensional, array of boolean values is used. The matrix is symmetric since we assume nodes to be connected bidirectionally.

Node dynamics are modeled by modifying the connectivity matrix. In order to reduce complexity, nodes either have or do not have connectivity. No intermediate state is possible as it would be in a more realistic link/physical layer model. It would be straightforward to model lower layers in a more detailed way, but this again increases complexity and reduces the chances of successful model checking because of the state space explosion problem.

Broadcasting. Due to the transient nature of radio communication, broadcast is heavily used in most ad hoc networking protocols and LUNAR is no exception. In our model, broadcast is modeled by unicasting to all nodes with whom the sending node presently has connectivity. A PROMELA macro has been constructed for this operation. This macro consults the corresponding row in the connectivity array for the sending node and sends to all connected nodes using the channel array. The unicast operations that represent a broadcast are implemented atomically to ensure that no connectivity interruptions occur part way through the process.

Limitations Imposed. In LUNAR, both remote and local selectors are randomly selected from different ranges. Since they are specified to be 64 bits long [23], the space of possible values is huge. In our PROMELA model we are therefore forced to pick the selectors from a few limited values.

The local selectors, as their name implies, do not have to be globally unique and are therefore selected from the same range for all nodes. However, the remote selectors are meant to be globally unique and are chosen from different ranges. When a new selector is needed, the selector port value is just monotonically increased and assertions are used to make sure that the bounds are not violated. The correct bounds to use are selected by experimentation. The abstraction of selector values to a fairly limited range thus has no impact on the verification since this range is set to accommodate the needed amount of values.

The abstraction of remote selector values could have had an influence on the verification result if there was a possibility that the random selector values in an implementation of the protocol were likely to coincide. However, because of the large value space, this possibility is so minor that we consider it to be insignificant.

Channel sizes, i.e. the number of outstanding messages in a channel at one time, are in general kept as small as possible. These are selected by experimentation to hold the required number of outstanding messages and do therefore not have any impact on the verification results.

Verification. The verification of the protocol is performed by setting up the model so that one node tries to send an IP packet to another node in the network. The topology and node transitions are selected so that the two nodes are always connected, possibly by traversing one or several other nodes. Initially, no routes are set up in the network. The sending node therefore needs to initiate a route discovery process and does so by sending out a LUNAR RREQ broadcast. If and when it receives a reply it thereafter tries to send the IP packet along the route that was set up. New RREQ:s are forced after topology changes and on timeouts.

A global boolean `message_delivered` is set to `true` when the correct receiving node has received the correct IP packet from the sending node (tagged accordingly). A hop counter keeps track of the nodes traversed by the packet before it reaches its destination and an assertion is used to verify that it does not traverse more nodes than theoretically possible in the absence of loops. This assertion is checked at the receiving node prior to setting `message_delivered`.

Finally, another assertion is used in a `timeout` statement in order to check that when one node times out because of inactivity, then `message_delivered` is `true` and the message has indeed been delivered. Using SPIN we also check for the absence of deadlocks and conformance to the LTL formula `<>message_delivered` which verifies that a message will eventually be delivered.

In total, this is sufficient to show that the protocol functions correctly in each situation studied according to the statement in Definition 1. In all our scenarios we have explicitly made certain that there is a possible path between the two communicating end nodes and that each transition maintains this property. If LUNAR had any looping behavior detectable in these situations, the LTL formula above would not be fulfilled.

In our initial approach, the number of nodes is specified and then a topology is generated nondeterministically. A recursive graph traversal is then performed to see if there is a communication path possible between nodes 0 and 1. If there is not, the program ends. If there is a possible path, then the node processes are initiated and the route discovery is started, etc. In this manner, all possible topologies are considered.

However, using this approach, the state space is already large without any node connectivity transitions. When node mobility is also added, it is no longer feasible to perform an exhaustive search even for a small number of nodes. Therefore, we choose to focus on a few especially interesting scenarios which are depicted in Figure 4. These scenarios have been selected in an attempt to capture situations that could cause problems for the protocol. In scenarios (a), (c), (d), (e), (g) and (h) a situation can occur in which a route has been set up, but is then broken before the packet could be delivered. In this case, a new route should successfully be set up and the packet delivered along that one instead. In (b), (d) and (f) an extra node suddenly appears, which could potentially cause confusion for a routing protocol.

For scenarios (a), (b), (c), and (e) we are able to verify correct operation. This effectively shows that LUNAR is loop free for these topologies (and node

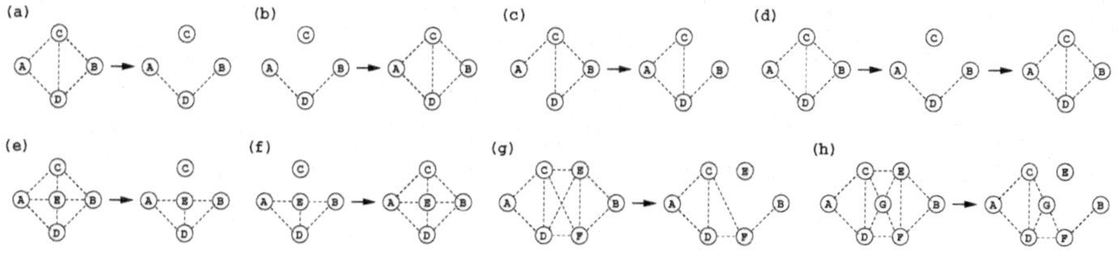

Fig. 4. Example classes of topology changes

transitions). For scenarios (d) and (f) we are not able to perform an exhaustive search because of the state space explosion (see further below). Scenarios (g) and (h) are not checked using SPIN.

Since we are doing brute force model checking it becomes important to utilize the most powerful hardware available. For this reason, we have used a Sun Fire 15k server with 36 UltraSPARC III+ CPUs at 900 MHz and 36 Gb of primary RAM to model check our scenarios. Unfortunately, SPIN models cannot currently be compiled to take full advantage of a multi-threaded architecture. There has been work on distributed LTL model checking algorithms for SPIN by Brim et al [1] and they have also implemented an experimental version. The performance increase is reported as promising. However, at this time there is no SPIN implementation with this feature publicly available.

Table 1 shows our results for scenarios (a)-(f). SPIN is here used in exhaustive search mode as opposed to the approximating bitstate hashing and hash-compact modes since we are interested in verifying correctness. Further note that both partial order reduction and COLLAPSE compression [7] are used everywhere. As a reference, the values with only partial order reduction are given within parentheses (where they differ). As can be seen, the state space rapidly grows with the number of nodes. Even using four nodes, when topology changes become just a bit more complex, the model checking fails because of memory restrictions (32 bit application). Interesting to note is that for both four and five nodes, the state space becomes much larger for the situation where one intermediate node comes up after a while, than when it goes down.

3.4   Using UPPAAL to Prove Timing Requirements

UPPAAL [15] is a tool that can be used to verify real time aspects of computer systems. The UPPAAL home page [25] provides the following definition: *"UP-PAAL is an integrated tool environment for modeling, validation and verification of real-time systems modeled as networks of timed automata, extended with data types (bounded integers, arrays, etc.)"*. The environment has a graphical user interface in which the automata are constructed by drawing them in a window on the screen. The tool contains a simulator and a verifier in which requirements are given as LTL formulae.

An UPPAAL model has been constructed in order to check timing requirements of LUNAR. The timing aspects that we focus on are to determine theoretical lower and upper bounds on the route formation and message delivery processes. We also check that the LUNAR model is deadlock free. In our UP-PAAL model we introduce more abstraction than in the SPIN model. The main reason for this is the unavailability of more complex data structures than arrays which becomes relevant in the handling of LUNAR callbacks and redirections.

Timing Constraints. As mentioned before, the setting up of routes in an ad hoc network is usually slower than in a conventional more static network. This is because the topology needs to be rediscovered (usually by broadcasting) at regular intervals. There is a tradeoff between the exchange of control packets (used for topology analysis) and the delivery of data packets in the network. We want to achieve an optimal balance that keeps the data packet delivery times as low as possible.

Connectivity and Dynamics. As in the SPIN model, the UPPAAL model uses arrays of booleans to represent inter-node connectivity. Either, there is connectivity between two nodes or there is not. Node connectivity transitions are modeled using a separate automaton, that can at any time move to its next state whereby it manipulates the (global) connectivity table.

Broadcasting. In our version of UPPAAL broadcast channels can be used for synchronization. However, communication can not be used for value passing in UPPAAL and instead a combination of global data holders and committed locations is the recommended procedure [25]. In our LUNAR UPPAAL model broadcasting is handled similarly to unicasting except that the sending node (i.e. the broadcast initiator) has to specify that a broadcast is intended. Then, the medium automaton will set a global parameter bc_sender specifying the sender's identity. This is, because in the case of broadcast, the connectivity check has been deferred to the receiving nodes.

Table 1. SPIN verification results

Scenario	States generated	Transitions	All states searched	Memory used [Mb]	Time used
(a)	5715	12105	Yes	4.242 (6.188)	0.20 (0.20) s
(b)	269886	731118	Yes	33.05 (124.7)	12.33 (10.48) s
(c)	53614	128831	Yes	8.836 (30.12)	2.19 (1.92) s
(d)	4.58e+07 (8.15e+06)	1.33e+08 (2.21e+07)	No	4083 (4083)	5 h:57 min (8 min:56 s)
(e)	1.41e+06	4.59e+06	Yes	170.4 (806.6)	1:36 (1:26) min:s
(f)	3.40e+07 (7.27e+06)	1.22e+08 (2.50e+07)	No	4083 (4083)	4 h:2 min (9 min:43 s)

Limitations Imposed. The limitations in the PROMELA model are also imposed on the UPPAAL model, for the same reasons. An additional limitation that becomes relevant in the UPPAAL model is that it does not take into account computation times in the nodes. The only places in which delays occur are in the communications. This has been modeled by using a range, [MIN_TRANSMIT_TIME, MAX_TRANSMIT_TIME] of possible delays. It provides a very rough approximation of wireless network conditions and can in future versions be exchanged for a more realistic Wireless Local Area Network (WLAN) model. There are such models available [13], but we here choose the simplistic approach for lower network layers in order to reduce complexity.

In current LUNAR implementations the RREQ resending is done in an elaborate way attempting first a limited discovery using a small network radius. After this, several attempts are made with a larger radius. A timeout value is specified per "ring", i.e. per number of hops from the source node. After each RREQ timeout there is an additional waiting period before making a new attempt. In our model, however, we have chosen to settle for two timeout triggered resends. This means that in total, three route formation attempts can be made. In combination with a properly chosen timeout value, this is theoretically enough to successfully set up a route (and deliver a packet) in the scenarios studied. Our selected timeout value of 75 ms corresponds to three times the "ring" timeout in current LUNAR implementations.

Verification. The verification is performed in a manner analogous to the one described in Section 3.3. Namely, one node tries to set up a route to another node after which it attempts to send a packet there. If the route could be set up, the initiating node goes into a state unic_rrep_rec. If and when the correct IP packet arrives at the receiver, it goes into a state ip_rec_ok. Using our UPPAAL model we then verify deadlock freedom as well as timely route formation and message delivery. The LTL formulae in Table 2 are used to verify the respective properties.

There has been work done on extending UPPAAL to perform parallel model checking by Behrmann et al [2]. The advantage gained is increased speed which would in our case e.g. enable checking a wider range of scenarios. However, the total required amount of memory is larger since the state space grows when exploration is parallelized [2]. We have chosen to just study the standard (non parallel) UPPAAL distribution here.

Table 2. LTL formulae used with UPPAAL model

Property	LTL formula
Deadlock freedom	A[] not deadlock
Route successfully set up	A<> Lunar0.unic_rrep_rec
IP packet delivered	A<> Lunar1.ip_rec_ok

Table 3. UPPAAL verification results

Scenario	Route formation time [ms]	Message delivery time [ms]	States searched	Search complet-ed	Memory used [Mb]	Time used
(a)	[8, 91]	[12, 99]	15072 (12789)	Yes	15.98 (16.10)	3.89 (3.23) s
(b)	[8, 16]	[12, 24]	12211 (9787)	Yes	11.42 (11.48)	2.85 (2.56) s
(c)	[8, 91]	[12, 99]	22783 (18613)	Yes	20.12 (17.28)	5.93 (5.01) s
(d)	[8, 91]	[12, 99]	50456 (41169)	Yes	37.37 (35.51)	14.91 (12.26) s
(e)	[8, 91]	[12, 99]	123196 (106257)	Yes	124.0 (109.0)	57.91 (50.44) s
(f)	[8, 16]	[12, 24]	134978 (109606)	Yes	77.39 (77.24)	47.58 (42.61) s
(g)	[12, 99]	[18, 111]	2.01e+06 (1.78e+06)	Yes	866.6 (779.4)	11:43 min:s (10:28)
(h)	-	-	2.97e+07 (2.63e+07)	No	4078 (4082)	1:59 h:min (1:50)

With the scenarios and hardware described in Section 3.3, the route forma-tion and message delivery times in Table 3 result. UPPAAL is here used with aggressive state space reduction [2, 14]. As a reference, the values for conserva-tive state space reduction (the default) are given within parentheses. In all our measurements the state space representation uses minimal constraint systems.

The memory and time usage in Table 3 pertains to the case where all three LTL formulae in Table 2 are checked. As communication delay we have used the range [2, 4] ms. These measurements cannot be directly compared to the ones in Table 1 for the SPIN verification because of the greater amount of ab-straction introduced in the UPPAAL model. The RREQ generation strategy also differs between the models because of the absence of timing in the SPIN model. However, similar observations can be made for UPPAAL to those made in SPIN, namely that the state space grows rapidly with the number of nodes. Also, the nature of the topology changes influences the state space in a way that may sometimes be difficulty to foresee. Further note in the timing values that the shortest possible path is always the one found because of the rough link/physical layer approximation with total determinism in packet delivery.

4   Related Work

The Verinet group [26] at the University of Pennsylvania have carried out formal validation of AODV [18] and identified a flaw that could lead to loop formation. This was done using the HOL [24] theorem prover and a SPIN model of AODV in a two node setup (with an AODV router environment). They have also suggested a modification and verified that, after this, the protocol was loop free. Their approach verified the general case, but the methodology involves substantial user interaction.

Das and Dill [5] have used predicate abstraction to prove the absence of routing loops in a simplified version of AODV. The method yields a general proof but requires human involvement in the construction of the abstraction predicates.

Engler et al [6] have studied three implementations of AODV and found 36 distinct errors, including a bug (routing loop) in the AODV specification itself. The authors used their own model checker called CMC, which checks C and C++ implementations directly, eliminating the need for a separate abstract description of the system behavior. The model checker performs its work automatically. However, prior to execution, in addition to specifying correctness properties, the user has to define an environment as well as providing guard functions for each event handler. Furthermore, their approach is not aimed at proving correctness, but rather as a method of finding bugs in the code since an exhaustive state space search can generally not be performed.

Chiyangwa and Kwiatkowska [3] have constructed an UPPAAL model of AODV in order to investigate timing properties of the protocol. To cope with the state explosion problem, a linear topology has been used with sender, receiver, and an intermediate n_nodes node. Using 12 intermediate nodes, the authors could conclude that the dependency of route life time on network size is undesirable and suggested a modification where it instead adapts as the network grows. This work is closely related to ours, but they have focused on UPPAAL and studied a single (linear) scenario type. The methodology involves manual consideration in constructing the specialized model. Apart from studying a different protocol, we have taken a broader view comparing two verification approaches with an emphasis on the modeling of connectivity, dynamics and broadcasting.

Xiong et al [29] have modeled AODV using colored Petri nets (CPN). To cope with the mobility problem they have proposed a topology approximation (TA) mechanism. Simulation results show that the TA mechanism can indeed simulate the mobility of a MANET without knowing its actual topology.

Theo Ruys' PhD thesis [22] discusses different methods for modeling broadcast in SPIN. An alternative to our connectivity array would be to use a matrix of channels. Furthermore, instead of a broadcast macro, a broadcast service process could have been used. Since we have utilized asynchronous channels with large enough capacity for the broadcasts, this choice has not had any impact on the asynchronous nature of the message delivery process.

5   Conclusions and Future Work

This work is to our knowledge the first to study a range of topologies in order to determine where the limit actually is when performing model checking on an ad hoc routing protocol. We demonstrate that LUNAR works correctly (according to our general definition) for a number of routing scenarios. We further provide bounds for route formation and message delivery times.

When verifying both the data and control aspects of the LUNAR protocol using SPIN and when verifying the timing properties using UPPAAL the size of network, i.e. the number of nodes involved, as well as the nature of the topological scenarios is limited due to state space storage overhead. Even if parallel model checking approaches were used, our conclusion is that it is at this point not feasible to provide a proof for topologies of any significant size by modeling the protocol directly. On the other hand, our study enables us not only to analyze the modeling considerations that have to be imposed, but also provides us with a solid starting point for the further work we intend to pursue in the direction of infinite-state verification of ad hoc routing protocols.

Our emphasis has been on automatic model checkers in which the user provides a system specification and a number of requirements to check. The construction of models for these tools naturally still involves a certain amount of manual consideration. However, now that many of the modeling considerations have been identified, constructing verifiable models for both tools can be made rather close to the engineering activity of programming. Ultimately our goal is for the whole process to require knowledge primarily of the application, namely the ad hoc routing protocol, and not of the model checking tool. At present it is still necessary to manually (experimentally) limit the topologies and devise LTL formulae. This can be remedied by introducing specialized macros in combination with an ad hoc routing protocol preprocessor. Standard formulae could thereby be used for common situations, e.g. route setup and packet delivered.

We aim to evaluate current and upcoming parallel model checking tools in order to see where the limit in terms of number of nodes and topology dynamics currently is. We will perform these analyses on a super computer which has a very large amount of primary memory available. Further studies are also planned which involve other ad hoc routing protocols such as the ones being considered for standardization by the MANET group.

In order to provide a general proof of correctness in an automatic way, it is however not enough to study just a limited set of topologies. We need to study all available permutations for any given number of nodes. Therefore we will focus on the following directions for future research:

- Isolate the critical aspects of the ad hoc routing protocol to hand and model check those. A theorem prover can then be used to construct a general proof. This requires significant user interaction. It would be a great advantage if this process can be made more automatic.
- Employ a formal construction method rather than a post-construction verification and evaluate if there are ways to make that process more user friendly.
- Attempt an automatized infinite-state verification approach.

We currently consider the last approach as the most promising in terms of simplifying the verification process while still being able to provide a general proof.

References

[1] Jiri Barnat, Lubos Brim, and Jitka Stribrna. Distributed LTL model-checking in SPIN. Technical report, Masaryk University, December 2000. 351

[2] Gerd Behrmann, Thomas Hune, and Frits Vaandrager. Distributed timed model checking - how the search order matters. In *Proc. of 12th International Conference on Computer Aided Verification*, Lecture Notes in Computer Science, Chicago, July 2000. Springer-Verlag. 353, 354

[3] Sibusisiwe Chiyangwa and Marta Kwiatkowska. Analysing timed properties of AODV with UPPAAL. Technical report, University of Birmingham, March 2004. Technical Report CSR-04-4. 355

[4] T. Clausen and P. Jacquet. Request for Comments: Optimized link state routing protocol (OLSR). http://www.ietf.org/rfc/rfc3626.txt, October 2003. 344

[5] Satyaki Das and David L. Dill. Counter-example based predicate discovery in predicate abstraction. In *Formal Methods in Computer-Aided Design*. Springer-Verlag, November 2002. 354

[6] Dawson Engler and Madanlal Musuvathi. Static analysis versus software model checking for bug finding. In *Proc. Verification, Model Checking, and Abstract Interpretation, 5th International Conference*, Lecture Notes in Computer Science, pages 191–210. Springer-Verlag, 2004. 355

[7] G.J. Holzmann. *The Spin Model Checker, Primer and Reference Manual*. Addison-Wesley, Reading, Massachusetts, 2003. 348, 351

[8] G.J. Holzmann and D. Peled. An improvement in formal verification. In *Proc. FORTE Conference*, 1994. 348

[9] IETF MANET Working Group. MANET charter. http://www.ietf.org/html.charters/manet-charter.html, 2004. 344

[10] Information Sciences Institute. The network simulator – ns-2 home page. http://www.isi.edu/nsnam/ns, 2004. 344

[11] David B. Johnson. Routing in ad hoc networks of mobile hosts. In *Proc. IEEE Workshop on Mobile Computing Systems and Applications*, pages 158–163, December 1994. 344

[12] David B. Johnson, David A. Maltz, and Yih-Chun Hu. Internet draft: The dynamic source routing protocol for mobile ad hoc networks (DSR). http://www.ietf.org/internet-drafts/draft-ietf-manet-dsr-09.txt, April 2003. 344

[13] Marta Kwiatkowska, Gethin Norman, and Jeremy Sproston. Probabilistic model checking of the IEEE 802.11 wireless local area network protocol. In *Proc. Second Joint International Workshop on Process Algebra and Probabilistic Methods, Performance Modeling and Verification*, pages 169–187, July 2002. 353

[14] Kim G. Larsen, Fredrik Larsson, Paul Pettersson, and Wang Yi. Efficient verification of real-time systems: Compact data structures and state-space reduction. In *Proc. 18th IEEE Real-Time Systems Symposium (RTSS)*, pages 14–24, December 1997. 354

[15] Kim G. Larsen, Paul Pettersson, and Wang Yi. UPPAAL in a Nutshell. *Int. Journal on Software Tools for Technology Transfer*, 1(1–2):134–152, October 1997. 351

[16] Henrik Lundgren. *Implementation and Real-world Evaluation of Routing Protocols for Wireless Ad hoc Networks*. Licentiate thesis, Uppsala University, 2002. 344

[17] Henrik Lundgren, David Lundberg, Johan Nielsen, Erik Nordström, and Christian Tschudin. A large-scale testbed for reproducible ad hoc protocol evaluations. In *Proc. 3rd annual IEEE Wireless Communications and Networking Conference (WCNC)*, pages 412–418. IEEE, March 2002. 344

[18] Davor Obradovic. *Formal Analysis of Routing Protocols*. Phd thesis, University of Pennsylvania, 2002. 345, 354

[19] R. Ogier, F. Templin, and M. Lewis. Internet draft: Topology dissemination based on reverse-path forwarding (TBRPF). `http://www.ietf.org/internet-drafts/draft-ietf-manet-tbrpf-11.txt`, October 2003. 344

[20] C. Perkins, E. Belding-Royer, and S. Das. Request for Comments: Ad hoc on-demand distance vector (AODV) routing. `http://www.ietf.org/rfc/rfc3561.txt`, July 2003. 344

[21] Charles E. Perkins and Elizabeth M. Royer. Ad hoc on-demand distance vector routing. In *Proc. 2nd IEEE Workshop on Mobile Computing Systems and Applications*, pages 90–100, February 1999. 345

[22] Theo C. Ruys. *Towards Effective Model Checking*. Phd thesis, University of Twente, March 2001. 355

[23] C. Tschudin, R. Gold, O. Rensfelt, and O. Wibling. LUNAR: a lightweight underlay network ad-hoc routing protocol and implementation. In *Proc. Next Generation Teletraffic and Wired/Wireless Advanced Networking (NEW2AN)*, February 2004. 344, 346, 348, 349

[24] University of Cambridge Computer Laboratory. Automated reasoning group HOL page. `http://www.cl.cam.ac.uk/Research/HVG/HOL/`, 2004. 354

[25] Uppsala University and Aalborg University. UPPAAL home page. `http://www.uppaal.com`, 2004. 351, 352

[26] Verinet group. Verinet home page. `http://www.cis.upenn.edu/verinet`, 2004. 354

[27] Oskar Wibling. LUNAR pseudo code description. `http://user.it.uu.se/ oskarw/lunar_pseudo_code/`, 2004. 348

[28] Wikipedia. Ad hoc protocol list. `http://en.wikipedia.org/wiki/Ad_hoc_protocol_list`, 2004. 344

[29] C. Xiong, T. Murata, and J. Tsai. Modelling and simulation of routing protocol for mobile ad hoc networks using coloured Petri nets. In *Proc. Workshop on Formal Methods Applied to Defence Systems in Formal Methods in Software Engineering and Defence Systems*, 2002. 355

A Temporal Logic Based Framework
for Intrusion Detection

Prasad Naldurg, Koushik Sen, and Prasanna Thati

Department of Computer Science, University of Illinois at Urbana-Champaign
Urbana, IL 61801, USA
{naldurg,ksen,thati}@cs.uiuc.edu

Abstract. We propose a framework for *intrusion detection* that is based
on runtime monitoring of temporal logic specifications. We specify intrusion patterns as formulas in an expressively rich and efficiently mon-
itorable logic called EAGLE. EAGLE supports data-values and parameterized recursive equations, and allows us to succinctly express security
attacks with complex temporal event patterns, as well as attacks whose
signatures are inherently statistical in nature. We use an online monitoring algorithm that matches specifications of the absence of an attack,
with system execution traces, and raises an alarm whenever the specification is violated. We present our implementation of this approach in
a prototype tool, called MONID and report our results obtained by applying it to detect a variety of security attacks in log-files provided by
DARPA.

Keywords: Intrusion detection, security, temporal logic, runtime monitoring

1 Introduction

Despite great progress in research on computer security, fully secure computer
systems are still a distant dream. Today any large and complex computer system
has many security flaws. *Intrusion detection* involves monitoring the system
under concern to identify the misuse of these flaws as early as possible in order
to take corrective measures.

There are two main approaches to intrusion detection: *signature-based* [10, 12]
and *anomaly-based* [1, 6, 14]. In the signature-based approach, system behavior
is observed for known patterns of attacks, while in the anomaly-based approach
an alarm is raised if an observed behavior deviates significantly from pre-learned
normal behavior. Both these approaches have relative advantages and disadvan-
tages. The signature-based approach has a low false-alarm rate, but it requires us
to know the patterns of security attacks in advance and previously unknown attacks would go undetected. In contrast, the anomaly-based approach can detect
new attacks, but has a high false-alarm rate.

In this paper, we adopt a *temporal logic* approach to signature-based intrusion detection. One can naturally specify the absence of a known attack pattern

D. de Frutos-Escrig and M. Núñez (Eds.): FORTE 2004, LNCS 3235, pp. 359–376, 2004.
© IFIP International Federation for Information Processing 2004

as a *safety* formula ϕ in a suitable temporal logic [5]. Such a temporal logic based approach was considered in [16] using a variant of linear temporal logic (LTL) with first order variables. However we consider a more expressive logic in which one can also express attack signatures involving real-time constraints and statistical properties. We show how to automatically monitor the specification ϕ against the system execution and raise an intrusion alarm whenever the specification is violated. We also show how this technique can be used for simple types of anomaly-based intrusion detection. The idea is to specify the intended behavior of security-critical programs as temporal formulas involving *statistical predicates*, and monitor the system execution to check if it violates the formula. If the observed execution violates the formula then an intrusion has occurred, and thus attacks can be detected even if they are previously unknown.

Our approach to intrusion detection is motivated by the success of the relatively new research area called *runtime verification* [8, 18, 20], a major goal of which is to use light-weight formal methods for system monitoring. We use EAGLE, introduced in [4], for specification of attack-safe behavior of a system. EAGLE supports recursively defined temporal formulas, parameterizable by both logical formulas and data-expressions, over a set of three primitive modalities "next", "previous", and "concatenation". The logic enables us to express temporal patterns that involve reasoning about the data-values observed in individual events, and thus allows us to specify attacks whose signatures are inherently statistical in nature. Examples include password guessing attacks or the ICMP-flood denial of service attack. For these attacks there is no clear distinction between an intrusion and a normal behavior, and their detection involves collecting temporal statistics at runtime and making a guess based on the collected statistics.

We use an online algorithm [4] to monitor EAGLE formulas that processes each event as soon as it occurs and modifies the monitored formula to store the relevant summary. If, after any event the modified formula becomes false, an intrusion alarm is raised. Thus the whole procedure works in real-time. We have implemented our proposed approach in a prototype tool called MONID which can detect intrusions either online or offline. Figure 1 illustrates the framework. Information about system-level events, obtained either from relevant log-files (offline) or generated by appropriately instrumented application code (online), are sent to a server. The server merges the events from various sources by timestamp and preprocesses them into an abstract intermediate form to generate a single event trace. Note that detecting certain attacks may require us to observe events from various sources. Our monitor subsequently monitors this event trace against a given specification, and raises an intrusion alarm if the specification is violated.

We show the effectiveness of our approach by specifying several types of attacks and by monitoring them using MONID. Specifically, we perform offline monitoring using the large log-files made available by DARPA exclusively for the task of evaluating intrusion detection systems [13]. We successfully detected the attacks specified with acceptable computational overheads for the monitor-

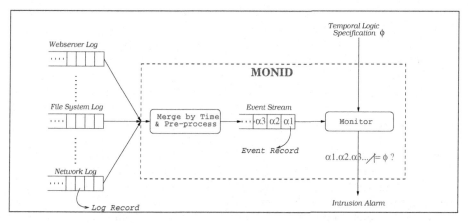

Fig. 1. MONID: A framework for intrusion detection

ing procedure. The experiments suggest that the proposed approach is a viable complement to existing intrusion detection mechanisms.

Following is the layout of the rest of this paper: In Section 2 we discuss related work in the area of intrusion detection and motivate our work. In Section 3, we briefly describe the syntax, semantics, and monitoring algorithm for EAGLE followed by Section 4 where we illustrate several common security-attack patterns specified in EAGLE. In Section 5, we describe the implementation of our tool MONID followed by a summary of our experimental results on DARPA log-files. We conclude in Section 6 with a brief discussion about future research directions.

2   Background and Motivation

The area of intrusion detection has seen synthesis of concepts and techniques from a variety of disciplines, including expert systems [1, 17], artificial neural networks [6], data mining [14], and static analysis [22]. A diverse collection of tools based on these various approaches have been deployed and tested [2, 7]. In the following, we elaborate on some of these approaches and clarify how our work fits in this context.

For signature-based approaches there are several languages with varying degrees of expressivity for specifying attack patterns. Roger et al. in [16] used temporal logic and model-checking based approach to detect intrusion. This work is closely related to ours; however, unlike [16] we can express more sophisticated signatures involving statistics and real-time by using powerful monitoring logic EAGLE. Ilgun *et al* [10] propose the use of finite state transition diagrams to specify sequences of actions that would lead the system from a secure initial state to a compromised final state. Ko *et al* [11] introduce a new class of grammars, called parallel environment grammars that are specifically suitable for specifying behavior (traces) of concurrent processes. The expected behavior of security critical programs is specified by a grammar, and an alarm is raised if the observed execution trace is not in the language defined by the grammar. Kumar *et al* [12] propose the use of Colored Petri nets for specifying attack patterns. We note that in comparison to the other approaches, temporal logic specifications of attack signatures tend to be much more compact and simpler to describe.

The state transition diagram and colored Petri net approaches can be seen as special cases of rule-based expert systems [9]. In rule-based expert systems, in general, knowledge about attacks is represented as a collection of `if-then` rules which are fired in response to the observed system execution. The main advantage of this approach is the clear separation of knowledge base from the control mechanism that applies the knowledge base for detecting intrusions.

In contrast to the signature-based approaches such as the above, the anomaly-based approach to intrusion detection does not require a priori knowledge of the attacks. One such approach is to collect statistical information [1, 15] about normal behavior into a user, group or target machine profile, and raise an alarm if the observed behavior deviates significantly from an estimated profile. One of the most rudimentary ones is *threshold detection*, where the idea is to record the number of occurrences of specific events and raise an alarm if the number is not within an expected range. As we will see in Section 3, such threshold detection policies can be elegantly expressed as temporal logic formulas.

Statistical profile-based anomaly detection can be seen as an instance of the general class of intrusion detection systems that *learn* the normal system behavior by constructing some model for it, and use the model to predict the system behavior and detect suspicious deviations. Other approaches in this category include that of time-based inductive generalization [21], artificial neural networks [6], and data-mining[14]. In time-based inductive generalization, the system behavior is modeled as a set of rules that are dynamically modified during the learning phase depending on how the predictions of the rules match with the observed system behavior. In the artificial neural networks approach, a neural net constitutes the model of system behavior and the net is trained with representative normal scenarios. In the data-mining approach, large audit trails are mined for patterns of normal or abusive behavior, which are then used for signature-based or anomaly-based intrusion detection. Self-learning capabilities such as the above are beyond the scope of our approach which is only intended for detecting attacks whose patterns are known a priori.

Anomaly-based intrusion detection systems have the disadvantage of having high false alarm rates due to inaccuracies in the learned model. In contrast, signature-based approaches such as ours have low false alarm rate, but would fail to detect attacks that differ even slightly from the given signature. Ideally, one would like a self-learning intrusion detection system with low false alarm rates. For now, the signature-based systems are quite popular because of their simplicity, accuracy, and ease of use. These systems would in any case be a valuable supplement to build more accurate anomaly-based systems.

3   EAGLE: An Expressive Temporal Monitoring Logic

The patterns for security attacks in software systems are specified formally in the logic EAGLE which is designed to support finite trace monitoring, and contains a small set of operators. The logic EAGLE introduced in [4] supports recursive parameterized equations, with a minimal/maximal fix-point semantics, together with three temporal operators: next-time ($\bigcirc$), previous-time ($\odot$), and concatenation ($\cdot$). Rules which are used to define new temporal operators can be parameterized with formulas and data-values, thus supporting specifications that can involve data, which can span an execution trace. The expressivity of EAGLE, which is indeed very rich, as shown in [3, 4], can express properties involving real-time, statistics and data-values. To make the paper self-contained, in this section, we give an informal introduction to EAGLE followed by its syntax, semantics, and the runtime monitoring algorithm for EAGLE as described in [4].

The logic EAGLE and its monitoring algorithm assumes the following:

1. There is a finite sequence of events σ generated by some executing system. An event is an instance of a record having a pre-specified schema. For example,

    LoginLogoutEvent $\{userId : \underline{\text{string}}, action : \underline{\text{int}}, time : \underline{\text{double}}\}$

    is the schema of an event and $\{userId = $ "Bob"$, action = $ login$, time = $ 18.7$\}$ is an event representing the fact that user "Bob" has logged in at time 18.7.

2. There is a formula F in EAGLE which specifies the condition for the absence of an attack.

We say that σ is free of the attack specified by F if and only if σ satisfies F.

Now, assume that we want to state a property that *"Whenever there is a login then eventually there is a logout"*. The property can be written in classical future time LTL: $\square(action = $ login $\rightarrow \Diamond(action = $ logout$))$. The formulas $\square F$ (always F) and $\Diamond F$ (eventually F), for some property F, satisfy the following equivalences, where the temporal operator $\bigcirc F$ stands for *next F* (meaning *'in next state F'*):

$$\square F \equiv F \wedge \bigcirc(\square F) \qquad \Diamond F \equiv F \vee \bigcirc(\Diamond F)$$

One can show that $\square F$ is a maximal solution of the recursive equivalence $X \equiv F \wedge \bigcirc X$, while $\Diamond F$ is the minimal solution of $X \equiv F \vee \bigcirc X$. In EAGLE one can write the following definitions for the two combinators Always and Eventually, and the formula to be monitored (M_1):

> $\underline{\text{max}}$ Always($\underline{\text{Form}}$ F) $= F \wedge \bigcirc$Always(F)
> $\underline{\text{min}}$ Eventually($\underline{\text{Form}}$ F) $= F \vee \bigcirc$Eventually(F)
> $\underline{\text{mon}}$ $M_1 = $ Always(($action = $ login) $\rightarrow$ Eventually($action = $ logout))

The Always operator is defined as having a maximal fix-point interpretation; the Eventually operator is defined as having a minimal interpretation. For further details the readers are referred to [4].

Let us complicate the above property a bit by stating that *"Whenever there is a login by any user x then eventually the user x logs out."* Thus, if "Bob" logs in then eventually "Bob" must logout. Similarly, the property must hold for any user such as "Tom", "Jim" or "Kelly". This property can be expressed by the following LTL formula with data-value bindings:

$$\Box((action = \texttt{login}) \rightarrow \underline{\text{let}}\ k = userId\ \underline{\text{in}}\ \Diamond(action = \texttt{logout} \wedge userId = k))$$

In this formula we use the operator $\underline{\text{let}}$ _ $\underline{\text{in}}$ _ to bind the value of $userId$ in the current event to the local variable k whenever $action = \texttt{login}$ in the current event. We then impose the condition that the value of $userId$ in some event in future must be same as the user id bound to k and that the action of the event must be $\texttt{logout}$. In EAGLE, we use a parameterized rule to express this property, capturing the value of $userId$ as a rule parameter:

$$\underline{\text{min}}\ \texttt{Bind}(\text{string}\ k) = \texttt{Eventually}(action = \texttt{logout} \wedge userId = k)$$
$$\underline{\text{mon}}\ M_2 = \texttt{Always}((action = \texttt{login}) \rightarrow \texttt{Bind}(userId))$$

Rule $\texttt{Bind}$ is parameterized with a string k, and is instantiated in M_2 when $action = \texttt{login}$, hence capturing the value of $userId$ at that moment. Rule $\texttt{Bind}$ replaces the binding operator $\underline{\text{let}}$ _ $\underline{\text{in}}$ _.

Indeed one can combine the two rules $\texttt{Bind}$ and $\texttt{Eventually}$ into a single rule $\texttt{EvLogout}$ with one parameter to get the same monitor as follows:

$$\underline{\text{min}}\ \texttt{EvLogout}(\text{string}\ k) = (action = \texttt{logout} \wedge userId = k) \vee \bigcirc\texttt{EvLogout}(k)$$
$$\underline{\text{mon}}\ M_2 = \texttt{Always}((action = \texttt{login}) \rightarrow \texttt{EvLogout}(userId))$$

Thus by allowing parameterized rules one gets the power of data-value binding in a formula. It can be argued that the introduction of the operator $\underline{\text{let}}$ _ $\underline{\text{in}}$ _ is sufficient to get the power of binding. However, parameterized rules can do more than simple data-binding. For example, suppose we want to express the property that *"Whenever there is a login by any user x then eventually the user x logs out within 100 units of time."* For this property we modify the rule $\texttt{EvLogout}$ by introducing two more parameters denoting the time at which the previous event took place and the time left. The modified rule and the monitor is given below:

$$\underline{\text{min}}\ \texttt{EvTimedLogout}(\text{string}\ k, \text{double}\ t, \text{double}\ \delta) = (\delta - (time - t) \geq 0)$$
$$\wedge((action = \texttt{logout} \wedge userId = k) \vee \bigcirc\texttt{EvTimedLogout}(k, time, \delta - (time - t)))$$
$$\underline{\text{mon}}\ M_3 = \texttt{Always}((action = \texttt{login}) \rightarrow \texttt{EvTimedLogout}(userId, time, 100))$$

Note that another simpler alternative to define the rule $\texttt{EvTimedLogout}$ is as follows:

$$\underline{\text{min}}\ \texttt{EvTimedLogout}(\text{string}\ k, \text{double}\ t, \text{double}\ \delta) = (time - t \leq \delta)$$
$$\wedge((action = \texttt{logout} \wedge userId = k) \vee \bigcirc\texttt{EvTimedLogout}(k, t, \delta))$$

A possible variation of our requirement for login and logout can be stated as *"Whenever there is a logout by any user x then in the past user x must have logged in"*. This property cannot be expressed concisely using the future time temporal operators only. However, the property can be expressed elegantly by a mixture of past-time and future-time temporal operators as follows:

$$\Box((action = \texttt{logout}) \rightarrow \underline{\text{let}}\ k = userId\ \underline{\text{in}}\ \diamondsuit\ (action = \texttt{login} \wedge userId = k))$$

where $\Diamond F$ denotes eventually in past F. This operator can be defined recursively in EAGLE using the primitive operator $\odot$ which is the past-time equivalent of $\bigcirc$. Thus the monitor definition can be written as follows:

$$\underline{\text{min}} \ \texttt{EventuallyInPast}(\underline{\text{Form}} \ F) = F \vee \odot \ \texttt{EventuallyInPast}(F)$$
$$\underline{\text{min}} \ \texttt{Bind}(\underline{\text{string}} \ k) = \texttt{EventuallyInPast}(action = \texttt{logout} \wedge userId = k)$$
$$\underline{\text{mon}} \ M_4 = \texttt{Always}((action = \texttt{login}) \rightarrow \texttt{Bind}(userId))$$

Thus rules in EAGLE allow us to define customized temporal operators with also the ability to bind and manipulate data. This capability proves to be indispensable for succinctly expressing attack-safe system executions. We recall the syntax and semantics of EAGLE to make the paper self-contained.

3.1   Syntax and Semantics

Syntax. A specification S consists of a declaration part D and an observer part O. D consists of zero or more rule definitions R, and O consists of zero or more monitor definitions M, which specify what is to be monitored. Rules and monitors are named (N).

$$
\begin{array}{lll}
S & ::= D \ O & D ::= R^* \qquad\qquad O ::= M^* \\
R & ::= \{\underline{\text{max}} \mid \underline{\text{min}}\} \ N(T_1 \ x_1, \ldots, T_n \ x_n) = F \\
M & ::= \underline{\text{mon}} \ N = F \\
T & ::= \underline{\text{Form}} \mid primitive \ type \\
F & ::= expression \mid \underline{\text{true}} \mid \underline{\text{false}} \mid \neg F \mid F_1 \wedge F_2 \mid F_1 \vee F_2 \mid F_1 \rightarrow F_2 \mid \\
& \quad\ \bigcirc F \mid \odot F \mid F_1 \cdot F_2 \mid N(F_1, \ldots, F_n) \mid x_i
\end{array}
$$

A rule definition R is preceded by a keyword indicating whether the interpretation is maximal or minimal. Maximal rules define safety properties (nothing bad ever happens), while minimal rules define liveness properties (something good eventually happens). For us, the difference only becomes important when evaluating formulas at the boundaries of a trace. To understand how this works it suffices to say here that monitored rules evolve as new events are appearing. Assume that the end of the trace has been reached (we are beyond the last event) and a monitored formula F has evolved to F'. Then all applications in F' of maximal fix-point rules will evaluate to true, since they represent safety properties that apparently have been satisfied throughout the trace, while applications of minimal fix-point rules will evaluate to false, indicating that some event did not happen.

The rule parameters are typed and can either be a formula of type $\underline{\text{Form}}$, or of a primitive type such as $\underline{\text{int}}$, $\underline{\text{long}}$, $\underline{\text{float}}$, etc., or any other composite types such as $\underline{\text{Set}}$, $\underline{\text{List}}$, etc.. The body of a rule (or monitor) is a boolean valued formula of the syntactic category $Form$ (with meta-variables F, etc.). Any recursive call on a rule must be strictly guarded by a temporal operator. The propositions of this logic are boolean expressions over fields of event. Formulas are composed using standard propositional logic operators together with a next-state operator $(\bigcirc F)$, a previous-state operator $(\odot F)$, and a concatenation-operator $(F_1 \cdot F_2)$. Finally, rules can be applied and their arguments must be type correct. That is, an argument of type <u>Form</u> can be any formula, with the restriction that if the argument is an expression, it must be of boolean type. An argument of a primitive type must be an expression of that type. Arguments can be referred to within the rule body (x_i).

In what follows, a rule N of the form

$$\{\underline{\max}|\underline{\min}\} \ N(\underline{\text{Form}} \ f_1, \ldots, \underline{\text{Form}} \ f_m, T_1 \ p_1, \ldots, T_n \ p_n) = B,$$

where $f_1, \ldots f_m$ are arguments of type <u>Form</u> and $p_1, \ldots p_n$ are arguments of primitive type, is written in short as: $\{\underline{\max}|\underline{\min}\} \ N(\overline{\underline{\text{Form}}} \ \bar{f}, \overline{T} \ \bar{p}) = B$, where $\bar{f}$ and $\bar{p}$ represent tuples of type <u>Form</u> and $\overline{T}$ respectively. Without loss of generality, in the above rule we assume that all the arguments of type <u>Form</u> appear first.

Semantics. An execution trace σ is a finite sequence of events $\sigma = s_1 s_2 \ldots s_n$, where $|\sigma| = n$ is the length of the trace. The i'th event s_i of a trace σ is denoted by $\sigma(i)$. The term $\sigma^{[i,j]}$ denotes the sub-trace of σ from position i to position j, both positions included; if $i \geq j$ then $\sigma^{[i,j]}$ denotes the empty trace. Given a trace σ and a specification $D \ O$, satisfaction is defined as follows:

$$\sigma \models D \ O \ \text{ iff } \ \forall \ (\text{mon } N = F) \in O \ . \ \sigma, 1 \models_D F$$

That is, a trace satisfies a specification if the trace, observed from position 1 (the first state), satisfies each monitored formula. The definition of the satisfaction relation $\models_D \ \subseteq \ (\textit{Trace} \times \textbf{nat}) \times \text{Form}$, for a set of rule definitions D, is presented below, where $0 \leq i \leq n+1$ for some trace $\sigma = s_1 s_2 \ldots s_n$. Note that the position of a trace can become 0 (before the first state) when going backwards, and can become $n+1$ (after the last state) when going forwards, both cases causing rule applications to evaluate to either true if maximal or false if minimal, without considering the body of the rules at that point.

$$
\begin{aligned}
\sigma, i \models_D \textit{expression} \ &\text{ iff } \ 1 \leq i \leq |\sigma| \text{ and } \textit{evaluate}(\textit{expression})(\sigma(i)) == \textit{true} \\
\sigma, i \models_D \underline{\text{true}} \ &\text{ iff } \ \sigma, i \not\models_D \underline{\text{false}} \\
\sigma, i \models_D \neg F \ &\text{ iff } \ \sigma, i \not\models_D F \\
\sigma, i \models_D F_1 \wedge F_2 \ &\text{ iff } \ \sigma, i \models_D F_1 \text{ and } \sigma, i \models_D F_2 \\
\sigma, i \models_D \bigcirc F \ &\text{ iff } \ i \leq |\sigma| \text{ and } \sigma, i+1 \models_D F \\
\sigma, i \models_D \bigodot F \ &\text{ iff } \ 1 \leq i \text{ and } \sigma, i-1 \models_D F \\
\sigma, i \models_D F_1 \cdot F_2 \ &\text{ iff } \ \exists j \text{ s.t. } i \leq j \leq |\sigma| + 1 \text{ and } \sigma^{[1,j-1]}, i \models_D F_1 \\
&\qquad\qquad\qquad\qquad \text{ and } \sigma^{[j,|\sigma|]}, 1 \models_D F_2
\end{aligned}
$$

$$
\sigma, i \models_D N(\overline{F}, \overline{P}) \quad \text{iff} \quad
\begin{cases}
\text{if } 1 \leq i \leq |\sigma| \text{ then:} \\
\quad \sigma, i \models_D B[\bar{f} \mapsto \overline{F}, \bar{p} \mapsto \textit{evaluate}(\overline{P})(\sigma(i))] \\
\quad \text{where } (N(\underline{\text{Form}} \ \bar{f}, \overline{T} \ \bar{p}) = B) \in D \\
\text{otherwise, if } i = 0 \text{ or } i = |\sigma| + 1 \text{ then:} \\
\quad \text{rule } N \text{ is defined as } \underline{\max} \text{ in } D
\end{cases}
$$

An expression (a proposition) is evaluated at the current event in case the position i is within the trace ($1 \leq i \leq n$). In the boundary cases ($i = 0$ and $i = n+1$) a proposition evaluates to false. Propositional operators have their standard semantics in all positions. A next-time formula $\bigcirc F$ evaluates to true if the current position is not beyond the last event and F holds in the next position. Dually for the previous-time formula. The concatenation formula $F_1 \cdot F_2$ is true if the trace σ can be split into two sub-traces $\sigma = \sigma_1 \sigma_2$, such that F_1 is true on σ_1, observed from the current position i, and F_2 is true on σ_2 (ignoring σ_1, and thereby limiting the scope of past time operators). Applying a rule within the trace (positions $1 \ldots n$) consists of replacing the call with the right-hand side of the definition, substituting arguments for formal parameters; if an argument is of primitive type its evaluation in the current state is substituted for the associated formal parameter of the rule, thereby capturing a desired freeze variable semantics.

3.2 The Monitoring Algorithm

We briefly describe the computation mechanism used to check if an EAGLE formula is satisfied by a sequence of events. We assume that the *propositions* or the *expressions* of an EAGLE formula are specified with respect to the fields of the event record. At every event the algorithm evaluates the monitored formula on the event and generates another formula. At the end of the event sequence, the value of the evolved formula is determined; if the value is true the formula is satisfied by the event sequence, otherwise, the formula is violated.

Formally, the evaluation of a formula F at an event $s = \sigma(i)$ results in an another formula $F' = eval(F, s)$ with the property that $\sigma, i \models F$ if and only if $\sigma, i + 1 \models F'$. At the end of the trace we compute the boolean function $value(F)$, where F is the evolved formula, such that $value(F)$ is true if and only if $\sigma, |\sigma| + 1 \models F$ and false otherwise. Thus for a given trace $\sigma = s_1 s_2 \ldots s_n$ and an EAGLE formula F, σ satisfies F if and only if $value(eval(\ldots eval(eval(F, s_1), s_2) \ldots, s_n)) = true$. The details of the algorithm can be found in [4] which gives the definition of the functions $eval$ and $value$ along with two other auxiliary functions $update$ and $init$. The definition of these four functions forms the calculus of EAGLE. For this paper, to help in understanding, we describe the algorithm informally through an example.

Suppose we want to monitor the following specification, described in Section 3

<u>max</u> Always(<u>Form</u> F) $= F \wedge \bigcirc$Always(F)
<u>min</u> EvTimedLogout(<u>string</u> k, <u>double</u> t, <u>double</u> δ) $= (time - t \leq \delta)$
$\qquad\qquad \wedge((action = \texttt{logout} \wedge userId = k) \vee \bigcirc$EvTimedLogout$(k, t, \delta))$
<u>mon</u> $M_3 = $ Always$((action = \texttt{login}) \rightarrow$ EvTimedLogout$(userId, time, 100))$

against the sequence of 2 events $e_1 = \{userId = $ "Bob", $action = \texttt{login}, time = 17.0\}$, $e_2 = \{userId = $ "Bob", $action = \texttt{logout}, time = 150.0\}$. At the first event the formula M_3 gets modified as follows:

$eval(M_3, e_1) = $ EvTimedLogout("Bob", 17.0, 100) $\wedge$
$\qquad\qquad$ Always$((action = \texttt{login}) \rightarrow$ EvTimedLogout$(userId, time, 100))$

Note that the relevant summary of the event, involving the user id "Bob" and the timestamp 17.0 has got assimilated into the modified formula. At the second event the predicate $(time - t \leq \delta)$ gets instantiated to $(150.0 - 17.0 \leq 100)$ which is false. Hence the whole formula becomes false, indicating that the two-event trace violates the property.

One point which is worth stressing on is that the logic EAGLE has a finite trace semantics. The monitoring algorithm as described above can determine the satisfaction or the violation of a formula at the end of a trace only. However, in intrusion detection, end of trace makes no sense as the sequence of events can be theoretically infinite. In that situation we want to raise an alarm as soon as a property is violated. This is done by checking after every event if the formula becomes unsatisfiable. Checking unsatisfiability of a formula in EAGLE is undecidable as it involves data-values. However, note that it is always possible to write a formula, corresponding to the absence of an attack, such that, whenever the attack pattern appears in the event sequence, the formula becomes false. The reason behind this is that we can always specify an attack pattern by a formula ϕ such that ϕ, when evaluated over a sequence of events representing the pattern becomes true. This is called *specifying-bad prefixes* [19]. Once we have the attack pattern specification in terms of ϕ, we can specify the safe behavior of the system as $\Box(\neg\phi)$. Note that this formula becomes false (hence unsatisfiable) whenever a sequence of events representing the attack is detected. Hence, checking unsatisfiability for the evaluation of this formula at any point simply reduces to checking if the evaluated formula is false.

3.3   EAGLE FLIER: Monitoring Engine

We use the monitoring engine EAGLE FLIER to implement our intrusion detection framework, called MONID. The engine EAGLE FLIER, written in Java, is available as a library. The library provides two basic methods that can be called by any client program for the purpose of monitoring. The first method **parse** takes a file containing a specification involving several monitors (sets of monitored formulas) written in EAGLE and compiles them internally into data structures representing monitors. After compilation, the client program calls the method **eval** iteratively for every event. This call internally modifies the monitors according to the definition of *eval* in Subsection 3.2. If at any step the monitored formulas become false, an error message is printed or a pre-specified method is invoked to take a corrective measure.

4   Example Attack Specifications

In this section, we present a few examples of how EAGLE can be used to specify formulas that correspond to desirable properties of execution traces of a system being monitored. An intrusion or an attack in this context is a trace that violates this specification. We draw our examples from real-world attacks to showcase the applicability of our framework. These examples highlight the expressive power of our formalism, as well as exemplify the various features of EAGLE. Moreover, we believe that many attack signatures in practice can be expressed using templates of our examples with minor modifications. In all the examples we use the rule **Always** defined in Section. 3.

Smurf Attacks

The first attack we describe is the Smurf IP Denial of Service (DoS) attack. An attacker creates a forged ICMP echo request message (also called a "ping" packet) with the victim's name as the sender and sets the destination IP address to a broadcast IP address. This attack can result in a large amount of ICMP echo reply packets being sent from broadcast hosts that respond to the request, to the victim, which can cause network congestion or outages.

In order to detect this attack, we need to look at network events from a log created by a network auditing tool such as *tcpdump*. The formula for the absence of this attack is given below:

$$\underline{\max} \; \texttt{Attack}() = (\mathit{type} = \text{``}ICMP\text{''}) \wedge \mathit{isBroadcast}(\mathit{ip})$$
$$\underline{\mathrm{mon}} \; \texttt{SmurfSafety} = \texttt{Always}(\neg\texttt{Attack}())$$

In the above example, the record schema of an event contains the *type* field that corresponds to the type of the network packet and the field *ip* that corresponds to the return IP address of a network packet. In the specification, we first specify the attack pattern by the rule **Attack** that checks if the type of the packet is *"ICMP"* and the destination address of the packet is a broadcast IP address (*isBroadcast*), where *isBroadcast* is a predicate over the event which checks if the last two bytes of the IP address provided as argument are 0 or 255. Then a good behavior of the system with respect to this attack can be stated as *"Always there is no attack"*.

Cookie-Stealing Scenario

The next example describes what is called the "cookie-stealing" attack. In order to monitor this attack we need to look at a web-server (application-level) log that contains a record of all sessions that the server participates in, along with session-specific state information.

A cookie is a session-tracking mechanism issued by a web-application server to a web-client and store client-specific session information. Clients automatically include these cookies that can act as authentication tokens in their requests. In this example we assume that a session is identified by its IP address. An attack occurs when a malicious user hijacks a session by reusing an old cookie issued to a different IP address. The formula below asserts that a particular cookie must always be used by the same IP address.

$$\underline{\min} \; \texttt{SafeUse}(\underline{\text{string}} \; c, \underline{\text{int}} \; i) = ((\mathit{name} = c) \rightarrow (\mathit{ip} = i)) \wedge \odot \texttt{SafeUse}(c, i)$$
$$\underline{\mathrm{mon}} \; \texttt{CookieSafe} = \texttt{Always}(\texttt{SafeUse}(\mathit{name}, \mathit{ip}))$$

A trace that violates this formula therefore encodes a cookie-stealing attack. In the above example, the record schema of an event contains the *name* field which corresponds to name of the cookie, and the *ip* field that corresponds to the IP address of the client using the cookie. The parameterized rule **SafeUse** checks whether the association between a particular cookie identified by the cookie name and an IP address (specified as arguments) is the same as this association in the past. This example highlights the use of value-binding and the previous operator to describe history-based intrusion signatures.

Multi-domain Buffer Overflows

The next example illustrates how we can combine information about events from different logs in a cross-domain intrusion detection exercise. This scenario examines both web-server's access logs, as well as network logs to infer when a buffer-overflow attack has been attempted against the server. Network packets are analyzed, looking for binary data. Subsequently, the web-server's access logs are checked to see if a matching event can be found, where the web-server closes the connection successfully after receiving some binary data. If no matching log record is found, within a specific timeout, then the buffer overflow attack was successful and the web-server is now executing the attackers code. This example is specified by the formula shown next.

$$\underline{\text{min}} \ \texttt{EventuallyClosed}(\underline{\text{long}} \ t, \underline{\text{long}} \ d, \underline{\text{long}} \ i1, \underline{\text{long}} \ i2) = (time - t < d) \wedge$$
$$((ip1 = i1 \wedge ip2 = i2 \wedge log = web \wedge type = closed) \vee$$
$$\bigcirc \texttt{EventuallyClosed}(t, d, i1, i2))$$
$$\underline{\text{mon}} \ \texttt{BufferSafe} = \texttt{Always}((log = network \wedge type = binary)$$
$$\rightarrow \texttt{EventuallyClosed}(time, 100, ip1, ip2))$$

The record schema for an event contains the *log* field which indicates the name of the log to which the event belongs, the *type* field which can be *binary*, *closed*, etc., the *time* field representing the time at which the event occurred, the *ip1* field representing the source IP address, and the *ip2* representing the destination IP address. In the rule `EventuallyClosed`, the arguments t, d, $i1$, and $i2$ represent the time at which the rule is invoked, the timeout period, the source IP address, and the destination IP address, respectively. The rule `EventuallyClosed` asserts that eventually within time d the connection involving IP addresses $i1$ and $i2$ must get closed. Finally, the monitor `BufferSafe` states that it is always the case that if there is a event of binary access in the network log then eventually within time 100 there must be a matching event in the web-server log that denotes the closing of the connection. Here a connection is identified by the source and destination IP addresses.

Password Guessing Attack

The next example illustrates the ability of EAGLE to collect statistics at runtime to detect a potential intrusion. In the password-guessing attack, an unauthorized user uses the *telnet* program to attempt to login into a machine over a network. If a user is allowed to guess an arbitrary number of passwords for a given user-name, it is only a matter of time before the password is broken. Most systems terminate a *telnet* session if a user makes more than three invalid password guesses over a short-time period. Some systems restrict the total number of invalid login attempts over the course of a longer time-period to prevent an attacker from succeeding by initiating multiple short sessions.

In order to detect this attack, we need to have access to the host's audit logs. On Solaris machines for example, auditing can be turned on by running Sun's Basic Security Monitoring (BSM) software. In order to encode this attack, we present a template that can be reused for any signature that specifies a threshold frequency of events of interest in a trace, which when exceeded constitutes an attack:

$$\underline{\max}\ \texttt{Failure}() = (type = login) \wedge \neg success$$
$$\underline{\max}\ \texttt{Guess}(\underline{\text{long}}\ i, \underline{\text{Form}}\ F) = (ip = i) \wedge \texttt{Failure}()$$
$$\underline{\max}\ \texttt{Counter}(\underline{\text{long}}\ t, \underline{\text{long}}\ d, \underline{\text{int}}\ c, \underline{\text{long}}\ i, \underline{\text{int}}\ C) = (time - t < d)$$
$$\rightarrow ((\texttt{Guess}(i) \rightarrow (c \leq C \wedge \bigcirc \texttt{Counter}(t, d, c+1, i, C)))$$
$$\wedge (\neg \texttt{Guess}(i) \rightarrow \texttt{Counter}(t, d, c, i, C)))$$
$$\underline{\text{mon}}\ \texttt{PassGuessSafe} = \texttt{Always}(\texttt{Failure}() \rightarrow \texttt{Counter}(time, 300, 1, ip, 3))$$

In the rule $\texttt{Counter}$, the arguments t, d, c, i, and C represent the rule invocation time, the timeout period, the current number of unsuccessful-guesses count, the source IP address doing the guess, and the threshold count. An attack occurs when the number-of-guess count c from the IP address i exceeds the threshold count C within the timeout period d. Whenever there is a $\texttt{Failure}()$ in login, the parameterized rule $\texttt{Counter}$ starts with the initial count set to 1. For every occurrence of an event, indicating login-failure from the same IP address within the timeout time d, the number-of-guess count is increased by one. The rule $\texttt{Counter}$ also checks if within time d whether c exceeds C; in which case the whole rule becomes false indicating an attack. The monitor $\texttt{PassGuessSafe}$ asserts that whenever there is a failure of login from an IP address then eventually within time 300 the number of login-failures from the same IP address must be less than or equal to 3.

Port-Sweep Attack

The Port-sweep attack is the most sophisticated example in this section. A port sweep is a surveillance scan through many ports on a single network host. Each port scan is essentially a message sent by the attacker to the victim's port and elicits a response from the victim that indicates the port's status. The aim of the attacker is to determine which services are supported on the host, and use this information to exploit vulnerabilities in these services in the future. Port scans may be legitimate, when a client is trying to determine if a service is being offered. However, when the number of port scans exceeds a certain threshold within a short time-period, the victim machine can assume that the scans are malicious. In order to detect this attack, once again, we need to include a time-period and a frequency explicitly in our formula, and can use the template from the previous example:

$\underline{\text{max}}$ NewPort(long $i1$, long $i2$, Set S) = $(i1 = ip1) \wedge (i2 = ip2) \wedge (port \notin S)$
$\underline{\text{max}}$ Counter(long t, long d, int c, long $i1$, long $i2$, Set S, int C) = $(time - t < d) \rightarrow$
    $((\text{NewPort}(i1, i2, S) \rightarrow (c \leq C \wedge \bigcirc \text{Counter}(t, d, c + 1, i1, i2, S \cup \{port\}, C)))$
    $\wedge (\neg \text{NewPort}(i1, i2, S) \rightarrow \bigcirc \text{Counter}(t, d, c, i1, i2, S, C)))$
$\underline{\text{mon}}$ PortScanSafe = Always(Counter($time$, 100, 1, $ip1$, $ip2$, $\{port\}$, 10))

As before, the arguments t, d, c and C in the Counter rule serve the same purpose as place holders for the initial time, the timeout period, the frequency count, and the threshold count. The parameterized Counter rule asserts that the number of port scans observed in a tcpdump record between a source and destination IP ($i1$ and $i2$) address pair never exceeds a certain threshold C within time d. Note that in the rule Counter we add every new port number scanned to the set S of all port numbers (involving $i1$ and $i2$) that are scanned within time d. The rule NewPort checks if the port number, involved in any communication between the IP addresses $i1$ and $i2$, exists in the set S of all port numbers (involved in all communications between $i1$ and $i2$) within the timeout period d. This example shows how we can use EAGLE to collect statistics by using a rich data-structure such as Set.

5   Implementation and Evaluation

5.1   MONID: Monitoring Based Intrusion Detection Tool

The intrusion detection tool, MONID, is designed to operate in both online and offline fashion. In the online mode, MONID runs as a server that receives streams of events from various sources. To generate these events, the different logging modules are instrumented so that they filter and send *relevant* events to the server. On receiving various events, the server merges them in increasing order of timestamps and generates a single event-stream, which is passed through a filter to get a projection of the events that are required for monitoring. The filtered event stream is fed to the EAGLE FLIER to see if the event stream violates the normal behavior of the system specified as a set of EAGLE formulas. Note that EAGLE FLIER never stores the event stream while monitoring; instead it collects the essential facts and assimilates them into the monitored formulas by transforming them into new formulas. This enables us to use EAGLE FLIER for online monitoring. In the offline mode, MONID reads various log files and sends an event corresponding each log entry to the server. The server then processes the event stream as before to detect intrusion. We perform most of our experiments in offline mode.

5.2   Evaluation

We test our MONID tool with the standard DARPA Intrusion Detection Evaluation data set [13] to study the overheads and explore the expressive power

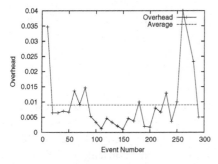

Fig. 2. Performance Overhead of Port-Sweep Attack

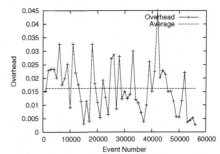

Fig. 3. Performance Overhead of Password-Guess Attack

of our logic with real-world examples. In our experiments with MONID, we focus on the data sets provided in the 1998 offline Intrusion Detection Evaluation plan [13]. This data set focuses on UNIX workstations. The experimental setup simulates a military base with a private network marked as "Inside" connected to the "Outside" world through a Cisco AGS+ router. Two types of logs are available for analysis. The *tcpdump* logs were collected by running *tcpdump* on this connecting router. This data contains the contents of every packet transmitted between computers inside and outside of the military base, and gives us network sessions of complete TCP/IP connections. The sessions were designed to reflect (statistically) traffic seen on military bases and contain explicit examples of different real attacks.

The other data available is from the Sun Basic Security Module (BSM) from the host *pascal*, which was the victim of the simulated attacks, located on the "Inside" network. This data contains audit information describing system calls made to the Solaris kernel.

We implemented and tested our tool against the smurf, port-sweep and password-guessing as discussed in Section 4, of which we report the results of last two experiments due to space limitation. We do not repeat the details of these attacks here. We ran our tool on a 2.0 GHz Pentium M laptop with 1GB RAM, simulating the behavior of a dedicated-monitor that passively observes traffic on the "Inside" network and processes events from our victim host offline. The aim of our experiments is to demonstrate that the tool can detect intrusions, and the monitoring and processing overheads of our prototype tool are very low.

Our experiments detected 5 password-guess attack and 2 port-sweep attack in the logs. The performance overheads for monitoring the Port-Sweep and Password-Attacks are given in Figure 2 and 3, respectively. The X-axis in both graphs shows the number of events we are monitoring, as they are obtained from our logs. Each data point is the average overhead calculated for intervals of 10 and 1000 events respectively. The Y-axis plots the ratio between the time spent by the monitor vs. the time between the generation of the events in the actual log. As long as this ratio is less than 1, our monitoring is feasible. The results, show that the average overhead, is around 0.009 for Port-Sweep attacks and 0.016 for Password-Guessing attacks, suggesting that online mode is feasible and efficient.

6   Conclusion

We have proposed a framework for intrusion detection using a temporal logic approach. In contrast to other such temporal logic based approaches [16], we use an expressively rich logic in which one can express both signature based and simple anamoly based attack specifications. We automatically monitor such attack specifications with respect to the system execution. An intrusion is detected when the observed execution violates the formula being monitored. We demonstrate this approach by specifying formulas for detecting several types of well-known attacks, and by testing a prototype implementation of our monitoring algorithm over large event-logs made available by DARPA for evaluation purposes. We believe that our examples are generic and can be used as template for specifying a large number of other attacks.

Our approach opens up several interesting directions for future research. We plan to conduct a more systematic performance study and categorize the overheads more precisely. With the aim to exploit the expressiveness of our logic, we plan explore the use of ideas introduced in [18, 19] for *predicting* security failures from successful executions in multi-threaded programs. Specifically, in addition to monitoring a given specification against the currently observed trace, we can also compare the specification with all the traces that correspond to different interleavings of the same partial order (causality relation) between the underlying events. Another problem of interest is to use the distributed monitoring framework introduced in [20] for detecting attacks that involve multiple hosts on a network. We believe that our approach can complement existing intrusion detection mechanisms and provide support for more expressive attack specifications.

References

[1] D. Anderson, T. Frivold, and A. Valdes. Next-generation intrusion detection expert system. Technical Report SRI-CSL-95-07, Computer Science Laboratory, SRI International, Menlo Park, CA, May 1995. 359, 361, 362

[2] S. Axelsson. Intrusion detection systems: A taxonomy and survey. Technical Report 99–15, Dept. of Computer Engineering, Chalmers University of Technology, Sweden, 2000. 361

[3] H. Barringer, A. Goldberg, K. Havelund, and K. Sen. Program monitoring with ltl in eagle. In *Workshop on Parallel and Distributed Systems: Testing and Debugging (PADTAD'04) (Satellite workshop of IPDPS'04)*, Santa Fe, New Mexico, USA, April 2004. (To Appear). 363

[4] H. Barringer, A. Goldberg, K. Havelund, and K. Sen. Rule-based runtime verification. In *Proceedings of 5th International Conference on Verification, Model Checking and Abstract Interpretation (VMCAI'04)*, volume 2937 of *Lecture Notes*

in *Computer Science*, pages 44–57, Venice, Italy, January 2004. Springer-Verlag. 360, 363, 367

[5] E. M. Clarke, O. Grumberg, and D. A. Peled. *Model Checking*. MIT Press, 1999. 360

[6] H. Debar, M. Becker, and D. Siboni. A neural network component for an intrusion detection system. In *IEEE Computer Society Symposium on Research on Security and Privacy*, pages 240–250, May 1992. 359, 361, 362

[7] H. Debar, M. Dacier, and A. Wespi. Towards a taxonomy of intrusion detection systems. *Computer Networks*, 31(8):805–822, April 1999. 361

[8] K. Havelund and G. Roşu. Monitoring Java Programs with Java PathExplorer. In *Proceedings of Runtime Verification (RV'01)*, volume 55 of *ENTCS*. Elsevier, 2001. 360

[9] J. P. Ignizio. *Introduction to Expert Systems-the Development and Implementation of Rule-Based Expert System*. McGraw-Hill Science, 1991. 362

[10] K. Ilgun, R. Kemmerer, and P. Porras. State transition analysis: A rule-based intrusion detection approach. *IEEE Transactions on Software Engineering*, 21(3):181–199, 1995. 359, 361

[11] C. Ko, M. Ruschitzka, and K. Levitt. Execution monitoring of security-critical programs in distributed systems: A specification-based approach. In *IEEE Symposium on Security and Privacy*, pages 175–187, May 1997. 361

[12] S. Kumar and E. Spafford. A pattern matching model for misuse intrusion detection. In *National Computer Security Conference*, pages 11–21, 1994. 359, 362

[13] MIT Lincoln Laboratory. DARPA intrusion detection evaluation. http://www.ll.mit.edu/IST/ideval/. 360, 372, 373

[14] W. Lee. A datamining framework for building intrusion detection models. In *IEEE Symposium on Security and Privacy*, pages 120–132, May 1999. 359, 361, 362

[15] P. Porras and P. Neumann. EMERALD: Event monitoring enabling responses to anomalous live disturbances. In *National Information Systems Security Conference*, 1997. 362

[16] M. Roger and J. Goubault-Larrecq. Log auditing through model-checking. In *14th IEEE Computer Security Foundations Workshop (CSFW'01)*. IEEE, 2001. 360, 361, 374

[17] M. Sebring, E. Shellhouse, M. Hanna, and R. Whitehurst. Expert systems in intrusion detection: A case study. In *National Computer Security Conference*, pages 74–81, 1998. 361

[18] K. Sen, G. Roşu, and G. Agha. Runtime Safety Analysis of Multithreaded Programs. In *9th European Software Engineering Conference and 11th ACM SIGSOFT International Symposium on the Foundations of Software Engineering (ESEC/FSE'03)*, pages 337–346, Helsinki, Finland, September 2003. ACM. 360, 374

[19] K. Sen, G. Roşu, and G. Agha. Online efficient predictive safety analysis of multi-threaded programs. In *Proceedings of 10th International Conference on Tools and Algorithms for the Construction and Analysis of Systems (TACAS'04)*, volume 2988 of *LNCS*, pages 123–138, Barcelona, Spain, March 2004. 368, 374

[20] K. Sen, A. Vardhan, G. Agha, , and G. Roşu. Efficient decentralized monitoring of safety in distributed systems. In *Proceedings of 26th International Conference on Software Engineering (ICSE'04)*, pages 418–427, Edinburgh, UK, May 2004. IEEE. 360, 374

[21] H. Teng, K. Chen, and S. Lu. Security audit trail analysis using inductively generated predictive rules. In *Conference on Artificial Intelligence Applications*, pages 24–29. IEEE Computer Society Press, March 1990. 362

[22] D. Wagner and D. Dean. Intrusion detection via static analysis. In *IEEE Symposium on Security and Privacy*, 2001. 361

Author Index